P9-CEG-757

EUSEBIUS

EUSEBIUS

BISHOP OF CÆSAREA

THE ECCLESIASTICAL HISTORY AND THE MARTYRS OF PALESTINE

TRANSLATED WITH INTRODUCTION
AND NOTES BY

HUGH JACKSON LAWLOR, D.D., Litt.D.

DEAN OF ST. PATRICK'S AND BERESFORD PROFESSOR OF ECCLESIASTICAL
HISTORY IN THE UNIVERSITY OF DUBLIN

AND

JOHN ERNEST LEONARD OULTON, B.D.

LECTURER ON THE BIBLE IN THE UNIVERSITY OF DUBLIN

VOLUME I
TRANSLATION

LONDON
SOCIETY FOR PROMOTING
CHRISTIAN KNOWLEDGE
NEW YORK AND TORONTO: THE MACMILLAN CO.

First published 1927

PRINTED IN GREAT BRITAIN BY RICHARD CLAY & SONS, LIMITED,
BUNGAY, SUFFOLK.

PREFACE

In the first volume of this work will be found a translation of the ten books of the *Ecclesiastical History* of Eusebius, and also of the two recensions of the *Martyrs of Palestine*.

As to our special treatment of the *Martyrs of Palestine*, we must refer our readers to the detailed account given in the Introduction (vol. ii); but it may be well to state at once our method and aim with regard to the *History*.

We have followed throughout the text of E. Schwartz (Leipzig, 1903–1909), except in a few passages in which we have stated our preference for variants noted in his *apparatus criticus*. It is hoped that the opportunity, denied to our predecessors, of using a finely-edited critical text will give this translation into English additional value.

In presenting the work to the reader, smaller type has been used for direct, formal quotations; while italics indicate that Eusebius has embodied in his own narrative words taken from other sources. Wherever the Bible is quoted, directly or indirectly, the wording of the Revised Version has been employed, as far as possible.

The style of Eusebius has failed to win the admiration of posterity, and, especially, of those who have attempted to translate him. A distinguished scholar describes it as " wearying the reader by a rhetoric at once turgid and obscure "; and although the *History* contains some powerful and eloquent passages from the pen of its author, it must be admitted that Dr. Swete's criticism is, on the whole, just. And herein, indeed, lies precisely the difficulty that besets a translator. To reproduce literally the long and involved periods of the Bishop of Cæsarea would, obviously, be impossible; but, on the other hand, in an historical work of such importance, where so much often turns upon the rendering of a phrase, the greatest care must be taken not to misrepresent the original. The present work aims at giving as readable a translation as is consistent with a strict regard to accuracy. But the translator feels that in the last resort he must fall back on the plea of one of his predecessors, who says : " nous ne pouvions donner au style d'Eusèbe les qualités qui lui manquent le plus."

Several passages in the *History* have given rise to many and varied interpretations on the part of scholars; but it has not been thought advisable to overload vol. i with numerous alternative renderings. If such, therefore, are omitted, it must not be inferred that they have not been considered.

In the preparation of this volume many translations of the *History* or of passages therein have been consulted, which it is impossible to mention here by name; but a special reference must be made to the well-known work of Dr. A. C. McGiffert in the Library of the Nicene and Post-Nicene Fathers; nor can we omit to acknowledge the kindness of Dr. J. Armitage Robinson in lending us the MS. of a translation, made by him, of a portion of Book vi. Unfortunately, Dr. Kirsopp Lake's translation of Books i–v (Loeb Classical Library) only reached us when this volume was already in print.

We think it well to state here that Mr. Oulton is responsible for the translation of the Greek text in vol. i, and Dr. Lawlor for the Introduction and Notes which comprise vol. ii. But each has criticized the work of the other.

Finally, we must express our sincere thanks for the help given us by two of our colleagues in Trinity College. Mr. William Kennedy performed the troublesome task of revising the translation of the Syriac text of the *Martyrs of Palestine* ; and Professor R. M. Gwynn undertook the larger, if somewhat less complicated, labour of reading and criticizing the translation of the Greek text of the *History*. We have gratefully accepted most of their many suggestions. Our thanks are also due to the Rev. H. M. Harriss for assisting us in the correction of the proofs.

H. J. L.
J. E. L. O.

January 1927.

ABBREVIATIONS AND EDITIONS USED

A.	Fragments of a Syriac Version of L.	S. E. Assemani, *Acta sanctorum Martyrorum*, 1748.
AA.SS.	Bollandist *Acta Sanctorum*.	
Acta Achatii	*Acta disputationis S. Achatii*.	*A.M.S.*, p. 115.
Acta Apoll.	Acts of Apollonius.	*A.M.S.*, p. 44. E.T., Conybeare, *Mon.*, p. 35.
	Acta Pauli et Theclæ.	Lipsius-Bonnet, i. p. 235. E.T., James, p. 272.
Acta Tarachi	*Acta Tarachi, Probi et Andronici*.	Ruinart, p. 419. E.T., Mason, p. 201.
	Acts of Peter.	Lipsius-Bonnet, i. p. 45. E.T., James, p. 300.
Afric., *ad Arist.*	Julii Africani, *Epistola ad Aristidem*.	Routh, *R.S.*, ii. p. 228; W. Reichardt (*T.U.* xxxiv. 3), 1909. E.T., *A.N.L.*, ix. 2, p. 164.
Allard	La Persécution de Dioclétien et le Triomphe de l'Église, par P. Allard, 1908.	
	Ambrose, *de Paradiso*.	C. Schenkl, 1897.
A.M.S.	O. von Gebhardt, *Acta Martyrum Selecta*, 1902.	
	Analecta Bollandiana.	
Anecd. Oxon.	*Anecdota Oxoniensia*, Classical Series.	
A.N.L.	Ante-Nicene Library.	
Anon. Vales.	*Anonymus Valesianus*.	T. Mommsen in *M.G.H.*, Chronica Minora, i. p. 1.
Append.	"Appendix to Book VIII," vol. i. p. 401.	
Arnobius, *adv. Nat.*	Arnobius, *adversus Nationes*.	A. Reifferscheid, 1875.
Ath., *Arian.*;	Athanasius, *Historia Arianorum ad Monachos;*	*P.G.*, xxv. pp. 695, 411; E.T., A. Robertson in *P.N.F.*, ser. 2, vol. iv.
Dec.	*Epistola de Nicænis Decretis.*	
Ath., *Fest. Lett.*	Athanasius, *Festal Letters.*	*P.N.F.*, 2. iv. (E.T.).
Athenag., *Supp.*	Athenagoras, *Supplicatio pro Christianis.*	Otto, vii. E.T., *A.N.L.*, ii.
Aubé.	B. Aubé, *Histoire des Persécutions de l'Église*, 1875, 1878.	

Aug., *Brev. Coll.*; *Hœr.*; *Epp.*	Augustinus, *Breviculus Collationis cum Donatistis*; *de Hœresibus*; *Epistolœ.*	M. Petschenig, 1910; *P.L.*, xlii., xliii; A. Goldbacher, 1895–1911.
Bardenhewer.	O. Bardenhewer, *Geschichte der Altkirchlichen Literatur*, 1913–1924.	
Bardy.	G. Bardy, *Paul de Samosate*, 1923.	
Benson.	E. W. Benson, *Cyprian, his Life, his Times, his Work*, 1897.	
Bethune-Baker.	J. F. Bethune-Baker, *Introduction to the Early History of Christian Doctrine*, 1903.	
Bingham.	J. Bingham, *Origines Ecclesiasticœ*, 1840.	
Bury, *R. E.*	J. B. Bury, *Student's Roman Empire*, 1896.	
C.	Syriac Version of L.	W. Cureton, 1861.
Cabrol.	Cabrol, *Dictionnaire d'Archéologie Chrétienne*, 1907.	
Cass., *Coll.*	Cassianus, *Collationes.*	M. Petschenig, 1886.
Chronicle.	Eusebius, *Chronica.*	J. K. Fotheringham, 1923 (for Hieronymian Version); A. Schoene, 1866, 1875.
Chron. Pasch.	*Chronicon Paschale.*	L. Dindorf, 1832.
C.I.G.	*Corpus Inscriptionum Grœcarum.*	
C.I.L.	*Corpus Inscriptionum Latinarum.*	
Clem., *Ep.*	First Epistle of Clement of Rome.	J. B. Lightfoot, 1890; E.T., J. A. F. Gregg (S.P.C.K.), 1899; K. Lake (*L.C.L.*), 1912.
Clem. Hom.	Clementine Homilies.	A. R. M. Dressel, 1853. E.T., *A.N.L.*, xvii.
Clem. Recog.	Clementine Recognitions.	J. B. Cotelier, 1672. E.T., *A.N.L.*, iii.
Clem., *Hypot.*; *Pœd.*; *Protrept.*; *Q.D.S.*; *Strom.*	Clement of Alexandria, *Hypotyposeis*; *Pœdagogus*; *Protrepticus ad Grœcos*; *Quis dives salvetur*; *Stromateis.*	O. Stählin, 1905–1909. E.T., *A.N.L.*, iv., xii., xxii. 2, xxiv; (*Protrept.* and *Q.D.S.*) G. W. Butterworth (*L.C.L.*), 1919; (*Strom.*) P. M. Barnard (S.P.C.K.), 1901. *Q.D.S.*, ed. by P. M. Barnard (*T.S.*, v. 2), 1897. *Strom.*, vii., ed. (with E.T.) by F. J. A. Hort and J. B. Mayor, 1902.
Const. Ap.	*Constitutiones Apostolorum.*	F. X. Funk, 1905. E.T., *A.N.L.*, xvii.

Conybeare, *Mon.*	F. C. Conybeare, *The Armenian Apology and Acts of Apollonius and other Monuments of Early Christianity,* 1896.	
Cramer, *Anecd.* ; *Cat.*	J. A. Cramer, *Anecdota Græca e manuscriptis Bibliothecæ Regiæ Parisiensis,* 1839–41 ; *Catenæ Græcorum Patrum in Nov. Test.,* 1844.	
Cyp., *de Unit.* ; *de Lapsis* ; *Epp.* ; *Sent. episc.*	Cyprian, *de Catholicæ Ecclesiæ Unitate* ; *de Lapsis* ; *Epistolæ* ; *Sententiæ Episcoporum.*	G. Hartel, 1868. E.T., *A.N.L.,* viii., xiii.
D. Addai.	*The Doctrine of Addai.*	G. Phillips (with E.T.), 1876.
D.C.A.	Smith-Cheetham, *Dict. of Christian Antiquities,* 1875, 1880.	
D.C.B.	Smith-Wace, *Dict. of Christian Biography,* 1877–1880.	
D.G.R.B. ; *D.G.R.G.*	W. Smith, *Dict. of Greek and Roman Biography,* etc., 1844–1849; *Dict. of Gr. and Rom. Geography* ; 1856–7.	
de Boor.	C. de Boor, *Neue Fragmente des Papias, Hegesippus und Pierius* (*T.U.*, v. 2, p. 165), 1888.	
de Labriolle, *Crise* ; *Sources.*	P. de Labriolle, *La Crise Montaniste* ; *Les Sources de l'Histoire du Montanisme,* 1913.	
Dion. Alex., *ul* *Herm.* ; *Prom.*	Dionysius of Alexandria, Epistle to Hermammon ; *On Promises.*	C. L. Feltoe, 1904. E.T., by same (S.P.C.K.), 1918.
Dittrich.	J. J. S. Dittrich, *Dionysius der Grosse,* 1867.	
Duchesne, *Hist. Ch.*	L. Duchesne, *Early History of the Christian Church* (E.T.). 1910– .	
Duruy.	V. Duruy, *History of Rome and the Roman People* (E.T.), 1882–1886.	
Encyc. Bib.	Cheyne-Black, *Encyclopædia Biblica,* 1899–1903.	
Epiph., *Anaceph.* ; *Hær.* ; *Mens.*	Ephiphanius, *Anacephalæosi* ; *Panarion* ; *de Mensibus et Ponderibus.*	W. Dindorf, 1859–1862.
E.R.E.	J. Hastings, *Encyclopædia of Religion and Ethics,* 1908–1921.	
E.T.	English Translation.	
Eus., *c. Marcell.*	Eusebius, *contra Marcellum.*	E. Klostermann, 1906.

ABBREVIATIONS AND EDITIONS USED

Eus., *Dem. Ev. ;* *Ecl. Proph.*	Eusebius, *Demonstratio Evangelica ; Eclogæ Propheticæ.*	T. Gaisford, 1852, 1842. E.T., *Dem. Ev.*, W. J. Ferrar (S.P.C.K.), 1920.
Eus., *Præp. Ev.*	Eusebius, *Præparatio Evangelica.*	E. H. Gifford (with E.T.), 1903.
Eus., *Theoph.*	Eusebius, *Theophania.*	S. Lee, 1842 ; H. Gressmann (Grk. Frags.), 1903. E.T., S. Lee, 1843.
Eus., *V.C.*	Eusebius, *Vita Constantini.*	J. A. Heikel, 1902. E.T., *P.N.F.*, i.
Euseb.	H. J. Lawlor, *Eusebiana,* 1912.	
Eutropius.	Eutropius, *Breviarium Historiæ Roma.*	A. J. Valpy, 1821.
Feltoe.	C. F. Feltoe, *The Letters and other Remains of Dionysius of Alexandria,* 1904.	
G.	Fragments of the Greek text of L.	E. Schwartz, 1908.
g.	Notices of Martyrs, in the Greek Menæa, etc., based on L.	
Gibbon.	E. Gibbon, *Decline and Fall of the Roman Empire,* ed. J. B. Bury, 1897–1900.	
Gregg.	J. A. F. Gregg, *The Decian Persecution,* 1897.	
Gregory, *Pan.*	Gregory, *Panegyric on Origen.*	P. Koetschau, 1894. E.T., W. Metcalfe (S.P.C.K.), 1907.
Gwatkin.	H. M. Gwatkin, *Early Church History to* A.D. 313, 1919.	
Harnack, *Uberlief. ; Chron.*	A. Harnack, *Geschichte der altchristlichen Litteratur,* Th. 1, 2, 1893–1904.	
Harnack, *Expansion.*	A. Harnack, *The Mission and Expansion of Christianity in the First Three Centuries* (E.T.), 1908.	
Hartel.	G. Hartel, *S. Cypriani Opera Omnia,* 1868–1871.	
Harvey.	W. W. Harvey, *S. Irenæi Libri Quinque adversus Hæreses,* 1857.	
H.E.	*Historia Ecclesiastica.*	
Hefele.	C. J. Hefele, *History of the Councils of the Church* (E.T.), 1871–1896.	
Heg.	Hegesippus, *Memoirs.* Hermas, *Shepherd.*	*Euseb.*, pp. 1–107. Lightfoot-Harmer, and K. Lake (*L.C.L.*) 1913 (both with E.T.). E.T., C. Taylor (S.P.C.K.), 1903, 1906.

Hippol., *Ref.*	Hippolytus, *Omnium Heresium Refutatio.*	Wendland, 1916. E.T., F. Legge (S.P.C.K.), 1921.
Hippol., *Syntag.*	Hippolytus, *Syntagma against Thirty-two Heresies.*	R. A. Lipsius, *Zur Quellenkritik des Epiphanios,* 1865.
Hist. Laus.	*Historia Lausiaca.*	C. Butler (*T.S.*), 1898, 1904. E.T., W. K. L. Clarke (S.P.C.K.), 1918.
Hort, *Jud. Christ.*	F. J. A. Hort, *Judaistic Christianity,* 1894.	
Ign.	Epistles of Ignatius.	J. B. Lightfoot (with E.T.), 1885. E.T., J. H. Srawley (S.P.C.K.), 1919; K. Lake (*L.C.L.*), 1912.
Iren.	Irenæus, *Against Heresies.*	W. W. Harvey, 1857. E.T., *A.N.L.*, v., ix.
James.	M. R. James, *The Apocryphal New Testament,* 1924.	
Jer., *Apol.* ; *Gal.* ; *Quæst.*	Hieronymus, *Apologia adversus libros Rufini* ; *Commentaria in Epistolam ad Galatos ; Quæstiones Hebraicæ.*	*P.L.*, xxiii., xxvi. E.T. (*Apol.*), *P.N.F.*, ser. 2, iii.
Jer., *Epp.* Jer., *V.I.*	Hieronymus, *Epistolæ.* Hieronymus, *Liber de Viris Illustribus.*	J. Hilberg, 1910, 1912. E. C. Richardson (*T.U.*, xiv. 1), 1896. E.T., *P.N.F.*, u.s.
Jos., *Ant.* ; *Ap.* ; *B.J.* ; *Vita.*	Josephus, *Antiquities of the Jews* ; *Treatise against Apion* ; *Wars of the Jews* ; *Autobiography.*	B. Niese, 1887–1895; S. A. Naber, 1888–1896. E.T., A. R. Shilleto, 1889, 1890; (*B.J.*, *Vita*) R. Traill, 1862.
Jul.	Julian, *Orationes.*	F. C. Hertlein, 1875, 1876. E.T., C. W. King, 1888.
Just., *Apol.* i, ii; *Dial.*	Justin Martyr, *First and Second Apologies ; Dialogue with Trypho.*	J. C. T. Otto, 1876, 1877; (*Apol.*) A. W. F. Blunt, 1911. E.T., *A.N.L.*, ii.
L. Lact., *Inst.* ; *Mort.*	Longer recension of *M.P.* Lactantius, *Divinæ Institutiones ; De Mortibus Persecutorum.*	S. Brandt, 1890. E.T., *A.N.L.*, xxi., xxii.
Lat.	Fragments of Latin Versions of L.	B. Violet, 1896.
L.C.L.	Loeb Classical Library. Liberian Catalogue.	T. Mommsen in *M.G.H.*, Chron. Min. ; Lightfoot, *Clem.*, i. 253.
Lightfoot, *Clem.* ; *Ign.* Lightfoot, *Col.* ; *Phil.* ; *S.R.*	J. B. Lightfoot, *The Apostolic Fathers,* Pt. I, 1890; Pt. II, 1889. *Epistles to Colossians and Philemon,* 1884; *to Philippians,* 1883; *Essays on Supernatural Religion,* 1889.	

Lightfoot-Harmer.	J. B. Lightfoot and J. R. Harmer, *Apostolic Fathers*, 1891.	
Lipsius-Bonnet.	R. A. Lipsius and M. Bonnet, *Acta Apostolorum Apocrypha* 1891–1893.	
Loofs.	F. Loofs, *Paulus von Samosata* (*T.U.*, xliv. 5), 1924.	
Macar. Mag.	Macarius Magnes, *Apocriticus*.	C. Blondel, 1876. E.T., T. W. Crafer (S.P.C.K.), 1919.
Mansi.	J. D. Mansi, *Sacrorum Conciliorum Collectio*.	
Marquardt-Mommsen.	J. Marquardt and T. Mommsen, *Handbuch der römischen Alterthümer*, 1878–1888.	
Mart. Pion.	Martyrdom of Pionius.	*A.M.S.*, 96.
Mart. Pol.	Martyrdom of Polycarp (the Epistle of the Smyrnæans).	Lightfoot in *Ign.*, iii. (with E.T.).
Mason.	A. J. Mason, *The Persecution of Diocletian*, 1876.	
Merrill.	E. T. Merrill, *Essays in Early Christian History*, 1924.	
M.G.H.	*Monumenta Germaniæ Historica*.	
Mommsen, *Prov.*	T. Mommsen, *The Provinces of the Roman Empire* (E.T.), 1886.	
M.P.	Eusebius, *Martyrs of Palestine*.	
N.P.F.	*Nicene and Post-Nicene Fathers*.	
Optatus.	Optatus, *De Schismate Donatistarum*.	C. Ziwsa, 1893.
Orig., *Cels.; Joh.; Mart.; Orat.; Princip.*	Origen, *Contra Celsum; Commentary on John; De Martyrio; De Oratione; De Principiis*.	P. Koetschau, E. Klostermann and F. Preuschen, 1899–1913. *Joh.*, also ed. by A. E. Brooke, 1896. E.T., *A.N.L.*, x., xxiii., and additional volume.
Orig., *Luc.; Matt.; Ep. ad African.*	Origen, *Homilies on Luke; Commentary on Matthew; Epistola ad Africanum*.	*P.G.*, xiii. 1801, 829; xi. 47. E.T., *A.N.L.*, additional volume and x. 371.
Orig., *Phil.*	Origen, *Philocalia*.	J. A. Robinson, 1893.
Otto.	J. C. T. de Otto, *Corpus Apologetarum Christianorum*, 1851–1881.	
Oxyr. Pap.	A. P. Grenfell and A. S. Hunt, *Oxyrhynchus Papyri*, 1898—.	

Paneg.	xii *Panegyrici Latini.*	A. Baehrens, 1874.
P.G.	Migne, *Patrologia Græca.*	
Philo, *D.V.C. ;* Leg.	Philo, *De Vita Contemplativa ; De Legatione ad Gaium.*	L. Cohn and S. Reiter, 1915. E.T., C. D. Yonge, 1854–5.
Photius.	Photius, *Bibliotheca.*	I. Bekker, 1824–5. E.T., J. H. Freese (S.P.C.K.), 1920– .
Pilg.	The Pilgrimage of Silvia (or Etheria).	J. F. Gamurrini, 1887. E.T., J. H. Bernard, 1891; M. L. McClure and C. L. Feltoe (S.P.C.K.), 1919.
P.L.	Migne, *Patrologia Latina.*	
P.N.F.	Library of Nicene and Post-Nicene Fathers.	
Pol., *Phil.*	Epistle of Polycarp to the Philippians.	J. B. Lightfoot, *Ign.*, iii. (with E.T.). K. Lake (*L.C.L.* with E.T.), 1912.
Ps.-Cyp., *Spect.*	Pseudo-Cyprianus (Novatianus), *De Spectaculis.*	G. Hartel, iii. E.T., *A.N.L.*, xiii.
Ps.-Tert., *Hær.*	Pseudo-Tertullianus, *Libellus adversus Omnes Hæreses.*	A. Kroymann, *Tertulliani Opera*, iii. 213, 1906. E.T., *A.N.L.*, xviii. 259.
Ramsay, *Phrygia ;* R.E. ; Discov.	W. M. Ramsay, *Cities and Bishoprics of Phrygia*, 1895, 1897; *The Church in the Roman Empire*, 1893; *The Bearing of Recent Discovery on the Trustworthiness of the New Testament*, 1915.	
R.E.	Pauly-Wissowa, *Real-Encyclopädie der classischen Altertumswissenschaft*, 1894.	
Routh, *R.S.*	M. J. Routh, *Reliquiæ Sacræ*, 1846–1848.	
Rufinus.	Rufinus, *Eusebii Ecclesiasticæ Historiæ.*	T. Mommsen in Schwartz.
Ruinart.	J. Ruinart, *Acta Primorum Martyrum Sincera et Selecta*, 1713.	
Salmon, *Infall. ;* Introd.	G. Salmon, *The Infallibility of the Church*, 1888; *A Historical Introduction to the Study of the Books of the New Testament*, 1889.	
Schürer.	E. Schürer, *History of Jewish People in the Time of Jesus Christ* (E.T.), 1890–1896.	
Schwartz.	E. Schwartz, *Eusebius Werke*, Bd. 2, *Die Kirchengeschichte*, 1903–1909.	

Smith, *Holy Land*	G. A. Smith, *Historical Geography of the Holy Land*, 1896.	
S.P.A.	Sitzungsberichte der Preussischen Akademie.	
Sueton.	Suetonius, *De Vita Cæsarum.*	C. L. Roth, 1893.
Swete.	H. B. Swete, *Introduction to the Old Testament in Greek*, 1900.	
Syriac Martyrology.	The Syriac Martyrology of 411.	H. Lietzmann (German translation), 1911.
Tac., *Ann.* ; *Hist.*	Tacitus, *Annales* ; *Historiæ.*	A. J. Valpy, 1821.
Tat., *ad Græc.*	Tatianus, *Oratio ad Græcos.*	E. Schwartz (*T.U.*, iv. 1), 1888. E.T., *A.N.L.*, iii.
Tat., *Diatess.*	Tatianus, *Diatessaron.*	J. H. Hill (E.T.), 1894.
Tert., *Marc.* ; *Prax.* ; *Res.* ; *Val.*	Tertullian, *Adversus Marcionem* ; *Adversus Praxeam* ; *De Resurrectione Carnis* ; *Adversus Valentinianos.*	A. Kroymann, 1906.
Tert., *An.* ; *Pud.*	Tertullian, *De Anima* ; *de Pudicitia.*	A. Reifferscheid and G. Wissowa, 1890.
Tert., *Apol.*	Tertullian, *Apologeticus.*	J. E. B. Mayor (with E.T., by A. Souter), 1917.
Tert., *Fug.* ; *Jud.* ; *Pal.* ; *Præsc.*	Tertullian, *De Fuga in Persecutione* ; *Adversus Judæos* ; *de Pallio* ; *De Præscriptionibus Hæreticorum.*	*P.L.*, ii.
		E.T. of all the above, *A.N.L.*, vii., xi., xv., xviii.; also of *Prax.* and *Res.* by A. Souter (S.P.C.K.), 1919, 1922; of *Præsc.* by T. H. Bindley (S.P.C.K.), 1914.
Theodoret, *H.E.* ; *H.F.*	Theodoret, *Historia Ecclesiastica* ; *Hæreticarum Fabularum Compendium.*	*P.G.*, lxxxii., lxxxiii.
Theoph., *Ad Autol.*	Theophilus, *Ad Autolycum.*	J. C. T. Otto, vii., 1861. E.T., *A.N.L.*, iii.
Tollinton.	R. B. Tollinton, *Clement of Alexandria*, 1914.	
T.S.	*Texts and Studies.*	
T.U.	*Texte und Untersuchungen.*	
Vict., *Cæs.* ; *Epit.*	Sextus Aurelius Victor, *Cæsarum Historia* ; *Epitome.*	A. J. Valpy, 1829.

Violet.	B. Violet, *Die Palästin-ischen Märtyrer* (*T.U.*, xiv. 4), 1896.	
Zahn, *Forsch.* ;	T. Zahn, *Forschungen zur Geschichte des neutesta-mentlichen Kanons,*	
K.G.	1881–1916; *Geschichte des neutestamentlichen Kanons,* 1888, 1892.	
Z.K.G.	*Zeitschrift für Kirchen-geschichte.*	
Zos.	Zosimus.	I. Bekker, 1837.

CONTENTS

	PAGE
PREFACE	V
ABBREVIATIONS AND EDITIONS USED . . .	vii
ECCLESIASTICAL HISTORY :	
BOOK I	1
BOOK II	33
BOOK III	63
BOOK IV	103
BOOK V	137
BOOK VI	175
BOOK VII	217
BOOK VIII	253
BOOK IX	277
BOOK X	297
MARTYRS OF PALESTINE	327
APPENDIX TO BOOK VIII	401

BOOK I

The First Book of the Ecclesiastical History contains the following:

1. The plan of the projected work.
2. A summary discussion of the pre-existence and divinity of our Saviour and Lord, the Christ of God.
3. That the name Jesus, and also the very name Christ, had been known from the beginning and honoured by the divinely inspired prophets.
4. That the nature of the religion proclaimed by Him to all the nations was not modern nor even strange.
5. On the time of His appearing among men.
6. That in His time, in accordance with the prophecies, those rulers who had formerly governed the nation of the Jews by right of succession from their forefathers came to an end; and that Herod was the first foreigner to be their king.
7. On the supposed discrepancy in the Gospels as to the genealogy of Christ.
8. On the attempt of Herod upon the children, and the manner of the death which overtook him.
9. On the times of Pilate.
10. On the high priests among the Jews, in whose day Christ taught.
11. The testimonies concerning John the Baptist and Christ.
12. On the disciples of our Saviour.
13. Narrative concerning the prince of the people of Edessa.

PREFACE

The Plan of the History.

1. THE successions from the holy apostles, together with the times that have elapsed from our Saviour's day down to our own; the important affairs that are said to have been transacted in the history of the Church, and those who took a prominent place in that history as leaders and presidents in such communities as were especially famous; those who in each generation were ambassadors of the divine word, either orally or by means of treatises also; the names, number and times of all those who through love of innovation fell into the most grievous error, and have proclaimed themselves as introducers of *knowledge falsely so called,*[1] unsparingly like 2 *grievous wolves* ravaging *the flock*[2] of Christ; the disasters, moreover, that fell upon the whole Jewish nation immediately after their plot against our Saviour; as also the extent, nature and times of the war which has been waged by the heathen against the divine word, and the noble men who as occasion offered endured death and torture in the conflict on its behalf; the martyrdoms, after these things, that took place in our day also, and the gracious and kindly succour of our Saviour at the end of all: these it is my purpose to commit to writing, yet my starting-point shall be none other than the beginning of the dispensation of Jesus, our Saviour and Lord, the Christ of God.

Difficulties of the Enterprise.

3 But our book in consequence must crave a lenient judgment from the indulgent. It acknowledges that it is beyond our powers to fulfil our promise completely and without omission, for we are the first to undertake this present project and to attempt, as it were, to travel along a lonely and untrodden path. We pray that we may have God as our guide, and the power of the Lord as our fellow-worker; but, as regards man, we can in no wise discover the clear tracks of those who have preceded us on the same path, but only faint traces, in which in their several ways they have bequeathed to us particular accounts of the times through which they passed, lifting up their voices like beacons from afar and crying from on high,

---

[1] 1 Tim. vi. 20. [2] Acts xx. 29.

3

as out of some watch-tower or from some outlook, to admonish us as to the path along which we ought to walk and direct the
4 course of our book so as to escape error and danger.   We have gathered, therefore, from among the things that these same persons have mentioned here and there, whatsoever we deemed profitable for the project in hand, and having plucked, as it were, from meadows of literature suitable passages from these authors of long ago, we shall attempt to embody them in an historical narrative : happy if we may preserve the successions from the apostles of our Saviour, if not in every case, at least the most renowned of them, in those churches that are still
5 pre-eminent and of note to this day.   And I consider that my labours in this project are most urgently needed, for among the ecclesiastical writers I know none who has hitherto given his attention to this department of writing; and I trust that they will also prove of the greatest benefit to those who are
6 eager for the useful learning afforded by history.   Indeed, I have already made an epitome of these things on a former occasion in the Chronological Canons which I drew up; but nevertheless in this present work I have set out to supply the
7 fullest account of them.   And my book will begin, as I said,[1] with the dispensation and divinity of Christ, a conception
8 too lofty and great for man's intelligence.   For he who would commit to writing the history that contains the Church's narrative, must needs begin from the first with the beginning of the dispensation of Christ Himself (since we have been deemed worthy to derive even our name from Him), a dispensation more divine than most men imagine.

INTRODUCTION

The Beginning of the Dispensation of the Word.

2.   Now since in Him there are two modes of being, and the one may be likened to the head of the body, in that He is conceived of as God, and the other may be compared to the feet, in that for our salvation He assumed human nature *of like passions with us* :[2] our statement of what follows will accordingly be complete, if we begin the narrative of His whole history with the chiefest and most important attributes of the Word.   And in this way also the antiquity and divine character that surround the beginnings of Christianity will be manifested to those who conceive of it as newfangled and outlandish in its origin, a creature of no earlier date than yesterday.
2   So then, no words could be sufficient to express the origin and worth, that is, the very essence and nature of the Christ, inasmuch as even the divine Spirit says in prophetic words,

[1] § 2.   [2] Cp. Acts xiv. 15; James v. 17.

Who shall declare his generation? [1]   For in truth *neither* did *anyone* know *the Father, save the Son* ; nor on the other hand did ever any worthily know *the Son, save* only *the Father* [2] who
3 begat Him. As for *the Light* which was before the world,[3] and the Wisdom, *quick of understanding* [4] and having essential being, which was before the ages,[5] and the *Word* which was living and *in the beginning* was *God* with the Father,[6] who except the Father can clearly conceive of Him ?—the first and only begotten of God before *every creature* and thing made, whether seen or *invisible*,[7] the *captain of the* spiritual and immortal *host* in *heaven*,[8] *the angel of mighty counsel*,[9] the attendant upon the ineffable will of the Father, the maker of all things with the Father, the second cause, after the Father, of the universe, the true and only-begotten Son of God, the Lord and God and King of all creatures, who has received from the Father the supreme authority and *dominion* together with deity and *power* and *honour* ; [10] for in truth, as the Scriptures bear witness to His divinity in mystic language,

In the beginning was the Word, and the Word was with God, and the Word was God. . . . All things were made by him; and without him was not anything made.[11]

4   Therefore the great Moses also, as the most ancient of all the prophets, in describing, under the influence of the divine Spirit, the coming into being and ordering of the whole, tells us of the Orderer and Creator of the universe conceding to the very Christ Himself, and to none other (it is plain) than His divine and first-begotten Word, the making of inferior creatures, and holding converse with Him on the begetting of man. For, says he, *God said, Let us make man in our image, and after*
5 *our likeness*.[12]   And to this word another of the prophets gives his surety, when he speaks of God on this wise in hymns : *He spake, and they were made ; He commanded, and they were created*.[13]   Thus he introduces the Father and Maker as giving commands like a universal ruler by His sovereign will ; and, holding the second place to Him, the divine Word—none other than He whom we proclaim—as doing service to His Father's behests.

[1] Isai. liii. 8.   [2] Matt. xi. 27.
[3] Cp. John i. 9.   [4] Wisdom vii. 22.
[5] Cp. Prov. viii. 23.   [6] John i. 1, 2.
[7] Col. i. 15, 16.   [8] Josh. v. 14; 1 Kin. xxii. 19.
[9] Isai. ix. 6 (LXX).   [10] Rev. v. 12, 13.
[11] John i. 1, 3.   [12] Gen. i. 26.
[13] Ps. xxxiii. 9; cxlviii. 5.

The Theophanies.

6   And even from the time when man was first begotten, all who are said to have excelled in righteousness and the virtue of reverence, namely, the followers of the great *servant Moses* [1] —yea, and before him Abraham first of all, his children, and as many just men and prophets as afterwards appeared— recognized the vision of Him which they perceived by the pure eyes of the mind, and accorded Him, as Son of God, fitting
7   honour.   And He, on His part, in no wise neglecting the piety due to His Father, became the teacher of them all in the knowledge of His Father.   For example, the Lord *God* is said to have *appeared* as an ordinary man to Abraham *as he sat by the oak of Mamre.*   And straightway he fell down, and, though it was a man that he saw with his eyes, *worshipped* Him as God, besought Him as Lord, and confessed that he was not ignorant who He was;   for he addressed Him in these words : *O Lord, shall not the Judge of all the earth do right ?* [2]
8   For if reason does not permit that the uncreated and immutable essence of God Almighty should be changed into the form of a man, or, on the other hand, should deceive the eyes of those who beheld it with the apparition of a created being that did not exist, or that the Scripture should falsely invent such things : what other name may be given to Him, the God and *Lord who judgeth all the earth* and *doeth right,* who is seen *in the fashion* of *a man* [3] (since we may not style Him the First Cause of the universe), except His only pre-existent Word ? Concerning whom it has also been said in the Psalms, *He sent his word, and healed them, and delivered them from their*
9   *destructions.* [4]   Him does Moses most clearly name as second Lord after the Father when he says, *The Lord rained upon Sodom and Gomorrah brimstone and fire from the Lord.* [5]   When He appeared also to Jacob once again *in the fashion* of a man, [3] the divine Scripture calls Him God;   when He said to Jacob, *Thy name shall be called no more Jacob, but Israel shall be thy name : for thou hast had power with God* ; [6] when also *Jacob called the name of that place Vision of God,* saying, *for I have seen God face to face, and my life was preserved.* [7]
10   And further, it is not permissible to regard the recorded theophanies as appearances of inferior angels and ministers of God, since when any of these appears to men, the Scripture uses no concealment, for it states that they are called by name, not " God " nor even " Lord," but " angels " ; as it would be
11   easy to prove by countless testimonies.   Joshua also, Moses'

[1] Num. xii. 7; Heb. iii. 5.   [2] Gen. xviii. 1, 2, 25.
[3] Phil. ii. 8.   [4] Ps. cvii. 20.
[5] Gen. xix. 24.   [6] Gen. xxxii. 28.
[7] Gen. xxxii. 30.

successor, when he beheld Him none otherwise than, once again, in *the form* and *fashion* of *a man*,[1] named Him *captain of the host of the Lord*,[2] as the leader of the celestial angels and archangels and of the supermundane hosts, and as being, so to speak, *the power and wisdom* [3] of the Father, and entrusted with
12 the second place in the kingdom and rule over all.   Thus it is written :

And it came to pass, when Joshua was at Jericho, that he lifted up his eyes and saw a man standing over against him, and his sword drawn in his hand; and Joshua went unto him and said, Art thou for us, or for our adversaries ?   And he said to him, I am the captain of the host of the Lord; now am I come.   And Joshua fell on his face to the earth, and said unto him, Lord, what commandest thou thy servant ?   And the captain of the Lord said unto Joshua, Put off thy shoes from off thy feet; for the place whereon thou standest is a holy place.[4]

13 Here also you will gather from these words that this was none other than He who had also given direction to Moses; for the Scripture employs the same words in this case also :

And when the Lord saw that he turned aside to see, the Lord called unto him out of the midst of the bush, saying, Moses, Moses.   And he said, What is it ?   And he said, Draw not nigh hither : put off thy shoes from off thy feet, for the place whereon thou standest is holy ground.   And he said unto him, I am the God of thy father, the God of Abraham and the God of Isaac and the God of Jacob.[5]

The Pre-existence of the Word.

14 And that there is a certain essence living and subsisting before the world, which ministered to the Father and God of the universe in the making of all created things, called the Word of God and Wisdom, we may perceive not only from the proofs already set forth, but further from the person of Wisdom herself; for by the mouth of Solomon she initiates us in the clearest manner into the things of herself, as follows :

I, wisdom, have made counsel my dwelling-place,
And I have invoked knowledge and discretion.

.   .   .   .

By me kings reign,
And princes decree justice.
By me great ones are made great,
And tyrants by me rule the earth.[6]

15 To this he adds :
The Lord created me as the beginning of his ways for his works,
Before the world he established me.
In the beginning, before he made the earth . . .

---

[1] Phil. ii. 7, 8.   [2] Josh. v. 14.   [3] Cp. 1 Cor. i. 24.
[4] Josh. v. 13–15.   [5] Ex. iii. 4–6.   [6] Prov. viii. 12, 15, 16 (LXX).

Before the fountains of waters sprang forth,
Before the mountains were settled,
Before all hills he brought me forth.

When he prepared the heaven, I was by his side,

And when he made fast the fountains of the region under heaven,

I was with him as his workman.
I was daily his delight,
And I rejoiced before him at all times,
When he rejoiced at the completion of the inhabited earth.[1]

16   So, then, that the divine Word was pre-existent and appeared to some, even if not to all, let this our brief account suffice to show.

Why He was not sooner manifested to all.

17   Why, then, He was not preached, as He is now, to all men and to all nations in former days of old, will appear from the following. Men as they lived in the olden days were unable to receive the all-wise and all-virtuous teaching of the Christ.

18 Indeed in the beginning, immediately after his original life of blessedness, the first man lightly regarded the divine commandment, fell to this mortal and perishable condition and received this earth, laid under a curse,[2] in exchange for his former God-given delights.

And this man's descendants filled the whole earth as we know it,[3] and turned out much worse with the exception of one or two, entering upon a beast-like, intolerable mode of existence.

19 And what is more, they took no thought for city or state, arts or sciences; they did not possess even the name of laws and ordinances, nor, still further, of virtue and philosophy; but passed a nomadic life in the desert like wild and fierce creatures. The powers of reasoning that nature gives for man's possession and the seeds of thought and culture implanted in the human soul, these they destroyed by an excess of self-chosen wickedness. They had wholly given themselves over to all kinds of unhallowed deeds : at one time they would corrupt, at another slay, each other; or, yet again, devour human flesh; they essayed battles with gods, and those battles with giants that were so universally famous; they planned to fortify earth against heaven, nay, in wild frenzy of mind prepared to war on Him who is over all.

20   Whereupon, as they conducted themselves on this wise, God, who watches over all things, visited them with floods and

---

[1] Prov. viii. 22–25, 27, 28, 30, 31 (LXX).
[2] Cp. Gen. iii. 17.   [3] καθ' ἡμᾶς.

conflagrations, as though they were a wild forest spread over the face of the whole earth; with continuous famines and plagues, and again with wars and thunder-bolts from on high, He cut them off, increasing His chastisements as if to check some dread and very dangerous disease of their soul.

21　So then at that time, when wickedness was overshadowing and darkening the souls of almost the whole human race, and, like a deep fit of drunkenness, spread its profound torpor over little short of all mankind, the first-born and first-created Wisdom of God and the pre-existent Word Himself in His abundant love for men showed Himself, at times by a vision of angels to the inferior order of beings, and at times by Himself as the saving power of God, to some one or another of those men of old whom God loved; yet not otherwise than in human form, because it was not possible for them [to see Him] in

22　another way. And when by this means the seeds of godliness had come to be implanted in a multitude of men, and a whole nation upon the earth, sprung from the primitive Hebrews, was found to adhere stedfastly to godliness, He imparted to them by His prophet Moses, as to multitudes still imbued with their ancient practices, images and symbols of a certain mystic sabbath, and introduced circumcision and other spiritual principles. But He did not initiate them into their meaning clearly.

The Incarnation.

23　And when the legislation of the Jews became famous and like a fragrant breeze was spread abroad among all men, then, thanks to them, the minds also of the majority of the nations were now softened by their law-givers and philosophers everywhere, and their wild and fierce brutality was changed to a gentler mood; so that also that profound peace which comes from mutual friendship and intercourse prevailed. And then finally there appeared, in the early days of the Roman Empire, to all mankind and the nations throughout the world— as to men who, so to speak, had been previously helped and were now fitted to receive the knowledge of the Father—once again that same Teacher of virtue, the Minister of the Father in all good things, the divine and heavenly Word of God, in a human body which in no point essentially differed from that which our nature wears. He did and suffered such things as were in accordance with the prophecies; for they predicted that One, both man and God, would come to this world to perform miraculous deeds, and that He would show Himself to all the nations as a Teacher of the piety due to His Father; they foretold also His miraculous birth, the new teaching and the wonders of His works; and, moreover, the manner of His

9

death, His resurrection from the dead, and finally His divine restoration to the heavens.

24 For example, Daniel the prophet, in the vision which the divine Spirit vouchsafed him of His final kingdom, was thus inspired by God to describe it in terms more suited to human comprehension :

> For I beheld, says he, till thrones were placed, and one that was ancient of days did sit : and his raiment was white as snow, and the hair of his head like pure wool : his throne was a fiery flame, and the wheels thereof burning fire. A fiery stream issued from before him : thousand thousands ministered unto him, and ten thousand times ten thousand stood before him : he held the court of judgment, and the books were opened.[1]

25 And afterwards :

> I beheld, says he, . . . and, lo, there came with the clouds of heaven one like unto a son of man, and he came even to the ancient of days, and was brought near before him. And there was given him the rule, and the honour, and the kingdom, and all the peoples, tribes, and languages shall serve him : his dominion is an everlasting dominion, such as shall not pass away, and his kingdom shall not be destroyed.[2]

26 Now these words should clearly be referred to none other than to our Saviour, to Him who was *in the beginning with God, God the Word*,[3] called *Son of Man* because of His incarnation 27 at the last. But since we collected in special memoirs those selections from the prophets that relate to our Saviour Jesus Christ, and in other writings arranged in more convincing form what is revealed concerning Him, on the present occasion we shall content ourselves with what has been said.

The Names Jesus and Christ in Moses.

3. But now it is time to show also that the very name of Jesus, and of Christ as well, had been honoured by those prophets 2 of old who were dear to God. Moses himself was the first to make known the name of Christ in the most revered and glorious manner possible. He gave *patterns* and symbols of *heavenly things*, and mystic images in accordance with the *warning of God* which *said* to him, *See that thou make all things according to the pattern that was shewed thee in the mount* ; [4] and in calling the high priest of God by the name of *Christ* [5] he gave him a name of as high omen as it was possible for man to bear, and thus upon the high-priestly dignity, which in his opinion surpassed every post of honour among men, he con-

---

[1] Dan. vii. 9, 10 (Theodotion).   [2] Dan. vii. 13, 14 (Theodotion).
[3] John i. 1.   [4] Heb. viii. 5 [Exod. xxv. 40].
[5] " Anointed " (χριστός): Lev. iv. 5, 16 and vi. 22 (LXX).

ferred the additional honour and glory of the name of Christ. So convinced was he, it would seem, that the title Christ was something divine.

3 And Moses also was inspired by the divine Spirit to foresee with perfect clearness the name of Jesus; and, once again, he deemed this name also worthy of a special privilege. Certainly it had never before been on the lips of men, until it was made known to Moses; and he conferred the designation of Jesus on him first of all, and on him alone, who he knew would succeed (once more in a type and symbol) after his death to
4 the supreme command.[1] Certainly his successor had not formerly borne the name of Jesus; but was called by another, that of Ause, which his parents had given him. Moses himself called him Jesus, bestowing on him the name as if it were some precious honour, far greater than a kingly diadem; for in truth Jesus the son of Nave himself bore the image of our Saviour, of Him who alone, after Moses and the completion of the symbolic service that Moses was the means of transmitting, succeeded to the command in that true and most pure religion.
5 Thus indeed did Moses confer upon those two men who in his day surpassed all the people in merit and distinction—that is, upon the high priest and him who should be the leader after him—the name of our Saviour Christ as an exceeding great honour.

The Name Christ in Later Prophets.

6 And the prophets also who came after clearly spoke beforehand of the Christ by name, and bore prophetic witness, both to the plot that the Jewish people were to lay against Him, and also to the calling of the nations through Him. Thus at one time Jeremiah speaks as follows :

The Spirit of our face, the Lord Christ, was taken in their corruptions;
Of whom we said, Under his shadow we shall live among the nations; [2]

at another, David utters his perplexity in these words :

Why did the nations rage,
And the peoples imagine vain things ?
The kings of the earth set themselves in array,
And the rulers were gathered together,
Against the Lord and against his Christ.[3]

To this, further on, he adds, speaking in the person of Christ :

The Lord said unto me, Thou art my son;
This day have I begotten thee.
Ask of me, and I will give thee the nations for thine inheritance,
And the uttermost parts of the earth for thy possession.[4]

---

[1] Num. xiii. 16; xxvii. 15 ff.
[2] Lam. iv. 20 (LXX).   [3] Ps. ii. 1, 2.   [4] Ps. ii. 7, 8.

7 So then, not only were those, who had been honoured with
the high-priesthood and symbolically anointed with prepared
oil, adorned among the Hebrews with the name of the Christ,
but also the kings; whom the prophets anointed at the divine
command and thus made, as it were, into representations of
Christ : for in truth they also bore in their own persons the
types of the royal and supreme authority of the only and true
Christ, the divine Word, the universal King.

The Relation of High Priests, Kings and Prophets to Christ.

8 And it has actually come down to us that some also of these
same prophets have by anointing become typically Christs,
so that they all may be referred to the true Christ, the divine
and heavenly Word, who is the only High Priest of the universe,
the only King of all creation, and the only supreme Prophet
9 among His Father's prophets.   A proof of this lies in the fact
that none of those who in days gone by have been symbolically
anointed, be he priest or king or even prophet, ever possessed
the power of divinely-given virtue to such a degree as that
which our Saviour and Lord, Jesus, the only and true Christ,
10 has displayed.   None at least of those men, distinguished
though they were for dignity and honour among their own
people for numberless generations, ever bestowed upon their
subjects the well-omened name of Christians after their own
symbolic title of Christ.   Nay, none of them ever received the
honour of worship from his subjects.   Nay, none excited
such affection after his death that men were ready to die on
behalf of him whom they honoured.   Nay, none of them in his
day was the cause of such a commotion among all the nations
of the world; for the power of the symbol was unable to
produce among them an effect equal to that caused by the
11 presentation of the truth as exhibited by our Saviour.   He
received no symbols or types of the high-priesthood from anyone; nay, He did not trace His earthly descent from those
who had been priests, nor was He advanced to a kingdom by
military power, nor was He made a prophet like those of old,
nor did the Jews confer on Him any dignity at all or eminence;
nevertheless the Father has honoured Him with them all, if
12 not with the symbols, at any rate with the truth itself.   And
if, after all, He did not possess like honours with those we have
mentioned before, He is more justly styled Christ than they
all, and since He is the only true Christ of God, He has filled
the whole world with Christians, that truly revered and sacred
title of His ; and He has committed to His followers no longer
types or symbols, but the very [1] virtues themselves and heavenly
13 life in principles of absolute truth.   And He has received the
oil, not that prepared of material substances, but the oil of the

---

[1] Lit. naked, clear.

divine Spirit as befits His divinity, by His participation in that
divine nature which is unbegotten and of the Father.   And
this again is the very thing that Isaiah teaches us, when he
cries aloud, as if from the lips of Christ, on this wise :

> The spirit of the Lord is upon me ;
> Wherefore he anointed me to preach good tidings to the poor,
> He hath sent me . . .
> To proclaim release to the captives,
> And recovering of sight to the blind.[1]

14   Yea, and not alone Isaiah, but David also addresses His
person, saying,

> Thy throne, O God, is for ever and ever :
> A sceptre of equity is the sceptre of thy kingdom.
> Thou hast loved righteousness and hated wickedness :
> Therefore, O God, thy God hath anointed thee
> With the oil of gladness above thy fellows.[2]

Wherein the Scripture calls Him God in the first line, while
15 in the second it honours Him with a kingly sceptre ; then
further on, after giving Him divine and kingly power, it
represents Him in the third place as having become Christ,
anointed, not with oil formed from earthly materials, but with
the divine *oil of gladness*.[3]   And thus it indicates His especial
honour, much superior to and differing from those who in days
of old had been symbolically anointed in more material
fashion.

16   And elsewhere too David declares the things concerning
Him, saying somewhat as follows :

> The Lord said unto my Lord, Sit thou at my right hand,
> Until I make thine enemies the footstool of thy feet,

and

> From the womb before the daystar I begat thee.
> The Lord sware, and will not repent himself.
> Thou art a priest for ever
> After the order of Melchizedek.[4]

17   Now *this Melchizedek* is introduced in the sacred Scriptures
as *priest of God Most High*,[5] consecrated by no kind of prepared
oil ; nay, not belonging by descent to the Hebrew priesthood.
For this reason, *after* his *order*,[6] but not after the order of the
others who had received symbols and types, our Saviour was
proclaimed Christ and *priest* [6] *with* the taking of *an oath*.[7]
18 Wherefore history does not record Him as anointed on the
body by the Jews, nor even as descended from a *tribe* of
priests,[8] but as called into being by God Himself *before the*

[1] Luke iv. 18 [Isai. lxi. 1].   [2] Ps. xlv. 6, 7.
[3] *Ib.*   [4] Ps. cx. 1, 3, 4 (LXX).
[5] Heb. vii. 1 ; cp. Gen. xiv. 18.   [6] Ps. cx. 4.
[7] Heb. vii. 21.   [8] Heb. vii. 14.

daystar,[1] that is, before the forming of the world, and as possessing a deathless and undecaying *priesthood* to endless *ages*.[2]

19   And that His unction was spiritual and divine, a great and clear proof lies in the fact that He alone of all men who ever existed up to the present day is called Christ by all the human race throughout the entire world, and is acknowledged and confessed by all under this title, and is had in memory by both Greeks and barbarians; and to this day He is honoured by His followers throughout the world as king, admired above a prophet, and glorified as the true and only high priest of God; and, in addition to all this, as the Word of God pre-existent and called into being before all ages, and as One who has received from the Father the honour of worship, He is also 20 worshipped as God.   Yet the most wonderful thing of all is that we honour Him, we who have dedicated ourselves to Him, not alone with voices and sounding words, but also with the whole soul's affection, insomuch that we prize our witness to Him before our very life.

Christianity as old as Creation.

4.   This, then, I have of necessity stated in the forefront of my history, lest any should think that our Saviour and Lord Jesus the Christ was only of yesterday, because of the time in which He lived in the flesh.   But that none should imagine that His teaching is recent and strange, put together (as it were) by one of recent origin, differing in no respect from the rest of mankind, let us now briefly discuss this question also.

2   Now though the brightness of the presence of our Saviour Jesus Christ but recently shone forth upon all men, it is acknowledged that a new nation has all of a sudden appeared at a time fixed in the secret counsels of God, a nation neither small nor weak nor established in some corner of the earth, but the most populous and god-fearing of all nations, indestructible and invincible in that it for ever receives the help that comes from God, a nation which has been honoured by all 3 with the name of Christ.   At it one of the prophets, when he foresaw with the eye of the divine Spirit what would come to pass, was so astonished that he broke forth into these words :

Who hath heard such things ?
And who hath spoken thus ?
Was a land in travail for one day ?
And was a nation brought forth at once ? [3]

And the same prophet indicates after a fashion the name also that was to be, when he says,

And my servants shall be called by a new name,
Which shall be blessed upon the earth.[4]

---

[1] Ps. cx. 3 (LXX).   [2] Heb. vii. 24.
[3] Isai. lxvi. 8.   [4] Isai. lxv. 15, 16.

4   And even though it is clear that we are recent in point of time, and that this undoubtedly *new name* of Christians has but lately become known among all nations, nevertheless we shall proceed to show as follows that our manner of life and mode of conduct, together with our religious principles, have not been just now invented by us, but from the first creation of man, so to speak, were established by the instinctive ideas
5 of those men of old whom God loved. The Hebrew nation is not recent; nay, it has been held in honour for its antiquity by all men, and to all men it is known. It is a fact that its books and writings speak within its pages of men of ancient times, scanty indeed and few in number, yet all the while excelling in piety and righteousness and every other virtue. Of these there were various examples before the Flood, while others came after it, for instance, some of the sons and descendants of Noah, yes and Abraham also, whom the children of the Hebrews boast as their own founder and fore-
6 father. All these, to whose righteousness witness has been borne, going back from Abraham to the first man, it would be no departure from the truth to style as Christians, in point
7 of fact if not in name. For surely, as regards the meaning of the name, that the Christian man should, through the knowledge and teaching of Christ, excel in self-mastery and righteousness, in stedfast conduct and manly virtue, in confession of piety towards the one and only God over all—all this
8 was their earnest endeavour no less than ours. They cared not, then, for bodily circumcision; neither do we: nor for the observance of sabbaths; neither do we: nay, nor for the abstention from certain kinds of food, nor for distinctions in other matters, the symbolic observance of which Moses was the very first to commit to subsequent generations; neither do Christians now observe such things. But they also knew clearly the Christ of God, since it has been shown before [1] that He appeared to Abraham, gave divine instructions to Isaac, spoke to Israel, and held converse with Moses and the later
9 prophets. Hence you will find that those same men whom God loved have been deemed worthy of even the name of the Christ, according to the voice which speaks thus of them:
10 *Touch not my Christs, and do my prophets no harm.*[2] So then, it is evident that we must regard as the first and most ancient and primitive of all that religion which was discovered by Abraham and his followers, men dear to God, and which has lately been proclaimed to all nations through the teaching of the Christ.
11   But if we are told that Abraham received a long time afterwards the command of *circumcision*, at any rate it is declared that previous to this he had received testimony for the

---

[1] 2. 7, 9, 22.   [2] Ps. cv. 15.

righteousness that is by *faith* ; [1] for thus the divine word speaks :

> And Abraham believed God, and it was reckoned unto him for righteousness.[2]

12   Such, then, was he before his circumcision, on the day when God (that is Christ Himself, the Word of God) manifested Himself to him, and in these words announced an oracle concerning those who should thereafter be justified in like manner as he :

> And in thee shall all the families of the earth be blessed; [3]

and that

> he shall become a great and mighty nation, and all the nations of the earth shall be blessed in him.[4]

13 And this we may note as having been fulfilled in us.   For he had been *justified by faith* in the Word of God, the Christ, who appeared to him.   He turned aside from the superstition of his fathers and the former error of his ways, confessed the supreme God as one and served Him, not with the formal worship of the subsequent *law* [5] of Moses, but with deeds of virtue ; and to such a one it was said that *all the families of*
14 *the earth* [3] and *all the nations shall be blessed in him.*[4]   And in deeds clearer than words Abraham's form of godliness is manifestly practised at present by Christians, and by them alone, throughout the whole world.

15   What obstacle, then, can remain to prevent the acknowledgment that we, the followers of Christ, have one and the same mode of life and manner of religion as those friends of God in days of old ?   So that we have shown that it is not recent and strange, but, if one must speak the truth, the first and only and true religion in perfect form, that which was committed to us by the teaching of Christ.   And let this suffice.

REIGN OF AUGUSTUS (B.C. 44—A.D. 14)

Date of the Birth of Christ.

5.   But come now, after this necessary preface to our proposed Ecclesiastical History, let us now enter upon our journey, as it were, starting from the appearance of our Saviour in the flesh ; having called upon God the Father of the Word, and Him of whom we are speaking, even Jesus Christ our Saviour and Lord, the heavenly Word of God, to aid and cooperate with the truth of our narrative.

[1] Rom. iv. 10, 11.   [2] Rom. iv. 3, cited from Gen. xv. 6.
[3] Gen. xii. 3.   [4] Gen. xviii. 18.
[5] Rom. iii. 28.

2   It was, then, the forty-second year of the reign of Augustus,
       the twenty-eighth after the subjugation of Egypt and
B.C. 2. the death of Antony and Cleopatra, with whom the
dynasty of the Ptolemies in Egypt came to a final end, in which
our Saviour and Lord Jesus the Christ, in the days of the *first
enrolment* at that time *when Quirinius was governor of Syria*,[1]
was born, in accordance with the prophecies concerning Him,
in Bethlehem of Judæa.[2]

3   And this enrolment under Quirinius is also mentioned by
Flavius Josephus, the most distinguished historian among the
Hebrews, who adds as well an account of the sect of the
Galilæans which sprang up at the same time; which also our
own writer Luke has mentioned in the Acts, as follows :

> After this man rose up Judas of Galilee in the days of the enrol-
> ment, and drew away some of the people after him: he also
> perished; and all, as many as obeyed him, were scattered abroad.[3]

4 Now, in agreement with this, the writer we have mentioned,
in the eighteenth book of the Antiquities, adds the following,
in these very words :

> Now Quirinius, a member of the Senate, a man who had reached
> consular rank after having performed the other offices and passed
> through them all, and one who held a high position in other
> respects, came with a few men to Syria, being sent by Cæsar to hold
> the office of judge of the nation, and assessor of property.

5   And, a little further on, he says,

> But Judas, a Gaulonite from a city called Gamala, took with
> him a Pharisee named Saddocus, and urged on a revolt; both of
> them saying that the assessment meant nothing but downright
> slavery; and exhorting the nation to the defence of their liberty.[4]

6   And in the second book of his Histories of the Jewish War
he writes on the same matter as follows :

> In his day a certain Galilæan named Judas stirred up his
> fellow-countrymen to revolt, reproaching them if they paid
> tribute to the Romans and tolerated mortal rulers after God.[5]

This is what Josephus says.

The Fulfilment of Gen. xlix. 10.

Now then also for the first time a person of foreign blood,
Herod, received the kingdom of the Jewish nation; and
thus the prophecy uttered by Moses received its fulfilment,[6]
which says that *there shall not be wanting a ruler from Judah*

---

[1] Luke ii. 2.   [2] Matt. ii. 1, 5, 6.   [3] Acts v. 37.
[4] Jos., *Ant.* xviii. i. 1 (1, 4).   [5] Jos., *B.J.* ii. 8. 1 (118).
[6] *Lit.* "determination," "limit."

nor a leader from his loins, until he come for whom it is reserved,
2 who, as he also shows, will be *the expectation of nations.*[1] The
words of the prediction were, to say the least, unfulfilled as
long as they were permitted to live under rulers of their own
nation, beginning from Moses himself and stretching right
down to the reign of Augustus, in whose day for the first time
a foreigner, Herod, was entrusted by the Romans with the rule
over the Jews. He, according to the account of Josephus,
was an Idumean by race on his father's side, and on his
mother's an Arabian; [2] but according to Africanus (and he was
no mean writer) those who are accurately informed as to his
affairs state that *Antipater* (that is, his father) was *the son of a
certain Herod* of *Ashkelon,* one of the *temple-slaves,* as they are
3 called, of the temple *of Apollo.* This Antipater, having been
taken *captive* when a little child by *Idumean robbers,* lived
with them, because his father *was unable,* through poverty,
to pay money down for him. *Brought up in* their *customs, he was
afterwards befriended by Hyrcanus the* Jewish *high priest.*[3]
And Herod, who lived in the time of our Saviour, was this
man's son.
4 When, therefore, the Jewish sovereignty had devolved
upon such a man, *the expectation of the nations* [4] was, conformably to the prophecy, already near, *at the doors,*[5] inasmuch
as from that time there was a cessation of those who had been
their rulers and leaders in succession from Moses himself.
5 Indeed, before their captivity and transportation to Babylon
they were under kings, beginning with Saul, the first, and
David. But before the kings they were governed by rulers,
those who were called judges; who ruled after Moses and his
6 successor Joshua. And after the return from Babylon they
did not cease to employ an aristocratic form of government
with an oligarchy (for the priests had charge of their affairs),
until *Pompey* the Roman general appeared and besieged
Jerusalem *in force.* He defiled the holy place, advancing as
far as the innermost sanctuary of the temple; and him who
by right of succession from his ancestors was both king and
high priest up to that time (his name was *Aristobulus*) Pompey
sent as a prisoner to Rome along with *his children.* He *gave
the high-priesthood to Hyrcanus,* Aristobulus' brother, and
made the whole Jewish nation from that day tributary to the
7 Romans.[6] So, to go no further, when *Hyrcanus,* the last to
hold the high-priestly succession, *was taken captive* by
Parthians,[7] *Herod* was the first foreigner (as, indeed, I said)

[1] Gen. xlix. 10. [2] Jos., *Ant.* xiv. 7. 3 (121); *B.J.* i. 6. 2 (123).
[3] Afric., *Ep. ad Arist.* (7. 11 below).
[4] Gen. xlix. 10. [5] Matt. xxiv. 33.
[6] Jos., *Ant.* xiv. 4. 1–4 (54 ff.), xx. 10 (244); *B.J.* i. 7. 6, 7 (152 ff.).
[7] Jos., *Ant.* xiv. 13. 10 (365); xv. 2. 1 (404); xx. 16 (245); *B.J.* i. 13. 5 (260).

to be entrusted by the Roman Senate and the Emperor Augustus
8 with the Jewish nation.[1] It is manifest that the coming of the
Christ took place in his day; and the expected salvation and
calling of the nations followed in accordance with the prophecy.

From that time indeed the rulers and leaders of Judah,
I mean those of the Jewish nation, ceased; and as a natural
consequence their high-priesthood, which from their ancestors
had descended in orderly fashion to the nearest successors
according to family, was immediately thrown into confusion.
9 Of these facts also you have a trustworthy witness in Josephus,
who shows that *Herod, when he received the kingdom at the
hands of the Romans, no longer appointed the high priests from
the* ancient *lineage, but assigned the honour to certain obscure
persons. And, with reference to the appointment of the priests,
a course of action similar to Herod's was taken by Archelaus,
his son, and after him by the Romans, when they had taken over*
10 *the government of the Jews.*[2] And the same writer tells us that
Herod had been the first to cause even *the high priest's sacred
robe* to be shut up *under* his private *seal*; and did not allow
the high priests to keep it any longer in their own possession.
And that *Archelaus* also, *and after* him *the Romans, did* the same.[3]
11 These things I have stated in order to prove that another
prophecy had its accomplishment in the appearing of our
Saviour Jesus Christ.

Thus in the book of Daniel the Scripture very clearly lays down
an express number of certain *weeks* (concerning which we have
treated distinctly elsewhere) [4] *until Christ rules*, and prophesies
that *after* the accomplishment of these the *unction* among the
Jews *will be utterly destroyed*.[5] And this is clearly shown as
fulfilled at the time of the birth of our Saviour Jesus Christ.
We have been obliged to premise these remarks in order to set
forth the correctness of the time.

Africanus on the Genealogies of Christ.

7.   But since Matthew and Luke in writing their Gospels have
presented to us the genealogy of Christ in different forms, and
most people imagine that they are discordant; and since every
believer through ignorance of the truth has been eager to
multiply words on these passages, we must quote the account
of them that has come down to us, which Africanus, of whom
we spoke a short time ago,[6] mentions in a letter he wrote to
Aristides on the harmony of the genealogy in the Gospels.
Having refuted the opinions of the others as unnatural and

---

[1] Jos., *Ant.* xiv. 14. 4 (385); xx. 10 (247); *B.J.* i. 14. 4 (284).
[2] Jos., *Ant.* xx. 10 (247, 249).
[3] *Ib.* xviii. 4. 3 (92 f.); cp. xv. 11. 4 (403 ff.); xx. 1. 1 (6 ff.).
[4] Eus. *Ecl. Proph.* iii. 45.   [5] Dan. ix. 25, 26 (Theod.).   [6] 6. 2.

utterly mistaken, he *sets forth the account* he himself had received,[1] in these very words :

2   For inasmuch as the names of the families in Israel used to be numbered either by nature or by law : by nature, when there was actual offspring to succeed; but by law, when another begat a son in the name of his brother who had died childless [2] (for as no clear hope of a resurrection had as yet been given, they represented the future promise under the figure of a mortal resurrection, so that the name of the departed one might never cease to exist)—

3   since, then, as regards those included in this genealogy, some succeeded by natural descent, the son to the father, while others, though born to one father, were assigned by name to another, mention was made of both, those who had [actually] begotten

4   sons, as well as those regarded as having begotten them. Thus neither of the Gospels says what is untrue, since there is a reckoning both by nature and by law. For the families, namely that which took its descent from Solomon and that from Nathan, became so mutually involved, by resurrections of childless men and second marriages and resurrection of offspring, that the same persons were justly considered to belong at one time to one, at another to another : now to their reputed fathers, now to their actual. So that both accounts are in accordance with the exact truth, and descend to Joseph in a complex, yet accurate, manner.

5   But to make clear what has been said, I shall give an account of the interchange of the families. If we reckon the generations from David through Solomon, the third from the end is found to be *Matthan*, who *begat Jacob*,[3] the father of Joseph. But if from *Nathan the son of David* [4] according to Luke the third from the end was, similarly, Melchi. For *Joseph* was *the son of Heli, the*

6   *son of Melchi*.[5] Joseph being, then, the object at which we aim, we must show how each of the two is recorded to be his father : namely Jacob, tracing his descent from Solomon, and Heli from Nathan; and, before that, how these same persons, namely Jacob and Heli, were two brothers; and, before that again, how their fathers, Matthan and Melchi, though of different families,

7   are declared to be Joseph's grandfathers. Well then, both Matthan and Melchi, marrying in turn the same wife, begat children who were brothers by the same mother, for the law does not prevent a widow marrying another, whether she be divorced

8   or her husband be dead. So then from Estha (for tradition asserts that this was the woman's name) first Matthan, who traced down his family from Solomon, begat Jacob; and, on the death of Matthan, Melchi, who traced his descent back to Nathan, married the widow, being of the same tribe but another family, as I said

9   before; and of her had a son Heli. Thus we shall find Jacob and Heli brothers with the same mother, though of two different families; of whom the former, Jacob, on the death without issue of his brother Heli, took his wife and from her in the third place [from Estha] begat Joseph, who according to nature was his own son (and also according to Scripture : for it is written, *and Jacob*

---

[1] Afric., *ad Arist.* (Reichardt, p. 53).
[2] Cp. Gen. xxxviii. 8; Deut. xxv. 6; Luke xx. 28.
[3] Matt. i. 15.   [4] Luke iii. 31.   [5] Luke iii. 23, 24.

begat Joseph); [1] but according to law he was the son of Heli.   For
10 Jacob, being his brother, *raised up seed* [2] to Heli.   Therefore also
the genealogy traced through him will not be rendered void,
though in reckoning it Matthew the evangelist says : *and Jacob
begat Joseph*; [1] and Luke on the other hand : *Who was, as was
supposed* (for indeed he adds this), *the son of Joseph, the son of
Heli, the son of Melchi.* [3]   For he could not express more distinctly
the descent according to law, and he abstains from using the word
" begat " with reference to this kind of procreation right up to the
end, tracing the genealogy up to *Adam, the son of God,* [4] backwards.

11   Nor is this a rash interpretation or incapable of proof.   At all
events, the Saviour's kinsmen according to the flesh, whether
stirred by the love of advertisement or by the single desire to
instruct—in any case telling the truth—have handed down this
tradition also.   [They say] that Idumean robbers attacked
Ashkelon, a city in Palestine, and from an idol temple of Apollo,
which was built near the walls, carried away captive, along with
the rest of their spoils, Antipater the son of a certain Herod a
temple-slave.   And since the priest was unable to pay down a
ransom for his son, Antipater was brought up in the customs of the
Idumeans, and was afterwards befriended by Hyrcanus the high
12 priest of Judæa.   He went as an ambassador to Pompey on behalf
of Hyrcanus, and having freed for him his kingdom from the grasp
of his brother Aristobulus, he fell in with good fortune, and bore
the title of superintendent of Palestine.   Antipater's great good
fortune cost him envy; he was treacherously murdered, and
succeeded by his son Herod, who afterwards by a decree of the
Senate under Antony and Augustus was chosen to be king of the
Jews.   His sons were Herod and the other tetrarchs.   These
facts, indeed, are also the common property of the histories of
the Greeks.

13   But there were still kept on record in their archives the genealogies of the Hebrews and of those who traced their origin back
to proselytes, such as Achior the Ammonite [5] and *Ruth the
Moabitess* [6] and the *mixed multitude* which came forth together
with them from Egypt.   So Herod, since the lineage of the
Israelites contributed nothing to his advantage, and he was
smitten by the consciousness of his lowly birth, burnt the registers
of their families; for he thought that he would appear nobly born
if no one else were able from a public record to trace his family
back to the patriarchs or to proselytes, and the *mixed multitude*
14 called *Giorae.* [7]   A few careful people had private records of their
own, either having remembered the names or otherwise securing
them from copies; who prided themselves on preserving the
memory of their noble birth.   Of such were the persons mentioned
above, [8] called Desposyni from their connexion with the Saviour's
family.   Coming from the Jewish villages of Nazareth and
Cochaba, they travelled over the rest of the land, explaining the
aforesaid genealogy, as far as they could trace it, [from records
15 and memory] and from the Book of the Days.   Whether, then,
it be so or otherwise, no clearer explanation could be found, as I
and every fair-minded person consider; and we should be content

---

[1] Matt. i. 16.   [2] Gen. xxxviii. 8.   [3] Luke iii. 23, 24.
[4] Luke iii. 38.   [5] Judith v. 5; xiv. 10.   [6] Ruth i. 16; ii. 2.
[7] Ex. xii. 19, 38.   [8] § 11

with it, even though it be unattested, for it is impossible to state a better or truer one. In fact the Gospel speaks the absolute truth.

16 And at the close of the same letter he adds as follows :

Matthan, who traced his descent from Solomon, begat Jacob. On the death of Matthan, Melchi, who traced his descent from Nathan, of the same wife begat Heli. Therefore Heli and Jacob were brothers with the same mother. Heli having died childless, Jacob raised up seed to him, and begat Joseph, who was by nature his own son, but by law Heli's. Thus Joseph was the son of both.

17 So much for Africanus. Moreover, now that the genealogy of Joseph is thus traced, Mary also has been virtually shown to belong to the same tribe as he, since according to the law of Moses intermarrying between different tribes was not permitted. For the command is to join in wedlock *with one of those from the* same *town* and the same *clan,* so that *the inheritance* of the family *should not remove from tribe to tribe.*[1] Thus, then, may these matters stand.

The Eastern Magi.

8. But indeed, *when* the Christ *was born,* agreeably to the prophecies, *in Bethlehem of Judæa* at the aforesaid time, Herod was not a little disturbed by the enquiry of the *wise men from the east,* who asked where he was *that was born King of the Jews,* for that they had *seen his star,* and for that reason had undertaken so long a journey in their earnest desire *to worship* as God Him that was born—Herod, I say, was not a little disturbed thereat, inasmuch as his throne was endangered, or so at least he thought. He *enquired,* therefore, of the doctors of the law among the nation *where* they expected *the Christ* to *be born.*[2] And when he became aware of the prophecy of Micah predicting Bethlehem,[3] by a single decree he commanded that *the male children* at the breast *in Bethlehem and in all the borders thereof, from two years old and under, according to the time carefully learned* by him *of the wise men,* should be *slain.*[4] For he supposed (as he might well do) that doubtless Jesus also would share a like fate with those of His own age.

2 Nevertheless the Child was conveyed into Egypt, and so escaped the plot, His parents being forewarned of what was impending by the appearance of an angel.[5]

The Divine Judgment on Herod.

Such, then, is the account given by the sacred book of the 3 Gospel. But it is worth while in addition to observe the

---

[1] Num. xxxvi. 7, 8.   [2] Matt. ii. 1, 2, 4.
[3] Mic. v. 2 (Matt. ii. 6).   [4] Matt. ii. 16.
[5] Matt. ii. 13, 14.

wages that Herod received for his act of daring against the
Christ and those of His age : how that straightway, without
even a slight delay, the divine Justice overtook him while still
alive, to give him a foretaste of what was awaiting him after
4 his departure hence. It is not possible to recount here how,
indeed, he sullied the supposed *prosperity* of his reign by the
successive calamities which overtook *his house* : by the murder
of wife, children and other members of his family who were
his *nearest* and dearest. Before such a subject every tragic
drama pales ; and Josephus has fully treated it in his Histories.[1]
5 But how a scourge wielded by a hand divine descended and
drove him on to death, just when he plotted against our
Saviour and the other infants, can best be learnt from the
words of that historian also, who in the seventeenth book of
the Jewish Antiquities writes thus of the end of his life, in
these very words :

But Herod's disease attacked him more severely, a requital
6 exacted by God for his wrong-doings. For indeed he suffered
from a slow fire, which did not so much betray its burning heat
to the touch as it increased the trouble internally. He had a
terrible longing for food, which could in no way be satisfied. His
intestines were ulcerated, and the colon especially attacked by
terrible pains ; and a running transparent humour settled on his
7 feet. He suffered also from similar trouble in his abdomen. Aye
indeed, his privy parts were putrefied, and gave forth worms ; his
breathing was only accomplished with difficulty and in an upright
position, and the heavy odour and quick respiration made it
exceedingly unpleasant. Every part of him was convulsed, so
8 that he became possessed of uncontrollable strength. So it used
to be said by those who practised divinations and such as were
possessed of wisdom to foretell these events, that God was exacting
a penalty from the king for his great impiety.[2]

Such is the conclusion drawn by the aforesaid writer in the
9 said work. And in the second of the Histories he gives a
similar account concerning the same person, writing somewhat
as follows :

From that time the disease seized upon his body as a whole,
over which it apportioned divers sufferings. A gentle fever
attacked him ; an intolerable itching spread over the entire
surface of the body ; the colon was racked with incessant pains ;
his feet swelled as with dropsy ; the abdomen was inflamed ;
the privy parts became putrid and bred worms ; and, in addition,
he could breathe only in an upright position and then with
difficulty ; and he had convulsions in all his limbs, so that those
who practised divinations said that his disorders were a penalty.
10 But although he was struggling with these terrible sufferings, he
nevertheless clung to life, hoped for recovery and bethought him
of cures. For instance, crossing the Jordan he used the hot

---

[1] Jos., *Ant.* xv. 6 (161 ff.); 7 (202 ff.); xvi. 11 (356 ff.); *B.J.* i. 22. 5
(443 ff.); 27. 6 (550 f.).   [2] Jos., *Ant.* xvii. 6. 5 (168 ff.).

springs of Callirrhoe, which flow into Lake Asphaltites, but are
11 sweet enough even to drink. There the physicians decided to
warm his whole body with hot oil, by letting him down into a tub
filled with it. But he grew weak and turned up his eyes like a
person in a faint.[1] However, he revived at the sound of the
commotion which his attendants made; and henceforth despairing of recovery ordered fifty drachmas apiece to be given to the
12 soldiers, and large money to his generals and friends. He himself
returned and came to Jericho, in a state of melancholy and all
but uttering threats at death itself. Then he proceeded to devise
an unhallowed deed. Collecting the notable men from each
village in all Judæa, he commanded them to be shut up in the
13 hippodrome, as it is called. Then summoning Salome his sister
and her husband Alexas, he said: "I know that the Jews will
celebrate my death by a festival; but I may be mourned by
others and have a splendid funeral, if you are willing to carry out
my commands. The moment I have breathed my last, surround
these men who are kept under guard with soldiers, and kill them;
that all Judæa and every house may weep because of me, even in
spite of themselves." [2]

14   And shortly afterwards he says,

And again (for indeed he was racked by want of food and a
convulsive cough), when the pains mastered him,[3] he planned to
anticipate Fate. Taking an apple, he asked for a knife as well.
For it was his custom to cut as he ate. Then, looking round to see
that there was no one to hinder him, he raised his right hand as if
to stab himself.[4]

15   Moreover, the same writer records that just before the end
of his life he ordered the death of another lawful son of his
(this was the third, for two had already been put to death);
and that straightway the thread of life was severed, not
without great pain.[5]

Archelaus.

16   Such, then, was the last end of Herod, who paid a just
penalty for the children whom he slew round about Bethlehem,
to further his design against our Saviour. After this *an angel*
appeared *in a dream to Joseph* while he was staying *in Egypt*,
and bade him depart with the child *and* His *mother* into
Judæa, revealing that *they are dead that sought the young child's
life.*[6] And then the evangelist goes on to say:

But when he heard that Archelaus was reigning in the room of
Herod his father, he was afraid to go thither; and being warned
of God in a dream, he withdrew into the parts of Galilee.[7]

---

[1] The text of Eusebius in this section is doubtful.
[2] Jos., *B.J.* i. 33. 5, 6 (656 ff.).
[3] Reading ἡσσηθείς, with some MSS. of Josephus, for ἡσθείς.
[4] Jos., *B.J.* i. 33, 7 (662).   [5] *Ib.* (663 f.); *Ant.* xvii. 7 (185 ff.).
[6] Matt. ii. 19, 20.   [7] Matt. ii. 22.

9.   And the aforesaid historian agrees with [the evangelist] that
Archelaus was appointed to the government after Herod;
and he describes the way in which the will of Herod his father
and the approval of Cæsar Augustus gave him the succession
to the kingdom over the Jews; and how, when he fell from the
government after ten years' time, his brothers *Philip and Herod*
the younger, together with Lysanias, ruled *their own tetrarchies.*[1]

REIGN OF TIBERIUS (14–37)

Date of Pilate : Forged Acts of Pilate.

2   The same writer tells us in the eighteenth book of the
Antiquities that in the twelfth year of the reign of *Tiberius*
36.   (for he *succeeded* to the supreme government after Augustus
had held *the principate for fifty-seven years*) Pontius
Pilate was entrusted with Judæa, and that he remained there
3 for *ten* entire *years*, almost until the death of Tiberius.[2]   Therefore the forgery of those who the other day published Memoirs
against our Saviour is clearly proved; in which the very date
noted at the beginning proves the falsity of those who forged
4 them.   The things they have dared to state about the Saviour's
Passion are placed, I say, in the fourth consulship of Tiberius,
that is, the seventh year of his reign; at which time it is shown
that Pilate was not yet in charge of Judæa, if at least we may
use the testimony of Josephus, who plainly indicates in his
aforesaid work that in the twelfth year of the reign of Tiberius
Pilate was appointed procurator of Judæa by that emperor.

The Period of Christ's Teaching.

10.   So then, in the time of these men, *in the fifteenth year*,
according to the evangelist, *of Tiberius Cæsar*, in the fourth
of *Pontius Pilate's* governorship, when *Herod* and *Lysanias* and
Philip were tetrarchs[3] of the rest of Judæa, our Saviour and
Lord, Jesus the Christ of God, *when beginning to be about
thirty years of age*,[4] *came to the baptism* of *John*,[5] and then
2 made a beginning of His *preaching* of *the Gospel.*[6]   Now the
divine Scripture says that He passed the entire time of His
teaching *in the high-priesthood of Annas and Caiaphas*; [7] thus
showing that the whole period during which He taught was
completed within the years bounded by these men's ministry.
Since He began, then, during the high-priesthood of Annas

---

[1] Jos., *B.J.* i. 33. 8 (668); ii. 6. 3 (93 f.); 7. 3 (111); 9. 1 (167);
Ant. xvii. 8. 1, 2 (188 ff.); 11. 4 (317 f.); 13. 2 (342 ff.).
[2] Jos., *Ant.* xviii. 2. 2; 4. 2 (32, 33, 35, 89).   [3] Luke iii. 1.
[4] Luke iii. 23.   [5] Matt. iii. 13.
[6] Cp. Matt. iv. 17; Mark i. 14.   [7] Luke iii. 2.

and remained until the rule of Caiaphas, the intervening period
3 is not a full four years. For indeed the ordinances which were
under the law had from that time been already abolished;
and that system was done away with, by which all that
appertained to the service of God was a charge for life, held by
hereditary succession; on the contrary, the Roman governors
assigned *the high-priesthood* now to one, now to another, and
4 these continued in office *not more* than one year. At all events
Josephus records that there were four high priests in succession
from Annas to Caiaphas, speaking somewhat on this fashion
in the same book of the Antiquities :

> . . . Valerius Gratus . . . deposed Ananus from acting as
> priest, and appointed Ishmael the son of Phabi high priest; but
> removed him not long afterwards, and nominated as high priest
> 5 Eleazar the son of Ananus the high priest. However, when a
> year had passed, he deposed him too, and handed the high-
> priesthood over to Simon the son of Camithus. But he likewise
> held office for no more than a year; and Joseph, who was also
> called Caiaphas, succeeded him.[1]

6 So, then, it has been shown that the whole period of our
Saviour's teaching did not comprise a full four years; four
high priests, from Annas to the appointment of Caiaphas,
having completed a ministry of a year apiece in four years.
In fact, the book of the Gospel has noted that *Caiaphas* was
high priest, as we might expect, that *year* in which the events
of the Saviour's Passion took place;[2] from which also it is
shown that the period of Christ's teaching is in harmony with
the foregoing investigation.

The Call of the Twelve and of the Seventy.

7 But indeed our Saviour and Lord, not very long after His
preaching began, called *the twelve apostles, whom* alone He
honoured, above the rest of His disciples, in an especial
manner by so *naming* them;[3] and, on another occasion, He
appointed seventy others, whom also He *sent two and two before his
face into every place and city, whither he himself was about to come.*[4]

John the Baptist.

11. But the divine book of the Gospels mentions that John the
Baptist was beheaded by the younger Herod not long after
this.[5] And Josephus also records the same fact, mentioning
Herodias by name, and how *Herod* married her though she was
his brother's *wife,* having put away his former lawful wife

[1] Jos., *Ant.* xviii. 2. 2 (33 ff.).
[2] John xi. 49; xviii. 13; cp. Matt. xxvi. 3, 57; John xviii. 24, 28.
[3] Matt. x. 1; Mark iii. 14; Luke vi. 13.
[4] Luke x. 1.   [5] Matt. xiv. 10; Mark vi. 27.

(who was the *daughter of Aretas king of Petrœa*), and separated
Herodias from her husband who was alive; and that on her
account also he put John to death and went to *war* with Aretas,
2 whose daughter he had dishonoured. And he says that *in a
battle which took place* in this war *Herod's whole army was
destroyed*, and that this disaster was due to the designs against
3 John.[1] And the same Josephus acknowledges that John was
without a superior in righteousness and a *baptist*;[2] and thus
his testimony agrees with what is written in the book of the
Gospels concerning him; and he also records the fact that Herod
lost his kingdom on account of the same Herodias, and that he
was driven into exile along with her, and condemned to make
4 Vienne, *a city of Gaul*, his home.[3] This information Josephus
has given us in the eighteenth book of the Antiquities, where
he writes thus concerning John, using these very words :

. . . but to some of the Jews it seemed that Herod's army had
been destroyed by God, as a most just requital for John who was
5 called the Baptist. For Herod put him to death, a good man who
bade the Jews practise virtue, use [4] righteous dealings among
themselves and piety towards God, and so come together for
baptism; for [he held] that thus indeed would the immersion
appear acceptable to Him, when men used it not to secure pardon
for certain sins, but to purify the body : inasmuch as the soul
6 had already been cleansed by righteousness. And when the others
rallied round him (for indeed they were greatly excited on listening
to his words), Herod became fearful lest his great powers of
persuasion with men might lead to some form of revolt (for they
seemed disposed to do anything at his advice). So he thought
it much better to anticipate any revolutionary action on John's
part by killing him, than to repent when involved in the
difficulties of an insurrection. Therefore, because of Herod's
suspicion, John was sent a prisoner to Machærus—the fortress we
mentioned before—and there put to death.[5]

The Statement of Josephus about Jesus.

7 Such is the account he gives of John. And he mentions
our Saviour also in the same narrative in the treatise, somewhat
after this fashion :

Now there lived about this time Jesus, a wise man, if indeed one
may call him a man. For he was a doer of marvellous works,
a teacher of such men as receive what is true with pleasure; and
many of the Jews, and many also of the Greeks, he won over to
8 himself. This was the Christ; and after that Pilate had condemned him to the cross on the indictment of the chief men
among us, they who had loved him at the first did not cease
[to do so]. For he appeared on the third day to them, living
again, the divine prophets having stated these and countless other
marvels concerning him. And even now the tribe of the Christians,
named after him, has not become extinct.[6]

---

[1] Jos., *Ant.* xviii. 5. 1, 2 (109 ff.).   [2] *Ib.* 5. 2 (§ 4 below).
[3] *Ib.* 7. 2 (252 ff.).   [4] Reading χρωμένοις with some MSS.
[5] Jos., *Ant.* xviii, 5. 2 (116 ff.).   [6] *Ib.* 3. 3 (63 f.).

9   When a writer belonging to the Hebrews themselves has
transmitted from primitive times in a work of his own this
record concerning John the Baptist and our Saviour, what
excuse can there be for not convicting as shameless those who
forged the Memoirs against them ?   However, let this suffice
here.

The Apostles and the Seventy Disciples.

12.   But to resume.   It is clear to everyone from the Gospels
what are the names of the apostles of the Saviour.[1]   But no
list of the seventy disciples [2] is extant anywhere ; Barnabas,
however, is said [3] to have been one of them, whom also the
Acts of the Apostles has mentioned in various places ; [4] and,
especially, Paul too, when writing to the Galatians.[5]   And it is
said that Sosthenes also was of their number, he who wrote,
2 along with Paul, to the Corinthians ; [6] and this is the record
of Clement in the fifth book of the Hypotyposeis ; in which
also he says that Cephas (of whom Paul says, *But when
Cephas came to Antioch, I resisted him to the face* [7]) was one of
the seventy disciples, being of the same name as Peter the
3 apostle.   And of Matthias too, who was numbered among the
apostles in the place of Judas, and of him who was honoured
by being voted on along with Matthias,[8] it is recorded that they
were deemed worthy of the same calling —that of the Seventy.
And it is said that Thaddæus was also one of them ; [9] concerning whom I shall presently recount a story that has come
4 down to us.[10]   And upon examination you will find that there
were evidently disciples of the Saviour over and above
the Seventy, if you take the testimony of Paul, who said that
after the rising from the dead *He appeared* first *to Cephas* ;
afterwards to the twelve ; and after them *to above five hundred
brethren at once, of whom* he stated that *some* had *fallen asleep,
but* that *the greater part remained* still alive at the time of
5 writing.   And *afterwards*, he says, *He appeared to James*.
The same was one of the Saviour's brethren, as they were called.
Then—since besides these there were very many apostles
indeed, in imitation of the Twelve, as also was Paul himself—
he adds thus : *Afterwards* He appeared *to all the apostles*.[11]

Thaddæus and Abgar.

13.   So much, then, for this.   But the story about Thaddæus
runs as follows.   When the divinity of our Lord and Saviour

---

[1] Matt. x. 2–4; Mark iii. 16–19; Luke vi. 14–16.
[2] Luke x. 1.   [3] Clem., *Hypot.* vii (ii. 1. 4 below).
[4] Acts iv. 36; ix. 27; xi. 22, 30; xii. 25; xiii–xv.
[5] Gal. ii. 1, 13.   [6] 1 Cor. i. 1.   [7] Gal. ii. 11.
[8] Acts i. 23, 26.   [9] *Thaddæus Legend* (13. 11 below).
[10] c. 13.   [11] 1 Cor. xv. 5–7.

Jesus Christ became noised abroad among all men, thanks to His wonder-working power, it attracted countless numbers even of persons in foreign lands very far distant from Judæa, who hoped to be cured of diseases and all kinds of disorders.
2 So it came about that when king Abgar, a most illustrious potentate of the nations beyond the Euphrates, being wasted by a terrible bodily *disorder*, incurable as far as human power goes, heard of the fame of Jesus' name and the unanimous testimony paid by all to His mighty works, he sent Him a message of entreaty by a despatch-bearer, asking that he
3 might be delivered from his disease. But Jesus did not at that time hearken to his request; howbeit He deemed him worthy of a personal letter, promising *to send one of* His *disciples to heal his disease* and, at the same time, bring
4 salvation to him and all who belonged to him.[1] And not long afterwards, it would seem, He fulfilled that which He had promised. At all events, *after* His resurrection from the dead and His ascent into the heavens, *Thomas*, one of the twelve apostles, was moved by a divine impulse to send forth *Thaddæus*—he too had been reckoned *among the seventy* disciples of Christ—to Edessa as a *herald* and evangelist of the teaching concerning Christ. And through him all that our Saviour had promised received its fulfilment.[2]
5   You have the proof of these facts also in writing, taken from the record office at Edessa, then a city ruled by kings. Thus, in the public documents there, which contain ancient matters and those connected with Abgar, these things have been found preserved from that day until now. But there is nothing like hearing the letters themselves, taken by us from the archives and literally translated from the Syriac, as follows :

Copy of a letter written by Abgar the Toparch to Jesus, and sent to Him at Jerusalem by the hand of Ananias a courier.

6   Abgar Uchama, toparch, to Jesus, gracious Saviour, who has appeared in the region of Jerusalem, greeting. I have heard of thee and of thy cures as having been wrought by thee without medicines or herbs. For by a word [3] thou dost make *the blind* to *receive their sight, the lame* to *walk, and* dost *cleanse the lepers*, cast out unclean *spirits* and devils, *heal* [4] them that are
7 *tormented* [5] with long sickness, and *raise up the dead*.[4] And when I heard all this concerning thee, I was convinced of one of two things : either that thou art God and doest these things, having come down from heaven ; or that, because thou doest them, thou
8 art the Son of God. Therefore for this cause I write and beseech thee to trouble thyself to come to me and heal the disorder which I have. For verily I have heard that even the Jews are murmur-

---

[1] *Thad. Leg.* (§§ 6–10 below).   [2] *Ib.* (§§ 11–20).
[3] Following the Syr.   [4] Luke vii. 21, 22.   [5] Matt. viii. 6.

ing at thee and wish to do thee harm. But I have a very small city, yet a stately one; which will suffice us both.

9 The written reply of Jesus to the Toparch Abgar [sent] by the hand of the courier Ananias.

10 *Blessed* art thou who *didst believe* in me, *not having seen me.*[1] For it is written of me that they who have seen me will not believe in me, even that they who have not seen me may themselves believe and live.[2] But as to that which thou didst write to me, that I should come to thee, I must fulfil all things for the which I was sent hither; and having fulfilled them, be *received up* [3] immediately to him that sent me.[4] And when I am received up, I will send thee one of my disciples, to heal thy disorder and bestow life on thee and those with thee.

11 To these letters there is also subjoined the following, in the Syriac language :

Now after *Jesus was received up,*[3] Judas, who was also called Thomas, sent unto him Thaddæus the apostle, one of the Seventy; who came and lodged with Tobias the son of Tobias. And when the news concerning him was heard, it was told Abgar, saying, " An apostle of Jesus is come hither, even as He wrote to thee."

12 Thaddæus, then, *began* in the power of God *to heal all manner of disease and sickness,*[5] so that *all wondered*. But when Abgar heard the mighty and *wonderful things that he did,*[6] and how he healed, he suspected that it was he of whom Jesus wrote, saying, " When I am received up, I will send thee one of my disciples,

13 who will heal thy disorder." He sent, therefore, for Tobias, with whom Thaddæus lodged, and said : " I have heard that a powerful man is come to lodge in thy house; bring him to me." So Tobias came to Thaddæus and said to him : " The toparch Abgar sent for me and bade me bring thee to him, that thou mightest heal him." Thaddæus replied : " I go before him; for I have

14 been sent unto him with power." So the next day Tobias rose up early, and took with him Thaddæus and came to Abgar. And when he appeared before him, his lords being present and standing round, immediately on his entry a great vision appeared to Abgar in the face of the apostle Thaddæus. Which when he saw, Abgar did obeisance to Thaddæus; and all they that stood by were filled with amazement : for they had not seen the vision, which

15 appeared to Abgar alone. He also asked Thaddæus : " Art thou of a truth a disciple of Jesus the Son of God, who said to me : ' I will send thee one of my disciples, who will heal thee and bestow upon thee life ' ? " And Thaddæus said : " Since thou hast mightily believed on Him that sent me, it was for this cause that I was sent unto thee. And moreover, if thou shalt believe on Him, even *as thou believest so* shall *the petitions of thine heart*

16 be granted." [7] And Abgar made him reply : " Such was my

---

[1] Cp. John xx. 29.
[2] Cp. Isai. vi. 9 ff.; Matt. xiii. 14 ff.; John xii. 39 ff.
[3] Acts i. 2, 11, 22; 1 Tim. iii. 16.   [4] Cp. John xvi. 5, etc.
[5] Matt. ix. 35, etc.; Mark v. 20.   [6] Matt. xxi. 15.
[7] Matt. viii. 13; Ps. xxxvii. 4.

belief in Him, that I even wished to take an army and destroy the Jews who crucified Him; howbeit I was checked from so doing by reason of the rule of the Romans." And Thaddæus said : " Our Lord hath fulfilled His Father's will; and having fulfilled

17 it was received up to His Father." Abgar said to him : " I also have believed on Him and on His Father." Thaddæus replied : " Therefore, I lay my hand upon thee in His name." And when he had done this, immediately he was healed of the disease and

18 disorder which he had. And Abgar was astonished that as he had heard concerning Jesus, so did he receive in very deed at the hand of His disciple Thaddæus; who healed him without the use of medicine or herbs, and not him alone but also Abdu the son of Abdu, who had gout. This man also came forward and fell at his feet; and was healed by his prayers with the imposition of his hand. And many others of their fellow-citizens were cured by Thaddæus, who did wonderful and mighty works, and preached the word of God.

19 Now after this Abgar said : " Thou, Thaddæus, doest these things by the power of God; and we ourselves did marvel. But besides all this, I beseech thee, declare unto me concerning the coming of Jesus, how it took place; and concerning His power; and by what power He did such things as I have heard tell of."

20 Then Thaddæus said : " Now indeed I will keep silence; but since I was sent to preach the word, to-morrow assemble me all thy citizens, and I will preach before them, and sow in them the word of life : namely, concerning the coming of Jesus, how it took place; concerning His mission, and why He was sent by the Father; concerning His power and works, and the mysteries which He spake in the world, and by what power He did these things; concerning His new preaching; concerning His littleness and humiliation; and how *he humbled himself,* and put aside and belittled His divinity; was crucified; [1] descended into Hades and rent asunder the barrier which from eternity had never been rent, and raised up the dead, and though He descended alone, yet ascended with a great multitude to His Father."

21 So then, Abgar bade his citizens assemble at dawn and hear the preaching of Thaddæus . . . and, after that, he ordered that gold and silver [2] should be given him. But he would not accept it, saying : " If we have left our own, how shall we take that which

22 is another's ? " These things took place in the three hundred and fortieth year.

Let this, then, translated literally from the Syriac language, be inserted here in its proper place, and, I trust, to some purpose.

[1] Phil. ii. 8.   [2] ἄσημον: cp. Job xlii. 11 (LXX).

BOOK II

The Second Book of the Ecclesiastical History contains the following:

1. On the course pursued by the apostles after the ascension of Christ.
2. How Tiberius was moved when Pilate informed him of the facts concerning Christ.
3. How in a short time *the word* which tells of Christ ran [1] throughout all the world.
4. That Gaius, succeeding Tiberius, appointed Agrippa king of the Jews, having punished Herod with perpetual exile.
5. That Philo went on an embassy on behalf of the Jews to Gaius.
6. The tide of misfortunes which flowed against the Jews after their crime against Christ.
7. That Pilate also committed suicide.
8. On the famine under Claudius.
9. Martyrdom of James the apostle.
10. That Agrippa, who was also called Herod, experienced the divine Justice the moment he attacked the apostles.
11. On Theudas the magician.
12. On Helena, queen of the Adiabeni.
13. On Simon the sorcerer.
14. On the preaching of Peter the apostle at Rome.
15. On the Gospel according to Mark.
16. That Mark was the first to preach the knowledge of Christ to those in Egypt.
17. The account which Philo gives of the ascetics in Egypt.
18. The treatises of Philo which have come into our hands.
19. The misfortunes which overtook the Jews in Jerusalem on the day of the Passover.
20. Also, what happened in Jerusalem in the time of Nero.
21. On the Egyptian, also mentioned in the Acts of the Apostles.
22. That Paul, when sent in bonds from Judæa to Rome, made his defence and was freed from every kind of accusation.
23. That James, who was called the Lord's brother, suffered martyrdom.
24. That, after Mark, Annianus was appointed as the first bishop of the church of the Alexandrians.
25. On the persecution under Nero, in whose day Paul and Peter were adorned, at Rome, with martyrdom on behalf of piety.
26. That the Jews were afflicted with countless evils, and started the final war with the Romans.

For this book we have taken as our sources the [works] of Clement, Tertullian, Josephus and Philo.

---

[1] 2 Thess. iii. 1.

Preface.

In the preceding book we discussed those subjects connected with the Ecclesiastical History which it was necessary to determine by way of introduction : such as the divinity of the saving Word,[1] the antiquity of the doctrines contained in our teaching, and the ancient character of the evangelical life as lived by Christians;[2] nor did we omit the facts concerning His recent appearing,[3] or the events before the Passion and those that have reference to the choice of the apostles;[4] in 2 all of which we supplied short proofs. But come, let us in the present book now examine also the events subsequent to His ascension—indicating some from the divine writings, and narrating others from such memoirs outside [the Scriptures] as we shall mention at the proper time.

The Beginnings of the Church.

1. The first, therefore, to be chosen by lot for the *apostleship* in the place of the traitor Judas was Matthias.[5] He also, as has been shown,[6] was one of the Lord's disciples. And there were appointed to the diaconate for the service of the community, by prayer and laying on of hands of the apostles, approved men numbering seven, namely, Stephen and his companions.[7] Stephen also was the first after the Lord—at the time of his ordination, as if he were promoted for this very purpose— to be stoned to death by the Lord's murderers.[8] Thus he was the first to carry off the crown—which name he himself 2 bore—of the martyrs of Christ to whom victory is due. Then, indeed, James also, the brother of the Lord as he was called (for he too was styled the son of Joseph, and Joseph the father of Christ; *to which Joseph* the Virgin *had been betrothed,* and *before they came together was found with child of the Holy Ghost,*[9] as the sacred book of the Gospel tells us)—this same *James,* then, whom the men of old *surnamed the Just on account of* his excellent virtue,[10] was the first, it is related, to be entrusted with the throne of the episcopate of the church at Jerusalem. 3 Clement establishes [this fact] in the sixth book of the Hypotyposeis, writing thus :

For he says that Peter and James and John after the ascension of the Saviour did not lay claim to glory, as men who had been preferred in honour by Him; but selected James the Just as bishop of Jerusalem.

---

[1] i. 2, 3.   [2] i. 4.   [3] i. 5, 6, 8.   [4] i. 9–13.
[5] Acts. i. 15–26.   [6] i. 12. 3.   [7] Acts. vi. 1–6.   [8] Acts vii. 58.
[9] Matt. i. 18.   [10] Heg. (23. 7 below).

4   And the same writer, moreover, also speaks thus concerning him, in the seventh book of the same work :

To James the Just and John and Peter the Lord after the resurrection committed the " gnosis "; they committed it to the other apostles, and the other apostles to the Seventy, of whom 5 Barnabas also was one. But there were two persons named James : one [called] the Just, he who was cast down from the pinnacle and beaten to death with a fuller's club; the other, he who was beheaded.

Paul also mentions " the Just " and none other, when he writes, *But other of the apostles saw I none, save James the Lord's brother*.[1]

6   At that time too the undertaking made by our Saviour to the king of the Osrhoëni was receiving its fulfilment. Certainly Thomas was moved by a divine impulse to send forth Thaddæus to Edessa as a *herald* and evangelist of the teaching of Christ, as we showed a little while back from the document 7 found there.[2] And when he arrived at those parts, he healed Abgar by the word of Christ, and astonished all the people there by his miraculous and marvellous works.[3] By this means also he mightily disposed their minds, and led them to reverence *the power* of Christ. Thus he made of them disciples of the teaching of salvation; and from that day to this *the whole city* of the Edessenes has been devoted to the name of Christ, and so contributes no ordinary proof of the beneficence of our Saviour towards them also.[4]

8   Enough, then, of these matters, which we have taken from an account given by men of olden time. Let us return once more to the divine Scripture. When the first and greatest *persecution* against *the church in Jerusalem arose* [5] at the hands of the Jews *about* the martyrdom of *Stephen*,[6] and when *all* the disciples *except the* twelve alone *were scattered* throughout *Judæa and Samaria*;[5] certain men, as the divine Scripture says, *travelled as far as Phœnicia and Cyprus and Antioch*, who could not yet venture to impart *the word* of the faith to Gentiles, 9 but proclaimed it *to Jews alone*.[6] At that time also, Paul then still *laid waste the church, entering houses* of the faithful, 10 *haling men and women* and *committing them to prison*. But *Philip*, one of those who, along with Stephen, were formerly elected to the diaconate, was among *them that were scattered abroad*, and went down *to Samaria*. Filled with divine power he was the first to *proclaim* the word to the people of that country;[7] and so mightily did the divine grace work with him, that even Simon the sorcerer, with very many others, 11 was won over by his words. Now Simon was at that time so famous, and had acquired by magic arts such an ascendancy

---

[1] Gal. i. 19.   [2] i. 13. 5.   [3] i. 13. 11–17.
[4] Cp. *D. Addai*, p. 17 ff.   [5] Acts viii. 1.
[6] Acts xi. 19.   [7] Acts viii. 3–5.

over his dupes, that he was held to be *the great power of God*. So then, on that occasion he too was astounded at the miracles wrought by the hand of Philip through the divine power, and stealthily *feigned faith* in Christ, even going as far as bap-
12 tism.[1]   And this amazing thing is done to this day by those who still even now follow the abominable heresy which he founded : after the manner of their forefather they steal into the Church like a pestilential and scabby disease, and cause the greatest mischief to such as they can infect [2] with the poison concealed in themselves, hard to cure and dangerous.   Already, in fact, many of them have been expelled, when the nature of their villainy was discovered; even as Simon himself paid the due penalty when Peter unmasked his true character.
13   But since the preaching of salvation went forward and increased from day to day, a divine dispensation brought from the land of the Ethiopians a principal man in the court of the queen of that country : it being an ancient custom, still to this day observed, that that nation should be ruled over by a woman.   It is recorded that this man (who was the first Gentile to partake of the sacred rites of the divine Word at the hands of Philip, to whom a revelation came,[3] thus becoming a firstfruits of the faithful throughout the world), on returning to his native land, was the first to preach the knowledge of the God of the universe and the life-giving sojourn of our Saviour among men.[4]   Thus by his means was fulfilled in truth the prophecy where it is said : *Ethiopia shall*
14 *haste to stretch out her hand unto God.*[5]   Moreover, Paul, the *chosen vessel,*[6] *not from men, neither through men, but through revelation of Jesus Christ* himself *and God the Father, who raised him from the dead,* was appointed *an apostle,*[7] being *counted worthy of* that *calling* [8] in a *vision, and in the voice that came from heaven* [9] with the revelation.

The Report of Pilate to Tiberius.

2.   And further, when the miraculous resurrection and ascension into the heavens of our Saviour had come to be very widely noised abroad, since the ancient custom still held that the governors of the provinces should indicate to the emperor then reigning any novelties that took place among them, in order that no occurrence might escape him, Pilate communicated to the Emperor Tiberius the facts, already on all men's lips throughout the whole of Palestine, concerning the resurrection
2 from the dead of our Saviour Jesus.   For Pilate had learnt of His other miraculous deeds, and how His rising again

---

[1] Acts viii. 10–13; Iren. i. 16. 1.   [2] *Lit.* " imprint upon."
[3] See Acts viii. 29.   [4] Iren. iii. 12. 10.   [5] Ps. lxviii. 31.
[6] Acts ix. 15.   [7] Gal. i. 1, 12.
[8] 2 Thess. i. 11.   [9] Acts xxii. 6–9; xxvi. 14, 19.

from the dead after death had caused many to believe in Him as God. Now it is said that, when Tiberius brought the matter before *the Senate*, that assembly *rejected it*, ostensibly because they had not first *approved* it (for an *ancient* law prevailed that no one should be deified among the Romans except by a decree and decision of the *Senate*); but in reality because the saving teaching of the divine message needed neither man's

3 approval nor commendation. At all events [it is said] that when the council of the Romans had thus rejected the report *which had been brought* concerning our Saviour, Tiberius maintained his former opinion and devised no evil against the teaching of Christ.

4 This is the account given by Tertullian, a man well versed in the laws of the Romans, of high repute in other respects and one of the most distinguished persons at Rome. He inserts it in the Apology for the Christians, which was written by him in Latin, and translated into Greek. His actual words run thus :

5 But that we may treat of such laws even from their origin, there was an ancient decree that no one should be elevated to the rank of deity by an emperor, except the matter were first approved by the Senate. This was the course adopted by Marcus Æmilius with reference to a certain idol Alburnus. And that with you divinity is conferred by man's approval is a fact in favour of our doctrine. If a god is not acceptable to men, he does not become a god. Thus on this principle man ought to be propitious to God.

6 Tiberius, then, in whose day the name "Christian" made its way into the world, communicated to the Senate this doctrine, the news of which had been brought him from Palestine, where first it began : being evidently, as they saw, pleased therewith. But the Senate rejected it, inasmuch as the approval had not come from itself. Howbeit Tiberius continued to abide by his own conclusion, and threatened with death those who accused the Christians.[1]

It was Providence on high which by a divine dispensation put this thought into the emperor's mind, to the end that *the word* of the Gospel might be without hindrance in its first stages, and so *run*[2] rapidly abroad throughout all the earth.

Expansion of the Church.

3. Thus verily, by the power and co-operation of heaven, the word of salvation like a ray of the sun flashed its light in a moment upon the whole world; and straightway, in accordance with the divine Scriptures, *the sound* of its inspired evangelists and prophets went forth through *all the earth, and their words to the*

2 *end of the world*.[3] And verily throughout every city and village, like unto a well-filled threshing floor,[4] churches thronged with multitudes sprang up all at once. They whose souls ancestral tradition and ancient error had long fettered with the old

[1] Tert., *Apol.* 5.   [2] 2 Thess. iii. 1.
[3] Ps. xix. 4 (LXX).   [4] Cp. Matt. iii. 12; Luke iii. 17.

disease of idolatrous superstition, were delivered from their
cruel masters, so to speak, by the power of Christ displayed
in both the teaching and miracles of His disciples, and found
release from their galling bonds; and as they renounced with
abhorrence every kind of devilish polytheism, so they acknowledged that there was one God alone, the Creator of the
universe; and Him they honoured with the ordinances of true
piety in that divine and chastened worship whose seeds were
sown in human life by our Saviour.

3   But indeed the grace of God *was* now being *poured on the
remaining Gentiles also*,[1] and *at Cæsarea* in Palestine *Cornelius with* his whole *house* [2] first received the faith of Christ
by means of a divine revelation and the agency of Peter;[3]
as did also a multitude of other *Greeks* at *Antioch*, to whom
they that were scattered abroad at the persecution connected
with *Stephen* preached.[4] The church at Antioch was now
flourishing and abounding : in it were to be found very many
prophets from Jerusalem,[5] and with them Barnabas and Paul
and another concourse of brethren too.   Thus the title
" Christians " then for the first time issued forth from thence,
4 as from a copious and fecund spring.[6] And *Agabus, one* of
the prophets with *them*, prophesied concerning the *famine*
which *should be*; while Paul *and Barnabas* were sent to render
their utmost service for the *relief* of *the brethren*.[7]

REIGN OF GAIUS (37–41)

Herod Agrippa I made King of Palestine.

1.   Tiberius, then, died after a reign of about two-and-twenty
years, and was succeeded in the government by *Gaius*, who
immediately *crowned Agrippa* ruler of the Jews, *making him
king of the tetrarchies of Philip and Lysanias*; and shortly
afterwards he also committed to him the tetrarchy of Herod as
well, when *he had punished* Herod and his wife Herodias *with
perpetual exile* on the ground of very many crimes.   (It was
this Herod who was a contemporary of the Saviour's Passion.)
Josephus is a witness to these facts also.[8]

Philo.

2   It was under this same Gaius that Philo came to be very
widely known : a man of very great note not only among
ourselves, but also among persons educated in paganism.   By
birth and origin a Hebrew, he was second to none of those illus-
3 trious men who held high office at Alexandria.   How exceedingly he laboured in divinity and the studies of his own people

---

[1] Acts x. 45.   [2] Acts x. 1, 2.   [3] Acts x. 3 ff.
[4] Acts xi. 19, 20.   [5] Acts xi. 27.   [6] Acts xi. 22, 26.
[7] Acts xi. 28–30.
[8] Jos., *Ant.* xviii. 6. 10; 7. 2 (237, 252); *B.J.* ii. 9. 6 (181 ff.).

is clear to all from the facts; and there is no need to speak of his proficiency in the philosophy and liberal studies of profane learning, since he is related to have been especially devoted to the school of Plato and Pythagoras, and therein to have surpassed all his contemporaries.

The Misfortunes of the Jews.

5.   And, moreover, he has handed down in five books the happenings to the Jews under Gaius : in which he tells of the mental derangement of the emperor, who proclaimed himself a god and wantonly abused his power again and again; and also of the afflictions of the Jews in his day; and of the embassy on which he went to the city of the Romans on behalf of his fellow-countrymen at Alexandria, and how that, on his appearance before Gaius to defend the laws of his fathers, he received nothing but ridicule and mockery, and all but ran the risk of losing his life.[1]

2   Josephus mentions these facts also, in the eighteenth book of his Antiquities.   The actual words which he writes are as follows :

And further, when faction arose at Alexandria between the Jews who lived there and the Greeks, three ambassadors were chosen from each party in the faction to appear before Gaius.
3 Now one of the deputation on the Alexandrian side was Apion, who brought many slanderous accusations against the Jews, saying among other things that they neglected the honours due to Cæsar : that, for instance, while all the subjects of the Roman Empire erected altars and temples to Gaius and in all other respects hailed him as they did the gods, the Jews alone thought it disgraceful to honour him with statues or swear by his name.
4 When Apion had uttered many grievous charges, by which he hoped, not unreasonably, that Gaius would be aroused, Philo, who was the head of the embassy of the Jews, a man in every respect distinguished, a brother of Alexander the Alabarch, and no tyro in philosophy, was capable of making a defence against
5 the accusations; but Gaius prevented him and bade him depart from his presence; for he was very angry, and it was plain that he meditated some severe measures against them.   So Philo went out grossly insulted, and told the Jews who were his colleagues to be of good courage, for that in his rage at them Gaius was in reality joining battle with God.[2]

6   Such is the account of Josephus.   And Philo himself, too, in his work The Embassy gives an accurate and detailed account of what he did at that time.   The greater part of this I shall pass over, and quote only so much as shall inform my readers clearly as to the misfortunes which befell the Jews then and shortly afterwards, because of their crimes against the Christ.   In the first place, then, Philo relates that, in the time of Tiberius, at the city of the Romans, Sejanus, a powerful member of the emperor's court, made every effort to

[1] Philo, *Leg.*, *passim*.   [2] Jos., *Ant.* xviii. 8. 1 (257 ff.).

secure the destruction of the whole [Jewish] nation root and branch ; while in Judæa Pilate, in whose day the crimes were committed against the Saviour, made an attempt with respect to the temple then still standing in Jerusalem which was contrary to Jewish law, and so aroused their fiercest frenzy.

6. But [he also relates] that, after the death of Tiberius, Gaius, who had received the principate, while making many persons the object of his numerous acts of violence, injured particularly the whole Jewish nation, and that to no small extent. This fact also we may briefly learn from his own language. He writes in these very words :

2   So capricious, then, was Gaius in his behaviour to everyone; but especially to the Jewish race, whom he hated so bitterly that he appropriated the places of prayer in the other cities, beginning with those in Alexandria, and filled them with images and statues representing himself (for he who allows others to set them up virtually erects them himself). And the temple in the Holy City, which had hitherto been untouched, being regarded as an unviolable sanctuary, he attempted to alter and transform into a temple of his own, so as to call it [the temple] of Zeus Incarnate, Gaius the Younger.[1]

3   In the second treatise of his work entitled On the Virtues the same writer relates that countless other events, terrible in character and surpassing all description, had happened to the Jews at Alexandria under the said emperor. And with him Josephus also is in agreement ; who likewise notes that the disasters which befell the whole nation began in the time 4 of Pilate and of their crimes against the Saviour. At all events, hear what he too tells us in the second book of the Jewish War. His actual words are as follows :

Now when Pilate was sent by Tiberius as procurator to Judæa, he secretly conveyed the images of Cæsar, called ensigns, veiled by night, into Jerusalem. This caused a tremendous disturbance among the Jews when it was day. For such as were near were astonished at the sight, since their laws had been trampled underfoot (for they allow no image to be set up in the city). . . .[2]

5   If you compare the foregoing with the book of the Gospels you will see that no long time elapsed before they were visited for the cry they uttered in the presence of Pilate himself, when they shouted that they had *no* other *king* save *Cæsar* [3] alone.
6 And then the same writer relates that after this they were visited by still another misfortune, in the following words :

But after this he raised another disturbance by spending the sacred treasure, called Corban, on an aqueduct, which conveyed water from a point three hundred stadia above. The multitude 7 was enraged at this, and, when Pilate came to Jerusalem, crowded

---

[1] Philo, *Leg.* 346.   [2] Jos., *B.J.* ii. 9. 2 (169 f.).   [3] John xix. 15.

around him, shouting against him all the while.   Pilate, however, foresaw the disturbance.   So he mingled armed soldiers, disguised in civilian dress, with the crowd; and, while forbidding the use of the sword, ordered them to strike those who made the outcry with batons.   Then he gave a preconcerted signal from the tribunal, and the Jews were smitten.   Many of them perished from the blows, many from being trampled underfoot by their friends in the panic; while the multitude was cowed and reduced to silence by the fate of those who were slain.[1]

8   Moreover, the same writer shows us that countless other revolutions were set on foot in Jerusalem itself, when he establishes the fact that, from that time on, the city and all Judæa were never free from factions, wars and wicked plots in quick succession, until finally the siege under Vespasian came upon them.   Such, then, was the punishment meted out by divine Justice upon the Jews for their crimes against Christ.

The Fate of Pilate.

7.   But it should be known that this very Pilate who lived in the time of the Saviour is recorded to have fallen into such misfortunes under Gaius (whose times we are now describing) that he was compelled to become his own murderer and execute himself with his own hand; for the divine Justice, as it would seem, was not long in overtaking him.   This is the account given by those Greeks who have drawn up a list of the Olympiads together with the events of each period.

REIGN OF CLAUDIUS (41–54)

8.   But indeed when Gaius had held the principate for less than four entire years, he was succeeded by the Emperor Claudius.

The Famine.

In his day the world was afflicted by a famine, a fact which even those writers who are strangers to our teaching have recorded in their histories.   And thus the prediction of *Agabus* the *prophet* in the Acts of the Apostles concerning the *famine* that *should be over all the world* received its fulfilment.

2   And Luke in the Acts has indicated the famine under *Claudius,* and placed it on record that *the brethren* in Antioch *sent* to those in *Judæa* by Paul *and Barnabas, every man* of *his ability.*[2]

Persecution of the Church.

9.   Then he goes on to say :

About that time

(evidently the time of Claudius)

Herod the king put forth his hands to afflict certain of the church. And he killed James the brother of John with the sword.[3]

---

[1] Jos., *B.J.* ii. 9. 4 (175 ff.).   [2] Acts xi. 27–30.   [3] Acts xii. 1, 2.

2 Now with reference to this James, in the seventh book of the Hypotyposeis Clement relates a further story worthy of mention, which he gives us on the strength of a tradition received from those before him. He states that

the person who led James to the judgment-seat was moved when he saw him bear witness, and confessed that he himself also was a 3 Christian. Thus both were led away together—

so he says—

and as they went he requested James to forgive him. James thought for a moment and then said : "Peace be to thee"; and kissed him. And thus they were both beheaded at the one time.

4 Then indeed, as the divine Scripture says, *when* Herod *saw,* after he had made away with James, that the deed caused *the Jews* pleasure, he attacked *Peter also.* And *when he had delivered him* to prison, he all but effected his murder as well : [which he would have done] had not Peter been miraculously released from his bonds, thanks to a divine visitation, *an angel* who *stood by him* [1] at night; and so he was set free for the ministry of preaching.

The Fate of Herod Agrippa I.

Thus, then, were the events of Peter's life divinely ordered.
10. But the consequences of the king's attempt upon the apostles were not long delayed; in fact the avenging minister of divine Justice overtook him at once. Immediately after his attack on the apostles, as the book of the Acts records, he had started for *Cæsarea*; and there on a noted feast *day* had *made an oration,* adorned with splendid and *royal apparel* and lifted high in front of the *throne.* And when *the people* to a man had received his oration with applause, as if it were *the voice of a god, and not of a man, immediately an angel of the Lord smote him,* as the oracle relates, *and he was eaten of worms, and gave up the ghost.* [2]

2 Now we may well wonder at the harmony that exists between the divine Scripture and the account given by Josephus in the case of this miraculous event also. It is evident that in it Josephus is witnessing to the truth, when, in the nineteenth tome of the Antiquities, he thus sets forth the wonderful tale in these very terms :

3 Now when the third year of his reign over all Judæa was com-
43-44. pleted, he came to the city of Cæsarea, which was formerly called Strato's Tower. And there he held public games in Cæsar's honour, having learnt that this was a certain festival observed on behalf of the emperor's safety; whereat a multitude of the officials in the province and men of high rank were assembled.

---

[1] Acts xii. 3, 4, 7.   [2] Acts xii. 19, 21–23.

4   But on the second day of the games he proceeded to the theatre
at daybreak, clad in a garment made wholly of silver, of a truly
marvellous texture.   There the silver was lit up by the first rays
of the sun as they struck it, and gave forth such a marvellous
reflection that its sheen filled those who gazed thereon with fear
5 and trembling.   And immediately his flatterers uttered from all
sides their shouts (though not to his good), addressing him as a
god, and adding : " Be thou gracious ; if until now we feared thee
as man, henceforth we acknowledge thee as superior to mortal
6 nature."   The king did not rebuke these words nor reject their
impious flattery.
     But after a little, on raising his eyes he saw an angel sitting above
his own head ; whom he immediately gathered to be an author
of evil, as he had once been of good : and anguish pierced his heart.
7 And all at once his belly was seized with a pain, violent from its
very start.   So, looking stedfastly at his friends, he said : " I
myself, who am your god, am under orders now to quit this life,
for destiny forthwith refutes the lying words ye uttered concerning
me.   I, whom ye called immortal, am now being led away to die.
Howbeit, fate must be accepted, even as God has willed it.   And
verily our life has in no wise been passed in sorry fashion, but
with that length of days which men call blessed."   So saying he
was overcome by an access of the pain.
8   Accordingly they conveyed him with haste to the palace, and
the rumour reached the ears of everyone that he would undoubtedly die before long.   And straightway the multitude,
with their wives and children, sat them down on sackcloth after
the custom of their fathers, and besought God for the king ; and
every place was filled with wailing and lamentations.   And when
the king, as he lay in a lofty chamber, looked down upon them
9 prostrate upon their faces, he too could not restrain a tear.   For
five days continually the pain in his belly wore him out, and then
he died, in the fifty-fourth year of his age, and the seventh of his
reign.
     So he reigned four years under the Emperor Gaius (ruling the
tetrarchy of Philip for a space of three years, and in the fourth
getting that of Herod as well) ; and three years besides during
the emperorship of Claudius Cæsar. . . .[1]

10   Here as elsewhere I marvel at the agreement of Josephus
with the truth of the divine Scriptures.   If, however, it may
seem to some that there is a discrepancy as regards the king's
name, in any case the time and the facts show that the same
person is in question.   Either the name has been changed
owing to a slip of the pen, or else, as happens frequently, he
was possessed of two names.

Theudas.

11.   Now since, once again, Luke in the Acts introduces Gamaliel
as saying, at the enquiry concerning the apostles, that about
the same time *rose up Theudas, giving himself out to be some-
body ; who* was put an end to, *and all, as many as obeyed him,*

---

[1] Jos., *Ant.* xix. 8. 2 (343 ff.).

were dispersed :[1] come, let us also quote what Josephus
writes about him. These, then, are the actual words of his
account, taken once more from the work of his which we have
just mentioned :

2   But when Fadus was procurator of Judæa, a certain magician
named Theudas persuaded the most of the populace to take up
their belongings, and follow him to the river Jordan. For he
said that he was a prophet, and that at his bidding the river
would divide in two and afford them an easy passage. And with
3 these words he deceived many. Howbeit Fadus did not allow
them to enjoy their folly, but sent out a troop of horse against
them, which fell upon them unawares, killing many and taking
many alive ; while they took captive Theudas himself, cut off
his head and brought it to Jerusalem.[2]

Helena, Queen of Adiabene.

Next after this, he mentions also the famine that took
place under Claudius, somewhat on this manner :

12.   Thereupon also it came to pass that the great famine took place
in Judæa, during which Queen Helena distributed among the
needy the corn which she had purchased at great expense from
Egypt. . . .[3]

2   Now you will find that this statement also accords with the
book of the Acts of the Apostles, where it tells us that *the
disciples* at Antioch, *every man according to his ability,
determined* to send *relief unto those that dwelt in Judæa :
which also they did, sending it to the elders by the hand of*
3 *Barnabas and* Paul.[4] In fact they still to this day point out
celebrated steles of this same Helena, whom the writer mentioned, in the suburbs of Ælia, as it now is. She was said to
have reigned over the people of Adiabene.[5]

Simon Magus.

13.   But since the faith of our Saviour and Lord Jesus Christ
was now being spread abroad among all men, the enemy of
man's salvation, in his endeavours to secure the first hold on
the imperial city, brought thither the aforesaid [6] Simon ; and,
moreover, joining forces with the man's clever magic, got into
his own possession, and led into error, many dwellers in Rome.
2 This fact is told us by Justin, who not long after the apostles
was a distinguished member of our faith ; concerning whom I
shall state what is necessary at the proper place. In his first
Apology to Antoninus on behalf of our doctrine he writes in
the following words :

[1] Acts v. 36.   [2] Jos., *Ant.* xx. 5. 1 (97 f.).   [3] *Ib.* 5. 2 (101).
[4] Acts xi. 29, 30.   [5] Jos., *Ant.* xx. 2. 1 (17).   [6] 1. 11.

3   And after the ascension of the Lord into heaven, the demons put forward certain men to say that they themselves were gods; who not only were not persecuted by you, but were even counted worthy of honours. Such was a certain Simon, a Samaritan, from the village of Gitta, as it is called; who in the days of Claudius Cæsar, thanks to the art of the demons who inspired him, wrought mighty works of magic in your imperial city of Rome, and so was reckoned as a god; and he has been honoured as a god by you with a statue . . . in the river Tiber between the two bridges, which bears this inscription in Latin : SIMONI DEO SANCTO,

that is, TO SIMON, HOLY GOD.

4 And almost all the Samaritans, and a few even of other nations, acknowledge and worship him as their chief god. And they call a certain Helena the Primary Thought that emanated from him— a woman who went round with him at that time, and formerly a public prostitute. . . .[1]

at Tyre in Phœnicia.[2]

5   Such is his account. But Irenæus also agrees with him, when in the first of his books Against the Heresies he gives a sketch of the man himself as well as of his profane and abominable teaching.[3] But this it would be superfluous for me to recount on the present occasion. For they who so desire may acquire an exact knowledge of the beginnings, the lives, the subject matters of the false opinions, of those heresiarchs who in turn succeeded Simon; as well as the practices of them all : since of these Irenæus has given us an account in the said book in no perfunctory manner.

6   That Simon, then, was the prime author of every kind of heresy is the tradition we have received. And from his day even to the present the followers of his heresy feign that sober Christian philosophy whose purity of conduct has won it universal fame. But none the less they continue to embrace that idolatrous superstition which they seemed to have done with, when they fall down before pictures and images of Simon himself and the said Helena his companion, and pursue the veneration of these with offerings of incense and 7 sacrifices and libations. And as for their esoteric practices, at which they say that a man, on first hearing them, will be amazed and " astonied "[4] (to use the written oracle in vogue among them)—for in truth they are full of amazement and frenzy and madness—they are of such a nature that not only may they not be committed to writing, but may not even so much as be found on the lips of modest men, so outrageously 8 vile and infamous is their character. For the foulest depths

---

[1] Just., *Apol.* i. 26.   [2] Iren. i. 16. 2.   [3] Iren. i. 16.
[4] θαμβόω (instead of the usual θαμβέω) : apparently the " correct " word in this circle.

of shame imaginable have all been surpassed by this filthiest
of heresies, which they follow who make a sport of wretched
women laden truly with all kinds of vices.[1]

14.   Of such vices Simon was at that time appointed the father
and creator—to be, as it were, the mighty adversary of
mighty men, the inspired apostles of our Saviour—by the
evil Power who hates the good and plots against the salvation of
2 men.   Howbeit the divine and super-celestial grace came to the
aid of her ministers, and through their appearing and presence
quenched with all speed the flame of the evil one as it was
kindling; by their means bringing low and *casting down every*
3 *high thing that is exalted against the knowledge of God.*[2]   Therefore neither on the part of Simon, nor of any other of those
who then sprung up, was any organized body formed in those
apostolic times.   For truly all things were subdued and over-
powered by the light of the truth and by the divine Word
Himself, who had just lately shone from God upon men, and
was in full force upon earth and dwelling in His own apostles.
4   No sooner was the said magician smitten in the eyes of his
mind by, as it were, a divine and miraculous flash of light, when
first in Judæa the apostle Peter unmasked his villany, than he
took a mighty journey across the sea from East to West and
fled away, deeming that thus alone might he live according
5 to his will.   So he came to the city of the Romans, and, with
the mighty assistance of the power which there lay in wait,
in a short time accomplished so much of what he endeavoured,
that the citizens *honoured him as a god*, even erecting *a*
6 *statue*.[3]   Nevertheless his affairs did not prosper for long.
Thus, in the same reign of Claudius, the all-good and gracious
Providence of the universe led Peter—the strong and great
apostle, marked out by his qualities as the spokesman of all
the rest—on Simon's heels to Rome, as if to oppose this
mighty bane of the world.   Having protected himself with
the divine armour like a noble captain of God, Peter conveyed the precious merchandise of the spiritual light from
the East to Western folk, preaching the good tidings of a
true light and a word which saves men's souls, to wit, the pro-
5.   clamation of the kingdom of heaven.   So then, when the
divine Word had thus come to sojourn among them, the power
of Simon was quenched and destroyed simultaneously with
the man himself.

The Origin of the Gospel of St. Mark.

But so brilliant was the light of piety that shone upon the
minds of Peter's hearers, that they were not content to be satisfied with hearing him once and no more, nor with the unwritten

[1] 2 Tim. iii. 6.   [2] 2 Cor. x. 5.
[3] Just., *Apol.* i. 26 (13. 3 above).

teaching of the divine message; but besought with all kinds
of entreaties Mark, whose Gospel is extant, a follower of
Peter, that he would leave them in writing also a memoir of
the teaching they had received by word of mouth; nor did
they relax their efforts until they had prevailed upon the man;
and thus they became the originators of the book of the
2 Gospel according to Mark, as it is called.   Now it is said that
when the apostle learnt, by revelation of the Spirit, what was
done, he was pleased with the men's zeal, and authorized the
book to be read in the churches—Clement has given the story
in the sixth book of the Hypotyposeis; [1] and the bishop of
Hierapolis also, Papias by name, corroborates his testimony.[2]
And [it is said] that Peter mentions Mark in his former
epistle; which also it is said he composed at Rome itself, and
indicates the fact when he calls the city, somewhat metaphoric-
ally, " Babylon," in these words : *She that is in Babylon, elect
together with you, saluteth you ; and so doth Mark my son.*[3]

Mark the Founder of the Church of Alexandria.

16.   Now it is said that this Mark journeyed to Egypt and was
the first to preach [there] the Gospel, which also he had
written; and that he was the first to form churches at
Alexandria itself.

Philo on the Early Christians of Alexandria.

2   And in consequence so large a multitude of believers, both
men and women, was there formed from the very start, living
in the most austere and rigorous discipline, that Philo
actually thought it worth while to describe in writing their
occupations, assemblies, repasts, as well as their whole manner
of life.

17.   It is recorded that he also conversed at Rome in the days
of Claudius with Peter, who at that time was preaching to the
people there.   Nor is this unlikely, for the very treatise of
which we speak, composed by him subsequently at a later
date, clearly contains the rules of the Church which are still
2 observed even to our own day.   And indeed, when he describes
with the utmost exactitude the manner of life of our ascetics,
it is plain that he not only knew, but also approved, extolled
and venerated the apostolic men of his day, who apparently
were of Hebrew race and therefore still observed most of the
ancient customs in a somewhat Jewish fashion.

3   In fact, after first assuring us, in his book entitled On the
Contemplative Life or On the Suppliants, that *of his own
invention* and of himself *he will add* to his proposed account
nothing that exceeds *the truth,* he says that they *were called*

---

[1] See vi. 14. 6, 7.   [2] See iii. 39. 15.   [3] 1 Pet. v. 13.

Therapeutæ, and the women of their company *Therapeutrides*. And he names the reasons for such a *title : either because* they cured and *healed* [1] *the souls* of those who came to them, thus ridding them, like a physician, of *disorders bred of evil ; or else* on account of the pure and sincere service [2] and worship which

4 they render to the Deity.[3] Whether, then, it is Philo himself who has thus designated them with a name adapted to the men's mode of life, or whether they were really so called from the very beginning, when the title " Christian " had not yet been universally given, we need not now argue.

5 In any case he testifies that first of all they renounce *their property*. He states that on beginning the philosophic life they make over their belongings to their relatives; then renouncing all the cares of this life go forth *outside city walls and make their dwelling in solitary fields and gardens, knowing* well *that intercourse with men unlike themselves is unprofitable and harmful*.[4] This, it would seem, the [Christians] of that day did, endeavouring with a spirited and fervent faith to

6 emulate the prophets' manner of life. For assuredly in the Acts of the Apostles also (an " acknowledged " book) it is similarly stated that *all* the disciples of the apostles, *selling off their possessions and goods, parted them to all, according as any man had need*,[5] so that *there was* not among *them any that lacked*. For example, *as many as were possessors of lands or houses*, as the word says, *sold them, and brought the prices of the things that were sold, and laid them at the apostles' feet :* so that *distribution was made unto each, according as anyone had need*.[6]

7 And when Philo has borne witness to facts similar to such as are here mentioned, he then goes on to use these very words :

So, then, this race is to be found in many places in the world. For it was right that both Greece and barbarian lands should share that which was perfectly good. But it is exceedingly numerous in Egypt, in each of the nomes, as they are called;

8 and especially in the neighbourhood of Alexandria. And the best men from every quarter set out to a colony—the fatherland, as it were, of the Therapeutæ—in a most suitable spot, which lies beyond the lake of Marea on a slightly elevated hillock, most conveniently situated on account of its security and mild climate.[7]

9 Then, after next describing the nature of their dwellings,[8] he speaks thus of the churches throughout the land :

Now in every house there is a sacred chamber, which is called the " holy place " or " monastery." In this they perform the mysteries of the religious life in solitude, bringing into it neither drink nor meat, nor any other thing necessary for their bodily

---

[1] θεραπεύειν.   [2] θεραπείας.   [3] Philo, *D.V.C.* 1, 2.
[4] *Ib*. 13, 18–20.   [5] Acts ii. 45.
[6] Acts iv. 34, 35.   [7] Philo, *D.V.C.* 21 f.   [8] *Ib*. 24.

needs, but laws, and inspired oracles from the lips of prophets, and hymns and all else by which knowledge and piety are increased and perfected.[1]

And later on he says :

10   Now the period between dawn and eventide is wholly occupied by them in diligent study. For as they read the sacred writings they meditate thereon, allegorizing the law [2] of their fathers, since they hold that the words in the literal sense are symbolical 11 of something hidden conveyed under the form of allegory. And they have also treatises of ancient men, past founders of their sect, who left behind many monuments of the allegorical method in its perfection, whom they adopt as archetypes, so to speak, and so imitate their manner and aim. . . .[3]

12   Such an account would naturally be given by the man after he had heard them expounding the sacred Scriptures. But it is highly probable that what he calls treatises of their ancient men are Gospels and the writings of the apostles and, it may be, expository discourses of the prophets of long ago, such as the Epistle to the Hebrews and many other epistles of Paul 13 contain. Then, again, he next writes as follows with reference to the fact that they composed new psalms :

    . . . so that they not only engage in contemplation, but also compose songs and hymns to God in all kinds of metres and melodies, which, of course, they write out in rhythms [4] of unusual solemnity.[5]

14   But of the many other matters, germane to our subject, of which he gives a full account in the same book, it appeared that we ought to choose such points as present to us the charac-15 teristic features of their mode of Church life. And if it should seem to anyone that what has been stated is not peculiar to the Gospel commonwealth, but might suit other persons better than the aforesaid, let him be convinced by the words of Philo which follow immediately. In these any fair-minded man will find indisputable testimony on this head. For he writes thus :

16   And self-control they first lay down as a kind of foundation of the soul, and then upon it build the other virtues. None of them may take food or drink before sunset, since they regard study as worthy of the light, but the bodily needs of the darkness. Therefore they have assigned the day to the one; but to the 17 other, a small part of the night. And some, in whom a greater longing for knowledge is implanted, only bethink them of food every three days; while others fare with such delight upon that sumptuous feast of wisdom which supplies their doctrines richly

---

[1] Philo, *D.V.C.* 25.
[2] Reading νομοθεσίαν, with Rufinus and the Armenian version of Philo.   .   [3] Philo, *D.V.C.* 28 f.
[4] Reading ἃ ῥυθμοῖς . . . χαράττουσιν with the MSS. of Philo.
[5] Philo, *D.V.C.* 29.

and without stint, that they actually refrain for a period twice
as long, and scarcely taste necessary food every six days; it
being their custom . . .[1]

18 Those statements of Philo in our opinion refer clearly and
indisputably to our co-religionists. But if after this there be
any man who still obstinately denies it, let such a one abandon
his incredulity under the persuasion of still plainer proofs,
which are to be found nowhere except in the Christian religion
19 conducted according to the Gospel. For he says that there
were *women also* in the company of the persons in question, of
whom the *greatest number* were aged *virgins,*

who have preserved their chastity not so much from necessity
(like some of the Greek priestesses) as of their own free will; since
their zeal and longing for wisdom, with whom they desired to live,
led them to despise the pleasures of the body and seek not for
mortal, but rather that immortal offspring which only the soul
that God loves can bear of itself. . . .[2]

20 Then, a little lower down, he tells us still more emphatically
the following :

They expound the sacred writings allegorically, according to
the deeper meaning. For the whole legislation, in the opinion of
these men, resembles a living organism, of which the ordinances
taken literally constitute the body, but the hidden sense under-
lying the words the soul. This sense was first made a special
object of study by this community,[3] which sees thoughts of
surpassing beauty reflected in the words as in a mirror. . . .[4]

21 Why need one add to this their *meetings* together; the
separate apartments of the men and women in the same
place ;[5] the spiritual exercises, which it is still our custom
to the present day to perform, and especially at the festival
of the Saviour's Passion, which it is our wont to spend in
fasting, vigil and meditation upon the divine Scriptures ?
22 These are the facts which the said person has told us in his own
work with unusual precision, indicating that very *method*
which we alone have preserved to this day. Thus he relates
the vigils [6] of the *great festival,*[7] the spiritual exercises therein
observed, the *hymns* it is our wont to recite ; and [describes]
how that while one man sings in strict time the others *listen
in silence* and only join in *chanting the refrain of each hymn ;* [8]
and [states] that on these said days they lie *upon the ground*
on *beds of rushes,*[9] and (to use the actual words he wrote) taste
absolutely no *wine* at all, nay, nor anything *which contains
blood ;* but *water* is their only *drink,* and *salt* and *hyssop the relish*
with their *bread.*[10]

[1] Philo, *D.V.C.* 34 f.   [2] *Ib.* 68.
[3] οἰκία.   The text of Eusebius has been followed in this section; but
it can scarcely be held to give us what Philo wrote. See Conybeare,
p. 250.   [4] Philo, *D.V.C.* 78.   [5] *Ib.* 32, 40.   [6] *Ib.* 83.
[7] *Ib.* 65.   [8] *Ib.* 80.   [9] *Ib.* 69.   [10] *Ib.* 73, 37.

23 In addition Philo describes the manner in which those to
whom the ministries of the Church had been entrusted performed their leadership : that is to say, the functions of the
deacon and the presidency of the bishop over all the rest.[1]
But anyone who is anxious for a careful examination of these
points may learn them from this man's account already
24 mentioned. It is plain to everyone, however, that when
Philo wrote this, he had in view the first heralds of the Gospel
teaching and the customs handed down by the apostles from
the beginning.

Philo's Writings.

18. But to resume. Copious in his language, broad in his conceptions, lofty and elevated in his views on the divine Scriptures, Philo has composed a varied and diverse exposition of
the sacred books. On the one hand, as regards Genesis he
has pursued the study of it in orderly sequence, in the books
which he entitled [1] Allegories of the Sacred Laws; on the
other hand, he has discussed, one by one, separate points
which are mooted in the Scriptures, and has given his observa-
tions and solutions, in those books on which he has bestowed
the title of [2] Questions and Solutions in Genesis and Exodus,
respectively.
2 As well as these he has composed special dissertations on
certain problems, such as the two books [3] On Husbandry,
and the same number [4] On Drunkenness; and certain others
to which he has given various and suitable titles, such as the
books [5] On what a Mind which has become sober desires
and detests, [6] On the Confusion of Tongues, [7] On Flight
and Discovery, [8] On the Coming Together for the sake
of Instruction, [9] On Who is the Heir to Things Divine or
On the Division into Equals and Opposites, and, moreover,
[10] On the Three Virtues which, with others, Moses has
described.
3 In addition to these there is the book [11] On those whose
Names were changed and Why they were changed, in which he
says that he also composed a [work] [11a] On Covenants,
4 Books i and ii.[2] And there are also his [works] [12] On Emigra-
tion and [13] the Life of a Wise Man who was perfected in
Righteousness, or Unwritten Laws; and, moreover, [14] On
Giants, or On the Immutability of the Deity; and [15] On
Dreams, that according to Moses they are sent by God, Books
i, ii, iii, iv, and v.
These are the books on Genesis which have come down to us.
5 But on Exodus we know his [16] Questions and Solutions,
Books i, ii, iii, iv and v; the [treatises] [17] On the Tabernacle;

---

[1] Cp. Philo, *D.V.C.* 75, 77, 79, 81.
[2] *De mut. nom.*, 53.

[18] On the Decalogue; [19] On the Special Laws which may be referred to the corresponding headings of the Ten Words, Books i, ii, iii and iv; [20] On the Animals appointed for the sacrificial Rites and What are the kinds of Sacrifices; and [21] On the Prizes set before the Good in the Law, and the Punishments and Curses set before the Wicked.

6 In addition to all these, there are also extant works of his, each in one book, such as [22] On Providence; the book he composed [23] On the Jews; [24] The Statesman; and, moreover, [25] Alexander, or That irrational animals possess reason.

Besides these there is [26] That every Wicked Man is a
7 Slave, followed by [27] That every Honest Man is Free. After these he has composed his book [28] On the Contemplative Life or The Suppliants, whence we have taken our account of the facts regarding the life of the apostolic men; and [29] The Interpretations of the Hebrew Names in the Law and the Prophets is also said to be his work.

8 Now Philo is stated to have come to Rome in the time of Gaius, and in the time of Claudius to have read before a full meeting of the Roman Senate what he had written concerning Gaius' hatred of God—a work which with characteristic irony he entitled [30] On Virtues. And so greatly, [it is stated,] they admired it, that his books were thought worthy of a place in libraries.

Aquila and Priscilla.

9 At this time, when Paul was completing his journey *from Jerusalem and round about even unto Illyricum,*[1] Claudius drove the Jews from Rome. So Aquila and Priscilla with the rest of the Jews left Rome and landed in Asia; and there they abode with Paul the apostle,[2] when he was *strengthening* [3] the foundations of the churches he had lately founded there. Our instructor in these matters also is the sacred book of the Acts.

Misfortunes of the Jews.

19.   Now while Claudius was still reigning, it came to pass that *so great a faction* and tumult broke out at *Jerusalem* during *the feast* of the *Passover,* that, *of* those *Jews* alone who *were forcibly crushed together around the exits* from *the temple,* thirty *thousand perished, trampled to death by one another.* So *the feast proved an occasion of grief to the people as a whole, and of lamentation to every house.* These are the very words em-
2 ployed by Josephus. But *Claudius appointed Agrippa,* the son *of Agrippa,* king of the Jews; and *sent Felix as procurator* of the whole district *of Samaria and Galilee, and of Peræa,*[4] as it is called, as well.

---

[1] Rom. xv. 19.   [2] Cp. Acts xviii. 2, 18, 19.   [3] Acts xviii. 23 (xv. 41).
[4] Jos., *B.J.* ii. 12. 1 (223 ff.), 8 (247); *Ant.* xx. 5. 3 (105 ff.).

REIGN OF NERO (54–68)

As for himself, when he had conducted the government for thirteen years and eight months, he died, leaving Nero to succeed to the principate.

Jewish Factions.

20.   Now Josephus, again, tells of the faction that took place among the priests themselves in the days of Nero, when Felix was procurator of Judæa.   He writes thus, in these very terms, in the twentieth book of the Antiquities :

2   And there actually arose a faction between the high priests on the one hand and the priests and leaders of the people of Jerusalem on the other. Each of them collected round him a band of the most reckless and revolutionary men, and put himself at their head; who when they met abused each other and threw stones.   Nor was there a single person to rebuke them : the thing was done
3 freely, as if in a city without a ruler.   And the high priests were possessed of such impudence and audacity, that they dared to despatch slaves to the threshing floors, to seize the tithes that were the priests' due; insomuch that needy priests might be seen perishing of want.   Thus did the violence of the factions prevail over all that is right.[1]

4   And, once more, the same writer records that a certain *kind of robbers sprang up* at the same time *in Jerusalem,* who, as he says, *used to murder* those they met *in broad daylight and*
5 *in the midst of the city.*   For [he states] that *especially at the festivals* they mingled *with the crowd and stabbed those that differed from them with short little swords, which they had previously concealed under their garments ;* and that *when* the men *fell, their murderers* actually *joined the ranks of the indignant, and so under this plausible disguise could in no way be detected.*
6 [He goes on to say] that while *Jonathan the high priest was the first to be murdered by them, after him many* were *killed every day, and* that *fear was a sorer burden than the evils themselves ; for, as in a battle, everyone was hourly expecting death.*[2]

The Egyptian False Prophet.

21.   After other remarks he next goes on to say :

But a greater blow than this was inflicted upon the Jews by the Egyptian false prophet.   For a wretched trickster arrived in the country, who by securing faith in himself as a prophet gathered together about thirty thousand of his dupes, and led them round from the desert to the mount of Olives, as it is called. From that point he was in a position to force his way into Jerusalem

---

[1] Jos., *Ant.* xx. 8. 8 (180 f.).   [2] Jos., *B.J.* ii. 13. 3 (254–256).

and overcome [1] the Roman garrison and the people with a high hand, with the aid of his body-guard of spearmen who were to
2 pour in with him.   But Felix anticipated his attack, and went to meet him with the Roman hoplites, while all the people lent a hand in the defence : so that, when the engagement took place, the Egyptian fled accompanied by a few, but the most of his followers perished or were taken captive. . . .[2]

3   Such is the account given by Josephus in the second of the Histories.   But it is worth while comparing the statements here made concerning the Egyptian with those in the Acts of the Apostles, where in the time of Felix it was said by *the chief captain* in Jerusalem to Paul, when *the multitude* of the Jews raised a disturbance against the apostle : *Art thou not then the Egyptian, which before these days stirred up to sedition and led out* into *the wilderness the four thousand men of the Assassins ?* [3]

Last Years of St. Paul.

So much, then, for the events that happened under Felix.
22. But, as his *successor*,[4] Nero sent Festus, in whose day Paul was brought in bonds to Rome, having first made his own defence. *Aristarchus* was with him,[5] whom also somewhere in his epistles he suitably calls a *fellow-prisoner*.[6]   And Luke, the same who delivered in writing the Acts of the Apostles, brought his history to a close at that point of time, after indicating that Paul spent *two whole years* at Rome without restraint, and *preached the* word *of God, none forbidding him*.[7]
2 Having, therefore, made his defence at that time, it is recorded that the apostle again journeyed on the ministry of preaching, and, having set foot for the second time in the same city, was perfected in his martyrdom.   While still in bonds he composed his second epistle to Timothy, mentioning both his former *defence* and also his imminent perfecting.
3   Hear his testimony on these matters also :

At my first defence, he says, no one took my part, but all forsook me : may it not be laid to their account.   But the Lord stood by me, and strengthened me ; that through me the message might be fully proclaimed, and that all the Gentiles might hear : and I was delivered out of the mouth of the lion.[8]

4   In these words he clearly establishes the fact that on the former occasion, to the end that *the message through* him *might be fully known*, he *was delivered out of the mouth of the lion :* [8] giving this name, it seems, to Nero, on account of his cruel

---

[1] Reading κρατῆσαι in place of κρατήσας.
[2] Jos., *B.J.* ii. 13. 5 (261 ff.).   [3] Acts xxi. 27-38.
[4] Acts xxiv. 27.   [5] Acts xxvii. 2.
[6] Col. iv. 10.   [7] Acts xxviii. 30, 31.
[8] 2 Tim. iv. 16, 17.

nature. Nor did he go on to add, " He will deliver me out of
the mouth of the lion " or anything similar; for he saw by
5 the Spirit that his end was just about to come.   Therefore,
after the words *and I was delivered out of the mouth of the lion*,[1]
he adds *The Lord will deliver me from every evil work, and will
save me unto his heavenly kingdom*,[2] indicating his imminent
martyrdom.   And this also he foretells still more clearly in the
same writing, when he says : *For I am already being offered,
6 and the time of my departure is come*.[3]   And then, in his second
epistle to Timothy, he informs us that at the time of writing
only Luke was present with him, but at *the* former *defence* [4]
not even he.   Probably it was for this reason that Luke used
that point of time as a terminus for the Acts of the Apostles,
having traced the course of the history so long as he was
7 present with Paul.   Now we have made these statements in
proof of the fact that Paul's martyrdom was not accomplished
8 during that stay at Rome which Luke has recorded.   In fact
it is probable that Nero received Paul's defence of the faith
more graciously, since at first he was of a milder disposition;
but that, when he proceeded to unhallowed crimes, he coupled
with his other deeds his attacks upon the apostles.

Martyrdom of James the Just.

23.   But to resume.   When Paul *appealed unto Cæsar* [5] and
was sent on his way to the city of the Romans by Festus, the
Jews were disappointed of the hope which led them to devise
the plot against him, and so turned to *James the Lord's brother*,
to whom *the apostles* had entrusted the throne of the episcopate
at Jerusalem.[6]   And they made their attempt against him in
2 the following way.   Bringing him forward they demanded of
him in the presence of all the people a denial of his faith in
Christ.   And when, contrary to the general opinion, he used
greater boldness and freedom of speech, before the whole
multitude, than they expected, and confessed that Jesus our
Saviour and Lord was the Son of God, they were unable to
endure the testimony of such a man; since the philosophy and
godliness, which his life displayed to so eminent a degree, was
the occasion of a universal belief in him as *the most just of men*.
So they *put him to death*,[7] seizing upon the fact that they were
without government as an opportunity for liberty of action;
for Festus died in Judæa at that very time, and the adminis-
3 tration there was without governor or procurator.   Now the
manner of James' death has already [8] been shown by the
words of Clement we have quoted, who has placed it on record
that he was *cast down* from *the pinnacle* and *beaten* to *death* with
a club.

---

[1] 2 Tim. iv. 17.   [2] 2 Tim. iv. 18.   [3] 2 Tim. iv. 6.
[4] 2 Tim. iv. 11, 16.   [5] Acts xxv. 11.   [6] Cp. Heg. (§ 4 below).
[7] Jos. (§ 20 below).   [8] See I. 5.

Nevertheless Hegesippus, who belonged to the first succession from the apostles, gives the most accurate record concerning him, in his fifth Memoir. He says as follows :

4   Together with the apostles James the Lord's brother succeeded to [the government of] the Church. He received the name of "the Just" from all men, from the time of the Lord even to our 5 own; for there were many called James. Now he was holy *from his mother's womb, drank no wine nor strong drink,*[1] nor ate anything in which was life; *no razor* came *upon his head,*[2] he anointed 6 himself not with oil, and used no bath. To him alone it was permitted to enter the holy place; for he wore nothing woollen, but linen garments. And alone he entered into the sanctuary, and was found on his knees asking forgiveness on behalf of the people, so that his knees became hard like a camel's, for he was continually bending the knee in worship to God, and asking 7 forgiveness for the people. In fact, on account of his exceeding great justice he was called "the Just" and "Oblias" which is in Greek "bulwark of the people" and "justice," as the prophets show concerning him.[3]
8   Certain, then, of the seven sects which are among the people, of which I have written before [4]

(in the Memoirs),

enquired of him, What is *the door* of Jesus ? [5] and he said that 9 He was the Saviour. Of these some [6] came to believe that Jesus is the Christ. But the above-mentioned sects did not believe either that He rose again or that He is *coming to render to every man according to his works.*[7] And as many as came to believe did so 10 through James. When, therefore, *many also of the rulers* were *believers,*[8] there was an uproar among the Jews and Scribes and Pharisees; for they said : "There is danger that the whole people should expect Jesus as the Christ."
Coming together, therefore, they said to James : "We beseech thee, restrain the people, for it is gone astray unto Jesus, [imagining] that He is the Christ. We beseech thee to persuade all who come for the day of the Passover concerning Jesus, for in thee do we all put our trust. For we bear thee witness, as do all the people, that thou art just and *that thou acceptest not the person of* 11 *any.*[9] Persuade, therefore, the multitude that they go not astray concerning Jesus. For of a truth the people and we all put our trust in thee. Stand, therefore, upon the pinnacle of the temple, that from thy lofty station thou mayest be evident, and thy words may easily be heard by all the people. For on account of the Passover all the tribes, with the Gentiles also, have come to-12 gether." Therefore the aforesaid Scribes and Pharisees set James upon the pinnacle of the temple,[10] and cried aloud to him, saying : "O just one, in whom we ought all to put our trust; inasmuch as the people is gone astray after Jesus who was crucified, tell us

---

[1] Luke i. 15; Lev. x. 9.   [2] Num. vi. 5.
[3] Cp. Isai. xxxiii. 15, 16 (Symmachus).
[4] Cp. Heg. (iv. 22. 7 below).   [5] Cp. John x. 1, 2, 7, 9.
[6] The text is corrupt, according to Schwartz.
[7] Rom. ii. 6; Rev. xxii. 12.   [8] John xii. 42.
[9] Luke xx. 21.   [10] Lit. "sanctuary."

13 what is *the door* of Jesus." [1]   And he replied with a loud voice:
" Why ask ye me concerning *the Son of Man,* since He *sitteth* in
heaven *at the right hand of the* mighty *power, and* shall *come on*
14 *the clouds of heaven ? "* [2]   And when many were fully persuaded
and gave glory at the testimony of James and said, " *Hosanna to
the son of David,"* [3] then once more the same Scribes and Pharisees
said among themselves : " We do ill in affording such a testimony
to Jesus.   Let us rather go up and cast him down, that being
15 affrighted they may not believe him."   And they cried aloud,
saying : " Ho, ho, even the just one has gone astray ! "   And they
fulfilled the scripture that is written in Isaiah : *Let us take away
the just one, for he is troublesome to us.   Therefore they shall eat
the fruit of their doings.*[4]   Going up therefore, they cast the just
16 one down.   And they said to each other, " Let us stone James the
Just."

And they began to stone him, for the fall did not kill him.   But
turning he kneeled down and said : " I beseech thee, O Lord
17 God, *Father, forgive them ; for they know not what they do."* [5]   And
while they thus were stoning him, one of the priests of the sons of
Rechab the son of *Rachabim,* who had witness borne to them by
Jeremiah the prophet,[6] cried aloud, saying : " Cease ye ; what do
18 ye ?   The just one is praying on your behalf."   And one of them,
a fuller, took the club with which he beat out the clothes, and
brought it down on the just one's head.   Thus he was martyred.
And they buried him at the spot beside the temple, and his monument still remains beside the temple.   He has become a true
witness both to Jews and Greeks that Jesus is the Christ.   And
immediately Vespasian attacked them.

19   Such is the account which Hegesippus gives at length, an
account which, in fact, agrees with that of Clement.   But it
would seem that James was so marvellous a person, and so
universally famed for justice, that the more sensible even of
the Jews thought that this was the cause of the siege of
Jerusalem which followed immediately after his martyrdom,
a siege which, in their opinion, happened to them for no other
20 reason than their guilty crime against James.   As a matter of
fact Josephus did not hesitate to testify to this in writing, when
he speaks in the following terms :

Now these things happened to the Jews to requite them for
James the Just, who was a brother of Jesus who was called Christ ;
inasmuch as the Jews put him to death, though the most just of
men.[7]

21   And the same person also tells us of his death in the
twentieth book of the Antiquities, as follows :

Now Cæsar sent Albinus as governor to Judæa, when he learnt
of the death of Festus. . . . But the younger Ananus, who, as
we stated, had received the high priesthood, was of a rash and

---

[1] John x. 1, 2, 7, 9.   [2] Matt. xxvi. 64.   [3] Matt. xxi. 9.
[4] Isai. iii. 10 (LXX, with variant).   [5] Luke xxiii. 34.
[6] Jer. xxxv.   [7] Jos. in Orig., *c. Cels.* i. 47.

exceedingly audacious disposition; he belonged to the sect of the
Sadducees, who surpass all the rest of the Jews in the cruelty of
22 their sentences, as we have already shown.   Inasmuch, then, as
Ananus was a man of this character, he convened the judicial
court of the Sanhedrin, deeming that he had a suitable opportunity
in the fact that Festus had died and that Albinus was still on his
way; and bringing before the court the brother of Jesus who was
called Christ, whose name was James, and certain others, he
accused them of breaking the law, and delivered them over to be
stoned.
23   But those in the city who had a reputation for greater fairness,
and strict observance of the laws, took this conduct very ill, and
sent secretly to the king, asking him to write to Ananus not to
continue such practices any longer; for he had not done rightly
even this first time.   And some of them also went to meet
Albinus as he was on his way from Alexandria, and informed him
that it was illegal for Ananus to convene a meeting of the
24 Sanhedrin without his consent.   Albinus was persuaded by what
they said, and wrote in anger to Ananus, threatening him with
punishment; and King Agrippa for this reason took the high
priesthood away from him, when he had ruled for three months,
and appointed Jesus the son of Dammæus.[1]

Such is the account given of James, who is stated to be the
author of the first of the epistles which are entitled " catholic."
25 But it should be known that it is considered spurious.   Certainly
not many of the ancients mentioned it : nor yet the Epistle of
Jude, as it is called ; which also is one of the seven " catholic "
epistles.   Nevertheless we know that these also, as well as the
others, have been read in public in most churches.

The First Bishop of Alexandria.

24.
63.
Now when Nero was in the eighth year of his reign, Annianus
succeeded, first after Mark the evangelist, to the ministry
of the community at Alexandria.

Persecution.

25.
But when the principate was now firmly secured for Nero,
he plunged into vile habits, and armed himself even against
piety towards the God of the universe.   Indeed, to describe
the nature of this man's depravity does not lie within our
2 present task.   Nevertheless, since many have given us the
facts about him in most accurate accounts, anyone who so
desires may perceive from them how stupid was the man's
outrageous madness.   Actuated by blind fury he perpetrated
the destruction of countless persons, and stained himself with
blood to such an extent that he spared not even his nearest

[1] Jos., *Ant.* xx. 9. 1 (197 ff.).

and dearest, but in like manner, by manifold forms of death, made away with mother, brothers and wife, together with countless other relatives as well, as if they were his enemies
3 and foes.   And it seems that in addition to all these crimes we must register this fact also to his credit, that he was the first emperor to be proclaimed as the foe of piety towards the Deity.
4   Once more it is the Roman Tertullian who mentions this, saying somewhat in this fashion :

Read your memoirs, and there you will find that Nero was the first to attack this opinion, when, after subduing all the East, he raged fiercely against all, but especially in Rome.   We glory that such a man was the author of our chastisement.   For anyone who knows him can understand that it could only have been something of great excellence that would have been condemned by Nero.[1]

The Martyrdom of Paul and Peter.

5   Thus, then, was he who was heralded as the very first antagonist of God stirred up to murder the apostles.   It is related that in his day Paul was beheaded at Rome itself, and that Peter likewise was crucified, and this story is accredited by the attachment, which prevails to this day, of the names of
6 Peter and Paul to the cemeteries there ; and in no less degree also by a churchman, named Gaius, who lived in the time of Zephyrinus, bishop of the Romans.   Gaius, in fact, when discoursing in writing with Proclus, a champion of the heresy of the Phrygians, speaks thus of the places where the sacred tabernacles of the said apostles have been laid :

7   But I myself can point out the trophies of the apostles.   For if it is thy will to proceed to the Vatican, or to the Ostian Way, thou wilt find the trophies of those who founded this church.

8   And that *they were martyred both on the same occasion*, Dionysius, bishop of the Corinthians, in a written communication to the Romans, proves in the following manner :

In these ways you also, by such an admonition, have united the planting that came from Peter and Paul, of both the Romans and the Corinthians.   For indeed both planted also in our Corinth, and likewise taught us; and likewise they taught together also in Italy, and were martyred on the same occasion.

These quotations I have made, in order to accredit still further the facts of the history.

[1] Tert., *Apol.* 5.

The Beginning of the Jewish War.

26. Now once more Josephus, in the very numerous details
that he gives concerning the disaster which fell on the whole
Jewish nation, shows in express terms that, in addition to very
many others, there were countless numbers of Jews of position
whom *Florus punished by scourging, and crucified* in Jerusalem itself.[1]   And [he says] that he was procurator of Judæa at
66.   the time when the flame of *war was first* kindled, *in the
twelfth year of Nero's government.*[2]

2 And he says that then a *terrible commotion* ensued, at the
revolt of the Jews, even throughout *the whole of Syria*, and
that everywhere the people of the [Jewish] nation were
pitilessly destroyed, as if they were foes, by the inhabitants of
each city; so that one saw *the cities full of unburied bodies, and
corpses scattered about, the old man and the babe together, and
women without even the covering that modesty demands; and*
that *while the whole province was full of indescribable calamities,*
the intense dread *of what was threatened was worse than the
actual cruelty in each case.*[3]   These are the express terms that
Josephus uses.   And such was the plight of the Jews at that
time.

[1] Jos., *B.J.* ii. 14. 9 (306).
[2] *Ib.* 14. 4 (284); *Ant.* 20. 11 (257).
[3] Jos., *B.J.* 18. 2 (462, 465).

BOOK III

The Third Book of the Ecclesiastical History contains the following :

1. In what parts of the world the apostles preached Christ.
2. Who was the first to preside over the church of the Romans.
3. On the epistles of the apostles.
4. On the first succession from the apostles.
5. On the final siege of the Jews after [the time of] Christ.
6. On the famine that pressed hard upon them.
7. On the predictions of Christ.
8. On the signs before the war.
9. On Josephus and the treatises he has left behind.
10. How he mentions the divine books.
11. That, after James, Symeon ruled the church at Jerusalem.
12. That Vespasian ordered the descendants of David to be sought out.
13. That Avilius was the second to rule the Alexandrians.
14. Also that Anencletus was the second bishop of the Romans.
15. That, after him, Clement was the third.
16. On the epistle of Clement.
17. On the persecution under Domitian.
18. On John the apostle and the Apocalypse.
19. That Domitian ordered the descendants of David to be put to death.
20. On the relatives of our Saviour.
21. That Cerdon was the third to rule the church of the Alexandrians.
22. That Ignatius was the second ruler of the church of the Antiochenes.
23. Story concerning John the apostle.
24. On the order of the Gospels.
25. On the divine Scriptures which are acknowledged, and those which are not so.
26. On Menander the magician.
27. On the heresy of the Ebionites.
28. On Corinthus the heresiarch.
29. On Nicolaus and those called after him.
30. On those apostles who were found to have lived in wedlock.
31. On the death of John and Philip.
32. How Symeon, the bishop at Jerusalem, was martyred.
33. How Trajan prevented the Christians being sought for.
34. That Evarestus was the fourth to rule the church of the Romans.
35. That Justus was the third ruler of the church at Jerusalem.
36. On Ignatius and his epistles.
37. On the evangelists who were still eminent at that time.
38. On the epistle of Clement, and on the writings falsely attributed to him.
39. On the treatises of Papias.

1. SUCH, then, was the plight of the Jews at that time. But when the holy apostles and disciples of our Saviour were dispersed over the whole world, Parthia was allotted to Thomas, according to tradition, while Scythia was allotted to Andrew, and Asia to John,

2 . . . with whom[1] also he lived, dying at Ephesus. But *Peter*, it seems, preached in *Pontus* and *Galatia* and *Bithynia*, in *Cappadocia* and *Asia*, to those Jews who were *of the Dispersion*.[2] He also at the last came to Rome, and was crucified head-down-
3 wards; for he requested that he might suffer thus. What need to speak of Paul, who *from Jerusalem even unto Illyricum has fully preached the gospel of Christ*,[3] and afterwards was martyred at Rome under Nero ?

These are the express terms which Origen uses in the third tome of his Commentaries on Genesis.

The First Bishop of Rome.

2. Now Linus was the first, after the martyrdom of Paul and Peter, to receive the episcopate of the church of the Romans. *Paul* mentions *him* when writing to *Timothy* from Rome, in the salutation at the close of the *epistle*.[4]

The Writings of Peter and Paul.

3. Of Peter, then, one epistle, his former as it is called, is acknowledged; and of this also the elders of olden time have made frequent use, as a work beyond dispute, in their own treatises. But as for the second extant [epistle], the tradition received by us is that it is not canonical; nevertheless, since it appeared profitable to many, store was set by it [5] along with
2 the other Scriptures. Yet as regards the book of his Acts, as it is entitled, and the Gospel named after him, and his Preaching, as it is called, and The Apocalypse (such is its name): we know that they were not handed down at all among the catholic [writings]; for no Church writer, either in ancient times or even in our day, used testimonies derived from them.

[1] Plural (οὓς).   [2] 1 Pet. i. 1.   [3] Rom. xv. 19.
[4] 2 Tim. iv. 21; cp. Iren. iii. 3. 2.
[5] *Or*, " it was diligently studied."

3   But as my history advances I shall deem it profitable to
indicate, along with the successions, what Church writers
in each period have made use of which of the disputed [books],
and what they have said about the canonical and acknowledged
writings, and anything that they have said about those
that are not such.

4   Now the writings that bear the name of Peter, of which I
recognize only one epistle as genuine and acknowledged by
5 the elders of olden time, are so many; while the fourteen
epistles of Paul are manifest and clear [as regards their genuine-
ness]. Nevertheless it is not right to be ignorant that some
have rejected the Epistle to the Hebrews, saying that it is
disputed by the church of the Romans as not being Paul's.
And I shall quote at the proper time what those who lived
before us have said with reference to this epistle also. Moreover, I have not received his Acts, as they are called, among
the undisputed writings.

6   But since the same apostle, in the concluding salutations
of the Epistle to the Romans, has mentioned among the others
Hermas also,[1] the author, it is said, of the book of The
Shepherd, it should be known that this too has been disputed
by some, on whose account it could not be placed among the
acknowledged [writings]; while it has been adjudged as most
essential by others, especially for those in need of an introduction of an elementary kind. Hence, as we know, it has
actually come to be read publicly in churches; and that some
of the oldest writers have used it is a fact which I have received
7 by tradition. So much, then, to show which of the divine
writings are unquestionable and which not acknowledged
by all.

The Preaching of Paul and Peter.

4.   That, indeed, in preaching to the *Gentiles* Paul had laid
the foundations of the churches *from Jerusalem and round
about even unto Illyricum*,[2] is an evident conclusion from his
own words and from what Luke has recorded in the Acts.
2 And from the language of Peter also—in how many provinces
he too used to preach the gospel to those of *the circumcision*,[3]
and deliver to them the word of the New Covenant, is clear
from what we have said to be his acknowledged epistle : in
which he writes to those of Hebrew parentage of *the Dispersion* in *Pontus* and *Galatia, Cappadocia* and *Asia and Bithynia*.[4]

Followers of Paul.

3   But how many and which of these became truly zealous
followers, and were accounted worthy to shepherd the churches

---

[1] Rom. xvi. 14.   [2] Rom. xv. 19.
[3] Gal. ii. 9.   [4] 1 Pet. i. 1.

founded by the apostles, it is not easy to say; except such
names as one might gather from expressions used by Paul.
4 For he had countless *fellow-workers and* (as he calls them)
fellow-soldiers; [1] the more part of whom he has deemed worthy
of undying remembrance, by the abiding testimony concerning them which he has included in his own epistles. Moreover,
Luke also in the Acts, in recording his disciples, mentions them
5 by name.   Nevertheless Timothy is stated to have been the
first to be allotted the episcopate of the community at
Ephesus; as also was Titus of the churches in Crete.[2]
6   Now Luke, who was by race an Antiochene and by profession
a physician, was very frequently in the company of Paul,
and had no merely casual acquaintanceship with the rest of
the apostles. So he has left us examples of that art of healing
souls which he acquired from them, in two inspired books.
These are, namely, the Gospel, which also he testified that he
penned in accordance with what *they delivered* unto him, *which
from the beginning were eye-witnesses and ministers of the word,
all* of whom, he also goes on to say, he had *followed closely
from the first;* [3] and the Acts of the Apostles, which he
composed, no longer from the evidence of hearsay but of his
7 own eyes. And it is said that Paul was wont to mention his
Gospel, whenever, in writing about some gospel of his own (as
it were), he used to say : *according to my gospel.*[4]
8   But of the other followers of Paul, he witnesses that *Crescens*
journeyed *to the Gauls;* while *Linus*, whom he mentions in the
Second Epistle to Timothy as being with him at Rome,[5]
was, as we have already shown,[6] the first after Peter to receive
9 the episcopate of the church of the Romans. Moreover,
Clement, who also was appointed over the church of the Romans
as its third bishop, according to Paul's own testimony was
10 his *fellow-worker* and *fellow-labourer.*[7]   In addition to these,
there is also that *Areopagite* named *Dionysius*, the first to
believe after Paul's speech to the Athenians *in Areopagus*,
according to the record of Luke in the Acts.[8]   Another
Dionysius, one of the ancients, pastor of the community of the
Corinthians, states that he was the first bishop of the church
11 at Athens.[9]   But indeed, as we go forward upon our way,
we shall mention at the proper place the events connected
with the succession from the apostles from time to time.   At
present let us proceed to the next stage of the history.

[1] Phil. ii. 25; Philem. 1, 2.   [2] 1 Tim. i. 3; Tit. i. 5.
[3] Luke i. 2, 3.   [4] Rom. ii. 10, xvi. 25, 2 Tim. ii. 8.
[5] 2 Tim. iv. 10, 21.   [6] c. 2.
[7] Phil. iv. 3.   [8] Acts xvii. 22, 34.
[9] Dionysius of Corinth (iv. 23. 3 below).

REIGN OF VESPASIAN (68–79)

5.　　After Nero had held the principate for thirteen years, and
Galba and Otho and their associates had continued in office
for a year and six months, Vespasian, who had distinguished
himself in the campaigns against the Jews, was made king
over Judæa itself, being proclaimed emperor by the armies
there.　He therefore set out immediately on the way to Rome,
entrusting the war against the Jews to his son Titus.

Departure of the Apostles from Judæa and the Christians from Jerusalem.

2　　But to resume.　After the ascension of our Saviour, the
Jews, in addition to their crime against Him, had devised
innumerable plots also against His apostles : first they put
Stephen to death by stoning; [1] and then, after him, *James,*
who was the son of Zebedee and *the brother of John,* was
beheaded; [2] and finally James, who was the *first,* after the
ascension of our Saviour, to receive *the throne* of the episcopate
there, departed this life in the manner we mentioned above.[3]
As for the other apostles, countless plots were laid against
their lives, and they were banished from the land of Judæa ;
but they journeyed to all the nations to teach the message,
in the power of *the Christ who said* [4] to them : *Go ye, and make*
3 *disciples of all the nations in my name.*[5]　Moreover, the people
of the church at Jerusalem, in accordance with a certain
oracle that was vouchsafed by way of revelation to approved
men there, had been commanded *to depart from the city* before
the war, and *to inhabit a certain city of Peræa.*　They called
it *Pella.*　And when *those who believed in Christ* had removed
from Jerusalem, as if holy men had utterly deserted both the
royal metropolis of the Jews itself and the whole land of
Judæa, the Justice of God then visited upon them all their
acts of violence to Christ and His apostles, by destroying that
generation of wicked persons *root and branch* from among
men.[6]

The Jewish War.

4　　How many evils, then, descended together at that time
in every place upon the whole nation; how the inhabitants
of Judæa especially were driven to the last extremity of misfortune; how many myriads of men from youth upwards,

---

[1] Acts vii. 58 ff.　　　　　　[2] Acts xii. 2.
[3] ii. 23.　　　　　　　　　　[4] Heg. in Epiph. *Hær.* 29. 7.
[5] Matt. xxviii. 19 (with variant).
[6] Heg. in Epiph. *Hær.* 29. 7; 30. 2; *Mens.* 15. 2–5.

together with women and children, fell by sword and famine and countless other forms of death ; the number and character of the sieges of Jewish cities that took place; nay more, what terrible, and worse than terrible, sights were seen by those who had fled to Jerusalem itself as to a most sure metropolis; the character of the whole war, and each of its happenings in detail; how at *the end the abomination of desolation* announced by the prophets took its *stand in* the once far-famed temple of God,[1] when it endured its utter ruin and final destruction by fire;—[all these things] he who wishes may gather with

5 exactitude from the history written by Josephus.[2] But it is necessary to indicate that this same writer records that a multitude, numbering about three million persons, of those who were assembled from the whole of Judæa at the season of the *feast* of *the Passover*, were *shut up* in Jerusalem *as in a*

6 *prison* (to use his very words). Certainly, it was fitting that on the days when they had inflicted His Passion upon the Saviour and Benefactor of all, the Christ of God—that on those very days they should be *shut up as in a prison*,[3] and receive at the hands of the divine Justice the destruction which came

7 upon them. Passing over, then, all those attempts upon them by the sword or in some other way which successively fell to their lot, I deem it necessary to set forth only those misfortunes that were caused by the famine, so that those who read this work may in part know that God's vengeance was not slow to descend upon them for their wickedness against the Christ of God.

6. Come, therefore, let us once more take into our hands the fifth book of the Histories of Josephus, and peruse the tragic records of the deeds of that time. He says :

But as for the wealthy, to remain [in the city] meant equally certain destruction. A man would be put to death for his possessions, on the pretext of desertion. The madness of the factious reached its height along with the famine, and day by day both

2 these terrible evils were inflamed more and more. Corn, indeed, was nowhere to be seen; but they used to burst in upon the houses, search them thoroughly, and then, if they found it, maltreat the inmates for denying its existence; or if they failed to find it, torture them for having concealed it too carefully. And the hapless people's bodies were used to decide whether or no they had the corn : if they were still robust, they were judged to be well off for food; but if wasted away already, they were passed by; and it seemed unreasonable to put to death those

3 who were about to perish immediately from want. And many secretly bartered their possessions for a single measure of wheat, if they happened to be of the richer sort; of barley, if of the

---

[1] Dan. ix. 27; Matt. xxiv. 14, 15; cp. Dan. xii. 11.
[2] Jos., *B.J.* vi. 4 (220 ff.); 6. 1 (316).
[3] *Ib.* 9. 3, 4 (423–428).

poorer. Then they would shut themselves up in the inmost recesses of their dwellings, and in some cases eat the grain raw under the pressure of direst want; in others, cook it in such
4 a manner as necessity and fear dictated. Nowhere was there a table set; but snatching the yet uncooked food from the fire they tore it in pieces. The fare was pitiable, and one might well weep to see the greed of the stronger, the lamentations of the weak.
5   In truth, famine is the worst of all misfortunes, but it destroys nothing so much as the sense of shame.[1] For that which in other circumstances is worthy of respect is in this case despised. Thus, wives would snatch the food out of the very mouths of their husbands, children from their fathers, and—most lamentable of all—mothers from their babes; and while their dearest were wasting away in their arms, they did not scruple to deprive them
6 of the drops that meant their life. Nevertheless such meals as these did not escape notice : the rioters everywhere swooped down even upon this loot. For whenever they spied a house shut up, it was a sign that its inmates were taking food; so they at once broke down the doors, burst in and carried off the morsels
7 which they had all but forced out of their throats. Old men who clung to their food were beaten, and women who concealed what was in their hands had their hair torn; there was no pity for grey hairs or for babes, nay they lifted up the little children, as they clutched their scraps of food, and dashed them to the ground. And to those who anticipated their entrance by swallowing beforehand the object of their plunder, they were still more
8 savage, as if they were the injured party. Terrible were the methods of torture that they devised to discover food : stopping up the hapless creatures' privy passages with bitter herbs, and piercing the fundament with sharp stakes. And sufferings horrible even to hear were inflicted upon men, to make them confess to a single loaf, or disclose a single handful of meal which they had concealed.
9   But as for the tormentors, they did not even suffer hunger (for undoubtedly the thing would have been less barbarous had it been done under necessity); nay, [they so acted] to keep their madness in exercise and to procure for themselves provisions
10 for the days to come. And they would go to meet those who under cover of night crept towards the Roman outposts to gather wild herbs or grass, and seize what they had secured, just when they thought to have escaped the enemy; and though they besought the robbers again and again, and invoked the most awful name of God, to give them some portion of what they had risked their lives to secure, not a single thing would they give them. Rather, they had to be content if they were not killed as well as robbed.[2]

11   To this, after other remarks, he adds as follows :

   So, with the closing of the ways out of the city, all hope of salvation was cut off for the Jews; and the famine strengthened its hold and battened on the people by houses and families.

---

[1] Reading αἰδῶ with Rufinus.
[2] Jos., *B.J.* v. 10. 2, 3 (424 ff.).

12 The upper rooms were filled with dying women and babes, the lanes with the corpses of old men; while children and young men swollen [with famine] crowded the market-places like phantoms, and fell down, each wherever the death-agony over-overtook him. But as for burying one's relatives, the sick had no strength to do so, and those who still retained it hesitated from the great number of the corpses and the uncertainty of their own fate. Many, indeed, followed in death those whom they were burying, and many proceeded to their graves before the destined

13 hour arrived. And neither lamentation nor wailing accompanied these calamities; but famine stifled the affections, and with dry eyes men in the throes of death contemplated those who had entered into their rest before them. Profound silence, and night big with death, enwrapped the city.

14 More grievous than they all were the robbers. For instance, they robbed the houses that now were tombs, plundered the dead, and stripping the coverings off the bodies went out with a laugh; they tested the points of their swords in the dead bodies, and in order to prove their weapon thrust through some who were still alive, prostrate on the ground; while such as besought them to use the right hand and sword they left in contempt to the famine. And everyone who was breathing his last turned his gaze fixedly towards the temple, leaving the rioters alive behind them.

15 These latter at first gave orders for the burial of the dead out of the public treasury, since they could not endure the stench. Afterwards, unequal to their task, they cast them from the walls into the ravines. And when Titus went around and beheld them filled with dead, and a thick discharge oozing from the decaying bodies, he groaned, and raising his hands on high called God to witness that it was not his work.[1]

16 To this, after some intervening remarks, he adds as follows :

I cannot refrain from saying what my feelings bid me. I think that had the Romans delayed their attack on these abominable sinners, the city would have been swallowed up by a yawning chasm,[2] or overwhelmed by a flood,[3] or struck with such thunder-bolts as destroyed the land of Sodom.[4] For it bore a generation far more godless than were those who thus suffered. At any rate, by their insensate fury the whole people was involved in destruction.[5]

17 And in the sixth book also he writes thus :

. . . but of those that were perishing by the famine in the city the multitude that fell was innumerable, while the miseries they underwent were indescribable. For in every house where there appeared a shadow of food, there was fighting; the dearest friends came to blows with each other, as they snatched away their miserable provisions for the support of life. Men would

18 not believe that even the dying lacked food; nay, the robbers searched those who were breathing their last, lest anyone should

---

[1] Jos., B.J. v. 12, 3 (512 ff.).
[2] Num. xvi. 30, 33.
[3] Gen. vi., vii.
[4] Gen. xix. 24 f.
[5] Jos., B.J. v. 13. 6 (566).

feign death while concealing food in his bosom. With mouths gaping from want, like mad dogs, they stumbled and staggered, reeling against the doors like drunken men; and in their dire distress they would burst in upon the same houses twice or thrice

19 in a single hour. Necessity compelled them to eat anything; and they gathered, and brought themselves to devour, food that was unfit even for the filthiest of brute beasts. For instance, in the end they did not refrain from belts and shoes, and they chewed the skins of which they had stripped their shields; and some found even in wisps of old hay an article of food. For there were certain who collected the fibres, and sold of them by weight a tiny amount for four Attic drachmas.

20 And why need one speak of the shamelessness that famine brings in what concerns inanimate objects? For I am now about to tell of a deed, the like of which has never been recorded either among Greeks or barbarians, a deed horrible to mention, incredible to hear. And I for my part would gladly even have omitted this sad event, not to appear to posterity a marvellous story-teller, had I not countless witnesses to it among my contemporaries. Besides, I would earn the cold thanks of my country were my

21 history to suppress the facts of her sufferings. There was a woman, living on the other side of Jordan, whose name was Mary, the daughter of Eleazar, of the village of Bathezor (which signifies "house of hyssop"). Distinguished alike for birth and wealth, she had fled in common with the rest of the multitude to Jeru-

22 salem and was, along with them, besieged. Now the tyrants had plundered her other effects, all that she had brought away with her from Peræa and transferred to the city; while the remnants of what she had stored up, and any food she had contrived to secure, were seized by the guards who rushed in upon her daily. The woman became terribly angry, and her frequent insults and

23 curses provoked the plunderers against her. But no one either from anger or pity would kill her, and she grew weary of seeking food for others to eat, while even to find it was now everywhere a matter of extreme difficulty. So when the hunger penetrated her heart and marrow, and angry passions burnt more fiercely even than the hunger, she took Wrath and Necessity as her fellow-counsellors, and made an onslaught upon Nature. Snatch-

24 ing the child (she had a boy at the breast), she said: "Wretched babe, in the midst of war and famine and faction, for what end do I preserve thee? From the Romans we may expect slavery, even if we should live to fall into their hands; but famine comes even before slavery, and the rioters are more grievous than both. Come, be thou my food, a Fury for the rioters and a tale for humanity, the only one lacking to the calamities of the Jews."

25 So speaking, she killed her son, then roasted him, ate the half and kept the remainder hidden. But the rioters were on the spot immediately, and catching the unhallowed odour threatened to cut her throat forthwith, unless she showed what she had prepared. But she said that she had kept a goodly portion

26 for them, and then disclosed the remainder of her child. They were seized with terror and amazement on the spot, and stood transfixed at the sight. "'Tis mine," said she, "this is my very child, and this my deed. Eat, for of a truth I myself have eaten. Be neither softer than a woman nor more compassionate than a mother. But if you from piety turn away from my sacrifice,

I myself have eaten on your behalf, and let the rest remain
27 mine." Thereupon the men went out trembling, cowards in
this one respect, yet with reluctance conceding this food to the
mother; but the whole city was straightway filled with the
story of this abominable thing, and everyone, as he pictured
28 the dreadful deed, shuddered as if the guilt lay with him. The
famished longed for death, and they were deemed happy who had
departed before hearing or beholding miseries like these.[1]

Such were the wages that the Jews received for their wicked-
7. ness and impiety towards the Christ of God; but it is right
to compare with these accounts also the unerring prediction
of our Saviour, in which He declares these very events. His
prophecy runs somewhat as follows :

But woe unto them that are with child and to them that give
suck in those days ! And pray ye that your flight be not in the
winter, neither on a sabbath : for then shall be great tribulation,
such as hath not been from the beginning of the world until now,
nor ever shall be.[2]

2   Now in adding up the whole *number* of the slain, the historian
says that *one million one hundred thousand persons* perished
by famine and sword,[3] and that the rest of *the rioters and
robbers were betrayed by each other* after the taking of the city,
and so were slain; that *the tallest and* handsomest *of the youths*
were *kept for* the *triumph ;* that, *of the multitude that remained,
those over seventeen* were *conveyed* in chains *to the works in
Egypt,* while still more were distributed *among the provinces
to perish in the theatres by sword or wild beasts ; that those
under seventeen were* carried off *and sold* as *slaves,*[4] and that
of these alone the *number amounted to ninety thousand male
persons.*[5]

3   Now these things took place after this manner *in the second
year of the* reign *of Vespasian,*[6] in accordance with the pre-
70–71. dictions foretold by our Lord and Saviour Jesus Christ;
who by divine power had foreseen them as if already
present, and who wept and *lamented,* according to the account
of the holy evangelists. They have quoted His very words, when
on one occasion, as if addressing Jerusalem herself, He said :

4   If thou hadst known, even thou, in this day the things which
belong unto thy peace ! but now they are hid from thine eyes.
For the days shall come upon thee, when thine enemies shall cast
up a bank about thee, and compass thee round, and keep thee in
on every side, and shall dash thee to the ground and thy
children. . . .[7]

---

[1] Jos., *B.J.* vi. 3. 3, 4 (193 ff.).   [2] Matt. xxiv. 19–21.
[3] Jos., *B.J.* vi. 9. 3 (420).   [4] *Ib.* 9. 2 (417 f.).
[5] *Ib.* 9. 3 (420).   [6] *Ib.* 10 (435).
[7] Luke xix. 42–44.

5   On another occasion, as if speaking concerning the people, [He says] :

... for there shall be great distress upon the land, and wrath unto this people.   And they shall fall by the edge of the sword, and shall be led captive into all the nations : and Jerusalem shall be trodden down of the Gentiles, until the times of the Gentiles be fulfilled.[1]

And again :

But when ye see Jerusalem compassed with armies, then know that her desolation is at hand.[2]

6   And when one compares the words of our Saviour with the other accounts of the historian concerning the whole war, how can one fail to be amazed, and to admit how truly divine and surpassingly marvellous our Saviour's prescience and foretelling were ?

The Long-suffering of God and the Signs before the War.

7   There is no need, therefore, to add anything to these accounts of the events which happened to the whole nation after the Saviour's Passion, and after those *voices* had been uttered in which the whole *multitude* of the Jews *asked* that the *robber* and *murderer* should be saved from death, but begged that
8 *the Prince of Life* [3] should be taken away from them.   But it may be right to mention as well those events which go to establish the loving-kindness of that all-gracious Providence, which for forty whole years after their crime against the Christ postponed their destruction.   During all these years the greater number of the apostles and disciples, and *James* himself, the first bishop there, who was called *the Lord's brother*, were still alive and made their abode in the city of Jerusalem itself, thus remaining, as it were, that place's most sure
9 bulwark.[4]   For the divine visitation was still long-suffering, if after all they might repent of what they had done, and so obtain pardon and salvation; and, besides this great long-suffering, marvellous signs were vouchsafed them by God of what was to happen to them should they not repent.   These matters also have been deemed worthy of mention by the aforesaid historian, and we cannot do better than lay them before the readers of this work.

8.   Take up, then, the sixth book of the Histories and read his statements therein.   They are as follows :

[1] Luke xxi. 23, 24.   [2] Luke xxi. 20.
[3] Matt. xxvii. 15 ff.; Mark xv. 6 ff.; Luke xxiii. 18 ff.; John xviii. 40; Acts iii. 14, 15.   [4] Cp. Heg. (ii. 23. 4, 7 above).

Thus were the wretched people prevailed upon at that time by these deceivers and false swearers by God; but to the clear portents that foretold the coming desolation they gave neither heed nor belief. Nay, like men thunderstruck, with neither sight nor understanding, they disregarded the proclamations of God.

2 So it was when on one occasion a star stood over the city like to a sword, and a comet which continued for a year. So again when, before the revolt and the movement in the direction of war, as the people were assembling at the feast of unleavened bread, on the eighth of the month Xanthicus at the ninth hour of the night, so brilliant a light shone around the altar and the sanctuary, that it seemed to be broad daylight; and this continued for half an hour. This seemed to the inexperienced to be a good portent; but the sacred scribes came at once to a decision about it, before

3 the events took place. And at the same feast a cow, on being led by the high priest to the sacrifice, brought forth a lamb in the

4 midst of the temple. And the eastern gate of the inner [court of the] temple, which was of brass and very massive, and was closed with difficulty every evening by twenty men, and moreover was secured by bolts bound with iron and had bars sunk to a great depth . . . was seen at the sixth hour of the night to have opened

5 of its own accord. . . . And not many days after the feast, on the twenty-first of the month Artemisius, there appeared a certain extraordinary apparition surpassing belief; yea, what we are about to say would seem fabulous, were it not for two facts : that it was narrated by those who beheld it, and also that the disasters which followed were worthy of the signs. For before sunset there appeared high up over all the land chariots and armed phalanxes darting through the clouds and encircling the cities.

6 And at the feast which is called Pentecost, the priests on passing into the temple by night, according to their custom, to perform the sacred offices, said that they were cognisant, first, of a commotion and noise; and then, of the voice as of a multitude, [saying] " We are departing hence."

7 But what follows is more terrible than these; for a certain Jesus by name, the son of Ananias, a rustic of the ignorant class, four years before the war, when the fullest peace and plenty reigned

62. in the city, came to that feast when it was the custom for all to erect tents in honour of God, and suddenly, in the precincts of the temple, began to cry aloud : " A voice from the east, a voice from the west, a voice from the four winds, a voice against Jerusalem and the sanctuary, a voice against bridegrooms and brides, a voice against all the people." Day and night he went

8 around all the alleys, crying this. And some citizens of note, vexed at his ill-omened cry, seized the man and punished him with many stripes. Yet he uttered not a syllable in self-defence or personally to those present, but continued to shout the same

9 words as before. And when the rulers came to think, as was the case, that the man was under some supernatural impulse, they brought him before the Roman governor. There, though torn to the bone with scourging, he neither uttered an entreaty nor shed a tear; but modulating his voice to the most lamentable tone possible, replied to each stroke, " Woe, woe to Jerusalem ! " [1]

---

[1] Jos., *B.J.* vi. 5. 3 (288–304).

10　Now the same writer relates a still more marvellous thing than this, when he states that a certain *oracle was found among their sacred writings*, to the effect that *at that time a man from their country should rule the world :* which oracle Josephus supposed to have been fulfilled in the case of 11 Vespasian.[1]　Yet he did not rule the whole world, but only that part which is under the Romans.　It would more justly be applied to Christ, to whom it was said by the Father :

Ask of me, and I will give thee the nations for thine inheritance, And the uttermost parts of the earth for thy possession.[2]

Yea, at that very time *the voice* of His holy apostles *went out into all the earth, and their words to the ends of the world.*[3]

Josephus and his Writings.

9.　In addition to all this it is right that we should know the origin and race of Josephus himself, who has contributed so largely to the history in hand.　Now he, once again, tells us this, in the following words :

. . . Josephus, son of Matthias . . . a native of Jerusalem, a priest, who myself at the first fought against the Romans, and perforce took part in the sequel.[4]

2　Now of the Jews at that time he was by far the most renowned man, not only among his own nation but also among the Romans; so that he was honoured by the erection of a statue in the city of the Romans, while the books composed by him were deemed worthy of being placed in the library.
3　This same writer has set down [1] the whole of the Jewish Antiquities in twenty entire treatises, and [2] the history of the contemporary Roman War in seven.　This latter work he himself testifies that he gave to posterity not only in Greek but also *in his native* tongue [5]—and he is worthy of credit 4 because of his truthfulness in other matters.　And there are extant of his [3] two other books which are worthy of study, those On the Antiquity of the Jews; in which also he has made *reply to Apion the grammarian*, who at that time composed *a book* against the Jews, and to others who also attempted to vilify the ancestral customs of the Jewish nation.[6]
5　In the former of these he gives the number of the canonical writings in the Old [Testament], as it is called.　He informs us in these very words, on the strength of an ancient tradition, which books are unquestionable among the Hebrews :

10.　We have not, therefore, multitudes of books at variance and conflicting with one another, but only two-and-twenty, contain- 2 ing the record of all time, justly believed to be divine.　And of

---

[1] Jos., *B.J.*, 5. 4 (312 f.).　　　[2] Ps. ii. 8.　　　[3] Ps. xix. 4 (LXX).
[4] Jos., *B.J.* i. Pref. 1 (3).　　　[5] *Ib.*　　　[6] Jos., *Ap.* ii. 1 (2, 6).

these five are Moses', which comprise the laws and the traditional history from [1] the origin of man down to the writer's death. The
3 period thus covered wants little of three thousand years. But from the death of Moses down to that of Artaxerxes, who succeeded Xerxes as king of the Persians, the prophets who came after Moses wrote the history of their own times in thirteen books. The remaining four books contain hymns to God and precepts of
4 life for men. From Artaxerxes up to our own time the several events have been written down, yet they have not been deemed worthy of the same credence as those before them, because the
5 exact succession of prophets had ceased. And our actions prove the nature of our attitude towards our own writings. For during so long a lapse of time no one has ever dared to add to, or take away from, or change them; but it is inbred in every Jew from the very day of his birth to regard them as the ordinances of God, to abide by them, and for them, if need be, gladly to die.[2]

6 But an end must be made of these useful quotations from our historian. Nevertheless he has composed [4] another, and no unworthy, work, On the Supremacy of Reason, entitled by some Maccabaicum, because it contains the conflicts of those Hebrews who contended valiantly for piety towards the Deity, to be found in the books of the Macca-
7 baica, as they are in like manner called. And at the close of the twentieth book of the Antiquities, the same writer indicates that he had *proposed to write a work in four books on God and His essence, according to the* traditional *beliefs of the Jews, and on the laws, why some* practices *were permitted therein, and others prohibited ;* [3] and he mentions in his own books that he had composed other works as well.

8 Moreover, it is fitting to record also the words which he has placed at the very close of his Antiquities, in order to accredit the testimony of our borrowings from him. In attacking, then, Justus of Tiberias (who, like him, had attempted to record the events of that same time) for not having written a true history, and having brought many other charges against the man, he goes on to add in these very words :

9 I for my part certainly was not afraid for my own writings, as you were for yours; but I presented the books to the emperors themselves, when the events were all but before men's eyes. For I was conscious of having preserved the true account, and did not
10 fail in my expectation of meeting with testimony to my accuracy. And I presented the history to many others, of whom also some had taken part in the war, such as King Agrippa and certain of
11 his kinsmen. For the emperor Titus indeed was so desirous that men should receive from them alone a knowledge of the facts, that he penned with his own hand an order for the publication of my

---

[1] Reading ἀπ', in place of τῆς, with the MSS. of Josephus.
[2] Jos., *Ap.* i. 8 (38–42).
[3] Jos., *Ant.* xx. 11. 2 (268).

books; while King Agrippa wrote sixty-two letters, in attestation
of the truth of my account.

From *these* also he quotes *two*.[1]   However, let this account
of him suffice; and let us proceed in order.

Succession of Bishops of Jerusalem: Vespasian's Persecution of the Jews.

11.   *After* the *martyrdom* of *James* and the taking of Jerusalem
which immediately ensued, it is recorded that those apostles
and disciples of the Lord who were still surviving met together
from all quarters and, together with our Lord's relatives after
the flesh (for the more part of them were still alive), took
counsel, all in common, as to whom they should judge worthy
to be the successor of James; and, what is more, that they
all with one consent approved *Symeon the son of Clopas*,[2]
of whom also the book of the Gospels makes mention,[3] as
worthy of the throne of the community in that place. He
was *a cousin*—at any rate so it is said—*of the* Saviour; [2] *for*
indeed Hegesippus relates *that Clopas was Joseph's brother*.[4]

12.   And [it is recorded], moreover, that Vespasian, after the
taking of Jerusalem, gave orders that all the members of the
family of David should be sought out, so that none of the
royal tribe might be left among the Jews; and that for this
reason a most terrible persecution once more hung over the
Jews.

REIGN OF TITUS (79–81)

13.   But when Vespasian had reigned for ten years, he was
succeeded by his son, the emperor Titus.

Succession of Bishops of Rome.

81.   In the second year of his reign, Linus, the bishop of the
church of the Romans, transmitted to Anencletus the
ministry which he had held for twelve years.

REIGN OF DOMITIAN (81–96)

When Titus had reigned for two years and the same number
of months, he was succeeded by his brother Domitian.

Succession of Bishops.

14.   In the fourth year, then, of Domitian, Annianus the first
85.   [bishop] of the community at Alexandria died, having
completed twenty-two years; and Avilius succeeded him
as second.

---

[1] Jos., *Vita*, 65 (361–364).   [2] Heg. (iv. 22. 4 below).
[3] John xix. 25.   [4] Heg. in Epiph., *Hær.* 78. 7.

15.
93. And in the twelfth year of the same government Anencletus, who had been bishop of the church of the Romans for twelve years, was succeeded by Clement; who is declared by the apostle, in writing to the Philippians, to be his *fellow-worker*. His words are :

. . . with Clement also, and the rest of my fellow-workers, whose names are in the book of life.[1]

Clement's Epistle.

16. Of this person, then, a single acknowledged epistle is extant, great and wonderful, which he composed as in the name of *the church* of the Romans to the church of the Corinthians, when *a dissension* took place at Corinth at that time.[2] And we know also that it has been read publicly in the presence of the congregation in very many churches for a long time back and in our own day. And of the fact that the dissension had broken out at Corinth under the [emperor] of whom we are speaking, Hegesippus is a trustworthy witness.

The Persecution of Domitian.

17. But to resume. *When Domitian had displayed great cruelty towards* many, and had put to death without a fair trial no small number of well-born and distinguished men at Rome, as well as punishing for no reason countless other notable men with banishment to a foreign land and confiscation of their property, he ended by making himself *Nero's* successor in his enmity and hostility towards God. Indeed he was *the second* to stir up *persecution against* us, albeit his father *Vespasian* made us the object of no evil designs.[3]

18. It is recorded that at that time *the apostle and evangelist John*, being still alive, was condemned to dwell in the island of *Patmos* for his testimony to the divine word.[4]

2 Indeed, Irenæus, in writing about the number of the name of the Antichrist which is to be found in the Apocalypse of John, as it is called,[5] uses these very words in the fifth book of his work Against the Heresies, with reference to John :

3 But if it were necessary that his name should be announced openly at this present time, it would have been stated by him who also saw the revelation. For it was seen not long ago, but almost in our own generation, at the close of the principate of Domitian.[6]

---

[1] Phil. iv. 3.   [2] Clem., *Ep.* Inscrip., 1.
[3] Heg. in J. A. Cramer, *Anecd. Græca*, ii. 88; and C de Boor, *T.U.* v. 2. 169.   [4] *Ib.*   [5] Rev. xiii. 18.
[6] Iren. v. 30. 3.

4   So conspicuous, then, had the teaching of our faith become at the time of the persons just mentioned, that even those writers who stood far apart from our doctrine did not hesitate to record in their histories both the persecution and the martyrdoms that took place in it.   Yes, and they also gave an exact indication of the date, for they have placed it on record that in the fifteenth year of Domitian, in company with *many* others, 96. *Flavia Domitilla, the daughter of a sister of Flavius Clemens* who was one of the *consuls* at Rome at that time, was committed by way of punishment *to the island of Pontia because of her testimony* for Christ.[1]

19.   Now when this Domitian gave orders that those who were of the family of David should be put to death, it is recorded in an ancient authority that some heretics brought an accusation against the descendants *of Jude*, who was the Saviour's *brother after the flesh, on the ground that* they were of *the family of David*, and that they bore kinship to Christ Himself.   This is shown by Hegesippus, who speaks as follows in these very words :

20.   But there still survived of the family of the Lord the grandsons of Jude, His brother after the flesh, as he was called.   These they informed against, as being of the family of David; and the " evocatus " brought them before Domitian Cæsar.   For he 2 feared the coming of the Christ, as did also Herod.   And he asked them if they were of David's line, and they acknowledged it.   Then he asked them what possessions they had or what fortune they owned.   And they said that between the two of them they had only nine thousand denarii, half belonging to each of them ; and this they asserted they had not in money, but only in thirty-nine plethra of land, so valued, from which by their own labours they both paid the taxes and supported themselves.

3   And [he adds] that then they showed also their hands, and put forward the hardness of their bodies and the callosities formed on their hands from continual working, as a proof of 4 personal labour.   And that when asked about Christ and His *kingdom*, its nature, and the place and time of its appearing, they tendered the reply that it was *not* of the *world* [2] nor earthly, but heavenly and angelic ; that it would appear at *the end of the world*,[3] when he should *come in glory* [4] and *judge the quick and the dead*,[5] and *render unto every man according to his* 5 conduct.[6]   And [he says] that after this Domitian in no way condemned them, but despised them as men of no account, let them go free, and by an injunction *caused the persecution* 6 *against* the Church *to cease*.[7]   And that when released they

[1] Bruttius in *Chronicle* 274.   [2] John xviii. 36.
[3] Cp. Matt. xiii. 40, 49.   [4] Matt. xvi. 27.
[5] 2 Tim. iv. 1.   [6] Matt. xvi. 27 ; Rom. ii. 6.
[7] Heg. in Cramer and de Boor, *ll. c.*

ruled the *churches*, inasmuch as they were both *martyrs and of the Lord's family ;* and, *when peace was established, remained alive until [the time of] Trajan.*[1]

7   Such is the account of Hegesippus.   Moreover, Tertullian too has mentioned Domitian in like terms :

Domitian also, with a share of Nero's cruelty, had tried on one occasion to do the same as Nero.   But being, as I imagine, possessed of some intelligence, he very soon ceased, and even recalled those whom he had banished.[2]

REIGN OF NERVA (96, 97)

8   Now after Domitian had ruled for fifteen years and Nerva had succeeded him in the principate, the Senate of the Romans decreed that Domitian's honours should be taken away, and that those unjustly banished should return to their own homes, and receive back their property as well.   This is recorded by
9 those who wrote the history of the period.   At that time, then, the record of our ancient men informs us that the apostle John also took up his abode once more at Ephesus after his exile on the island.

REIGN OF TRAJAN (98–117)

21.   But when Nerva had reigned little more than a year, he was succeeded by Trajan.

Succession of Bishops.

It was in his first year that Cerdon succeeded Avilius, who for thirteen years had ruled the community at
98–9.   Alexandria.   Cerdon was the third that presided over the people of that place, in succession to Annianus who was the first.

At that time Clement was still ruling the Romans, and he also occupied the third place of those who were bishops after Paul and Peter.   But Linus was the first, and after him Anencletus.

22.   And—to proceed—after Euodius, the first [bishop] of those at Antioch, Ignatius was known to have been the second, at that said time.

Similarly, Symeon was the second to hold the ministry of the church at Jerusalem, in the time of those persons, in succession to the brother of our Lord.

[1] Heg. (32. 6 below).   [2] Tert., *Apol.* 5.

Last Days of St. John.

23.   Moreover, there was still alive in Asia and directing the churches there, he *whom Jesus loved*,[1] apostle alike and evangelist, even John, having returned from his exile on the island
2 after the death of Domitian.   And that he survived up to their day—this account is sufficiently accredited by two witnesses, who may be considered worthy of credit, as men who were ambassadors of the orthodoxy of the Church : seeing that such
3 were Irenæus and Clement the Alexandrian.   The former of these indeed writes thus in the second book of his work Against the Heresies, in these very words :

> . . . and all the elders who have come in contact with John, the disciple of the Lord, in Asia testify that John delivered. . . . For he remained with them until the time of Trajan.[2]

4   And in the third book of the same work he states this same thing, as follows :

> Yea also the church at Ephesus, founded by Paul, and where John remained with them until the time of Trajan, is a truthful witness of the tradition of the apostles.[3]

5   But Clement both indicated the time, and also adds a story which such as delight in hearing what is beautiful and helpful should most certainly know.   It is in his treatise which he entitled Who is the rich man who is being saved ?   Take and read this writing of his also; it runs as follows :

6   . . . hear a tale that is no mere tale, but a true account of John the apostle, which has been handed down and preserved in memory.   For when on the death of the tyrant he removed from the island of Patmos to Ephesus, he used to go off, when requested, to the neighbouring districts of the Gentiles also, to appoint bishops in some places, to organize whole churches in others, in others again to appoint to an order some one of those who were
7 indicated by the Spirit.   He came, then, also to a certain city at no great distance, whose very name is told by some, and having otherwise refreshed the brethren, he finally looked at the bishop who presided (for he saw a young man of powerful physique, refined appearance and ardent temperament), and said : " This youth I entrust to thee in all earnestness in the presence of the Church and Christ as witnesses."   On the bishop accepting him and making all promises, the apostle again addressed and adjured him in the same words.
8   Then he went back to Ephesus, while the presbyter took home his youthful charge, brought him up, kept him by his side, cherished and finally enlightened him.   After that he relaxed his excessive

---

[1] John xiii. 23; xxi. 7, 20.
[2] Iren. ii. 33. 3.   [3] *Ib*. iii. 3. 4.

care and guardianship, thinking that he had placed over him the
9 perfect guard, the seal of the Lord. But the youth grasped his
freedom too soon, and to his ruin fell in with certain idle and
dissolute fellows of his own age, of evil habits. First they led him
on by costly entertainments; then also they would perhaps take
him with them as they sallied forth at night to rob; then they
10 urged him to join them in some even greater crime. He for his
part little by little adopted their habits; and like a hard-mouthed
and powerful horse he left the straight path, took the bit between
his teeth,[1] and rushed down the precipice, the more violently
11 because of his strength of character. And completely despairing
of his salvation in God, he was no longer minded to commit some
slight offence; but, since he had lost his soul once and for all,
determined to do a big thing and suffer a like fate with the rest.
So he took these same companions and got together a robber
band, of which he was an active chief, the most violent, bloody
and cruel of them all.
12   Time passed, and, some necessity having arisen, they called
John back; who, when he had set in order the business that
brought him thither, said : " Come now, bishop, return us the
deposit, which both Christ and I have committed to thee, in the
presence of the church over which thou presidest as witness."
13 At first the bishop was amazed, thinking that he was being falsely
accused with regard to money which he had not received; and he
could neither believe a charge about what he did not possess,
nor disbelieve John. But when the latter said, " It is the youth
that I demand, and the soul of our brother," the old man heaved
a deep sigh, and even shed some tears. " That youth," said he,
" is dead." " How; and by what kind of death ? " " He is
dead to God," he replied; " for he turned out a wicked and
abandoned person, in short, a robber; and now he has left the
Church to haunt the mountain with a troop of men like himself."
14 The apostle rent his clothes and smote his head with loud lamentation : " A fine guardian," said he, " I left of our brother's soul !
Howbeit, provide me with a horse at once, and let me have someone to guide the way."
15   He rode right from the church, just as he was; and when he
came to the spot and was captured by the robbers' sentry, he
neither made to fly nor protested, but cried aloud : " To *this*
16 *end am I come*;[2] bring me to your leader." The latter for a while
awaited them, armed as he was. But when he recognized John
as he approached, he was filled with shame and turned to flee.
Forgetful of his years John followed after him with all his might,
17 crying aloud : " Why dost thou fly from me, my child; from thy
own father, from one unarmed and aged ? Have pity on me, my
child, fear not. Thou hast still hopes of life. I myself *will give
account* to Christ *on* thy *behalf*.[3] If need be, I will willingly
endure thy death, as the Lord the death which He suffered on
behalf of us. For thy sake I will give my own life in place of
18 thine. Stand, believe; Christ has sent me." On hearing this
the robber at first stood still with downcast eyes, then he threw
away his arms, then trembled and *wept bitterly*.[4] But when the

---

[1] Cp. Plato, *Phædrus* 254 D.   [2] John xviii. 37.
[3] Heb. xiii. 17.   [4] Matt. xxvi. 75.

old man drew near he embraced him, pleading his cause, as best
he could, with groans; being baptized a second time in his tears,
19 and concealing only his right hand. But the apostle gave his
pledge and solemn assurance that he had found forgiveness for
him from the Saviour; and praying he kneeled down and kissed
that same right hand as if it were now purified by his repentance.
Thus he brought him back to the church. And making intercession
for him with copious prayers, striving with him in continual
fastings, subduing his mind with the varied siren-spell of words, he
did not depart, as it is said, until he had set him over [1] the church,
thus affording a notable example of true repentance and a notable
token of regeneration, a trophy of a resurrection that all might see. [2]

24.   I have placed here this extract from Clement both for its
historical interest and for the profit of such as shall read it.

St. John's Writings, and the Order of the Gospels.

But come, let us now indicate also the unquestionable
2 writings of this apostle. And let his Gospel, recognized by the
churches under heaven, be first acknowledged. That indeed
it has with good reason been reckoned by the ancients in the
fourth place after the other three, may be made clear in this
way.
3   Those inspired and truly divine men, I mean the apostles
of Christ, had purified their lives exceedingly and adorned
their souls with every virtue; but in speech they were un-
cultivated. They verily placed their confidence in the divine,
wonder-working *power* truly bestowed upon them by the
Saviour; [3] they neither knew how, nor attempted, to present
the teachings of the Master in *persuasive* and skilful *words*,
but they used only the *demonstration of the* divine *Spirit* which
was working with them, and the wonder-working *power* [4] of
Christ which found its fulfilment through them.   Thus they
published the knowledge of the kingdom of heaven throughout
the whole world, paying little heed to the desire for writing
4 books.   And such was their practice, inasmuch as they were
aided by a greater and more than human ministry.   For
instance, Paul, who excelled them all in the power of composition and in fertility of thought, has committed to writing
nothing but the briefest of epistles; [5] although he had countless unutterable things to relate, since he had attained to the
sights even of *the third heaven*, and *was caught up* to the divine
Paradise itself, and deemed worthy to *hear* the *unspeakable*
5 *words* there. [6]   And, indeed, the rest of the followers of our
Saviour—the twelve apostles, the seventy disciples, and

[1] ἐπιστῆσαι : the reading adopted by Stählin and Schwartz. A less
well-attested reading is ἀποκατέστησε, "restored him to."
[2] Clem., *Q.D.S.* 42. 1–15.   [3] Acts i. 8.   [4] 1 Cor. ii. 4.
[5] Cp. Orig., *Joh.* (vi. 25. 7. below).   [6] 2 Cor. xii. 2, 4.

countless others as well—were not without these same
experiences.

Yet out of them all Matthew and John alone have left us
memoirs of the Lord's discourses; and they, it is recorded,
6 only came to write under compulsion. For Matthew first of
all preached to Hebrews; and when he was about to go also
to others he committed his Gospel to writing in his native
tongue : thus he made his writing compensate those from whom
7 he was departing for the lack of his bodily presence. And when
Mark and Luke had already published their Gospels, it is said
that John, who all the time had used unwritten preaching,
at last came also to write, for the following reason. Those
three which we mentioned above having come already into the
hands of all, including his own, it is said that he accepted
them and attested their truth; but [expressed the opinion]
that the narrative only lacked, it seems, an account of what
had been done by Christ first of all and at the beginning of the
preaching.
8   And this statement is indeed true. For instance, one can
see at a glance that the three evangelists have only recorded
the deeds of the Saviour for one year after the shutting up
in prison of John the Baptist, and that they indicated this
9 very fact at the beginning of their account. Thus, after the
forty days' fast and the temptation that ensued, Matthew
informs us as to the chronology of his work by saying, *Now
when he heard that John was delivered up, he withdrew* from
10 Judæa *into Galilee ;* [1] and Mark likewise says, *Now after that
John was delivered up, Jesus came into Galilee ;* [2] and Luke too,
before he begins the acts of Jesus, makes a similar observation,
declaring that *Herod,* in *adding* to the *evil things* he had committed, *shut up John in prison.*[3]
11   It is said, then, that the apostle John for these reasons
was called upon to give in his Gospel the period which the
former evangelists had passed over in silence, and the deeds
of the Saviour during that period (and these were before the
shutting up of the Baptist) ; and that he indicated this very
fact, when on one occasion he said, *This beginning of his*
marvels *did Jesus,*[4] and when on another he mentioned the
Baptist, in the midst of an account of the acts of Jesus, as still
at that time *baptizing in Aenon near to Salim ;* and that he
shows this clearly when he says, *For John was not yet cast into
prison.*[5]
12   Therefore John in writing his Gospel gives us the things
which Christ did before the Baptist was cast into prison; but
the remaining three evangelists mention those done after the
13 shutting up of the Baptist in the dungeon. And anyone who

[1] Matt. iv. 12.   [2] Mark i. 14.   [3] Luke iii. 19, 20.
[4] John ii. 11.   [5] John iii. 23, 24.

understands this can no longer imagine that the Gospels are at variance with one another, because the Gospel according to John contains the first acts of Christ, but the remaining Gospels contain the record of what He did at the close of the period; but would therefore regard it as natural that, while John passed over in silence the genealogy according to the flesh of our Saviour, inasmuch as it had been previously set down by Matthew and Luke, he should begin with the doctrine of His divinity, since the divine Spirit had reserved that for him as their superior.

14   This, then, must suffice as to the writing of the Gospel according to John; and we have stated above the cause which
15 led to the writing of that according to Mark.[1] But Luke has himself at the beginning of his treatise prefixed the cause which had led him to its composition : showing that *many* others had somewhat rashly taken it upon them to compose *a narrative* of those *things* of which he had *been fully persuaded*; and so, feeling himself bound to free us from our doubt and suspicion as to the others, he gave us in his own Gospel the *certain* record of those events whose truth he had firmly grasped by the aid of his intercourse and stay with Paul and his converse with
16 the other apostles.[2] So much for our own account of these things. But in a more suitable place we shall endeavour to show by means of quotations from the ancients what others also have said about them.

17   And as to the treatises of John, the former of the epistles, as well as the Gospel, has been acknowledged as undisputed, both by the men of to-day and by the ancients also; but
18 the remaining two are disputed. As to the Apocalypse, the opinion of the majority is still to this day divided one way or the other. But at the proper time this question also will be likewise decided by the testimony of the ancients.

DIGRESSION ON THE APOSTOLIC AGE

The Books of the New Testament.

25.   But now that we have reached this point, it is reasonable to sum up the writings of the New Testament already mentioned. Well then, we must set in the first place the holy quaternion of the Gospels; which are followed by the book
 2 of the Acts of the Apostles. After this we must reckon the epistles of Paul; following which we must pronounce genuine the extant former epistle of John, and likewise the epistle of Peter. After these we must place, if it really seem right, the Apocalypse of John, the views that have been held as to

---

[1] ii. 15.   [2] Luke i. 1–4.

3 which we shall set forth at the proper time. These, then, [are to be placed] among the acknowledged writings. But of those which are disputed, nevertheless familiar to the majority, there is extant the epistle of James, as it is called; and that of Jude; and the second epistle of Peter; and the second and third of John, so named, whether they belong to the evangelist 4 or perhaps to some other of the same name as he. Among the spurious writings there are to be placed also the book of the Acts of Paul, and the Shepherd, as it is called, and the Apocalypse of Peter; and, in addition to these, the extant epistle of Barnabas, and the Teachings of the Apostles, as it is called; and, moreover, as I said, the Apocalypse of John, if it seem right. (This last, as I said, is rejected by some, but 5 others give it a place among the acknowledged writings.) And among these some have reckoned also the Gospel of the Hebrews, a work which is especially acceptable to such Hebrews as received the Christ. Now all these would be 6 among the disputed writings; but nevertheless we have been compelled to make a catalogue of these also, distinguishing those writings which the tradition of the Church has deemed true and genuine and acknowledged, from the others outside their number, which, though they are not canonical but even disputed, yet are recognized by most churchmen. [And this we have done] in order that we might be able to know both these same writings and also those which the heretics put forward in the name of the apostles, whether as containing Gospels of Peter and Thomas and Matthias, or even of some others besides these, or as containing Acts of Andrew and John and the other apostles. None of these has been deemed worthy of any kind of mention in a treatise by a single member 7 of successive generations of churchmen; and the character of the style also is far removed from the apostolic manner, and the thought and purport of their contents is so absolutely out of harmony with true orthodoxy, as to establish the fact that they are certainly the forgeries of heretics. For this reason they ought not even to be placed among the spurious writings, but refused as altogether monstrous and impious. Let us now proceed with the history in due course.

Heretics : 1. Menander.

26.   Simon the sorcerer *was succeeded by Menander*, whose conduct showed him to be a second instrument of the devil's working, not inferior to the former. He also was *a Samaritan*, and no whit behind his master in *reaching the summit* of charlatanry, while he abounded in still more marvellous tales. For he *said* that he himself was, forsooth, *the Saviour*, proceeding *from invisible* æons and *sent* down from somewhere on high *for* 2 *the salvation of mankind*. And he taught that no one could

overcome even the world-creating angels themselves, unless he were first to go *through the practice of magic* which he *transmitted*, and *the baptism* imparted *by him ;* and that such as were deemed worthy of this baptism would partake of ever-lasting immortality in this present life, *no longer subject to death, but* destined to *remain* alive here for ever in a kind of *ageless and immortal* existence. These facts, then, may also
3 be discovered from the writings of Irenæus.[1] And Justin, too, in the same passage in which he mentions Simon, also adds his account of Menander, as follows :

> . . . and such was a certain Menander, he too a Samaritan, who was from the village of Caparattæa and a disciple of Simon : we know that he, like Simon, was driven frantic by the demons, and came to Antioch and deceived many by his magical art. He also persuaded those who followed him that they would not die ; and there are still some to this day who follow him in asserting this. . . .[2]

4 It was, therefore, part of the devil's working to employ these charlatans who assumed the name of Christians ; so eager was he to misrepresent the *great mystery* of godliness [3] in the interests of sorcery, and by their means to ridicule the doctrines of the Church as to the immortality of the soul and the resurrection of the dead. But they that have enrolled themselves under the patronage of these saviours have fallen from the true hope.

2. *Ebionites.*

27.　　But there were others, whom that evil demon was unable to detach from their devotion to the Christ of God, yet found accessible from another direction, and so made his own. Ebionites was the suitable name given them from the first,
2 since they held poor and low opinions about Christ. For indeed they regarded Him as a simple, ordinary person ; a man whom progress [4] in character, and this alone, had justified ; the fruit of a man's intercourse with Mary. And in their opinion the worship [of God] enjoined by the Law was abso-lutely necessary for them,[5] since faith in Christ by itself and a corresponding life would not secure their salvation.
3 But there were others besides these, who went by the same name, yet escaped the outlandish absurdity of the persons mentioned. They did not deny that the Lord was *born of a Virgin and* the Holy *Spirit* ; *nevertheless*, like the others, they *refused* to acknowledge that, being *God* the *Word* and Wisdom, He pre-existed ; and so the impiety of the former was their overthrow also, especially as they set great store by the

---

[1] Iren. i. 17.　　　　　[2] Just., *Apol.* i. 26.
[3] 1 Tim. iii. 16.　　　[4] προκοπήν ; cp. Luke ii. 52 (προέκοπτε).
[5] Orig., *Matt.* xvi. 12 ; *Cels.* v. 61.

observance of the carnal worship prescribed by the Law, as

4 did the others. These were of the opinion that *the epistles of the apostle* [1] ought altogether to be *disowned, calling him a renegade from the Law*; but they *used only the Gospel of the Hebrews*, as it is called,[2] and made little account of the rest.

5 And they observed the sabbath and the other Jewish customs, as did the former; yet, on the other hand, each Lord's day they celebrated rites similar to ours, in memory of the Saviour's

6 resurrection. Therefore, as a result of such a proceeding, they were given the title they possess : the name of Ebionites suggesting the *poverty of their understanding, for* this *is the term that the Hebrews employ for a poor man*.[3]

3. *Cerinthians.*

28.   It has been handed down to us that in the times of which we have been speaking Cerinthus was the author of another heresy. Gaius, whose words I have already quoted on a former occasion,[4] writes of him, in his extant Discussion, as follows :

2   Yea, Cerinthus also,[5] by means of revelations purported to be written by a great apostle, fraudulently foists marvellous tales upon us, on the ground that they were shown him by angels. He says that after the resurrection the kingdom of Christ will be on earth, and that the flesh, dwelling at Jerusalem, will once more *serve lusts and pleasures*.[6] And—enemy that he is of God's Scriptures—in his wish to deceive he says that there will be a period of a thousand years, to be spent in wedding festivities.[7]

3   And Dionysius too (who in our day was in possession of the episcopate in the community at Alexandria), when making certain statements, in the second book of his Promises, about the Apocalypse of John, on the strength of primitive tradition, mentions the same man in the following words :

4   . . . but Cerinthus, the same who created the sect called "Cerinthian" after him, since he desired to affix to his own forgery a name worthy of credit. For that this was the doctrine which he taught, that *the kingdom of Christ* would *be on earth;*

5 and he dreamed that it would consist in those things which formed the object of his own desires (for he was a lover of the body and altogether carnal), in the full satisfaction of the belly and lower lusts, that is, in feasts and carousals and *marriages*, and (as a means, he thought, of procuring these under a better name) in *festivals* and sacrifices and slayings of victims.[8]

---

[1] Orig., *Cels.* v. 65.   [2] Iren. i. 22.
[3] Orig., *Princip.* iv. 3. 8.   [4] ii. 25. 7.
[5] Omitting ὁ with Schwartz.   [6] Tit. iii. 3.
[7] This is the sense obviously needed, but the Greek is corrupt.
[8] Dion. Alex., *Prom.* (vii. 25. 3 f. below) : cp. § 2.

6   Such is the account of Dionysius.   But Irenæus, who in the first treatise of his work Against the Heresies set forth certain false opinions of a more esoteric nature which Cerinthus held,[1] has in the third treatise also placed on record a story which deserves to be remembered.   He states, on the authority of a tradition of *Polycarp*, that once upon a time *John* the apostle entered a *bath-house* for the purpose of *taking a bath*, but that when he found that *Cerinthus* was within, he sprang out of the place and fled outside, since he could not endure to be under the same roof as he;   and that he advised those also that were with him to do the same, saying :   " *Let us flee, lest even the bath-house fall in ;   for within is Cerinthus, the enemy of the truth.*" [2]

4. *Nicolaitans.*

29.   It was in their day, to be sure, that the heresy of the Nicolaitans, as it is called, also arose, for a very brief time. It is mentioned in the Apocalypse of John.[3]   These persons made their boast of Nicolaus, one of those deacons, Stephen's companions, who had been chosen by the apostles to look after the needy.[4]   Indeed the Alexandrian Clement, in the third book of the Stromateis, gives the following account of him, and in these very words :

2   This man, it is said, had a young and lovely wife.   And when he was reproached by the apostles, after the ascension of the Saviour, for jealousy, he brought her into their midst and bade anyone marry her who wished.   For this action, it is said, was in accordance with that saying [of his], " One ought to abuse the flesh " ;   and, as a matter of fact, the members of his sect have followed both example and precept absolutely and without
3 question, and commit fornication freely.   But for my part, I understand that Nicolaus had intercourse with no woman except his wife ; and that, as regards his children, the daughters grew old in a state of virginity, while his son preserved his chastity. Such being the case, when he brought the wife, whom he jealously loved, publicly into the midst of the apostles, it was to renounce his passion ; and it was self-control, in the face of pleasures men eagerly seek, that taught him to say " abuse the flesh."   For, I imagine, in accordance with the Saviour's command, he did not
4 wish to *serve two masters*,[5] pleasure and the Lord.   At all events, they say that Matthias also thus taught : to fight against and abuse the flesh, and in no way to give in to it for the sake of pleasure, but to develop the soul by faith and knowledge.[6]

      Let this, then, suffice to be said concerning those who at the said times attempted to pervert the truth ; who neverthe-less, in less time than it takes to say it, were completely extinguished.

[1] Iren. i. 21.   [2] Iren. iii. 3. 4 (iv. 14. 6 below).
[3] Rev. ii. 6.   [4] Acts vi. 1-6.
[5] Matt. vi. 24; Luke xvi. 13.   [6] Clem., *Strom.* iii. 4. 25 f.

Married Apostles.

30. Indeed Clement, whose words we have just read, follows up what he said above by giving a list, for the benefit of such as set at nought marriage, of those apostles who were proved to have lived in wedlock. This is what he says :

Or will they reject even the apostles ? For Peter, indeed, and Philip begat children, while Philip also gave his daughters in marriage to husbands; and as for Paul, he does not hesitate in a certain epistle to address his *yokefellow*,[1] whom he did not carry about [2] in order to avoid encumbrance in his ministry.[3]

2 But since we have mentioned these things, it can cause no tedium to quote as well another story of the same writer that is worth the telling, which he has inserted in the seventh book of the Stromateis. It runs as follows :

It is said, for instance, that when the blessed Peter beheld his own wife led away to die, he rejoiced in that the call had come and she was returning home; and that he addressed her by name in words of very great encouragement and comfort : " O do thou remember the Lord." Such was the marriage of those blessed ones; such their perfect affection for their dearest.[4]

Let me insert here, as in their proper place, these remarks, which are germane to the work in hand.

The Deaths of John and Philip.

31. Now indeed as regards Paul and Peter, we have already on a former occasion [5] shown both the time and manner of their death, and, as well, the spot where their tabernacles were **2** laid after they departed this life. But as for John, while we have already stated after a fashion the time [of his death],[6] we must go to the epistle of Polycrates (who was bishop of the community at Ephesus) to show us the place where his tabernacle lies. In writing this epistle to Victor, bishop of the Romans, he mentions John and, together with him, Philip the apostle and his daughters, somewhat as follows :

3 For indeed in Asia great luminaries have fallen asleep, such as shall rise again at the last day, the day of the Lord's appearing, when He comes with glory from heaven to seek out all His saints : to wit, Philip, one of the twelve apostles, who has fallen asleep in Hierapolis, [as have] also his two daughters who grew old in virginity, and his other daughter who lived in the Holy Spirit and rests at Ephesus; and, moreover, [there is] John too, who *leant back on* the Lord's *breast*,[7] who was [8] a priest, wearing the sacerdotal plate, both martyr and teacher. He has fallen asleep at Ephesus.

---

[1] Phil. iv. 3.   [2] Cp. 1 Cor. ix. 5.
[3] Clem., *Strom.* iii. 6. 52 f.   [4] *Ib.*, vii. 11. 63 f.
[5] ii. 25. 5 ff.   [6] 23. 1–4.   [7] John xiii. 25.   [8] Or " became."

4   So much, then, for the end of these persons also. And in
the Dialogue of Gaius too, whom we mentioned a little while
ago,[1] Proclus, against whom he conducted the Discussion, is
in agreement with what has been set forth, when he speaks on
this wise of the death of Philip and his daughters :

But after him there were at Hierapolis in Asia four prophetesses,
daughters of Philip.   Their tomb is there, and that of their father.

5   So much for Proclus.   But Luke in the Acts of the Apostles
mentions the daughters of Philip as living with their father at
Cæsarea in Judæa, and as having been accounted worthy of a
prophetic gift.   He speaks thus, in these very words :

We came unto Cæsarea : and entering into the house of Philip
the evangelist, who was one of the seven, we abode with him.
Now this man had four daughters, virgins, which did prophesy.[2]

Summary of the Preceding Chapters.

6   Having, therefore, stated distinctly in these pages what has
come to our knowledge concerning the apostles and the times
of the apostles ; concerning the sacred writings they have left
us, and regarding such as are disputed yet publicly read by
many in most churches, and such as are completely spurious
and foreign to apostolic orthodoxy—having stated this, let us
proceed with the history of those events that follow.

REIGN OF TRAJAN (resumed).

Persecution : 1. *At Jerusalem.*

32.   After Nero and Domitian, under the emperor whose times
we are now reviewing, it is recorded that persecution against
us was stirred up here and there and in cities, as a result of
popular risings.   It has been handed down to us that therein
Symeon, the son of Clopas, who, as we showed,[3] *was appointed
second bishop* of the church at Jerusalem,[4] ended his life by
2 martyrdom.   And the witness to this fact is that very person
whose words we have already employed on various former
occasions,[5] Hegesippus.   In telling of certain heretics,[6] he
goes on to show that the said Symeon underwent *an accusation*
at their hands at that time ; and when he *had been tortured* in
various ways and *for* very *many days for being a Christian,* and
had filled the judge himself and his attendants with the greatest
amazement, he was at the last awarded an end similar to that
3 which the Lord suffered.[7]   But there is nothing like hearing

---

[1] 28. 1.   [2] Acts xxi. 8, 9.
[3] c. 11.   [4] Heg. (iv. 22. 4 below).
[5] ii. 23. 4–18; iii. 11; 12; 16; 17; 18. 1; 19; 20. 1–6, 9.
[6] Heg. (iv. 22. 5, 6; cp. c. 19).   [7] §§ 3, 6.

the writer himself; he gives his account somewhat as follows, in these very words :

Certain of these

(plainly, the heretics)

accused Simon the son of Clopas of being of the house of David and a Christian; and so he was martyred at the age of a hundred and twenty years, when Trajan was Cæsar and Atticus consularis.

4 And the same author says that it so happened that actually his accusers also were taken prisoner, in the search that was then being made for such Jews as were of the royal tribe, on the ground that they belonged to it.

And one might further reasonably conclude that Symeon was an eye-witness and actual hearer of the Lord, judging by the length of time that he lived, and from the fact that the passage in the Gospels mentions *Mary the wife of Clopas*,[1] who was the father of Symeon, as the record on a former occasion showed.[2]

5 And the same writer says that there were also other descendants of one of the Saviour's reputed brethren, whose name was Jude; they survived until this same reign, after they had given their testimony before Domitian to their faith in Christ, as we have already previously recorded.[3] He writes as follows :

6 They came, therefore, and ruled every church, as being martyrs and of the Lord's family; and, when profound peace was established in every church, they remained until [the time of] Trajan Cæsar : until the son of an uncle of the Lord, the aforesaid Simon son of Clopas, was informed against by the sects, and was likewise also accused on the same charge before Atticus the consularis. And he bore witness through tortures of many days' duration, so that all, including the consularis, marvelled exceedingly how an old man of a hundred and twenty years could thus endure. And orders were given for him to be crucified.

7 In addition, the same man, in describing what happened in the time of the said persons, goes on to say that up to that time *the Church* remained *a virgin*, pure and *undefiled*; [4] that if there were any who were trying to corrupt the sound standard of the preaching of salvation, they were still then lurking, as it
8 were, in some obscure and dark hole.✳But when the sacred band of the apostles had ended their lives in various ways, and the generation of those who had been privileged to listen to the divine Wisdom with their own ears had passed away, then godless error began to take its rise, and form itself through the deceit of those who taught another doctrine; who now also

---

[1] John xix. 25. [2] c. 11.
[3] 20. 1-6. [4] Heg. (iv. 22. 5 below).

threw off the mask, since none of the apostles any longer
remained, and tried to counter the preaching of the truth by
preaching *the knowledge which is falsely so called.*[1]

Persecution : 2. In other places.

33.   But to resume.   To such an extent was the persecution of
that day intensified against us in most places, that *Pliny
Secundus,* a most distinguished governor, was moved by *the
number* of the martyrs to *communicate with* the *emperor* with
reference to the number of those who were put to death for
the faith ; *and* in the same letter he *informed* him as well that
he had detected them in *no criminal* or unlawful practices,
saving only this : that they rose as soon as it was dawn to
sing hymns to Christ as to a god, and also that they abjured
adultery, murder, and all such nefarious crimes, and in all their
2 practices conformed to the laws.   *In answer to* this [we are
told] that *Trajan* laid down the following decree : *that the
tribe of Christians was not, indeed, to be sought out, but punished
if met with.*   By this means [it came about] that the threat of
persecution which hung so very terribly over us was in a certain
measure checked, yet there were just as many pretexts left
for those who would do us evil ; sometimes it was the people,
at others the local rulers, who laid their plots against us : so
that, even without there being open persecutions, partial
ones in particular provinces sprang up, and numbers of the
faithful endured the conflict of martyrdom under various
forms.
3   Now our account has been taken from the Latin Apology
of Tertullian, of which we spoke above.[2]   The translation
thereof runs after this fashion :

   And yet we have found that even search for us has been forbidden.   For when Pliny Secundus, the governor of a province,
had condemned certain Christians and driven them out of office,
he was alarmed by the number ; and, in his ignorance as to what
else he could do, he communicated with the emperor Trajan, saying
that, apart from the unwillingness to worship idols, he had found
no crime in them.   And he also informed him to this effect :
that the Christians rose at dawn and sang hymns to Christ as to a
god ; and that, with a view to maintaining their discipline, murder,
adultery, fraud, robbery *and such like*[3] were forbidden them.
In answer to this Trajan wrote a reply that the tribe of Christians
was not, indeed, to be sought out, but punished if met with.[4]

---

[1] 1 Tim. vi. 20.   [2] ii. 2. 4 ff.; 25. 4.
[3] Gal. v. 21.   [4] Tert., *Apol.* 2.

Succession of Bishops.

34. Such, then, were the happenings in those times. But of the
bishops at Rome, in the third year of the principate of the
101. aforesaid emperor, Clement departed this life and left
the ministry to Evarestus. He had presided over the
teaching of the divine word for nine years in all.

35. And when Symeon had been perfected in the manner
described,[1] a certain Jew of the name of Justus, who also was
one of those countless numbers of the circumcision who had
then believed in Christ, succeeded to the throne of the
episcopate at Jerusalem.

The First Succession from the Apostles. 1. Ignatius and Polycarp.

36. But to resume. In their day in Asia a companion of the
apostles, Polycarp, was in eminence : he had been entrusted
with the episcopate of the church at Smyrna by the *eye-witnesses*
2 *and ministers* [2] of the Lord. In his day Papias was well known,
also a bishop, but of the community at Hierapolis ; as was also
Ignatius, he whose name is still to this day on the lips of very
many, who was the second in the succession from Peter at
Antioch to receive the episcopate.

3 Now it is recorded that he was sent *from Syria* to the city
of the Romans,[3] and became *food for wild beasts* [4] because of
4 his testimony to Christ. And what is more, while he was
making the journey through Asia under the strictest military
surveillance,[5] he confirmed the communities in the several
cities where he stopped by verbal instructions and exhortations, *counselling* them above all things *to guard beforehand*
against the *heresies* which were just then for the first time
becoming common,[6] and urging them to cling closely to the
tradition *of the apostles* ; [7] which tradition, as his martyrdom
was now at hand, he considered should of necessity be given
5 a fixed form, for safety's sake, in writing also. So then,
when he came to *Smyrna*, where *Polycarp* was, *he wrote* one
letter to *the church* at *Ephesus*,[8] mentioning its pastor
Onesimus; [9] and another to *the* church *at Magnesia on the
Maeander*,[10] where, again, he has made mention of *the bishop
Damas;* [11] and still another *to the church at Tralles*, whose
6 ruler at that time, as he records, was *Polybius*.[12] In addition

---

[1] 32. 2, 3.   [2] Luke i. 2.   [3] Ign., *Eph.* 1, 21; *Rom.* 5, 10.
[4] Ign., *Rom.* 4 (Greek).   [5] Cp. Ign., *Rom.* 5.
[6] Ign., *Magn.* 11; *Trall.* 6, 7; *Philad.* 3; *Smyrn.* 4.
[7] Ign., *Magn.* 13; *Trall.* 7.   [8] Ign., *Eph.* Pref., 21.   [9] *Ib.* 1, 2, 6.
[10] Ign., *Magn.* Pref., 15.   [11] *Ib.* 2.   [12] Ign., *Trall.* Pref., 1, 12.

to these, he wrote also *to the church of the Romans*,[1] in which [letter] he implores them not to beg him off his martyrdom and thus deprive him of the *hope* he longed for.[2]

To illustrate what I have said, it is fitting to make even the briefest quotations from these letters. He writes, then, in these very words :

7   From Syria to Rome I fight with wild beasts by land and sea, by night and day, being bound to ten leopards (that is, a company of soldiers), who, the better they are treated, the worse they become. But by their evil deeds I am becoming the more a
8 disciple, *yet am I not* on this account *justified*.[3] May I have joy of the wild beasts that are ready for me ; and I pray that I may find them prompt. I shall even coax them to devour me promptly, not as has happened to some whom they refused to touch through fear ; and if they are unwilling of themselves
9 and have no wish, it is I who will compel them. Pardon me ; I know what is expedient for me ; now I am beginning to be a disciple. May naught of things visible or invisible envy me ; that I may attain unto Jesus Christ. Come fire and cross and conflicts with wild beasts, wrenching of bones, hacking of limbs, grinding of the whole body, tortures of the devil upon me ; if only I may attain unto Jesus Christ.[4]

10   Now these words were penned from the aforesaid city to the churches which we have recounted. But when he was now beyond Smyrna, from *Troas* he communicated, once more in *writing*, to those *at Philadelphia, to the church of the Smyrnœans*, and, personally, *to* its leader *Polycarp*.[5] And knowing full well that he was a truly apostolic man, like a true and kind shepherd Ignatius commits to his charge *the* flock at *Antioch*, requesting him to take earnest thought for it.[6]
11 And the same person, in writing to the Smyrnæans, has made use of a saying taken from I know not what source, giving the following account concerning Christ :

But I for my part know and believe that He was in the flesh even after His resurrection. And when He came to Peter and those who were with him, He said to them : " Lay hold and handle me, and see that I am not a bodiless demon." And straightway they touched Him, and believed. . . .[7]

12   And Irenæus too knew his martyrdom, and mentions his epistles. His words are as follows :

As one of our people said, when condemned to the wild beasts for his testimony to God : " I am God's wheat, and I am ground by the teeth of wild beasts, that I may be found pure bread." [8]

---

[1] Ign. *Rom.* Pref., 10.   [2] Ign., *Rom. passim* (cp. *Eph.* 1).
[3] 1 Cor. iv. 4.   [4] Ign., *Rom.* 5.
[5] Ign., *Philad.* Pref., 11; *Smyrn.* Pref., 12; *Pol.* Pref., 8.
[6] Ign., *Pol.* 7.   [7] Ign., *Smyrn.* 3.   [8] Iren. v. 28. 3; cp. Ign., *Rom.* 5.

13   And Polycarp too mentions these same letters in his extant
letter to the Philippians.   These are the very words in which
he does so :

> I exhort you all, therefore, to obey, and to practise every kind
> of *endurance,* which you saw before your *eyes* not only in the
> blessed ones, Ignatius and Rufus and Zosimus, but also in others
> who were your own, and in Paul himself and the rest of *the apostles* ;[1]
> being persuaded that all these *did not run in vain,*[2] but in faith and
> righteousness, and that they are gone *to the place which is* their
> *due,*[1] by the Lord's side *with* whom also *they suffered.*[3]   For they
> *loved* not *this present world,*[4] but *Him who died for us* and *for our
> sakes was raised* [5] by God.[6]

And afterwards he adds :

14   You wrote to me, both you yourselves and Ignatius, that if
anyone should go hence to Syria, he might also carry to its destina-
tion the letter from you.   And this I shall do, if I find a fitting
opportunity, whether it be I, or he whom I send to be an ambassador
15 on your behalf also.   The epistles of Ignatius which were sent by
him to us, and as many others as we had by us, we send to you,
even as you gave us charge.   These are subjoined to this epistle ;
and from them you will be able to derive great profit.   For they
contain faith and endurance, and every kind of edification which
pertains to our Lord.[7]

So much, then, for Ignatius.   He was succeeded in the
episcopate of Antioch by Heros.

2. *Quadratus.*

37.   Now among the illustrious persons in the time of these men
was *Quadratus.*   It is recorded that he, as well as *the daughters
of Philip,* was distinguished for *the prophetical gift.*[8]

3. *Clement of Rome.*

And moreover many others besides were well known in their
day, occupying the first step in the succession from the apostles.
And these also, inasmuch as they were godly disciples of such
great men, *built upon the foundations* of the churches which in
every place had been already laid down by *the apostles,*[9]
extending still further the preaching [of the Gospel], and
scattering far and wide throughout the whole world the saving
2 seeds of the kingdom of heaven.   For in very truth numbers
of the disciples of that day felt their souls smitten by the
divine word with a more ardent passion for philosophy, and

---

[1] Clem. *Ep.* 5.   [2] Phil. ii. 16.
[3] Rom. viii. 17 ; 2 Tim. ii. 12.   [4] 2 Tim. iv. 10.
[5] Ign., *Rom.* 6.   [6] Pol., *Phil.* 9.
[7] *Ib.* 13.   [8] Anon. (v. 17, 3, 4 below).
[9] Cp. 1 Cor. iii. 10 ; Eph. ii. 20.

so at first fulfilled the Saviour's command, by distributing
their goods to the needy.[1]   Afterwards they set out on journeys
from home and performed *the work of evangelists*,[2] *making it*
their *aim* to preach to such as had not yet heard the word of
the faith at all,[3] and to give them the book of the divine
3 Gospels.   But they were content to lay the foundations only
of the faith in some foreign places, appointing others as
pastors to whom they entrusted the care [4] of those lately
brought in; then they would depart to other lands and
nations, with the grace and co-operation of God : for the
divine Spirit still to that day worked mightily through them in
many miraculous powers, insomuch that at the first hearing
whole multitudes in a body eagerly embraced in their souls
piety towards the Creator of the universe.

4   But since it is impossible for us to enumerate by name all
who at that time, in the first succession from the apostles,
were pastors or even evangelists in the churches throughout
the world, we have naturally preserved in writing by name
the memory of those alone whose presentation of the apostolic
38.   teaching is even to our day extant in memoirs.   Such, of
course, are Ignatius, in the letters we have recounted, and
Clement, in the letter acknowledged by all, which he penned
in the name of the church of the Romans to the church of the
Corinthians.   In it he gives many thoughts from the Epistle
to the Hebrews, and even quotes verbally when using certain
passages from it : thus most clearly establishing the fact that
2 the treatise was no recent thing.   For this reason it has seemed
right and reasonable to reckon it among the other letters of the
apostle.   For, Paul having communicated in writing with the
Hebrews in their native tongue, some say that the evangelist
Luke, others that this Clement himself, translated the writing.
3 The latter statement is the more probably true; because both
the Epistle of Clement and that to the Hebrews maintain the
same character from the point of view of style, and because the
thoughts in each of the two treatises are not divergent.

4   But it should be known that there is said to be also a
second epistle of Clement; yet we understand that this is
not as well known as the former, for we are not aware that
5 the ancients have made any use of it.   And now certain
persons have brought forward just recently other wordy and
lengthy treatises purporting to be his, containing dialogues of
Peter, forsooth, and Apion.   These are not so much as even
mentioned by the men of old, nor do they preserve the stamp
of apostolic orthodoxy intact.

---

[1] Cp. Matt. xix. 21.   [2] 2 Tim. iv. 5.
[3] Cp. Rom. xv. 20, 21.   [4] Lit. " tillage."

4. *Papias.*

The acknowledged writing, then, of Clement is clearly
genuine; and we have spoken also of the writings of Ignatius
39. and Polycarp.[1] But of Papias there are five treatises extant,
which also have been entitled Expositions [2] of the Dominical
Oracles. These Irenæus also mentions as his only writings,
saying somewhat as follows:

> And these things Papias also, who was a hearer of John and a
> companion of Polycarp, a man of primitive times, attests in
> writing in the fourth of his books. For there are five books
> composed by him.[3]

2   So, indeed, says Irenæus. Nevertheless Papias himself,
in the preface to his discourses, makes it plain that he was
in no sense a hearer and eye-witness of the holy apostles; but
tells us, by the language he uses, that he had received the
things pertaining to the faith from those who were their
pupils:

3   But I will not hesitate also to set down for thy benefit, along
with the interpretations, all that ever I carefully learnt and
carefully recalled from the elders, guaranteeing its truth. For I
did not take delight, as most men do, in those who have much to
say, but in those who teach what is true; not in those who recall
foreign commandments, but in those who recall the commandments
given by the Lord to faith, and reaching us from the truth itself.
4 And if anyone chanced to come who had actually been a follower
of the elders, I would enquire as to the discourses of the elders,
what Andrew or what Peter said, or what Philip, or what Thomas
or James, or what John or Matthew or any other of the Lord's
disciples; and the things which Aristion and John the elder,
disciples of the Lord, say. For I supposed that things out of
books did not profit me so much as the utterances of a voice
which liveth and abideth.[4]

5   Here it is worth while noting that twice in his enumeration
he mentions the name John: the former of these Johns he
puts in the same list with Peter and James and Matthew and
the other apostles, clearly indicating the evangelist; but the
latter he places with others, in a separate clause,[5] outside the
number of the apostles, placing Aristion before him; and he
6 clearly calls him "elder." So that he hereby also proves their
statement to be true who have said that two persons in *Asia*
have borne the same name, *and that there were two tombs at
Ephesus, each of which is* still to this day *said to be John's.*[6]
And to these details one must needs pay attention, for it is

---

[1] c. 36.   [2] Reading ἐξηγήσεις.
[3] Iren. v. 33. 4.   [4] 1 Pet. i. 23.
[5] Or "with a distinction in the phrase."
[6] Dion. Alex., *Prom.* vii. 25. 16, below.

likely that the second (if one is unwilling to admit that it was
the first) saw the Revelation which is extant under the name
7 of John.   And Papias, of whom we are now speaking, acknowledges that he received *the discourses of the* apostles from those
who had been their *followers*, but says that he was himself an
actual hearer of *Aristion and* of *John the elder*.[1]   Certainly he
mentions them by name frequently in his treatises and sets
forth their traditions.

8   So much, then, for these points which, it is hoped, we have
not adduced to no purpose.   But it is right to add to the words
of Papias which we have quoted other sayings, in which he
relates some other miraculous events likewise, as having come
9 down to him by tradition.   It has been shown, indeed, by
what has gone before,[2] that Philip the apostle resided in
Hierapolis with his daughters ; but now it must be pointed
out that Papias, their contemporary, mentions that he had a
wonderful story from *the daughters of Philip*.   For he relates
that the *resurrection* of a dead body took place in his day ;
and, on the other hand, he tells of another miraculous happening, concerned with *Justus who was* surnamed *Barsabbas* :
that he *drank* a deadly poison [3] and, by the grace of the Lord,
suffered no unpleasant effects.

10   The book of the Acts records that, after the ascension of
the Saviour, the holy apostles *put forward* this *Justus* along
with *Matthias and prayed* as to *the lot* [which was to be taken]
to fill up the place in their number vacated by the traitor
Judas.   The passage runs somewhat as follows :

And they put forward two, Joseph called Barsabbas, who was
surnamed Justus, and Matthias.   And they prayed and said . . .[4]

11   And the same writer has quoted other things also, as coming
to him from unwritten tradition ; for instance, certain strange
parables of the Saviour and teachings of His, and some other
12 things of a rather mythical character.   And among these is
his statement that there will be a certain period of a thousand
years after the resurrection from the dead, when the kingdom
of Christ will be set up in a material order upon this earth.   I
imagine that he got these ideas through a misinterpretation
of the apostolic accounts, for he did not understand what they
13 said mystically and in figurative language.   For he evidently
was a man of exceedingly small intelligence, as one might say
judging from his discourses ; nevertheless it was owing to him
that so very many churchmen after him adopted a like opinion,
taking their stand on the fact that he was a man of primitive
times : as, for example, Irenæus and all others who have given

[1] Papias in § 4 above.   [2] 31. 1–4.
[3] See Philip of Side in *T.U.* v. 2, p. 170 ; cp. [Mark] xvi. 18.
[4] Acts i. 17, 23, 24.

14 evident expression to like views. And, besides, Papias gives us in his work accounts of the aforesaid Aristion of the sayings of the Lord, and traditions of John the elder.

While we refer scholars to these, we shall now of necessity add to the words of his already quoted a tradition which he has set forth concerning Mark who wrote the Gospel. It is in these words :

15 This also the elder used to say. Mark, indeed, having been the interpreter of Peter, wrote accurately, howbeit not in order, all that he recalled of what was either said or done by the Lord. For he neither heard the Lord, nor was he a follower of His, but, at a later date (as I said), of Peter ; who used to adapt his instructions to the needs [of the moment], but not with a view to putting together the Dominical oracles in orderly fashion : so that Mark did no wrong in thus writing some things as he recalled them. For he kept a single aim in view : not to omit anything of what he heard, nor to state anything therein falsely.

16 Such, then, is Papias' account of Mark. But the following is the statement concerning Matthew :

So then, Matthew compiled the oracles in the Hebrew language ; but everyone interpreted them as he was able.

17 And the same writer has used testimonies drawn from the former epistle of John, and likewise from that of Peter ; and he has set forth, as well, another story about a woman accused falsely of many sins before the Lord, which the Gospel of the Hebrews contains. So much, then, for these things which of necessity we have noted, in addition to what has been already set forth.

BOOK IV

The Fourth Book of the Ecclesiastical History contains the following:

1. The persons who were bishops of the Romans and Alexandrians in the reign of Trajan.
2. The sufferings of the Jews in his day.
3. Those who wrote apologies for the faith in the time of Hadrian.
4. The bishops of the Romans and Alexandrians in his day.
5. The bishops of Jerusalem from the first, from the time of the Saviour right down to the [emperors] of whom we are speaking.
6. The final siege of the Jews in the time of Hadrian.
7. The persons who were leaders of the *knowledge which is falsely so called* [1] at that time.
8. Those who were ecclesiastical writers.
9. A letter of Hadrian, ordering that we ought not to be persecuted without trial.
10. The persons who were bishops of the Romans and the Alexandrians in the reign of Antoninus.
11. On the heresiarchs of their day.
12. On the apology of Justin to Antoninus.
13. A letter of Antoninus to the Common Assembly of Asia in regard to our doctrine.
14. The facts related concerning Polycarp the disciple of the apostles.
15. How, under Verus, Polycarp along with others suffered martyrdom at the city of the Smyrnæans.
16. How Justin the philosopher, presenting the word of Christ at the city of the Romans, suffered martyrdom.
17. On the martyrs whom Justin mentions in a treatise of his own.
18. The works of Justin which have come down to us.
19. The persons who presided over the church of the Romans and of the Alexandrians in the reign of Verus.
20. Those who [presided over] the [church] of the Antiochenes.
21. On the ecclesiastical writers who were conspicuous in their day.
22. On Hegesippus, and the things which he mentions.
23. On Dionysius bishop of the Corinthians, and the epistles which he wrote.
24. On Theophilus, bishop of the Antiochenes.
25. On Philip and Modestus.
26. On Melito, and the things which he mentions.
27. On Apollinarius.
28. On Musanus.
29. On the heresy of Tatian.
30. On Bardesanes the Syrian and his extant works.

---

[1] 1 Tim. vi. 20.

Succession of Bishops.

1.

110. Now about the twelfth year of the reign of Trajan, the bishop of the community at Alexandria, whom we mentioned a little while ago,[1] departed this life; and Primus, the fourth from the apostles, was appointed to the ministry of the people there.

At that time also, when Evarestus had completed his eighth year, Alexander received the episcopate at Rome, holding the fifth place in the succession from Peter and Paul.

The Jewish Revolt.

2.

116. And while everything connected with our Saviour's teaching and Church daily flourished and went forward more and more, the calamities of the Jews were at their height, and disaster followed upon disaster. For instance, when the emperor was approaching the eighteenth year [of his reign], another disturbance arose on the part of the Jews,

2 causing the destruction of very large numbers of them. For in Alexandria and the rest of Egypt, and in Cyrene as well, a violent spirit of revolt, so to speak, fanned their passions into flame, so that they rushed into an open rising against their fellow-inhabitants the Greeks. And when the faction had greatly extended, in the following year they began a war on no small scale, Lupus being then governor of all Egypt.

3 And indeed in the first engagement it so happened that the Jews had the advantage over the Greeks, who in their turn fled to Alexandria, and captured and slew the Jews in the city. But the Jews in Cyrene, though deprived of their aid, continued to plunder the land of Egypt and devastate its nomes, under the leadership of Lucuas. Against them the emperor sent Marcius Turbo with a force of infantry and a

4 naval contingent, and with cavalry as well. And he diligently prosecuted the war with them in many battles and for no brief period, killing immense numbers of Jews, not only of those from Cyrene, but also of those from Egypt who had come to the assistance of their king Lucuas.

5 But the emperor suspected that the Jews in Mesopotamia also would attack the inhabitants of that country. So he ordered Lusius Quietus to clear the province of them. And he in turn marched against them and killed an immense number of those that dwelt there; for which success the emperor appointed him governor of Judæa. These events have also been recorded in the same terms by such Greeks as have handed down in writing an account of those times.

[1] iii. 21.

REIGN OF HADRIAN (117–138)

3.   Now when Trajan had held the principate for twenty entire years all but six months, Ælius Hadrianus succeeded to the government.

Two Apologists : Quadratus and Aristides.

To him Quadratus dedicated and addressed a discourse, which he had composed in defence of our religion, because certain wicked men were endeavouring to molest our people. The treatise is still to be found in the hands of very many of the brethren, as indeed it is in ours also. From it we may gather striking proofs of the author's understanding and of
2 his apostolic soundness in the faith.[1] But he himself reveals the early date at which he lived in the following account, given by him in these very words :

But the works of our Saviour were always present (for they were genuine) : namely, those who were healed, those who rose from the dead; who were not only seen in the act of being healed or raised, but were also always present ; and not merely when the Saviour was in earth, but after His departure as well, they lived for a considerable time; insomuch that some of them survived even to our own day.

3   Such a one was he. And Aristides too, a faithful follower of our religion, has left behind him an Apology which, like Quadratus, he dedicated to Hadrian on behalf of the faith. And his book also is to this day preserved in the hands of very many.

Succession of Bishops.

4.   Now in the third year of the same government, Alexander,
120. bishop of the Romans, died, having completed the tenth year of his administration.[2] Xystus was his successor. And in the community of the Alexandrians also, Primus departed this life about the same time, in the twelfth year of his presidency, and was succeeded by Justus.

5.   As to the bishops at Jerusalem, however, I have quite failed to find their dates preserved in writing (for indeed it is
2 recorded that they were exceedingly short-lived); but this much I have learnt from writings : that up to the siege of the Jews under Hadrian there had been fifteen bishops in succession, all of whom, it is said, were of Hebrew origin, but received the knowledge of Christ with a sincere heart, insomuch that the persons capable of judging such matters approved them as worthy of the ministry of a bishop; for [it is said]

---

[1] ὀρθοτομία : cp. 2 Tim. ii. 15.   [2] οἰκονομία.

that their whole church at that time consisted of believing Hebrews, who continued from the days of the apostles right down to that siege in which the Jews, having again revolted from the Romans, were conquered after severe fighting.

3 It will be right, then, since the bishops of the circumcision came to an end at that time, to give here a list of them from the first. The first, therefore, was James, the Lord's brother, as he was called; after him the second, Symeon; the third, Justus; Zacchæus, the fourth; the fifth, Tobias; the sixth, Benjamin; John, the seventh; the eighth, Matthias; the ninth, Philip; the tenth, Seneca; the eleventh, Justus; Levi, the twelfth; Ephres, the thirteenth; the fourteenth,

4 Joseph; last of all, the fifteenth, Judas. Such is the number of the bishops in the city of Jerusalem, from the apostles to the time of which we are now speaking. All of them were of the circumcision.

5 Now in the twelfth year of [Hadrian's] government, Xystus, **129.** having completed a period of ten years as bishop of the Romans, was succeeded by Telesphorus, the seventh from the apostles.

And after a lapse of a year and some months, Eumenes succeeded in the sixth place [1] to the presidency of the community of the Alexandrians. His predecessor had continued [in office] for eleven years.

Bar Cochba and the founding of Ælia.

6. The revolt of the Jews once more grew to be a great and large movement; so Rufus the governor of Judæa took unsparing advantage of their folly, and advanced against them with the military reinforcements which the emperor had sent him. At a single stroke he destroyed tens of thousands of them, men, children and women alike; and in accordance

2 with the rules of warfare confiscated their lands. Now the commander of the Jews at that time was a man named Bar Cochba, which means a star. He was nothing but an assassin and a robber; nevertheless he used his name to impress his servile followers with the belief that he was in truth a luminary come down from heaven to shine upon their evil plight.

3 The war was at its height in the eighteenth year of the rule [of **135.** Hadrian], round about Beth-ther, a small but very strong town not very far from Jerusalem, where a protracted siege brought the revolutionaries to utter destruction through hunger and thirst, and the author of their folly paid the just penalty. From that time forward the whole nation was wholly prohibited from setting foot upon the country round about Jerusalem, by the decree and ordinances of a law of Hadrian, which forbade them even from afar to gaze on the

[1] κλήρῳ.

soil inherited from their fathers.　Such is the account given
4 by Aristo of Pella.　So when the city was thus emptied of the
nation of the Jews and its old inhabitants utterly destroyed,
and when it was peopled with an alien race, the Roman city
which then arose changed its name, and was called Ælia in
honour of him who was ruling, Ælius Hadrianus.

And moreover, since the church there was [now] composed
of Gentiles, the first to be entrusted with the ministry of its
members, in succession to the bishops of the circumcision,
was Mark.

Heresies.

7.　　　As the churches throughout the world were now resplendent
like brilliant luminaries, and as faith in our Saviour and Lord
Jesus Christ was now flourishing wherever man was to be
found, the demon who hates the good—that enemy of the
truth, that ever deadly foe of man's salvation—pondered all
sorts of devices against the Church.　In days of old he used to
2 arm himself against her with external persecutions; but when
that course lay no longer open to him, he employed men who
were villains and cheats as instruments for the destruction of
souls and as ministers of perdition, and adopted another plan
of campaign.　For he left no stone unturned to secure that
cheats and deceivers, by assuming the very name of our
religion, should bring such of the faithful as became their
victims to the lowest depths of perdition, and also, by their
own actions and practices, turn aside those ignorant of the
faith from the path that leads to the word of salvation.

Satorninus.

3　　So *from* Menander (who, as we have already stated,[1] was
Simon's successor) there proceeded a power with, as it were,
the double jaws and twin heads of a serpent, which produced
the authors of two *different* heresies : *Satorninus an Antiochene
by race, and Basilides an Alexandrian.*　Of these *the one in
Syria, the other in Egypt,* established schools of God-hating
4 heresies.　Irenæus tells us that for the most part *Satorninus*
gave utterance to *the same* falsehoods *as Menander,*[2] but that
Basilides, *under the pretence of profounder mysteries, set no
bounds to the sweep of his ideas,*[3] so monstrous were the fictions
which he invented to form his impious heresy.

5　　Therefore very many churchmen contended at that time
for truth, and with unusual eloquence championed the doctrine
of the apostles and of the Church.　And some of these by means
of treatises also provided subsequent generations with methods
of guarding against these very heresies of which we spoke.

[1] iii. 26. 1.　　　　[2] Iren. i. 18.　　　　[3] *Ib.* 19. 1.

Basilides.

6   Among those which have come down to us, there is a most
powerful refutation of Basilides by a writer of the greatest
renown at that time, Agrippa Castor, which unmasks the man's
7 cunning imposture. In exposing his hidden mysteries, he
says that Basilides composed four and twenty books on the
Gospel, and on the other hand that he named Barcabbas and
Barcoph as his prophets, providing himself likewise with
certain others who never existed, whom he called by barbarous
names in order to strike amazement into those who marvel at
such things ; that he taught that to taste meat offered to idols,
and to renounce without reservation the faith in times of
persecution, were matters of indifference ; and that he imposed
upon his followers a five years' silence after the manner of
8 Pythagoras. And the writer of whom we have spoken has
collected other similar facts about Basilides, and thus openly
laid bare the error of the said heresy in no unworthy fashion.

Carpocrates.

9   Now Irenæus also writes that *Carpocrates* was a contemporary of these men, the father of another heresy, that of
the *Gnostics, as* it was *called.*[1] These latter also claimed to
hand down the *magic* arts of Simon, yet not secretly like
Basilides, but now even openly. Thus, they almost prided
themselves, as if forsooth it were something great, on the
spells which they composed with excessive care, and on certain
demons *that send dreams and act as familiar spirits*, and on
other like practices. And [Irenæus says] that consequently
they teach that every kind of infamy must be done by those
who are about to enter upon the final stage of their initiation
(or, rather, of their abomination), for that they may not
escape the " *cosmic powers* " (so they say) except by discharging
to them all their due payment of infamous conduct.[2]

Slanders against the Christians.

10   So it came to pass that, by the use of these ministers, the
demon who rejoices in evil enslaved and brought to ruin
their pitiable dupes, while supplying the heathen with abundant
material of speaking ill of the divine word : for their fame
spread, and brought infamy upon the whole Christian nation.[3]
11 And so it was chiefly for this reason that that impious and
outrageous suspicion came to be circulated among the unbelievers of that day concerning us, namely, that we indulged in
unlawful intercourse with mothers and sisters, and in unhallowed
feasts.

[1] Iren. i. 20. 4.   [2] *Ib.* 20. 2.   [3] Cp. *ib.* 20. 2.

12   These efforts of his, however, did not long achieve success;
      since the truth established herself, and as time advanced
13 became a brilliant and powerful light. For by her action the
   machinations of her enemies were exposed and checked
   immediately : new heresies being successively devised, since
   the previous ones were ever passing away and losing themselves
   in forms of diverse character and shape, now in one way, now
   in another. But the splendour of the Catholic and only true
   Church, ever the same and ever alike, grew in magnitude and
   power, as it cast upon every race both of Greeks and barbarians the light of all that is venerable, unsullied and free,
   all that is modest and pure, in her divine life and philosophy.
14 So then, in the process of time there was quenched also the
   slander against the Faith as a whole; and in consequence
   our teaching alone remained victorious on all sides, and was
   acknowledged as superior without a rival in gravity and
   sobriety and in divine and philosophic doctrines. Hence no
   one to-day may dare to utter vile calumny against our faith,
   nor any such slander as they who conspired against us were
   formerly wont to use in days of yore.

Champions of the Faith.

15   Nevertheless, in the time of the [heretics] of whom I am
      speaking, the truth again brought forward many champions
      of her cause, who made war on the godless heresies, not with
      oral refutations alone, but also with proofs in writing.

Hegesippus.

8.   Among these Hegesippus was well known, he whose words
      we have already previously employed on very many occasions,[1]
      in order to set forth from his tradition certain facts relating to
   2 apostolic times. Now, he has noted down in five treatises,
      written in the simplest style, the unerring tradition of the
      apostolic preaching; and he indicates the time at which he
      flourished when he writes thus of those who first set up idols :

      . . . to whom they erected cenotaphs and temples, as they do
      to this day. One of these was Antinous, a slave of Hadrian
      Cæsar, in whose honour also the Antinoean games are held, who
      lived in our day. Indeed [the emperor] founded a city named
      after Antinous and [appointed] prophets. . . .

Justin Martyr.

3   In his day Justin also, a genuine lover of the true philosophy,
     was still engaged in studying the learning of the Greeks.   He

   [1] ii. 23. 4–18; iii. 11; 12; 16; 17; 18. 1; 19; 20. 1–6, 9; 32.

too indicates this time, when writing thus in his Apology to Antoninus :

> And we do not deem it out of place to mention here Antinous also, who lived just lately ; and whom all were driven by fear to worship as a god, though they knew who he was and whence he came.[1]

4   And, speaking of the war that was then being waged against the Jews, the same writer makes the following statement :

> For indeed in the Jewish war which was waged just lately, Bar Cochba, the leader of the Jewish revolt, ordered the Christians —and them alone—to be led off to terrible punishments, unless they denied that Jesus was the Christ and blasphemed Him.[2]

5   And in the same [volume] also he shows that his change from Greek philosophy to Christianity[3] was made not groundlessly but deliberately. He writes as follows :

> For indeed at the time when I took delight in the doctrines of Plato, I used to hear the Christians slandered ; but for my part, when I saw them fearless in the face of death and all that men deem fearful, I gradually came to the conclusion that they could not possibly be living in vice and the love of pleasure. For who is there that loves pleasure, or is licentious, or thinks it a good thing to feed on human flesh, who would embrace death, and so lose the satisfaction of his own lusts ; and would not rather at all costs endeavour to continue his present existence permanently and escape the notice of the rulers, instead of giving himself up to be put to death ?[4]

Rescript to Minucius Fundanus.

6   And the same writer also records that when Hadrian received a letter on behalf of the Christians from that most distinguished governor, Serenius Granianus, to the effect that it was not right to put them to death without any charge or trial in order to gratify popular outcries, the emperor sent a rescript to Minucius Fundanus, the proconsul of Asia, ordering that no one should be tried without a charge or reasonable 7 accusation.   And he has given a copy of the letter, preserving the original Latin.   He prefaces it with the following remarks :

> And although a letter of the most mighty and noble Cæsar, Hadrian, your father, supplies us with grounds for asking you to order that the trials should take place, even as we requested ; we have not made this request because it was ordered by Hadrian, but rather from the conviction that we request what is right[5] . . . our address.   However, we have subjoined the copy of Hadrian's letter, that you may know that we speak the truth in this matter also ; and here it is.[6]

---

[1] Just., *Apol.* i. 29.   [2] *Ib.* 31.
[3] θεοσέβεια.   [4] Just., *Apol.* ii. 12.
[5] Reading δίκαια for δικαίαν.   [6] Just., *Apol.* i. 68.

8   Therewith the said author gives the actual Latin rescript;
while we have translated it into Greek to the best of our ability.
It runs as follows :

9.   To Minucius Fundanus. I received a letter, written to me
by thy illustrious predecessor Serenius Granianus. I do not
think it right, therefore, to let the matter pass without examination, lest the men should be harassed and the informers supplied
2 with opportunity of villainy.   So then, if the provincials can so
clearly sustain this petition against the Christians as to give answer
in a court of law, let them have recourse to this method alone, and
not to petitions and mere outcries.   For it were much more fitting
that thou shouldest decide concerning any accusations which may
3 be made. If, therefore, any bring an accusation and show that they
are breaking the law in any particular, do thou pass judgment
according to the gravity of the offence.   But, by Hercules ! should
anyone prefer a suit of the kind through mere calumny, arrest him
for his sharp practice, and see to it that thou inflict punishment.[1]

Such, then, are the terms of Hadrian's rescript.

REIGN OF ANTONINUS (138–161)

10.   But when Hadrian had paid the debt of nature,[2] after [a reign
of] one and twenty years, Antoninus, called Pius, succeeded to
the principate of the Romans.

Succession of Bishops of Rome.

Now in his first year Telesphorus departed this life in the
eleventh year of his ministry, and Hyginus received
138-9. the office of the episcopate of the Romans.   Irenæus
records that Telesphorus adorned his death by martyrdom.[3]

Heretics : Valentinus and Cerdon.

In the same [passage] he shows that, in the time of the said
bishop of the Romans Hyginus, Valentinus, the founder of a
sect [4] of his own, and Cerdon, the author of the Marcionite error,
were both of them well known at Rome.   He writes thus :

11.   For Valentinus came to Rome under Hyginus, flourished under
Pius, and remained until Anicetus.   But Cerdon, the predecessor
of Marcion—he too came to the church under Hyginus (who was
the ninth bishop) and making public confession continued therein
on this manner : now teaching in secret, now making public
confession anew, now being convicted of false teaching and
removed from the assembly of the brethren.[5]

---

[1] Just., *Apol.* i. 68.   [2] τὸ χρεών.   [3] Iren. iii. 3. 3.
[4] Or " heresy."   [5] Iren. iii. 4. 2.

2   Now he says this in his third book Against the Heresies. In
the first book, however, he gives this further account of
Cerdon :

> Now a certain Cerdon, who went back for his material to the
> followers of Simon, and who came to stay at Rome under Hyginus
> (the holder of the ninth place from the apostles in the episcopal
> succession), taught that the God proclaimed by the law and the
> prophets was not the Father of our Lord Jesus Christ : for that
> the one was known, the other unknown ; the one was just, the
> other good.   And his successor, Marcion of Pontus, enlarged his
> school, blaspheming unblushingly. . . .[1]

3   And the same Irenæus, having unfolded with the greatest
vigour the unfathomable Depth of Valentinus' much-erring
Matter, lays bare the fact that his villainy was concealed and
4 hidden like a reptile in a hole.[2] Moreover he says that in
their day there was also *another past-master in the art of magic
trickery, whose name was Marcus.*[3] And he writes these very
words describing also their purposeless perfectings and
abominable initiations :

> 5   For some of them prepare a nuptial chamber and perform a rite
> of initiation accompanied by invocations over those who are being
> perfected ; and they assert that this which they do is a spiritual
> marriage after the likeness of the heavenly unions.   Others lead
> [the candidates] to water, and as they baptize them say the
> following words : " Into the name of the unknown Father of the
> universe, into Truth the Mother of all things, into Him that
> descended upon Jesus. . . ."   Others, again, use Hebrew ex-
> pressions with a view to impressing those who are being per-
> fected with still greater astonishment. . . .[4]

Succession of Bishops.

6   But to resume. Hyginus having died after an episcopate
of four years, Pius was entrusted with the ministry at Rome.
In Alexandria, however, Mark was appointed pastor, after
Eumenes had completed thirteen years in all ; and when
Mark rested from his ministry after ten years, Celadion
received the ministry of the church of the Alexandrians.
7   And in the city of the Romans too, when Pius had departed
this life in the fifteenth year of his episcopate, Anicetus
presided over the Christians of that place. Hegesippus
records that he himself took up his abode at Rome in his day,
and remained there until the episcopate of Eleutherus.[5]

Justin Martyr (continued).

8   But Justin was in his fullest prime in the time of these men,
presenting the divine word in the garb of a philosopher, and

[1] Iren. i. 24 ; 25. 1.   [2] *Ib.* 1. 8(?).   [3] *Ib.* 7. 1.
[4] *Ib.* 14. 2.   [5] Heg. (22. 3 below).

contending for the faith in his treatises. He wrote also a treatise against Marcion, in which he mentions that at the time when he composed it the man was alive and well known. He speaks thus :

9   . . . and [such was] a certain Marcion of Pontus, who is even now still teaching his followers to believe in some other God greater than the Creator.   And with the aid of the demons he has also persuaded many throughout the whole human race to utter blasphemies, and to deny that the Maker of this universe is the Father of Christ : yea, to confess that some other, greater than He, has made it.[1]   And *all* the followers of these men are called *Christians*, as we said ; [2] just as philosophers *share the name* they bear *in common*, although they may have no *beliefs* in common.[3]

10   Then he goes on to say :

Now we have also composed a work against all the heresies that have ever been ; which we will give you, should you wish to read it.[4]

11   And this very Justin, besides the most excellent work against the Greeks, also *addressed* other discourses containing an Apology for our faith to the emperor *Antoninus* (the same who was called *Pius*) and *the Senate of the Romans*.   For indeed he was staying at Rome.   And he makes it plain who and whence he was, in the Apology in the following words :

12.   To the emperor Titus Ælius Hadrianus Antoninus Pius Cæsar Augustus, and to Verissimus his son the philosopher, and to Lucius, own son of Cæsar the philosopher, and adopted son of Pius, a lover of learning ; and to the sacred Senate and the whole people of the Romans : I Justin, son of Priscus the son of Bacchius, of Flavia Neapolis in Syria Palestina, have composed this address and petition on behalf of those men of every race who are unjustly hated and reviled, I myself being one of them.[5]

Rescript to the Commune Asiæ.

And the same emperor, on being petitioned by other brethren in Asia who were suffering from all kinds of injuries at the hands of the peoples of that country, thought it right to address the following ordinance to the Common Assembly of Asia :

13.   The emperor Cæsar Marcus Aurelius Antoninus Augustus, Armenius, Pontifex Maximus, holding the Tribunician Power for the fifteenth time, Consul for the third : to the Common 2 Assembly of Asia, greeting.   I for my part indeed know that the gods also are careful that such persons should not escape detection. For theirs it is, much rather than yours, to punish such as will not 3 worship them.   Whom if ye bring into trouble, accusing them as

---

[1] Text corrupt : see note.   [2] Just. *Apol.* i. 7.
[3] *Ib.* 26.   [4] *Ib.*   [5] *Ib.* 1.

atheists, ye will but confirm in the opinion which they hold.[1] For when accused it were preferable in their eyes to appear [2] to die for their own god rather than to live. Wherefore also they come off victorious when they give up their own lives rather than 4 obey your behests. But as to the earthquakes which have taken, and are still taking, place, it is not improper to admonish you who lose heart whensoever they occur, and compare our condition with 5 theirs. They indeed become the more confident towards their god; but ye during all the time (in which ye are seemingly ignorant) neglect both the other gods and the worship of the Immortal.[3] And the Christians, because they worship Him, ye 6 harass and persecute unto death. Now, with regard to such persons, many also of the provincial governors wrote in times past to our divine father too; to whom also he sent a rescript that they should in no wise annoy such persons, unless they were manifestly making some attempt upon the government of the Romans. And to me also many have given information concerning such persons; to whom also I sent a rescript in agreement with my 7 father's decision. But if anyone persist in bringing to trial any of such persons as such : let him who is accused be acquitted of the charge, even though he be manifestly such; but the accuser shall be liable to be punished. Published at Ephesus in the Common Assembly of Asia.

8   That such was the course of these events is a fact further testified by Melito, bishop of the church at Sardis, who was well known at that time : as is clear from what he has said in the Apology for our faith which he addressed to the emperor Verus.[4]

Polycarp.

14.   Now Irenæus records that in the time of the said persons, while Anicetus was ruling the church of the Romans, Polycarp, who was still alive, was at Rome and held converse with Anicetus on a certain question relating to the day of the 2 Pascha.[5] And the same writer tells us another story about Polycarp, which must needs be added to our present account of him. It runs as follows :

From the Third Book of Irenæus Against the Heresies.

3   And Polycarp too, who not only was instructed by apostles and held intercourse with many who had seen the Lord, but also received in Asia his appointment from apostles as bishop in the church at Smyrna, whom we ourselves also have seen in 4 our early manhood (for he survived long and departed this life at a very great age by a glorious and most notable martyrdom), always taught [6] these very things which he had learnt from the

---

[1] A slight emendation of Schwartz has been adopted.
[2] Reading τό for τῷ.
[3] It is difficult to get an intelligible meaning out of § 5.
[4] Melito, *Apol.* (26. 10 below).
[5] Iren. *ad Victor.* (v. 24. 16 below).
[6] Reading ἐδίδαξεν with the Latin of Irenæus (*docuit*) for διδάξας.

apostles, which the Church hands down, which alone are true.
5 To these witness is borne by all the churches in Asia and by
the successors of Polycarp up to this day, who was a much more
trustworthy and surer witness to the truth than Valentinus and
Marcion and all such wrong-minded men. He also, when he
came to stay at Rome in the days of Anicetus, converted many
followers of the aforesaid heretics to the Church of God, proclaiming that he had received from the apostles as the one and
6 only truth that which is handed down by the Church. And
there are those who have heard him tell how that John the
disciple of the Lord, when at Ephesus he went to take a bath
and saw Cerinthus within, rushed out of the bath-house without
taking it, with the words, " Let us flee, lest even the bath-house
7 fall in, for within is Cerinthus the enemy of the truth." And
Polycarp himself too, when Marcion on one occasion confronted
him and said, " Recognize us," replied : " I recognize, I recognize, the first-born of Satan." So great precaution did the
apostles and their disciples take to avoid communication, even
by word, with any of those who were falsifying the truth ; as
Paul also said : *A man that is heretical after a first and second
admonition refuse ; knowing that such a one is perverted, and
8 sinneth, being self-condemned.*[1] Now there is also an epistle
of Polycarp written to the Philippians, of a most adequate
kind ; from which such as so desire, and have a care for their
own salvation, can learn both the character of his faith and the
message of the truth.[2]

9   Such is the account of Irenæus. Now Polycarp, in the
said writing of his to the Philippians, extant to this day,
has employed certain testimonies taken from the former
epistle of Peter.

REIGN OF MARCUS AURELIUS (161–180)

10   When Antoninus—the same who was called Pius—had
completed the twenty-second year of his principate, he
was succeeded by his son Marcus Aurelius Verus, also called
Antoninus, together with his brother Lucius.

Polycarp (continued)

15.   Now at this time, when the greatest persecutions again
threw Asia into turmoil, Polycarp was perfected by martyrdom ; and I deem it absolutely necessary that [the account
of] his end, which is still extant in writing, should be recorded
2 in this history. There is in existence the letter written in
the name of *the church* over which he ruled, indicating in the
following words to the *communities*[3] *in each place the events
which befell* him :

3   The church of God which sojourns at Smyrna to the church
of God which sojourns at Philomelium and to all the sojourn-

---

[1] Tit. iii. 10, 11.   [2] Iren. iii. 3. 4.   [3] παροικίαις.

ings [1] of the holy Catholic Church in every place : *mercy, peace and love* from God the Father and our Lord Jesus Christ *be multiplied*.[2] We write unto you, brethren, the story of that which befell them that suffered martyrdom and the blessed Polycarp, who by his martyrdom caused the persecution to cease, having, as it were, set thereon his seal.[3]

4   Next, before they tell the story of Polycarp, they relate the events which befell the other martyrs, describing the stedfastness they displayed under the agonies. For they say that *the* encircling *bystanders* were amazed to behold them, now *torn with scourges* even *to the* innermost *veins and arteries*, so that actually the hidden, secret parts of the body, their entrails and members, became visible ; now *laid upon a couch of* sea *shells* and a kind of sharp pointed spit ; and, after going through every kind of *punishment and torture*, at last committed as *food to the wild beasts*.[4]

5   But they relate that *the right noble Germanicus* was especially pre-eminent, *encouraging*, with the help of the divine grace, the natural *shrinking* of the body from death [which some displayed]. In fact *when the proconsul wished to persuade him*, urging *his years*, and entreating one who was in the full bloom of early youth to take *pity* on himself, [they go on to say] that he did not hesitate but eagerly *dragged the wild beast* towards *him*, all but *using violence* [5] and irritating it, to the intent that he might *the more speedily be released from*

6 *their unrighteous and lawless life.* And [they add] that after his glorious death *the whole multitude, marvelling* at the bravery of the martyr *beloved of God* and at the fortitude of the *people of the Christians* as a whole, began with one consent to *cry aloud : " Away with the atheists ; let search be made for Polycarp."* [6]

7   Further, [they say] that when these cries were the occasion of a very great tumult, a certain *Phrygian* by race, *named Quintus*, lately arrived from *Phrygia*, on *seeing the wild beasts* and the threatened tortures to follow, lost heart and courage,

8 and at last gave up his salvation. Yet the account given by the aforesaid letter shows that this man rushed forward along with others to the tribunal with unusual eagerness, howbeit without proper discretion ; but that notwithstanding when seized he gave a clear example to all, that one ought not to venture on such conduct in a fool-hardy and indiscreet manner. Such, then, was the end that overtook these men.[7]

9   But to resume. [They go on to say] that the *most marvellous Polycarp, when first he heard these things*, remained *undismayed*, preserving a stedfast and unshaken mien, and *wished* to *remain* on the spot *in the city ;* but that he *yielded* to the

---

[1] παροικίαις.   [2] Jude 2.   [3] *Mart. Pol.*, Inscr. 1.
[4] *Mart. Pol.* 2 (Ign. *Rom.* 4).   [5] Ign., *Rom.* 5.
[6] *Mart. Pol.* 3.   [7] *Ib.* 4.

entreaties and advice of his friends that he should *quietly
withdraw ;* and so *went* out *to a farm* at *no* great distance from
the city and there *abode* with *a few companions,* doing *nothing
else night and day* but continuing in stedfast prayers [1] to the
Lord ; and that therein he asked for peace for *the churches
throughout the* whole *world* with entreaty and supplication :
10 which thing *it had* ever *been his wont to do. And,* further,
[they say] that *as he prayed* he *saw in a trance* at night, *three
days* before his *apprehension,* the pillow under his head burst
into flame and all in a moment consumed *by fire ;* and that
on arousing from sleep thereupon, he immediately interpreted
the appearance to those present, prophesying the future, as
it were, and plainly declaring to his companions that *he must*
11 for Christ's sake depart this life by fire.[2]   So then, they say
that as *those who were seeking him* prosecuted the search with
all eagerness, he was once more compelled by the love and
affection of the brethren to *depart* to *another farm ;* whither
not long afterwards his pursuers came, and *seized two* of the
servants on the spot : *one of whom* they tortured, and through
12 him discovered where Polycarp lodged.[3]   And that *arriving
late in the evening* they *found* him *in bed in an upper room ;*
whence he *might* have departed to *another* house, but *would*
13 not, *saying, " The will of* God *be done."* [4]   And moreover,
when he heard of *their arrival,* as the account says, he *went
down and conversed with them* with a right cheerful and gentle
countenance ; so that those to whom the man was until then
unknown thought they actually beheld a miracle, as they
observed *his* advanced *years* and the gravity and *firmness*
of his bearing, and wondered *why* there was *so much ado to*
14 *apprehend an old man like him.*   But he without delay ordered
that a table *should immediately be set before* them ; then
requested them to partake freely of food, and *asked* of *them*
one *hour* that he might *pray unmolested. To this they con-
sented ;* and *he stood* up *and prayed, being* filled *with the grace
of the* Lord, *so that those who* were present *were amazed* when
they heard him praying, *and many* of them now *repented* that
such a grave and *venerable old man* was to be put to death.[5]
15   After this the letter concerning him proceeds with the
story somewhat on this manner and in these very words :

But when at length he had finished his prayer, having called
to mind all, even those who at any time had come in his way,
both small and great, both famous and obscure, and the whole
Catholic Church throughout the world, *the hour* for departure
came,[6] and they set him on an ass and brought him to the city,
it being a great sabbath.   And there met him Herod the captain
of the police and his father Nicetes ; who also transferred him

---

[1] Cp. Rom. xii. 12.   [2] *Mart. Pol.* 5.   [3] *Ib.* 6.
[4] Acts xxi. 14.   [5] *Mart. Pol.* 7.   [6] Cp. John xvii. 1.

to their vehicle, and strove to persuade him, sitting beside him and saying, "Why, what harm is there in saying, 'Cæsar is

16 Lord,' and in sacrificing, and saving thyself?'" At first he made no reply, but when they persisted he said : "I am not going to do what you counsel me." So, failing to persuade him, they uttered threatening words; and made him dismount so speedily that he scraped his shin as he was getting down from the vehicle. But indeed, without turning round, as if none the worse, he went on his way promptly and speedily. Thus was he

17 conducted to the arena.[1] Now though there was such a tumult therein that many could not even so much as hear, a *voice out of heaven came* [2] to Polycarp as he entered it, "*Be strong*, Polycarp, *and play the man*." [3] And though no one saw the speaker, many of our people heard the voice.

18 When, therefore, he was brought forward, there was a great tumult when they heard that Polycarp had been apprehended. At last when he came forward the proconsul asked him if he were Polycarp; and when he admitted it, tried to persuade him to deny, saying, "Have respect to thy years," and making similar remarks as it is their wont to say; "Swear by the genius of Cæsar:

19 repent and say, 'Away with the atheists.'" But Polycarp with a grave countenance looked upon the whole multitude that was in the arena, and waving his hand at them he *sighed* and

20 *looked up to heaven* [4] and said : "Away with the atheists." The governor pressed him and said : "Swear, and I will release thee; revile Christ." But Polycarp replied : "Eighty and six years am I His servant, and He hath done me no wrong. How then

21 can I blaspheme my King who saved me?" [5] And on his persisting again and saying : "Swear by the genius of Cæsar," Polycarp answered : "If thou vainly thinkest that I will swear by the genius of Cæsar, as thou sayest, pretending to be ignorant who I am, hear my plain speech : I am a Christian. And if thou wouldest learn the doctrine of Christianity, appoint a day

22 and give it a hearing." The proconsul said : "Persuade the people." Polycarp replied : "As for thyself, I have deemed thee worthy of discourse; for we have been taught to render, as is meet, to *rulers and powers ordained of God* such *honour* [6] as does not harm us. But them I count not worthy, that I should

23 make my defence before them." [7] So the proconsul said : "I have wild beasts; to them I will throw thee, except thou repent." But he said : "Call for them; for repentance from better to worse is a change we cannot make; but it is a noble thing to

24 change from cruel to righteous deeds." So he again said to him : "I will have thee consumed by fire, shouldest thou despise the wild beasts; except thou repent." Polycarp said : "Thou threatenest a fire that burns for a season, and after a little is quenched; for thou art ignorant of that fire of the judgment to come and of *eternal punishment*,[8] reserved for the ungodly. But why dost thou delay? Come, do according to thy will." [9]

25 Now in saying these things and much else as well, he was filled with courage and joy, and his countenance was full of grace;

---

[1] *Mart. Pol.* 8.   [2] Luke iii. 22.
[3] Josh. i. 6, 7, 9 (LXX).   [4] Cp. Mark, vii. 34.
[5] *Mart. Pol.* 9.   [6] Rom. xiii. 1, 7; cp. 1 Pet. ii. 13.
[7] *Mart. Pol.* 10.   [8] Matt. xxv. 46.   [9] *Mart. Pol.* 11.

so that not only did it not fall in dismay at the things which were said to him, but on the contrary the proconsul was astounded, and sent the herald to proclaim in the midst of the arena : " Thrice has Polycarp confessed himself to be a Christian."

26 When this statement had been made by the herald, the whole multitude of heathen and of Jews who dwelt in Smyrna shouted aloud in ungovernable rage : " This fellow is the teacher of Asia, the father of the Christians, the destroyer of our gods,
27 he who teaches many not to sacrifice or even worship."   So saying, they cried out and asked the Asiarch Philip to let loose a lion on Polycarp.   But he said that it was *unlawful* for him to do this, seeing that he had closed the sports.   Then they thought good with one consent to cry out that he should burn Polycarp
28 alive.   For it must be that the matter of the vision which appeared to him concerning the pillow should *be fulfilled* : [1] when, as he prayed, he saw it in flames, and turning to the faithful who
29 were with him said prophetically, " I must be burnt alive." [2]   So speedily, then, did these things happen, more quickly than it takes to say it—the crowds straightway collecting from the workshops and baths timber and faggots ; in which work the Jews especially
30 lent a ready hand, as is their wont.   But when the pyre was prepared, he stripped him of all his outer garments, loosened his girdle and endeavoured even to take off his shoes, although not in the habit of doing this formerly, because at all times every one of the faithful vied, which should be before another in touching his flesh.   For he had received all honour because of his holy
31 life, even before the gray hairs came.   Immediately, then, they placed about him the instruments prepared for the pyre.   But as they were for nailing him as well, he said : " Let me be ; for He who gives the power to endure the fire will give the power to remain at the pyre without shrinking, even without the security ye seek from the nails." [3]   So they did not nail him, but bound
32 him to [the stake].   And he put his hands behind him, and was bound like a choice ram taken from a mighty flock and offered
33 as a burnt-offering acceptable to Almighty God ; and said : " O Father of Thy beloved and blessed Child, Jesus Christ, through whom we have received the knowledge of Thee, the God of angels and powers and of all creation, and of the whole family of the righteous who live before Thee ; I bless Thee that Thou hast deemed me worthy of this day and hour, that among the number of the martyrs I may have a share in *the cup* of Thy Christ,[4] *unto the resurrection of eternal life*,[5] both of soul and body
34 in the incorruptibility of the Holy Spirit.   And may I be received to-day among them before Thee, as a rich and acceptable sacrifice, even as Thou hast before prepared it, Thou *true God* [6] *who canst not lie*,[7] who both didst manifest it beforehand and didst fulfil.
35 Therefore also I praise Thee for all things, I bless Thee, I glorify Thee, through *the eternal High Priest* [8] Jesus Christ, Thy beloved Child ; through whom with Him in the Holy Spirit be glory to Thee both now and for the ages that are to come.   Amen." [9]

---

[1] Cp. John xviii. 31, 32.   [2] *Mart. Pol.* 12.
[3] *Ib.* 13.   [4] Matt. xx. 23, etc.
[5] John v. 29 ; Tit. i. 2.   [6] John xvii. 3.
[7] Tit. i. 2.   [8] Pol., *Phil.* 12.   [9] *Mart. Pol.* 14.

36 Now when he had offered up the Amen and completed the
prayer, the men who were in charge of the fire lit it; and when
a great flame blazed forth, those of us to whom it was given to
see it—who also were preserved to tell to the others what happened
37 —saw a marvellous thing. For the fire formed into the likeness
of a vaulted room, as it were a boat's sail filled with the wind,
and made a wall about the body of the martyr; and it was in
the midst, not as burning flesh, but . . . as gold or silver refined
in a furnace. For verily we perceived such a fragrant odour, as
if it were the scent of frankincense or of some other costly spice.[1]
38 So at length the lawless men, seeing that the body could not be
consumed by the fire, ordered a confector to approach and stab
39 him with a sword; which when he did, *there came out* a quantity
of *blood*,[2] so that the fire was quenched and all the multitude
marvelled that there was so much difference between the unbelievers and the elect. Of the number of these was also this
man, who was the most marvellous apostolic and prophetical
teacher in our time, bishop of the Catholic Church in Smyrna.
For every word which he uttered from his mouth both was and
shall be accomplished.[3]
40 But the jealous and envious evil one, the adversary of the
family of the righteous, seeing the greatness of his martyrdom
and his blameless life from the beginning, and that he had been
wreathed with the crown of incorruptibility and had carried off
a prize which none could gainsay, took care that not even his
poor body should be taken away by us, although many longed
41 to do this and to have fellowship with his holy flesh. So certain
persons instigated Nicetes, the father of Herod and the brother
of Alce, to petition the governor not to give up his body, " lest,"
it was said, " they should leave the Crucified and begin to worship
this man." And this they said at the instigation and strong
pressure of the Jews; who also watched when we were going to
take him out of the fire. For they were ignorant that we shall
never be able either to desert Christ, who suffered for the salvation of those who are being saved in the whole world, or worship
42 any other. For Him, being the Son of God, we adore; but the
martyrs, as disciples and imitators of the Lord, we love as they
deserve for their matchless affection towards their own King and
Teacher. God grant that we too may be partakers and fellow-
43 disciples with them.[4] When, therefore, the centurion saw the
contention caused by the Jews, he set him in the midst, as their
custom is, and burnt him. And so we on our part afterwards
took up his bones, more valuable than precious stones and purer
44 than wrought gold, and laid them in a fitting place. And when
we assemble there according to our power in gladness and joy,
the Lord will permit us to celebrate the birthday of his martyrdom, both in memory of those who have already contended, and
for the training and preparation of such as shall hereafter do the
same.[5]
45 Such were the events that befell the blessed Polycarp. Including those who came from Philadelphia, he was the twelfth to be
martyred at Smyrna, yet he alone is held in especial memory by

---

[1] *Mart. Pol.* 15.   [2] John xix. 34.   [3] *Mart. Pol.* 16.
[4] *Ib.* 17.   [5] *Ib.* 18.

all, so that his name is on the lips even of the heathen in every
place. . . .[1]

46   Such, then, was the issue bestowed upon the events that
befell the marvellous and apostolic Polycarp; the account
of which the brethren of the church of the Smyrnæans have
set forth in their letter of which I have spoken.

Metrodorus and Pionius.

But in the same volume concerning him other martyrdoms
as well were subjoined, which took place in the same Smyrna
about the same period of time with Polycarp's martyrdom.
Among them *Metrodorus* also, who was accounted *a presbyter*
of the Marcionite error, was put to death, being committed
47 to the fire.[2] Of those of that day, however, there was a
certain celebrated martyr, Pionius, who was well known.
The several *confessions* made by this man; [3] his boldness of
speech; his *apologies* for the faith before the people and the
rulers; [4] his instructive harangues; moreover, his kindly
help to those who had succumbed to the temptation that
persecution brings; [5] the exhortations which he addressed to
the brethren who came to visit him in prison; [6] the tortures
which he subsequently endured; [7] the agonies that were
consequent thereupon; the nailings [8] and the endurance on
the pyre; [9] the end which crowned his marvellous deeds : [10] of
these the writing concerning him contains a very full account;
and to it, which has been given a place in the Martyrdoms of
the Ancients collected by us, we shall refer such as so desire.

Carpus, Papylus and Agathonice.

48   And, following this, there are extant memoirs of others also
who suffered martyrdom in Pergamum, a city in Asia : Carpus
and Papylus and a woman, Agathonice, who were perfected
gloriously after very many magnificent confessions.

Justin Martyr (continued)

16.   Now in their day Justin, of whom we spoke a little before,[11]
when he had addressed a second book on behalf of our doctrines
to the aforesaid rulers, was adorned with a divine martyrdom,
in consequence of the plot against him which was devised
by a philosopher, Crescens, a man who eagerly pursued the
manner of life and conduct of a Cynic—that name so aptly

---

[1] *Mart. Pol.* 19.   [2] *Mart. Pion.* 21. 6 ff.   [3] *Ib.* 20. 7.
[4] *Ib.* 4. 2.   [5] *Ib.* 12. 2; 14. 16.   [6] *Ib.* 11.
[7] *Ib.* 20. 1, 2.   [8] *Ib.* 21. 2, 3.   [9] *Ib.* 21. 7–9.
[10] *Ib.* 22. 2–4.   [11] 8. 3–5; 11. 8–11; 12.

given—since Justin had again and again refuted Crescens in dialogues in the presence of an audience. So at the last by his martyrdom he was wreathed with the triumphal crown 2 of the truth of which he was an ambassador. And this event that truly devoted lover of wisdom himself also indicated quite clearly in the aforesaid Apology before it came to pass, even as it was destined very shortly to happen to him. His words are as follows :

3 I, too, therefore, expect to be plotted against and thrust into the stocks by one of those named, or, it may be, by Crescens, that lover of display rather than wisdom.[1] For we ought not to call that man a lover of wisdom who, in matters which he does not understand, bears adverse testimony in public, declaring that the Christians are atheists and ungodly persons. And this he does in order to please and gratify the masses who have been 4 led astray. For if he attacks us without having read the teachings of Christ, he is a scoundrel, and much worse than ignorant people, who frequently avoid the discussion and condemnation of matters which they do not understand. And if he has read them but not grasped their grandeur; or, grasping it, adopts this course in order to avoid the suspicion of being a Christian : he is a low scoundrel to a far greater extent, the slave of ignorant, 5 unreasoning opinion and fear. For indeed I would have you know that when I put forward, and asked him, certain questions of this kind, I discovered and proved that he really was without understanding; and, to show that I speak the truth, if our discussions have not been brought before you, I am ready to discuss the questions again even in your presence also. For this would 6 be a matter worthy of emperors. But if my questions and his replies have actually been made known to you, it is manifest to you that he understands nothing about our affairs; or, if he understands, but has not the courage to speak because of those who hear him, he is plainly no lover of wisdom, as I said before, but a lover of glory: for he does not even honour that admirable saying of Socrates [2]

7 This, then, is what Justin says. But that he was perfected, as he himself predicted, in consequence of the machinations of Crescens, is recorded by Tatian, a man who for the first part of his life gave lectures on Greek studies, wherein he had won no small reputation, and who left behind him in treatises very much that will cause him to be remembered. In his work Against the Greeks he states the above fact, thus :

And Justin, that marvellous man, rightly declared that the aforesaid were like robbers.[3]

8 Then, after making some further statements about the philosophers, he thus continues :

Crescens, for example, who made his nest in the great city,

---

[1] τοῦ ἀφιλοσόφου καὶ φιλοκόμπου.   [2] Just. *Apol.* ii. 3.
[3] Tat., *ad Græc.* 18.

surpassed all in sodomy, and was wholly attached to the love of money. And he who was counselling men to despise death himself so feared it, that he exerted himself to compass the death of Justin, as though it were some great evil; because in proclaiming the truth Justin proved the philosophers to be gluttons and impostors.[1]

Such, then, was the cause of Justin's martyrdom.

17.   Now the same man, previously to his own conflict, in the former Apology calls to mind others who suffered martyrdom before he did; and the account he gives is also useful for our 2 purpose. He writes as follows :

A certain woman lived with a dissolute husband. She herself too had formerly been of like habits; but when she came to know the teachings of Christ, she learnt sobriety, and endeavoured to persuade her husband likewise to be sober-minded, repeating His teachings and telling of the *punishment* in *eternal fire* [2] which is to come upon such as do not live soberly and with right reason. 3 But he pursued the same licentious conduct, and by his actions estranged his wife. For the woman deemed it wrong to continue to share the bed of a man whose aim it was to provide himself with pleasures from any and every source, contrary to the law of nature and what is right. So she wished to be separated from the union.

4   And when she was earnestly entreated by her friends, who counselled her still to remain with him in the hope that some day her husband would change, she did violence to herself and 5 remained. But when her husband went to Alexandria and was reported to be conducting himself still worse: in order that she might not be a partaker of his crimes and infamies by remaining in the union and sharing his bed and board, she gave him the "repudium," as you call it, and so was separated.

6   But that fine fellow of a husband—instead of being glad, as he ought, that she had done with all that giddy conduct of the old days, when in the company of servants and hirelings she delighted in revellings and every kind of vice, and that she now wished him too to be done with the like—because she had left him against his wishes, brought an accusation to the effect that 7 she was a Christian. And she addressed a petition to thee, the emperor, requesting that she might be permitted first to set her affairs in order, and then, after the settlement thereof, to make her defence as regards the accusation. Which thing thou didst 8 grant. But he who was once her husband, being unable for the moment to say anything further against her, turned his attention to one Ptolemy, whom Urbicius had punished, her former teacher 9 in Christian doctrine. This was his method. He persuaded a centurion, who was his friend, to cast Ptolemy into bonds; then to seize and ask him one question and one alone, whether he were a Christian. And when Ptolemy, who was a lover of truth and in no way disposed to deceit or falsehood, had confessed himself to be a Christian, the centurion had caused him to be kept in bonds, and for a long time punished him as he lay in the

---

[1] Tat., *ad Græc.*, 19.   [2] Matt. xviii. 8; xxv. 41, 46.

10 prison.   And finally, when the man was brought before Urbicius,
he was examined as before on one point and on that alone,
whether he were a Christian.   And again, conscious of the
benefits he enjoyed through the teaching of Christ, he confessed
11 that he had been schooled in the divine virtue.   For he who
denies anything whatsoever either does so because he has decided
against it; or else avoids confession, feeling himself unworthy
and out of place as regards the matter.   But neither of these
things can be the case with the true Christian.
12   And when Urbicius ordered him to be led away, a certain
Lucius, who himself also was a Christian, on seeing judgment so
unreasonably passed, said to Urbicius : " Why is it that thou hast
punished this man, who is neither an adulterer nor fornicator
nor murderer nor thief nor robber nor convicted of any wrong-
doing at all, but because he confesses to the name of Christian ?
Thou dost not give such judgment, O Urbicius, as befits the
emperor Pius, or the philosopher the son of Cæsar, or the sacred
13 Senate."   And he, without making any other answer, said also
to Lucius : " Methinks thou also art such a one."   And on his
replying " Most certainly," he again ordered that he too should
be led away.   But Lucius professed his thanks; for that he was
rid, he added, of such evil masters, and was going to a good
Father and King, even God.   And there was a third also as well
who came forward and was condemned to punishment.[1]

To this Justin naturally and suitably adds those words of
his which we have already recalled, saying :

I, too, therefore expect to be plotted against by one of those
named,

and so forth.[2]

Writings of Justin.

8.   Now Justin has left us very many monuments [3] of a cultured
mind keenly interested in divine things, which are replete
with profitable matter of every kind.   And to these we shall
refer scholars, when we have performed the useful task of
2 indicating such as have come to our knowledge.   There is
[1] one book of his on behalf of our doctrines, addressed to
Antoninus who was called Pius, and his sons and the Senate
of the Romans; and [2] another, containing a second defence
of our faith, which defence he had made to the successor and
namesake of the aforesaid emperor, Antoninus Verus, the
events of whose time we are at the present moment describ-
3 ing.   And [3] there is another, the book Against the Greeks,
in which, having discussed at great length very many of the
questions investigated by us and the philosophers of the
Greeks, he treats distinctly of the nature of demons.   These
4 things there is no urgent necessity to quote at present.   And,
again, [4] another treatise of his against the Greeks has
come down to us; and this he entitled Refutation.   And

---

[1] Just., *Apol.* ii. 2.   [2] 16. 3 ff.   [3] ὑπομνήματα.

besides these there is [5] another treatise On the Monarchy
of God, which fact he establishes not only from our Scriptures
5 but also from the Greek books.   After these [6] [there is the
treatise] entitled Harper ; and [7] another, in the manner of
the schools, On the Soul, in which after propounding various
questions on the problem before him, he gives the opinions
of the Greek philosophers ; and these he promises to con-
trovert, as well as to give his own opinion, in another treatise.
6 And he also composed [8] a Dialogue against the Jews, which
he had held at the city of the Ephesians with Trypho, a most
distinguished Hebrew of that day.   In it he shows the way
in which the divine grace impelled him towards the word of
faith, as well as the great zeal which in former days he had
bestowed upon the study of philosophy, and the whole-
hearted search for the truth which he pursued.[1]
7   And he records of the Jews in the same work that they
formed a plot against the teaching of Christ, when he aims
these very words at Trypho :

> And not only did ye not repent of your evil deeds, but chose
> picked men at that time and sent them out from Jerusalem over
> all the earth, saying that a godless sect, the Christians, had
> made its appearance, and recounting the things that all those
> who do not know us say against us ; so that not only are ye to
> blame for your own iniquity, but also for that of absolutely the
> whole human race as well.[2]

8   And he writes also that *even as late as* his day *prophetical
gifts* were a conspicuous feature in the Church.[3]   And he
mentions the *Apocalypse* of *John,* saying clearly that it was
the *apostle's.*[4]   And he also calls to mind certain prophetic
utterances, proving as against Trypho that the Jews had
indeed *cut them out of* the Scripture.[5]   And many other fruits
9 of his labours are still in the hands of many brethren.   And
so worthy of study did the man's books seem, even to the
men of olden time, that Irenæus calls to mind his sayings.
Thus in one place, in the fourth book Against the Heresies,
he adds these very words :

> And well does Justin say in his work against Marcion : " I
> would not have believed the Lord Himself, had He preached
> another God besides the Creator. . . ."[6]

and in another place, in the fifth book of the same work, as
follows :

> And well did Justin say that before the coming of the Lord
> Satan never dared to blaspheme God, inasmuch as he did not
> yet know his condemnation. . . .[7]

---

[1] Just., *Dial.* 1–8.   [2] *Ib.* 17.   [3] *Ib.* 82.   [4] *Ib.* 81.
[5] *Ib.* 71–73.   [6] Iren. iv. 11. 2.   [7] *Ib.* v. 26. 3.

10   So much, then, for these things, which I have of necessity stated that I may urge scholars to a diligent regard for his books. And such were the facts concerning him.

Succession of Bishops.

169. But when the government of which we are at present speaking was now in its eighth year, Soter succeeded Anicetus, when he had completed his episcopate of the church of the Romans in eleven years in all.

But when Celadion had presided over the community of the Alexandrians for fourteen years, Agrippinus took up the succession.

And in the church of the Antiochenes also Theophilus was well known as the sixth from the apostles, since Cornelius, who came after Heron, was the fourth [bishop] of the Christians there, and, after him, Eros succeeded to the episcopate in the fifth step.

Other Ecclesiastical Writers.

Now there flourished in the Church in those days Hegesippus, whom we know from what has gone before,[1] and Dionysius, bishop of the Corinthians, and Pinytus, a bishop too, but of the people of Crete, and, moreover, Philip and Apollinarius and Melito, and Musanus and Modestus, and finally Irenæus; of these also the orthodoxy and sound faith, derived from the apostolic tradition, have come down in writing even to us.

Hegesippus (continued).

Now Hegesippus, in the five Memoirs which have come down to us, has left behind a very complete record of his personal views. And in his Memoirs he tells us that on a journey as far as *Rome he associated with* very many bishops, and that he had received the same teaching from all.[2] In fact, we may listen to what he says, when, after some remarks on the epistle of Clement to the Corinthians, he adds as follows :

2   And the church of the Corinthians continued in the true doctrine until Primus was bishop at Corinth. . . . With them I associated on my voyage to Rome, and I abode with the Corinthians many days; during which we were refreshed together 3 in the true doctrine. But when I came to Rome, I made for myself a succession-list as far as Anicetus; whose deacon was Eleutherus. And from Anicetus Soter received the succession; after whom came Eleutherus. And in every succession and in every city that which the Law and the Prophets and the Lord preach is faithfully followed.

---

[1] See 8. 1.   [2] Heg. (§ 2).

4   And the same writer also touches upon the beginnings of the heresies in his day, in the following words :

And after James the Just had suffered martyrdom, as had also the Lord, on the same account . . . again . . . the son of His [1] uncle, Symeon the son of Clopas, was appointed bishop; whom all put forward, being a cousin of the Lord, as the second [bishop]. . . . For this reason they used to call the church a virgin : for she had not yet been corrupted by vain teachings.

5 But Thebuthis, because he was not made bishop, began secretly to corrupt her from the seven sects among the people, to which he himself belonged; from which came Simon (whence the Simonians) and Cleobius (whence the Cleobians) and Dositheus (whence the Dositheans) and Gorthæus (whence the Goratheni) and the Masbotheans.   Springing from these, the Menandrianists and Marcianists and Carpocratians and Valentinians and Basilidians and Satornilians, each by themselves and each in different

6 ways, introduced their own peculiar opinions.   From these sprang false Christs, false prophets, false apostles, those who have divided the unity of the church by injurious words *against* God *and against his Christ.* [2]

7   And, moreover, the same writer also records the sects that have been of old time among the Jews, saying :

Now these were the different opinions in the circumcision, among the sons of the Israelites, against the tribe of Judah and the Christ : Essenes, Galilæans, Hemerobaptists, Masbotheans, Samaritans, Sadducees, Pharisees.

8   And he wrote very much else besides, which in part we have already mentioned previously, giving the accounts at suitable points. [3]   And he sets down certain things from the Gospel of the Hebrews and the Syriac [Gospel] and, in particular, from [writings in] the Hebrew tongue, thus showing that he was himself a believer of Hebrew origin.   And he relates other matters as well, on the strength of unwritten

9 Jewish tradition.   And not only he, but Irenæus also and the whole company of the ancients, used to call the Proverbs of Solomon " All-virtuous Wisdom."   And in treating of the Apocryphal [books], as they are called, he records that some of them were fabricated by certain heretics in his own time. But now we must pass on to another matter.

Dionysius of Corinth.

23.   And first of all it should be said of Dionysius, that he had been entrusted with the throne of the episcopate of the community at Corinth, and that he used to communicate without stint of his inspired industry, not only with those under his charge but also with those in foreign lands, rendering himself of the greatest service to all in the catholic epistles

---

[1] Or " his."   [2] Ps. ii. 2; Acts iv. 26.   [3] See p. 110, note [1].

2 which he penned to the churches.   Of these [1] one is addressed
to the Lacedæmonians, containing instruction in orthodoxy
and exhorting to peace and unity; [2] another to the Athenians, stirring them up to faith and that conduct which is in
accordance with the Gospel, which conduct he convicts them
of esteeming lightly, in that they had all but apostatized
from the Word from the time that it befell their president
Publius to suffer martyrdom in the persecutions of that day.
3 And he mentions that Quadratus was appointed their bishop
after the martyred Publius, and testifies that by his zeal
they were brought together again and had their faith
rekindled.   And, moreover, he informs us that *Dionysius the
Areopagite*, whom the apostle Paul converted to the faith
according to the account in the Acts,[1] had been the first
to be entrusted with the episcopate of the community at
Athens.
4   And there is extant [3] another epistle of his, to the Nicomedians; in which he attacks the heresy of Marcion and
defends the canon of the truth.
5   And in writing also [4] to the church which sojourns in
Gortyna together with the other communities in Crete, he
commends their bishop Philip, because the church under
him had witness borne to it for very many deeds of bravery;
and reminds him of the need of guarding against the perversion
of the heretics.
6   And in writing also [5] to the church which sojourns in
Amastris together with the churches in Pontus, he mentions
that Bacchylides and Elpistus had urged him to write; and
he has set out expositions of the divine Scriptures, indicating
their bishop Palmas by name.   And he gives the same people
much exhortation on the subjects of marriage and chastity;
and orders that those who come back from any falling away
whatsoever, whether it be a fault [of conduct] or even a
wandering into heresy, should be welcomed.
7   With these has been included [6] another epistle, to the
Cnossians; in which he counsels Pinytus, the bishop of the
community, not to *lay* a *heavy burden*, that of chastity, as a
necessary thing, upon the brethren,[2] but to have an eye to
8 the weakness of the many.   In his reply to this Pinytus
admires and commends Dionysius, but in his turn counsels
him to impart on some future occasion more *solid food*, and
nourish his people with a further letter for *men* more *fully
grown;* so that from continual converse with doctrines of
milk they might not grow old imperceptibly under a training
fit for *babes.*[3]   And in this epistle also Pinytus' orthodoxy
in the faith, his care for the profit of his hearers, his learning

---

[1] Acts xvii. 34.
[2] Acts xv. 28 combined with Matt. xxiii. 4.
[3] Heb. v. 12–14.

and understanding of divine things, are revealed, so to speak, under the most perfect of images.

9   Moreover, there is also extant [7] an epistle of Dionysius to the Romans, addressed to Soter, the then bishop. There is nothing like quoting passages from it too; in which he writes thus in commendation of the custom of the Romans which was observed down to the persecution in our day :

10   For this has been your custom from the beginning : to do good in divers ways to all the brethren, and to send supplies to many churches in every city : now relieving the poverty of the needy, now making provision, by the supplies which ye have been in the habit of sending from the beginning, for brethren in the mines; and thus as Romans ye observe the hereditary custom of Romans, which your blessed bishop Soter has not only maintained, but even advanced, by providing in abundance the help that is distributed for the use of the saints, and by *exhorting* with blessed words, *as a* loving *father his children*,[1] the brethren who come up [to Rome].[2]

11   Now in this same epistle he mentions also the epistle of Clement to the Corinthians, showing that it was an ancient custom dating from primitive times to read it in the church. At all events he says :

This day, therefore, we spent as a holy Lord's day, in which we read your epistle; from the reading of which we shall always be able to obtain admonition, as also from the former epistle written to us through [3] Clement.

12   And, moreover, the same person also speaks thus of the fact that his own epistles were tampered with :

For when the brethren desired me to write epistles, I did so. And these the apostles of *the devil* have filled with *tares*,[4] cutting out some things and adding others : for whom the woe is reserved.[5] It is not marvellous, therefore, if some have set themselves to tamper with the Dominical Scriptures as well, since they have also laid their designs against writings that do not class as such.

13   And, besides these, there is also [8] another epistle of Dionysius extant, which he wrote to a most faithful sister Chrysophora. In it he writes what is suitable, and imparts to her also the fitting spiritual food.

Theophilus.

24.   The writings, then, of Dionysius are so many. But of Theophilus, who, as we have shown, was bishop of the church of the Antiochenes,[6] [1] the three elementary treatises To

---

[1] 1 Thess. ii. 11.
[2] The text of the earlier part of this extract is almost certainly corrupt.   [3] διά.   [4] Matt. xiii. 25, 39.
[5] Cp. Rev. xxii. 18, 19.   [6] c. 20.

Autolycus are extant; as is also [2] another, with the title
Against the heresy of Hermogenes, in which he has made use
of testimonies drawn from the Apocalypse of John. And
[3] certain catechetical books of his are extant as well.

But since the heretics, in no less degree at that time also,
were spoiling like *tares* the pure seed of the apostolic teaching,[1]
the *pastors* of the churches everywhere, as if they were scaring
wild beasts away from the *sheep* of Christ,[2] endeavoured to
ward them off : at one time by warning and counsel to the
brethren; at another, delivering a more open attack upon
them in oral discussions and refutations in person; or yet
again, by means of written memoirs completely refuting their
opinions with the most rigorous proofs.

In fact, that Theophilus along with the others entered the
field against them is evident from [4] a certain book of uncom-
mon merit which he composed against Marcion; which book
has itself been preserved even to this day along with the
others of which we have spoken.

Succession of Bishops of Antioch.

Now Theophilus was succeeded by Maximin, the seventh
[bishop] from the apostles of the church of the Antiochenes.

Other Writers against Marcion.

25.   But to resume.   Philip, who, as we learnt from the words
of Dionysius,[3] was bishop of the community at Gortyna,
also composed a most weighty book against Marcion; as
likewise did Irenæus and Modestus. The last-named also
was more successful than the others in unmasking the man's
error and making it plain to all. And many others too
[wrote with the same object], whose labours are still to this
day preserved in the hands of many of the brethren.

Melito and Apollinarius.

6.   In their day also Melito and Apollinarius, bishops respectively of the communities at Sardis and Hierapolis, flourished
with distinction; and they addressed, each of them separately, books in defence of the faith to the aforesaid emperor
2 of the Romans at that time. Of these writers there have
come to our knowledge the works that are set out below.
Of Melito : [1] the two [treatises] On the Pascha, [2] the
treatise On Conduct and the Prophets, the books [3] On the
Church, and [4] On the Lord's Day; and, further, [5] the book
On the Faith of Man, [6] On Creation, [7] On the Subjection

---

[1] Matt. xiii. 25.   [2] Cp. John x. 12 f.   [3] 23. 5.

of the Senses to Faith; and, in addition to these, [8] the book On Soul and Body or Mind,[1] [9] On Baptism [2] and Truth and Faith and the Birth of Christ, and [10] his book of Prophecy and [11] that On Soul and Body, and [12] the book On Hospitality, and [13] The Key, and [14] the [treatises] On the Devil and the Apocalypse of John, and [15] the book On the Corporeality of God; and, finally, [16] the petition To Antoninus.

3   Now at the beginning of his work On the Pascha he indicates the time at which he composed it, in the following words :

> When Servillius Paulus was proconsul of Asia, at the season when Sagaris suffered martyrdom, there arose a great discussion in Laodicea concerning the Pascha, which fell in due season in those days.   And these things were written. . . .

4   Now Clement the Alexandrian mentions this book in his own book On the Pascha, which he says he composed because of Melito's work.

5   And in the petition addressed to the emperor, Melito records that under him the following misfortunes befell us :

> For the race of the godly—a thing that never before happened —is now persecuted, being harassed in Asia by recent decrees. For the shameless informers and lovers of other men's goods, taking advantage of the ordinances, plunder openly, day and night pillaging innocent persons.

6   And, further on, he says :

> And if this action is taking place at thy bidding, well and good.   For a just emperor would never make an unjust decision ; and we for our part gladly accept the honour of such a death. Howbeit, this request only we present to thee, that thou wouldest thyself first note the workers of such strife, and so judge aright as to whether they are worthy of death and punishment, or of safety and quiet.   But if this decision and this fresh ordinance —not fit for use even against barbarian enemies—come not from thee, we beseech thee all the more earnestly not to abandon us to such spoliation at the hands of the people.

7   Again, in addition to this, he goes on to say :

> For our philosophy at first flourished among barbarians ; but after it had appeared among thy peoples during the mighty principate of thy ancestor Augustus, it became to thy Empire especially an auspicious boon.   For from that time the power of the Romans increased to something great and splendid.   And to this thou hast become the successor whom men desired ; yea, and such shalt thou continue to be, along with thy son, if thou protectest the philosophy which was nursed in the cradle of the Empire and saw the light along with Augustus, which also thy
8 ancestors honoured, as they did the other religions.   And this is

---

[1] Reading, with Schwartz, ἢ νόος.   [2] λουτροῦ.

the greatest proof of the fact that it was for the good that our
doctrine flourished alongside of the Empire in its happy incep-
tion : that [1] from the time of the principate of Augustus no evil
has befallen it, but, on the contrary, all things have been splendid
9 and glorious in accordance with the prayers of all. Nero and
Domitian, alone of all [the emperors], persuaded by certain
malignant persons, desired to bring our doctrine into ill repute ;
and since their day, by an unreasonable custom, lying information
10 about the Christians has come to be prevalent. But thy pious
fathers have corrected their ignorance, many a time rebuking
in writing as many as dared to raise disturbances concerning
them. Thus it is clear that thy grandfather Hadrian wrote to
the proconsul Fundanus, governor of Asia, as well as to many
others besides ; and thy father, when thou also wast ruling the
world with him, wrote to the cities, and, among others, to the
people of Larissa and Thessalonica and Athens, and to all the
Greeks, that they should raise no disturbances concerning us.
11 But as for thee, we are the more persuaded that thou wilt do all
whatsoever we ask of thee, inasmuch as thou art of the same
mind on these matters as they ; aye, and with a far greater love
for mankind and for wisdom.

12   These words, then, are to be found in the aforesaid book.
But in [17] his book of Extracts, the same writer, in the
introduction at the beginning, gives a catalogue of the acknowledged Scriptures *of the Old Covenant*. This also we must
needs set down here. He writes thus :

13   Melito to Onesimus the brother, greeting. Since thou didst
oft-times request, in thy zeal for the word, that thou mightest
have extracts from the Law and the Prophets concerning the
Saviour and our faith as a whole ; and moreover didst desire
also to learn the exact truth as to the ancient books, what is
their number and what their order : I was zealous to perform
such a task, knowing thy zeal for the faith and love for the study
of the word, and that thou, in thy yearning for God, esteemest
these things above all else, contending for the prize of eternal
14 salvation. Having, therefore, gone up to the East and come
to the place where these things were proclaimed and done, and
having exactly learnt which are the books of the Old Covenant,
I send thee the list of them as given below. These are their
names. Of Moses, five books : Genesis, Exodus, Numbers,
Leviticus, Deuteronomy ; Jesus Nave, Judges, Ruth ; four
[books] of Kings, two of Chronicles ; [the book] of Psalms of
David ; of Solomon, Proverbs, also called Wisdom, Ecclesiastes,
Song of Songs ; Job ; of prophets, [the books] of Isaiah, Jeremiah,
[the book] of the twelve [prophets] in a single roll, Daniel,
Ezekiel ; Esdras. From these also I have made the extracts,
dividing them into six books.

7.   The writings, then, of Melito are so many. But of Apollinarius many are preserved in the hands of many persons, and
the following have come down to us : [1] the discourse
addressed to the aforesaid emperor ; [2] five treatises Against

----

[1] Reading τό in place of ἐκ τοῦ.

the Greeks; [3] On Truth, i and ii; [4] Against the Jews, i and ii; and [5] what after these he wrote against the heresy of the Phrygians (a novelty devised not long afterwards, but at that time beginning, as it were, to shoot forth) while Montanus with his false prophetesses was still taking the first steps in his error.

Musanus, Tatian and the Severians.

28.   And of Musanus too, whom we included in the foregoing list of persons,[1] there is extant a certain book in the nature of a very sharp rebuke, written by him to some brethren who were inclining towards the heresy of the Encratites, as they are called, a heresy which at that time was beginning to spring up, and was introducing a strange, pernicious, false doctrine into the world.   It is recorded [2] that the author of
29.   this error was Tatian, whose remarks about the *marvellous Justin* we quoted a little further back,[3] relating that he was a disciple of the martyr.

Now Irenæus tells us this fact in his first book Against the Heresies.   He writes thus, both with regard to the man and his heresy :

2   . . . from Satorninus and Marcion those who are called Encratites preached celibacy, setting at naught the primitive creation of God, and tacitly censuring Him who *made male and female* [4] for the generation of mankind; and they introduced abstinence from such things as they call " animate," thus showing ingratitude to God who has made all things.[5]   And they deny the
3 salvation of the first-created man.   And this last point was a recent invention of theirs, a certain Tatian having first introduced this blasphemy.   He had been a hearer of Justin, and, as long as he was with him, gave vent to no such doctrine; but after Justin's martyrdom he broke away from the Church, and, elated at the thought of being a teacher and puffed up with the idea that he was superior to the rest, formed a school with a distinctive character of its own.   For while he invented certain invisible æons, as did the followers of Valentinus; while he proclaimed marriage to be corruption and fornication, in a manner similar to Marcion and Satorninus : his own contribution was to deny the salvation of Adam.[6]

4   Thus did Irenæus write at that time.   But a little later a certain man, Severus by name, put fresh strength into the aforesaid heresy; and so it came to pass that its adherents
5 went by the name—derived from him—of Severians.   Now these persons make use of the Law and the Prophets and Gospels, but interpret in a way peculiar to themselves the thoughts contained in the sacred Scriptures.   But they revile

[1] c. 21.   [2] Iren. i. 26. 1 (§ 3).   [3] 16. 7–9.
[4] Gen. i. 27.   [5] Cp. 1 Tim. iv. 3, 4.   [6] Iren. i. 26. 1.

the apostle Paul, and reject his epistles; nor do they receive even the Acts of the Apostles.

6   Their former leader, however, Tatian, arranged a kind of joining together and compilation of the Gospels, I know not how, to which he gave the title The Diatessaron; and it is still to this day to be found in the hands of some.   But it is said that he dared to alter certain of the apostle's expressions, with a view to correcting the style in which they were 7 composed.   Now this writer has left behind him a great number of treatises, of which his famous book Against the Greeks is chiefly remembered by many.   Speaking in it of primitive times, he has shown that Moses and the prophets of the Hebrews were earlier than all *the* famous men *among the Greeks*.[1]   And this work also seems to be the best and most useful of all his treatises.   So was it with regard to these men.

Bardesanes.

30.   Now in the same reign, when the heresies were multiplying in Mesopotamia, Bardesanes, a most able man and an exceedingly skilled disputant in the Syriac language, having composed dialogues against the Marcionites and certain other leaders of various doctrines, committed them to writing in his own tongue, along with very many other treatises of his. These dialogues his disciples (of which he had very many : for he was a powerful defender of the faith) translated from 2 Syriac into Greek.   And among them is that able dialogue of his On Fate, to [2] Antoninus, and all the others which, it is said, he composed because of the persecution of that day. 3 Now he formerly belonged to the Valentinian school; but, having abjured it and refuted a great part of this heretic's fictions, he imagined somehow that he had come over to the more correct opinion.   Howbeit he did not completely cleanse himself from the filth of the ancient heresy.

Now at that time Soter, the bishop of the church of the Romans, ended [his life].

[1] Tat., *ad Græc.* 31, 36–41.   [2] Or " against."

BOOK V

The Fifth Book of the Ecclesiastical History contains the following :

1. The number of those who endured to the end the conflict for religion in Gaul under Verus; and the manner of that conflict.
2. How the martyrs dear to God received and tended those who had fallen in the persecution.
3. The vision which appeared in a dream to the martyr Attalus.
4. How the martyrs commended Irenæus by letter.
5. How God sent rain from heaven for Marcus Aurelius Cæsar in answer to the prayers of our people.
6. List of those who were bishops at Rome.
7. How even down to those times miraculous powers were exercised by the faithful.
8. How Irenæus mentions the divine Scriptures.
9. Those who were bishops under Commodus.
10. On Pantænus the philosopher.
11. On Clement of Alexandria.
12. On the bishops at Jerusalem.
13. On Rhodo and the disagreement which he mentioned in the matter of Marcion.
14. On the false prophets of the Phrygians.
15. On the schism of Blastus which took place at Rome.
16. What is related concerning Montanus and the false prophets with him.
17. On Miltiades and the books which he composed.
18. In what respects Apollonius also refuted the Phrygians, and the persons he mentioned.
19. Serapion on the heresy of the Phrygians.
20. The converse that Irenæus held in writing with the schismatics at Rome.
21. How Apollonius was martyred at Rome.
22. What bishops were well known in the times of those persons.
23. On the question as to the Pascha which arose at that time.
24. On the disagreement in Asia.
25. How all agreed upon one decision concerning the Pascha.
26. The elegant works of Irenæus which have come down to us.
27. The works, too, of the others who flourished at that time.
28. On those who at the first advanced the heresy of Artemon; their manner of life, and how they dared to corrupt the Holy Scriptures.

ref. So then, Soter, bishop of the church of the Romans, ended this life during the eighth year of his leadership. He was succeeded by Eleutherus, the twelfth from the apostles, in the seventeenth year of the emperor Antoninus Verus.

The Martyrs of Gaul.

In this year the fire of persecution against us was fanned

178. anew to a still fiercer flame in some parts of the world, and the myriads of martyrs who distinguished themselves, as a result of popular attacks in the cities, may be conjectured from the events in a single province, events which, as it happens, have been transmitted in writing to posterity, as being

2 in truth worthy of undying remembrance. Now the treatise which gives the most complete account of them has been inserted in its entirety in our Collection of Martyrs, comprising a narrative not only of historical value, but also full of teaching; yet I will now quote at any rate so many extracts as may be germane to the present work.

3 Other writers, indeed, of historical narratives would have transmitted in writing, to the exclusion of all else, victories won in war and conquests over enemies, the prowess of generals and brave deeds of warriors defiled with blood of myriads whom they slew for the sake of children and fatherland and

4 other possessions; but our narrative of God's commonwealth will inscribe on everlasting monuments the record of most *peaceful wars* fought for the very *peace* of the soul,[1] and of those who therein contended valiantly for truth rather than fatherland, for religion rather than their dearest; it will proclaim for everlasting remembrance the stedfastness of the *champions* of religion, their deeds of bravery and much endurance, the conquests, too, over devils, and *victories* won over invisible adversaries, and the *crowns* gained when all was done.[2]

1. Gaul, then, was the country where the arena was thronged with the said persons. Its capital cities are Lyons and Vienne, whose fame surpasses that of the other cities of that land; and the river Rhone flows through them both, its

2 ample streams traversing the entire country. Now, the most illustrious of the churches there sent around an account in

[1] Cp. 2. 7.   [2] Cp. 1. 36.

writing of their martyrs to the churches in Asia and Phrygia, recording after this fashion what had happened with them 3 (I shall quote their words) :

> The servants of Christ who sojourn at Vienne and Lyons in Gaul to the brethren in Asia and Phrygia *who* have the same *faith* and hope *as we* of redemption : *peace and grace* and glory *from God* the Father, *and* Christ *Jesus our* Lord.[1]

4   Then, having proceeded to mention some other matters by way of preface, they begin their account in the following terms :

> Indeed we are unable, and it is beyond the power of pen, to state with exactitude the greatness of the affliction here, the mighty rage of the heathen against the saints, and all that the 5 blessed martyrs endured. For the adversary fell upon us with all his might, and gave us *already* a foretaste of what *his coming* in the future without restraint would be ; [2] he left nothing undone to train and exercise beforehand his own against the servants of God, insomuch that not only were we excluded from houses and baths and market-place, but they even forbade any of us to be 6 seen at all in any place whatsoever. Nevertheless the grace of God was our captain on the other side, rescued the weak, and ranged against the foe firm pillars,[3] able by their endurance to draw upon themselves the whole attack of the evil one. And these joined battle, enduring every kind of reproach and punishment ; yea, regarding their many trials as little, they hastened to Christ, truly showing *that the sufferings of this present time are not worthy to be compared with the glory which shall be revealed to us-ward.*[4]
7   First of all they nobly endured the attacks which the whole mass of the people heaped upon them, clamours, blows, halings, plunderings, stonings and confinements, and all that an infuri-8 ated mob is wont to employ against foes and enemies. Then they were conducted to the market-place by the tribune and the authorities presiding over the city; and when they had been questioned before the whole multitude, and given their testimony, 9 they were shut up in prison until the governor's arrival. But afterwards, when they were brought before the governor, who used all his savagery against us, Vettius Epagathus, one of the brethren, a man filled with the fulness of love towards God and his neighbour, came forward. His conduct had reached such a degree of perfection that, young though he was, his reputation equalled that of the elder Zacharias; for he had *walked in all the commandments and ordinances of the Lord blameless ;* [5] in every service to his neighbour he was untiring, *having a great zeal for God* [6] and *fervent in spirit.*[7] Such a man could not endure the passing of so groundless a judgment against us; but was exceeding angry, and requested that he himself might be heard in defence of the brethren, that there is nothing godless or impious among us.

---

[1] Cp. 2 Pet. i. 1, 2.   [2] Cp. 2 Thess. ii. 7–9.
[3] Cp. 1 Tim. iii. 15 ; Gal. ii. 9.   [4] Rom. viii. 18.
[5] Luke i. 6.   [6] Rom. x. 2.
[7] Acts xviii. 25 ; Rom. xii. 11.

10 Those around the tribunal cried out against him (for he was indeed a man of note), and the governor would not listen to the just request he had thus put forward, but asked him this one question, if he too were a Christian. And having confessed in a very clear voice, he also attained to the inheritance of the martyrs, being called the advocate of Christians, but having the *Advocate* [1] *in himself, the Spirit of Zacharias ;* [2] which Spirit he showed in the fulness of *his love,* in that he was *well pleased* to *lay down even his own life for* the defence of *the brethren.* [3] For he was and is a true disciple of Christ, *following the Lamb whithersoever he goeth.* [4]

11 Henceforward the rest were divided; some were manifestly ready for martyrdom, [5] and fulfilled with all zeal the confession wherein they gave witness; but others were manifestly unready and untrained and still weak, unable to bear the strain of a mighty conflict : of which number some ten proved abortions. These last wrought in us great sorrow and immeasurable mourning, and hindered the zeal of the remainder who had not yet been seized, and who in spite of every terrible suffering nevertheless

12 attended the martyrs and would not leave them. But then we were all greatly affrighted at the uncertainty of confession ; not that we feared the punishments inflicted, but we looked to the

13 issue and dreaded lest any should fall away. Nevertheless those who were worthy were seized day by day, thus filling up the number of the former class, so that from the two churches were gathered all the zealous members, by whose means our position

14 here [6] had been mainly established. And there were seized also certain of our heathen household servants, since the governor gave an official order that we should all be sought out. And they too, thanks to *the snares* of Satan, [7] in their fear of the tortures which they saw the saints enduring, and at the instigation of the soldiers, falsely accused us of Thyestean banquets and Œdipodean intercourse, and things of which it is not right for us to speak or think, nay, not even to believe that the like was

15 ever done by man. But these rumours spread, and all were infuriated at us, insomuch that those who had formerly acted with moderation, on the ground of kinship, were now greatly incensed and *cut to the heart* [8] against us. Thus was fulfilled that which was said by the Lord : *The* time will *come,* when *whosoever*

16 *killeth you shall think that he offereth service unto God.* [9] From that time on the holy martyrs endured punishments beyond all description, Satan earnestly endeavouring to elicit from their lips also some of the slanders.

17 But the entire fury of the crowd, governor and soldiers fell upon Sanctus, the deacon from Vienne, and upon Maturus, a noble combatant though but lately baptized, and upon Attalus, a native of Pergamum, of which church [10] he had been always *the pillar and ground,* [11] and upon Blandina, through whom Christ showed that things which appear mean and unsightly and despicable in the eyes of men are accounted worthy of great glory in

---

[1] παράκλητος (comforter). [2] John xiv. 16 f., 26; Luke i. 67.
[3] 1 John iii. 16; 1 Thess. ii. 8. [4] Rev. xiv. 4.
[5] The translation follows the Greek as emended by Schwartz.
[6] τὰ ἐνθάδε. [7] Ign. *Trall.* 8; *Philad.* 6. [8] Acts v. 33; vii. 54.
[9] John xvi. 2. [10] τῶν ἐνταῦθα. [11] 1 Tim. iii. 15.

141

the sight of God,[1] through love towards Him, a love which showed
18 itself in power and did not boast itself in appearance.[2] For when
we were all afraid, and her mistress according to the flesh [3] (who
was herself also a combatant in the ranks of the martyrs) was in
a state of agony, lest the weakness of her body should render her
unable even to make a bold confession, Blandina was filled with
such power that those who by turns kept torturing her in every
way from dawn till evening were worn out and exhausted, and
themselves confessed defeat from lack of aught else to do to her ;
they marvelled that the breath still remained in a body all mangled
and covered with gaping wounds, and they testified that a single
form of torture was sufficient to render life extinct, let alone
19 such and so many.   But the blessed woman, like a noble champion,
in confession regained her youth ; [4] and for her, to say " I am a
Christian, and with us no evil finds a place " was refreshment
and rest and insensibility to her lot.
20   Now as for Sanctus, he also nobly endured with surpassing and
superhuman courage all the torments that human hands could
inflict, and though the wicked men hoped that the continuance and
severity of the tortures would cause him to utter something that
he ought not, he set the battle against them with such firmness
that he would not state even his own name, or the people or city
whence he came, or whether he were bond or free.   But to
every question he replied in Latin : " I am a Christian."   This
he confessed again and again, instead of name and city and race
and all else, and no other word did the heathen hear from his
21 lips.   Hence there actually arose great contention on the part of
the governor and the torturers against him, with the result that
finally, when nothing else was left to inflict upon him, they applied
22 red-hot brazen plates to the most tender parts of his body.   And
though these were burning, Sanctus himself remained unbending
and unyielding, and firm in his confession ; for he was bedewed
and strengthened by the heavenly *fountain of the water of life* [5]
23 which issues from the bowels of Christ.[6] But his poor body was a
witness to what he had undergone—one whole wound and bruise,
contracted, having lost the outward form of a man—in which
body Christ suffered and accomplished mighty wonders, bringing
the adversary to nought and *showing* for the *ensample* of those
that remained [7] that nothing is to be feared where there is the love of
the Father is,[8] nothing is painful where there is the *glory of*
24 *Christ.*[9]   For the wicked men after certain days again tortured
the martyr, thinking to overcome him when they applied the
same instruments to limbs so swollen and enflamed that he could
not bear even the hand to touch them ; or that he would die
under the tortures and so cause terror to the rest.   Yet not only
did nothing of the kind occur in his case, but, contrary to all
human expectation, the poor body actually arose and became
erect under the subsequent tortures, and regained its former
shape and the use of its limbs.   Thus by the grace of Christ the
second torturing proved for him not punishment but healing.

---

[1] Cp. 1 Cor. i. 28   [2] Cp. 2 Cor. v. 12.
[3] Cp. Eph. vi. 5; Col. iii. 22.   [4] Or " her strength."
[5] Rev. xxi. 6.   [6] Cp. John vii. 38; xix. 34.
[7] Cp. 1 Tim. i. 16.   [8] Cp. 1 John iv. 18.
[9] 2 Cor. viii. 23.

25 And Biblis too, one of those who had denied, *the devil* supposed
that he had already *devoured ;* [1] but wishing to use her slander
as a further ground of condemnation, he brought her to punishment, that he might compel an already fragile and craven woman
26 to state impieties concerning us. She, however, regained her
senses under the torture and awoke, so to speak, out of a deep sleep,
when the passing retribution recalled to her mind the *eternal
punishment* [2] in hell ; and she directly contradicted the slanderers,
saying : "How could they eat their children, who may not eat
blood even of creatures without reason ? " [3] And henceforth she
confessed herself a Christian, and joined the inheritance of the
martyrs.
27   Now when the tyrant's instruments of torture were brought to
nought by Christ through the endurance of the blessed ones, the
devil began to invent other devices : close confinement in prison,
in darkness and its most noisome spot ; stretching the feet in the
stocks, and keeping them stretched five holes apart ; and all
those other torments which his servants when enraged—aye, and
filled with their master—are wont to inflict upon prisoners. So
that the more part were stifled in the prison, as many as the
Lord willed thus to depart, that He might manifest *His glory*.[4]
28 For some, though tortured so cruelly that it seemed they could
no longer live even with every attention, remained alive in the
prison, destitute indeed of human care, but fortified afresh by
the Lord and *strengthened* [5] both in body and soul, cheering on
and encouraging the rest. But others who were young and just
recently apprehended, whose bodies had not been previously
tortured, could not endure the rigour of their confinement, and
29 died within its walls. Now the blessed Pothinus, to whom had .
been committed the ministry of the episcopate at Lyons, was
above ninety years of age, and very frail in body. He breathed
with difficulty because of the bodily *weakness* which was laid
upon him, but the earnest desire for martyrdom filled him with
that renewed strength which a *willing spirit* [6] supplies. He too
was haled to the tribunal, and though his body was weakened
both by age and disease, his life was preserved within him, that
30 through it Christ might *triumph*.[7] He was conveyed to the
tribunal by the soldiers, escorted by the city authorities and
the whole multitude,[8] who gave utterance to all sorts of cries, as
if he were Christ Himself ; [9] and so he gave *the good* witness.[10]
31 Being examined by the governor as to who the God of the
Christians was, he replied, "If thou art worthy, thou shalt know",
and thereupon he was haled without mercy, and received blows
of every kind : those close by heaped on him all manner of
insult with blows of hands and feet, regardless of his age, while
those at a distance made him the object of whatever missile came
to their hand ; and all considered it a grievous fault and impiety
to be behindhand in their wanton violence to him. For thus
indeed they thought to avenge their gods. Scarcely breathing
he was cast into prison, and after two days gave up the ghost.
32   Then in truth a mighty dispensation of God came to pass,

---

[1] 1 Pet. v. 8.   [2] Matt. xxv. 46.   [3] Cp. Acts xv. 29.
[4] Cp. John ii. 11.   [5] 2 Tim. iv. 17.   [6] Cp. Mark xiv. 38.
[7] Cp 2 Cor. ii. 14; Col. ii. 15.   [8] Luke xxiii. 1.
[9] Cp. Luke xxiii. 18 ff.   [10] Cp. 1 Tim. vi. 13.

and the measureless compassion of Jesus was displayed, in a manner rarely vouchsafed among the brethren, but not beyond
33 the art of Christ.   For they who had denied when the Christians were first arrested were also confined with [the others] and shared their sufferings; for on this occasion their denial had profited them nothing.   On the contrary, those who confessed what they really were, were confined as Christians, no other charge being brought against them; while the others were detained thenceforward as murderers and scoundrels, and were punished twice
34 as much as the rest.   For the burden of the confessors was lightened by the joy of martyrdom, the hope of the promises, their love to Christ, and the Spirit of the Father; but the others were grievously tormented by their conscience, insomuch that their countenances could be clearly distinguished from all the rest
35 as they passed by.   For they went forth with joy, great glory and grace blended on their countenances, so that even their *chains* hung around them like a *goodly* ornament,[1] as a bride adorned *with golden fringes of divers colours*,[2] perfumed the while with the *sweet savour of Christ;* [3] hence some supposed that they had been anointed with earthly ointment as well.   But the others were dejected, downcast, unsightly and covered with every kind of confusion; reproached, moreover, by the heathen for baseness and cowardice; under the charge of murder, and having lost the one precious, glorious and life-giving Name.   The rest beholding this were stablished, and those who were apprehended confessed without doubting, nor did they bestow even a thought upon the persuasion of the devil.

36   After some intervening remarks they again go on to say :

After this their martyrdoms henceforth embraced every different form of death.   For having *woven* a single *crown* [4] of divers colours and variegated flowers they offered it to the Father.   And so it was fitting that the noble champions, after having endured a varied conflict and mightily conquered, should receive as their
37 due the mighty *crown* of incorruptibility.[5]   Maturus, then, and Sanctus and Blandina and Attalus were led to contend with wild beasts to the amphitheatre, and to the public spectacle of heathen inhumanity, a day for contests with wild beasts being granted
38 of set purpose for our benefit.   And Maturus and Sanctus passed once more through every kind of torture in the amphitheatre, as if they had suffered absolutely nothing before, or rather as if they had already vanquished their antagonist in many rounds, and were now contending for the crown itself.   Again they ran the gauntlet of scourges, as is the custom of the place; they were dragged by wild beasts; they endured all that the cries of a maddened populace ordered, now from this side, now from that; and last of all, the iron chair, which fried their bodies and choked them
39 with smoke.   Nor even at this point did the heathen stop, but were still further maddened, in their desire to conquer the Christians' endurance; nevertheless nothing escaped the lips of Sanctus save that word of confession which it had been his wont
40 from the very first to utter.   So then, these men, whose life had

---

[1] Cp. Ign., *Eph.* 11.   [2] Ps. xlv. 13 (LXX).   [3] 2 Cor. ii. 15.
[4] Cp. Ign., *Magn.* 13 (Phil. iv. 1; 1 Thess. ii. 19).   [5] 1 Cor. ix. 25.

lasted long through a mighty conflict, were finally sacrificed, being *made* throughout that day *a spectacle unto the world* [1] in place of all the varied show that single combats offered.

41 Now Blandina, suspended on a stake, was exposed as food to wild beasts which were let loose against her. Even to look on her, as she hung cross-wise in earnest prayer, wrought great eagerness in those who were contending, for in their conflict they beheld with their outward eyes in the form of their sister Him who was crucified for them, that He might persuade those who believe in Him that all who suffer for the glory of Christ have
42 unbroken fellowship with the living God. And as none of the wild beasts then touched her, she was taken down from the stake and cast again into prison, being kept for another conflict, that she might conquer in still further contests, and so both render irrevocable the sentence passed on *the crooked serpent*,[2] and encourage the brethren—she the small, the weak, the despised, who had *put on Christ* [3] the great and invincible Champion, and who in many rounds vanquished the adversary and through conflict was crowned with the *crown* of incorruptibility.[4]

43 As for Attalus, he too was loudly called for by the crowd (for he was indeed a man of repute), and entered the arena a ready combatant by reason of his good conscience, since he had been truly exercised in the Christian discipline, and always a *witness*
44 among us of *truth*.[5] He was conducted round the amphitheatre, preceded by a board, on which was written in Latin " This is Attalus the Christian," the people bursting with vehement indignation against him. But when the governor learnt that he was a Roman, he ordered him to be taken back to the prison, where also were the others concerning whom he wrote to Cæsar and was awaiting his sentence.

45 But the intervening time proved *not idle nor unfruitful* [6] in their case; nay, through their endurance the measureless compassion of Christ was displayed. For by the living the dead were quickened, and martyrs forgave those who were not martyrs, and the virgin mother rejoiced greatly to receive alive those whom her
46 womb had brought forth dead. For by their means the more part of those who had denied traversed once more life's road,[7] were conceived again, were rekindled into life, and learnt to confess; full now of life and vigour they approached the tribunal, for their trial was made sweet by God, who *hath no pleasure in the death of the sinner*, but is kind towards *repentance;*[8] that they
47 might be again questioned by the governor. For Cæsar had written that they should be tortured to death,[9] but that any who denied should be set free. And as the national festival held in that place [10] was then at its commencement—a festival largely attended by visitors from all the tribes [11]—the governor had the blessed ones conducted to the tribunal, to make of them a spectacle, and to form a procession for the benefit of the crowds. Therefore he again examined them; and those who appeared to possess Roman citizenship he beheaded, but sent the others to

---

[1] 1 Cor. iv. 9.
[2] Isai. xxvii. 1.
[3] Rom. xiii. 14; Gal. iii. 27.
[4] 1 Cor. ix. 25.
[5] Cp. John xviii. 37.
[6] 2 Pet. i. 8.
[7] ἀνεμετροῦντο : cp. § 55.
[8] Ezek. xxxiii. 11; 2 Pet. iii. 9.
[9] ἀποτυμπανισθῆναι : cp. Heb. xi. 35.
[10] ἐνθάδε.
[11] ἐθνῶν.

48 the wild beasts. And Christ was mightily glorified in those who
formerly denied Him, but then confessed, contrary to the expectation of the heathen. Indeed they were examined privately,
presumably as a prelude to their release; but confessing, were
added to the inheritance of the martyrs. And there remained
outside those who had never even a trace of faith, or an idea of the
marriage *garment*,[1] or a thought for the fear of God, nay rather,
blaspheming the Way by their manner of life [2]—in fact, *the sons of*
49 *perdition*.[3] But all the rest *were added* [4] to the Church.

While these were being examined, a certain Alexander, a
Phrygian by race and a physician by profession, who had lived for
many years in the Gauls, and was known almost to everyone for
his love to God and *boldness* for *the word* (for he too was not
destitute of the apostolic gift),[5] stood by the tribunal and by signs
encouraged them to confess. To the bystanders there he
50 appeared to be, as it were, in travail. The crowd were enraged
that those who had formerly denied should afterwards confess,
and cried out against Alexander as the cause of this. Thereupon
the governor summoned him and asked him who he was; and
angry at his reply " A Christian," condemned him to the wild
beasts. And on the following day he entered [the amphitheatre]
in the company of Attalus as well; for indeed the governor, to
please the crowd, had delivered Attalus too again to the wild
51 beasts. These men experienced in turn every instrument that
has been devised for torture in the amphitheatre, and, having
endured a mighty conflict, at last were sacrificed like the rest.
Alexander *neither groaned nor uttered* the slightest *cry*,[6] but held
52 converse with God in his heart. But Attalus, when he was placed
in the iron chair and scorched, so that the fumes rose from his
body, addressed the multitude in Latin : " Behold, this which ye
do is devouring men ; but we neither devour men nor practise
any other wickedness." And on being asked the name of God, he
53 replied, " God has not a name as a man has." And after all these,
finally on the last day of the single combats Blandina was again
brought in, in the company of Ponticus, a lad about fifteen years
old. They had also been fetched in every day to view the tortures
of the others. The heathen tried to force them to swear by their
idols, and as they remained firm and set them at nought, the
multitude was so infuriated at them that it had neither compassion
for the youth of the boy nor respect for the sex of the woman.
54 Nay, they exposed them to every cruelty and brought them
through the entire round of tortures, again and again trying to
force them to swear. But this they were unable to accomplish ;
for Ponticus, encouraged by his sister (so that the heathen themselves saw that it was she who was urging him on and strengthening him), having nobly endured every kind of torture *gave up his*
55 *spirit*.[7] But the blessed Blandina last of all, having, like a high-
born mother, exhorted her children and sent them forth victorious
to the King,[8] travelled herself along the same path [9] of conflicts
as they did, and hastened to them, rejoicing and exulting at her
departure, like one *bidden to* a marriage *supper*,[10] rather than

---

[1] Cp. Matt. xxii. 11.   [2] Cp. 2 Pet. ii. 2 ; Acts xix. 9, etc.
[3] John xvii. 12; 2 Thess. ii. 3.   [4] Acts ii. 41.
[5] Cp. Acts iv. 29–31.   [6] *Mart. Pol.* 2.
[7] John xix. 30.   [8] Cp. 2 Macc. vii. 20–23, 27–29, 41.
[9] ἀναμετρουμένη.   [10] Rev. xix. 9.

56 cast to the wild beasts. And after the scourging, after the wild
beasts, after the frying-pan, she was at last thrown into a basket
and presented to a bull. For a time the animal tossed her, but
she had now lost all perception of what was happening, thanks to
the hope she cherished, her grasp of the objects of her faith, and
her intercourse with Christ. Then she too was sacrificed, and even
the heathen themselves acknowledged that never in their experience had a woman endured so many and terrible sufferings.

57 Nevertheless not even thus were their madness and cruelty
towards the saints satisfied. For wild and barbarous tribes when
incited by a wild beast were not easily checked; and their wanton
violence found another distinct outlet with regard to the corpses.

58 That they had been worsted did not put them out of countenance, since for them man's gift of reason did not exist; nay
rather, in them as in a wild beast the fact inflamed anger, and the
governor and people were at one in displaying an unjust hatred
towards us, that the Scripture might be fulfilled : *He that is lawless,
let him do lawlessness still : and he that is righteous, let him be
59 accounted righteous still.*[1] For indeed they cast those suffocated
in prison to the dogs, and kept a careful guard by night and day
lest any should receive funeral rites at our hands. And then
they actually exposed what the wild beasts and the fire had left
behind—mangled or charred, as the case might be—and the
heads of the others together with their severed trunks, and guarded
them likewise from burial, with a military watch, for many days.

60 And some were moved with indignation and *gnashed on* them
with their teeth,[2] seeking to take still further vengeance upon them;
while others laughed and jeered, at the same time exalting their
own idols, to whom they attributed the punishment of the Christians; others again, of a more forbearing nature and seeming
to extend to them a measure of fellow-feeling, uttered many
reproaches, saying, " *Where is* their *god ?*[3] and what profit has their
religion brought them, which they have preferred to their own
61 life ? " So varied, then, was their attitude; but as for us, we were
plunged in great grief, in that we could not bury the bodies in
the earth. For neither did night avail us for this purpose, nor
did money persuade or prayers move them. But in every possible
way they kept guard, as if the prevention of burial would bring
them great gain.

62 After some other remarks they go on to say :
The bodies, then, of the martyrs, which for six days were displayed and exposed to the elements in every way possible, the lawless
men afterwards burnt and reduced to ashes. Then they swept them
down into the river Rhone which flows close by, so that not even
a trace of them might remain upon the earth. And this they
63 did, thinking that they could conquer God and deprive them of
the regeneration,[4] " in order," as they themselves said, " that they
may not even have hope of a resurrection, in faith of which they
introduce into our midst a certain strange and new-fangled cult,
and despise dread torments, and are ready to go to their death,
and that too with joy. Now let us see if they will rise again,
and if their *god can* help them, and *deliver them out of* our *hands.*"[5]

---

[1] Rev. xxii. 11 : for the unusual reading in this text cp. Dan. xii. 10
(Theod.).   [2] Acts vii. 54.   [3] Ps. xlii. 3, 10.
[4] Matt. xix. 28.   [5] Dan. iii. 15; vi. 20 (Theod.).

2.   Such, then, were the events that happened to the churches
of Christ under the aforesaid emperor; from which one may
reasonably conjecture also the occurrences in the other
provinces.   It is right to subjoin to these extracts other
passages from the same document, in which the forbearance
and humanity of the aforesaid martyrs have been placed on
record in the following words :

2   . . . who also *were* such emulators and *imitators of Christ,*[1]
*who being in the form of God, counted it not a prize to be on an equality
with God,*[2] that, though being in such glory and having borne
witness [3] not once nor twice but many times, though brought
back to prison from the wild beasts and all covered with burns
and weals and wounds, they neither proclaimed themselves
martyrs, nor indeed did they permit us to address them by this
name ; nay, they severely rebuked any one of us who so styled them
3 in letter or conversation.   For they gladly conceded the title of
martyr to *Christ, the faithful and true martyr* and *firstborn of the
dead and Prince of the life of God ;* [4] and they bethought them
of the martyrs now departed, and said : " They are now martyrs,
whom Christ deemed worthy to be taken up in their confession,
setting upon them the seal of martyrdom by their departure ;
but we are ordinary and lowly confessors."   And with tears they
besought and entreated the brethren for their earnest [5] prayers
4 that they might be perfected.   And the power of martyrdom
they showed in deed, using great boldness towards the heathen,
and by endurance, fearlessness and dauntlessness made manifest
their noble spirit ; but from the brethren they refused the title
of martyrs, being *filled with the fear of God.*[6]

5   And a little further on they say :

They *humbled* themselves *under the mighty hand,* by which they
are now greatly *exalted.*[7]   And then they made their defence before
all, but accused no one.   They *loosed* all, but *bound* no one.[8]   And
they prayed for those who entreated them cruelly, as did Stephen
the perfect martyr, *Lord, lay not this sin to their charge.*[9]   And
if he made supplication for those who stoned him, how much
more for the brethren ?

6   And further on they say again :

For this, their greatest, war was waged by them against him
out of genuine love, to the intent that the wild beast when choked
might vomit forth alive those whom he thought to have already
devoured.[10]   For they did not indulge in boasting against the
fallen, but with a mother's compassion supplied the more needy
with that wherein they themselves abounded ; and pouring forth
7 many tears on their behalf to the Father, they *asked life, and* he
gave it them.[11]   And this life also they shared with their neigh-

---

[1] Cp. 1 Cor. xi. 1 ; 1 Thess. i. 6.   [2] Phil. ii. 6.
[3] Or " suffered martyrdom " (μαρτυρήσαντες).
[4] Rev. i. 5 ; iii. 14 ; Acts iii. 15.   [5] ἐκτενεῖς : cp. Acts xii. 5.
[6] Cp. Isai. xi. 3 (LXX).   [7] 1 Pet. v. 6.   [8] Cp. Matt. xvi. 19.
[9] Acts vii. 60.   [10] 1 Pet. v. 8.   [11] Ps. xxi. 4.

bours, when, victorious in everything, they departed to God.
Ever lovers of peace, they also commended peace to us, and accompanied by peace journeyed to God, leaving no sorrow to their
mother, no dissension and war to their brethren, but rather *joy
and peace* and concord and *love.*[1]

8 This record of the affection of those blessed ones for the
brethren who had fallen may profitably be set forth, on
account of the inhuman and merciless temper displayed by
those who afterwards behaved so harshly towards the members
of Christ.

3. Now the same document of the aforesaid martyrs contains
also another story which deserves to be remembered, nor can
there be any objection to my bringing it before the knowledge
2 of my readers. It runs thus. There was one of them, a certain
Alcibiades, who lived in absolute squalor, partaking formerly
of nothing whatever save bread and water only; and he
essayed to continue this mode of existence in prison also.
But it was revealed to Attalus, after his first conflict in the
amphitheatre was completed, that Alcibiades was not doing
well in refusing the *creatures of God* and leaving an example
3 whereat others might stumble. So Alcibiades was persuaded,
and began to *receive all* things freely and *give thanks* to God.[2]
For they were not unvisited by the grace of God, but had the
Holy Spirit for their Counsellor.

Montanism.

4 So much, then, for these matters. But just then for the
first time the disciples of Montanus and Alcibiades and Theodotus in the region of Phrygia were winning a wide reputation for prophecy (for indeed numerous other miracles of the
gift of God, still at that time performed in various churches,
caused a widespread belief that they too were prophets).
And when a dissension arose about these said persons, the
brethren in Gaul once more submitted a pious and most
orthodox judgment of their own on this matter also, issuing
as well various letters of martyrs who had been perfected among
them—letters that they penned while still in bonds to the
brethren in Asia and Phrygia, and moreover to Eleutherus the
then bishop of the Romans, negotiating for the peace of the
churches.

4. And the same martyrs too commended Irenæus, already at
that time a presbyter of the community at Lyons, to the said
bishop of Rome, rendering abundant testimony to the man,
as their expressions, which are as follows, show :

2 Once more and always we pray that thou mayest rejoice in
God, father Eleutherus. This letter we have charged our *brother*

---

[1] Gal. v. 22.   [2] 1 Tim. iv. 3, 4.

and companion [1] Irenæus to convey to thee, and we beseech thee to hold him in commendation, as zealous for the covenant of Christ.　For if we knew that place ever brought a man righteousness, we would have commended him first and foremost as a presbyter of the Church, which office indeed he holds. [2]

The List of Martyrs.

3　Why need we transcribe the list of the martyrs in the said letter—the separate lists of those perfected by decapitation, of those thrown for food *to the wild beasts*, and, again, of *those who* fell asleep *in prison*—and the number of the confessors then still surviving? [3]　For anyone who so wishes may easily obtain the fullest knowledge of these matters also, by taking up the treatise itself, which we have inserted, as I said, [4] in the Collection of Martyrs.

The Thundering Legion.

5.　But these events took place under Antoninus.　It is recorded that his brother Marcus Aurelius Cæsar, when about to engage in battle with the Germans and Sarmatians, was in despair because his army was in great distress with thirst; but that the soldiers of the legion of Melitene, as it is called, with a faith that has subsisted from that day until now, when they were drawn up before the enemy, kneeled on the ground, as is our familiar custom in prayer, and turned to God in supplica-
2 tion.　And it is recorded that, though a sight like this appeared marvellous to the enemy, a still more marvellous thing followed immediately : that a thunderbolt drove the enemy to flight and destruction, while a shower descended on the army of those who had called upon the Divine Being, and refreshed it when just on the point of entirely perishing with
3 thirst.　Now this story is to be found even in writers alien to our faith, [5] whose care it has been to write the history of the times of the said emperors ; but it has also been told by our own writers.　Pagan historians, however, being strangers to the faith, have stated the marvellous occurrence without acknowledging that it was in answer to the prayers of Christians ; but ours, being lovers of truth, have told the event in a simple and artless manner.
4　To this latter class belongs Apollinarius, who said that from that time the legion which had wrought the marvel by its prayers received from the emperor a title appropriate to the event, being styled, in Latin, the Thundering Legion.
5　And a trustworthy witness of these facts is Tertullian : who in a Latin Apology for the Faith addressed to the Senate,

---

[1] Rev. i. 9.
[2] ὅπερ ἐστὶν ἐπ᾽ αὐτῷ : lit. " which office (*or* title) attaches to him."
[3] *Eccl. Lugdun. Epist.* (see note).　　　[4] Pref. 2.　　　[5] λόγου.

which also we mentioned above,[1] confirms the story by a
6 stronger and clearer proof. He writes to the effect that *a
letter of that wisest of emperors, Marcus, was still extant in his
day, in which the emperor testifies that his army had been saved
in Germany by the prayers of the Christians*, when it was on
the point of destruction through *want of water ;* and Tertullian
says that he also threatened with death those who were
7 attempting to *accuse* us. Then the said person goes on to add
the following remarks :

Of what sort, then, are these laws—impious, unjust, cruel laws,
which pursue us alone ? These did not Vespasian observe,
although he had conquered the Jews; these did Trajan partly
set aside, forbidding Christians to be sought for; these did neither
Hadrian, although a busybody in all curious arts, nor he who
was called Pius, ratify.[2]

However, let each one regard these matters as he pleases.
8 But we must pass on to what follows in due course.

Irenæus' List of Roman Bishops.

When Pothinus, together with the martyrs in Gaul, had
been perfected when full ninety years of age, Irenæus succeeded to the episcopate of the community at Lyons of which
Pothinus was the leader. We discovered that in his early
9 years Irenæus was a hearer of Polycarp.[3] In the third book
of his work Against the Heresies, having set forth the succession of the bishops of Rome, he stops his list at Eleutherus
(the events of whose time we are now considering) since, to
be sure, the work was in course of composition by Irenæus
in his day. He writes thus :

6.   So then, the blessed apostles, having founded and built the
church, entrusted the ministry of the episcopate to Linus. This
Linus Paul mentions in his epistles to Timothy.[4] He was succeeded
2 by Anencletus. After him, in the third place from the apostles,
Clement was allotted the episcopate, he who had seen the blessed
apostles and conversed with them; in whose ears the preaching
of the apostles still sounded, before whose eyes was still present
their tradition. Nor was he alone in this. For many still
remained at that date who had been instructed by the apostles.
3 Now, in the time of this Clement, when no small dissension had
arisen among the brethren in Corinth, the church in Rome wrote
at great length to the Corinthians, to reconcile them in peace and
revive their faith, and [to proclaim] the tradition it had lately
received from the apostles. . . .[5]

4   And a little further on he says :

But this Clement was succeeded by Evarestus, and Evarestus
by Alexander. Next, Xystus was appointed, who thus was the

---

1 ii. 2, 4; 25, 4; 20. 7; 33, 3.   2 Tert., *Apol.* 5.
3 Iren., *ad Florin.* (20. 5 f. below).
4 2 Tim. iv. 21.   5 Iren. iii. 3, 2.

sixth from the apostles; and after him Telesphorus, who also
suffered a glorious martyrdom. Then Hyginus; next, Pius;
and after him Anicetus. And Soter having succeeded Anicetus,
Eleutherus now holds in the twelfth place the office of the epis-
5 copate which came down from the apostles. In the same order
and succession the tradition from the apostles in the Church and
the preaching of the truth have come down to us.[1]

Irenæus on Miraculous Gifts.

7.   In agreement with the accounts previously given by us,
Irenæus has indicated these facts in the five books which he
entitled Refutation and Overthrow *of the Knowledge falsely
so called ;*[2] and in the second book of the same work he points
out that even to his day manifestations of the divine and
miraculous power continued in some churches. His words
are as follows :

2   . . . but so far are they from raising the dead (as the Lord
raised them, and the apostles by prayer; and in the brotherhood
frequently, when necessity required it and the whole church in
one place or another craved it with much fasting and supplication, the spirit of the departed has returned, and the person been
given to the prayers of the saints) . . .[3]

And again, further on, he says :

3   But if they say that even the Lord only appeared to do such
things, we will bring them back to the writings of the prophets,
and from them show that thus it was predicted of Him in every
respect, and thus it surely came to pass, and that He alone is
the Son of God. Therefore also in His name His true disciples,
receiving grace from Him, perform them for the benefit of the rest
of mankind, according as each one has received the gift from
4 Him. For some cast out devils surely and truly, insomuch that
frequently they themselves who were cleansed from the evil spirits
believe and are in the Church; others have knowledge of future
events, and visions and prophetical utterances; others, again,
heal the sick through the laying-on of hands and restore them
whole; and actually, as we said, even the dead were raised, and
5 remained with us many years. And, assuredly, it is not possible
to tell the number of the gifts which throughout all the world the
Church, having received them from God in the name of Jesus
Christ who was crucified under Pontius Pilate, exercises every
day for the benefit of the heathen, neither deceiving any nor
using her gifts for gain. For as she has *received* from God *freely*,
so also *freely* [4] she ministers.[5]

6   And in another place the same person writes :

. . . even as we also hear of many brethren in the Church
having prophetical *gifts*, and speaking with all kinds of *tongues*

---
[1] Iren. iii. 3, 3.   [2] 1 Tim. vi. 20.   [3] Iren. ii. 48, 2.
[4] Matt. x. 8.   [5] Iren. ii. 49, 3.

by means of the Spirit, and bringing to light the secrets of men to *their profit,*[1] and expounding the mysteries of God. . . .[2]

So much, then, for the fact that differences of gifts[3] remained in the possession of fit persons even until the times in question.

Irenæus on the Scriptures.

8.   But since at the beginning of our work we made a promise to quote at the proper time the words of the ancient elders and writers of the Church, in which they have transmitted in writing those traditions respecting the canonical Scriptures which came down to them;[4] and since Irenæus also was one
2 of these : come, let us quote his sayings too, and first of all those which concern the sacred Gospels.   They run thus :

Matthew published a Gospel in writing also, among the Hebrews in their own language, while Peter and Paul were preaching the
3 Gospel and founding the church in Rome.   But after their decease Mark, the disciple and interpreter of Peter—he also transmitted to us in writing the things which Peter used to preach.   And Luke too, the attendant of Paul, set down in a book the Gospel
4 which Paul used to preach.   Afterwards John, the disciple of the Lord, the same who *leant back on His breast*[5]—he too set forth the Gospel, while residing at Ephesus in Asia.[6]

5   Such, then, are his remarks in the afore-mentioned third book of the said work ; but in the fifth he makes the following distinct statement about the Apocalypse of John and the number of the name of the antichrist :

But since these things are so and this number is found in all good and ancient copies, and since those very persons who have seen John face to face testify to it, and since reason[7] teaches us that the number of the name of the beast, when calculated after the Greek manner by means of the letters contained in the name,[8] . . .

is shown.

6   And a little lower down he says with reference to the same subject :

. . . we, then, for our part are not so bold as to pronounce with certainty

as to the name of the antichrist.

For if it were necessary that his name should be announced openly at this present time, it would have been stated by him who also saw the revelation.   For it was seen not long ago, but almost in our generation, at the close of the principate of Domitian.[9]

---

[1] Cp. 1 Cor. xii. 7–10; xiv. 25.   [2] Iren. v. 6, 1.
[3] Cp. Rom. xii. 6 ; 1 Cor. xii. 4.   [4] iii. 3. 3.
[5] John xiii. 25.   [6] Iren. iii. 1. 2.   [7] Or, " calculation."
[8] Iren. v. 30. 1.   [9] *Ib.* v. 30. 3.

7   This is also the record of the said person concerning the
Apocalypse. And he mentions, too, the first epistle of John,
adducing testimonies from it on very many occasions; and,
in like manner also, the former epistle of Peter. And he not
only knows but also receives The Shepherd, saying,

Well, then, does the Scripture say, *First of all believe that God
is one, who made and framed* [1] *all things,* [2]

and so forth.

8   And he uses, too, certain texts from the Wisdom of
Solomon, saying somewhat thus :

Now the vision of God confers *incorruption ; and incorruption
bringeth near unto God.* [3]

And he mentions also memoirs of a certain apostolic elder,
whose name he bequeaths to silence, and has cited his exposi-
9 tions of divine Scriptures. Moreover he has made mention
too of Justin the martyr and Ignatius, employing in their
case also testimonies drawn from their writings; and he has
promised to *answer Marcion out of his own treatises,* in a special
work. [4]

10   And with reference to the translation of the inspired Scriptures made by the Seventy, these are the actual words which
he employs :

God, therefore, became man and the Lord Himself saved us,
giving the sign of the virgin; but not as some say who now dare
to translate the Scripture thus : *"Behold, the young woman* [5] *shall
be with child and shall bear a son* "; [6] as Theodotion of Ephesus
translated it, and Aquila of Pontus, both Jewish proselytes, whom
the Ebionites have followed, alleging that He was begotten by
Joseph. . . . [7]

11   Shortly afterwards he goes on to say :

For before the Romans had established their empire, while the
Macedonians were still holding Asia, Ptolemy the son of Lagus,
being desirous of adorning the library he had built in Alexandria
with such treatises by every author as were at least of importance,
asked the people of Jerusalem that he might acquire their Scrip-
12 tures, translated into the Greek language. And they (now they
were at that time still subject to the Macedonians) sent to Ptolemy
seventy elders, the most skilled in the Scriptures and in both
languages that they possessed. Thus God accomplished His
13 purpose. Now Ptolemy wished to make trial of them privily,
fearful lest, after all, they should conspire together in some way
to hide the truth contained in the Scriptures, by means of the
translation. So he separated them, the one from the other, and
bade them all write the same translation. This he did in the case

----

[1] Cp. Heb. xi. 3.   [2] Iren. iv. 34. 2 ; Hermas, *Shepherd*, Mand. 1.
[3] Iren. iv. 63. 2 ; Wisdom vi. 18 f.   [4] Iren. i. 25. 2 ; iii. 12. 15.
[5] ἡ νεᾶνις (LXX, ἡ παρθένος).   [6] Isai. vii. 14.   [7] Iren. iii. 23.

14 of all the books. But when they came together into the presence
of Ptolemy and compared their several translations, God was
glorified and the Scriptures were recognized as truly divine, for
all had expressed the same things in the same phrases and the
same words from beginning to end; so that even the heathen who
were present recognized that the Scriptures had been translated
15 through the inspiration of God. Nor is it a strange thing that God
should have done this, seeing that, when the people were taken
captive under Nebuchadnezzar and the Scriptures were destroyed,
and when the Jews had returned after seventy years to their own
land, He afterwards inspired Ezra the priest of the tribe of Levi,
in the time of Artaxerxes king of the Persians, to rehearse all the
words of the prophets of days gone by,[1] and to restore to the
people the law as given by Moses.[2]

THE REIGN OF COMMODUS (180–192)

9. Such are the words of Irenæus. But after Antoninus had
continued emperor for nineteen years, Commodus received the
government.

Succession of Bishops at Alexandria.

In his first year Julian was entrusted with the episcopate
of the churches at Alexandria, Agrippinus having com-
180–1. pleted his ministry after twelve years.

Pantænus.

0. Now at that time there was a man of great renown for
learning named Pantænus, who had charge of the school of the
faithful at Alexandria, where it has been a primitive custom
that a school for sacred studies should exist. This school
has continued even to our day, and although we understand
that it was filled with men of great learning and zeal for
divinity, it is recorded that the said person was especially
distinguished at that time, inasmuch as he had come from
2 that sect of philosophers who are called the Stoics. Now,
it is said that he displayed such ardent love and zeal for the
divine word that he was appointed as a herald of the Gospel
of Christ to the nations of the East, and that he journeyed even
as far as the land of the Indians. For there were, yes, even
still at that time, many evangelists of the word, desirous to
contribute an inspired zeal, after the manner of the apostles,
3 for the increase and building up of the divine word. Pantænus
also was one of these, and is mentioned as having gone to
India; and the story goes that there he found, in the hands of
some persons who had come to know Christ in that land, the

[1] 1 Esd. ix. 38–41; 2 Esd. xiv. 1–26. [2] Iren. iii. 24. 1.

Gospel according to Matthew, which had anticipated his arrival; for that Bartholomew, one of the apostles, had preached to them and left behind the writing of Matthew in the actual Hebrew characters, and that it was preserved up 4 to the said time. But to resume. Pantænus after many good deeds ended by becoming head of the school at Alexandria, where he expounded the treasures of the divine doctrines both orally and by means of treatises.

Clement of Alexandria.

11.   In his time Clement was well known at Alexandria for his thorough training in the divine Scriptures. He was a namesake of that disciple of the apostles who long ago was at the 2 head of the church of the Romans. In his work the Hypotyposeis he expressly mentions Pantænus by name as his teacher; and, in my opinion, hints at this same person also in the first treatise of the Stromateis, when, after indicating the more eminent men of the apostolic succession to which he had reached back, he speaks thus :

3   Now this work is not a writing artfully composed for display; but memoirs which I have stored up against old age, a remedy for forgetfulness, an artless image and outlined sketch of those clear and living words which I was privileged to hear, and of those 4 blessed and truly remarkable men. Of these, one—the Ionian—was in Greece, others in Magna Græcia (the one of them came from Coele-Syria, the other from Egypt); there were others in the East, and, in this quarter, the one was from the country of the Assyrians, the other a Hebrew by origin, in Palestine.[1] But when I fell in with the last (who in ability proved to be the first), having run down my quarry as it lay concealed in Egypt—I 5 took my rest. . . . Now these men, preserving the true tradition of the blessed teaching straight from the holy apostles Peter and James, John and Paul, as son inheriting from father (howbeit few sons are like their fathers), came under God even to our time, to deposit those seeds of their ancestors the apostles.[2]

Bishops of Jerusalem.

12.   In their time a bishop of the church at Jerusalem, namely Narcissus, who even to this day enjoys widespread fame, was well known. He occupied the fifteenth [place in the] succession, which dates from the siege of the Jews under Hadrian, that is to say, from the time when first, as we have shown,[3] the church there was composed of Gentiles (following on those of the circumcision), and Mark was the first Gentile bishop 2 to be their head. The succession-lists of the [bishops] of that place show that Cassian came after him in the episcopate, and,

[1] The text of Eusebius is unsatisfactory in this section; and the above translation follows the text of Clement (ed. Stählin).
[2] Clem., *Strom.* i. 1. 11.   [3] iv. 5. 2, 3; 6. 4.

after Cassian, Publius; then Maximus, and after these Julian; then Gaius, after whom came Symmachus, and another Gaius, and again another Julian; and, besides these, Capito and Valens and Dolichianus; and, last of all, Narcissus, the thirtieth from the apostles according to the list of the successive [bishops].

Rhodo and Apelles.

13.   At that time also, Rhodo, an Asian by race, a disciple, as he himself records, at Rome of Tatian (whose acquaintance we have previously made),[1] composed various books, and thus ranged himself along with the rest in opposition to the heresy of Marcion. He records the fact that in his day this heresy was divided up into various opinions; he describes for us who they were who caused the division, and carefully refutes 2 the falsehoods devised by each of them. But hear what he writes :

Therefore disagreement has broken out even among themselves, since they contend for an inconsistent opinion. For one of their herd, Apelles, he who plumes himself on his mode of life and old age, acknowledges a single principle, but says that the prophecies come from an enemy spirit—putting his trust in the utterances of a maiden possessed of a devil, named Philumene. 3 But others, as also the sailor Marcion himself, introduce two prin- 4 ciples; of whom are Potitus and Basilicus. These last, having followed the wolf of Pontus, and failing, as he did, to find the division of things, became reckless, and without any proof baldly asserted two principles. While others, again, of their number, drifting into a worse error, assume not only two, but even three natures. Their leader and chief is Syneros, according to those who shelter themselves behind his school.

5   Now the same person writes that he also conversed with Apelles. His words are as follows :

For the old man Apelles, when he talked with us, was refuted in many wrong statements. Therefore he went on to allege that one ought not to examine doctrine at all, but that everyone should remain in his own belief. For he asserted that they who have placed their hopes in the Crucified will be saved, if only they be found in good works. But he held that the most obscure thing of all was, as I have said, the question of God. For he spoke of a single principle, as also our doctrine does.

6   Then, after fully stating the views of Apelles, Rhodo goes on to say :

But when I said to him, "Whence do you get this proof ? or how can you say that there is a single principle ? tell us," he replied that the prophecies refute themselves, being absolutely devoid of truth; for they are inconsistent and lying and self-

---

[1] iv. 16. 7; 28; 29.

contradictory.   But as to how there is a single principle, he said
7 he did not know, but that it was merely his impression.[1]   Then,
on my adjuring him to tell what was true, he swore that he was
speaking the truth when he said that he did not understand
how there was one uncreated God, but that this was his belief.
For my part I laughed, and reproved him, because he said he was
a teacher, and yet was unable to establish what he taught.

8   Now in the same treatise, in addressing Callistio the same
writer acknowledges that he had been a disciple of Tatian at
Rome.   And he says too that a book of Problems was composed by Tatian.   And as its author undertook to present
therein the obscure and hidden parts of the divine Scriptures,
Rhodo himself promises to give the solutions of Tatian's
problems in a special treatise.   And there is also extant a
memoir of his on the Hexaemeron.
9   In fact Apelles—that notorious fellow—gave utterance to
countless impieties against the law of Moses : in very many
treatises blaspheming the divine words, on whose refutation
(as he thought) and overthrow he had bestowed no small
amount of zeal.

Heresies.

14.   So much, then, for these matters.   But to resume.   The
enemy of the Church of God, who has no superior in his hatred
of good and love of evil, having left untried no manner of craft
against men, set himself to cause strange heresies to spring
up once more to the Church's hurt.   Some followers of these
crawled over Asia and Phrygia like venomous reptiles, boasting
of the Paraclete Montanus, and of the women in his train,
Priscilla and Maximilla, inasmuch as they had been prophet-
15. esses of Montanus.   But others flourished at Rome, led by
Florinus, who had fallen from the presbyterate of the Church,
and, with him, Blastus, the subject of a similar fall.   These
drew away many members of the Church and enticed them to
their purpose, the one and the other endeavouring to innovate
upon the truth in his own way.

Montanism.

16.   To contend, therefore, with the heresy of the Phrygians,
as it is called, the power which champions the truth raised
up, as a strong and invincible weapon at Hierapolis, Apollinarius (whom our history has mentioned before),[2] and along
with him many learned men of that time ; who have left us
the amplest supply of historical material.

---

[1] οὕτως δὲ κινεῖσθαι μόνον : the meaning is doubtful.   [2] iv. 27.

1. *The Anonymous.*

2 For instance, at the beginning of his work against them, a certain one of the said persons indicates first of all that he had also attacked and refuted them orally. Thus, he premises after this fashion :

3 It is a very long and considerable time, beloved Avircius Marcellus, since I was charged by thee to write some kind of treatise against the heresy of the followers of Miltiades, as they are called. Yet I have somehow held back until now, not through lack of ability to refute falsehood and bear witness to the truth, but from fear and extreme caution, lest perchance I might seem to some to be *adding* a new article or clause to the word of the New *Covenant*[1] of the Gospel, to which no one who has purposed to *live* according to *the* simple *Gospel*[2] may add, from which no
4 one may *take away*.[3] But when I recently came to Ancyra in Galatia, and found the local church ringing with the noise of this new (not, as they themselves say, prophecy; but much rather, as will be shown) false prophecy : with the help of the Lord we discoursed, to the best of our ability, for many days in the church on every one of these same points, as well as on those which they put forward; insomuch that the church rejoiced exceedingly and was confirmed in the truth, while they of the contrary part were for the moment discomfited, and the opposers put to grief.
5 So when the local presbyters requested us to leave behind some memorandum of what had been said against *them that oppose themselves*[4] to the word of truth (and there was present also our fellow-presbyter Zoticus of Otrus), though we did not do this, we promised to write it here, should the Lord permit us, and send it to them speedily.

6 Having stated these and, subsequently, other facts at the beginning of the work, he proceeds to tell of the author of the aforesaid heresy, after the following manner :

Their opposition, then, and their recent schismatical heresy as
7 regards the Church, arose thus. There is reported to be a certain village in that Mysia which borders on Phrygia, called by the name of Ardabau. There it is said that a certain recent convert to the faith named Montanus (while Gratus was proconsul of Asia), in the immeasurable longing of his soul for the pre-eminence, first gave the adversary a passage into his heart; and that moved by the spirit he suddenly fell into a state of possession, as it were, and abnormal ecstasy, insomuch that he became frenzied and began to babble and utter strange sounds, that is to say, prophesying contrary to the manner which the Church had received from generation to generation by tradition from the
8 beginning. Some of those who heard at that time his spurious utterances were incensed at him, as at one possessed and tormented with a devil, the prey of a *spirit of error*[5] and a disturber of the people. So they rebuked and strove to check his babblings, mindful of the injunction and warning of the Lord to guard

---

[1] Gal. iii. 15.   [2] Phil. i. 27.   [3] Cp. Rev. xxii. 18, 19.
[4] 2 Tim. ii. 25.   [5] 1 John iv. 6.

watchfully against the coming of *false prophets.*[1] But others
were puffed up, as if at a prophetical gift of the Holy Spirit, and
filled with no mean conceit, and forgetful of the injunction of
the Lord. Therefore they called forth this maddening and
cajoling spirit which was deceiving the people, by which they
were beguiled and deceived, so that it could no longer be checked
9 to silence. And by some art, or rather by the employment of
such an evil artifice, the devil secretly stirred up and enflamed
the minds, which had lost in sleep the true faith, of those dis-
obedient persons whose ruin he had devised, and by whom—a
strange requital !—he was honoured. So that he raised up two
women as well, and so filled them with the spurious spirit that
they too chattered in a frenzied, inopportune and unnatural [2]
fashion, like him whom we mentioned above. And the spirit
pronounced them blessed who rejoiced and prided themselves
in him, and puffed them up with the greatness of his promises;
yet at times he would administer shrewd and plausible rebukes
to their face, that he might seem capable of reproving also.
Howbeit there were few who were thus deceived by the Phrygians.[3]
Moreover, this arrogant spirit taught them to blaspheme the entire
universal Church under heaven, because the spirit of false prophecy
10 received neither honour nor admission into it. For when the
faithful throughout Asia had met frequently and at many places
in Asia for this purpose, and on examination of the new-fangled
teachings had pronounced them profane, and rejected the heresy,
these persons were thus expelled from the Church and shut off
from its communion.

11   Having related these facts at the outset, and having deve-
loped the refutation of their error throughout the entire
treatise, in the second [book] he speaks thus of the end of the
aforesaid persons :

12   Since, therefore, they also used to dub us *slayers* of the *prophets* [4]
because we did not receive their *prophets* of unbridled tongue
(for these, they say, are they whom the Lord promised to send
to the people), let them answer us before God : Is there a single
one, my good sirs, of these followers of Montanus or of the women
who began to chatter, who was *persecuted* by Jews or *killed* by
lawless men ? Not one. Or, were any of them seized and
crucified [5] *for the sake of the Name ?* [6] Not so. Or even, were any
of the women ever *scourged in the synagogues* [5] of the Jews or
13 *stoned ?* [7] Never, in any wise. Nay, it was another death that
Montanus and Maximilla are reported to have died. For report
says that a maddening spirit drove both of them to hang themselves, though not at the same time ; and a persistent rumour
at the time of each death [asserted] that thus they died and
14 ended their life, after the manner of the traitor Judas.[8] In like
manner also, as concerning that marvellous fellow, the first
steward, as it were, of their so-called prophecy, Theodotus,
common report has it that once upon a time, on being lifted and

---

[1] Matt. vii. 15.   [2] ἀλλοτριοτρόπως.
[3] A conjectural emendation of Schwartz has been adopted.
[4] Matt. xxiii. 31.   [5] Matt. xxiii. 34.
[6] 3 John 7.   [7] Cp. Matt. xxiii. 37.   [8] Matt. xxvii. 5.

raised heavenwards, he fell into abnormal ecstasy, and, entrusting himself to *the spirit of* error,[1] was whirled to the ground, and so met a miserable end.   At any rate, this is how they say it hap-
15 pened.   But, my dear sir, do not let us imagine that we can be certain of a fact of this kind, when we did not see it.   Perhaps it was thus, perhaps it was not thus, that Montanus and Theodotus and the aforesaid woman met their end.

16   Again, in the same work he says that the holy *bishops* of that day had endeavoured *to refute* utterly *the spirit* that dwelt in Maximilla, but were prevented by others, who were mani-
17 festly in league with the spirit.   He writes thus :

> And let not the spirit which spoke in the person of Maximilla say in the same book According to Asterius Urbanus, "I am driven as a wolf from the sheep.   I am not a wolf.   I am word and *spirit and power*."[2]   But let him show clearly the power that is in the spirit, let him bring convincing proof of it, and by the spirit let him force an acknowledgment from those who were then present to prove and discourse with the talkative spirit : approved men and bishops, Zoticus from the village of Cumana and Julian from Apamea, whose mouths Themiso and his crew muzzled, and would not allow them to refute the false spirit which was deceiving the people.

18   And once more in the same work, after some intervening remarks in refutation of the false prophecies of Maximilla, he both indicates the time when he wrote this account, and also mentions her predictions, in which she foretold *wars and tumults*,[3] the falsity of which he goes on to expose.   This is what he says :

19   And surely this falsehood too is now evident.   For it is more than thirteen years to-day since the woman died, and there has been neither a partial nor a universal war in the world.   Nay rather, by the mercy of God the Christians have enjoyed continuous peace.

20   The above is taken from the second treatise.   And I shall quote short passages from the third also, in which he thus replies to those who were boasting that they too had many martyrs in their ranks :

> So then, when worsted in all their arguments they are at a loss, they endeavour to take refuge in the martyrs, saying that they have many martyrs, and that this is a reliable proof of the power of that which is called among them the prophetical spirit.   But
21 this, as it appears, proves to be absolutely untrue.   For it is a fact that some of the other heresies have immense numbers of martyrs, yet surely we shall not for this reason give them our assent, nor acknowledge that they possess the truth.   To take them first, those called Marcionites from the heresy of Marcion say that they have immense numbers of martyrs of Christ, but as regards Christ Himself they do not truly acknowledge Him.

---

[1] Cp. 1 John iv. 6.   [2] 1 Cor. ii. 4.   [3] Luke xxi. 9.

And shortly afterwards he goes on to say :

22   It is doubtless for this reason that, whenever those called from the Church to martyrdom for the true faith meet with any so-called martyrs from the heresy of the Phrygians, they sever themselves from them and are perfected, without holding communion with them, for they do not wish to assent to the spirit [that spoke] through Montanus and the women.   And that this is true, and that it took place in our time at Apamea on the Mæander among those martyrs of Eumenia who were the companions of Gaius and Alexander,[1] is an evident fact.

17.   Now in this treatise he also mentions a writer Miltiades : that he too had written a certain book against the aforesaid heresy.   Thus, having quoted certain of their sayings, he goes on to say :

I found these things in a certain treatise of theirs, wherein they attack that treatise of our brother Alcibiades, in which he shows that a prophet ought not to speak in a state of ecstasy ; and I abridged them.

2   And a little further on in the same treatise he gives a list of those who had prophesied *under the new* Covenant, among whom he enumerates a certain *Ammia* and *Quadratus*.   His words are as follow :

. . . but the false prophet in abnormal ecstasy, upon whom follow licence and fearlessness.   For while he begins with voluntary ignorance, he ends with involuntary madness of soul, as has
3 been stated.   But they cannot show any prophet under either the Old or the New [Covenant] who was moved by the Spirit after this manner, neither Agabus nor Judas nor Silas nor the daughters of Philip, nor Ammia in Philadelphia nor Quadratus, nor can they make their boast of any others whatever not belonging to their number.

4   And, once again, he shortly afterwards goes on to say :

For if, as they say, the women in Montanus' train succeeded to the prophetical gift after Quadratus and Ammia of Philadelphia, let them show which of their number, who were followers of Montanus and the women, succeeded to it.   For the Apostle lays it down that the prophetical gift ought to continue in the whole Church until the final coming.   But they cannot produce anyone, though it is the fourteenth year or thereabouts since the death of Maximilla.

5   Such are the remarks of this writer.   Now Miltiades, whom he has mentioned, has also left us other monuments of his personal zeal for the divine oracles, both in [1] the discourses which he composed against the Greeks and in [2] those against the Jews, dealing with each subject separately in two treatises ; and moreover [3] he has addressed a defence of the philosophy which he followed to the rulers of this world.

[1] Or " those martyrs who were the companions of Gaius and Alexander of Eumenia."

2. *Apollonius.*

18.   But an ecclesiastical writer called Apollonius also undertook to refute the Phrygian heresy, as it is called, when it was then still at its height in Phrygia; and he has written a special treatise against them, exposing in detail the falsity of the prophecies they circulated, and thoroughly examining the kind of life lived by the leaders of the heresy. But listen to the very words he uses when speaking of Montanus:

2   But his works and teaching show of what kind is this new-fangled teacher. This is he who taught dissolutions of marriages; who laid down laws on fasting; who named Pepuza and Tymion (small towns in Phrygia) Jerusalem, in his desire to gather to them people from all quarters; who appointed agents for collecting money; who has devised his scheme for receiving gifts, under the name of "offerings"; who has supplied salaries to those who preach his doctrine, so that by means of gluttony the teaching thereof may be made more effective.

3   This is what he says of Montanus. And a little lower down he writes thus of his prophetesses also:

We show, therefore, that these prophetesses were the very first, from the time when they were filled with the spirit, who left their husbands. How, then, did they speak falsehood, calling Priscilla a virgin?

4   Next, he goes on to say:

Does not every Scripture seem to thee to forbid a prophet to receive gifts and money? [1] Therefore, when I see the prophetess possessed of gold and silver and costly apparel, must I not eschew her?

5   And once more, a little lower down, he speaks thus of one of their confessors:

Moreover, Themiso also, he who is clothed with plausible covetousness, who did not bear the sign of confession, but put off his chains, thanks to a large sum of money, and (though this fact should have made him humble) boasts himself a martyr—this man, aping the Apostle, dared to compose a "catholic epistle," and therein to instruct those whose faith has surpassed his, to contend with empty-sounding words, and to utter blasphemy against the Lord, the apostles and the holy Church.

6   And of another also—one of those whom they honoured as martyrs, forsooth—he again writes thus:

But not to speak of many, let the prophetess tell us about Alexander, who calls himself a martyr, with whom she banquets, to whom also many do reverence. It is not for us to speak of his robberies, and the other deeds of daring for which he has been

---

[1] Cp. *Didache* 11, 12.

7 punished; nay, the record office preserves their tale. Which, then, of the two forgives the other's sins? Does the prophet forgive the martyr his robberies, or the martyr the prophet his deeds of covetousness? For though the Lord has said, *Get you no gold, nor silver, neither two coats*,[1] they, in complete contradiction, have transgressed as regards the getting of these forbidden things. For we shall show that they whom they call prophets and martyrs get their petty gains not only from the rich but also from poor
8 people and orphans and widows. And if they are confident, let them take their stand on this, and come to a definite agreement on this understanding, that if convicted they may at least for the future cease to transgress. For one ought to prove the fruits
9 of the prophet: *for the* tree *is known* by *its fruit*.[2] But, that those who wish may know about Alexander, he has been judged by Æmilius Frontinus, proconsul at Ephesus, not because of the Name, but because of the robberies he committed, being already an apostate. Next, he made a false appeal to the Name of Christ and was released, having deceived the faithful in that city. And his own community, whence he came, would not receive him, because he was a robber. Those who have a mind to learn about
10 him have the public archives of Asia. And yet the prophet knows nothing of him with whom he associated many years! In exposing this man we also expose, by means of him, his claim to be a prophet. We can show the same in the case of many; and, if they have the courage, let them stand the exposure!

11   And again, in another place in the treatise, he adds this with reference to their vaunted prophets:

If they deny that their prophets have received gifts, let them agree on this point: that if they are convicted of having received them, they are not prophets; and we will furnish countless demonstrations of the fact. But one must needs prove all the fruits of a prophet. Tell me, does a prophet dye his hair? Does a prophet paint his eyelids? Does a prophet love adornment? Does a prophet play at gaming-tables and dice? Does a prophet lend money at interest? Let them agree as to whether these things are permitted or not, and I for my part will show that they took place among them.

12   Now this same Apollonius in the same treatise records that at the date of writing his treatise it was the fortieth year
13 since Montanus had begun his pretended prophesying. And, again, he says that Zoticus, whom also the former writer mentioned,[3] arrived at Pepuza when Maximilla was pretending, forsooth, to prophesy, and attempted to refute the spirit that was working in her; howbeit he was prevented by her partizans.
14 And he also mentions one Thraseas as a martyr at that time. And he says too, relying on tradition, that the Saviour had ordered His apostles *not to depart* from *Jerusalem* [4] for twelve years; and he also makes use of testimonies drawn from the Apocalypse of John; and he records that a dead man had,

---

1 Matt. x. 9, 10.   2 Matt. xii. 33.
3 16. 17.   4 Acts i. 4.

through the divine power, been raised at Ephesus by John himself; and he makes certain other statements in which he gives in the fullest manner a satisfactory exposure of the error of the aforesaid heresy. Such is the account of Apollonius.

3. *Apollinarius.*

19.   The [works] of Apollinarius against the said heresy have been mentioned by Serapion, who, it is recorded, succeeded Maximin as bishop of the church of the Antiochenes at the time of which we are speaking. He mentions him in a personal epistle to Caricus and Pontius, in which he too exposes the same heresy, and then goes on to say as follows:

2   But that you may know this also, that the working of this lying organization [1] called the New Prophecy is held in abomination by the whole brotherhood in the world, I have sent unto you a letter also of Claudius Apollinarius, the late most blessed bishop at Hierapolis in Asia.

3   And in this epistle of Serapion are extant signatures also of various bishops, one of whom has subscribed after this fashion:

I, Aurelius Quirinius, a martyr, pray that ye may fare well.

And another, on this manner:

Ælius Publius Julius, a bishop from Develtum a colony in Thrace. As God in heaven liveth, I swear that the blessed Sotas of Anchialus wished to cast out Priscilla's demon, and the hypocrites would not allow it.

4   And the autograph signatures of a large number of other bishops, in agreement with the foregoing, are extant in the said letter.

Blastus and Florinus.

20.   So much, then, for these persons. But in opposition to those at Rome who were falsifying the sound rule of the Church, Irenæus composed various letters: one he entitled To Blastus, On Schism; another To Florinus, On Monarchy or That God is not the Author of Evil. For indeed Florinus seemed to defend this opinion. And because he was being dragged, on another occasion, into the error of Valentinus, Irenæus also composed his [work] On the Ogdoad, in which also he indicates that he himself had reached back to the first succession from the apostles. At the close of this treatise we found a most charming note of his, which also we are constrained to insert in this work. It runs as follows:

[1] τάξεως.

I adjure thee who mayest transcribe this book, by our Lord Jesus Christ and by His glorious advent, when He cometh to *judge the quick and the dead*,[1] to compare what thou hast transcribed, and to correct it carefully by this copy, whence thou hast transcribed it; and likewise to transcribe this adjuration and insert it in the copy.

3   Let us note for our profit this saying of his which we have recorded, to the end that we may have those ancient and truly holy men as a supreme example of most painstaking carefulness.

4   But to resume. In the aforesaid letter of Irenæus to Florinus, he again mentions his intercourse with Polycarp, saying :

These opinions, Florinus, to say no more, are not of sound judgment; these opinions are not in harmony with the Church, involving those who adopt them in the greatest impiety; these opinions not even the heretics outside the Church ever dared to espouse openly; these opinions the elders before us, who also
5 were disciples of the apostles, did not hand down to thee. For when I was still a boy I saw thee in lower Asia in the company of Polycarp, faring brilliantly in the imperial court and endeavouring to secure his favour. For I distinctly recall the events of that
6 time better than those of recent years (for what we learn in childhood keeps pace with the growing mind and becomes part of it), so that I can tell the very place where the blessed Polycarp used to sit as he discoursed, his goings out and his comings in, the character of his life, his bodily appearance, the discourses he would address to the multitude, how he would tell of his intercourse with John and with the others who had seen the Lord, how he would relate from memory their words; and what the things were which he had heard from them concerning the Lord, His mighty works and His teaching, Polycarp, as having received them from the *eyewitnesses of the life of the Word*, would *declare* [2]
7 altogether in accordance with the Scriptures. To these things I used to listen diligently even then, by the mercy of God which was upon me, noting them down not on paper but in my heart. And by the grace of God I constantly ruminate upon them faithfully; and I can testify before God that if that blessed and apostolic elder had heard the like, he would have cried aloud and stopped his ears and said, as was his wont : " Good God, for what sort of times hast Thou kept me, that I should endure these things ? " and he would have fled the very place where, sitting
8 or standing, he had heard such words. And this can be shown from his letters too which he wrote, whether to the neighbouring churches, confirming them, or to some of the brethren, admonishing and exhorting them.

Such are the words of Irenæus.

---

[1] 2 Tim. iv. 1; cp. Acts x. 42, 1 Pet. iv. 5.
[2] Cp. 1 John i. 1, 2; Luke i. 2.

Apollonius the Martyr.

21.   Now at the same time, that is, during the reign of Commodus, our affairs took an easier turn, and, thanks to the divine grace, peace embraced the churches throughout the whole world. Then also the word of salvation was gently leading every soul from every race of men towards the devout worship of the God of the universe; insomuch that already large numbers even of those at Rome, highly distinguished for wealth and birth, were advancing towards their own salvation
2 with all their households and kindred. But, as one might expect, the demon who hates the good, being by nature envious, could not endure this. At all events he stripped himself once more for the contest, and varied were the contrivances he devised against us. For instance, in the city of the Romans he brought Apollonius before the court, one of the faithful of that day, a man famed for culture and philosophy; having stirred up one of his ministers, who were
3 well fitted for that task, to accuse him. But the wretched man preferred his suit at an inauspicious time, for by an imperial decree informers of such things might not live. So *his legs* were *broken* [1] immediately. It was a judge named
4 Perennius who pronounced this sentence upon him. But as for the martyr most dearly beloved of God, in response to many earnest entreaties of the judge, who asked him to render an account before the Senate, he made a most eloquent defence before them all of the faith to which he bore witness, and was perfected by decapitation in accordance with *a decree of the Senate ;* [2] for an ancient law prevails among them that once men had appeared before the court and refused in any
5 way to recant, they should not be lightly [3] released. Now, this man's words before the judge, the answers he made in reply to the questions of Perennius, and the defence in full which he delivered to the Senate, may be learnt, by anyone who wishes to know them exactly, from the record we have collected of the ancient martyrdoms.

Succession of Bishops.

22.   But to resume. In the tenth year of the reign of Commodus, Victor succeeded Eleutherus, who had ministered
190. in the episcopal office for thirteen years; in which year also, when Julian had completed his tenth year, Demetrius was entrusted with the ministry of the communities at Alexandria. In their day also Serapion, already mentioned before,[4] was at that time still well known as the eighth bishop from the

---

[1] Cp. *Acta Apoll.* (Grk.), 45.   [2] *Acta Apoll.* (Armen.), 45.
[3] Or, " on any other terms."   [4] c. 19.

↯ apostles of the church of the Antiochenes. Theophilus ruled at Cæsarea in Palestine, and likewise Narcissus, of whom we made mention previously in this book,[1] still held the ministry of the church at Jerusalem. In their time Bacchyllus was bishop of Corinth in Greece, and Polycrates of the community at Ephesus. And, in addition to them, numberless others, as one might imagine, were prominent in the time of these [bishops]. Howbeit we have, naturally, recounted those by name, the orthodoxy of whose faith has come down to us in writing.

The Paschal Controversy.

23. Now a question of no small importance arose in their time. For the communities of the whole of Asia, relying on a tradition of great antiquity, thought that they ought to observe the fourteenth day of the moon—the day on which the Jews were ordered to sacrifice the lamb—as the day for the festival of the Saviour's Pascha; since they deemed it necessary at all costs to put an end to their fast on that day, no matter on what day of the week it should fall. But it was not the custom for the churches throughout all the rest of the world thus to celebrate it, preserving as they did by an apostolic tradition the custom which had obtained hitherto, that it was not proper to end the fast on any other day than
2 on the day of the resurrection of our Saviour. So then, synods and assemblages of bishops came together, and unanimously drew up in letters an ecclesiastical decree for the faithful everywhere, to the effect that the mystery of the Lord's resurrection from the dead should never be celebrated on any other but the Lord's day, and that on that day alone we
3 should observe the close of the paschal fast. Now there is still extant to this day a letter from those who were then assembled in Palestine, over whom Theophilus, bishop of the community at Cæsarea, and Narcissus, of Jerusalem, presided; and likewise another also from those at Rome, on the same question, which indicates that Victor was bishop; [another] too from the bishops in Pontus, over whom Palmas, as the oldest, had presided; and also [another] from the communities in Gaul, over which Irenæus was bishop;
4 [another] moreover from the bishops in Osrhoëne and the cities in that part; as well as a personal letter from Bacchyllus, bishop of the church of the Corinthians, and from great numbers of others who pronounced one and the same opinion and judgment, and gave the same decision. And the one decree which they made was that which we have stated.

24. But of those bishops in Asia who confidently affirmed that they ought to keep to the custom which they had received

[1] 12. 2.

from days of yore, Polycrates was the leader.   And he too
sets forth the tradition which had come down to him, in the
letter he penned to Victor and the church of the Romans, in
the following words :

2   As for us, then, we keep the day without tampering with it,
neither adding, nor subtracting.   For indeed in Asia great
luminaries have fallen asleep, such as shall rise again on the day
of the Lord's appearing, when He comes with glory from heaven
to seek out all his saints : to wit, Philip, one of the twelve apostles,)
who has fallen asleep in Hierapolis, [as have] also his two daughters
who grew old in virginity, and his other daughter who lived in
3 the Holy Spirit and rests at Ephesus ;   and, moreover, [there is]
John too, he who *leant back on* the Lord's *breast*,[1] who was [2] a priest,
wearing the sacerdotal plate, both martyr and teacher.   He
4 has fallen asleep at Ephesus.   Moreover, Polycarp too at Smyrna,
both bishop and martyr ;   and Thraseas, both bishop and martyr,
5 of Eumenia, who has fallen asleep at Smyrna.   And why need I
mention Sagaris, bishop and martyr, who has fallen asleep at
Laodicea ?   or the blessed Papirius, or Melito the eunuch who
in all things lived in the Holy Spirit, who lies at Sardis, awaiting
the visitation [3] from heaven, when he shall rise from the dead ?
6 These all observed the fourteenth day for the Pascha according to
the Gospel, in no way deviating therefrom, but following the rule
of faith.   And moreover I also, Polycrates, the least of you all,
[do] according to the tradition of my kinsmen, some of whom
also I have followed closely.   Seven of my kinsmen were bishops,
and I am the eighth.   And my kinsmen always kept the day
7 when the people [4] put away the leaven.   Therefore I for my part,
brethren, who number sixty-five years in the Lord and have conversed with the brethren from all parts of the world and traversed
the entire range of holy Scripture, am not *affrighted* [5] by threats.
For those better than I have said, *We must obey God rather than
men.*[6]

8   Then he goes on to add as follows, with reference to the
bishops present at his writing who held the same view as he
did :

But I could mention the bishops present with me, whom I
summoned when ye yourselves desired that I should summon
them.   And if I were to write their names, the number thereof
would be great.   But they who know my littleness approved my
letter, knowing that I did not wear my grey hairs in vain, but that
I have ever lived in Christ Jesus.

9   Thereupon Victor, the president of the [church] of the
Romans, endeavoured to cut off by a single stroke the communities of the whole of Asia, together with the neighbouring
churches, from the common union, on the ground of un-
orthodoxy ;   and, indeed, denounced them in letters, proclaiming that the brethren in those parts were all wholly excom-

---

[1] John xiii. 25.   [2] Or " became."
[3] ἐπισκοπήν.   [4] ὁ λαός : the Jews.
[5] Phil. i. 28.   [6] Acts v. 29.

10 municate. Howbeit this did not please all the bishops without exception. On the contrary, they exhorted him in reply
to have a mind for *the things which make for peace* [1] and neigh-
bourly union and charity. And their words are extant also,
11 in which they censure Victor with unusual severity. One of
these was Irenæus, who wrote in the name of the brethren in
Gaul, whose leader he was; and, while holding that the mystery
of the Lord's resurrection should be celebrated on the Lord's
day and on that alone, he nevertheless gives Victor much
suitable counsel besides, not to cut off whole churches of God
for observing an ancient custom handed down to them.
Then he goes on to add, in these very words :

12   For not only is there a controversy about the day, but also about
the very manner of the fast. For some think they ought to fast
a single day, but others two, others again even more. And in the
opinion of others, the "day" amounts to forty continuous [2]
13 hours. And this variety of observance did not originate in our
time, but much further back, in the times of those before us, who,
no doubt mistakenly, held closely, in their simplicity and ignorance, to this custom, and have transmitted it to posterity. Yet
none the less they all lived in peace, and we live in peace, with one
another; and the difference concerning the fast enhances the
unanimity of our faith.

14   To these remarks he also adds the following account, which
it will not be out of place for me to quote :

. . . among whom the elders before Soter, who presided over
the church of which thou art now the leader—we mean Anicetus
and Pius, Hyginus and Telesphorus and Xystus—neither themselves observed it nor permitted those [residing] with them
[to do so]; and none the less, though themselves not observing it,
were they at peace with the members of those communities where
it was observed, when the latter came to them. And yet the
observance was the more obnoxious to those who did not observe
15 it. And none were ever cast out because of this course of action,
but those very elders before thee, though they did not observe
it, would send the eucharist to members of those communities
16 who observed it. And when the blessed Polycarp stayed at
Rome in the time of Anicetus, although they had some trifling
disagreements on other matters, they immediately made peace,
nor did they care to quarrel on this head. For neither could
Anicetus persuade Polycarp not to observe what he had always
observed with John the disciple of our Lord and the other apostles
with whom he consorted; nor yet did Polycarp persuade Anicetus
to observe it, for he said that he ought to hold to the custom of
17 the elders before him. And though such was the case, they held
communion with one another, and in the church Anicetus yielded
the [celebration of the] eucharist to Polycarp, manifestly out of
respect. So they parted from one another in peace, and the
whole Church was at peace, both they who observed and they
who did not observe.

---

[1] Rom. xiv. 19.   [2] Lit. "during the day and night."

18   Thus, then, did Irenæus entreat and negotiate on behalf of
the peace of the churches; a man well-named, for he was a
peace-maker both in name and character. And he corre-
sponded by letter not only with Victor, but also with very
many and various rulers of churches, in a fitting manner, on
the question which had been raised.

25.   But to resume. The [bishops] in Palestine, of whom we
lately spoke,[1] that is to say, Narcissus and Theophilus, and
with them Cassius, bishop of the church at Tyre, and Clarus
of the [church] at Ptolemais, and those assembled with them,
having treated at length of the tradition concerning the
Pascha that had come down to them in succession from the
apostles, at the close of their letter speak thus, in these very
words :

But do ye endeavour to send copies of our letter round every
community, that we be not chargeable for those who lightly
deceive their own souls. Howbeit we declare unto you that they
of Alexandria do also hold it on the same day as do we. For
they receive letters from us, and we from them, to the end that
we may keep the holy day in concord and at the one time.

The Writings of Irenæus.

26.   But indeed, in addition to the treatises and letters of
Irenæus which have been cited,[2] there is extant [1] a most concise and exceedingly cogent work of his against the Greeks,
entitled On Science; and [2] another, which he has dedicated
to a brother named Marcian, regarding the Demonstration of
the Apostolic Preaching; and [3] a certain book of various
discourses, in which he mentions the Epistle to the Hebrews
and the Wisdom of Solomon, as it is called, quoting certain
passages from them. These, then, are the works of Irenæus
which have come to our knowledge.

REIGN OF SEPTIMIUS SEVERUS (193–211)

But when Commodus had brought his principate to an end
after thirteen years, the emperor Severus became the ruler,
for Pertinax did not continue six entire months in office after
the death of Commodus.

Writers.

27.   So then, large numbers of memoirs, composed with virtuous
diligence by the ancient churchmen of that time, are still to
this day preserved by many. Among those, however, of which
we have personal knowledge, are the [memoirs] of Heraclitus

---

[1] 23. 3.   [2] See v. 5. 8, 9; 6–8; 20; 24. 12–17.

On the Apostle; those of Maximus on that much-discussed question among the heretics, the Origin of Evil and That Matter had a Beginning; of Candidus On the Hexaemeron; of Apion on the same subject; of Sextus, likewise, On the Resurrection; and another work, of Arabianus; as well as the works of countless others, in whose case the lack of data prevents us from recording the times in which they lived or making any mention of their history. And the works also of many others, of whom we cannot recount even the names, have reached us : orthodox churchmen, as their several interpretations of the divine Scripture show, but nevertheless unknown to us, since such do not bear the names of their authors.

The Little Labyrinth.

28.   In a work composed by one of these against the heresy of Artemon (which heresy Paul of Samosata has endeavoured to revive again in our day) there is extant a narrative germane
2 to our historical investigations. For indeed the book exposes the allegation of the said heresy that the Saviour was a mere man, and plainly shows that it was a recent novelty, since they who introduced it wished to clothe it with the grave garb of antiquity. And after many other quotations in refutation of their blasphemous falsehood, it gives the following account in these very words :

3   For they say that all the men of former days, and the apostles themselves, received and taught the things which these men now say, and that the truth of the preaching was preserved until the times of Victor, who was the thirteenth bishop at Rome from Peter; but that the truth was falsified from the days of his
4 successor, Zephyrinus. Now what they say might perhaps have carried weight, were it not, in the first place, that the divine Scriptures were opposed to them. And there are writings of certain of the brethren too, older than the times of Victor, which they wrote both against the Gentiles on behalf of the truth and also against the heresies of that day—I mean [the writings] of Justin and Miltiades and Tatian and Clement and many others—
5 in all of which Christ is spoken of as God. For who does not know the books of Irenæus and Melito and the rest, proclaiming as they do that Christ is God and man; or all the psalms or songs written from the beginning by faithful brethren, which celebrate the Word of God, even Christ, and speak of Him as
6 God ? How then, when the mind of the Church has been thus declared for so many years back, can it be that Christians up to the time of Victor preached in the way that they assert ? And how are they not ashamed to ascribe these things falsely to Victor, when they certainly know that Victor excommunicated Theodotus the cobbler, the prime mover and father of this God-denying apostasy, when he was the first to say that Christ was a mere man ? For if Victor was of their way of thinking, as their slander affirms, how could he have cast out Theodotus the inventor of this heresy ?

Succession of Bishops of Rome.

7   So much in regard to the happenings in the time of Victor.
But when he had presided over the ministry for ten years,
202.   Zephyrinus was appointed to succeed him, about the
ninth year of the reign of Severus.

The Little Labyrinth (continued).

Now the author of the aforesaid book dealing with the
founder of the said heresy adds also another event which took
place under Zephyrinus. He writes somewhat as follows,
using these very words :

8   For example, I shall remind many of the brethren of an event
which took place in our day, the which, if it *had been done in
Sodom,*[1] would, in my opinion, have perchance admonished even
that people.   There was a certain confessor named Natalius,
9 who lived not long ago, but in our own time.   Once upon a time
this man was deceived by Asclepiodotus and another Theodotus, a
banker.   Both these last were pupils of Theodotus the cobbler,
who was the first to be excommunicated by Victor, as I said,
the then bishop, on account of this sentiment or, rather, senseless-
10 ness.   So Natalius was persuaded by them to take the title of
bishop of this heresy at a salary, and to be paid by them one
11 hundred and fifty denarii a month.   When, therefore, he became
one of them, he was frequently admonished by the Lord in visions.
For our compassionate God and Lord, Jesus Christ, did not wish
that a witness to His own sufferings should perish outside the
12 Church.   But when he paid less regard to the visions, being
ensnared by having the first place among them, and by the greed
of filthy lucre which destroys many, he was finally scourged by
the holy angels, and suffered no light punishment the whole night
long; insomuch that he arose at dawn, put on sackcloth, covered
himself with ashes, and with all haste prostrated himself in tears
before Zephyrinus the bishop; and, rolling at the feet not only
of the clergy but also of the laity, he moved with his tears the
compassionate Church of the merciful Christ.   And though he
used much entreaty and showed the weals of the stripes he had
received, scarcely was he taken back into communion.

13   To this we shall subjoin also other remarks of the same writer
on the same subject.   They are as follows :

They have tampered with the divine Scriptures without fear;
they have set aside the rule of the primitive faith; they have not
known Christ.   For they seek not for what the divine Scriptures
declare, but laboriously set themselves to find a form of syllogism
which may support their godlessness.   And if one puts before
them a text of divine Scripture, they try whether a conjunctive
14 or disjunctive form of syllogism can be made out of it.   And
deserting the holy Scriptures of God, they pursue the study of
geometry, since they *are of the earth and speak the things of the earth*

---

[1] Matt. xi. 23.

and know not *him that cometh from above*.[1] Thus, to study Euclid
is for some of them a labour of love; Aristotle and Theophrastus
are admired; aye, Galen in like manner by some is even wor-
15 shipped. But, that those who use to the full the arts of unbelievers to establish their heretical opinions, and *corrupt* the
simple faith of the divine Scriptures [2] with the craftiness of godless
men—what need is there even to say that such are nowhere near
the faith? ∣ Therefore they laid hands fearlessly on the divine
16 Scriptures, saying that they had corrected them. And whosoever
desires can find out that in saying this I do not falsely accuse
them. For anyone who will collect their several copies together
and compare them, one with another, will discover marked dis-
crepancies. For instance, Asclepiades' copies do not agree with
17 those of Theodotus. ∣ And you may get possession of many of
those of Theodotus. ∣ And you may get possession of many of
them, because their disciples have vied in copying their several
corrections (as they call them), that is, disfigurements. And,
again, those of Hermophilus are not in accordance with the first-
named. Aye, and those of Apolloniades do not even agree
among themselves. For you may compare the copies they made
at an earlier date with those they again altered later, and find
18 great divergence. Nor is it likely that they themselves are
ignorant of the audacity of this offence. For either they do not
believe that the divine Scriptures were spoken by the Holy Spirit,
and, therefore, are unbelievers; or they consider themselves wiser
than the Holy Spirit, and what is that but devil-possession?
For they cannot deny that the audacious act is their own, since
the copies have been written in their own hand; and, since they
received [3] no such Scriptures from their instructors, they are
19 unable to show any copies whence they transcribed them. But
some of them disdained even to falsify them, and absolutely denied
the law and the prophets. Thus under the cover of a lawless and
impious teaching [4] they have sunk down to the lowest depths of
perdition.

So much, then, for this account.

[1] John iii. 31.   [2] Cp. 2 Cor. ii. 17.
[3] A conjectural emendation of Schwartz has been adopted.
[4] Omitting χάριτος, which is probably corrupt.

BOOK VI

The Sixth Book of the Ecclesiastical History contains the following:

1. On the persecution under Severus.
2. On Origen's training from boyhood.
3. How he set forth the word of Christ when quite young.
4. How many of those instructed by him were elevated to the rank of martyrs.
5. On Potamiæna.
6. On Clement the Alexandrian.
7. On Judas, a writer.
8. On Origen's rash act.
9. On the miracles of Narcissus.
10. On the bishops at Jerusalem.
11. On Alexander.
12. On Serapion and his extant works.
13. On the treatises of Clement.
14. What Scriptures he mentioned.
15. On Heraclas.
16. How Origen laboured at the divine Scriptures.
17. On Symmachus the translator.
18. On Ambrose.
19. What things are mentioned concerning Origen.
20. What books of the men of that day are extant.
21. What bishops were well known in the time of these persons.
22. What works of Hippolytus have reached us.
23. On Origen's zeal, and how he was deemed worthy of the presbyterate in the Church.
24. The commentaries he wrote at Alexandria.
25. How he mentioned the Canonical Scriptures.
26. How the bishops regarded him.
27. How Heraclas succeeded to the episcopate of the Alexandrians.
28. On the persecution under Maximin.
29. On Fabian, how he was miraculously designated bishop of the Romans by God.
30. What pupils of Origen there have been.
31. On Africanus.
32. The commentaries that Origen wrote at Cæsarea in Palestine.
33. On the error of Beryllus.
34. What happened under Philip.
35. How Dionysius succeeded Heraclas in the episcopate.
36. Other works composed by Origen.
37. On the dissension of the Arabians.
38. On the heresy of the Helkesaites.
39. On what happened under Decius.
40. On what befell Dionysius.
41. On those that suffered martyrdom at Alexandria itself.
42. On the other martyrdoms which Dionysius relates.
43. On Novatus, his manner of life, and his heresy.
44. A story of Dionysius about Serapion.
45. Letter of Dionysius to Novatus.
46. On the other letters of Dionysius.

1. Now when Severus also was stirring up persecution against the churches, in every place splendid martyrdoms of the champions of piety were accomplished, but with especial frequency at Alexandria. Thither, as to some great arena, were escorted from Egypt and the whole Thebais God's champions, who, through their most stedfast endurance in divers tortures and modes of death, were wreathed with the crowns laid up with God. Among these was Leonides, known as " the father of Origen," who was beheaded, leaving his son behind him quite young. It will not be out of place to describe briefly how deliberately his mind was set on the Divine Word from that early age, especially as the story about him has **2.** received exceedingly widespread notoriety. Many things, indeed, would there be to say, if one were to attempt at leisure to hand down in writing the man's life, and the narrative concerning him would require also a work of its own. Nevertheless, on the present occasion abridging most things as briefly as may be, we shall state some few of the facts concerning him, gathering what we set forth from certain letters and information derived from pupils of his, whose lives have been preserved even to our day.

2 In the case of Origen I think that even the facts from his very cradle,[1] so to speak, are worthy of mention. For Severus **203.** was in the tenth year of his reign, and Lætus was governor of Alexandria and the rest of Egypt, and Demetrius had just then received the episcopate of the communities 3 there in succession to Julian. When, therefore, the flame of persecution was kindled to a fierce blaze, and countless numbers were being wreathed with the crowns of martyrdom, Origen's soul was possessed with such a passion for martyrdom, while he was still quite a boy, that he was all eagerness to come to close quarters with danger, and to leap forward and 4 rush into the conflict. In fact, it were but a very little step and the end of his life was at hand, had not the divine and heavenly Providence, acting for the general good through his 5 mother, stood in the way of his zeal. She, at all events, at first had recourse to verbal entreaties, bidding him spare a mother's feelings; then, when he learnt that his father had been captured and was kept in prison, and his whole being was set on the desire for martyrdom, perceiving that his purpose

---

[1] Lit. " swaddling-clothes."

was more resolute than ever, she hid all his clothes, and so laid
6 upon him the necessity of remaining at home. And since
nothing else remained for him to do, and a zeal, intense beyond
his years, suffered him not to be quiet, he sent to his father
a letter on martyrdom most strongly urging him on, in which
he advises him in these very words, saying :

Take care not to change thy mind on our account.

Let this be recorded as the first proof of Origen's boyish
7 readiness of mind and genuine love of godliness. For indeed
in the study of the faith also he had already laid down a
good foundation, having been trained in the divine Scriptures
from the time that he was still a boy. Certainly it was no
ordinary amount of labour that he bestowed on these, since
his father, in addition to the customary curriculum, took pains
that these also should be for him no secondary matter.
8 On all occasions, for example, before he applied himself to
his secular [1] lessons, he kept urging him to train himself in the
sacred studies, exacting from him each day learning by heart
9 and repetition. And this the boy did with no lack of willing-
ness, nay, he worked with even excessive zeal at these studies,
so that he was not satisfied with reading the sacred words in a
simple and literal manner, but sought something further, and
busied himself, even at that age, with deeper speculations,
troubling his father by his questions as to what could be the
10 inner meaning of the inspired Scripture. And his father would
rebuke him ostensibly to his face, counselling him to seek
nothing beyond his years nor anything further than the manifest meaning ; but secretly in himself he rejoiced greatly, and
gave profound thanks to God, the Author of all good things,
that He had deemed him worthy to be the father of such a
11 boy. And it is said that many a time he would stand over the
sleeping boy and uncover his breast, as if a divine spirit were
enshrined therein, and kissing it with reverence count himself
happy in his goodly offspring. These are the stories, and
others akin to these, that they tell about Origen's boyhood.
12   But when his father had been perfected by martyrdom,
he was left destitute with his mother and six smaller brothers,
13 when he was not quite seventeen. His father's property
was confiscated for the imperial treasury, and he found himself,
along with his relatives, in want of the necessaries of life. Yet
he was deemed worthy of divine aid, and met with both
welcome and refreshment from a certain lady, very rich
in this world's goods and otherwise distinguished, who
nevertheless was treating with honour a well-known person,
one of the heretics at Alexandria at that time. He was an
Antiochene by race, but the lady we have mentioned kept him

---

[1] Ἑλληνικῶν.

at her house as her adopted son, and treated him with especial
14 honour. But although Origen of necessity had to consort
with him, he used to give clear proofs of his orthodoxy, at
that age, in the faith. For though very great numbers, not
only of heretics but also of our own people, were gathered
together with Paul (for that was the man's name), attracted
by his apparent skilfulness in speech, Origen could never be
persuaded to associate with him in prayer, keeping the rule
of the Church, even from boyhood, and "loathing"—the
very word he himself uses somewhere—the teachings of the
15 heresies. His father had brought him forward in secular
studies, and after his death he applied himself wholly with
renewed zeal to a literary training, so that he had a tolerable
amount of proficiency in letters; and, not long after his
father's perfecting, by dint of application to these studies, he
was abundantly supplied, for a person of his years, with the
necessaries of life.

3.　　And while he was devoting himself to teaching, as he himself
informs us somewhere in writing, since there was no one at
Alexandria set apart for catechetical instruction (for all had
been driven away by the threat of the persecution), some of
2 the heathen approached him to hear the word of God. Of these
Plutarch is pointed out as being the first, who after a noble
life was adorned also with a divine martyrdom; and the
second, Heraclas, Plutarch's brother. He also, in his own
person, afforded a fine example of a philosophic life and of
discipline, and was deemed worthy of the bishopric of the
3 204. Alexandrians in succession to Demetrius. Origen was
in his eighteenth year when he came to preside over the
catechetical school, and at this time also he came into pro-
minence when the persecutions were going on under Aquila
the governor of Alexandria. Then also he won for himself an
exceedingly wide reputation among all those who were of
the faith, by the kindly help and goodwill that he displayed
towards all the holy martyrs, unknown and known alike.
4 For he was present not only with the holy martyrs who were
in prison, not only with those who were under examination
right up to the final sentence, but also when they were being
led away afterwards to their death, using great boldness
and coming to close quarters with danger; so that, as he
courageously drew near and with great boldness greeted the
martyrs with a kiss, many a time the heathen multitude round
about in its fury went near to stoning him, but for the fact
that time after time he found the divine right hand to help
5 him, and so escaped marvellously; and this same divine and
heavenly grace on other occasions again and again—it is impossible to say how often—preserved him safely, when plots were
laid against him at that time because of his excessive zeal and
boldness for the word of Christ. And so great, then, was the

war of unbelievers against him, that soldiers were placed in
groups for his protection [1] round the house where he abode,
because of the number of those who were receiving instruction
6 from him in the sacred faith. Thus day by day the persecution against him blazed, so that there was no longer any place
for him in the whole city; from house to house he passed, but
was driven from all sides, on account of the numbers who
through him came over to the divine teaching. For in his
practical conduct were to be found to a truly marvellous
7 degree the right actions of a most genuine philosophy (for—as
the saying goes—as *was his speech*, so *was the manner of life* [2]
that he displayed, and as his manner of life, so his speech), and
it was especially for this reason that, with the co-operation of
the divine power, he brought so very many to share his zeal.
8   And when he saw still more pupils coming to him (for the
task of instruction had been entrusted by Demetrius, the
president of the church, to him alone), considering that the
teaching of letters [3] was not consonant with training in the
divine studies, without more ado he broke off the task of
teaching letters,[3] as being unprofitable and opposed to sacred
9 study; and then for a fitting reason, that he might never be
in need of others' assistance, he disposed of all the volumes
of ancient literature which formerly he so fondly cherished,
content if he who purchased them brought him four obols a
day. For a great number of years he continued to live like a
philosopher in this wise, putting aside everything that might
lead to *youthful lusts* [4]; all day long his discipline was to
perform labours of no light character, and the greater part
of the night he devoted himself to studying the divine
Scriptures; and he persevered, as far as possible, in the most
philosophic manner of life, at one time disciplining himself by
fasting, at another measuring out the time for sleep, which he
10 was careful to take, never on a couch, but on the floor. And
above all he considered that those sayings of the Saviour in
the Gospel ought to be kept which exhort us *not* [to provide]
two coats nor to use *shoes*,[5] nor, indeed, to be worn out with
11 thoughts about the future.[6] Yea, he was possessed of a zeal
beyond his years, and by persevering *in cold and nakedness* [7]
and going to the extremest limit of poverty, he greatly
astounded his followers, causing grief to numbers who besought him to share their goods, when they saw the labour
that he bestowed on teaching divine things. But he was not
12 one to slacken endurance. He is said, for example, to have
walked for many years without using a shoe of any description,
yea more, to have refrained for a great many years from the

---

[1] Or "with a view to capturing him."
[2] Cp. Plato, *Repub.* 400 D.   [3] Or "literature."
[4] 2 Tim. ii. 22.   [5] Matt. x. 10.
[6] Cp. Matt. vi. 34.   [7] 2 Cor. xi. 27.

usc of wine and all except necessary food, so that he actually
incurred the risk of undermining and destroying his con-
stitution.[1]

Origen's Pupils.

13   And by displaying proofs such as these of a philosophic
life to those who saw him, he naturally stimulated a large
number of his pupils to a like zeal, so that, even among the
unbelieving Gentiles and those from the ranks of learning and
philosophy, some persons of no small account were won by his
instruction.   By his agency these very persons received the
faith of the divine Word truly in the depths of the soul, and
were conspicuous at the persccution then taking place;
insomuch that even some of them were arrested and perfected
by martyrdom.

4.   The first of these, then, was Plutarch, he whom we mentioned
a little while ago.[2]   As this man was being led on the way to
death, he of whom we have been speaking, being present with
him to the very end of his life, was again almost killed by his
fellow-citizens, as being clearly responsible for his death.
But on that occasion also he was kept by the will of God.[3]
2 And, after Plutarch, Serenus was the second of Origen's
pupils to show himself a martyr, after he had given through
3 fire the proof of the faith he had received.   From the same
school Heraclides was the third martyr, and after him Hero,
the fourth; the former of these was still a catechumen, the
latter lately baptized.   Both were beheaded.   Further, in
addition to these, from the same school was proclaimed a
fifth champion of piety, one Serenus, a different person from
the first-mentioned of that name.   It is recorded that after
very great endurance of torture his head was taken off.
And, among the women, Herais, who was still under instruction
for baptism, as Origen himself says somewhere,

        received the baptism by fire,

and so ended her life.

5.   Seventh among them must be numbered Basilides, who led
away the famous Potamiœna.   The praise of this woman is
to this day still loudly sung by her fellow-countrymen, as of
one who on behalf of the chastity and virginity of her body,
in which she excelled, contended much with lovers (for
assuredly her body, as well as her mind, was in the full bloom
of its youthful beauty) ; as of one who endured much, and at
the end, after tortures that were terrible and fearful to relate,
2 was perfected by fire, along with her mother Marcella.   It is
said, in fact, that the judge, whose name was Aquila, after

----

[1] τοῦ θώρακος.   [2] 3. 2.   [3] Cp. 3. 4, 5.

inflicting severe tortures upon her entire body, at last threat
ened to hand her over to the gladiators for bodily insult,
and that, when after a brief period of reflection she was asked
what her decision was, she made a reply which involved from
3 their point of view something profane.   No sooner had she
spoken than she received the sentence, and Basilides, being
one of those serving in the army, took her and led her away
to death.   And as the crowd tried to annoy her, and insult
her with shameful words, he kept restraining them and driving
away the insulters, displaying the greatest pity and kindness
towards her.   She on her part accepted his fellow-feeling
for her and bade him be of good cheer, for that she would
ask him from her Lord, when she departed, and before long
4 would requite him for what he had done for her.   Thus
speaking, [it is said], she right nobly endured the end, boiling
pitch being poured slowly and little by little over different
5 parts of her body from head to toe.   Such was the contest
waged by this maiden celebrated in song.   And not long afterwards, when Basilides was asked by his fellow-soldiers to
swear for some reason or other, he stoutly affirmed that
swearing was absolutely forbidden in his case,[1] for that he
was a Christian and acknowledged it openly.   At first, indeed,
for a time they thought he was jesting, but when he continued stedfastly to affirm it, they brought him to the judge.
And when he admitted the constancy [of his profession] in his
6 presence, he was committed to prison.   When his brethren
in God came to him and enquired the reason of this sudden
and incredible impulse, it is said that he stated that three
days after her martyrdom Potamiæna appeared to him by
night, wreathing his head with a crown and saying that she
had called upon the Lord for him, and obtained what she
requested, and that before long she would take him to herself.
Thereupon the brethren imparted to him the seal in the Lord,
and on the day afterwards he gave notable testimony for the
7 Lord and was beheaded.   And it is related that many others
of those at Alexandria came over all at once to the word of
Christ in the time of the persons mentioned, because Potamiæna appeared to them in dreams and invited them.   But
this must suffice.

Clement of Alexandria.

6.   Pantænus was succeeded by Clement, who directed the
instruction at Alexandria up to such a date that Origen also
was one of his pupils.   In fact Clement, when compiling his
Stromateis, in the first book displays a chronological table,
using the death of Commodus as a terminus in measuring

[1] Op. Matt. v. 33, 34.

his dates;[1] so that it is clear that the work was composed by him under Severus, whose time this present account is describing.

Judas.

7. At this time Judas also, another writer, composed a written discourse on the *seventy weeks* in the book of Daniel[2]; he stops his record of time at the tenth year of the reign of Severus. 203. He also was of the opinion that the much talked of coming of the antichrist was then already near. So strongly did the persecution which was then stirred up against us disturb the minds of the many.

The Rash Act of Origen and its Consequences.

8. At that time, while Origen was performing the work of instruction at Alexandria, he did a thing which gave abundant proof of an immature and youthful mind, yet withal of faith 2 and self-control. For he took the saying, *There are eunuchs which made themselves eunuchs for the kingdom of heaven's sake*,[3] in too literal and extreme a sense, and thinking both to fulfil the Saviour's saying, and also that he might prevent all suspicion of shameful slander on the part of unbelievers (for, young as he was, he used to discourse on divine things with women as well as men), he hastened to put into effect the Saviour's saying, taking care to escape the notice of the 3 greater number of his pupils. But, wishful though he might be, it was not possible to hide a deed of this nature. Naturally Demetrius got to know of it later, since he was presiding over the community at that place; and while he marvelled exceedingly at him for his rash act, he approved the zeal and the sincerity of his faith, bade him be of good cheer, and urged him to attach himself now all the more to the work of instruction.

4 Such indeed was his attitude at that time. But not long afterwards, when the same person saw that he was prospering and a great man and distinguished and famous in the sight of all, overcome by a human weakness, he attempted to describe the deed as monstrous to the bishops throughout the world, when the most highly approved and distinguished bishops in Palestine, namely those of Cæsarea and Jerusalem, deeming Origen worthy of privilege and the highest honour, ordained 5 him to the presbyterate by laying on of hands. So, as he had then advanced to a position of great esteem, and had acquired no small reputation and fame for his virtue and wisdom in the eyes of all men everywhere, through lack of any other ground of accusation Demetrius spread grave scandal about the deed

[1] Clem., *Strom.* i. 21 (139, 140, 144).
[2] Dan. ix. 24.   [3] Matt. xix. 12.

that he had committed long ago when a boy, and had the temerity to include in his accusations those who raised him to the presbyterate.

6   This happened a little while afterwards. At that time, however, Origen was engaged at Alexandria in the work of divine instruction for all, without reserve, who came to him by night and in the course of the day, devoting his whole time untiringly to the divine studies and his pupils.

REIGN OF CARACALLA (211–217)

7   When Severus had held the principate for eighteen years, he was succeeded by his son Antonius.

Narcissus and Alexander.

At this time Alexander (being one of those who played the man during the persecution and after contending for the faith by their confessions were preserved by the Providence of God), whom we have mentioned lately as bishop of the church at Jerusalem,[1] was deemed worthy of the said bishopric, distinguished as he was for his confessions on behalf of Christ; Narcissus his predecessor being still alive.

9.   Many other miracles, indeed, of Narcissus do the citizens of the community call to mind, as handed down by the brethren in succession, and among these they relate that the following 2 wonder was performed by him. Once at the great all-night vigil of the Pascha it is said that the oil failed the deacons, and that when deep despondency seized the whole multitude, thereupon Narcissus commanded those who were preparing 3 the lights to draw water and bring it to him; that when this was no sooner said than done, he then prayed over the water, and bade them pour it down into the lamps with unfeigned faith in the Lord. And that when they did this, contrary to all reason by miraculous and divine power its nature was changed in quality from water into oil; and that for a very long time, from that day even to ours, a little was preserved as a proof of that wonder of former days by very many of the brethren there.

4   And they enumerate a great many other things about the life of this man worthy of mention, among which is the following. Certain miserable characters, not being able to endure his energy and the firmness of his conduct, and fearing that they could not stand a trial if captured (for they were conscious of many evil deeds), anticipated the event by devising an intrigue against him and spreading a certain grave slander

[1] § 4.

5 to his hurt.   Then, with a view to securing the belief of their
hearers, they strove to confirm their accusations by oaths;
one swore, " [if this is not true] may I be destroyed by fire ";
another, " may my body be wasted by an untoward disease ";
and the third, "may my eyes be blinded ".   But, swear
though they might, none of the faithful gave heed to them,
because the fame of Narcissus' sobriety and virtuous manner of
6 life was always well known to all.   He, nevertheless, could not
brook the wickedness of what had been said, and, besides, had
for a long time been pursuing the ascetic life; so he escaped
the whole company of the church, and spent many years
7 secretly in deserts and obscure parts of the country.   Yet the
great eye of Justice did not remain quiet at these deeds, but
with utmost speed visited upon those godless men the curses
with which in their perjury they had bound themselves.   So
the first was burnt to death with all his family, the house in
which he was staying being wholly set on fire one night from
absolutely no other cause than a small spark which happened
to fall on it; as for the second, his body was covered, all at
once, from head to toe with the disease that he had assigned
8 to himself as a penalty; and the third, perceiving the hap
of the other two, and fearing the inevitable judgment of
God who seeth all, made public confession of what they had
plotted together in common.   Yet, in the act of his repentance, so great were the lamentations by which he was wasted,
so many were the tears that he unceasingly poured forth, that
both eyes were destroyed.

10.   Such were the punishments that these men suffered for
their falsehood.   But as Narcissus had retired and no one
knew where he might be, it seemed good to those presiding over
the neighbouring churches to proceed to the appointment of
another bishop.   His name was Dius.   After a brief presidency he was succeeded by Germanion, and he in turn by
Gordius.   In his day Narcissus appeared from somewhere, as
if come to life again, and was once more summoned to the
presidency by the brethren, for all admired him to a still
greater degree because of his retirement and philosophic life,
and especially because of the punishment with which God had
deemed it meet to avenge him.

11.   And when he was no longer able to perform the ministry
on account of ripe old age, the above-mentioned [1] Alexander,
being bishop of another community, was called by a dispensation of God to a joint ministry with Narcissus, by a revelation
2 which appeared to him in a vision at night.   Whereupon, as
if in obedience to some oracle, he made the journey from the
land of the Cappadocians, where he was first deemed worthy
of the episcopate, to Jerusalem, for the purpose of prayer and

[1] 8. 7.

investigation of the [sacred] places. The people there gave him the most cordial welcome, and suffered him not to return home again, in accordance with another revelation which was seen by them also at night, and which vouchsafed an identical utterance of the clearest kind to those of them who were peculiarly zealous. For it indicated to them to go forth outside the gates and welcome as their bishop him who was fore-ordained of God. And doing this, with the common consent of the bishops who were administering the churches round about, they compelled him of necessity to remain.

3 And in fact Alexander himself in a personal letter to the Antinoites, which is still to this day preserved with us, mentions Narcissus as holding the chief place along with him, writing as follows, in these very words, at the close of the letter :

> Narcissus greets you, who before me was holding the position of bishop here, and now is associated with me in the prayers, having completed 116 years ; and exhorts you, as I do likewise, to be of one mind.

Bishops of Antioch.

4 So was it with these matters. But when Serapion entered upon his rest, Asclepiades succeeded to the bishopric of the church at Antioch, and he was himself distinguished for his 5 confessions in the persecution. Alexander also mentions his appointment, writing thus to the Antiochenes :

> Alexander, a slave and prisoner of Jesus Christ, to the blessed church of the Antiochenes, greeting in the Lord. Light and easy did the Lord make my bonds, when I learnt at the time of my imprisonment that by the Divine Providence Asclepiades, whose worthy faith makes him most suitable, had been entrusted with the bishopric of your holy church of the Antiochenes.

6 This epistle he indicates had been sent by the hand of Clement, writing at the close in this manner :

> But this letter I send unto you, my dear brethren, by the hand of Clement the blessed presbyter, a man virtuous and approved, of whom ye yourselves also have heard, and with whom ye will become acquainted ; who, when he was present here in the providence and oversight of the Master, both stablished and increased the Church of the Lord.

Serapion Bishop of Antioch.

12. Now it is likely, indeed, that other memoirs also, the fruit of Serapion's literary studies, are preserved by other persons, but there have come down to us only [1] those addressed To Domnus, one who had fallen away from the faith of Christ, at the time of the persecution, to Jewish *will-worship* [1] ; and

---

[1] Cp. Col. ii. 23.

[2] those To Pontius and Caricus, churchmen, and other
2 letters to other persons; and [3] another book has been composed by him Concerning what is known as the Gospel of
Peter, which he has written refuting the false statements in it,
because of certain in the community of Rhossus, who on the
ground of the said writing turned aside into heterodox teachings. It will not be unreasonable to quote a short passage
from this work, in which he puts forward the view he held about
the book, writing as follows :

3   For our part, brethren, we *receive* both Peter and the other
apostles *as Christ*,[1] but the writings which falsely bear their
names we reject, as men of experience, knowing that such were
4 not handed down to us. For I myself, when I came among you,
imagined that all of you clung to the true faith; and, without
going through the Gospel put forward by them in the name of
Peter, I said : If this is the only thing that seemingly causes
captious feelings among you, let it be read. But since I have
now learnt, from what has been told me, that their mind was
lurking in some hole of heresy,[2] I shall give diligence to come
5 again to you; wherefore, brethren, expect me quickly. But we,
brethren, gathering to what kind of heresy Marcianus belonged
(who [3] used to contradict himself, not knowing what he was saying,
6 as ye will learn from what has been written to you), were enabled [4]
by others who studied this very Gospel, that is, by the successors
of those who began it, whom we call Docetæ (for most of the ideas
belong to their teaching)—using [the material supplied] by them,
were enabled to go through it and discover that the most part
indeed was in accordance with the true teaching of the Saviour,
but that some things were added, which also we place below for
your benefit.

The Writings of Clement of Alexandria.

13.   Such are the writings of Serapion. But of Clement [1] the
Stromateis, all the eight books, are preserved with us, upon
which he bestowed the following title : "Titus Flavius
Clement's Stromateis of Gnostic Memoirs according to the
2 True Philosophy"; and of equal number with these are [2]
his books entitled Hypotyposeis, in which he mentions
Pantænus by name as his teacher, and has set forth his inter-
3 pretations of the Scriptures and his traditions. There is also
a book of his, [3] the Exhortation to the Greeks, and [4] the
three books of the work entitled Pædagogus, and [5] Who is
the Rich Man that is being Saved ? (such is the title of another
book of his), and [6] the treatise On the Pascha, and discourses
[7] On Fasting and [8] On Slander, and [9] the Exhortation to
Endurance, or To the Recently Baptized, and [10] the [book]

---

[1] Gal. iv. 14.
[2] Schwartz supposes that Serapion wrote : "was halting by reason
of some heresy."   [3] Reading ὅς, with Schwartz.
[4] Omitting γάρ, with Schwartz.

entitled the Ecclesiastical Canon, or Against the Judaizers,[1]
which he has dedicated to Alexander, the bishop mentioned
above.[2]

4 Now in [1] the Stromateis he has composed a patch-work,[3]
not only of the divine Scripture, but of the writings of the
Greeks as well, if he thought that they also had said anything
useful, and he mentions opinions from many sources, explaining
5 Greek and barbarian alike, and moreover sifts the false
opinions of the heresiarchs; and unfolding much history he gives
us a work of great erudition.   With all these he mingles also the
opinions of philosophers, and so he has suitably made the title
6 of the Stromateis to correspond to the work itself.   And in
them he has also made use of testimonies from the disputed
writings, the book known as the Wisdom of Solomon, and the
Wisdom of Jesus the Son of Sirach, and the Epistle to the
Hebrews, and those of Barnabas, and Clement, and Jude;
7 and he mentions Tatian's book Against the Greeks, and
Cassian, since he also had composed a chronography,[4] and
moreover Philo and Aristobulus and Josephus and Demetrius
and Eupolemus, Jewish writers, in that they would *show*, all
of them, in writing, that *Moses* and *the Jewish race* went back
8 further in their origins *than the Greeks*.[5]   And the books of
Clement, of which we are speaking, are full of much other
useful learning.   In the first of these he shows with reference
to himself that he came very near to the successors of the
Apostles [6];   and he promises in them also to write a commentary on Genesis.[7]

9 And in [6] his book On the Pascha he professes that he was
compelled by his companions to commit to writing traditions
that he had heard from the elders of olden time, for the
benefit of those that should come after;   and he mentions in it
Melito and Irenæus and some others, whose accounts also of
the matter he has set down.

14.   And in [2] the Hypotyposeis, to speak briefly, he has
given concise explanations of all the Canonical Scriptures, not
passing over even the disputed writings, I mean the Epistle of
Jude and the remaining Catholic Epistles, and the Epistle of
2 Barnabas, and the Apocalypse known as Peter's.   And as for
the Epistle to the Hebrews, he says indeed that it is Paul's,
but that it was written for Hebrews in the Hebrew tongue,
and that Luke, having carefully [8] translated it, published it for
the Greeks; hence, as a result of this translation, the same
complexion of style is found in this Epistle and in the Acts:

---

[1] Or, "To the Judaizers."   [2] 8. 7; 11.
[3] καταστρωσιν.   [4] Clem., *Strom.* i. 21 (101. 2).
[5] *Ib.* 15 (72. 4), 22 (150. 1), 21 (147. 2; 141. 1 ff.), 23 (153. 4).
[6] Lit., "the succession from the apostles."   *Ib.* 1 (11. 3), quoted v.
11. 5.   [7] Clem., *Strom.* iii. 14 (95. 2); iv. 1 (3. 3); vi. 18 (168. 4).
[8] φιλοτίμως.

3 but that the [words] " *Paul an apostle* " [1] were naturally not prefixed. For, says he,

in writing to Hebrews who had conceived a prejudice against him and were suspicious of him, he very wisely did not repel them at the beginning by putting his name.

4 Then lower down he adds :

But now, as the blessed elder used to say, since the Lord, being the *apostle*[2] of the Almighty, was sent to the Hebrews, Paul, through modesty, since he had been *sent to* the *Gentiles*,[3] does not inscribe himself as an apostle of the Hebrews, both to give due deference to the Lord and because he wrote to the Hebrews also out of his abundance, being *a preacher and apostle of the Gentiles*.[4]

5 And again in the same books Clement has inserted a tradition of the primitive elders with regard to the order of the Gospels, as follows. He said that those Gospels were first written which 6 include the genealogies, but that the Gospel according to Mark came into being in this manner : [5] When Peter had publicly preached the word at Rome, and by the Spirit had proclaimed the Gospel, that those present, who were many, exhorted Mark, as one who had followed him for a long time and remembered what had been spoken, to make a record of what was said ; and that he did this, and distributed the Gospel 7 among those that asked him. And that when the matter came to Peter's knowledge he neither strongly forbade it nor urged it forward. But that John, last of all, conscious that the outward [6] facts had been set forth in the Gospels, was urged on by his disciples, and, divinely moved by the Spirit, composed a spiritual Gospel. This is Clement's account.

Clement, Pantænus, Origen and Alexander.

8 And again Alexander, of whom we spoke before,[7] mentions Clement, and at the same time also Pantænus, in a certain letter to Origen, as men who had been known to him. He writes as follows :

For this also has proved to be the will of God, as thou knowest, that the friendship that comes to us from our forbears should remain unshaken, nay rather grow warmer and more stedfast. 9 For we know as fathers those blessed ones who went before us, with whom we shall be ere long : Pantænus, truly blessed and my master, and the holy Clement, who was my master and profited me, and all others like them. Through these I came to know thee, who art the best in all things, and my master and brother.

---

[1] Gal. i. 1, etc. [2] Heb. iii. 1. [3] Acts xxii. 21.
[4] 1 Tim. ii. 7 ; 2 Tim. i. 11 ; Rom. xi. 13.
[5] Lit., " had this dispensation."
[6] Lit., " bodily." [7] c. 11, etc.

Origen's Visit to Rome and his Work at Alexandria.

10   Thus do these matters stand. Now Adamantius (for this also was Origen's name), when Zephyrinus was at that time ruling the church of the Romans, himself states in writing somewhere that he stayed at Rome. His words are :

> Desiring to see the most ancient church of the Romans.

11   After spending a short time there, he returned to Alexandria, and indeed continued to fulfil in that city his customary work of instruction with all zeal, Demetrius, the bishop of the people there, still exhorting and well-nigh entreating him to ply diligently his task of usefulness for the brethren.

15.   But when he saw that he was becoming unable for the deeper study of divine things, namely, the examination and translation of the sacred writings, and in addition for the instruction of those who were coming to him and did not give him time to breathe (for one batch of pupils after another kept frequenting from morn to night his lecture room), he made a division of the numbers. Selecting Heraclas from among his pupils, a man who was zealous of divine things, and, as well, a very learned person and no tyro in philosophy, he gave him a share in the task of instruction, assigning to him the preliminary studies of those who were just learning their elements, and reserving for himself the teaching of the experienced pupils.

16.   And so accurate was the examination that Origen brought to bear upon the divine books, that he even made a thorough study of the Hebrew tongue, and got into his own possession the original writings in the actual Hebrew characters, which were extant among the Jews. Thus, too, he traced the editions of the other translators of the sacred writings besides the Seventy ; and besides the beaten track of translations, that of Aquila and Symmachus and Theodotion, he discovered certain others, which were used in turn, which, after lying hidden for a long time, he traced and brought to light, I know not from 2 what recesses. With regard to these, on account of their obscurity (not knowing whose in the world they were) he merely indicated this : that the one he found at Nicopolis, 3 near Actium, and the other in such another place. At any rate, in the Hexapla of the Psalms, after the four well-known editions, he placed beside them not only a fifth but also a sixth and a seventh translation ; and in the case of one of these he has indicated again that it was found at Jericho in a 4 jar in the time of Antoninus the son of Severus. All these he brought together, dividing them into clauses and placing them one over against the other, together with the actual Hebrew text ; and so he has left us the copies of the Hexapla, as it is called. He made a further separate arrangement of the edition

of Aquila and Symmachus and Theodotion together with that
of the Seventy, in the Tetrapla.

17.   Now as regards these same translators it is to be noted
that Symmachus was an Ebionite. Those who belong to the
heresy of the Ebionites, as it is called, affirm that the Christ
was born of Joseph and Mary, and suppose Him to be a mere
man, and strongly maintain that the law ought to be kept in a
more strictly Jewish fashion, as also we saw somewhere from
the foregoing history.[1] And memoirs too of Symmachus are
still extant, in which, by his opposition to the Gospel according
to Matthew, he seems to hold the above-mentioned heresy.
These, along with other interpretations of the Scriptures by
Symmachus, Origen indicates that he had *received* from a
certain *Juliana*, who, he says, inherited in her turn the books
from Symmachus himself.[2]

18.   At this time also Ambrose, who held the views of the heresy
of Valentinus, was refuted by the truth as presented by
Origen, and, as if his mind were illuminated by light, gave his
  2 adhesion to the true doctrine as taught by the Church. And
many other cultured persons, since Origen's fame was noised
abroad everywhere, came to him to make trial of the man's
sufficiency in the sacred books. And numbers of the heretics,
and not a few of the most distinguished philosophers, gave
earnest heed to him, and, one might almost say, were instructed
  3 by him in secular philosophy as well as in divine things. For
he used to introduce also to the study of philosophy as many
as he saw were naturally gifted, imparting geometry and arithmetic and the other preliminary subjects, and then leading
them on to the systems which are found among philosophers,
giving a detailed account of their treatises, commenting upon
and examining into each, so that the man was proclaimed as a
  4 great philosopher even among the Greeks themselves. And
many persons also of a more ignorant character he urged to
take up the ordinary elementary studies, declaring that they
would derive no small advantage from these when they came
to examine and study the divine Scriptures. For this reason
he deemed especially necessary even for himself a training in
secular and philosophic studies.

Origen's Study of Profane Literature.

9.   Now, as witnesses also to his achievements in this direction,
we have the Greek philosophers themselves who flourished in
his day, in whose treatises we find frequent mention of the
man. Sometimes they would dedicate their books to him,
sometimes submit their own labours to him for judgment,
  2 as to a master. But why need one say this, when even
Porphyry, who settled in our day in Sicily, issued treatises

[1] iii. 27. 2.   [2] Annotation of Origen (see note).

against us, attempting in them to slander the sacred Scriptures, and mentioned those who had given their interpretations of them ? And since he could not by any means bring any base charge against our opinions, for lack of argument he turned to deride and slander their interpreters also, and among these
3 Origen especially. He says that in his early manhood he had known him ; and he tries to slander the man, but unknown to himself really commends him, telling the truth in some cases, where he could not speak otherwise, in others telling lies, where he thought he could escape detection ; and at one time accusing him as a Christian, at another describing his devotion to the study of philosophy.
4   But hear the very words that he uses :

Some, in their eagerness to find an explanation of the wickedness of the Jewish writings rather than give them up, had recourse to interpretations that are incompatible and do not harmonize with what has been written, resulting in approval and praise of their own, rather than in a defence of foreign, goods. For they boast that the things said plainly by Moses are riddles, treating them as divine oracles full of hidden mysteries, and bewitching the mental judgment by their own pretentious obscurity; and so they put forward their interpretations.

5   Then, after other remarks, he says :

But this kind of absurdity must be traced to a man whom I met when I was still quite young, who had a great reputation, and still holds it, because of the writings he has left behind him, I mean Origen, whose fame has been widespread among the teachers of
6 this kind of learning. For this man was a hearer of Ammonius, who had the greatest proficiency in philosophy in our day; and so far as a grasp of knowledge was concerned he owed much to his master, but as regards the right choice in life he took the
7 opposite road to him. For Ammonius was a Christian, brought up in Christian doctrine by his parents, yet, when he began to think and study philosophy, he immediately changed his way of life conformably to the laws; but Origen, a Greek educated in Greek learning, drove headlong towards barbarian recklessness; and making straight for this he hawked himself and his literary skill about; and while his manner of life was Christian and contrary to the law, in his opinions about material things and the Deity he played the Greek, and introduced Greek ideas into
8 foreign fables. For he was always consorting with Plato, and was conversant with the writings of Numenius and Cronius, Apollophanes and Longinus and Moderatus, Nicomachus and the distinguished men among the Pythagoreans; and he used also the books of Chæremon the Stoic and Cornutus, from whom he learnt the figurative interpretation, as employed in the Greek mysteries, and applied it to the Jewish writings.

9   These statements were made by Porphyry in the third treatise of his writings against Christians. And while he tells the truth about the man's training and erudition, he clearly

lies (for what is the opponent of Christians not prepared to do ?) where he says that Origen came over from the Greeks, and that Ammonius lapsed from a godly life into paganism.

10 For Origen kept safely the Christian teaching which he had from his parents, as the history above made clear [1]; and Ammonius maintained his inspired philosophy pure and unshaken right up to the very end of his life. To this fact the man's works witness to the present day, and the widespread fame that he owes to the writings he left behind him, as, for example, that entitled On the Harmony of Moses and Jesus, and all the other works that are to be found in the possession of lovers of literature.

11 Let these things be stated to prove at once the false one's calumny and Origen's great knowledge of Greek learning. With regard to such learning also he writes as follows in a certain epistle, defending himself against those who found fault with him for his zeal in that direction :

12 But as I was devoted to the word, and the fame of our proficiency was spreading abroad, there approached me, sometimes heretics, sometimes those conversant with Greek learning, and especially philosophy, and I thought it right to examine both the opinions of the heretics, and also the claim that the philosophers 13 make to speak concerning truth. And in doing this we followed the example of Pantænus, who, before us, was of assistance to many, and had acquired no small attainments in these matters, and also Heraclas, who now has a seat in the presbytery of the Alexandrians, whom I found with the teacher of philosophy, and who had remained five years with him before I began to attend 14 his lectures. And though he formerly wore ordinary dress, on his teacher's account he put it off and assumed a philosophic garb, which he keeps to this day, all the while studying Greek books as much as possible.

Origen Visits Arabia and Palestine.

This, indeed, is what he wrote in defence of his Greek training. 15 But at this time, while he was living at Alexandria, one of the military appeared on the scene and delivered letters to Demetrius, the bishop of the community, and to the then governor of the province of Egypt, from the ruler of Arabia, to the intent that he should send Origen with all speed for an interview with him. He duly arrived in Arabia, but soon accomplished the object of his journey thither, and returned 16 again to Alexandria. But after the lapse of some time no small warfare broke out again in the city, and leaving Alexandria secretly he went to Palestine and abode at Cæsarea. And although he had not yet received ordination to the presbyterate, the bishops there requested him to discourse and expound the divine Scriptures publicly in the church.

[1] 2. 7 ff.

17 That this is so is clear from what Alexander, the bishop of
Jerusalem, and Theoctistus, the bishop of Cæsarea, write with
reference to Demetrius.   They make their defence somewhat as
follows :

And he added to his letter that such a thing had never been
heard of, nor taken place hitherto, that laymen should preach
in the presence of bishops ; though I do not know how he comes to
18 say what is evidently not true.   For instance, where there are
found persons suited to help the brethren, they also are invited to
preach to the people by the holy bishops, as, for example, in
Laranda Euelpis by Neon, and in Iconium Paulinus by Celsus,
and in Synnada Theodore by Atticus, our blessed brother bishops.
And it is likely that this thing happens in other places also without our knowing it.

In this way honour was paid to the man of whom we are
speaking, while he was still young, not only by his fellow-
countrymen [1] but also by the bishops in a foreign land.
19 But since Demetrius once again recalled him by letter, and by
men who were deacons of the Church urged him to come back
with speed to Alexandria, he returned and continued to labour
with his accustomed zeal.

The Literature of this Period.

20.   Now there flourished at that time many learned churchmen, and the letters which they penned to one another are
still extant and easily accessible.   They have been preserved
even to our day in the library at Ælia, equipped by Alexander,
then ruling the church there ; from which also we have been
able ourselves to gather together the material for our present
work.
2   Of these Beryllus has left behind him, as well as letters,
varied and beautiful compositions.   He was bishop of the
Arabians at Bostra.
And likewise also Hippolytus, who also presided over another
church somewhere.
3   And there has reached us also a Dialogue of Gaius, a very
learned person (which was set a-going at Rome in the time
of Zephyrinus), with Proclus the champion of the heresy of
the Phrygians.   In which, when curbing the recklessness and
audacity of his opponents in composing new Scriptures, he
mentions only thirteen epistles of the holy Apostle, not
numbering the Epistle to the Hebrews with the rest ; seeing
that even to this day among the Romans there are some who
do not consider it to be the Apostle's.

---

[1] τῶν συνήθων.

REIGNS OF MACRINUS (217–218) AND ELAGABALUS (218–222)

*1.   But indeed when Antoninus had reigned for seven years and six months he was succeeded by Macrinus; and when he had continued in office for a year, again another Antoninus received the Roman government.

Roman Bishops.

In the first year of the latter, Zephyrinus, the bishop of the Romans, departed this life, having held the ministry
2 **218–9.** for eighteen entire years. After him Callistus was entrusted with the episcopate; he survived five years and then left the ministry to Urban.

REIGN OF ALEXANDER SEVERUS (222–235)

After this the Emperor Alexander succeeded to the principate of the Romans, Antoninus having continued in office for only four years.

Bishops of Antioch.

At this time also Philetus succeeded Asclepiades in the church of the Antiochenes.

Origen and Mamœa.

3   Origen's fame was now universal, so as to reach the ears of the Emperor's mother, Mamæa by name, a religious woman if ever there was one. She set great store on securing a sight of the man, and on testing that understanding of divine things
4 which was the wonder of all. She was then staying at Antioch, and summoned him to her presence with a military escort. And when he had stayed with her for some time, and shown her very many things that were for the glory of the Lord and the excellence of the divine teaching, he hastened back to his accustomed duties.

The Writings of Hippolytus.

2.   At that very time also Hippolytus, besides very many other memoirs, composed the treatise On the Pascha, in which he sets forth a register of the times and puts forward a certain canon of a sixteen-years [cycle] for the Pascha, using the first
222–3. year of the Emperor Alexander as a terminus in measuring his dates. Of his other treatises the

following have reached us : [1] On the Hexaemeron, [2] On what followed the Hexaemeron, [3] Against Marcion, [4] On the Song, [5] On Parts of Ezekiel, [6] On the Pascha, [7] Against All the Heresies ; and very many others also might be found preserved by many people.

How Ambrose Assisted Origen.

23.   Starting from that time also Origen's commentaries on the divine Scriptures had their beginning, at the instigation of Ambrose, who not only plied him with innumerable verbal exhortations and encouragements, but also provided him 2 unstintingly with what was necessary. For as he dictated there were ready at hand more than seven shorthand-writers, who relieved each other at fixed times, and as many copyists, as well as girls skilled in penmanship ; for all of whom Ambrose supplied without stint the necessary means. Nay further, he contributed to Origen a vast amount of zeal in the earnest study of the divine oracles, a zeal which more than anything else acted as an incentive to him to compose his commentaries.

Succession of Bishops.

3   Such was the state of affairs when Pontianus succeeded Urban, who had been bishop of the church of the Romans for eight years, and Zebennus came after Philetus as [bishop] of the [church] of the Antiochenes.

Origen visits Cæsarea and Greece.

4   In their day Origen journeyed to Greece through Palestine because of an urgent necessity in Church matters, and received the laying-on of hands for the presbyterate at Cæsarea from the bishops there. The agitation that was set on foot concerning him on this account, and the decisions made by those who presided over the churches on the matters agitated, as well as the other contributions that he made as he was reaching his prime to the study of the divine Word, require a separate composition, and we have given a fairly full account of them in the second [book] of the Apology that we have written on his behalf.

Books written by Origen at Alexandria.

24.   But to that information it is necessary to add that in the sixth of his Expositions on the [Gospel] according to John he indicates that he composed the first five while he was still at Alexandria ; but of this work on the whole of the self-same Gospel only

2 twenty-two tomes have come our way.   And [we must also state] that in the ninth of those On Genesis (there are twelve in all) he shows that not only were those before the ninth written at Alexandria, but also [his commentary] on the first twenty-five Psalms, and, as well, those on Lamentations, of which there have come to us five tomes.   In these he mentions also those

3 On the Resurrection, of which there are two.   Moreover he wrote his De Principiis before his removal from Alexandria, and he composed the [books] entitled Stromateis, ten in number, in the same city in the reign of Alexander, as is shown by the annotations in his own hand in front of the tomes.

Origen's Statements about the Scriptures.

25.   Now while expounding the first Psalm he has set forth the catalogue of the sacred Scriptures of the Old Testament, writing somewhat as follows in these words :

But it should be known that there are twenty-two canonical books, according to the Hebrew tradition; the same as the number of the letters of their alphabet.

2   Then further on he adds as follows :

These are the twenty-two books according to the Hebrews : That which is entitled with us Genesis, but with the Hebrews, from the beginning of the book, Brēsith, that is " In the beginning." Exodus, Ouelle smōth, that is, " These are the names." Leviticus, Ouikra, " And he called." Numbers, Ammes phekōdoim. Deuteronomy, Elle addebareim, " These are the words." Jesus the son of Nave, Iōsoue ben noun. Judges, Ruth, with them in one book, Sōphteim.   Of Kingdoms i, ii, with them one, Samuel, " The called of God." Of Kingdoms iii, iv, in one, Ouammelch david, that is, " The kingdom of David."   Chronicles i, ii, in one, Dabrē iamein, that is, " Words of days." Esdras i, ii, in one, Ezra, that is, "Helper."   Book of Psalms, Sphar thelleim. Proverbs of Solomon, Melōth. Ecclesiastes, Kōelth. Song of Songs (not, as some suppose, Songs of Songs), Sir assireim. Esaias, Iessia.   Jeremiah with Lamentations and the Letter, in one, Jeremia.   Daniel, Daniēl.   Ezekiel, Ezekiēl.   Job, Jōb. Esther, Esthēr.   And outside these there are the Maccabees, which are entitled Sar bēth sabanai el.

3   These things he inserts in the above mentioned treatise. But in the first of his [Commentaries] on the Gospel according to Matthew, defending the canon of the Church, he gives his testimony that he knows only four Gospels, writing somewhat as follows :

4   . . . as having learnt by tradition concerning the four Gospels, which alone are unquestionable in the Church of God under heaven, that first was written that according to Matthew, who was once a tax-collector but afterwards an apostle of Jesus Christ, who published it for those who from Judaism

197

came to believe, composed as it was in the Hebrew language.
5 Secondly, that according to Mark, who wrote it in accordance with
Peter's instructions, whom also Peter acknowledged as his son in
the catholic epistle, speaking in these terms : *She that is in
Babylon, elect together with you, saluteth you; and so doth Mark my
6 son.*[1]   And thirdly, that according to Luke, who wrote, for
those who from the Gentiles [came to believe], *the Gospel* that
was *praised* by Paul.[2]   After them all, that according to John.

7   And in the fifth of his Expositions on the Gospel according
to John the same person says this with reference to the
epistles of the apostles :

But he who was *made sufficient* to become a *minister of the new
covenant, not of the letter but of the spirit,*[3] even Paul, who *fully
preached the Gospel from Jerusalem and round about even unto
Illyricum,*[4] did not so much as write to all the churches that he
taught; and even to those to which he wrote he sent but a few
8 lines.   And *Peter, on* whom the *Church* of Christ is *built, against
which the gates of Hades shall not prevail,*[5] has left one acknowledged epistle, and, it may be, a second also; for it is doubted.
9 Why need I speak of him who *leaned back on Jesus' breast,*[6] John,
who has left behind one Gospel, confessing that he could write so
many *that even the world itself* could *not contain them*;[7] and he
wrote also the Apocalypse, being ordered to keep silence *and not
10 to write the voices of seven thunders* ?[8]   He has left also an epistle
of a very few lines, and, it may be, a second and a third; for not
all say that these are genuine.   Only, the two of them together
are not a hundred lines long.

11   Furthermore, he thus discusses the Epistle to the Hebrews,
in his Homilies upon it :

That the character of the diction of the epistle entitled To the
Hebrews has not the apostle's rudeness in speech, who confessed
himself *rude in speech,*[9] that is, in style, but that the epistle is
better Greek in the framing of its diction, will be admitted by
12 everyone who is able to discern differences of style.   But again,
on the other hand, that the thoughts of the epistle are admirable,
and not inferior to the acknowledged writings of the apostle, to
this also everyone will consent as true who has given attention
to reading the apostle.

13   Further on, he adds the following remarks :

But as for myself, if I were to state my own opinion, I should
say that the thoughts are the apostle's, but that the style and
composition belong to one who called to mind the apostle's
teachings and, as it were, made short notes of what his master
said.   If any church, therefore, holds this epistle as Paul's, let
it be commended for this also.   For not without reason have
14 the men of old time handed it down as Paul's.   But who wrote

---

[1] 1 Pet. v. 13.   [2] See 2 Cor. viii. 18.
[3] 2 Cor. iii. 6.   [4] Rom. xv. 19.
[5] Matt. xvi. 18.   [6] John xiii. 25.
[7] John xxi. 25.   [8] Rev. x. 3, 4.
[9] 2 Cor. xi. 6.

the epistle, in truth God knows. Yet the account which has
reached us [is twofold], some saying that Clement, who was bishop
of the Romans, wrote the epistle, others, that it was Luke, he
who wrote the Gospel and the Acts. . . .

Origen migrates to Cæsarea.

26.
232.
But this must suffice on these matters. Now it was in the
tenth year of the above-mentioned reign that Origen removed from Alexandria to Cæsarea, leaving to Heraclas
the Catechetical School for those in the city.

Bishops of Alexandria.

And not long afterwards Demetrius, the bishop of the
church of the Alexandrians, died, having continued in the
ministry for forty-three entire years. He was succeeded by
Heraclas.

Origen in Cappadocia and Palestine.

27.
Now at this time Firmilian, bishop of Cæsarea in Cappadocia, was distinguished; he displayed such esteem for
Origen, that at one time he would summon him to his own
parts for the benefit of the churches; at another, journey
himself to Judæa, and spend some time with him for his own
betterment in divine things. Nay further, Alexander, who
presided over the [church] of Jerusalem, and Theoctistus, [who
presided] at Cæsarea, continued their attendance on him the
whole time, as their only teacher, and used to concede to
him the task of expounding the divine Scriptures, and the
other parts of the Church's instruction.

REIGN OF MAXIMIN (235–238)

28.
But to resume. When Alexander the Emperor of the
Romans had brought his principate to an end after thirteen
years, he was succeeded by Maximin Cæsar.

Origen and the Persecution.

He, through ill will towards the house of Alexander, since
it consisted for the most part of believers, raised a persecution,
ordering the leaders of the Church alone to be put to death, as
being responsible for the teaching of the Gospel. Then also
Origen composed his work On Martyrdom, dedicating the
treatise to Ambrose and Protoctetus, a presbyter of the
community at Cæsarea; for in the persecution no ordinary
distress had befallen them both, in which distress it is recorded

that these men were distinguished for the confession they
made during the period, not more than three years, that the
reign of Maximin lasted. Origen has noted this particular
time for the persecution, in the twenty-second of his Expositions of the Gospel according to John, and in various letters.

REIGN OF GORDIAN (238–244)

Succession of Bishops.

29.   Gordian having succeeded to the Roman government after
Maximin, Pontianus, when he had been bishop of the church
of Rome for six years, was succeeded by Anteros; who
exercised his ministry for a month, and was succeeded by
2 Fabian. It is said that Fabian, after the death of Anteros,
came from the country along with others and stayed at Rome,
where he came to the office in a most miraculous manner,
3 thanks to the divine and heavenly grace. For when the
brethren were all assembled for the purpose of appointing
him who should succeed to the episcopate, and very many
notable and distinguished persons were in the thoughts of
many, Fabian, who was there, came into nobody's mind. But
all of a sudden, they relate, a dove flew down from above and
settled on his head, in clear imitation of the descent of *the*
4 *Holy Ghost in the form* of a *dove upon* the Saviour; [1] whereupon the whole people, as if moved by one divine inspiration,
with all eagerness and with one soul cried out " worthy,"
and without more ado took him and placed him on the
episcopal throne.

At that very time also Zebennus, bishop of Antioch, departed
this life and Babylas succeeded to the rule ; and in Alexandria,
Heraclas, having received the ministry after Demetrius, was
succeeded in the Catechetical School there by Dionysius,
who had also been one of Origen's pupils.

Origen's pupils at Cæsarea.

Now while Origen was plying his accustomed tasks at
Cæsarea, many came to him, not only of the natives, but also
numbers of foreign pupils who had left their *own countries*.
Among these as especially distinguished we know to have been
Theodore, who was the self-same person as that renowned
bishop in our day, Gregory, and his brother Athenodore. Both
of them were strongly enamoured of Greek and Roman
studies, but Origen instilled into them *a passion for philosophy*
and *urged* them to exchange their former love for the study of
divine truth.[2] Five whole years they continued with him,

[1] Luke iii. 22.   [2] Gregory, *Pan.* 6. 78, 83, 84.

and made such progress in divine things that while still young both of them were deemed worthy of the episcopate in the churches of Pontus.

Africanus.

31. At that time Africanus also, the author of the books entitled Cesti, was well known. A letter of his, written to Origen, is extant; he was at a loss as to whether the story of Susanna in the book of Daniel were a spurious forgery. Origen makes a 2 very full reply to it. And of the same Africanus there have reached us as well five books of Chronographies, a monument of labour and accuracy. In these he says that he himself made a journey to Alexandria because of the great fame of Heraclas; who, as we have stated, was greatly distinguished for philosophy and other Greek learning, and was entrusted with the 3 bishopric of the church there.[1] And another letter of the same Africanus is extant, to Aristides, On the supposed discord between the Genealogies of Christ in Matthew and Luke. In it he establishes very clearly the harmony of the evangelists from an account that came down to him, which by anticipation I set forth in the proper place in the first book of the present work.[2]

Works written by Origen.

32. And Origen too at this time was composing his Commentaries on Isaiah, and at the same time those also on Ezekiel. Of the former, thirty tomes have come our way on the third part of Isaiah, up to *the vision of the beasts in the desert*;[3] and on Ezekiel five and twenty, the only ones that he has written on 2 the whole prophet. And having come at that time to Athens, he finished the commentary on Ezekiel, and began that on the Song of Songs, carrying it forward there up to the fifth book. And returning to Cæsarea he brought these also to an end, 3 numbering ten. Why should one draw up the exact catalogue of the man's works here and now, seeing that such would require a special study? And we did record it in our account of the life of Pamphilus, that holy martyr of our day, in which, in showing the extent of Pamphilus' zeal for divine things, I quoted as evidence the lists in the library that he had brought together of the works of Origen and of other ecclesiastical writers; and from these anyone who pleases can gather the fullest knowledge of the works of Origen that have reached us. But we must now proceed with our history.

[1] 3. 2; 15; 19. 13 f.; 26.   [2] i. 7.   [3] Isai. xxx. 6 (LXX).

Origen and Beryllus.

33.   Beryllus, who, as we have mentioned a little above,[1] was bishop of Bostra in Arabia, perverting the Church's standard, attempted to introduce things foreign to the faith, daring to say that our Saviour and Lord did not pre-exist in an individual existence of His own before His coming to reside among men, nor had He a divinity of His own, but only the Father's
2 dwelling in Him. Whereupon, after a large number of bishops had held questionings and discussions with the man, Origen, being invited along with others, entered in the first place into conversation with the man to discover what were his opinions, and when he knew what it was that he asserted, he corrected what was unorthodox, and, persuading him by reasoning, established him in the truth as to the doctrine, and restored
3 him to his former sound opinion. And there are still extant to this very day records in writing both of Beryllus and of the synod that was held on his account, which contain at once the questions Origen put to him and the discussions that took place in his own community, and all that was done on that occasion.
4 And a great many other things about Origen have been handed down to memory by the older men of our day, which I think it well to pass over, as they do not concern the present work. But all that it was necessary to know of his affairs, these also one may gather from the Apology that was written on his behalf by us and Pamphilus, that holy martyr of our day, a work that we were at pains to compose conjointly because of the fault-finders.

REIGN OF PHILIP (244–249)

34.   When after six whole years Gordian brought his government of the Romans to an end, Philip along with his son Philip succeeded to the principate.

A Story About Philip.

It is recorded that he, being a Christian, wished on the day of the last paschal vigil to share along with the multitude the prayers at the church, but was not permitted to enter by him who was then presiding, until he confessed and numbered himself among those who were reckoned to be in sins and were occupying the place of penitence; for that otherwise, had he not done so, he would never have been received by [the president] on account of the many charges made concerning him. And it is said that he obeyed readily, displaying by his actions how genuine and pious was his disposition towards the fear of God.

[1] 20. 2.

Bishops of Alexandria.

35.
247. It was the third year of his reign when Heraclas departed this life, after presiding for sixteen years over the churches at Alexandria; Dionysius took up the episcopal office.

Works of Origen.

36. Then indeed, as was fitting, when the faith was increasing and our doctrine was boldly proclaimed in the ears of all, it is said that Origen, who was over sixty years of age, inasmuch as he had now acquired immense *facility* from long *preparation*,[1] permitted shorthand-writers to take down the discourses delivered by him in public, a thing that he had never before allowed.

2   At that time also he composed the treatises, eight in number, in answer to the work against us, entitled True Discourse of Celsus the Epicurean, and his twenty-five tomes on the Gospel according to Matthew, and those on the twelve

3 prophets, of which we found only five and twenty. And there is extant also a letter of his to the Emperor Philip himself, and another to his wife Severa, and various other letters to various persons. As many of these as we have been able to bring together, preserved as they were here and there by various persons, we arranged in separate roll-cases,[2] so that they might no longer be dispersed. These letters number

4 more than a hundred. And he wrote also to Fabian the bishop of Rome, and to very many other rulers of churches, with reference to his orthodoxy. You will find these facts also established in the sixth book of the Apology we wrote on the man's behalf.

Origen and the Arabian Dissension.

37. Once more in Arabia at the above-mentioned time other persons sprang up, introducing a doctrine foreign to the truth, and saying that the human soul dies for a while in this present time, along with our bodies, at their death, and with them turns to corruption; but that hereafter, at the time of the resurrection, it will come to life again along with them. Moreover, when a synod of no small dimensions was then assembled together, Origen was again invited, and there opened a discussion in public on the subject in question, with such power that he changed the opinions of those who had formerly been deluded.

[1] Gregory, *Pan.* 2. 10.   [2] τόμων περιγραφαί.

Origen on the Helkesaites.

38.   At that time also another perverse opinion had its beginning, the heresy known as that of the Helkesaites, which no
sooner began than it was quenched. Origen mentions it in
a public address on the eighty-second Psalm, in some such
words as these :

There has come just now a certain man who prides himself on
being able to champion a godless and very impious opinion, of
the Helkesaites, as it is called, which has lately come into opposition with the churches. I shall lay before you the mischievous
teachings of that opinion, that you may not be carried away by
it. It rejects some things from every Scripture ; again, it has
made use of texts from every part of the Old Testament and the
Gospels ; it rejects the Apostle entirely. And it says that to
deny is a matter of indifference, and that the discreet man will
on occasions of necessity deny with his *mouth, but* not *in his
heart.*[1] And they *produce a certain book* of which they say that
it has fallen from heaven, and that he who has *heard* it *and
believes* will *receive forgiveness of his sins* [2]—a forgiveness other
than that which Christ Jesus has bestowed.

REIGN OF DECIUS (249–251)

39.   But to resume. When Philip had reigned for seven years
he was succeeded by Decius.

The Persecution : 1. Successors of Martyred Bishops.

He, on account of his enmity towards Philip, raised a
persecution against the churches, in which Fabian was perfected by martyrdom at Rome, and was succeeded in the
episcopate by Cornelius.

2   In Palestine, Alexander, the bishop of the church of Jerusalem, appeared once more for Christ's sake at Cæsarea
before the governor's courts, and for the second time distinguished himself by the confession he made ; he underwent the trial of imprisonment, crowned with the venerable
3 hoary locks of ripe old age.   And when after the splendid and
manifest testimony that he gave in the governor's courts he
fell asleep in prison, Mazabanes was proclaimed as his successor
in the episcopate at Jerusalem.

4   And when at Antioch Babylas, in like manner to Alexander,
after confession departed this life in prison, Fabius was made
president of the church there.

---

[1] Book of Helkesai (see note).   [2] *Ib.*

The Persecution : 2. The sufferings of Origen.

Now the nature and extent of that which happened to Origen at the time of the persecution, and what was the end thereof; how the evil demon marshalled all his forces in rivalry against the man, how he led them with every device and power, and singled him out, above all others upon whom he made war at that time, for special attack; the nature and extent of that which he endured for the word of Christ, chains and tortures, punishments inflicted on his body, punishments as he lay in iron and in the recesses of his dungeon; and how, when for many days his feet were stretched four spaces in that instrument of torture the stocks, he bore with a stout heart threats of fire and everything else that was inflicted by his enemies; and the kind of issue he had thereof, the judge eagerly striving with all his might on no account to put him to death; and what sort of sayings he left behind him after this, sayings full of help for those who needed uplifting—[of all these matters] the man's numerous letters contain both a true and accurate account.

The Persecution : 3. The sufferings of Dionysius, the Alexandrians and the Egyptians.

40.   As to that which befell Dionysius, I shall quote from a letter of his against Germanus, where, speaking of himself, he gives the following account :

Now I for my part speak also *before God*, and He knows if *I lie*.[1] Acting not on my own judgment nor apart from God
2 have I taken flight; but on a former occasion also, when the persecution under Decius was publicly proclaimed, that selfsame hour Sabinus sent a " frumentarius " to seek me out, and on my part I remained four days at my house, expecting the arrival of the "frumentarius"; but he went around searching everything, the roads, the rivers, the fields, where he suspected I was hidden or walking, but was holden with blindness and did not find the house. For he did not believe that, pursued as I
3 was, I was staying at home. And after the fourth day, when God bade me depart, and miraculously made a way, with difficulty did I and the boys and many of the brethren set out together. And that this was the work of the Divine Providence, the sequel showed, in which we proved helpful, it may be, to some.

4   Then, after some intervening remarks, he tells what happened to him after the flight, adding as follows :

For I, indeed, falling about sunset into the hands of the soldiers, together with those who were with me, was brought to Taposiris, but Timothy by the Divine Providence happened to

---

[1] Gal. i. 20.

be absent and to escape being seized; but coming afterwards
he found the house deserted and servants guarding it, and us
completely taken captive.

5   And further on he says :

And what was the way in which He wonderfully brought it
about ? For the truth shall be told. One of the country folk
met Timothy fleeing and distraught, and inquired the reason of
6 his haste. And he spoke out the truth, and when the other
heard it (now he was off to take part in a marriage feast, for it
is their custom to spend the entire night in such gatherings) he
went in and told those who were reclining at table. And they
all, with a single impulse, as if at a preconcerted signal, rose up,
and came running with all speed; and bursting in upon us they
gave a shout, and when the soldiers that were guarding us
straightway took to flight, they came up to us, lying as we were
7 on pallets without bedding. And I—God knows that at first I
thought they were robbers coming to plunder and steal—stayed
on the bed, naked save for my linen shirt, and the rest of my
garments that were lying by I held out to them. But they bade
8 me get up and go out with all speed. And then, gathering why
they were come, I cried out, begging and beseeching them to go
away and leave us alone; and I asked them, if they wished to
do me a good turn, to anticipate those who were leading me
away and to cut off my head themselves. And while I was
thus shouting, as those who were my companions and partakers
in everything know, they raised me up forcibly. And I let
myself fall on my back on the ground, but they seized me by
9 the hands and feet and dragged and brought me outside. And
there followed me the witnesses of all these things, Gaius, Faustus,
Peter and Paul; who also took me up in their arms and brought
me out of the little town, and setting me on the bare back of
an ass led me away.

Such is the account Dionysius gives concerning himself.
41. But the same person in a letter to Fabius, bishop of the
Antiochenes, gives the following account of the contests of
those who suffered martyrdom at Alexandria under Decius :

It was not with the imperial edict that the persecution began
amongst us, but it preceded it by a whole year; and that prophet
and creator of evils for this city, whoever he was, was beforehand in stirring and inciting the masses of the heathen against
2 us, fanning anew the flame of their native superstition. Aroused
by him and seizing upon all authority for their unholy deeds,
they conceived that this kind of worship of their gods—the
thirsting for our blood—was the only form of piety.
3   First, then, they seized an old man named Metras, and bade
him utter blasphemous words; when he refused to obey they
belaboured his body with cudgels, stabbed his face and eyes
with sharp reeds, and leading him to the suburbs stoned him.
4   Then they led a woman called Quinta, a believer, to the idol
temple, and were for forcing her to worship. But when she
turned away and showed her disgust, they bound her by the

feet and dragged her through the whole city over the rough pavement, so that she was bruised by the big stones, beating her all the while; and bringing her to the same place they stoned 5 her to death. Then with one accord they all rushed to the houses of the godly, and, falling each upon those whom they recognized as neighbours, they harried, spoiled and plundered them, appropriating the more valuable of their treasures, and scattering and burning in the streets the cheaper articles and such as were made of wood, until they gave the city the appear- 6 ance of having been captured by enemies. But the brethren gave way and gradually retired, and, like those of whom Paul also testified, they *took joyfully the spoiling of* their *possessions*.[1] And I know not if there be any—save, it may be, a single one who fell into their hands—who up to the present has denied the Lord.

7 Moreover, they seized then that marvellous aged virgin Apollonia, broke out all her teeth with blows on her jaws, and piling up a pyre before the city threatened to burn her alive, if she refused to recite along with them their blasphemous sayings. But she asked for a brief space, and, being released, without flinching [2] she leaped into the fire and was consumed.

8 Serapion they laid hold of at his own home, broke all his limbs by the severe tortures they inflicted, and cast him down head foremost from the upper storey.

Now there was no way, no thoroughfare, no alley by which we could go, either by night or during the day: always and everywhere all were shouting, that he who did not join in the chorus of blasphemy must immediately be dragged off and burnt. 9 And thus this state of things continued at its height for a long time. But the strife and civil war came upon the wretched men, and turned on themselves the fury of which we had been the object; and for a brief space we breathed again, since they had no time to indulge their anger against us. Immediately, however, the news was spread abroad of the change from that rule that had been more kindly to us, and great was the fear of threatened 10 punishment that hung over us. And, what is more, the edict arrived, and it was almost like that which was predicted by our Lord, well nigh the most terrible of all, *so as, if possible*, to cause 11 to stumble *even the elect*.[3] Nevertheless all cowered with fear. And of many of the more eminent persons, some came forward immediately through fear, others in public positions were compelled to do so by their business, and others were dragged by those around them. Called by name they approached the impure and unholy sacrifices, some pale and trembling, as if they were not for sacrificing but rather to be themselves the sacrifices and victims to the idols, so that the large crowd that stood around heaped mockery upon them, and it was evident that they were by nature cowards in everything, cowards both to die and to 12 sacrifice. But others ran eagerly towards the altars, affirming by their forwardness that they had not been Christians even formerly; concerning whom the Lord very truly predicted that they shall *hardly* be saved.[4] Of the rest, some followed one or

---

[1] Heb. x. 34. [2] Or, "eagerly."
[3] Matt. xxiv. 24. Eus. has σκανδαλίσαι for Matthew's πλανᾶσθαι.
[4] A very free reference to Matt. xix. 23; cp. Mark x. 23; Luke xviii. 24.

13 other of these, others fled; some were captured, and of these some went as far as *bonds and imprisonment*,[1] and certain, when they had been shut up for many days, then forswore themselves even before coming into court, while others, who remained firm for a certain time under tortures, subsequently gave in.

14　But the firm and blessed pillars of the Lord, being strengthened by Him, and receiving power and stedfastness in due measure according to the mighty faith that was in them, proved them-

15 selves admirable martyrs of His kingdom. Of these the first was Julian, a man who suffered from gout, unable to stand or walk. He was brought up with two others who carried him, of whom the one straightway denied; the other, Cronion by name, but surnamed Eunus, and the old man Julian himself, confessed the Lord, and were carried upon camels through the whole city, very large in extent as ye know, and thus uplifted were beaten, and in the end, surrounded by all the people, burnt in quick-

16 lime. A soldier who stood by as they were being led off, opposed those who insulted them; and, when the crowd cried out, Besas, that brave warrior of God, was brought up, and after excelling

17 in the great war of piety was beheaded. And another, a Libyan by race, Macar,[2] true both to his name and the [Lord's] bene-diction,[3] though the judge urged him strongly to deny, was not induced, and so was burnt alive. And after these Epimachus and Alexander, when they had remained a long time in prison, enduring to the end countless agonies from scrapers and scourges, were also burnt in quicklime.

18　And with them four women: Ammonarion, a holy virgin, though tortured vigorously by the judge for a very long time, inasmuch as she had made it plain beforehand that she would not utter anything of what he bade her, kept true to her promise, and was led away. And as to the rest, Mercuria, an aged woman of reverend mien, and Dionysia, the mother indeed of many children, who yet did not love them above the Lord, when the governor was ashamed to ply continued tortures all to no end, and to be worsted by women, were put to death by the sword, and so had trial of no further tortures. For these Ammonarion, true champion, had taken upon herself on behalf of all.

19　Hero and Ater and Isidore, Egyptians, and with them a young boy of about fifteen named Dioscorus were delivered up. And at first [the governor] tried to wheedle the lad by words, as one easily led astray, and to compel him by tortures, as one that would easily give in; but Dioscorus neither obeyed nor yielded.

20 The rest he savagely tore in pieces, and, when they endured, committed them also to the flames. But, marvelling at the splendid bearing of Dioscorus in public and the wise answers he made to his questions in private, he let him off, saying that he granted him a period of delay to repent, on account of his youth. And now the most godly Dioscorus is with us, having remained for a still longer contest and a more lasting conflict.

21　A certain Nemesion, he also an Egyptian, was falsely accused of consorting with robbers, and when he had cleared himself before the centurion of that charge so foreign to his character, he was informed against as being a Christian, and came bound before the governor. He most unjustly inflicted on him twice

---

[1] Heb. xi. 36.　　　[2] " Blessed."　　　[3] See Matt. v. 10, 11.

as many tortures and scourgings as he did on the robbers, and burnt him between them, thus honouring him, happy man, with a likeness to Christ.[1]

22 A whole band of soldiers, Ammon and Zeno and Ptolemy and Ingenuus, and with them an old man Theophilus, had taken their stand before the court. Now a certain man was being tried as a Christian, and at that moment was inclining towards denial, when these men standing by ground their teeth, cast looks at him, stretched out their hands and made gestures with

23 their bodies. And when all turned towards them, before anyone could otherwise seize them, they ran of their own accord to the prisoner's dock, saying that they were Christians; so that both the governor and his assessors were filled with fear, and those who were on their trial appeared very courageous in the face of their future sufferings, while the judges were affrighted. So these men marched from the court in proud procession, exulting in their witness, *God spreading abroad their fame* [2] gloriously.

42. And many others throughout the cities and villages were torn in pieces by the heathen, of whom I shall mention one as an example. Ischyrion was acting as the hired steward of one of the rulers. His employer bade him sacrifice; when he refused he insulted him, when he abode by his refusal he abused him foully; and as he still remained firm he took a very large stick, thrust it through his bowels and vital organs, and so killed him.

2 What need is there to speak of the multitude of those who *wandered in deserts and mountains*,[3] and perished by hunger and thirst and frost and diseases and robbers and wild beasts? Such of them as survive bear testimony to their election and victory; but one fact in connexion with these men also I shall adduce as

3 evidence. Chæremon was bishop of the city called Nilopolis, and of extreme age. He fled to the Arabian mountain with his wife,[4] and never returned, nor could the brethren ever lay eyes again either on them or their bodies, although they made a long

4 and thorough search. But many in that same Arabian mountain were reduced to utter slavery by barbarian Saracens. Of these some were with difficulty ransomed for large sums, others have not yet been, up to this day.

And I have not given this account, brother, to no purpose, but that you may know all the terrible things that happened with us. Those who have had a larger experience of them would know more examples.

5 Then, after a little, he adds as follows:

Therefore the divine martyrs themselves among us, who now are assessors of Christ, and share the fellowship of His kingdom, and take part in His decisions and judge along with Him,[5] have espoused the cause of certain of the fallen brethren who became answerable for the charge of sacrificing; and seeing their conversion and repentance, they judged it had the power to prove acceptable to Him who *hath no pleasure* at all *in the death* of the sinner, *but rather* his *repentance ;* [6] and so they received and

---

[1] Cp. Matt. xxvii. 38; Mark xv. 27; Luke xxiii. 33; John xix. 18.
[2] 2 Cor. ii. 14.   [3] A free ref. to Heb. xi. 38.   [4] συμβίῳ.
[5] Cp. Matt. xix. 28; 1 Cor. vi. 2, 3; Rev. xx. 4.
[6] Cp. Ezek. xxxiii. 11; 2 Pet. iii. 9.

admitted them to the worship of the Church as " consistentes," and
6 gave them fellowship in their prayers and feasts. What do ye
counsel us, brethren, on these matters ?   What are we to do ?
Are we to be of like opinion and mind with them, uphold their
decision and concession, and deal kindly with those they pitied ?
Or shall we esteem their decision unjust, and set ourselves up as
critics of their opinion, cause grief to kindness, and do away with
their arrangement ?

Novatianism.

Now these words Dionysius suitably added, raising the
question about those who had proved weak in the time of
43. persecution, since Novatus, a presbyter of the church of the
Romans, being lifted up by arrogance against these, as if
there was no longer any hope of salvation for them, not
even if they were to perform everything that a genuine conversion and a pure confession demand, became the leader of a
separate sect of those who, in their pride of mind, styled
themselves Puritans.
2   Whereupon a very large synod was assembled at Rome, of
sixty bishops and a still greater number of presbyters and
deacons, while in the rest of the provinces the pastors in
their several regions individually considered the question as
to what was to be done. It was unanimously decreed that
Novatus, together with the partners of his arrogance, and
those who decided to agree with the man's brother-hating
and most inhuman opinion, should be considered as strangers
to the Church,[1] but that such of the brethren as had fallen
into the misfortune should be treated and restored with the
medicines of repentance.
3   Now there have reached us [1] a letter of Cornelius, bishop
of the Romans, to Fabius, bishop of the church of the Antiochenes, telling the facts concerning the Roman Synod, and
what was decreed by them of Italy and Africa and the regions
thereabout ; and, again, [2] another of Cyprian and of those
with him in Africa, composed in the Latin language, in which
it was made clear that they also agreed that those who had
suffered trial should meet with succour, and that in the
reason of things it was fitting that the leader of the heresy
should be excommunicated from the Catholic Church, and
4 likewise all those who were led away with him. To these
was subjoined [3] a certain other letter of Cornelius, on the
resolutions of the synod ; and, again, [4] another on the doings
of Novatus. There is nothing to prevent me from quoting
parts of this last, so that those who read this book [2] may
5 know about him. In explaining, then, to Fabius what kind
of manner of man Novatus was, Cornelius writes these very
words :

[1] ἀλλοτρίοις τῆς ἐκκλησίας.   [2] γραφή.

But that you may know that for a long time back this marvellous fellow has been *seeking the office of a bishop*,[1] and has succeeded in concealing in his heart this his violent desire, using as a veil for his insane folly the fact that he had the confessors
6 with him from the beginning, I wish to speak. Maximus, one of our presbyters, and Urban, both of whom twice reaped the highest meed of renown by confession, and Sidonius, and Celerinus, a man who, by the mercy of God, bore with the utmost endurance all kinds of tortures, and by the strength of his faith strengthened the weakness of his body, and so has mightily overcome the adversary—these men marked him, and detecting the craftiness and duplicity that was in him, his perjuries and falsehoods, his unsociability and wolf-like friendship, returned to the holy Church. And all the knavish tricks and devices that he had long dissembled in his heart, they made known in the presence both of a number of bishops, and also of very many presbyters and laymen, bewailing and repenting of the fact that for a brief space they had left the Church under the persuasion of this treacherous and malicious wild beast.

7 Then shortly afterwards he says :

How extraordinary a change and transformation, brother beloved, we have beheld to have taken place in him in a little while! For in sooth this highly distinguished person, who was in the habit of pledging himself by some terrible oaths in no wise to *seek the office of a bishop*,[1] of a sudden appears as a bishop
8 as if he were cast into our midst by some contrivance.[2] For in sooth this master of doctrine, this champion of the Church's discipline, when he was attempting to wrest and filch away the episcopate that was not given him from above, chose to himself two companions who had renounced their own salvation, that he might send them to a small and very insignificant part of Italy, and entice thence by some made-up device three bishops, rough and very simple men. He confidently maintained and affirmed the necessity of their coming quickly to Rome, on the pretext that any dissension whatsoever that had arisen might be ended by their activity as mediators, conjointly with other
9 bishops. When they arrived, inasmuch as they were too simple, as we said before, for the unscrupulous devices of the wicked, they were shut up by certain disorderly men like himself, and at the tenth hour, when they were drunk, and sick with the after effects, he forcibly compelled them to give him a bishop's office by a counterfeit and vain laying on of hands, an office that he assumed by crafty treachery since it did not fall to his lot.
10 One of the bishops not long afterwards returned to the Church, bewailing and confessing his fault; with whom we had communion as a layman, all the laity present interceding for him. And as for the remaining bishops, to these we appointed successors, whom we sent into the places where they were.
11 This vindicator, then, of the Gospel did not know that there should be one bishop in a catholic church, in which he was not ignorant (for how could he be ?) that there are forty-six presbyters, seven deacons, seven sub-deacons, forty-two acolytes, fifty-two

---

[1] 1 Tim. iii. 1. [2] μαγγάνου.

exorcists, readers and door-keepers, above fifteen hundred widows and persons in distress, all of whom are supported by the grace
12 and loving kindness of the Master. But not even did this great multitude, so necessary in the Church, that number who by God's providence were rich and multiplying, nor an immense and countless laity, turn him from such a desperate failure and recall him to the Church.

13 And again, further on, he adds to these remarks as follows :

But come, let us next say in what deeds or in what kind of conduct he placed his confidence so as to aspire to the episcopate. Was it because from the beginning he had been brought up in the Church, and had fought many conflicts on her behalf, and had been through the midst of dangers, many and great, for the
14 sake of religion ? Not so. The occasion of his acceptance of the faith was Satan, who resorted to him and dwelt in him for a long time. While he was being healed by the exorcists he fell into a grievous sickness, and, as he was considered to be all but dead, received baptism by affusion on the very bed in which he
15 lay, if indeed one may say that such a man has received it. Nor yet indeed did he obtain the other things, when he recovered from his sickness, of which one should partake according to the rule of the Church, or the sealing by the bishop. And as he did not obtain these, how could he obtain the Holy Spirit ?

16 And shortly afterwards he says again :

. . . he who through cowardice and love of life at the time of persecution denied that he was a presbyter. For when he was requested and exhorted by the deacons to leave the cell in which he shut himself, and bring all the help to the brethren that it is right and possible for a presbyter to bring to brethren who are in danger and in need of succour, so far was he from obeying the deacons' exhortations, that he even went away and departed in anger. For he said that he no longer wished to be a presbyter, since he was enamoured of a different philosophy.

17 Passing over a few things, he again adds as follows :

For when this illustrious person deserted the Church of God, in which, when he came to believe, he was deemed worthy of the presbyterate through the favour of the bishop, who laid his hand on him to confer that order (meeting the opposition of all the clergy and many lay persons as well—since one who has received clinical baptism by affusion owing to sickness, as Novatus had, might not be ordained to an order—with the request that he should be allowed to ordain this man alone). . . .

18 Then he adds something else, the worst of all the man's offences, saying thus :

For when he has made the offerings, and is distributing to each his portion, as he gives it [into their hands] he compels the wretched persons to utter an oath instead of the blessing, taking in both his hands those of him who had received, and not letting go until they swear saying thus (for I shall use his

very words): "Swear to me by the Blood and Body of our Lord Jesus Christ never to forsake me and turn to Cornelius."
19 And the miserable person does not taste until he first calls down a curse upon himself, and instead of saying the Amen as he receives that bread, he says, "I will not return to Cornelius."

20 And after other remarks he again says as follows :

But know that now he has become bare and desolate, for every day the brethren desert him and go back to the Church. And Moses, that blessed martyr who just now bore a goodly and marvellous testimony amongst us, while he was still in the world, perceiving his insane arrogance, broke off communion with him and with the five presbyters who, along with him, had separated themselves from the Church.

21 And at the close of the letter he has made a catalogue of the bishops present at Rome who condemned the stupidity of Novatus, indicating at once both their names and the name
22 of the community over which each one presided; and of those who were not present, indeed, at Rome, but who signified in writing their assent to the judgment of the aforesaid, he mentions the names and, as well, the city where each lived and from which each wrote.

A story of Serapion.

This is what Cornelius wrote for the information of Fabius,
44. bishop of Antioch. But to this same Fabius, when he was inclining somewhat towards the schism, Dionysius also, he of Alexandria, wrote, making many other remarks with reference to repentance in his letter to him, and describing the conflicts of those lately martyred at Alexandria. In the course of his narrative he tells a certain astonishing tale, which must needs be handed down in this work. It is as follows :

2 But this one example that happened amongst us I shall set forth for thee. There was a certain Serapion amongst us, an old man and a believer, who lived blamelessly for a long time, but in the trial fell. This man oftentimes besought [absolution], and no one paid him heed. For indeed he had sacrificed. And, falling sick, he continued for three successive days speechless and
3 unconscious; but on the fourth he rallied a little, and calling his grandson to him, he said : "How long, my child, do ye hold me back ? Haste ye, I pray, and grant me a speedy release ; do thou summon me one of the presbyters." And having said
4 this he again became speechless. The boy ran for the presbyter. But it was night, and he was unwell and could not come. Yet since I had given an order that those who were departing this life, if they besought it, and especially if they had made supplication before, should be absolved, that they might depart in hope, he gave the little boy a small portion of the eucharist, bidding him soak it and let it fall in drops down into the old man's mouth.

5 Back came the boy with it, and when he was near, before he entered, Serapion revived again and said, "Hast thou come, child ? The presbyter could not come, but do thou quickly what he bade thee, and let me depart." The boy soaked it and at the same time poured it into his mouth, and when he had 6 swallowed a little he straightway gave up the ghost. Was it not plain that he was preserved and remained until he obtained release, that, with his sin blotted out, he might be acknowledged for all the good deeds he had done ?

Letter of Dionysius to Novatian.

45.   Such is the account of Dionysius. But let us see the kind of letter that the same person wrote also to Novatus, who was then disturbing the Roman brotherhood. Since, then, he put forward some of the brethren as an excuse for his defection and schism, as having been compelled by them to proceed to this length, see how Dionysius writes to him :

Dionysius to Novatianus a brother, greeting. If thou wast led on unwillingly, as thou sayest, thou wilt prove it by retiring willingly. For a man ought to suffer anything and everything rather than divide the Church of God, and it were not less glorious to incur martyrdom to avoid schism than to avoid idolatry, nay, in my opinion it were more. For in the one case a man is a martyr for the sake of his own single soul, but in the other for the sake of the whole Church. And if thou wert even now to persuade or compel the brethren to come to one mind, thy recovery will be greater than thy fall, and the one will not be reckoned, while the other will be praised. But if they obey thee not, and thou hast no power, *by all means save thine own soul.*[1] I pray that thou mayest fare well and cleave to peace in the Lord.

Letters of Dionysius.

46.   This also [he wrote] to Novatus. And he wrote also [1] to the Egyptians a letter On Repentance, in which he has set forth his opinions with reference to those who had fallen, 2 outlining degrees of failures. And [2] to Colon (he was bishop of the community of the Hermopolitans) a personal letter of his is extant On Repentance, and [3] another in the nature of a rebuke [2] to his flock at Alexandria. Among these there is also [4] the letter written to Origen On Martyrdom ; and [5] to the brethren at Laodicea over whom Thelymidres presided as bishop ; and he wrote [6] to those in Armenia, likewise 3 On Repentance, whose bishop was Meruzanes. In addition to all these he wrote also [7] to Cornelius of Rome, when he received his letter against Novatus, in which also he clearly indicates that he had been invited by Helenus, bishop at Tarsus in Cilicia, and the rest of the bishops with him, namely Firmilian in Cappadocia and Theoctistus in Palestine, to

[1] Gen. xix. 17 (LXX).   [2] ἐπιστρεπτική.

attend the synod at Antioch, where certain were attempting
4 to strengthen the schism of Novatus. Moreover he writes
that he had received information that Fabius had fallen
asleep, and that Demetrian was appointed his successor in
the episcopate of Antioch. And he writes also with reference
to the bishop of Jerusalem, saying in these very words :

For Alexander, that wonderful man, being put in prison,
happily entered into his rest.

5   Next to this there is also [8] another extant, a " diaconic "
letter of Dionysius to those in Rome through Hippolytus.
To the same people he composed [9] another letter On Peace,
and [10] likewise On Repentance, and again [11] another to
the confessors there while they were still in agreement with
the opinion of Novatus. And to these same persons he
wrote [12, 13] two more, after they had returned to the
Church. And in his communications with many others, likewise by letter, he has left behind a varied source of profit to
those who still to this day set store by his writings.

BOOK VII

The Seventh Book of the Ecclesiastical History contains the following :

1. On the evil disposition of Decius and Gallus.
2. The bishops of Rome in their day.
3. How Cyprian, along with the bishops on his side, was the first to hold the opinion that those who were turning from heretical error ought to be cleansed by baptism.
4. How many letters Dionysius composed on this subject.
5. On the peace after the persecution.
6. On the heresy of Sabellius.
7. On the abominable error of the heretics and the God-sent vision of Dionysius, and the rule of the Church which he had received.
8. On the heterodoxy of Novatus.
9. On the ungodly baptism of the heretics.
10. On Valerian and the persecution in his day.
11. On the things that then happened to Dionysius and those in Egypt.
12. On those who were martyred at Cæsarea in Palestine.
13. On the peace under Gallienus.
14. The bishops who flourished at that time.
15. How Marinus was martyred at Cæsarea.
16. The story of Astyrius.
17. On the signs at Paneas of the mighty working of our Saviour.
18. On the throne of James.
19. On the festal letters of Dionysius, where also he draws up a canon concerning the Pascha.
20. On the happenings at Alexandria.
21. On the disease that visited it.
22. On the reign of Gallienus.
23. On Nepos and his schism.
24. On the Apocalypse of John.
25. On the letters of Dionysius.
26. On Paul of Samosata and the heresy put together by him at Antioch.
27. On the illustrious bishops who were well known at that time.
28. How Paul was refuted and excommunicated.
29. On the perverse heterodoxy of the Manicheans, which began precisely at that time.
30. On the distinguished churchmen of our own day, and which of them remained until the attack upon the churches.

Preface.

In the composition of the seventh book of the Ecclesiastical History Dionysius, the great bishop of the Alexandrians, will again assist us in our task by his own words, indicating in turn each of the things that were done in his day, by means of the letters he has left behind. From that point of time my record will take its beginning.

THE REIGN OF GALLUS (251–253)

1.   When Decius had reigned for an entire period of less than two years, he was forthwith murdered along with his sons, and Gallus succeeded him. At this time Origen died, having completed the seventieth year save one of his life. Now when writing to Hermammon, Dionysius speaks as follows, with reference to Gallus :

But not even did Gallus recognize the fault [in the policy] of Decius, nor yet did he look to that which caused his fall, but he stumbled against the same stone that was before his eyes. For when his reign was prospering, and matters were going according to his mind, he drove away the holy men who were supplicating God for his peace and health. Therefore along with them he banished also their prayers on his behalf.

Succession of Bishops of Rome.

2.   So much, then, concerning him. But in the city of the Romans, when Cornelius brought his episcopate to an end after about three years, Lucius was appointed his successor ; but he exercised his ministry for less than eight entire months, and dying transmitted his office to Stephen.

The Controversy about Baptism.

To him Dionysius indited the first of his letters On Baptism, no small question having then arisen as to whether it were necessary to cleanse by means of baptism those who were turning from any heresy whatsoever. A custom, which was at any rate old, having prevailed in such cases to use only 3. prayer with the laying on of hands, Cyprian, pastor of the community at Carthage, was the first of those of his day to consider that they ought not to be admitted otherwise than by having been first cleansed from their error by baptism. But Stephen, thinking that they ought not to make any innovation contrary to the tradition that had prevailed from the beginning, was full of indignation thereat.

219

Extracts from the Epistles of Dionysius on Baptism.

4. Dionysius, therefore, having communicated with him on this point at very great length in a letter, at its close shows that with the abatement of the persecution the churches everywhere, rejecting the innovation of Novatus, had resumed peace among themselves. He writes thus :

5. But know now, brother, that all the churches in the East and still further away, which were formerly divided, have been united, and all their presidents everywhere are of like mind, rejoicing above measure at the unexpected arrival of peace : Demetrian at Antioch, Theoctistus at Cæsarea, Mazabanes at Ælia, Marinus at Tyre (Alexander having fallen asleep), Heliodorus at Laodicea (for Thelymidres has entered into his rest), Helenus at Tarsus and all the churches of Cilicia, Firmilian and all Cappadocia. For I name only the more eminent bishops, 2 to avoid making my letter long and my discourse tedious. Nevertheless, the Syrias as a whole and Arabia, which ye constantly help and to which ye have now written, and Mesopotamia and Pontus and Bithynia, and, in a word, all everywhere rejoice exceedingly in their concord and brotherly love, giving glory to God.

Bishops of Rome.

3 Such is the account of Dionysius. But when Stephen had fulfilled his ministry for two years, he was succeeded by Xystus.

Extracts (continued).

To him Dionysius penned a second letter on baptism, showing the opinion and decision both of Stephen and of the other bishops. About Stephen he speaks thus :

4 Now he had written formerly with reference both to Helenus and Firmilian and all those from Cilicia and Cappadocia and, in fact,[1] Galatia and all the provinces that border on these, to the effect that he would not hold communion in future with them either, for this same reason ; since, says he, they rebaptize heretics. 5 And look thou at the importance of the matter. For decrees on this question have been actually passed in the largest synods of bishops, as I learn, so that those who come over from heresies are first placed under instruction, then *washed* [2] and *purged* again from the filth of *the old* and impure *leaven*.[3] And I wrote beseeching him on all these matters.

6 And, after other remarks, he says :

And to our beloved fellow-presbyters also, Dionysius and Philemon, who had formerly been of the same opinion as Stephen and wrote [some letters] to me about the same matters, at first I wrote briefly, but now at greater length.

---

[1] δῆλον ὅτι.   [2] 1 Cor. vi. 11.   [3] 1 Cor. v. 7.

So much with regard to the question of which I am speaking. But when indicating in the same letter, with reference to the followers of the Sabellian heresy, that they were prevalent in his day, he speaks thus :

For as to the doctrine now set on foot at Ptolemais in the Pentapolis, an impious doctrine which contains great blasphemy concerning the Almighty God, Father of our Lord Jesus Christ, and great unbelief as to His only-begotten Son, the *firstborn of all creation*,[1] the Word who was made man, and which is without perception of the Holy Spirit,—when there came to me from both sides both documents and also the brethren who were ready to discuss the question, I wrote some letters, as I was able by the help of God, giving an exposition of the matter in a somewhat didactic manner ; of which I send thee the copies.

And in the third of those on baptism, which the same Dionysius wrote to Philemon the Roman presbyter, he relates the following :

But as for me, I read both the compositions and the traditions of the heretics, polluting my soul for a little with their abominable thoughts, yet all the while deriving this advantage from them, that I could refute them for myself and loathed them far more.
2 And indeed a certain brother, one of the presbyters, attempted to dissuade and frighten me from becoming involved in the mire of their wickedness, for he said that I should injure my own
3 soul ; and said truly, as I perceived. But a vision sent by God came and strengthened me, and a word of command was given me, saying expressly : "Read all things that may come to thy hand. For thou art able to sift and *prove* each matter ;[2] which thing was originally the cause of thy faith." I accepted the vision, as agreeing with the apostolic saying addressed to the stronger : "Be approved money-changers."

4 Then, making certain remarks about all the heresies, he goes on to say :

This rule and pattern I myself received from our blessed pope [3] Heraclas. For those who came over from the heresies, although they had departed from the Church (or rather, had not even done that, but, while still reputed members of the congregation, were charged with frequenting some false teacher) he drove from the Church, and refused to listen to their entreaties until they publicly declared all that they had heard from *them that oppose themselves*,[4] and then he admitted them to the congregation, without requiring of them a second baptism. For they had formerly received the holy [baptism] from him.

5 And again, after a protracted discussion of the question, he adds as follows :

I have learnt this also, that the Africans did not introduce this practice now for the first time, but that long before, in the

---

[1] Col. i. 15.   [2] Cp. 1 Thess. v. 21.
[3] πάπα.   [4] 2 Tim. ii. 25.

days of the bishops that were before us, in the most populous churches and the synods of the brethren, in Iconium and Synnada and in many places, this course was adopted. And I do not dare to overturn their decisions and involve them in strife and contention. *For thou shalt not remove*, he says, *thy neighbour's landmarks, which thy fathers* placed.[1]

6   The fourth of his letters on baptism was written to Dionysius of Rome, who at that time had been deemed worthy of the presbyterate, but not long afterwards received also the episcopate there. From it one may learn how that he too had witness paid him by Dionysius of Alexandria for his learning and admirable qualities. In the course of his letter to him he mentions the affair of Novatus in the following terms :

8.   For it is with good reason indeed that we feel enmity towards Novatian, who caused a division in the Church and drew away some of the brethren to impieties and blasphemies, and introduced as well most profane teaching about God, and falsely accuses our most compassionate Lord Jesus Christ of being without mercy; and above all this, he sets at naught the holy washing, and overturns the faith and confession that precede it, and entirely banishes the Holy Spirit from them, even though there was some hope of His remaining with or even returning to them.

9.   And his fifth letter was written to Xystus, bishop of the Romans. In it, speaking much against the heretics, he sets forth the following thing that happened in his day, saying :

Of a truth, brother, I have need of counsel, and ask an opinion of thee. The following matter has come before me, and I am 2 fearful lest after all I be mistaken. Of the brethren who meet together for worship there is one, reckoned faithful, of long standing, a member of the congregation before my ordination, and, I think, before the appointment of the blessed Heraclas. Having been present with those who were recently being baptized, and having heard the questions and answers, he came to me in tears, bewailing himself and falling before my feet; confessing and swearing that the baptism with which he had been baptized by the heretics, was not such as this and had nothing in common with it inasmuch as it had been full of impieties and 3 blasphemies. He said that he was now altogether *pricked* in heart [2] and had not courage *so much as to lift up his eyes* to God,[3] after beginning with those unholy words and deeds; and therefore he begged that he might receive this most pure cleansing 4 and reception and grace. This I for my part did not dare to do, saying that his long-standing communion with us had been sufficient for this purpose. For since he had heard the Thanksgiving and joined in saying the Amen, and stood beside the Table and stretched forth his hands to receive the holy food, and had received it and partaken of the Body and Blood of our Lord for a long time, I should not dare to build him up

---

[1] Deut. xix. 14 (LXX).   [2] Cp. Acts ii. 37.
[3] Luke xviii. 13.

again from the beginning. But I kept exhorting him to be of
good courage, and to approach for the participation of the holy
5 things with firm faith and good hope. But he never ceases his
lament, and shudders to approach the Table, and scarcely,
though invited, does he dare to take his stand with the " consistentes " at the prayers.[1]

6   In addition to the above-mentioned letters, there is extant
also another of his on baptism, addressed by him and the
community over which he ruled to Xystus and the church
at Rome, in which with a long proof he gives a protracted
discussion of the subject in question. And, after these, there
is yet another letter of his extant, to Dionysius at Rome,
that with reference to Lucian. So much for these matters.

REIGN OF VALERIAN (253–260)

But to resume. Gallus and his associates held the principate
for less than two entire years, and then were removed out of
the way ; and Valerian along with his son Gallienus succeeded
to the government.

The Cause of the Persecution.

2   Once more we may learn from his letter to Hermammon
the description that Dionysius gives of him also ; in which he
gives an account of the following kind :

And to John also it is likewise revealed. Thus : *And there
was given to him*, says he, *a mouth speaking great things and blasphemy, and there was given to him authority and forty and two
3 months.*[2] One may *wonder* [3] at both of these things under
Valerian, and of them note especially the nature of his previous
conduct,[4] how mild and friendly he was to the men of God.
For not a single one of the emperors before him was so kindly
and favourably disposed towards them, not even those who were
said to have been openly Christians, as he manifestly was, when
he received them at the beginning in the most intimate and
friendly manner ; indeed all his house had been filled with godly
4 persons, and was a church of God. But the master and ruler
of the synagogue of the Egyptian magicians persuaded him to
get rid of them, bidding him slay and pursue the pure and holy
men, as being rivals and hinderers of his abominable and disgusting incantations (for indeed they are and were capable by
their presence and sight, and by merely breathing on them and
uttering words, of scattering the designs of the baneful demons).
And he advised him to perform unhallowed rites, and abominable juggleries and ill-omened sacrifices, such as cutting the
throats of wretched boys and sacrificing children of hapless

---

[1] συνεστάναι ταῖς προσευχαῖς.
[2] Rev. xiii. 5. (The text differs somewhat from that of A.V. and
R.V.)   [3] Rev. xiii. 3.
[4] Reading τὰ πρῶτα, with three MSS.

parents and opening up the entrails of new-born babes, and
cutting up and mincing the handy-work of God, as if all this
would bring them divine favour. . . .

5　And in addition he goes on to say :

Goodly at all events were the thankofferings that Macrianus
made to them for the Empire of his hopes.　Formerly when he
was regarded as minister over the imperial accounts [1] as a whole,[2]
he displayed neither a reasonable nor a catholic [3] mind.　But
he has fallen under the prophetic curse which says : *Woe unto them*
6 *that prophesy from their heart, and see not the whole.*[4]　For he
did not understand the universal Providence, nor did he suspect
the judgment of Him who is *before all and through all and over
all.*[5]　Therefore he has come to be at enmity with His Catholic
Church, and so alienated and estranged himself from God's
mercy and banished himself as far as possible from his own
salvation, in this proving true his name.[6]

7　And again, after other remarks, he says :

For Valerian, being induced by him to this course of action,
was given over to insults and reproaches, according to that
which was said to Isaiah : *And these have chosen their own ways
and abominations, in which their soul delighteth, and I will choose
8 their mockings, and their sins I will recompense them.*[7] . . . Now
this man, in his mad desire for the imperial rule of which he was
not worthy, and unable to deck his maimed body with the
imperial robes, put forward his two sons, who thus received their
father's sins.　For in them was clearly fulfilled the prophecy
that God spake : *Visiting the sins of fathers upon children, until
9 the third and fourth generation in them that hate me.*[8]　For his own
evil desires, in which he failed, he heaped upon the heads of his
sons, and so wiped off on them his own wickedness and his hatred
toward God.

The Sufferings of Dionysius in the Persecution.

This is the account given by Dionysius concerning Valerian.
11.　But with regard to the storm of persecution that raged
fiercely in his day, what the same Dionysius, and others with
him, underwent for their piety toward the God of the universe
will be made plain by his own words which he wrote at length
against Germanus, one of the bishops of his day who was
attempting to defame him.　He makes his statement in the
following manner :

[1] λόγων.
[2] καθόλου : a tedious play upon this word follows, which cannot be
reproduced in English.
[3] εὔλογον οὐδὲ καθολικόν.
[4] Ezek. xiii. 3 (LXX) : in order to maintain the play on words
Dionysius takes τὸ καθόλου as the object of the sentence, instead of
adverbially (" not at all ").　　　　　　[5] Cp. Eph. iv. 6; Col. i. 17.
[6] Another play upon words : Macrianus and μακρός (" far off ").
[7] Isai. lxvi. 3, 4.　　　　　　[8] Ex. xx. 5.

2   But I am in danger of falling, in truth, into great foolishness [1]
and stupidity, being forced to the point of compulsion to recount
the wonderful dispensation of God concerning us.   But since, he
says, *it is good to keep close the secret of a king, but glorious to reveal
the works of God*,[2] I will join issue with the violence of Germanus.
3 I came before Æmilianus, not alone, but there followed me my
fellow-presbyter Maximus, and Faustus, Eusebius, Chæremon,
deacons; and one of the brethren who had come from Rome
4 entered in along with us.   And Æmilianus did not lead off
with the words "Do not hold assemblies."   For that would have
been superfluous for him to say, and the last thing [to be men-
tioned] by one who was going back to the very beginning.   For
his discourse was not about not assembling others, but about
not being Christians ourselves, and from that he ordered me to
desist, thinking that if I were to change, the others also would
5 follow me.   But I gave a reply that was not inappropriate, nor
far from *We must obey God rather than men*[3]; yea, I testified
outright that I worship the only God and none other, nor would
I change or ever cease to be a Christian.   Thereupon he bade us
depart to a village near the desert, called Cephro.
6   But hear the things themselves that were spoken on both sides,
as they were placed on record: When Dionysius and Faustus
and Maximus and Marcellus and Chæremon were brought into
court, Æmilianus, the deputy-prefect, said, ". . . . And verbally
I discoursed with you concerning the kindness that our lords
7 have displayed on your behalf.   For they gave you the opportunity of safety if ye were willing to turn to that which is
according to nature and worship the gods which preserve their
Empire, and forget those gods which are contrary to nature.
What, therefore, say ye to these things?   For I do not expect
that ye will be ungrateful for their kindness, forasmuch as
8 they urge you on to the better course."   Dionysius replied:
"Not all men worship all gods, but each one certain whom he
regards as such.   We therefore both worship and adore the one
God and Maker of all things, who also committed the Empire
to the Augusti, most highly favoured of God, Valerian and
Gallienus; and to Him we unceasingly pray for their Empire,
9 that it may remain unshaken."   Æmilianus, the deputy-prefect,
said to them: "And who prevents you from worshipping this
god also, if he be a god, along with the natural gods?   For ye
were bidden to worship gods, and gods whom all know."   Diony-
10 sius replied: "We worship no other God."   Æmilianus, the
deputy-prefect, said to them: "I see that ye are at once ungrateful and insensible of the clemency of our Augusti.   Wherefore
ye shall not be in this city, but ye shall betake yourselves to the
parts of Libya and [remain] in a place called Cephro.   For this
is the place I chose in accordance with the command of our
Augusti.   And it shall in no wise be permitted either to you or
to any others either to hold assemblies or to enter the ceme-
11 teries, as they are called.   If anyone be proved not to have
gone to the place that I commanded, or be found at any assembly,
he will bring the peril upon himself, for there shall be no lack
of the necessary observation.   Be gone therefore whither ye
were bidden."

---

[1] Cp. 2 Cor. xi. 1, 17.   [2] Tobit xii. 7.   [3] Acts v. 29.

And even though I was sick, he hurried me away without granting me a single day's respite. What spare time had I then remaining either for holding or not holding an assembly?

Then after other remarks he says :

12   But we did not abstain from even the visible assembling of ourselves with the Lord; nay, I strove the more earnestly to gather together those in the city, as if I were with them, *being absent in body*, as he says, *but present in spirit*,[1] and at Cephro a large church also sojourned with us, some brethren following 13 us from the city, others joining us from Egypt. And there God *opened unto us a door for the word*.[2] And at first we were pursued, we were stoned, but afterwards not a few of the heathen left their idols and turned to God. Then for the first time was the word sown through our agency among those who had not formerly received it.

14   It was, as it were, for this that God took us away to them, and, when we *had fulfilled* this *ministration*,[3] took us away again. For Æmilianus wished to remove us to rougher, as he thought, and more Libyan-like places, and he bade those [who were scattered] in every direction to stream together to the Mareotian [nome], assigning separate villages in the district for each party; but us he posted more on the road, so that we should be the first to be arrested. For he evidently was managing and arranging it, that, whenever he wished to seize us, he might find us 15 all easy of capture. As for me, when I had been bidden to depart to Cephro, I did not even know in what direction the place lay, scarcely having heard so much as the name before; nevertheless I departed with a good grace and made no disturbance. But when it was told me that I was to remove to the parts of Colluthion, those who were present know how I was 16 affected (for here I shall be my own accuser). At first I was vexed and exceedingly angry. For although the places happened to be better known and more familiar to us, yet it was affirmed that the district was without brethren or persons of good character, and exposed besides to annoyances of travellers and 17 incursions of robbers. But I found encouragement when the brethren reminded me that it was nearer the city, and that, while Cephro used to bring us much intercourse with brethren from Egypt, so that there was a wider area from which to gather a congregation, yet there, from the nearer position of the city, we should enjoy seeing more constantly those really beloved and most intimate and dear. They would come, they said, and stay the night, and, as in the more remote suburban districts, there would be sectional assemblies. And so it proved.

18   And, after other remarks with reference to what happened to him, he writes again as follows :

Many, to be sure, are the confessions on which Germanus prides himself, many the happenings to his hurt of which he has to tell. Can he reckon up in his case as many as we can in ours : sentences, confiscations, proscriptions, *spoiling of*

---

[1] 1 Cor. v. 3.   [2] Col. iv. 3.   [3] Acts xii. 25.

possessions,[1] losses of dignities, despisings of worldly glory, disdainings of commendations and the reverse from prefect and council, endurance of threats, outcries, *perils, persecutions,* wanderings, *anguish* and divers *tribulations,*[2] such as happened to me under Decius and Sabinus, up to the present time under
19 Æmilianus? But where did Germanus appear? What talk was there about him? But I must cease from the great folly into which I am falling on account of Germanus; wherefore also I forbear to give in detail to the brethren who know them an account of the events.

20 The same Dionysius, in the letter also to Domitius and Didymus, mentions again the happenings of the persecution, as follows :

But it is superfluous to recount by name our people, since they are numerous and unknown to you. Only understand that men and women, both old men and lads, both girls and aged women, both soldiers and civilians, both every race and every age, some enduring scourgings and fire, others the sword, conquered in the
21 fight and have received their crowns. But in the case of some, a very long time was not sufficient to show them acceptable to the Lord, as indeed it is still seemingly not sufficient in my case ; wherefore I have been put off, until that suitable time that He knows, by Him that saith : *At an acceptable time I hearkened*
22 *unto thee, and in a day of salvation did I succour thee.*[3] For since ye make inquiries as to our affairs and desire to be told how we pass our time, ye have heard of course how that when we were being led away prisoners by a centurion and duumvirs with their soldiers and servants—I and Gaius and Faustus and Peter and Paul—certain of the nome of Marea came up, dragged us by force and carried us away, against our will and in the face of
23 our refusal to follow them. And now I and Gaius and Peter only, bereft of the other brethren, have been shut up in a lonely, parched spot in Libya, a three days' journey from Parætonium.

24 And a little further down he says :

But in the city there have concealed themselves, secretly visiting the brethren, of the presbyters Maximus, Dioscorus, Demetrius, Lucius. For those who are better known in the world, Faustinus and Aquila, are wandering about in Egypt. As to the deacons, they who survived those that died in the island are Faustus, Eusebius, Chæremon : that Eusebius, whom from the beginning God strengthened and prepared to render with all energy the services to the confessors that were in prison, and at no small risk to perform the task of laying out the corpses
25 of the blessed and perfect martyrs. For even to this day the prefect does not cease from putting to a cruel death, as I have said before, some of those who are brought before him, while others he mutilates with tortures, or allows to pine away in imprisonment and chains, giving his orders that no one is to go near them, and investigating whether any has been found so doing ; nevertheless God gives some respite to those who are sorely pressed, through the zeal and stedfastness of the brethren.

---

[1] Heb. x. 34. [2] Cp. Rom. viii. 35.
[3] Isai. xlix. 8 = 2 Cor. vi. 2.

Careers of the Companions of Dionysius.

26   Such is the account given by Dionysius. It should be observed, however, that Eusebius, whom he calls a deacon, shortly afterwards was appointed bishop of Laodicea in Syria; and Maximus, of whom he speaks as a presbyter then, succeeded Dionysius himself in his ministry to the brethren in Alexandria; but that Faustus, who along with him was distinguished at that time for his confession, was preserved until the persecution in our day, and, when quite an old man and full of days, was perfected by martyrdom in our own time, being beheaded.

Martyrs at Cæsarea.

12.   So it happened to Dionysius at that time. But during the persecution of Valerian, of which we are speaking, three persons at Cæsarea in Palestine, conspicuous for their confession of Christ, were adorned with a divine martyrdom, becoming food for wild beasts. Of these one was called Priscus, the second Malchus, and the name of the third was Alexander. It is said that these men, who were living in the country, at first reproached themselves for their carelessness and sloth, because, instead of hastening to secure the crown of martyrdom, they were proving contemptuous of prizes, though the present opportunity was bestowing them upon such as yearned with a heavenly desire. But that when they had taken counsel thereon, they started for Cæsarea, appeared before the judge and met the above-mentioned end. Moreover they relate that, besides these, a certain woman during the same persecution and in the same city endured to the end a like conflict. But it is recorded that she belonged to the sect of Marcion.

REIGN OF GALLIENUS (261–268)

The Peace.

13.   But not long afterwards Valerian underwent slavery at the hands of the barbarians, and his son, succeeding to the sole power, conducted the government with more prudence, and immediately by means of edicts put an end to the persecution against us. He granted free power to those who presided over the word to perform their accustomed duties, by a rescript which runs as follows :

The Emperor Cæsar Publius Licinius Gallienus Pius Felix Augustus to Dionysius and Pinnas and Demetrius and the other bishops. I have given my order that the benefit of my bounty should be published throughout all the world, to the intent that the places of worship should be given up, and therefore ye also may use the ordinance contained in my rescript, so that none may molest you.   And this thing which it is within your power to accomplish has long since been conceded by me; and therefore Aurelius Quirinius, who is in charge of the Exchequer, will observe the ordinance given by me.

Let this, which for the sake of greater clearness was translated from the Latin, be inserted.   And there is also extant another of the same emperor's ordinances, which he addressed to other bishops, giving them permission to recover the sites of the cemeteries, as they are called.

Successions of Bishops.

14.   At that time Xystus was still ruling the church of the Romans, Demetrian, who came after Fabius, the church at Antioch, and Firmilian at Cæsarea in Cappadocia; and moreover Gregory and his brother Athenodore were ruling the churches of Pontus, pupils of Origen.   As to Cæsarea in Palestine, on the death of Theoctistus, Domnus succeeded to the episcopate, but after he had continued in office a short time Theotecnus, our contemporary, was appointed to succeed him.   He also was of the school of Origen.   But at Jerusalem, when Mazabanes had entered into his rest, Hymenæus succeeded to the throne, the same who was distinguished for very many years in our day.

Marinus and Astyrius.

15.   In the time of those persons, when the churches everywhere were at peace, a man at Cæsarea in Palestine called Marinus, honoured by high rank in the army and distinguished besides by birth and wealth, was beheaded for his testimony to 2 Christ, on the following account.   There is a certain mark of honour among the Romans, the vine-switch, and those that obtain it become, it is said, centurions.   A post was vacant, and according to the order of promotion Marinus was being called to this advancement.   Indeed he was on the point of receiving the honour, when another stepped forward before the tribunal, and stated that in accordance with the ancient laws Marinus could not share in the rank that belonged to Romans, since he was a Christian and did not sacrifice to the emperors; but that the office fell to himself.   And [it is 3 said] that the judge (his name was Achæus) was moved thereat, and first of all asked what views Marinus held; and then, when he saw that he was stedfast in confessing himself a Christian, gave him a space of three hours for consideration.

4   When he came outside the court Theotecnus, the bishop
there, approached and drew him aside in conversation, and
taking him by the hand led him forward to the church.
Once inside, he placed him close to the altar [1] itself, and
raising his cloak a little, pointed to the sword with which he
was girded; at the same time he brought and placed before
him the book of the divine Gospels, and bade him choose
which of the two he wished. Without hesitation he stretched
forth his right hand and took the divine book. " Hold fast
then," said Theotecnus to him, " hold fast to God; and,
strengthened by Him, mayest thou obtain that thou hast
chosen. Go in peace."

5   As he was returning thence immediately a herald cried
aloud, summoning him before the court of justice. For the
appointed time was now over. Standing before the judge he
displayed still greater zeal for the faith; and straightway,
even as he was, was led away to death, and so was perfected.

16.   In that place Astyrius also is commemorated for the boldness which is dear to God. He was a member of the Roman
Senate, a favourite of emperors, and well known to all both
for birth and wealth. He was present with the martyr when
he was being perfected, and raising the corpse [2] upon his
shoulder he placed it upon a splendid and costly robe, and
laying it out with great magnificence gave it a fitting burial.

A great many other facts are mentioned about this man
by his friends, who have survived to our day, and also the
17.   following wonderful event. At Cæsarea Philippi, which
Phœnicians call Paneas, it is said that on a certain festival
a victim is thrown down among the springs that are shown
there, on the slopes of the mountain called Paneion, from
which the Jordan takes its source; and that it becomes
invisible in some miraculous way through the demon's power,
a circumstance, they say, that is looked upon by those present
as a far-famed marvel. Now [the story goes] that once
Astyrius was there when this was being done, and when he
saw the multitude struck with amazement at the affair, in
pity for their error he looked up toward heaven and besought
God who is over all,[3] through Christ, to confound the demon
who was causing the people to err, and put an end to the
deception of these men. And it is said that, when he had
thus prayed, of a sudden the sacrifice floated on the surface
of the springs; and thus their miracle came to an end, and
no further marvel ever took place in connection with that
spot.

[1] Or " sanctuary " : τῷ ἁγιάσματι.
[2] Lit. " tabernacle " (σκῆνος).   [3] Rom. ix. 5.

The Image of Christ at Cæsarea Philippi.

18.   But since I have come to mention this city, I do not think
it right to omit a story that is worthy to be recorded also
for those that come after us. For they say that she *who
had an issue of blood*,[1] and who, as we learn from the sacred
Gospels, found at the hands of our Saviour relief from her
affliction, came from this place, and that her house was
pointed out in the city, and that marvellous memorials of
the kindness, which the Saviour wrought upon her, still
2 remained.   For [they said] that there stood on a lofty stone
at the gates of her house a brazen figure in relief of a woman,
bending on her knee and stretching forth her hands like a
suppliant, while opposite to this there was another of the
same material, an upright figure of a man, clothed in comely
fashion in a double cloak and stretching out his hand to the
woman; at his feet on the monument itself a strange species
of herb was growing, which climbed up to *the border*[1] of the
double-cloak of brass, and acted as an antidote to all kinds
3 of diseases.   This statue, they said, bore the likeness of
Jesus.   And it was in existence even to our day, so that we
4 saw it with our own eyes when we stayed in the city.   And
there is nothing wonderful in the fact that those heathen,
who long ago had good deeds done to them by our Saviour,
should have made these objects, since we saw [2] the likenesses
of His apostles also, of Paul and Peter, and indeed of Christ
Himself, preserved in pictures [3] painted in colours.   And this
is what we should expect, for the ancients were wont, according to their pagan habit, to honour them as saviours, without
reservation, in this fashion.

The Throne of James.

19.   Now the throne of James, who was the first to receive
from the Saviour and the apostles the episcopate of the
church at Jerusalem, who also, as the divine books show,[4] was
called a brother of Christ, has been preserved to this day;
and by the honour that the brethren in succession there pay
to it, they show clearly to all the reverence in which the holy
men were and still are held by the men of old time and those
of our day, because of the love shown them by God.   So much
for these matters.

The Festal Epistles of Dionysius.

20.   But to resume.   Dionysius, in addition to the letters of
his that were mentioned, composed at that time also the festal
letters which are still extant, in which he gives utterance to

[1] Matt. ix. 20.   [2] ἱστορήσαμεν.
[3] Or, " books " (γραφαῖς).   [4] Gal. i. 19.

words specially suited to a solemn occasion with reference
to the festival of the Pascha. Of these he addressed [1] one
to Flavius, [2] another to Domitius and Didymus in which also
he sets forth a canon based on a cycle of eight years, proving
that it is not proper to celebrate the festival of the Pascha
at any other time than after the vernal equinox. In addition
to these he penned also [3] another letter to his fellow-presbyters at Alexandria, and to others at the same time in different
places. And these [he wrote] while the persecution was still
proceeding.

21.   Peace had all but arrived, when he returned to Alexandria.
But when faction and war broke out there once more, since it
was not possible for him to discharge his oversight over all
the brethren in the city, separated as they were into one or
other part of the faction, he again [4] at the festival of the
Pascha communicated with them by letter, as if he were
2 someone in a foreign country, from Alexandria itself. And
[5] to Hierax, after this, a bishop of those in Egypt, he writes
another festal letter, mentioning in the following terms the
faction prevailing among the Alexandrians in his day :

But as for me, what wonder is it if I find it difficult to communicate even by letter with those who live at some distance, seeing
that it has become impossible even for myself to converse with
3 myself, or to take counsel with my own soul ? Certainly, I have
need to write by letter to *my very heart*,[1] that is, the brethren that
are of the same household and mind with me, and citizens of the
same church; and there seems no possible way of getting this
correspondence through. For it were easier for a man to pass, I do
not say to a foreign country, but even from East to West, than to
4 traverse Alexandria from Alexandria itself. For the street that
runs through the very centre of the city is harder to traverse and
more impassable than that great and trackless desert through
which Israel journeyed for two generations. And our calm and
waveless harbours have become an image of the sea, which, split
up and made into a wall on either side, was for them a carriage
road, in whose thoroughfare [2] the Egyptians were drowned; and
from the murders that take place in them they oftentimes appeared
like a Red Sea. And the river that flows on past the city at one
time appeared drier than the waterless *desert*, and more arid than
that in whose crossing Israel so *thirsted* that Moses cried out, and
there *flowed* to them, from Him *who alone doeth wonders*, drink
out of the rock of flint.[3] At another time it overflowed to such an
extent that it submerged the whole neighbourhood, both the roads
and the fields, threatening to bring upon us the rush of waters
that took place in the days of Noah. And always its course is
defiled with blood and murders and drownings, such as it became
for Pharaoh by the hand of Moses, when *it was turned to blood* and
stank.[4] And what other water could there be to cleanse the water

---

[1] Philem. 12.   [2] Omitting ὧν, as Schwartz suggests.
[3] Deut. viii. 15; Ps. lxxviii. 20; cxxxvi. 4; Wisdom xi. 4.
[4] Ex. vii. 20, 21.

that cleanses all things ? How could the great ocean that men cannot pass, if it were poured upon it, purge this horrid sea ? Or how could the great *river* that *goeth out of Eden*, if it were to divert the *four heads*, into which it *is parted*, into one, the
8 *Gihon*,[1] wash away this gore ?   Or when might the air, made foul by the vile exhalations on all sides, become pure ? For such are the vapours that are given off from the land, winds from the sea, breezes from the rivers and mists from the harbours, that the dews are discharges from corpses rotting in all their constituent elements.
9 Yet men marvel and are at a loss as to whence come the constant plagues, whence the grievous diseases, whence the various forms of death, whence the manifold and great human mortality, why this greatest of cities no longer contains within it so great a multitude of inhabitants, from infant children up to those extremely advanced in years, as it used formerly to support of those known as men of green old age ! Nay, those of forty years old and up to seventy were then so numerous, that the full total of their number is not to be reached now, when those from fourteen to eighty years have been registered and reckoned together for the public food-ration ; and the youngest in appearance have become of equal
10 age, so to speak, with those who long ago were the oldest.   And though the human race upon earth is thus ever diminishing and consuming away before their eyes, they do not tremble, as its total disappearance draws nearer and nearer.

22.   After this, when the war was followed by a pestilential disease, and the feast was at hand, [6] he communicated once more by letter with the brethren, indicating the sufferings of the calamity, as follows :

2   To other men the present would not seem to be a time for festival, nor for them is this or any other time of such a nature ; I speak not of times of mourning, but even of any time that might be thought especially joyful. Now indeed all is lamentation, and all men mourn, and wailings resound throughout the city because of the number of dead and of those that are dying day by day.
3 For as it is written of the first-born of the Egyptians, so also it is now : *There was a great cry ; for there is not a house where there is not one dead :*[2] and would indeed that it were but one !

   For of a truth many and terrible were the things also that
4 happened to us before this. At first they drove us out, and alone we kept our festival at that time also, persecuted and put to death by all, and every single spot where we were afflicted became for us a place of festive assembly, field, desert, ship, inn, prison ; but the brightest of all festivals was kept by the perfect martyrs, when they feasted in heaven.
5   And, after that, war and famine came upon us, which we bore along with the heathen. Alone we endured all the injuries they inflicted upon us, while we had the benefit besides of what they wrought upon each other and what they suffered ; and we found our joy once more in the peace of Christ, which He has given to us alone.
6   But when the briefest breathing-space had been granted us and them, there descended upon us this disease, a thing that

---

[1] Gen. ii. 10, 13.   [2] Ex. xii. 30.

is to them more fearful than any other object of fear, more cruel than any calamity whatsoever, and, as one of their own writers declared, *the only thing of all that proved worse than what was expected.*[1] Yet to us it was not so, but, no less than the other misfortunes, a source of discipline and testing. For indeed it did not leave us untouched, although it attacked the heathen with great strength.

7   Following these remarks he adds as follows :

The most, at all events, of our brethren in their exceeding love and affection for the brotherhood were unsparing of themselves and clave to one another, visiting the sick without a thought as to the danger, assiduously ministering to them, tending them in Christ, and so most gladly departed this life along with them; being infected with the disease from others, drawing upon themselves the sickness from their neighbours, and willingly taking over their pains. And many, when they had cared for and restored to health others, died themselves, thus transferring their death to themselves, and then in very deed making good the popular saying, that always seems to be merely an expression of courtesy : for in departing they became their " devoted servants."
8 In this manner the best at any rate of our brethren departed this life, certain presbyters and deacons and some of the laity, receiving great commendation, so that this form of death seems in no respect to come behind martyrdom, being the outcome of
9 much piety and strong faith. So, too, the bodies of the saints they would take up in their open hands to their bosom, closing their eyes and shutting their mouths, carrying them on their shoulders and laying them out; they would cling to them, embrace them, bathe and adorn them with their burial clothes, and after a little receive the same services themselves, for those that were left behind were ever following those that went before.
10 But the conduct of the heathen was the exact opposite. Even those who were in the first stages of the disease they thrust away, and fled from their dearest. They would even cast them in the roads half-dead, and treat the unburied corpses as vile refuse, in their attempts to avoid the spreading and contagion of the death-plague; a thing which, for all their devices, it was not easy for them to escape.

11   And also after this letter, when peace reigned in the city, he once more sent [7] a festal letter to the brethren in Egypt, and following this he again indited others. And there is extant, also, [8] a certain letter of his on the Sabbath, and [9] another on Exercise.
12   Communicating by a letter [10] again with Hermammon and the brethren in Egypt, he recounts in full many other things about the wickedness of Decius and his successors, and men-
23. tions the peace under Gallienus. But there is nothing like hearing the nature of these happenings also.

He then, after inciting one of his emperors and attacking the other, of a sudden disappeared altogether, root and branch with

---

[1] Thuc. ii. 64. 1.

all his family, and Gallienus was proclaimed and acknowledged by all, being at once an old and a new emperor, for he was before
2 and came after them; for in accordance with that which was spoken to the prophet Isaiah : *Behold, the former things are come to pass, and new things which shall now spring forth.*[1] For as when a cloud speeds underneath the rays of the sun, and for a short time screens and darkens it, and appears instead of it, but when the cloud passes by or is melted away, the sun that shone before again shines forth and once more appears; so Macrianus, after coming forward and getting for himself access to the imperial power that belonged to Gallienus, is no more, since indeed he
3 never was, while Gallienus is like as he was before; and the monarchy has, as it were, put aside its old age and cleansed itself from its former wickedness, and now blossoms forth in fuller bloom, is seen and heard more widely and spreads abroad everywhere.

4   Then, following on this, he indicates also the time at which he wrote this, in these words :

And it occurs to me once more to observe the days of the imperial years. For I perceive that those wicked persons, though they were named with honour, after a short time have become nameless; while he, who is holier and filled with more love to God, has passed the period of seven years, and is now completing a ninth year, in which *let us keep the feast.*[2]

Dionysius on Chiliasm.

24.   Besides all these, the two treatises On Promises were also composed by him. The occasion was supplied him by the teaching of Nepos, a bishop of those in Egypt, that the promises which had been made to the saints in the divine Scriptures should be interpreted after a more Jewish fashion, and his assumption that there will be a kind of millennium on this
2 earth [3] devoted to bodily indulgence. Thinking, for example, to establish his own peculiar opinion from the Apocalypse of John, he composed a certain book on the subject and entitled
3 it Refutation of the Allegorists. Dionysius attacked him in the books On Promises, in the first of which he sets out the view that he himself held with regard to the doctrine, and in the second treats of the Apocalypse of John. There, at the beginning, he mentions Nepos, writing as follows about him :

4   But since they bring forward a certain composition of Nepos, on which they rely greatly as proving indisputably that the kingdom of Christ will be on earth, [let me say that] in many other respects I approve and love Nepos, for his faith and devotion to work, his diligent study of the Scriptures and his abundant psalmody, by which many of the brethren have till this day been cheered; and I am full of respectful regard for the man, all the

---

[1] A mixed quotation from Isai. xlii. 9 and xliii. 19.
[2] 1 Cor. v. 8.   [3] ξηρᾶς.

more for that he has gone to his rest already. But *truth* is *dear* and to be *honoured above* all things,[1] and one must give ungrudging praise and assent to whatever is stated rightly, but examine and
5 correct whatever appears to be unsoundly written. And if he were present and putting forward his opinions merely in words, conversation, without writing, would be sufficient, persuading and instructing by question and answer *them that oppose themselves*.[2] But when a book is published, which some think most convincing, and when certain teachers, who consider the law and the prophets of no value and disregard the following of the Gospels and depreciate the epistles of the apostles, yet make promises concerning the teaching of this treatise as if it were some great and hidden mystery, and do not suffer the simpler of our brethren to have high and noble thoughts, either about *the* glorious and truly divine *appearing of our Lord*,[3] or of our resurrection from the dead and our *gathering together* and being made *like* unto *Him*,[4] but persuade them to hope for what is petty and mortal and like the present in the kingdom of God—then we also are compelled to argue with Nepos our brother as if he were present.

6   After other remarks he adds as follows :

Now when I came to the [nome] of Arsinoe, where, as thou knowest, this doctrine had long been prevalent, so that schisms and defections of whole churches had taken place, I called together the presbyters and teachers of the brethren in the villages (there were present also such of the brethren as wished), and I urged
7 them to hold the examination of the question publicly. And when they brought me this book as some invincible weapon and rampart, I sat with them and for three successive days from morn
8 till night attempted to correct what had been written. On that occasion I conceived the greatest admiration for the brethren, their firmness, love of truth, facility in following an argument, and intelligence, as we propounded in order and with forbearance the questions, the difficulties raised and the points of agreement ; on the one hand refusing to cling obstinately and at all costs (even though they were manifestly wrong) to opinions once held ; and on the other hand not shirking the counter-arguments, but as far as possible attempting to grapple with the questions in hand and master them. Nor, if convinced by reason, were we ashamed to change our opinions and give our assent ; but conscientiously and unfeignedly and with hearts laid open to God we accepted whatever was established by the proofs and teachings of the holy
9 Scriptures. And in the end the leader and introducer of this teaching, Coracion, as he was called, in the hearing of all the brethren present, assented, and testified to us that he would no longer adhere to it, nor discourse upon it, nor mention nor teach it, since he had been sufficiently convinced by the contrary arguments. And as to the rest of the brethren, some rejoiced at the joint conference, and the mutual deference and unanimity which all displayed. . . .

25.   Then, in due course, lower down he speaks thus, with reference to the Apocalypse of John :

[1] Cp. Aristotle, *Eth. Nic.*, i. 1096 A.   [2] 2 Tim. ii. 25.
[3] 1 Tim. vi. 14.   [4] Cp. 2 Thess. ii. 1 ; 1 John iii. 2.

Some indeed of those before our time rejected and altogether impugned the book, examining it chapter by chapter and declaring 2 it to be unintelligible and illogical, and its title false. For they say that it is not John's, no, nor yet an apocalypse (unveiling), since it is veiled by its great thick curtain of unintelligibility; and that the author of this book was not only not one of the *apostles*, nor even one of the saints or those belonging to the Church, but *Cerinthus*, the same who created the sect called "Cerinthian" after him, since he desired to affix to his own forgery a name 3 worthy of credit. For that this was the doctrine which he taught, that *the kingdom of Christ* would *be on earth;* and he dreamed that it would consist in those things which formed the object of his own desires (for he was a lover of the body and altogether carnal), in the full satisfaction of the belly and lower lusts, that is, in feasts and carousals and *marriages*, and (as a means, he thought, of procuring these under a better name) in *festivals* and sacrifices 4 and slayings of victims.[1] But for my part I should not dare to reject the book, since many brethren hold it in estimation; but, reckoning that my perception is inadequate to form an opinion concerning it, I hold that the interpretation of each several passage is in some way hidden and more wonderful.[2] For even although I do not understand it, yet I suspect that some deeper 5 meaning underlies the words. For I do not measure and judge these things by my own reasoning, but, assigning to faith the greater value, I have come to the conclusion that they are beyond my comprehension, and I do not reject that which I have not grasped, but I marvel the more because I did not even see it.

6 Moreover, after closely examining the whole book of the Apocalypse and demonstrating that it cannot be understood in the literal sense, he adds as follows :

After completing the whole, one might say, of his prophecy, the prophet calls those blessed who observe it, and indeed himself also. For he says : *Blessed is he that keepeth the words of the prophecy of this book, and I John, he that saw and heard these things.*[3] 7 I will not gainsay the fact that he was certainly named John and that this book is by one John, for I fully allow that it is the work of some holy and inspired person. But I should not readily agree that he was the apostle, the son of Zebedee, the brother of James, whose are the Gospel entitled According to John and the Catholic 8 Epistle. For I form my judgment from the character of each and from the nature of the language and from what is known as the general construction of the book, that [the John therein mentioned] is not the same. For the evangelist nowhere adds his name, nor yet proclaims himself, throughout either the Gospel or the Epistle.

9 Then lower down he again speaks thus :

. . . But John nowhere, either in the first or the third person. But he who wrote the Apocalypse at the very beginning puts himself forward : *The Revelation of Jesus Christ, which he gave him to shew unto his servants quickly, and he sent and signified it by his angel unto his servant John; who bare witness of the word of God*

---

[1] Cp. Gaius (iii. 28. 2 above).
[2] *i.e.* than appears on the surface.   [3] Rev. xxii. 7, 8.

10 *and his testimony, even of all things that he saw.*[1] Then he also
writes an epistle : *John to the seven churches which are in Asia :
Grace to you and peace.*[2]   But the evangelist did not write his name
even at the beginning of the Catholic Epistle, but without anything superfluous began with the mystery itself of the divine
revelation : *That which was from the beginning, that which we have
heard, that which we have seen with our eyes.*[3]   It was in respect of
this revelation that the Lord also called Peter blessed, saying :
*Blessed art thou, Simon Bar-Jonah : for flesh and blood hath not
11 revealed it unto thee, but my heavenly Father.*[4]   Nay, not even in
the second or third extant epistles of John, although they are
short, is John set forth by name; but he has written *the elder,*[5]
without giving his name.   But this writer did not even consider
it sufficient, having once mentioned his name, to narrate what
follows, but he takes up his name again : *I John, your brother and
partaker with you in the tribulation and kingdom and in the patience
of Jesus, was in the isle that is called Patmos, for the word of God and
the testimony of Jesus.*[6]   Moreover at the close he speaks thus :
*Blessed is he that keepeth the words of the prophecy of this book, and I
John, he that saw and heard these things.*[7]

12   That the writer of these words, therefore, was John, one must
believe, since he says it.   But what John, is not clear.   For he did
not say that he was, as is frequently said in the Gospel, the
disciple loved by the Lord, nor he *which leaned back on his breast,*[8]
nor the brother of James, nor the eye-witness and hearer of the
13 Lord.   For he would have mentioned some one of these aforesaid
epithets, had he wished to make himself clearly known.   Yet he
makes use of none of them, but speaks of himself as our *brother
and partaker with* us, and a *witness of Jesus,*[9] and *blessed* in seeing
14 and *hearing* [10] the revelations.   I hold that there have been many
persons of the same name as John the apostle, who for the love
they bore him, and because they admired and esteemed him and
wished to be *loved,* as he was, of the Lord,[11] were glad to take also
the same name after him; just as Paul, and for that matter Peter
15 too, is a common name among boys of believing parents.   So then,
there is also another *John* in the Acts of the Apostles, *whose
surname was Mark,* whom *Barnabas and* Paul *took with* themselves,[12] concerning whom also the Scripture says again : *And they
had also John as their attendant.*[13]   But as to whether it were he
who was the writer, I should say No.   For it is written that he did
not arrive in Asia along with them, but *having set sail,* the Scripture says, *from Paphos Paul and his company came to Perga in
Pamphylia ; and John departed from them and returned to Jeru-*
16 *salem.*[14]   But I think that there was a certain other [John] among
those that were in Asia, since it is said both that there were two
tombs at Ephesus, and that each of the two is said to be John's.

17   And from the conceptions too, and from the terms and their
arrangement, one might naturally assume that this writer was a

---

[1] Rev. i. 1, 2.   [2] Rev. i. 4.
[3] 1 John i. 1.   [4] Matt. xvi. 17.
[5] 2 John 1; 3 John 1.   [6] Rev. i. 9.
[7] Rev. xxii. 7, 8.   [8] John xiii. 25.
[9] Rev. i. 9.   [10] Rev. xxii. 7, 8.
[11] John xxi. 20, etc.   [12] Acts xii. 25.
[13] Acts xiii. 5.   [14] Acts xiii. 13.

18 different person from the other. For there is indeed a mutual agreement between the Gospel and the Epistle, and they begin alike. The one says : *In the beginning was the Word ;* [1] the other : *That which was from the beginning.* [2] The one says ; *And the Word became flesh, and dwelt among us (and we beheld his glory, glory as of the only-begotten from the Father)* ; [3] the other, the same words slightly changed : *That which we have heard, that which we have seen with our eyes, that which we beheld, and our hands handled,*
19 *concerning the Word of life ; and the life was manifested.* [4] For these words he employs as a prelude, since he is aiming, as he shows in what follows, at those who were asserting that the Lord had not come in the flesh. [5] Therefore he was careful also to add : *And that which we have seen, we bear witness, and declare unto you the life, the eternal life, which was with the Father, and was manifested unto us ; that which we have seen and heard, declare we unto you also.* [6]
20 He is consistent with himself [7] and does not depart from what he has proposed, but proceeds throughout under the same heads and
21 expressions, certain of which we shall mention concisely. But the attentive reader will find frequently in one and the other " the life," [8] " the light," [9] " turning from darkness "; continually " the truth," [10] " the grace," [11] " the joy," [12] " the flesh [13] and blood [14] of the Lord," " the judgment," [15] " the forgiveness of sins," [16] " the love of God toward us," [17] the " commandment " that we should " love one another," [18] that we should " keep all the commandments "; [19] the " conviction " of " the world," [20] of " the devil," [21] of " the antichrist "; [22] the promise of the Holy Spirit ; [23] the adoption of the sons of God ; [24] the " faith " [25] that is demanded of us throughout ; " the Father " and " the Son " : [26] these are to be found everywhere. In a word, it is obvious that those who observe their character throughout will see at a glance that the Gospel and Epistle have one and the same
22 complexion. But the Apocalypse is utterly different from, and foreign to, these writings ; it has no connexion, no affinity, in any way with them ; it scarcely, so to speak, has even a syllable in
23 common with them. Nay more, neither does the Epistle (not to

---

[1] John i. 1.
[2] 1 John i. 1.
[3] John i. 14.
[4] 1 John i. 1, 2.   [5] 1 John iv. 2.
[6] 1 John i. 1, 2, 3.   [7] The text is probably corrupt.
[8] John i. 4, and *passim* ; 1 John ii. 25 ; iii. 14 f., etc.
[9] John i–xii. *passim* ; 1 John i. 5, 7 ; ii. 8–10.
[10] John i. 14, and *passim* ; 1 John i. 8 ; iii. 19, etc.
[11] John i. 14, 16, 17 ; 2 John 3.
[12] John iii. 29, etc. ; 1 John i. 4 ; 2 John 12 ; 3 John 4 (v.l. " grace ").
[13] John i. 13, 14 ; vi. 53, 56, etc. ; 1 John iv. 2.
[14] John vi. 53–56 ; xix. 34 ; 1 John i. 7 ; v. 6, 8.
[15] John iii. 19, etc. ; 1 John iv. 17 ; cp. ii. 18, etc.
[16] Cp. John xx. 23 ; 1 John i. 9 ; ii. 12 ; cp. iii. 5.
[17] John iii. 16 ; xiv. 23 ; xvii. 23 ; 1 John iii. 1 ; iv. 11, etc.
[18] John xiii. 34 ; xv. 12, 17 ; 1 John iii. 23, etc.
[19] John xv. 10 ; 1 John ii. 3 ; iii. 22 ff., etc.
[20] John xvi. 8 ; 1 John ii. 16 f.
[21] 1 John iii. 8 ; cp. ii. 14, etc.
[22] 1 John ii. 18 f.
[23] John xiv. 16, etc. ; 1 John iii. 24 ; iv. 13 ; cp. ii. 20.
[24] John i. 12 ; xi. 52 ; 1 John iii. 1, 2, etc.
[25] John i. 7, etc. ; 1 John v. 4.
[26] John iii. 36 and *passim* ; 1 John iv. 14, etc.

speak of the Gospel) contain any mention or thought of the Apocalypse, nor the Apocalypse of the Epistle, whereas Paul in his epistles gave us a little light also on his revelations,[1] which he did not record separately.

24　And further, by means of the style one can estimate the difference between the Gospel and Epistle and the Apocalypse.

25　For the former are not only written in faultless Greek, but also show the greatest literary skill in their diction, their reasonings, and the constructions in which they are expressed.　There is a complete absence of any barbarous word, or solecism, or any vulgarism whatever.　For their author had, as it seems, both kinds of word, by the free gift of the Lord, *the word of knowledge*

26　and *the word* [2] of style.　But I will not deny that the other writer had seen *revelations* and received *knowledge* and *prophecy;* [3] nevertheless I observe his language and his inaccurate Greek usage, employing, as he does,[4] barbarous idioms and in some places com-

27　mitting downright solecisms.　These there is no necessity to single out now.　For I have not said these things in mockery (let no one think it), but merely to establish the dissimilarity of these writings.

Dionysius on Sabellianism.

26.　In addition to these letters of Dionysius there are extant also many others, as for example those against Sabellius to Ammon bishop of the church at Bernice, and that to Teles- phorus, and that to Euphranor and Ammon (again) and Euporus.　And he composed on the same subject also four other treatises, which he addressed to his namesake at Rome, Dionysius.

Other Writings of Dionysius.

2　And we have many letters of his besides these, and moreover lengthy books written in epistolary form, such as those on Nature, addressed to Timothy his boy, and that on Tempta-

3　tions, which also he dedicated to Euphranor.　In addition to these, in writing also to Basilides, bishop of the communities in the Pentapolis, he says that he himself had written an exposition of the beginning of Ecclesiastes; and he has left behind for our benefit various other letters addressed to this person.

So much for Dionysius.　But come now, after recording these things, let us hand down for the information of posterity the character of our own generation.

Successions of Bishops.

27.　When Xystus had presided over the church of the Romans for eleven years, he was succeeded by Dionysius, namesake of him of Alexandria.　At this time also, when Demetrian had

---

[1] 2 Cor. xii. 1–4.　　　[2] 1 Cor. xii. 8.　　　[3] 1 Cor. xiv. 6.
[4] Dionysius' own grammar seems to go astray here.

departed this life at Antioch, Paul of Samosata received the episcopate.

The Heresy of Paul of Samosata.

2   As this person espoused low and mean views as to Christ, contrary to the Church's teaching, namely, that He was in His nature an ordinary man, Dionysius of Alexandria was invited to attend the synod, but, pleading as his excuse both old age and bodily weakness, he postponed his coming, and furnished by letter the opinion that he held on the subject in question.   But the rest of the pastors of the churches, from various quarters, all hasted to Antioch, and assembled as against a spoiler of the flock of Christ.

28.   Among those who were the most distinguished were Firmilian, bishop of Cæsarea in Cappadocia; the brothers Gregory and Athenodore, pastors of the communities in Pontus; and in addition to these, Helenus, [bishop] of the community at Tarsus, and Nicomas, of the [community] at Iconium; nor must we omit Hymenæus, of the church at Jerusalem, and Theotecnus, of this neighbouring church of Cæsarea; and moreover there was Maximus also, who was ruling with distinction the brethren at Bostra; and one would not be at a loss to reckon up countless others, together with presbyters and deacons, who were gathered together in the above-mentioned city for the same cause.   But these were the 2 most famous among them.   When all, then, were coming together frequently on different occasions, arguments and questions were mooted at each meeting,[1] the Samosatene and his party attempting to keep still concealed and to cloak what was heterodox, while the others were earnestly engaged in laying bare and bringing into the open his heresy and blasphemy against Christ.

Bishops of Alexandria.

3   At that time Dionysius died in the twelfth year of the reign
265.   of Gallienus, having presided in the episcopate at Alexandria for seventeen years.   He was succeeded by Maximus.

REIGNS OF CLAUDIUS AND AURELIAN
(268—275)

4   Gallienus having held the principate for fifteen entire years, Claudius was appointed his successor.   When he had completed his second year, he gave over the government to Aurelian.

---

[1] σύνοδον.

Proceedings against Paul of Samosata.

29.   In Aurelian's day a final synod of an exceedingly large
number of bishops was assembled, and the leader of the heresy
at Antioch, being unmasked and now clearly condemned of
heterodoxy by all, was excommunicated from the Catholic
2 Church under heaven.   The person foremost in calling him
to account and in utterly refuting his attempts at concealment
was Malchion, a learned man, who also was head of a school
of rhetoric, one of the Greek educational establishments at
Antioch; and, moreover, for the surpassing sincerity of his
faith in Christ he had been deemed worthy of the presbyterate
of that community.   In fact, this man had stenographers to
take notes as he held a disputation with Paul, which we know
to be extant even to this day; and he, alone of them all, was
able to unmask that crafty and deceitful person.

30.   The pastors, then, who had been assembled together,
indited unanimously a single letter personally to Dionysius,
bishop of Rome, and Maximus, of Alexandria, and sent it
throughout all the provinces.   In it they make manifest to all
their zeal, and also the perverse heterodoxy of Paul, as well as
the arguments and questions that they addressed to him; and
moreover they describe the man's whole life and conduct.
From which, by way of memorial, it may be well on the present
occasion to give an account of these their utterances.

2   To Dionysius and Maximus and to all our fellow-ministers
throughout the world, bishops, presbyters and deacons, and to
the whole Catholic Church under heaven, Helenus and Hymenæus
and Theophilus and Theotecnus and Maximus, Proclus, Nicomas
and Ælianus and Paul and Bolanus and Protogenes and Hierax
and Eutychius and Theodore and Malchion and Lucius and all
the others who, with us, sojourn in the adjacent cities and
provinces, bishops and presbyters and deacons and the churches
of God, as to brethren beloved in the Lord send greeting.

3   A little further on they proceed thus :

And we wrote [1] inviting many even of the bishops at a distance
to come and heal this deadly doctrine, as for example, both
Dionysius at Alexandria and Firmilian of Cappadocia, those
blessed men.   The former of these wrote to Antioch, [not to the
bishop,] neither deeming the leader of the heresy worthy of being
addressed nor writing to him personally, but to the whole com-
4 munity; of which letter also we subjoin a copy.   Firmilian, on
the other hand, even came twice, and condemned Paul's new-
fangled ideas, as we who were present know and bear witness,
and many others know as well; but, on his promising to change,
he adjourned [the proceedings], hoping and believing that the
matter would be fittingly concluded without any reproach to the
Word; for he was deceived by him who both *denied* his *God and*

---

[1] The Greek (imperf.) implies a continued correspondence.

Lord, and also did not preserve *the faith* [1] that he himself formerly
5 held.   And Firmilian was now again on his way to cross over to
Antioch and had got as far as Tarsus, for he had had experience
of the villainy of this denier of God.   But while we had come
together and were actually calling him and awaiting his arrival,
in the midst of it all he reached life's end.

6   Again, after other remarks they describe the manner of his
life, in the following terms :

But whereas he departed from the canon [of truth], and has
turned aside to spurious and bastard doctrines, we are under no
7 obligation *to judge* the actions of him *that is without,* [2] not even
because, though he was formerly poor and penniless, neither
having received a livelihood from his fathers nor having got it from
a trade or any occupation, he has now come to possess abundant
wealth, as a result of lawless deeds and sacrilegious plunderings
and extortions exacted from the brethren by threats ; for he
deprives the injured of their rights, and promises to help them for
money, yet breaks his word with these also, and with a light heart
makes his harvest out of the readiness of persons engaged in
lawsuits to make an offer, for the sake of being rid of those that
trouble them ; seeing that he considers that *godliness is a way of*
8 *gain.* [3]   Neither [do we judge him] because he *sets* his *mind on
high things* [4] and is lifted up, clothing himself with worldly honours
and wishing to be called " ducenarius " rather than bishop, and
struts in *the market-places,* [5] reading and dictating letters as he
walks in public, and attended by a body-guard, some preceding,
some following, and that too in numbers : with the result that the
faith is ill thought of and hated because of his conceit and the
9 overweening pride of his heart.   Nor [do we judge] the quackery
in church assemblies that he devises, courting popularity and
posing for appearance sake, and thus astonishing the minds of the
simpler folk, with the tribunal and lofty throne that he prepared
for himself, not befitting a disciple of Christ, and the " secretum,"
which, in imitation of the rulers of the world, he has and so styles.
Also, he smites his hand on his thigh and stamps the tribunal
with his feet ; and those who do not applaud or wave their hand-
kerchiefs, as in a theatre, or shout out and jump up in the same
way as do the men and wretched women who are his partizans
and hearken in this disorderly fashion, but who listen, as in God's
house, with orderly and becoming reverence, he rebukes and
insults.   And towards the interpreters of the Word who have
departed this life he behaves in an insolent and ill-bred fashion
in the common assembly, and brags about himself as though he
10 were not a bishop but a sophist and charlatan.   And as to psalms,
he put a stop to those addressed to our Lord Jesus Christ, on the
ground that they are modern and the compositions of modern
men, but he trains women to sing psalms to himself in the middle
of the church on the great day of the Pascha, which would make
one shudder to hear.   Such also is the kind of discourse that he
permits the bishops of the neighbouring country and towns, who
fawn upon him, and the presbyters as well, to deliver in their

[1] Jude 3, 4.   [2] 1 Cor. v. 12.
[3] 1 Tim. vi. 5.   [4] Rom. xii. 16; 1 Tim. vi. 17.
[5] Cp. Demosthenes, κατὰ Μειδίου, 158.

11 sermons to the people. For he is not willing to acknowledge with us that the Son of God has come down from heaven (to anticipate something of what we are about to write; and this will not be merely asserted, but is proved from many passages of the notes that we send, and not least where he says that *Jesus Christ is from below* [1]); while they who sing psalms to him and utter his praises in the congregation say that their impious teacher has come down an angel from heaven. And he does not prevent this, but is even present when such things are said, arrogant fellow that he is.

12 And as to the " subintroductæ," as the Antiochenes call them, his own and those of the presbyters and deacons in his company, with whom he joins in concealing both this and the other incurable sins (though he knows of, and has convicted, them), that he may have them under obligation to him, and that they may not dare, through fear for themselves, to accuse him of his misdemeanours in word and deed; yea, he has even made them rich, for which cause he is the beloved and admired of those who affect such

13 conduct—why should we write of these things? But we know, beloved, that the bishop and the priesthood as a whole should be a pattern to the people *of all good works ;* [2] and we are not ignorant of this : how many have fallen through procuring " subintro- ductæ " for themselves, while others are under suspicion; so that even if it be granted that he does nothing licentious, yet he ought at least to guard against the suspicion that arises from such a practice, lest he cause someone to stumble, and induce others

14 also to imitate him. For how could he rebuke another, or counsel him not to consort any further with a woman and so guard against a slip, as it is written,[3] seeing that he has sent one away already, and has two in his company in the flower of youth and beauty, and even if he go away anywhere, he brings them around

15 with him, living all the while in luxury and surfeiting? Where- fore, though all groan and lament in private, so fearful have they become of his tyranny and power, that they dare not accuse him.

16 Yet, as we have said before,[4] one might call to account for these matters a man who has at any rate a catholic mind and is num- bered along with us; but as for one who burlesqued *the mystery,*[5] and strutted about in the abominable heresy of Artemas (for why should we not bring ourselves to declare his father ?)—from such a one we think that we are under no obligation to demand a reckon- ing for these things.

17 Then at the close of the letter they add as follows :

We were compelled therefore, as he opposed himself to God and refused to yield, to excommunicate him, and appoint another bishop in his stead for the Catholic Church, [choosing] by the providence of God, as we are persuaded, Domnus the son of the blessed Demetrian, who formerly presided with distinction over the same community; he is adorned with all the noble qualities suitable for a bishop, and we notify [this his appointment] unto you that ye may write to him, and from him receive letters of communion. But let this fellow write to Artemas, and let those who side with Artemas hold communion with him.

---

[1] Paul, frag. ii. l. 4; frag. x. 3 (*J.T.S.* vol. xix. pp. 22, 37).
[2] Tit. ii. 7.   [3] Cp. Ecclus. ix. 8, 9.
[4] § 6.   [5] Cp. 1 Tim. iii. 16

Bishops of Antioch.

18 When Paul, then, had fallen from the episcopate as well as
from his orthodoxy in the faith, Domnus, as has been said,
succeeded to the ministry of the church at Antioch.

Further Proceedings against Paul.

19 But as Paul refused on any account to give up possession of
the church-building, the emperor Aurelian, on being petitioned,
gave an extremely just decision regarding the matter, ordering
the assignment of the building to those with whom the bishops
of the doctrine [1] in Italy and Rome should communicate in
writing. Thus, then, was the aforesaid man driven with the
utmost indignity from the church by the ruler of this world.

Later years of Aurelian.

20 Such indeed was the disposition of Aurelian towards us at
that time.   But as his reign advanced, he changed his mind
with regard to us, and was now being moved by certain counsels
to stir up persecution against us; and there was great talk
21 about this on all sides.   But as he was just on the point of
so doing and was putting, one might almost say, his signature
to the decrees against us, the divine Justice visited him, and
pinioned his arms, so to speak, to prevent his undertaking.
Thus it was clearly shown for all to see that the rulers of this
world would never find it easy to proceed against the churches
of Christ, unless the hand which champions us were to permit
this to be done, as a divine and heavenly judgment to chasten
and turn us, at whatsoever times it should approve.

REIGNS OF PROBUS, CARUS AND DIOCLETIAN
(276–305)

22 At all events, when Aurelian had reigned for six years, he
was succeeded by Probus. He held the government for
something like the same number of years, and Carus with his
sons Carinus and Numerianus succeeded him; and when they
in their turn had remained in office for not three entire years,
the government devolved on Diocletian and on those who were
brought in after him; and under them was accomplished the
persecution of our day and the destruction of the churches
therein.

Bishops of Rome.

23 But a short time before this, Felix succeeded in the ministry
Dionysius, bishop of Rome, who had completed nine years.

[1] τοῦ δόγματος, i.e. the Christian religion : probably a translation of the
actual words used by Aurelian.

Manes.

31.   At that time also the madman, named after his devil-possessed heresy, was taking as his armour mental delusion; for the devil, that is Satan himself, the adversary of God, had put the man forward for the destruction of many. His very speech and manners proclaimed him a barbarian in mode of life, and, being by nature devilish and insane, he suited his endeavours thereto and attempted to pose as Christ : at one time giving out that he was *the Paraclete* and *the* Holy *Spirit*[1] Himself, conceited fool that he was, as well as mad; at another time choosing, as Christ did, *twelve disciples*[2] as
2 associates in his new-fangled system. In short, he stitched together false and godless doctrines that he had collected from the countless, long-extinct, godless heresies, and infected our empire with, as it were, a deadly poison that came from the land of the Persians; and from him the profane name of Manichæan is still commonly on men's lips to this day.

Succession of Bishops.
Rome.

Such, then, was the foundation on which rested this *knowledge which is falsely so called*,[3] which sprang up at the time we have
32.   mentioned. At that time Felix, who had presided over the church of the Romans for five years, was succeeded by Euty-chianus. This person did not survive for even ten entire months; he left the office to Gaius our contemporary. And when he had presided for about fifteen years, Marcellinus was appointed his successor, the same whom the persecution has overtaken.

Antioch : Dorotheus.

2   In the time of these persons, in succession to Domnus, Timæus was in charge of the episcopate of Antioch, whom our contemporary Cyril succeeded.

During Cyril's episcopate we came to know Dorotheus, a learned man, who had been deemed worthy of the presbyterate at Antioch. In his zeal for all that is beautiful in divine things, he made so careful a study of the Hebrew tongue that he read with understanding the original Hebrew Scriptures.
3 And he was by no means unacquainted with the most liberal studies and Greek primary education; but withal he was by nature a eunuch, having been so from his very birth, so that even the emperor, accounting this as a sort of miracle, took him into his friendship and honoured him with the charge of

---

[1] John xiv. 16 f.   [2] Matt. x. 1, etc.   [3] 1 Tim. vi. 20.

4 the purple dye-works at Tyre. We heard him giving a measured exposition of the Scriptures in the church.

After Cyril, Tyrannus succeeded to the episcopate of the community of the Antiochenes, in whose day the attack upon the churches was at its height.

Laodicea : Eusebius, Anatolius, Stephen and Theodotus.

5 After Socrates as head of the community at Laodicea came Eusebius, being a native of the city of Alexandria. The reason of his migration was the affair of Paul. For when he had come to Syria on business connected with Paul, he was prevented from returning home by those who had divine things at heart. He was a goodly example of piety among our contemporaries, as it will be easy to discover from the expressions of Dionysius quoted above.[1]

6 Anatolius was appointed his successor, one good man, as they say, following another. He also was by race an Alexandrian, who for his learning, secular education and philosophy had attained the first place among our most illustrious contemporaries; inasmuch as in arithmetic and geometry, in astronomy and other sciences, whether of logic or of physics, and in the arts of rhetoric as well, he had reached the pinnacle. It is recorded that because of these attainments the citizens there deemed him worthy to establish the school of the

7 Aristotelian tradition [2] at Alexandria. Now countless other of his deeds of prowess are related during the siege of the Pyrucheum at Alexandria, seeing that he was deemed worthy by all of an extraordinary privilege among the officials; but as an example I shall make mention of the following one only.

8 It is said that when the wheat failed the besieged, so that hunger was now a more intolerable thing than their enemies without, the person of whom we are speaking, being present, adopted the following device. The other part of the city was fighting in alliance with the Roman army, and thus was not besieged. Among these latter was Eusebius (for [it is said] that he was still there at that time before his migration to Syria), who had won so great fame and so widespread a reputation that it reached the ears even of the Roman general To him Anatolius sent, and informed him as to those that were perish-

9 ing of hunger in the siege. When he learnt it, he asked the Roman commander as a very great favour to grant safety to deserters from the enemy; and having obtained his request acquainted Anatolius of the fact. The moment Anatolius received the promise, he assembled a council of the Alexandrians, and at first requested all to extend the right hand of fellowship to the Romans. But when he perceived that they

---

[1] II. 3, 24.   [2] Lit. " succession."

were getting angry at the proposal, " At any rate," said he,
" I do not think you would contradict me if I were to counsel
that those who were superfluous and in no wise useful to us
ourselves, old women and young children and old men, should
be permitted to go outside the gates whithersoever they wish.
Why keep we these persons with us to no purpose, seeing they
are all but on the point of death ?   Why destroy we with
hunger the maimed and crippled in body, when we should
support only men and youths, and husband the necessary
10 wheat for such as are required to guard the city ? "   With
some such arguments he persuaded the assembly, and was
the first to rise and give his vote that the whole body of those
who were not required for the army, whether men or women,
should depart from the city, because were they to remain and
uselessly stay therein, there would be no hope of safety for
11 them, since they would perish with hunger.   And when all the
rest of those in the assembly assented to this proposal, he went
within a little of saving the whole of them that were besieged ;
he took care that first of all those belonging to the Church, and
then the rest remaining in the city, of all ages, should escape,
not only those who came under the terms of the vote, but also
great numbers of others, passing themselves off as such, who
secretly donned women's attire, and by his management left
the gates by night and hastened to the Roman army.   Eusebius was there to receive them all, and, like a father and
physician, restore them, in evil plight after their long siege,
with every kind of forethought and attention.
12   Such were the two pastors that the church of Laodicea
was deemed worthy to have successively, who by divine
providence, after the above-mentioned war, had left the city
of the Alexandrians to come there.
13   Not a very great many works, indeed, were composed by
Anatolius, but enough have reached us to enable us to perceive
both his eloquence and his great erudition.   In these he
presents, especially, his opinions with reference to the Pascha ;
from which it may be necessary on the present occasion to give
the following passage.

From the Canons of Anatolius on the Pascha.

14   It has therefore in the first year the new moon of the first
month, which is the beginning of the whole nineteen-year cycle,
on the 26th of Phamenoth according to the Egyptians, but according to the months of the Macedonians the 22nd of Dystrus, or, as
the Romans would say, the 11th before the Kalends of April.
15 The sun is found on the aforesaid 26th of Phamenoth not only to
have arrived at the first sign of the zodiac, but already to be
passing through the fourth day within it.   This sign is commonly
called the first of the twelve divisions and the equinoctial [sign]
and the beginning of months and head of the cycle and the starting-point of the planetary course.   But the preceding [sign] is

the last of the months and the twelfth sign and the last of the twelve divisions and the end of the planetary circuit. Therefore we say that they who place the first month in it, and determine the fourteenth day of the Pascha accordingly,[1] are guilty of no
16 small or ordinary mistake. And this is not our own statement, but the fact was known to the Jews, those of old time even before Christ, and it was carefully observed by them. One may learn it from what is said by Philo, Josephus and Musæus, and not only by them but also by those of still more ancient date, the two Agathobuli, surnamed the Masters of Aristobulus the Great.[2] He was reckoned among the Seventy who translated the sacred and divine Hebrew Scriptures for Ptolemy Philadelphus and his father; and he dedicated books exegetical of the Law of Moses
17 to the same kings. These [writers], when they resolve the questions relative to the Exodus, say that all equally ought to sacrifice the passover after the vernal equinox, at the middle of the first month; and that this is found to occur when the sun is passing through the first sign of the solar, or, as some have named it, the zodiacal cycle. And Aristobulus adds that at the feast of the passover it is necessary that not only the sun should be passing
18 through an equinoctial sign, but the moon also. For as the equinoctial signs are two, the one vernal, the other autumnal, diametrically opposite each to other, and as the fourteenth of the month, at evening, is assigned as the day of the passover, the moon will have its place in the station that is diametrically opposed to the sun, as may be seen in full moons; and the one, the sun, will be in the sign of the vernal equinox, while the other, the moon,
19 will of necessity be in that of the autumnal. I know many other statements of theirs, some of them probable, others advanced as absolute proofs,[3] by which they attempt to establish that the Feast of the Passover and of unleavened bread ought without exception to be held after the equinox. But I refrain from demanding proofs thus composed from those for whom *the veil upon* the law of *Moses* has been *taken away*, and for whom it now remains *with unveiled face* ever *to behold as in a mirror*[4] Christ and the things of Christ, both what He learned and what He suffered.[5] But that the first month with the Hebrews lies around the equinox is shown also by the teachings in the Book of Enoch.[6]

20 And the same person has left behind Introductions to Arithmetic also in ten complete treatises, and, as well, evidences
21 of his study and deep knowledge of divine things. Theotecnus, bishop of Cæsarea in Palestine, first had ordained him to the episcopate, seeking to procure him as his successor in his own community after his death, and indeed for some short time both presided over the same church. But, the synod with reference to Paul summoning him to Antioch, as he was

---

[1] The Greek (κατ' αὐτήν) is unintelligible.
[2] τοῦ πάνυ: the punctuation of Schwartz has been kept, but a more probable translation is, " the two Agathobuli, surnamed the Masters, and Aristobulus the Great "—three separate authorities.
[3] The translation is uncertain.   [4] 2 Cor. iii. 15, 16, 18.
[5] μαθήματα παθήματα: Herod. i. 207; cp. Heb. v. 8.
[6] Enoch 72. 6, 9, 31, 32.

passing by the city of the Laodiceans he was retained there by the brethren, Eusebius having fallen asleep.

22   And when Anatolius also departed this life, Stephen was appointed over the community there, the last bishop before the persecution.   He won widespread admiration for his knowledge of philosophy and other secular learning, but he was not similarly disposed towards the divine faith, as the progress of the persecution clearly proved, demonstrating that the man was more of a dissembler, more of a craven and coward, than a true philosopher.

23   But indeed the church and her affairs were not destined to perish because of him; they were set to rights by one who was immediately proclaimed bishop of that community by God Himself, the Saviour of all, even Theodotus, a man whose deeds themselves proved true his title to his own name and that of a bishop.   He had reached, indeed, the first rank in the science of healing bodies, but in that of curing souls he was second to none among men, because of his benevolence, sincerity, fellow-feeling and zeal towards those that sought his aid; and he was also greatly devoted to the study of divinity.

Cæsarea : Pamphilus.

24   Such a one was he.   But at Cæsarea in Palestine Theotecnus, after exercising his episcopal office in the most zealous fashion, was succeeded by Agapius, whom also we know to have laboured much, displaying a most genuine regard for the government of his people, and with a liberal hand caring
25   especially for all the poor.   In his day we came to know Pamphilus, a most eloquent man and a true philosopher in his mode of life, who had been deemed worthy of the presbyterate of that community.   It would be no small undertaking to show the kind of man he was and whence he came.   But of each particular of his life and of the school that he established, as well as his contest in various confessions during the persecution, and the crown of martyrdom with which he was wreathed at the end of all, we have treated separately in a special work concerning him.

Pierius and Meletius.

26   Truly he was the most admirable of those of that city; but as men possessed of especially rare qualities in our day we know Pierius, one of the presbyters at Alexandria, and
27   Meletius, bishop of the churches in Pontus.   The former of these had been noted for his life of extreme poverty and for his learning in philosophy.   He was exceedingly well practised in the deeper study of divine things and in expositions thereof, as well as in his public discourses in church.   Meletius (edu-

cated persons used to call him the honey of Attica) was such
as one would describe as a most accomplished scholar in all
respects.   It is impossible to admire sufficiently his skill in
oratory, yet this might be said to be his by a natural gift.
But who could surpass the excellence of his great experience
28 and erudition as well, because you would say, even on a single
trial, that he was the most skilful and learned man in all
branches of literature ?   Equally, too, was his life distinguished
for its virtues.   We took note of him during the period of
the persecution, as for seven whole years he was fleeing in the
regions of Palestine.

Jerusalem.

29   In the church at Jerusalem, after the bishop Hymenæus
mentioned shortly before, Zabdas received the ministry.
After no great time he fell asleep, and Hermo, the last of the
bishops up to the persecution in our day, succeeded to the
apostolic throne that has still been preserved there to the
present day.

Alexandria : Achillas.

30   And at Alexandria too, Maximus, who had held the episcopate for eighteen years after the death of Dionysius, was
succeeded by Theonas.   In his day at Alexandria Achillas,
deemed worthy of the presbyterate along with Pierius, was
well known ; he had been entrusted with the school of the
sacred faith, having displayed a wealth of philosophy most
rare and inferior to none, and a manner of life that was truly
31 in accordance with the Gospel.   After Theonas had given his
utmost service for nineteen years, Peter succeeded to the
episcopate of the Alexandrians, and he too was especially
prominent for twelve entire years ; he ruled the church for
less than three entire years before the persecution, and for the
remainder of his days practised a life of severer discipline,
and cared in no hidden manner for the general good of the
churches.   For this reason, therefore, in the ninth year of the
persecution he was beheaded, and so adorned with the crown
of martyrdom.

Conclusion.

32   In these books having concluded the subject of the successions, from the birth of our Saviour to the destruction of the
places of prayer—a subject that extends over three hundred
and five years—come, let us next leave in writing, for the
information of those also that come after us, what the extent
and nature have been of the conflicts in our own day of those
who manfully contended for piety.

BOOK VIII

The Eighth Book of the Ecclesiastical History contains the following:

1. On the events before the persecution in our day.
2. On the destruction of the churches.
3. On the nature of the conflicts endured in the persecution.
4. On the famed martyrs of God, how they filled every place with their memory, being wreathed with varied crowns for piety.
5. On those in Nicomedia.
6. On those in the imperial palaces.
7. On the Egyptians in Phœnicia.
8. On those in Egypt.
9. On those in the Thebais.
10. Accounts [1] in writing of Phileas the martyr concerning what had taken place at Alexandria.
11. On the martyrs in Phrygia.
12. On very many others, both men and women, who endured various conflicts.
13. On the presidents of the Church who displayed in their own blood the genuineness of the piety of which they were ambassadors.
14. On the character of the enemies of piety.
15. On the events which happened to those without [the Church].
16. On the change of affairs for the better.
17. On the recantation of the rulers.

---

[1] διδασκαλίαι.

ref. HAVING concluded the succession from the apostles in seven entire books, in this eighth treatise we regard it as one of our most urgent duties to hand down, for the knowledge of those that come after us, the events of our own day, which are worthy of no casual record; and from this point our account will take its beginning.

The Prosperity of the Church.

1. It is beyond our powers to describe in a worthy manner the measure and nature of that honour as well as freedom which was accorded by all men, both Greeks and barbarians, before the persecution in our day, to that word of piety toward the God of the universe which had been proclaimed through 2 Christ to the world. Yet proofs might be forthcoming in the favours granted by the rulers to our people; to whom they would even entrust the government of the provinces, freeing them from agony of mind as regards sacrificing, because of the great friendliness that they used to entertain 3 for their doctrine. Why need one speak of those in the imperial palaces and of the supreme rulers, who allowed the members of their households—wives, children and servants—to practise openly to their face the divine word and conduct, and—one might say—permitted them even to boast of the freedom accorded to the faith? And these they used to regard with especial esteem and more favourably than their 4 fellow-servants. Such a one was the famous Dorotheus, who surpassed all in his devotion and faithfulness to them, and for this reason was more highly honoured than men who held positions as rulers or governors. With him was the celebrated Gorgonius and all those who, like them, had been deemed 5 worthy of the same honour because of the word of God. With what favour one might note that the rulers in every church were honoured by all procurators and governors! And how could one fully describe those assemblies thronged with countless men, and the multitudes that gathered together in every city, and the famed concourses in the places of prayer; by reason of which they were no longer satisfied with the buildings of olden time, and would erect from the foundations churches of spacious dimensions throughout all the cities? 6 And as these things went forward with the times, and day by day increasingly grew mightier, no envy could stop them, nor was any evil spirit able to cast its spell or hinder them by human devices, so long as the divine and heavenly hand was sheltering and guarding, as a worthy object, its own people.

The Sins of the Church the Cause of Persecution.

7   But when, as the result of greater freedom, a change to pride and sloth came over our affairs, we fell to envy and fierce railing against one another, warring upon ourselves, so to speak, as occasion offered, with weapons and spears formed of words; and rulers attacked rulers and laity formed factions against laity, while unspeakable hypocrisy and pretence pursued their evil course to the furthest end : until the divine judgment with a sparing hand, as is its wont (for the assemblies were still crowded), quietly and moderately began to exercise its oversight, the persecution commencing
8 with the brethren in the army. But when in our blindness we took not the least care to secure the goodwill and propitious favour of the Deity, but, like some kind of atheists, imagined that our affairs escaped all heed and oversight, we went on adding one wickedness to another; and those accounted our pastors, casting aside the sanctions of the fear of God, were enflamed with mutual contentions, and did nothing else but add to the strifes and threats, the jealousy, enmity and hatred that they used one to another, claiming with all vehemence the objects of their ambition as if they were a despot's spoils; then indeed, then according to the word spoken by Jeremiah, *the Lord hath darkened the daughter of Zion in his anger*, and *hath cast down from heaven the glory of Israel ; he hath not remembered his footstool in the day of his anger ;* but *the Lord hath* also *swallowed up all the beauty of*
9 *Israel* [1] and *hath broken down all his hedges.* [2] And according to what has been foretold in the Psalms, *He hath overturned the covenant of his servant* and *hath profaned to the ground,* through the destruction of the churches, *his sanctuary* and *hath broken down all his hedges, he hath made his strongholds cowardice. All that pass by the way have spoiled* the multitudes of the people, yea more, *he hath become a reproach to his neighbours. For he hath exalted the right hand of his adversaries,* and *hath turned back the help of his sword and hath not taken his part in the battle. But he hath* also *made his purification to cease,* and *hath cast his throne down to the ground,* and *hath shortened the days of his time* and, last of all, *he hath covered him with shame.* [3]

2.   All things in truth were fulfilled in our day, when we saw with our very eyes the houses of prayer cast down to their foundations from top to bottom, and the inspired and sacred

---

[1] Lam. ii. 1, 2 (with variations from LXX).
[2] Ps. lxxxix. 40.   [3] Ps. lxxxix. 39–45.

Scriptures committed to the flames in the midst of the market-places, and the pastors of the churches, some shamefully hiding themselves here and there, while others were ignominiously captured and made a mockery by their enemies; when also, according to another prophetic word, *He poureth contempt upon princes, and causeth them to wander in the waste, where there is no way.*[1]

2   But as to these, it is not our part to describe their melancholy misfortunes in the issue, even as we do not think it proper to hand down to memory their dissensions and unnatural conduct to one another before the persecution. Therefore we resolved to place on record nothing more about

3   them than what would justify the divine judgment. Accordingly, we determined not even to mention those who have been tried by the persecution, or have *made* utter *shipwreck*[2] of their salvation, and of their own free will were plunged in the depths of the billows; but we shall add to the general history only such things as may be profitable, first to ourselves, and then to those that come after us. Let us proceed, therefore, from this point to give a summary description of the sacred conflicts of the martyrs of the divine Word.

The First, Second and Third Edicts.

4   It was the nineteenth year of the reign of Diocletian, and

303.   the month Dystrus, or March, as the Romans would call it, in which, as the festival of the Saviour's Passion was coming on, an imperial letter was everywhere promulgated, ordering the razing of the churches to the ground and the destruction by fire of the Scriptures, and proclaiming that those who held high positions would lose all civil rights, while those in households, if they persisted in their profession

5   of Christianity, would be deprived of their liberty. Such was the first document against us. But not long afterwards we were further visited with other letters, and in them the order was given that the presidents of the churches should all, in every place, be first committed to prison, and then afterwards compelled by every kind of device to sacrifice.

Results of the Third Edict.

3.   Then indeed, then very many rulers of the churches contended with a stout heart under terrible torments, and displayed spectacles of mighty conflicts; while countless others, whose souls cowardice had numbed beforehand, readily proved weak at the first assault; while of the rest, each underwent a series of varied forms of torture : one would

[1] Ps. cvii. 40.   [2] 1 Tim. i. 19.

have his body maltreated by scourgings; another would be punished with the rack and torn to an unbearable degree,
2 whereat some met a miserable end to their life. But others, again, emerged from the conflict otherwise : one man was brought to the abominable and unholy sacrifices by the violence of others who pressed round him, and dismissed as if he had sacrificed, even though he had not; another who did not so much as approach or touch any accursed thing, when others had said that he had sacrificed, went away bearing the false accusation in silence. A third was taken up half-dead and
3 cast aside as if he were a corpse already; and, again, a certain person lying on the ground was dragged a long distance by the feet, having been reckoned among those who had voluntarily sacrificed. One cried out and with a loud voice attested his refusal to sacrifice, and another shouted aloud that he was a Christian, glorying in his confession of the saving Name. Another stoutly maintained that he had not sacri-
4 ficed, and never would. Nevertheless these also were struck on the mouth and silenced by a large band of soldiers drawn up for that purpose, and with blows on their face and cheeks driven forcibly away. So great store did the enemies of godliness set on seeming by any means to have accomplished their purpose.

Persecution in the Army.

But even such methods did not avail them against the holy martyrs. What word of ours could suffice for an
4. accurate description of these ? For one might tell of countless numbers who displayed a marvellous zeal for piety to the God of the universe ; not only from what time the persecution was stirred up against all, but long before, during the period
2 when peace was still firmly established. For when he who had received the authority was just now awakening, as it were, from profound torpor, though he was in a secret and hidden manner already making attempts against the churches during the time that came after Decius and Valerian, and did not get himself in readiness for the war against us all at once, but as yet made an attempt only upon those in the camps (for in this way he thought that the rest also could easily be taken, if first of all he were to get the better in the conflict with these) : then one could see great numbers of those in the army most gladly embracing civil life, so that they might not prove renegades in their piety toward the
3 Creator of the universe. For when the " magister militiæ," [1] whoever he was, was just making his first attempt at persecuting the soldiers—separating into classes and thoroughly sifting out those serving in the camps, giving them a choice

---

[1] στρατοπεδάρχης : see note.

whether they would obey and enjoy the rank they held,
or else be deprived of it, if they continued to disobey the
commandment—a great many soldiers of Christ's kingdom,
without hesitation, unquestionably preferred to confess Him
than retain the seeming glory and prosperity that they
4 possessed. And already in rare cases one or two of these
were receiving not only loss of honour but even death in
exchange for their godly stedfastness, for as yet the instigator
of the plot was working with a certain moderation and daring
to proceed *unto blood* [1] only in some instances; fearing, presumably, the multitude of believers, and hesitating to plunge
into the war against us all at once.

An Edict torn down.

5 But when he prepared himself still further for battle, it
is quite impossible to recount the number or the splendour of
God's martyrs that it was given to the inhabitants throughout
all the cities and country parts to see.

5. To begin with, the moment that the decree against the
churches was published at Nicomedia, a certain person by no
means obscure, but most highly honoured as the world counts
pre-eminence, moved by zeal towards God and carried away
by his burning faith, seized and tore it to pieces, when posted
up in an open and public place, as an unholy and profane
thing; [and this he did] while two emperors were present in the
same city, the senior of them all, and he who held the fourth
place in the government after him. But this man was the first
of those at that time who thus distinguished himself; and, at
the same time, in his endurance of such results as naturally
followed a daring act of this kind, he maintained an untroubled
and undisturbed demeanour to his very last breath.

Martyrs at Nicomedia.

6. But above all those whose praises have ever yet been sung
as worthy of admiration and famed for courage, whether
by Greeks or barbarians, this occasion produced, as divine
and outstanding martyrs, Dorotheus and the imperial servants
that were with him. These persons had been deemed worthy
of the highest honour by their masters, who loved them no
less than their own children; but they *accounted* the
reproaches and sufferings for piety and the many forms of
death that were newly devised against them, as truly *greater
riches* [2] than the fair fame and luxury of this life. We shall
mention the kind of death that one of them met, and leave
our readers to gather from that instance what happened to
the others.

[1] Heb. xii. 4.   [2] *Ib*. xi. 26.

2   A certain man was publicly brought forward in the city of which we have spoken above, under the rulers we have mentioned. He was ordered to sacrifice; and, as he refused, the command was given that he should be raised on high naked, and have his whole body torn with scourges, until he should give in, and even against his will do what was bidden 3 him. But when he remained unmoved even under these sufferings, they proceeded to mix vinegar and salt together and pour them into the mangled parts of his body, where the bones were already showing. And as he despised these pains also, a gridiron and fire were then produced, and the remnants of his body, just as if it were flesh for eating, were consumed by the fire, not all at once, in case he might find immediate release, but little by little; nor were those who placed him on the pyre allowed to desist, until, after such sufferings, he 4 should signify his assent to what was commanded. But he clung fixedly to his purpose, and triumphantly gave up the ghost in the midst of his tortures. Such was the martyrdom of one of the imperial servants, who truly was worthy of his name. For he was called Peter.

5   But we shall pass by the martyrdoms of the rest, though they were not inferior, having regard to the due proportions of the book; only placing it on record that Dorotheus and Gorgonius, together with many others of the imperial household, after conflicts of various kinds, departed this life by strangling, and so carried off the prizes of the God-given victory.

6   At that time Anthimus, who then presided over the church at Nicomedia, was beheaded for his witness to Christ. And with him was associated a large number of martyrs all together; for, I know not how, in the palace at Nicomedia a fire broke out in those very days, and through a false suspicion the rumour went around that it was the work of our people : and by the imperial command the God-fearing persons there, whole families and in heaps, were in some cases butchered with the sword; while others were perfected by fire, when it is recorded that men and women leaped upon the pyre with a divine and unspeakable eagerness. The executioners bound a multitude of others, and [placing them] on boats threw 7 them into the depths of the sea. As to the imperial servants, whose bodies after death had been committed to the ground with fitting honours, their reputed masters, starting afresh, deemed it necessary to exhume them and cast them also into the sea, lest any, regarding them as actually gods (so at least they imagined), should worship them as they lay in their tombs.

Sedition in Melitene and Syria : Second Edict.

Such were the things that were done in Nicomedia at the
8 beginning of the persecution. But not long afterwards, when
some in the district known as Melitene, and, again on the
other hand when others in Syria, had attempted to take
possession of the Empire, an imperial command went forth
that the presidents of the churches everywhere should be
9 thrown into prison and bonds. And the spectacle of what
followed surpasses all description ; for in every place a
countless number were shut up, and everywhere the prisons,
that long ago had been prepared for murderers and
grave-robbers, were then filled with bishops and presbyters
and deacons, readers and exorcists, so that there was no
longer any room left there for those condemned for wrong-
doing.

The Third Edict.

10   Moreover, the first letter was followed by others, wherein
the order had been given that those in prison should be
allowed to go in liberty if they sacrificed, but if they refused,
should be mutilated by countless tortures. And then, once
more, how could one here number the multitude of the martyrs
in each province, and especially of those in Africa and Mauri-
tania,[1] and in Thebais and Egypt ? From this last country
also some departed into other cities and provinces and were
distinguished in their martyrdoms.

Egyptians at Tyre.

7.   We know at any rate those of them who were conspicuous
in Palestine, and we know also those at Tyre in Phœnicia.
Who that saw them was not struck with amazement at the
numberless lashes and the stedfastness displayed under them
by these truly marvellous champions of godliness ; at the
conflict with man-eating wild beasts that followed immediately
on the lashes ; the attacks that then took place of leopards
and different kinds of bears, of wild boars and bulls goaded
with hot iron ; and the marvellous endurance of these noble
2 persons when opposed to each of the wild beasts ? We
ourselves were present when these things were happening,
what time we beheld the present, divine power of our Saviour,
Jesus Christ Himself, the Object of their witness, and the
clear manifestation of that power to the martyrs. The man-
eating beasts for a considerable time did not dare to touch
or even approach the bodies of those who were dear to God,
but made the attacks on the others who presumably were

---

[1] Lit. " the province (ἔθνος) of the Moors."

261

provoking and urging them on from the outside; while the
holy champions were the only persons they did not reach at
all, though they stood naked, waving their hands to draw
them on to themselves (for this they were commanded to
do); and sometimes, when the beasts would make a rush at
them, they would be checked by, as it were, some divine
3 power and once again retreat to the rear. And when this
happened for a long time, it occasioned no small astonishment
among the spectators, so that, as the first beast did nothing,
a second and a third were let loose against one and the same
martyr.

4   One might be astounded at the fearless and valiant bearing
of those holy persons in the face of these trials, and the steady,
inflexible endurance to be found in young bodies. For
example, you might have seen a youth, not twenty years old
in all, standing unbound, his hands spread in the form of a
cross, and, with a mind undismayed and unmoved, most
leisurely engaged in earnest prayer to the Deity; never a whit
changing his ground or retreating from the place where he
had taken his stand, while bears and leopards, breathing
anger and death, almost touched his very flesh. And yet,
by a divine and mysterious power I cannot explain, their
mouths were muzzled, so to speak, and they ran back again
5 to the rear. Such a one was he.

Again you might have seen others (for they were five in all)
thrown to a maddened bull, who, when others approached
from the outside, tossed them into the air with his horns and
mangled them, leaving them to be taken up half-dead; but
when he rushed in threatening anger at the holy martyrs as
they stood unprotected, he was unable even to approach
them, though he pawed with his feet and pushed with his
horns this way and that; and though the goading irons
provoked him to *breathe* anger *and threatening* [1] he was
dragged away backwards by Divine Providence; so that
other wild beasts were let loose against them, since the bull
6 in no way did them the slightest injury. Then at last, after
the terrible and varied assaults of these beasts, they were all
butchered with the sword, and instead of being buried in the
earth were committed to the waves of the sea.

Martyrs in Egypt.

8.　　　Such was the contest of the Egyptians who at Tyre displayed their conflicts on behalf of piety. But one must
admire those of them also that were martyred in their own
land, where countless numbers, men, women and children,
despising this passing life, endured various forms of death
for the sake of our Saviour's teaching. Some of them were

----

[1] Acts ix. 1.

committed to the flames after being torn and racked and
grievously scourged, and suffering other manifold torments
terrible to hear, while some were engulfed in the sea; others
with a good courage stretched forth their heads to them that
cut them off, or died in the midst of their tortures, or perished
of hunger; and others again were crucified, some as malefactors usually are, and some, even more brutally, were
nailed in the opposite manner, head-downwards, and kept
alive until they should perish of hunger on the gibbet.

Martyrs in the Thebais.

9.   But it surpasses all description what the martyrs in the
Thebais endured as regards both outrages and agonies. They
had the entire body torn to pieces with sharp sherds instead
of claws, even until life was extinct. Women were fastened
by one foot and swung aloft through the air, head-downwards,
to a height by certain machines, their bodies completely
naked with not even a covering; and thus they presented
this most disgraceful, cruel and inhuman of all spectacles to
2 the whole company of onlookers. Others, again, were
fastened to trees and trunks, and so died. For they drew
together by certain machines the very strongest of the
branches, to each of which they fastened one of the martyr's
legs, and then released the branches to take up their natural
position : thus contriving the rending asunder all at once of
3 the limbs of those who were the objects of this device. And
indeed all these things were done, not for a few days or for
some brief space, but for a long period extending over whole
years—sometimes more than ten, at other times above twenty
persons being put to death; and at others not less than
thirty, now nearer sixty, and again at other times a hundred
men would be slain in a single day, along with quite young
children and women, being condemned to manifold punishments which followed one on the other.
4   And we ourselves also beheld, when we were at these places,
many all at once in a single day, some of whom suffered
decapitation, others the punishment of fire; so that the
murderous axe was dulled and, worn out, was broken in pieces,
while the executioners themselves grew utterly weary and
5 took it in turns to succeed one another. It was then that we
observed a most marvellous eagerness and a truly divine
power and zeal in those who had placed their faith in the
Christ of God. Thus, as soon as sentence was given against
the first, some from one quarter and others from another
would leap up to the tribunal before the judge and confess
themselves Christians; paying no heed when faced with
terrors and the varied forms of tortures, but undismayedly
and boldly speaking of the piety towards the God of the

universe, and with joy and laughter and gladness receiving
the final sentence of death; so that they sang and sent up
hymns and thanksgivings to the God of the universe even to
the very last breath.

Philoromus and Phileas.

6   And while these indeed were marvellous, those especially
were marvellous who were distinguished for wealth, birth
and reputation, as also for learning and philosophy, and yet
put everything second to true piety and faith in our Saviour
7 and Lord Jesus Christ. Such was Philoromus; who had
been entrusted with an office of no small importance in the
imperial administration at Alexandria, and who, in connection with the dignity and rank that he had from the
Romans, used to conduct judicial enquiries every day,
attended by a body-guard of soldiers. Such also was Phileas,
bishop of the church of the Thmuites, a man who was distinguished for the services he rendered to his country in
8 public positions, and also for his skill in philosophy. And
though great numbers of relatives and other friends besought
them, as well as many officials of high rank, and though the
judge himself exhorted them to take pity on themselves and
spare their children and wives, they could in no wise be
induced by this strong pressure to decide in favour of love of
life and despise the ordinances of our Saviour as to confessing
and denying; [1] but with a brave and philosophic resolution,
nay rather, with a pious and godly soul, they stood firm
against all the threats and insults of the judge, and both
were beheaded.

A Letter of Phileas.

10.   But since we said [2] that Phileas deserved a high reputation
for his secular learning as well, let him appear as his own
witness, to show us who he was, and at the same time to relate,
more accurately than we could, the martyrdoms that took
place at Alexandria. Here are his words :

From the Writings of Phileas to the Thmuites.

2   Since all these examples and patterns and goodly tokens are
placed before us in the divine and sacred Scriptures, the blessed
martyrs with us did not hesitate, but directed the eye of the
soul sincerely towards the God who is over all, and with a mind
resolved on death for piety they clung fast to their calling, finding
that our Lord Jesus Christ became man for our sakes, that He
might destroy every kind of sin, and provide us with the means
of entering into eternal life. For *he counted it not a prize to be
on an equality with God, but emptied himself, taking the form of a
servant ; and being found in fashion as a man, he humbled himself*

---

[1] Matt. x. 32 f.; Lk. xii. 8 f.   [2] 9. 7.

3 *unto death, yea, the death of the cross.*[1] Wherefore also, *desiring earnestly the greater gifts,*[2] the Christ-bearing martyrs endured every kind of suffering and all manner of devices of torture, not once, but even a second time in some cases; and though their guards vied in all kinds of threats against them, not only in word but also in deed, they refused to give up their resolution, because

4 *perfect love casteth out fear.*[3] What account would suffice to reckon up their bravery and courage under each torture ? For when all who wished were given a free hand to insult them, some smote them with cudgels, others with rods, others with scourges;

5 others, again, with straps, and others with ropes. And the spectacle of their tortures was a varied one with no lack of wickedness therein. Some with both hands bound behind them were suspended upon the gibbet, and with the aid of certain machines stretched out in every limb; then, as they lay in this plight, the torturers acting on orders began to lay on over their whole body, not only, as in the case of murderers, punishing their sides with the instruments of torture, but also their belly, legs and cheeks. Others were suspended from the porch by one hand and raised aloft; and in the tension of their joints and limbs experienced unequalled agony. Others were bound with their face towards pillars, their feet not touching the ground, and thus their bonds were drawn tight by the pressure upon them of

6 the weight of the body. And this they would endure, not while the governor conversed or was engaged with them, but almost throughout the entire day. For when he went away to others, he would leave the agents of his authority to watch the first, if perchance anyone should be overcome by the tortures and seem to give in; and he bade them approach mercilessly with bonds also,[4] and, when they were at the last gasp after all this, take

7 them down to the ground and drag them off. For [he said] that they were not to have the least particle of regard for us, but to be so disposed and act as if we were no longer of any account. Such was the second torture that our enemies devised in addition

8 to the stripes. And some, even after the tortures, were placed in the stocks, and had both feet stretched out to the fourth hole, so that they were compelled to lie on their back therein, being unable [to sit upright] because of the recent wounds they had from the stripes over the whole body. Others were thrown to the ground and lay there, by reason of the wholesale application of the tortures; presenting to those who saw them a sight more terrible than did the actual punishment, in that they bore on their bodies marks of the manifold and varied tortures that were devised.

9 In this condition of affairs, some died under their tortures, having shamed the adversary by their endurance; while others were shut up half dead in prison, and after not many days perfected by reason of their agonies; the remainder recovered under treatment, and as the result of time and their stay in prison gained

10 confidence. So then, when the order was given and the choice held out, either to touch the abominable sacrifice and be unmolested, receiving from them the accursed freedom; or not to sacrifice and be punished with death : without hesitation they

---

[1] Phil. ii. 6–8.   [2] 1 Cor. xii. 31.   [3] 1 John iv. 18.
[4] The text gives no good sense : perhaps we should read " he bade them actually add to their bonds without mercy."

gladly went to their death. For they knew what had been prescribed for us by the sacred Scriptures. For he says, *He that sacrificeth unto other gods shall be utterly destroyed ;* [1] and, *Thou shalt have none other gods but me.* [2]

11   Such are the words of the martyr, true lover both of wisdom and of God, which he sent to the brethren in his community before the final sentence, when he was still in a state of imprisonment, at one and the same time showing the conditions in which he was living, and also stirring them up to hold fast to the fear of God in Christ, even after his death who
12 was just about to be perfected. But why need one make a long story and add fresh instance upon instance of the conflicts of the godly martyrs throughout the world, especially of those who were assailed no longer by the common law, but as if they were enemies ?

Martyrs in Phrygia.

11.   For instance, at this time armed soldiers surrounded a little town in Phrygia, of which the inhabitants were all Christians, every man of them, and setting fire to it burnt them, along with young children and women as they were calling upon the God who is over all. The reason of this was, that all the inhabitants of the town to a man, the curator himself and the duumvirs [3] with all the officials and the whole assembly, confessed themselves Christians and refused to give the least heed to those who bade them commit idolatry.
2   And there was a certain other person who had attained to a high position under the Romans, Adauctus by name, a man of illustrious Italian birth ; who had advanced through every grade of honour under the emperors, so as to pass blamelessly through the general administration of what they call the magistracy and ministry of finance. And besides all this, having distinguished himself by his noble deeds of godliness and his confessions of the Christ of God, he was adorned with the crown of martyrdom, enduring the conflict for piety while actually engaged as finance minister.

Martyrs in Arabia, Cappadocia, Mesopotamia, and Alexandria.

12.   Why need I now mention the rest by name, or number the multitude of the men, or picture the varied tortures inflicted upon the wonderful martyrs ? Sometimes they were slain with the axe, as was the case with those in Arabia ; at other times they had their legs broken, as happened to those in Cappadocia ; on some occasions they were suspended on high by the feet, head-downwards, while a slow fire was kindled

---

[1] Ex. xxii. 20.   [2] Ex. xx. 3.   [3] στρατηγοί.

beneath, so that when the wood was alight they were choked by the rising smoke—a treatment meted out to those in Mesopotamia; on others, the noses, ears and hands were mutilated, and the remaining limbs and parts of the body cut up, as was done at Alexandria.

Martyrs of Antioch.

2 Why need one rekindle the memory of those at Antioch, who were roasted on heated gridirons, not unto death, but with a view to lengthy torture; and of others who put their right hand into the very fire sooner than touch the accursed sacrifice? Some of them, to escape such trials, before they were caught and fell into the hands of those that plotted against them, threw themselves down from the tops of lofty houses, regarding death as a prize snatched from the wickedness of evil men.

3 And a certain holy person, admirable for strength of soul yet in body a woman, and famed as well by all that were at Antioch for wealth, birth and sound judgment, had brought up in the precepts of piety her two unmarried daughters, distinguished for the full bloom of their youthful beauty. Much envy was stirred up on their account, and busied itself in tracing in every manner possible where they lay concealed; and when it discovered that they were staying in a foreign country, of set purpose it recalled them to Antioch. Thus they fell into the soldiers' toils. When, therefore, the woman saw that herself and her daughters were in desperate straits, she placed before them in conversation the terrible things that awaited them from human hands, and the most intolerable thing of all these terrors—the threat of fornication. She exhorted both herself and her girls that they ought not to submit to listen to even the least whisper of such a thing, and said that to surrender their souls to the slavery of demons was worse than all kinds of death and every form of destruction. So she submitted that to flee to the Lord was the 4 only way of escape from it all. And when they had both agreed to her opinion, and had arranged their garments suitably around them, on coming to the middle of their journey they quietly requested the guards to allow them a little time for retirement, and threw themselves into the river that flowed by.

5 Thus were these their own executioners. But another pair of maidens, also at Antioch, godly in every respect and true sisters, famous by birth, distinguished for their manner of life, young in years, in the bloom of beauty, grave of soul, pious in their deportment, admirable in their zeal, the worshippers of demons commanded to be cast into the sea, as if the earth could not endure to bear such excellence.

Martyrs in Pontus.

6 Thus it happened with these martyrs. And others in
Pontus suffered things terrible to hear : sharp reeds were
driven through their fingers under the tips of the nails; in
the case of others, lead was melted down by fire, and the
boiling, burning stuff poured down their backs, roasting the
7 most essential parts of their body; others endured in their
privy parts and bowels sufferings that were disgraceful,
pitiless, unmentionable, which the noble and law-abiding
judges devised with more than usual eagerness, displaying
their cruelty as if it were some great stroke of wisdom;
striving to outdo one another by ever inventing novel tortures,
as if contending for prizes in a contest.

8 But the end of these calamities came when they were now
worn out with their excessive wickedness, and were utterly
weary of killing and surfeited and sated with shedding blood,
and so turned to what they considered merciful and humane
conduct; so that they no longer thought that they were doing
9 any harm to us. For it was not fitting, they said, to pollute
the cities with the blood of their own people, or to involve
in a charge of cruelty the supreme government of the rulers,
a government that was well-disposed and mild towards all;
but rather that the beneficence of the humane and imperial
authority should be extended to all, and the death penalty
no longer inflicted. For [they declared] that this their
punishment of us had been stopped, thanks to the humanity
10 of the rulers. Then orders were given that their eyes should
be gouged out and one of their legs maimed. For this was
in their opinion humanity and the lightest of punishments
inflicted upon us. Hence, because of this humanity on the
part of godless men, it is now no longer possible to tell the
incalculable number of those who had their right eye first
cut out with a sword and then cauterized with fire, and the
left foot rendered useless by the further application of branding
irons to the joints, and who after this were condemned to
the provincial copper mines, not so much for service as for
ill-usage and hardship, and withal fell in with various other
trials, which it is not possible even to recount; for their
brave and good deeds surpass all reckoning.

Martyred Rulers of Churches.

11 In these conflicts verily the magnificent martyrs of Christ
were conspicuous throughout all the world, and, as was
natural, everywhere filled with amazement the eye-witnesses
of their bravery; while in their own persons they furnished
a clear proof that the power of our Saviour is truly divine and

inexpressible. To mention, indeed, each by name would be a long task, not to say an impossibility.

13. Of those rulers of the churches who were martyred in well-known cities, the first name that we must record on the monuments to holy men, as a martyr of the kingdom of Christ, is that of Anthimus, bishop of the city of the Nicomedians, who was beheaded.

2 Of the martyrs at Antioch the best in his entire life was Lucian, a presbyter of that community; the same who in Nicomedia, where the emperor was, proclaimed the heavenly kingdom of Christ, first by word of mouth in an Apology, and afterwards also by deeds.

3 Of the martyrs in Phœnicia the most famous would be the pastors of the spiritual flocks of Christ, beloved of God in all things, Tyrannion, bishop of the church at Tyre, and Zenobius, presbyter of the church at Sidon, and, moreover,

4 Silvanus, bishop of the churches about Emesa. The last-named became food for wild beasts, along with others, at Emesa itself, and so was received up into the choirs of martyrs; the other two *glorified the word of God* [1] at Antioch by their endurance unto death; one of them, the bishop, being committed to the depths of the sea, while that best of physicians, Zenobius, died bravely under the tortures that were applied to his sides.

5 Of the martyrs in Palestine, Silvanus, bishop of the churches about Gaza, was beheaded at the copper mines at Phæno, with others, in number forty save one; and Egyptians there, Peleus and Nilus, bishops, together with others, endured death

6 by fire. And among these we must mention the great glory of the community of Cæsarea, Pamphilus, a presbyter, the most marvellous man of our day; the merit of whose brave and good deeds we shall record at the proper time.

7 Of those at Alexandria and throughout all Egypt and the Thebais who were perfected gloriously, the first that must be recorded is Peter, bishop of Alexandria itself, a divine example of the teachers of godliness in Christ; and of the presbyters with him Faustus, Dius and Ammonius, perfect martyrs of Christ; and Phileas, Hesychius, Pachymius and Theodore, bishops of the churches in Egypt; and countless other famous persons as well, who are commemorated by the communities in their own district and locality.

It is not our part to commit to writing the conflicts of those who fought throughout the world on behalf of piety towards the Deity, and to record in detail each of their happenings; but that would be the especial task of those who witnessed the events. Yet I shall make known to posterity in another

8 work those with whom I was personally conversant. In this present book, however, I shall subjoin to what has been said

[1] Acts xiii. 48.

the recantation of the things that were wrought concerning us, and the results of the persecution since the beginning, most profitable as they are to my readers.

The Empire before the Persecution.

9   Now as concerns the state of the Roman government before the war against us, during all the periods that the rulers were friendly and peaceably disposed towards us, no words could sufficiently describe how bountiful and plenteous was its harvest of good things; when also those who held the chiefest places in a world-empire completed the decennalia and vicennalia of their principate, and used to pass their days in festivals and public games, in the most joyous feasts and gaieties, possessing complete, well-established peace.

The Empire during the Persecution.

10   But as their authority thus increased without let or hindrance and day by day waxed greater, all at once they departed from their peaceful attitude towards us and stirred up an internecine war. And the second year of this kind of movement on their part had not fully expired, when a sort of revolution affecting the entire principate took place and threw
11 the whole of public life into confusion. For a fateful disease fell upon him who stood first among those of whom we spoke, which caused his mind to become deranged; and, along with him who had been honoured with the second place after him, he resumed the ordinary life of a private citizen. And this had not yet taken place, when the whole principate was rent in twain, a thing that had never even been recorded as having happened at any time in days gone by.
12   But after no very great interval of time the Emperor Constantius, who all his life long was most mildly and favourably disposed towards his subjects, and most friendly towards the divine word, died according to the common law of nature, leaving his lawful son Constantine Emperor and Augustus in his stead; and was the first [of the new tetrarchy] to be proclaimed among the gods by them, being deemed worthy of every honour after death that might be due to an emperor,
13 kindest and mildest of emperors that he was. He indeed was the only one of our contemporaries who passed the whole period of his principate in a manner worthy of his high office; and in other respects displayed himself in a most favourable and beneficent light towards all; and he took no part in the war against us, but even preserved the God-fearing persons among his subjects from injury and harsh treatment; neither did he pull down the church-buildings nor employ any other new device against us. So he has had as his reward a happy

and thrice-blessed issue of his life; for he alone enjoyed a
favourable and glorious end while he was still emperor, with
a lawful son, in all respects most prudent and godly, to
succeed him.

14 His son Constantine from the very first was proclaimed
by the armies most perfect Emperor and Augustus, and, long
before them, by God Himself, the King Supreme; and he set
himself to be an emulator of his father's piety towards our
doctrine.

Such was he. And afterwards Licinius was declared
Emperor and Augustus by a common vote of the rulers.
15 These things caused great vexation to Maximin, since up to that
time he was still entitled only Caesar by all. Therefore, being
above all things a tyrant, he fraudulently seized the honour
for himself, and became Augustus, appointed such by himself.
At this time he who had resumed office again after his abdication, as we have shown, was discovered devising a plot to
secure the death of Constantine, and died a most shameful
death. He was the first [emperor] whose honorific inscriptions [1] and statues and all such things as it has been customary
to set up publicly they threw down, as belonging to an
infamous and utterly godless person.

14. His son Maxentius, who secured for himself the tyranny
at Rome, at the beginning counterfeited our faith in order to
please and fawn upon the Roman populace; and for this
reason ordered his subjects to give over the persecution against
Christians; for he was feigning piety and endeavouring to
appear favourable and very mild above his predecessors.
2 Yet his deeds have not shown him to be such as it was hoped
he would be. On the contrary, he drove headlong into every
form of wickedness, and there is not a single abominable and
dissolute act that he has left undone, committing adulteries
and all kinds of rape. In fact he used to separate from their
husbands lawfully married women, insult them with the
utmost dishonour, and send them back again to their
husbands; and he made it his business thus to assail persons
neither undistinguished nor obscure, but the most eminent
of those who had attained the highest rank in the assembly of
the Roman Senate were the very and especial objects of his
3 offensive behaviour. All cowered before him, people and
rulers, famous and obscure, and were worn out by his terrible
tyranny; and even though they remained quiet and endured
the bitter servitude, still there was no escape from the
tyrant's murderous cruelty. Once, for example, on a small
pretence he gave the people over to his bodyguard to be
slaughtered, and immense numbers of the Roman people
were killed, in the midst of the city, by the spears and arms,
not of Scythians nor even of barbarians, but of their very

[1] τὰς ἐπὶ τιμῇ γραφάς.

4 fellow-citizens. Of a truth it would not even be possible to reckon how many senators were slaughtered because of designs on their wealth, for countless numbers were done away with 5 for feigned reasons, varying according to circumstances. But the finishing touch of all the tyrant's evil deeds was when he resorted to witchcraft : bent upon magic, at one time he would rip up pregnant women, at another explore the entrails of the new-born babes, slaughter lions, and invent certain abominable actions to invoke demons, and a sacrifice to avert war. For all his hope lay in these means of securing victory.

6 Indeed, one cannot even mention the kind of things that this tyrant at Rome did to enslave his subjects; so that they were actually reduced to such extreme scarcity and lack of even necessary food, as has never been known, according to our contemporaries, either at Rome or elsewhere.

7 But the tyrant in the East, Maximin, secretly forming a friendly alliance with the tyrant at Rome, as with a brother in wickedness, for a very long time thought that it was unknown. As a matter of fact, afterwards he was detected 8 and paid the just penalty. It was marvellous how he acquired a family likeness and kinship with the villainy of the tyrant at Rome, nay rather, carried off the first prize for wickedness and the reward of victory over him. For it was the principal charlatans and magicians who were deemed worthy by him of the highest honour; he became exceedingly frightened at every noise and superstitious, and attached great importance to error with regard to idols and demons. For instance, without divinations and oracles he could not dare to move 9 even a nail's breadth, as they say. Accordingly, he applied himself to the persecution against us with more energy and persistence than those before him, ordering temples to be erected in every city and the sacred groves that had been destroyed through long lapse of time to be restored with all diligence; and he appointed idol priests in every locality and city, and over them as high priest of each province one of those engaged in state-craft, who was the most manifestly distinguished in every branch of the public service, with an escort and body-guard of soldiers; and he recklessly bestowed governments and the greatest privileges on all charlatans, as 10 if they were pious and dear to the gods. Henceforward he vexed and oppressed, not a single city nor even district, but the provinces under him completely and as a whole, by exactions of gold and silver and unspeakably large amounts of goods, and by the heaviest assessments [1] and varied fines. Taking away from the wealthy the possessions they had gotten from their ancestors, he bestowed upon his train of 11 flatterers riches and heaps of goods in a single gift. In truth he carried his drunken excesses to such a point that he became

[1] ἐπισκήψεσιν.

mad and deranged in his cups, and when drunk would give
such orders as he would repent of next day when he was
sober. In debauchery and riotous living he suffered none to
surpass him, but appointed himself instructor in villainy to
those around him, rulers and ruled alike. He induced the
army to become enervated as a result of every kind of wanton
excess; encouraging governors and commanders to proceed
against their subjects with rapacity and extortion, almost as
12 if they were his fellow tyrants. Why need one recall the
man's disgraceful deeds of passion or reckon up the multitude
of those whom he debauched? In fact, he could not pass by
a city without continually ravishing women and abducting
13 virgins. And in this he was successful with all, save only with
Christians. They who despised death set at naught this his
fierce tyranny. For the men endured fire and sword and
nailings; wild beasts and engulfing in the sea; cutting off
and burning of limbs, stabbing and digging out of eyes, and
mutilation of the whole body; and, in addition to these,
hunger and mines and bonds: thus showing on all occasions
that they preferred to endure for the sake of piety rather than
14 transfer to idols the honour due to God. And the women,
on the other hand, showed themselves no less manly than the
men, inspired by the teaching of the divine Word: some,
undergoing the same contests as the men, won equal rewards
for their valour; and others, when they were being dragged
away to dishonour, yielded up their souls to death rather than
15 their bodies to seduction. A certain Christian lady, for
example, most famous and distinguished among those at
Alexandria, alone of those whom the tyrant ravished, conquered the lustful and licentious soul of Maximin by her
brave spirit. Renowned though she was for wealth, birth
and education, she had put everything second to modest
behaviour. Many a time he importuned her, yet was unable
to put her to death though willing to die, for his lust over-
mastered his anger; but punishing her with exile he possessed
16 himself of all her property. A great number of others, unable
even to listen to a threat of fornication, underwent every
form of torture and racking and mortal punishment at the
hands of the provincial governors.

These indeed were wonderful, yet most surpassingly wonderful was that woman at Rome, truly the most noble and chaste of
all those towards whom the tyrant there, Maxentius, in conduct
17 like Maximin, attempted to act offensively. For when she
learnt that at her house were those who ministered to the
tyrant in such deeds (and she also was a Christian), and that
her husband, and he too a prefect of the Romans, through
fear had permitted them to take and lead her off, she begged
to be excused for a brief space, as if forsooth to adorn her
person, entered her chamber, and when alone transfixed

herself with a sword. And straightway dying she left her
corpse to her procurers; but by deeds that themselves were
more eloquent than any words she made it known to all men,
both those present and those to come hereafter, that a Christian's virtue is the only possession that cannot be conquered
18 or destroyed.   To such an extent, in truth, did the two tyrants,
who had divided among them East and West, carry the
wickedness that they wrought at one and the same time.
But who is there, in search for the reason of such evils, who
would be at a loss to find it in the persecution against us?
Especially as there was no cessation of this great state of
confusion until Christians recovered their rights of freedom.

15.   In fact, during the whole period of ten years of persecution
there was no respite in their plotting and warfare against each
other. The seas were unnavigable, and none, no matter
whence they sailed, could escape being subjected to all kinds
of torments : stretched on the rack and having their sides
torn, and examined under all sorts of tortures in case they
should possibly be coming from the enemy of the contrary
part, and in the end subjected to crucifixion or punishment
2 by fire.   Moreover, every place was busy with the preparation
of shields and armour, the getting ready of darts and spears
and other warlike accoutrements, and of triremes and naval
gear; and no one expected anything but an enemy attack
all day long. And subsequently the famine and pestilence
broke out among them, about which we shall recount what is
necessary at the proper time.

The Recantation.

16.   Such was the state of affairs that continued throughout the
whole persecution; which came completely to an end, by the
grace of God, in the tenth year, though indeed it began to
abate after the eighth year. For when the divine and
heavenly grace showed that it watched over us with kindly
and propitious regard, then indeed our rulers also, those very
persons who had long time committed acts of war against us,
changed their mind in the most marvellous manner, and gave
utterance to a recantation, quenching the fire of persecution
that had blazed so furiously, by means of merciful edicts and
2 the most humane ordinances.   But this was not due to any
human agency nor to the pity, as one might say, or humanity
of the rulers. Far from it. For from the beginning up to
that time they were daily plotting further and severer measures
against us; from time to time they were inventing fresh
assaults upon us by means of still more varied devices. But
it was due to the manifestation of the Divine Providence itself,
which, while it became reconciled to the people, attacked the
perpetrator of these evils, and was wroth with him as the

chief author [1] of the wickedness of the persecution as a whole.
3 For verily, though it was destined that these things should
come to pass as a divine judgment, yet the Scripture says,
Woe, through whomsoever the offence cometh. [2] A divinely-sent
punishment, I say, executed vengeance upon him, beginning
4 at his very flesh and proceeding to the soul. For all at once
an abscess appeared in the midst of his privy parts, then a
deeply-seated fistular ulcer; which could not be cured and
ate their way into the very midst of his entrails. Hence there
sprang an innumerable multitude of worms, and a deadly
stench was given off, since the entire bulk of his members
had, through gluttony, even before the disease, been changed
into an excessive quantity of soft fat, which then became
putrid and presented an intolerable and most fearful sight to
5 those that came near it. As for the physicians, some of them
were wholly unable to endure the exceeding and unearthly
stench, and were butchered; others, who could not be of any
assistance, since the whole mass had swollen and reached a
point where there was no hope of recovery, were put to death
without mercy.

17. And wrestling with such terrible misfortunes he was con-
science-stricken for the cruel deeds he had perpetrated against
the godly. Collecting, therefore, his thoughts, he first openly
confessed to the God of the universe; then he called those
around him, and commanded them without delay to cause
the persecution against Christians to cease, and by an imperial
law and decree to urge them to build their churches and to
perform their accustomed rites, offering prayers on the
2 Emperor's behalf. Action immediately followed his word,
and imperial ordinances were promulgated in each city,
containing the recantation of the [persecution edicts] of our
time, after this manner :

3 The Emperor Cæsar Galerius Valerius Maximianus Invictus
Augustus, Pontifex Maximus, Germanicus Maximus, Ægyptiacus
Maximus, Thebaicus Maximus, Sarmaticus Maximus five times,
Persicus Maximus twice, Carpicus Maximus six times, Armeniacus
Maximus, Medicus Maximus, Adiabenicus Maximus, holding the
Tribunician Power for the twentieth time, Emperor for the nine-
teenth time, Consul for the eighth, Father of his country, Proconsul :
4 . . . And the Emperor Cæsar Flavius Valerius Constantinus
Pius Felix Invictus Augustus, Pontifex Maximus, holding the
Tribunician Power, Emperor for the fifth time, Consul, Father
5 of his country, Proconsul : And the Emperor Cæsar Valerius
Licinianus Licinius Pius Felix Invictus Augustus, Pontifex
Maximus, holding the Tribunician Power for the fourth time,
Emperor for the third time, Consul, Father of his country, Pro-
consul : to the people of their provinces, greeting.

---

[1] πρωτοστάτῃ.
[2] Luke xvii. 1 (inexact quotation). The words, " and was wroth . . .
cometh " are omitted in several important MSS.

6   Among the other measures that we frame for the use and profit
of the state, it had been our own wish formerly that all things
should be set to rights in accordance with the ancient laws and
public order of the Romans; and to make provision for this,
namely, that the Christians also, such as had abandoned the
persuasion of their own ancestors, should return to a sound
7 mind; seeing that through some reasoning they had been possessed of such self-will and seized with such folly [1] that, instead
of following the institutions of the ancients, which perchance their
own forefathers had formerly established, they made for themselves,
and were observing, laws merely in accordance with their own
disposition and as each one wished, and were assembling various
8 multitudes in divers places : Therefore when a command of ours
soon followed to the intent that they should betake themselves
to the institutions of the ancients, very many indeed were subjected to peril, while very many were harassed and endured all
9 kinds of death; And since the majority held to the same folly,
and we perceived that they were neither paying the worship due
to the gods of heaven nor honouring the god of the Christians;
having regard to our clemency and the invariable custom by
which we are wont to accord pardon to all men, we thought it
right in this case also to extend most willingly our indulgence :
That Christians may exist again and build the houses in which
they used to assemble, always provided that they do nothing
contrary to order. In another letter we shall indicate to the
10 judges how they should proceed. Wherefore, in accordance with
this our indulgence, they will be bound to beseech their own god
for our welfare, and that of the state, and their own; that in
every way both the well-being of the state may be secured, and
they may be enabled to live free from care in their own homes.

11   Such is the character of this edict in the Latin tongue,
translated into Greek as well as may be. Now it is time to
consider carefully what happened subsequently.

[1] The words, " and . . . folly " are omitted in some important
MSS. of Eusebius, but are in the original Latin.

BOOK IX

The Ninth Book of the Ecclesiastical History contains the following :

1. On the feigned relaxation.
2. On the change for the worse that ensued.
3. On the new-made idol at Antioch.
4. On the petitions against us.
5. On the forged memoirs.
6. On those who were martyred at this time.
7. On the document against us set up on tablets.
8. On the subsequent events, the famine and pestilence and wars.
9. On the close of the tyrants' lives, and what expressions they made use of before the end.
10. On the victory of the God-beloved Emperors.
11. On the final destruction of the enemies of godliness.

The Letter of Sabinus.

1. THE recantation of the imperial will set forth above [1] was promulgated broadcast throughout Asia and in the neighbouring provinces. After this had thus been done, Maximin, the tyrant of the East, a monster of impiety if ever there was one, who had been the bitterest enemy of piety towards the God of the universe, was by no means pleased with what was written, and instead of making known the letter set forth above gave verbal commands to the rulers under him to relax the war against us. For since he might not otherwise gainsay the judgment of his superiors, he put in a corner the law set forth above; and, taking measures how it might never see the light of day in the districts under him, by an oral direction he commanded the rulers under him to relax the persecution against us. And they intimated to each 2 other in writing the terms of the order. Sabinus, for instance, whom they had honoured with the rank of most excellent prefect, made known the Emperor's decision to the provincial governors in a Latin epistle. The translation of the same runs as follows :

3 With a most earnest and devoted zeal the Divinity of our most divine masters, the Emperors, has for a long time determined to lead all men's thoughts into the holy and right path of life, so that those also who seemed to follow customs foreign to the Romans should perform the acts of worship due to the immortal gods. 4 But the obstinacy and most unyielding determination of some was carried to such a length, that neither could they be turned back from their own purpose by just reasoning embodied in the 5 order, nor did they fear the punishment that threatened. Since therefore it has come about that many by such conduct endanger themselves, in accordance with the noble piety that is theirs, the Divinity of our masters, the most mighty Emperors, deeming it foreign to their divine purpose that for such a reason they should so greatly endanger these men, gave commandment through my Devotedness to write to thy Intelligence, that if any of the Christians be found following the religion of his nation, thou shouldest set him free from molestation directed against him and from danger, nor shouldest thou deem anyone punishable on this charge, since so long a passage of time has proved that they can in no wise be persuaded to abandon such obstinate conduct. 6 Let it be thy Solicitude's duty, therefore, to write to the curators and the duumvirs and the magistrates of the district of every city, that they may know that it is not beseeming for them to take any further notice of that letter.

---

[1] viii. 17.

A Temporary Peace.

7 Whereupon the rulers of the provinces, having concluded that the purport of what had been written to them was a genuine expression, made known by means of letters the imperial resolve to curators, duumvirs and rural magistrates. And not only did they further these measures by writing, but also much more so by action. With a view to carrying out the imperial will, as many as they kept shut up in prisons for their confession of the Deity they brought into the light of day and set free, releasing such of these same persons as were consigned to the mines for punishment. For this, in truth, they mistakenly conceived to be the Emperor's wish.

8 And when these things had thus been carried into effect, as though some *light shined* forth all at once *out of* a gloomy night,[1] one might see churches thronged in every city, and crowded assemblies, and the rites performed thereat in the customary manner. And every single one of the unbelieving heathen was in no small degree amazed at these happenings, marvelling at the miracle of so great a change, and extolling

9 the Christians' God as alone great and true. Of our own people, those who had faithfully and bravely contended throughout the conflict of persecutions once more resumed their confident bearing in the sight of all; but those whose faith had been diseased and souls storm-tost eagerly strove for their own healing, beseeching and begging the strong for the right hand of safety, and supplicating God to be merciful

10 to them. And then also the noble champions of godliness, freed from their evil plight in the mines, returned to their own homes. Proudly and joyously they went through every city, full of unspeakable mirth and a boldness that cannot even be

11 expressed in words. Yea, thronging crowds of men went on their journey, praising God in the midst of thoroughfares and market-places with songs and psalms; and you might see those who shortly before had been prisoners undergoing the harshest punishment and driven from their native lands, now regaining with gay and joyful countenances their own hearths, so that even those who formerly were thirsting for our blood, seeing the wondrous thing contrary to all expectation, rejoiced with us at what had happened.

Renewed Persecution : the Petitions from the Cities.

2. This the tyrant could no longer endure, hater as he was of that which is good, and plotter against every virtuous man (he was the ruler, as we said,[2] of the eastern parts); nor did he suffer matters thus to be carried on for six entire months. Numerous, therefore, were his devices to overturn the peace :

---

[1] 2 Cor. iv. 6; cp. *M.P.* (S) 3. 7.   [2] 1. 1.

at first he attempted on some pretext to shut us out from
November 311. assembling in the cemeteries, then through the
medium of certain evil men he sent embassies
to himself against us, having urged the citizens of Antioch to
request that they might obtain from him, as a very great
boon, that he should in no wise permit any of the Christians
to inhabit their land, and to put it into the minds of others
to do the same thing. The originator of all this sprang up at
Antioch itself in the person of Theotecnus, a clever cheat and
an evil man, and quite unlike his name. He was accounted
to hold the post of curator in the city.

3.   This man, then, many times took the field against us; and,
having been at pains by every method to hunt our people
out of hiding-places as if they were unholy thieves, having
employed every device to slander and accuse us, having been
the cause even of death to countless numbers, he ended by
erecting a statue of Zeus Philius with certain *juggleries* and
sorceries, and having devised *unhallowed rites* for it and
ill-omened initiations and *abominable* purifications,[1] he
exhibited his wonder-working by what oracles he pleased,
even in the Emperor's presence. And moreover this fellow,
in order to flatter and please him who was ruling, stirred up
the demon against the Christians, and said that the god,
forsooth, had given orders that the Christians should be driven
away beyond the borders of the city and country round about,
since they were his enemies.

4.   This man was the first to act thus of set purpose, and all
the other officials who lived in the cities under the same rule
hastened to make a like decision, the provincial governors
having seen at a glance that it was pleasing to the Emperor,
and having suggested to their subjects to do the very same
2 thing. And when the tyrant had given a most willing assent
May 312. to their petitions [2] by a rescript, once more the
persecution against us was rekindled.

A Pagan Hierarchy.

Maximin himself appointed as priests of the images in each
city and, moreover, as high priests, those who were especially
distinguished in the public services and had made their mark
in the entire course thereof. These persons brought great
zeal to bear on the worship of the gods whom they served.
3 Certainly, the outlandish superstition of the ruler was inducing,
in a word, all under him, both governors and governed, to do
everything against us in order to secure his favour; in return
for the benefits which they thought to secure from him, they

---

[1] Dion. Alex. (vii. 10. 4 above).
[2] We have thus translated ψηφίσματα here and wherever it occurs in
this book.

bestowed upon him this greatest of boons, namely, to thirst for our blood and to display some more novel tokens of malice towards us.

Forged Acts of Pilate.

5. Having forged, to be sure, Memoirs of Pilate and our Saviour, full of every kind of blasphemy against Christ, with the approval of their chief they sent them round to every part of his dominions, with edicts that they should be exhibited openly for everyone to see in every place, both town and country, and that the primary teachers should give them to the children, instead of lessons, for study and committal to memory.

Slanders against the Christians.

2 While this was thus being carried out, another person, a commander,[1] whom the Romans style " dux," caused certain infamous women to be abducted from the market-place at Damascus in Phœnicia, and, by continually threatening them with the infliction of tortures, compelled them to state in writing that they were once actually Christians, and privy to their unhallowed deeds, and that the Christians practised in the very churches lewdness and everything else that he wished these women to say in defamation of our faith. He also made a memorandum of their words and communicated it to the Emperor, and moreover at his command published this docu-
6. ment also in every place and city. But not long afterwards he, that is to say, the commander, died by his own hand, and thus paid the penalty for his wickedness.

Martyrs.

But as for us, banishments and severe persecutions were again renewed, and the rulers in every province once more rose up cruelly against us, with the result that some of those eminent in the divine Word were taken, and received the sentence of death without mercy.

Of these, three in Emesa, a city of Phœnicia, were consigned to wild beasts as food, having declared themselves Christians. Among them was a bishop, Silvanus, exceedingly advanced in age, who had exercised his ministry for forty entire years.

2 At the same time Peter also, who presided with the greatest distinction over the communities at Alexandria—a truly divine example of a bishop on account of his virtuous life and his earnest study of the holy Scriptures—was seized for no reason at all and quite unexpectedly; and then immediately

---

[1] στρατοπεδάρχης.

and unaccountably beheaded, as if by the command of
Maximin. And along with him many others of the Egyptian
bishops endured the same penalty.

3 Lucian, a most excellent man in every respect, of temperate
life and well versed in sacred learning, a presbyter of the community at Antioch, was brought to the city of Nicomedia,
where the Emperor was then staying; and, having made his
defence before the ruler on behalf of the doctrine which he
professed, he was committed to prison and put to death.

The Rescript to the Cities.

4 So mightily, indeed, did that hater of the good, Maximin,
contrive against us in a short space, that this persecution
which he had stirred up seemed to us much more severe than

7. the former one.   In fact, in the midst of the cities—a thing
that had never happened before—petitions presented against
us by cities, and rescripts containing imperial ordinances in
reply, were set up, engraved on brazen tablets; while the
children in the schools had every day on their lips the names
of Jesus and Pilate and the Memoirs forged to insult us.

2 At this point I think it necessary to insert this same document of Maximin that was set up on tablets, so as to make
manifest at once the boastful, overweening arrogance of this
hater of God, and the divine Justice that followed close upon
his heels with its sleepless hatred of the evil in wicked men.
It was this which smote him; and not long afterwards he
reversed his policy with regard to us, and made a decree by
laws in writing.

3   Copy of a Translation of the Rescript of Maximin in
answer to the Petitions against us, taken from the Tablet
at Tyre.

Now at length the feeble boldness of the human mind has
shaken off and dispersed all blinding mists of error, that error
which hitherto was attacking the senses of men not so much
wicked as wretched, and was wrapping them in the baneful
darkness of ignorance; and it has been enabled to recognize
that it is governed and established by the benevolent providence

4 of the immortal gods.   It passes belief to say how grateful, how
exceeding pleasant and agreeable, it has proved to us that you
have given a very great proof of your godly disposition; since
even before this none could be ignorant what regard and piety
you were displaying towards the immortal gods, in whom is
manifested a faith, not of bare and empty words, but constant

5 and admirable [1] in its noble deeds.   Wherefore your city might
worthily be called a temple [2] and dwelling-place of the immortal
gods.   Certainly, by many signs it appears that it flourishes

---

[1] Reading συνεχὴς καὶ παράδοξος.   [2] Omitting φόβον.

6 because there the immortal gods sojourn. Behold therefore, your city put away all thought for its own private advantage and neglected former requests for its own affairs, when once again it perceived that the followers of that accursed folly were beginning to spread, as a neglected and smouldering pyre which, when its fires are rekindled into flame, forms once more a mighty conflagration. Then immediately and without any delay it had recourse to our piety, as to a metropolis of all religious feeling,

7 requesting some healing and help. It is evident that the gods have placed in your heart this saving thought on account of your faith and godly fear. Accordingly it was he, the most exalted and mighty, even Zeus, he who presides over your far-famed city, he who protects your ancestral gods and women and children and hearth and home from all destruction, who inspired your hearts with this saving purpose; it was he who plainly showed how excellent and splendid and saving a thing it is to draw nigh to the worship and sacred rites of the immortal gods with due

8 reverence. For who can be found so senseless or bereft of all intelligence as not to perceive that it is by the benevolent care of the gods that the earth does not refuse the seeds committed to it, and thus disappoint the husbandmen of their hope with vain expectation? Or, again, that the spectre of unholy war does not plant itself without opposition upon the earth, so that squalid bodies are dragged off to death, while the wholesome air of heaven is polluted? Or, indeed, that the sea does not toss and swell under the blasts of immoderate winds? Or that hurricanes do not burst without warning and stir up a death-dealing tempest? Or, still further, that the earth, the nurse and mother of all, does not sink from its deepest hollows with fearful tremor, and the mountains that lie upon it crash into the resulting chasms? For all these evils, and evils even more terrible, have happened

9 many a time before this, as everyone knows. And all these things happened at once because of the baneful error and vain folly of those unhallowed men, when that error took possession of their souls, and, one might almost say, oppressed the whole world everywhere with its deeds of shame.

10 After other remarks he adds :

Let them behold in the broad plains the crops already ripe with waving ears of corn, the meadows, thanks to opportune rains, brilliant with plants and flowers, and the weather that has

11 been granted us temperate and very mild; further, let all rejoice since through our piety, through the sacrifices and veneration we have rendered, the most powerful and intractable air has been propitiated,[1] and let them take pleasure in that they therefore enjoy the most serene peace securely and in quiet. And let as many as have been wholly rescued from that blind folly and error and returned to a right and goodly frame of mind rejoice indeed the more, as if they were delivered from an unexpected hurricane or severe illness and were reaping life's sweet enjoyment for the

12 future. But if they persist in their accursed folly, let them be separated and driven far away from your city and neighbour-hood, even as you requested; that so, in accordance with your

---

[1] The text of this clause is hopelessly corrupt.

praiseworthy zeal in this respect, your city may be separated from all pollution and impiety, and, following its natural desire, may respond with due reverence to the worship of the immortal gods.

13   And that you may know how pleasing this your request has been to us, and how fully disposed to benevolence our soul is, of its own accord apart from petitions and entreaties : we permit your Devotedness to ask whatsoever bounty you wish, in return for this your godly intent. And now let it be your resolve so to
14 do and receive. For you will obtain your bounty without delay, the granting of which to your city will furnish a testimony for evermore of our godly piety towards the immortal gods, and a proof to your sons and descendants that you have met with the due meed of reward from our benevolence on account of these your principles of conduct.

15   This was emblazoned against us in every province, excluding every ray of hope from our condition, at least as far as human help is concerned ; so that, in accordance with the divine oracle itself, *if possible - even the elect* [1] themselves should be caused to stumble at these things.

The Retribution.

16   In truth, *expectation* was already almost *failing* [2] in very many souls, when all at once, while those serving the writ set forth against us were on their way and had not yet finished their journey in some districts, the Champion of His own Church, even God, stopping,[3] as it were, the proud boasting of the tyrant against us, displayed His heavenly aid on our behalf.

8.   The customary rains, indeed, and showers of the then prevailing winter season were withholding their usual downpour upon the earth, and we were visited with an unexpected famine, and on top of this a plague and an outbreak of another kind of disease. This latter was an ulcer, which on account of its fiery character was called an anthrax. Spreading as it did over the entire body it used to endanger greatly its victims; but it was the eyes that it marked out for special attack, and so it was the means of blinding numbers of men as well as women and children.

2   In addition to this, the tyrant had the further trouble of
c. November 312. the war against the Armenians, men who from ancient times had been friends and allies of the Romans; but as they were Christians and exceedingly earnest in their piety towards the Deity, this hater of God, by attempting to compel them to sacrifice to idols and demons, made of them foes instead of friends, and enemies instead of allies.

---

[1] Matt. xxiv. 24 (cp. vi. 41. 10 above).   [2] Luke xxi. 26.
[3] ἐπιστομίζων : lit. " gagging."

285

3   The fact that all these things came together all at once, at
one and the same time, served to refute utterly the tyrant's
insolent boasting against the Deity; for he used to affirm
insolently that, on account of his zeal for the idols and his
attack upon us, neither famine nor pestilence nor even war
took place in his time.   These things, then, coming upon him
together and at the same time had constituted the prelude
4 of his overthrow.   He himself, therefore, was worn out along
with his commanders in the Armenian war; while the rest of
the inhabitants of the cities under his rule were so terribly
wasted by both the famine and the pestilence, that two
thousand five hundred Attic drachmas were given for a single
5 measure of wheat.   Countless was the number of those who
were dying in the cities, and still larger of those in the country
parts and villages, with the result that the registers, which
formerly contained the names of a numerous rural population,
were now all but entirely wiped out; for one might almost
say that the entire population perished all at once through
6 lack of food and through plague.   Some, indeed, did not
hesitate to barter their dearest possessions for the scantiest
supply of food with those better provided; others sold off their
goods little by little and were driven to the last extremity of
want; and others again injured their bodily health, and died
from chewing small wisps of hay and recklessly eating certain
7 pernicious herbs.   And as for the women, some well-born
ladies in cities were driven by their want to shameless necessity, and went forth to beg in the market-places, displaying a
proof of their noble upbringing in their shamefacedness and
8 the decency of their apparel.   And some, wasted away like
ghosts of the departed, and at the last gasp, stumbled and
tottered here and there from inability to stand, and fell down;
then, stretched out prone in the midst of the streets they
would beg for a small morsel of bread to be handed them, and
with the last breath in their body cry out that they were
hungry, finding strength for this most anguished of cries
9 alone.   Others, such as were regarded as belonging to the
wealthier classes, amazed at the multitude of beggars, after
giving countless doles, henceforth adopted a hard and pitiless
frame of mind, since they expected that before very long they
would be suffering the same misery as the beggars; so that
in the midst of market-places and alleys dead and naked
bodies lay scattered here and there unburied for many days,
presenting a most piteous spectacle to those who saw them.
10 Some actually became food even for dogs; and chiefly for
this reason those who were alive turned to killing dogs, for
fear lest they might become mad and turn to devouring men.
11 But worst of all, the pestilence also battened upon every
house, especially those whom the famine could not completely
destroy because they were well provided with food.   Men,

for example, in affluent circumstances, rulers and governors
and numbers of officials, who had been left, as it were, of set
purpose by the famine for the benefit of the plague, endured
a sharp and very speedy death. So every place was full of
lamentations; in every alley and market-place and street
there was nothing to be seen but funeral dirges, together with
12 the flutes and noises [1] that accompany them. Thus waging
war with the aforesaid two weapons, pestilence and famine,
death devoured whole families in a short time, so that one
might actually see the bodies of two or three dead persons
carried out for burial in a single funeral train.

The Conduct of the Christians.

13 Such were the wages received for the proud boasting of
Maximin and for the petitions presented by the cities against
us; while the proofs of the Christians' zeal and piety in every
14 respect were manifest to all the heathen. For example, they
alone in such an evil state of affairs gave practical evidence
of their sympathy and humanity : all day long some of them
would diligently persevere in performing the last offices for
the dying and burying them (for there were countless numbers,
and no one to look after them); while others would gather
together in a single assemblage the multitude of those who
all throughout the city were wasted with the famine, and dis-
tribute bread to them all, so that their action was on all
men's lips, and they glorified the God of the Christians, and,
convinced by the deeds themselves, acknowledged that they
alone were truly pious and god-fearing.

The Heavenly Succour.

15 After these things were thus accomplished, God, the great
and heavenly Champion of the Christians, when He had displayed His threatening and wrath against all men by the
aforesaid means, in return for their exceeding great attacks
against us, once again restored to us the bright and kindly
radiance of His providential care for us. Most marvellously,
as in a thick darkness, He caused the light of peace to shine
upon us from Himself, and made it manifest to all that God
Himself had been watching over our affairs continually, at
times scourging and in due season correcting His people by
means of misfortunes, and again on the other hand after
sufficient chastisement showing mercy and goodwill to those
who fix their hopes on Him.

Thus in truth Constantine, who, as aforesaid,[2] was Emperor
and sprung from an Emperor, pious and sprung from a most
pious and in every respect most prudent father, and Licinius,

[1] Or " beating (of breasts)."   [2] viii. 13. 12 f.

who ranked next to him—both honoured for their understanding
and piety—were stirred up by the King of kings, God of the
universe and Saviour, two men beloved of God, against the
two most impious tyrants; and when war was formally
engaged, God proved their ally [1] in the most wonderful
manner, and Maxentius fell at Rome at the hands of Constantine; while he of the East did not long survive him, for
he too perished by a most disgraceful death at the hands of
Licinius, who had not yet become mad.

2   But to resume.   Constantine, the superior of the Emperors
in rank and dignity, was the first to take pity on those subjected to tyranny at Rome; and, calling in prayer upon God
who is in heaven, and His Word, even Jesus Christ the Saviour
of all, as his ally, he advanced in full force, seeking to secure
3 for the Romans their ancestral liberty. Maxentius, to be
sure, put his trust rather in devices of magic than in the
goodwill of his subjects, and in truth did not dare to advance
even beyond the city's gates, but with an innumerable multitude of heavy-armed soldiers and countless bodies of legion-
aries secured every place and district and city that had been
reduced to slavery by him in the environs of Rome and in
all Italy. The Emperor, closely relying on the help that
comes from God, attacked the first, second and third of the
tyrant's armies, and capturing them all with ease advanced
over a large part of Italy, actually coming very near to Rome
4 itself. Then, that he might not be compelled because of
the tyrant to fight against Romans, God Himself as if with
chains dragged the tyrant far away from the gates; and
those things which were inscribed long ago in the sacred
books against wicked men—to which as a myth very many
gave no faith, yet were they worthy of faith to the faithful
—now by their very clearness found faith, in a word, with all,
faithful and faithless, who had the miracle before their eyes.
5 As, for example, in the days of Moses himself and the ancient
and godly race of the Hebrews,

> Pharaoh's chariots and his host hath he cast into the sea,
>   his chosen horsemen, even captains,
> They were sunk in the Red Sea, the deep covered them;

in the same way also Maxentius and the armed soldiers and
guards around him *went down into the depths like a stone*,[2]
when he turned his back before the God-sent power that
was with Constantine, and was crossing the river that lay in
his path, which he himself had bridged right well by joining

---

[1] The shorter text of Eusebius runs as follows : " Thus in truth
Constantine . . . most prudent father, was stirred up by the . . .
Saviour, against those most impious tyrants . . . God proved his
ally. . . ."   [2] Ex. xv. 4, 5.

of boats, and so formed into an engine of destruction against
6 himself. Wherefore one might say :

> He hath made a pit, and digged it,
> And shall fall into the ditch which he made.
> His work shall return upon his own head,
> And his violence shall come down upon his own pate.[1]

7   Thus verily, through the breaking of the bridge over the
27 October, 312.   river, the passage across collapsed, and down
went the boats all at once, men and all, into
the deep; and first of all he himself, that most wicked of men,
and then also the shield-bearers around him, as the divine
8 oracles foretell, *sank as lead in the mighty waters.*[2] So that
suitably, if not in words at least in deeds, like the followers
of *the* great *servant Moses*,[3] those who had won the victory
by the help of God might in some sort hymn the very same
words which were uttered against the wicked tyrant of old,
and say :

> Let us sing unto the Lord, for gloriously hath he been
>   glorified :
> The horse and his rider hath he thrown into the sea.
> The Lord is my strength and protector,
> He is become my salvation ;

and

> Who is like unto thee, O Lord, among the gods ?
> Who is like thee, glorified in saints,
> Marvellous in praises, doing wonders ? [4]

9   These things, and such as are akin and similar to them,
Constantine by his very deeds sang to God the Ruler of all
and Author of the victory ; then he entered Rome with hymns
of triumph, and all the senators and other persons of great
note, together with women and quite young children and
all the Roman people, received him in a body with beaming
countenances to their very heart as a ransomer, saviour and
10 benefactor, with praises and insatiable joy. But he, as one
possessed of natural piety towards God, was by no means
stirred by their shouts nor uplifted by their praises, for well
he knew that his help was from God ; and straightway he
gave orders that a memorial of the Saviour's Passion should
be set up in the hand of his own statue ; and indeed when
they set him in the most public place in Rome holding
the Saviour's sign in his right hand, he bade them engrave
this very inscription in these words in the Latin tongue :

[1] Ps. vii. 15, 16.   [2] Ex. xv. 10.
[3] Ex. xiv. 31.   [4] Ex. xv. 1, 2, 11.

11 BY THIS SALUTARY SIGN, THE TRUE PROOF OF BRAVERY,
I SAVED AND DELIVERED YOUR CITY FROM THE YOKE OF THE
TYRANT; AND MOREOVER I FREED AND RESTORED TO THEIR
ANCIENT FAME AND SPLENDOUR BOTH THE SENATE AND THE
PEOPLE OF THE ROMANS.

The Ordinance of Constantine and Licinius, and the Epistle to Sabinus.

12 And after this Constantine himself, and with him the
emperor Licinius, whose mind was not yet deranged by the
madness into which he afterwards fell, having propitiated
God as the Author of all their good fortune, both with one
will and purpose drew up a most perfect law in the fullest
January 313. terms on behalf of the Christians; and to Maximin, who was still ruler of the provinces of the
East and playing at being their friend, they sent on an account
of the marvellous things that God had done for them, as well
13 as of their victory over the tyrant, and the law itself.   And he,
tyrant that he was, was greatly troubled at the intelligence;
but, not wishing to seem to yield to others, nor yet to
suppress the command through fear of those who had enjoined
it, as if of his own motion he penned perforce this first letter
c. 10 February, 313. on behalf of the Christians to the governors under him; in which he belies him-
self, and feigns that he had done things he never had.

Copy of a Translation of the Epistle of the Tyrant.

9a. Jovius Maximinus Augustus to Sabinus.   I am persuaded that
it is manifest both to thy Firmness and to all men that our
masters Diocletian and Maximian, our fathers, when they perceived that almost all men had abandoned the worship of the
gods and associated themselves with the nation of the Christians,
rightly gave orders that all men who deserted the worship of their
gods, the immortal gods, should be recalled to the worship of the
2 gods by open correction and punishment.   But when under happy
auspices I came for the first time to the East, and learnt that in
certain places very many persons who were able to serve the public
good were being banished by the judges for the aforesaid reason, I
gave orders to each of the judges that none of them in future was
to deal harshly with the provincials, but rather by persuasive
words and exhortations to recall them to the worship of the
3 gods.   It came to pass at that time, therefore, when in accordance with my injunction the judges observed what was commanded, that no one in the eastern provinces was either banished
or suffered insult, but rather was recalled to the worship of the
gods, because no severe measures were employed against them.
4 But afterwards, when last year under happy auspices I had
September 311. gone to Nicomedia and was staying there, there
came to me citizens of the same city with images of
the gods, earnestly requesting that on no account should such a
5 nation be permitted to dwell in their city.   But when I learnt

that very many of the same religion dwelt in those very parts,
I thus made them reply : That I was gratified, and thanked them
for their request, but I perceived that this request did not come
from all.   If, then, there were some that persevered in the same
superstition, let each one keep thus his resolve according as he
personally wished ; and if they so desired it, let them acknowledge
6 the worship of the gods.   Nevertheless to these same Nicomedians
and the rest of the cities, who themselves have so very earnestly
addressed me a similar request, namely, that no Christian should
inhabit their cities, I was compelled to reply in a friendly manner,
because the Emperors of old time had carefully observed this
very thing, and it was pleasing to the gods themselves, by whom [1]
all men and the government itself of the state subsist, that [2]
I should confirm such a request as they were making on behalf
of the worship of their Deity.

7   Therefore, although special letters have been written to thy
Devotedness before this time, and likewise it has been laid down
by ordinances that no harsh measures should be adopted against
provincials who have a mind to persevere in such a custom, but
that men should deal with them in a long-suffering and adapt-
able spirit : nevertheless that they may not suffer insults or
extortions at the hands of the "beneficiarii" or any others
whatsoever, I think it right by this letter also to put thy Firmness in mind that thou shouldest cause our provincials to recognize the attention they owe to the gods rather by persuasive
8 words and exhortations.   Wherefore if any should make it his
resolve that the worship of the gods should be recognized, it is
fitting to welcome such persons ; but if some desire to follow their
9 own worship, thou shouldest leave it in their own power.   For
this reason it behoves thy Devotedness to observe carefully that
which is commanded thee, and that authority be given to none to
afflict our provincials with insults and extortions, since, as we
wrote above, it is fitting to recall our provincials to the worship
of the gods rather by exhortations and persuasive words.   And
that this our injunction may come to the knowledge of all our
provincials, it behoves thee to make known that which has been
enjoined in an ordinance put forth by thyself.

10   Since he issued these commands under the compulsion of
necessity and not of his own free will, no one any longer
regarded him as truthful or even trustworthy, because after
a similar concession he had already on a former occasion
showed himself to be changeable and false of disposition.
11 None of our people therefore dared to convene an assembly
or to present himself in public, because the letter did not
allow him even this.   This alone it laid down, that we should
be kept from harsh treatment, but it gave no orders about
holding meetings or erecting church buildings or practising
12 any of our customary acts.   And yet the advocates of peace
and piety, Constantine and Licinius, had written to him to
allow this, and had conceded it to all their subjects by means

---

[1] δι᾽ οὕς : probably representing *per quos* in the original.
[2] Omitting οὖν, as suggested by Schwartz.

of edicts and laws. In truth, this monster of iniquity had resolved not to give in as regards this matter; until he was smitten by the divine Justice, and at the last against his will forced to do so.

The Overthrow of Maximin.

10.   The following were the circumstances that hemmed him in. He was unable to carry on the vast government with which he had been undeservedly entrusted; but, lacking a prudent and imperial mind, he managed his affairs tactlessly; and, above all, his soul was uplifted in an absurd manner by an overweening arrogance, actually against his colleagues in the Empire, men who were in every way his superiors in birth and upbringing and education, in worth and intelligence, and—what is most important of all—in sobriety and piety towards the true God. So he began to venture to act with

2 insolence, and publicly to style himself first in rank. Then he pushed his madness to the length of insanity, and, breaking the treaty he had made with Licinius, raised an internecine war. Next, in a short time he threw everything into confusion, greatly disturbed every city, and, gathering together all the army, an innumerable multitude of men, went forth to fight him in battle array, his soul uplifted by the hopes he placed in demons, whom, forsooth, he regarded as gods, and in his myriads of armed soldiers.

3 But when he joined battle, he found himself bereft of

30 April, 313.   divine Providence, for, by the direction of Him who is the one and only God of all, the victory

4 was given to Licinius who was then ruling. First of all, the armed soldiers in whom he had trusted were destroyed; and when his body-guard had left him defenceless and wholly deserted, and had gone over to him who was ruling, the wretched man divested himself with all speed of the imperial insignia that ill became him, and in a cowardly, base and unmanly way quietly slipt into the crowd. Then he ran about here and there, hiding himself in the fields and villages; and for all his courting of safety he escaped with difficulty the hands of his enemies, his deeds themselves proclaiming how very trustworthy and true are the divine oracles, in which it has been said :

5   There is no king saved by much power,
  And a giant will not be saved by his great strength.
  A horse is a vain thing for safety,
  And will not be saved by his great power.
  Behold, the eyes of the Lord are upon them that fear him,
  Upon them that hope in his mercy;
  To deliver their souls from death.[1]

---

[1] Ps. xxxiii. 16–19.

6   Thus, then, did the tyrant, filled with shame, come to his own territory. And first in his mad fury he put to death many priests and prophets of those gods who had formerly been his admiration, and whose oracles had incited him to begin the war, on the ground that they were charlatans and deceivers and, above all, betrayers of his safety. Next, he gave glory to the Christians' God, and drew up a law on behalf of their liberty in the most complete and fullest manner. Then straightway, no respite being granted him, he ended his life by a miserable death.

The Edict of Maximin.

Now the law issued by him was as follows :

> Copy of a Translation of the Ordinance of the Tyrant on behalf of the Christians, made from the Latin tongue into the Greek.

7   The Emperor Cæsar Gaius Valerius Maximinus Germanicus, Sarmaticus, Pius Felix Invictus Augustus. We believe that no one is ignorant, nay that every man who has recourse to the facts knows and is conscious that it is manifest, that in every way we take unceasing thought for the good of our provincials, and desire to grant them such things as are best calculated to secure the advantage of all, and whatsoever things are advantageous and useful to their common weal, and such as are suitable to the
8   public advantage and agreeable to every mind. Since, therefore, before this it has been evident to our knowledge that, on the plea that the most divine Diocletian and Maximian, our fathers, had given orders for the abolishment of the Christian assemblies, many extortions and robberies have been practised by the officials, and that this increased as time went on to the detriment of our provincials (for whose good it is our especial desire that there should be due thought), and that their own personal possessions were being destroyed : we addressed a letter to the governors in each province last year, laying it down that if any should wish to follow such a custom or the same religious observances, such a one should adhere to his purpose without hindrance, and be hindered or prevented by no one ; and that they should have a free hand, without fear and suspicion, to do whatsoever each
9   one pleases. But it cannot escape our notice even now that some of the judges misinterpreted our injunctions, and caused our people to have doubts with regard to our commands, and made them somewhat backward in joining in those religious observances that were pleasing to them.
10   That, therefore, for the future all suspicion or doubt arising from fear may be removed, we have decreed that this ordinance be published, so that it may be plain to all that those who desire to follow this sect and religious observance are permitted, in accordance with this our bounty, as each one wishes or finds it pleasing, to join in that religious observance which from choice he was wont to practise. And permission has also been granted
11   them to build the Lord's houses. Nevertheless, that our bounty

may be even greater, we have decided to decree this also : that
if any houses or lands, which used formerly to belong by right
to the Christians, have by the injunction of our parents passed
into the right of the public treasury or have been seized by any
city—whether a sale of these has taken place, or they have
been handed over to anyone as a gift—we have given orders
that all these be restored to the Christians as their original right,
so that in this also all may perceive our piety and solicitude.

12   These are the words of the tyrant that came less than a whole
year after the ordinances against the Christians, set up by
him on tablets ; and he who a short while previously looked
upon us as impious and godless and the pests of society, so
that we were not permitted to dwell in, I will not say, a city,
but even a spot in the country or a desert—this same person
drew up ordinances and legislation on behalf of the Christians ;
and those who shortly before were being destroyed by fire and
sword and given to wild beasts and birds for food before his
eyes, and were enduring every kind of chastisement and punishment and loss of life in the most pitiable manner, as if they
were godless and wicked, these he now allows both to observe
their form of worship and to build churches ; and the tyrant
himself confesses that they possess certain rights !

The Death of Maximin.

13   And when he had made these confessions, as if meeting
with some kind of reward on this very account—that is,
suffering less, to be sure, than it behoved him to suffer—
he was smitten all at once by a stroke of God, and perished
14 in the second encounter of the war.   But the circumstances
of his death were not such as fall to the lot of generals on a
campaign, who time after time contend bravely on behalf
of virtue and friends, and with a good courage meet a glorious
end in battle ; but he suffered his due punishment like an
impious enemy of God, skulking at home while his army was
still stationed in battle array on the field.   All at once he
was smitten by a stroke of God over his whole body, with
the result that he fell prone under the onslaught of terrible
pains and agonies ; he was wasted by hunger, and his flesh
entirely consumed by an invisible, divinely-sent fire ; the
form which his body once possessed wasted away and
vanished, and there remained only a form of dry bones, like
some phantom shape long since reduced to a skeleton, so
that those present could not but think that his body had
become the tomb of his soul, which had been buried in what
15 was now a corpse and completely wasted away.   And as the
heat consumed him still more fiercely in the very depths of
his marrow, his eyes projected, and falling from their sockets
left him blind.   Yet he still breathed in this condition, and

making confession to the Lord invoked death. So with his last breath he acknowledged that he suffered thus justly because of his violence against Christ; and then gave up the ghost.

October (?) 313.

The Sequel.

11. When Maximin was thus removed—he who was the only one left of the enemies of godliness, and showed himself the worst of all—by the grace of Almighty God the renewal of the churches from the foundation was set on foot, and the word of Christ received a due increase upon its former freedom, and was clearly heard to the glory of the God of the universe; while the impiety of the enemies of godliness was covered 2 with the most abject shame and dishonour. For Maximin himself was the first to be proclaimed by the rulers as a common enemy of all, and posted in public edicts on tablets as a most impious, most hateful and God-hating tyrant. As to the portraits which were set up in every city to his honour and that of his children, some were hurled from a height to the ground and smashed to pieces, others had their faces blackened over with dark-coloured paint and so rendered useless; the statues likewise, as many as had been set up in his honour, were cast down and broken in the same manner, and lay as an object of merriment and sport to those who wished to insult or abuse them. 3 Next, all the honours of the other enemies of godliness also were taken away, and all who were of the party of Maximin were slain, especially those in high government positions who had been honoured by him, and who indulged in violent 4 abuse against our doctrine in order to fawn upon him. Such was Peucetius, a man whom he honoured and respected above all, the truest of his friends, consul a second and a third time, and appointed by him general finance minister; such likewise was Culcianus, who had gone through every grade of office in the government, the same person who gloried in the murder of countless Christians in Egypt; and in addition to these not a few others, who were the chief means of confirming and increasing Maximin's tyranny. 5 So it was that Theotecnus also was summoned by Justice, who in no wise consigned to oblivion what he did against the Christians. For after he had set up the idol at Antioch, he seemed to be prospering, and had actually been deemed 6 worthy of a governorship by Maximin; but when Licinius came to the city of the Antiochenes, he made a search for charlatans, and plied with tortures the prophets and priests of the new-made idol, to find out by what contrivance they were practising this deceit. And when the infliction of the tortures made concealment impossible for them, and they revealed that the whole mystery was a deceit manufactured by the art of Theotecnus, he inflicted a just punishment upon them all, putting to death, after a long series of tortures, first Theotecnus himself, and then also the partners in his charlatanry.

7   To all these were added also the sons of Maximin, whom he had already caused to share the imperial dignity and to be set up in paintings and pictures. And those who formerly boasted kinship with the tyrant and were moved by pride to lord it over all men underwent the same sufferings, accompanied by the most abject disgrace, as those mentioned above; for they *received not correction*,[1] nor did they know or understand the exhortation in the sacred books which says:

8   Put not your trust in princes,
          In the sons of men, in whom there is no help.
          His breath shall go forth and he shall return to his earth.
          In that day all his thoughts shall perish.[2]

9   [3] Thus verily when the impious ones had been purged away, the kingdom that belonged to them was preserved stedfast and undisputed for Constantine and Licinius alone; who, when they had made it their very first action to purge the world of enmity against God, conscious of the good things that He had bestowed upon them, displayed their love of virtue and of God, their piety and gratitude towards the Deity, by their enactment on behalf of the Christians.

---

[1] Zeph. iii. 2.   [2] Ps. cxlvi. 3, 4.

[3] The following conclusion is found in some authorities in place of the above: "Thanks be to God, the Almighty and King of the universe, for all things; and abundant thanks be also to the Saviour and Redeemer of our souls, Jesus Christ, through whom we pray continually that peace from troubles without and troubles in the heart may be preserved for us stedfast and undisturbed."

BOOK X

The Tenth Book of the Ecclesiastical History contains the following :

1. On the peace vouchsafed to us from God.
2. On the restoration of the churches.
3. On the dedications in every place.
4. Panegyric on the joyful condition of affairs.
5. Copies of imperial laws having reference to the Christians.
6. On the exemption from public service granted to the clerics.
7. On the subsequent wickedness of Licinius and his tragic end.
8. On the victory of Constantine and the blessings which he was the means of procuring for the subjects of the Roman Empire.

1.   THANKS be to God, the Almighty and King of the universe,
for all things ; and abundant thanks be also to the Saviour
and Redeemer of our souls, Jesus Christ, through whom we
pray continually that peace from troubles without and
troubles in the heart may be preserved for us stedfast and
undisturbed.

2   And having now added, while we pray, the tenth tome also
of the Ecclesiastical History to those which preceded it, we
shall dedicate this tome to thee, my most holy Paulinus,
3 invoking thee as the seal of the whole work ; and fitly in a
perfect number we shall here place the perfect and panegyrical discourse on the restoration of the churches, in
obedience to the divine Spirit who thus exhorts us :

O sing unto the Lord a new song;
For he hath done marvellous things :
His right hand, and his holy arm, hath wrought salvation
   for him.
The Lord hath made known his salvation :
His righteousness hath he revealed in the sight of the heathen.[1]

The Peace.

4   And verily, in accordance with the oracle which thus bids
us, let us now cry aloud the *new song*, since, after those terrible
and gloomy spectacles and narratives, we were accounted
worthy now to behold and to celebrate in panegyric such
things as of a truth *many righteous men* and martyrs of God
before us *desired to see* upon earth *and saw them not, and to*
5 *hear, and heard them not.*[2]   But they indeed, hasting with
all speed, obtained *far better* things *in the heavens* themselves [3] and were *caught up* into a *paradise* [4] of divine pleasure ;
while we, acknowledging that even these present things are
beyond our deserts, have been utterly astounded at the
munificence of the bounty of which He is the Author, and
with our whole soul's might fittingly render Him our awe
and worship, attesting the truth of the written predictions,
6 wherein it is said :

Come and behold the works of the Lord,
What wonders he hath made in the earth,
Making wars to cease unto the ends of the earth.
He will break the bow and shatter the armour,
And the shields he will burn with fire.[5]

---

[1] Ps. xcviii. 1, 2.   [2] Matt. xiii. 17.
[3] Cp. Phil. i. 23 ; Heb. x. 34 (A.V.).   [4] 2 Cor. xii. 4.
[5] Ps. xlvi. 8, 9.

Rejoicing that these things have been clearly fulfilled to us-ward, let us proceed to take up our narrative.

7   The whole race of God's enemies had verily been removed even as we have stated,[1] and in a moment blotted out of men's sight; so that once more a divine saying *hath fulfilment*,[2] that which says :

> I have seen the wicked in great power,
> And lifted up like the cedars of Lebanon.
> And I passed by, and, lo, he was not :
> And I sought his place, and it was not found.[3]

8 And now henceforth a day bright and radiant with rays of heavenly light, overshadowed by never a cloud, shone down upon the churches of Christ throughout the whole world ; nor were even those outside our society [4] grudged, if not the equal enjoyment of our divinely-sent blessings, at any rate a share in their effluence and a participation thereof.

The Churches rebuilt.

2.   So the whole human race was freed from the oppression of the tyrants.   And, delivered from his former ills, each one after his own fashion acknowledged as the only true God Him who was the Champion of the pious.   But we especially, who had fixed our hopes upon the Christ of God, had gladness unspeakable, and a divine joy blossomed in the hearts of us all as we beheld every place, which a short time before had been laid in ruins by the tyrants' evil deeds, now reviving as if after a long and deadly destruction, and temples rising once more from their foundations to a boundless height, and receiving in far greater measure the magnificence of those that formerly had been destroyed.

Imperial Ordinances.

2   Yea, and Emperors, the most exalted, by successive enactments on behalf of the Christians, confirmed still further and more widely God's bounty towards us ; and bishops constantly received even personal letters from the Emperor, and honours and gifts of money.   It may not be unfitting at the proper place in this work, as on a sacred tablet, to insert in this book the text of these documents, translated from Latin into Greek, so that they may also be preserved in remembrance by all those who come after us.

The Dedication of the Churches.

3.   After this there was brought about that spectacle for which we all prayed and longed : festivals of dedication in

---

[1] ix. 11.   [2] Luke xxii. 37.
[3] Ps. xxxvii. 35, 36.   [4] θιάσου.

the cities and consecrations of the newly-built houses of prayer, assemblages of bishops, comings together of those from far off foreign lands, kindly acts on the part of laity towards laity, union between the members of Christ's body 2 as they met together in complete harmony. Certainly, in accordance with a prophetic prediction that mystically signified beforehand what was for to come, *there came together bone* to bone and joint *to joint,* and all that the oracular 3 utterance in dark speech truly foretold. One was the power of the divine *Spirit* that spread through all the members; all were *of one soul,*[1] and displayed the same zeal for the faith; one hymn of praise to God came from the lips of all. Yea verily, our leaders conducted perfect ceremonies, and the consecrated priests performed the sacred rites and stately ordinances of the Church, here with psalmody and recitation of such other words as have been given us from God, there with the ministering of divine and mystic services; and the ineffable symbols of the Saviour's Passion were 4 present. And all together, of every age, male and female, with the whole power of their mind gave honour to God the Author of their good fortune, in prayer and thanksgiving with joyful heart and soul.

The Discourse in the Church of Tyre.

Moreover every one of the Church's rulers that were present, according to his ability, delivered panegyrical orations, inspiring the assembly.

4. And a certain one of moderate parts advanced into the midst, having composed a discourse; and, in the presence of very many pastors who gave it a quiet and orderly hearing as in a church assembly, he delivered the following oration, addressed personally to a single bishop who was in every respect most excellent and beloved of God, by whose zeal and enthusiasm the temple in Tyre, surpassing in splendour all others in Phœnicia, had been erected :

Panegyric on the building of the churches, addressed to Paulinus, bishop of the Tyrians.

2 O friends of God and priests who are clothed with the holy robe and the celestial crown of glory, the divine unction and the priestly garb of the Holy Spirit; and thou, O youthful pride of God's holy temple, honoured indeed by God with revered wisdom, yet noted for the choice deeds and acts of a youthful virtue that cometh to its prime, upon whom He who compasseth the whole world hath bestowed the especial honour of building His house upon earth, and restoring it for Christ His only-begotten and 3 first-born Word and for Christ's holy and reverend Bride—whether

---

[1] See Ezek. xxxvii. 7, 10; Acts iv. 32.

one should call thee a new Bezalel the architect of a divine tabernacle,[1] or Solomon the king of a *new* and far goodlier *Jerusalem*,[2]
or even a new Zerubbabel who bestowed upon the temple of
4 God that *glory* which greatly exceeded the former; [3] and you also,
ye nurslings of the sacred flock of Christ, dwelling-place of goodly
words, school of sobriety, auditory of godliness grave and dear
5 to God: Long ago, as we listened to the reading aloud of those
passages of Holy Writ which told of the miraculous signs that
God gave and the wondrous deeds that the Lord wrought for the
service of men, we could raise hymns and songs to God and say,
even as we were taught:

> We have heard with our ears, O God, our fathers have
> told us,
> What work thou didst in their days, in the days of old.[4]

6 But now indeed no longer by hearing or by report do we learn
of the *stretched out arm* [5] and the heavenly right hand of our
all-gracious God and universal King; nay, by deeds, as one
might say, and with our very eyes do we behold that those
things committed to memory long ago are faithful and true;
and so we can sing a second hymn of victory, and raise our
voices aloud and say:

> As we have heard, so have we seen
> In the city of the Lord of hosts, in the city of our God.[6]

7 And in what city, if it be not the new-made city that God hath
builded, *which is the church of the living God, the pillar and ground
of the truth*; [7] of which also another divine oracle speaketh good
tidings, somewhat on this manner: *Glorious things are spoken
of thee, O city of God*? [8]   To which city since the all-gracious God
hath gathered us, through the grace of His Only-begotten, let
each of the guests sing, yea all but shout, and say

> I was glad when they said unto me,
> We will go unto the house of the Lord; [9]
and
> Lord, I have loved the beauty of thy house,
> And the place where thy glory dwelleth.[10]

8 And let not only each one by himself, but also all together with
one spirit and one soul, give honour and praise, saying:

> Great is the Lord, and highly to be praised,
> In the city of our God, in his holy mountain.[11]

Yea verily, He is truly great, and *great is His house, lofty and
large*; [12] and *more lovely in beauty than the sons of men*.[13]   *Great
is the Lord who only doeth wondrous things*.[14]   Great is He *who
doeth great things and past finding out; yea, glorious and marvellous
things of which there is no number*.[15]   Great is He *who changeth
the times and the seasons, removing kings and setting them up*,[16]

---

[1] Ex. xxxv. 30 ff.   [2] 1 Kin. vii. f.; 2 Chr. iii. ff.; Rev. xxi. 2.
[3] Hag. ii. 4, 9.   [4] Ps. xliv. 1.   [5] Ps. cxxxvi. 12.
[6] Ps. xlviii. 8.   [7] 1 Tim. iii. 15.   [8] Ps. lxxxvii. 3.
[9] Ps. cxxii. 1.   [10] Ps. xxvi. 8.   [11] Ps. xlviii. 1.
[12] Baruch iii. 24, 25.   [13] Ps. xlv. 2.   [14] Ps. lxxii. 18.
[15] Job ix. 10.   [16] Dan. ii. 21.

raising up the poor from the ground, and from the dunghill setting up the needy.[1] *He hath put down princes from their thrones, and hath exalted them of low degree* from the ground. *The hungry he hath filled with good things,*[2] and he *hath broken the arms of the*
0 *proud.*[3] Since, therefore, He hath confirmed not only for the faithful but also for the faithless the record of the ancient narratives, even the Doer of wonders, the Doer of great things, the Lord of the universe, the Maker of the whole world, the Almighty, the All-gracious, the one and only God : let us sing to Him the *new song,*[4] supplying in thought this also :

> To him who alone doeth great wonders :
> For his mercy endureth for ever.
>
> To him which smote great kings,
>
> And slew mighty kings ;
> For his mercy endureth for ever.
>
> For he remembered us in our low estate,
>
> And hath delivered us from our adversaries.[5]

10 And may we never cease to praise aloud in these words the Father of the universe. But as for Him who is the second cause of our good things, who brought men to the knowledge of God, the Teacher of true piety, the Destroyer of the wicked, the Slayer of tyrants, the Emender of human life, our Saviour when we were in despair, even Jesus, let us honour His name
11 upon our lips ; for He alone, as being the one only, all-gracious Son of an all-gracious Father, since the Father in His love for man so ordained it, right willingly put on the nature of those who lay in corruption somewhere beneath Him, even of us. And like some excellent physician, who, to save those who are sick, though *he sees the ills* yet *touches the foul spots, and for another's misfortunes reaps suffering for himself,*[6] so He by Himself saved from the very abyss of death us, who were not merely sick or oppressed by grievous sores and wounds already putrifying, but even lying among the dead ; for none other in heaven possessed such strength as to minister unscathed for the salvation
12 of so many. He, then, it was who alone laid hold upon the grievous suffering of our corruption, alone endured our sorrows, alone took upon Himself the penalty for our wickednesses ;[7] and when we were, I will not say, half dead, but even *by this time* altogether foul and *stinking*[8] in tombs and graves, He raised us up, and saveth us now as in the days of old, in His earnest love for man, beyond the hope of anyone, even of ourselves, and imparteth to us freely a share of the good things of His Father—He who is the Giver of life, the Enlightener, our great Physician and King
13 and Lord, the Christ of God. Yea at that time, when He beheld[9] the whole human race lying sunk in gloomy night and darkness

---

[1] Ps. cxiii. 7. [2] Luke i. 52, 53. [3] Job xxxviii. 15.
[4] Ps. xcviii. 1. [5] Ps. cxxxvi. 4, 17, 18, 23, 24.
[6] Hippocrates, Περὶ φυσῶν 1. [7] Cp. Isai. liii. 4, 5.
[8] John xi. 39. [9] Supplying ὁρῶν, as Schwartz suggests.

profound through the deceit of baneful demons and the opera-
tions of God-hating spirits, by naught save His appearing He
broke asunder once for all the many-fettered chains of our
wickednesses, *as wax is melted* [1] by the rays of His light.

14   And when at this great grace and benefaction the envy that
hateth the good, even the demon that loveth the evil, was torn
asunder with wrath, so to speak, and was marshalling all his
death-dealing forces against us, at first raging like a dog which
gnaweth with his teeth at the stones hurled at him and venteth
on the lifeless missiles his fury against those who would drive him
away, he directed his ferocious madness against the stones of
the houses of prayer and the lifeless materials of which the
buildings were composed, to work (as at least he thought within
himself) the ruin of the churches; then he emitted his dread
hissings and serpent-like sounds, at one time by the threats of
wicked tyrants, at another by blasphemous ordinances of impious
rulers; yea further, he vomited forth the death that was his,
and bewitched the souls he captured by his baneful and soul-
destroying poisons, all but causing their death by his death-
fraught sacrifices to dead idols, and secretly stirring up every wild
beast in shape of man, and every kind of savage thing, against us.

15   But now, now again once more the *Angel of mighty counsel*,[2]
the great *Captain of the host of* God,[3] after that the greatest soldiers
in His kingdom had given sufficient proof of their full training
by their endurance and stedfastness in all things, by naught save
His sudden appearing caused to vanish into nothingness whatsoever was adverse and hostile, so that it seemed never to have
had even a name; howbeit, whatsoever was friendly and dear
to Him, that He advanced beyond all glory in the sight of all,
not only of men, but even also of the powers of heaven, the sun

16 and moon and stars, and of the whole heaven and earth; so that
now—a thing unknown heretofore—the most exalted Emperors
of all, conscious of the honour which they have received from
Him, spit upon the faces of dead idols, trample upon the unhallowed rites of demons, and laugh at the old deceits they
inherited from their fathers: but Him who is the common
Benefactor of all and of themselves they recognize as the one
and only God, and confess that Christ the Son of God is sovereign
King of the universe, and style Him as Saviour on tablets, inscrib-
ing in an imperishable record His righteous acts and His victories
over the impious ones, in imperial characters in the midst of
the city that is Empress among the cities of the world. Thus
Jesus Christ our Saviour, alone of those who have ever been,
is acknowledged, even by the most exalted on the earth, not as
an ordinary king taken from among men, but is worshipped as
the very Son of the God of the universe, and as Himself God.

17   And rightly so. For what king ever attained to so much
virtue as to fill the ears and tongues of all mankind upon earth
with his name? What king, when he had laid down laws so good
and wise, was powerful enough to cause them to be published from
the ends of the earth even to the bounds of the whole world in

18 the hearing of all mankind? Who abolished the barbarous and
uncivilized customs of uncivilized nations by his civilized and
most humane laws? Who, when warred on by all men for

---

[1] Cp. Ps. lviii. 8 (LXX).   [2] Isai. ix. 6 (LXX).   [3] Josh. v. 14.

whole ages, gave such proof of superhuman might as to flourish
19 daily and remain young throughout his entire life ? Who established a nation never even heard of since time began, which
now lieth not hidden in some obscure corner of the earth but
extendeth wherever the sun shineth ? Who so defended his
soldiers with the weapons of piety that their souls proved harder
than adamant when they contended with their adversaries ?
20 Which of the kings exerciseth so great a sway, taketh the field
after death, triumpheth over enemies, and filleth every place
and district and city, both Greek and barbarian, with votive
offerings of his royal houses and divine temples, such as the fair
ornaments and offerings that we see in this temple ? Truly
venerable and great are these same things, worthy of amazement
and wonder, and in themselves clear proofs of the sovereignty
of our Saviour : *for even now he spake, and they were made*; *He
commanded, and they were created* : [1] for what could resist the
will of the universal King and Ruler and the Word of God
Himself ?

Such things would require a discourse of their own, were one
21 carefully to examine and expound them at leisure. Yet indeed
the zeal of those who have laboured is not so great or so noble
in the judgment of Him whom we address as God, when He
looketh into the lively *temple* [2] which we all compose, and vieweth
the house formed of *living* and firmly set *stones*,[3] well and securely
grounded *upon the foundation of the apostles and prophets, Jesus
Christ himself being the chief corner stone* ; [2] *which* stone the master-
builders *rejected*,[3] not only of that old building which is no more,
but also of that *building* [2] which compriseth the more part of
mankind to the present day, evil workmen as they were of evil
things ; but the Father approved it, and then and now builded
22 it *into the head of the corner* [3] of this our common Church. This
living *temple*, then, *of* a living *God* [4] formed out of ourselves, I
mean the greatest sanctuary and truly reverend, whose innermost shrine may not be seen by the common eye, for verily holy
it is and a holy of holies—who that viewed it would dare to
describe ? Who is able even to peer into the temple buildings
that surround it, save only the *great High Priest* [5] of the universe,
to whom alone it is permitted to search the hidden mysteries
23 of every rational soul ? But perchance it is possible for another
also, and for one alone among equals, to take the second place
after Him, namely, for the commander who presideth over this
army, whom the first and *great High Priest* [5] Himself hath honoured
with the second place in the priestly ministries of this place,
the pastor of your divine flock who was allotted and adjudged
your people by the Father, as if He Himself had appointed him
His attendant and interpreter, the new Aaron, or Melchizedek
made like unto the Son of God, abiding and kept by Him *continually* [6]
24 by the common prayers of you all. To him, therefore, let it be
permitted alone, after the first and greatest High Priest, if not
in the first at any rate in the second place, to behold and inspect
the inmost recesses of your souls ; since through experience and
length of time he hath proved each one accurately, and by his

---

[1] Ps. xxxiii. 9 = cxlviii. 5 (LXX).   [2] Eph. ii. 20, 21.
[3] 1 Pet. ii. 5, 7.   [4] Cp. 1 Cor. iii. 16.
[5] Heb. iv 14.   [6] Heb. vii. 3.

zealous care he hath disposed you all in a godly order and doctrine; and he best of all is able to *give* such an *account* [1] as will match his deeds, of those things that he himself hath wrought by the power of God.

25   Now our first and *great High Priest* [2] saith that whatsoever things *he seeth the Father doing, these the Son also doeth in like manner.* [3] And this one also, *looking unto* [4] the first as unto a master with the pure eyes of the mind, whatsoever *he seeth Him doing,* these he useth as patterns and archetypes, and by his workmanship hath wrought their images, as far as in him lieth, into the closest likeness; thus in no wise doth he come behind that *Bezalel,* whom God Himself *filled with the spirit of wisdom and under-standing and* with the knowledge as well of crafts and *sciences,* and *called* [5] him to be the workman that should construct the

26 temple of heavenly types in symbolic fashion. [6] After this manner, then, this man also, bearing in his own soul the image of Christ entire, the Word, the Wisdom, the Light, hath formed this magnificent temple of God most high, answering in its nature to the pattern of that which is better, even as the visible answereth to the invisible; nor could one describe with what noble-minded-ness, with what a liberal hand—whose will to give was insatiable—and with what emulation on the part of you all, ye nobly vied with one another by the large-heartedness of your contributions in no respect to come behind him in this self-same purpose. And this place—which thing also is worthy to be mentioned first of all—which by the evil designs of our enemies had been covered with all kinds of vile rubbish, he did not overlook nor surrender to the malice of those who did this, though he might have lighted upon another spot (for the city supplied countless other sites), and thus found relief from toil and freedom from trouble.

27 Nay, he first of all aroused himself to the work; then by his zeal he strengthened the whole people, and gathering together all into one great body, entered upon the first contest; for he deemed that she especially who had been destroyed by the enemy, she who had been aforetime afflicted and had endured the same persecutions as we and before us, even the church who like a mother had been bereft of her children, should have her share in the enjoyment of the bounty of the all-gracious God.

28   For since once more *the great shepherd,* [7] having driven away the wild beasts and the wolves and every kind of cruel and savage creature, and *having broken the great teeth of the lions,* [8] as the divine oracles say, once more had vouchsafed to bring His sons together, it was most meet that he should also set up the fold of the flock, that he might put to shame *the enemy and the avenger,* [9] and openly rebuke the evil deeds of impious men

29 fighting against God. And now these men, the haters of God, are no more, for they never were; but after troubling and being troubled for a little while, then they paid to Justice no con-temptible penalty, accomplishing the utter overthrow of them-selves, their friends and houses; so that the predictions which long ago had been inscribed on sacred records are confessedly

---

[1] Heb. xiii. 17 (inexact quotation).   [2] Heb. iv. 14.
[3] John v. 19.   [4] Heb. xii. 2.
[5] Ex. xxxi. 2, 3 = xxxv. 30, 31.   [6] Cp. Heb. viii. 5.
[7] Heb. xiii. 20.   [8] Ps. lviii. 6.   [9] Ps. viii. 2.

proved trustworthy by the facts, in which, among other true
things that the divine word speaketh, this also it declareth
concerning them :

30   The wicked have drawn out the sword, and have bent their
        bow;
      To cast down the poor and needy,
      To slay the upright in heart :
      May their sword enter into their own hearts,
      And may their bones be broken; [1]

and again :

      Their memorial is perished with a sound,

and

      Their name hath been blotted out for ever and for ever and
        ever; [2]

for verily when they also were in trouble

      They cried, and there was none to save :
      Unto the Lord, and he did not hear them; [3]

yea, they indeed

      Had their feet bound together and fell,
      But we rose and stood upright; [4]

and that which was predicted in these words,

      Lord, in thy city thou shalt set at naught their image, [5]

hath been shown to be true before the eyes of all.

31   But they verily, engaging like giants in battle against God,
have thus brought their lives to a miserable end; while the issue
of that godly endurance on the part of her who was deserted [6]
and rejected by men was such as we have seen; so that the
prophecy of Isaiah calleth aloud unto her in these words :

32   Be glad, O thirsty desert; [7]
      Let the desert rejoice and blossom as a lily;
      And the desert places shall blossom forth and rejoice. . . .
      Be strong, ye hands that hang down,
      And ye palsied knees.
      Be of good courage, ye feeble-hearted,
      Be strong, fear not;
      Behold, our God recompenseth judgment,
      And will recompense;
      He will come and save you. . . .
      For, saith he, water broke out in the desert,
      And a stream in thirsty ground.
      And the waterless place shall become marsh-meadows,
      And upon the thirsty ground shall be a fountain of water. [8]

33   Now these things, foretold long ago, had been recorded in the
sacred books in words; howbeit the deeds have come down to
us no longer by hearsay, but in actual fact. This *desert*, this

[1] Ps. xxxvii. 14, 15.   [2] Ps. ix. 6, 5 (LXX).
[3] Ps. xviii. 41.   [4] Ps. xx. 8 (LXX).
[5] Ps. lxxiii. 20.   [6] ἐρήμου   [7] ἔρημος.
[8] Isai. xxxv. 1–4, 6, 7 (LXX).

waterless place, this widowed and defenceless one, whose gates *they cut down with axes as in a thicket of trees*; *whom together with hatchet and hammer* they brake down; whose books also they destroyed and *set on fire the sanctuary* of God; *they profaned the dwelling place of* His *name to the ground*; [1] whom *all they which pass by the way* did *pluck,* having before *broken down her fences,* whom *the boar out of the wood did ravage* and on whom the *solitary wild beast did feed*: [2] now by the miraculous power of Christ, when He willeth it, hath become *as a lily.*[3] For at that time also by His command, as of a careful father, she was chastened. *For whom the Lord loveth he chasteneth, and scourgeth every son whom*
34 *he receiveth.*[4] So then, after being corrected in due measure, once more again she is bidden anew to *rejoice,* and she *blossoms forth as a lily* and breathes upon all men of her divine, sweet odour; *for,* saith he, *water broke out in the desert,*[3] the streams of the divine *regeneration* that the *washing* [5] of salvation bestoweth; and that which a short time before was *desert* hath now become *marsh-meadows,* and *a fountain of* living *water* hath burst forth *upon the thirsty ground*; and in very truth *hands* that before *hung down* have become *strong,* of the strength of which hands these great and manifest works are tokens. Yea, and the *knees* [3] that long ago were diseased and relaxed have recovered their natural movement, and go straight forward upon the way of the knowledge of God, hasting to the *flock* of the all-gracious *Shep-*
35 *herd,*[6] their true home. But if through the threats of the tyrants the souls of some have waxed numb, not even these doth the saving Word pass by as incurable, but right well He healeth them also and urgeth them on towards the divine encouragement,
36 saying : *Be of good courage, ye feeble-hearted, be strong, fear not.*[3]

The word which prophesied that she whom God had made desert was to enjoy these blessings, this our new and goodly Zerubbabel heard with the sharp hearing of his mind, after that bitter captivity and *the abomination of desolation*; [7] nor did he pass by the corpse as dead, but first of all with entreaties and prayer he propitiated the Father with the common consent of you all; and taking as his Ally and Fellow-worker Him who alone can quicken the dead,[8] he raised up her that had fallen, having first cleansed and healed her of her ills; and he clothed her with a garment, not the old one that she had from the beginning, but with such a one as he was once more instructed by the divine oracles, which thus clearly say :

And the latter glory of this house shall be greater than the former.[9]

37 Thus, then, the whole area that he enclosed was much larger.[10] The outer enclosure he made strong with the wall surrounding the whole, so that it might be a most secure defence thereof;
38 while he spread out a porch, great and raised aloft, towards the rays of the rising sun, and even to those standing far out-side the sacred precincts supplied no scanty view of that which

---

[1] Ps. lxxiv. 5–7.   [2] Ps. lxxx. 12, 13.
[3] Isai. xxxv. (see above).   [4] Heb. xii. 6.   [5] Tit. iii. 5.
[6] John x. 16.   [7] Matt. xxiv. 15.
[8] Cp. Rom. iv. 17.   [9] Hag. ii. 9.
[10] *sc.* than that occupied by the previous church.

is within; thus, one might say, turning the gaze, even of
strangers to the faith, towards the first entrances, so that none
might hastily pass by without first having his soul mightily struck
by the memory of the former desolation and the wondrous miracle
of to-day; struck by which he hoped that perchance such a one
would also be impelled, and have his steps turned forwards by
30 the bare sight, towards the entrance. Now he hath not permitted him that passeth inside the gates to tread forthwith with
unhallowed and unwashen feet upon the holy places within;
but hath left a space exceeding large between the temple and the
first entrances, and adorned it all around with four transverse
colonnades, fencing the place into a kind of quadrangular figure,
with pillars raised on every side, and filling the spaces between
them with wooden barriers of lattice-work rising to a convenient
height; and in the midst thereof he hath left an open
space where men can see the sky, thus providing it with
40 air bright and open to the rays of light. And here he hath
placed symbols of sacred purifications, by erecting fountains
right opposite the temple, whose copious streams of flowing
water supply cleansing to those who are advancing within the
sacred precincts. And this is the first stopping-place for those
that enter; supplying at once adornment and splendour to the
whole, and a place of sojourn suited to such as are still in need of
their first instructions.

41 But verily, passing by this spectacle, he hath thrown open
passages to the temple by means of innermost porches in still
greater numbers, once again under the rays of the sun placing
three gates on one side, upon the middle one of which he hath
bestowed a height and size that far surpasseth the two on either
side, and hath singled it out for special adornment with bronze
fastenings bound with iron and varied embossed work, making
the others a body-guard, as it were, beneath it as their queen.

42 And after the same manner he hath also ordered the number
of the porches for the colonnades on either side of the entire temple;
and above them hath devised as well separate openings into the
building to give still further light; and for these also he hath
wrought a varied adornment with delicately-carved wood.

Now as to the royal house, he hath builded it of abundant
and still richer materials, eagerly desiring to spare no expenses.

43 I deem it superfluous for me to describe here the length and
breadth of the edifice, to recount in full the brilliant beauty, the
magnitude no words can express, and the dazzling appearance of
the workmanship, yea, and the loftiness that reacheth heaven,
and the costly cedars of Lebanon that are placed above; the
mention of which even the divine oracle doth not pass over in
silence, saying :

> The trees of the Lord shall be glad,
> Even the cedars of Lebanon which he hath planted.[1]

44 Why need I now speak more particularly of the perfect wisdom
and art with which the building hath been ordered, and the
surpassing beauty of every part, when the witness of the eyes
leaveth no place for the instruction that cometh through the

---

[1] Ps. civ. 16 (with variant).

ears ? Nevertheless, having thus completed the temple he
adorned it with thrones, very lofty, to do honour unto the presidents, and likewise with benches arranged in order throughout
in a convenient manner; and after all these he hath placed in
the midst the holy of holies even the altar, and again surrounded
this part also, that the multitude might not tread thereon, with
a fence of wooden lattice-work, delicately wrought with the
craftsman's utmost skill, so as to present a marvellous spectacle
to those that see it.

45   Nor did even the pavement, as one might suppose, escape his
care. This also, for example, he hath made exceeding brilliant
with every kind of fair marble; and then, finally, passing on outside the temple as well, he hath constructed chambers and
buildings on either side, very large, the which he hath skilfully
joined together to the sides of the royal [house], and united
with the openings into the central building. These also were
wrought by our most peaceful Solomon, who builded the temple
of God, for those who still have need of cleansing and sprinkling
with *water and the* Holy *Spirit*,[1] insomuch that the aforesaid
46   prophecy [2] is no longer a word only, but is become a fact. For
the latter glory of this house hath become, and in truth even now
is, *greater than the* former.[3]

For it was meet and right that, as her Shepherd and Lord
had suffered once for all death on her behalf, and after the Passion
had changed the foul body with which He had clothed Himself
for her sake into His splendid and glorious body,[4] and brought
the very flesh that was dissolved from *corruption* into *incorruption*,[5] she also likewise should enjoy the fruits of the dispensa-
tions of the Saviour. For verily having received from Him a
promise of much *better*[6] things than even these, she longeth to
receive as her due, lastingly and for the ages that are to come,
the much greater glory of the new birth in the resurrection of an
incorruptible body, in the company of the choir of the angels
of light in the kingdoms of God beyond the heavens, with Christ
47   Jesus Himself her supreme Benefactor and Saviour. But mean-
while in the present time she who hath long been a widow and
deserted hath been robed by the grace of God with these blossoms,
and is become in truth *as a lily*,[7] as saith the prophecy; and
having received again the garb of a bride and put on the garland
of beauty, she is taught by Isaiah to dance, as it were, presenting
her thank-offering to the glory of God the King in words of
praise. Let us listen to her as she saith :

48   Let my soul rejoice in the Lord;
For he hath clothed me with the garment of salvation
And the cloke of gladness,
He hath put a chaplet upon me as a bridegroom,
And hath adorned me with adornment as a bride.
And as the earth that maketh her flower to grow,
And as the garden causeth the things that are sown in it to
spring forth;

John iii. 5.   [2] § 36.   [3] Hag. ii. 9.
[4] Cp. Phil. iii. 21; Heb. ii. 9.   [5] Cp. 1 Cor. xv. 42.
[6] Cp. Heb. xi. 39, 40.   [7] Isai. xxxv 1.

> So the Lord, the Lord, will cause righteousness and rejoicing
> to spring forth
> Before all the nations.[1]

49   With these words, then, she danceth. But with what words the Bridegroom also, even the heavenly Word, Jesus Christ Himself, answereth her, hear the Lord as He saith:

> Fear not for that thou hast been put to shame;
> Neither dread for that thou hast been put to reproach:
> For thou shalt forget thy everlasting shame,
> And the reproach of thy widowhood shalt thou remember no
> more. . . .
> Not as a wife forsaken and faint-hearted hath the Lord
> called thee,
> Nor as a wife hated from her youth,
> Saith thy God.
> For a little time I forsook thee;
> And with great mercy I will have mercy on thee.
> In a little wrath I hid my face from thee,
> And with everlasting mercy I will have mercy on thee,
> Saith the Lord who delivered thee.[2]

50
> Awake, awake, . . .
> Thou who hast drunk at the hand of the Lord the cup of his
> fury;
> For the cup of staggering, the bowl of fury, thou hast drunk
> and drained it.
> And there was none to comfort thee among all thy sons whom
> thou hast brought forth;
> And there was none to take thee by the hand. . . .
> Behold I have taken out of thine hand the cup of staggering,
> The bowl of my fury;
> And thou shalt no more drink it again:
> And I will put it into the hands of them that did thee wrong
> And of them that humbled thee. . . .

51
> Awake, awake, put on strength, . . .
> Put on thy glory. . . .
> Shake off the dust and arise. Sit thee down . . .
> Loose the band from thy neck.[3]
> Lift up thine eyes round about,
> And behold thy children gathered together.
> Behold they were gathered together and came to thee.
> As I live, saith the Lord,
> Thou shalt clothe thee with them all as with an ornament,
> And gird thyself with them as with the ornament of a bride.
> For thy desolate and destroyed and ruined places
> Will now be too strait by reason of them that inhabit thee,
> And they that swallow thee up shall be far away from thee.

52
> For thy sons whom thou hast lost
> Shall say in thy ears,
> The place is too strait for me:
> Give place to me that I may dwell.
> And thou shalt say in thine heart,
> Who hath begotten me these?

---

[1] Isai. lxi. 10, 11.   [2] Isai. liv. 4, 6–8.
[3] Isai. li. 17, 18, 22, 23; lii. 1, 2.

> I am childless and a widow,
> But as for these, who hath brought me them up ?
> I was left alone,
> But these, where had I them ? [1]

53   These things Isaiah prophesied, these things had of old been
recorded concerning us in sacred books; but it was necessary
that somehow we should come to learn their truthfulness at some
54 time by facts.   Moreover, since the Bridegroom, even the Word,
thus addresseth His Bride, the sacred and Holy Church, fittingly
did this paranymph [2] stretch out your hands in the common
prayers of you all, and *awake* [3] and raise up her who was *desolate*,[4]
who lay like a corpse, of whom men despaired, by the will of
God the universal King and the manifestation of the power of
Jesus Christ; and having raised he restored her to be such as
he learnt from the record of the sacred oracles.
55   A mighty wonder truly is this, and surpassing all amazement,
especially in the eyes of such as take heed only to the appearance
of outward things.   But more wonderful than wonders are the
archetypes, the rational prototypes of these things and their
divine models, I mean the renewal of the God-given, spiritual
56 edifice in our souls.   This edifice the Son of God [5] Himself
created *in* His own *image*,[6] and everywhere and in all things hath
bestowed upon it the divine likeness, an incorruptible nature, an
essence incorporeal, spiritual, a stranger to all earthy matter and
endowed with intelligence of its own; once for all at the first He
formed it into being from that which was not, and hath made it a
holy bride and an all-sacred temple for Himself and the Father.
And this also He Himself clearly showeth, when He thus
confesseth :

> I will dwell in them, and walk in them; and I will be their God,
> and they shall be my people.[7]

Such, then, is the perfect and purified soul, thus begotten from
the beginning so as to bear the image of the heavenly Word.
57   But when through the envy and jealousy of the demon which
loveth evil she became of her own free choice a lover of that which
is sensual and evil, and the Deity departed from her, leaving her
bereft of a protector, she fell an easy capture and prey to the
snares of those who long had envied her; and, laid low by the
engines and machines of her invisible enemies and spiritual foes,
she fell a tremendous fall, so that *not* even *one stone upon another* [8]
of her virtue remained standing in her; nay, she lay her full
length upon the ground, absolutely dead, altogether deprived of
58 her inborn thoughts concerning God.   Yea, verily, as she lay
fallen there, she who was made *in the image of God*,[9] it was not
that *boar out of the wood* which we can see that *ravaged* her, but
some death-dealing demon and spiritual *wild beasts*,[10] who also
have inflamed her with their passions as with *fiery darts* of their

---

[1] Isai. xlix. 18–21.   [2] νυμφοστόλος.
[3] Isai. lii. 1.   [4] Isai. xxxv. 1.
[5] θεόπαις.   [6] Gen. i. 26.   [7] 2 Cor. vi. 16.
[8] Luke xxi. 6.   [9] Gen. i. 27.   [10] Ps. lxxx. 13.

own wickedness,[1] and *have set the* truly divine *sanctuary* of God *on fire,* and *have profaned the dwelling-place of* His *name to the ground ;* [2] then they buried the hapless one in a great heap of earth, and brought her to a state bereft of all hope of salvation.

59 But her Guardian, the Word, the divinely-bright and saving One, when she had paid the just penalty for her sins, once more again restored her, hearkening to the loving-kindness of an all-

60 gracious Father. First, then, choosing unto Himself the souls of the supreme Emperors, by means of these men most dearly beloved of God He cleansed the whole world of all the wicked and baneful persons and of the cruel God-hating tyrants themselves. And then those men that were His disciples, who all their life long had been consecrated to Him, yet secretly concealed, as in a storm of evils, by His sheltering care, these He brought out openly and honoured worthily with the great gifts of His Father's bounty. And by their means He once more purified and cleansed with pickaxes and mattocks, namely, the penetrating teachings of His instruction, those souls which a short time before had been befouled and overlaid with every sort of matter and rubbish

61 contained in impious decrees ; and when He had made bright and clear the place of the understanding of all of you, He then for the future consigned it to this all-wise and God-beloved ruler. He, discerning and prudent as he is in all else, distinguisheth also and discerneth the understanding of the souls committed to his charge ; and from the first day, so to speak, even unto now he hath never ceased to *build,* and among you all to fit into its place, at one time the radiant *gold,* at another the approved and purified *silver* and the *precious* and costly *stones ;* [3] so as once more to fulfil in his deeds to you-ward the sacred and

62 mystic prophecy, in which it hath been said :

Behold I prepare for thee thy stone of carbuncle,
And thy foundations of sapphire,
And thy battlements of jasper,
And thy gates of crystals,
And thy wall of choice stones,
And all thy sons taught of God,
And in great peace thy children:
And in righteousness shalt thou be built.[4]

63 *Building* verily *in righteousness,* he duly divided the whole people according to their several abilities ; with some he fenced the outer enclosure and this alone, surrounding it with a wall of unerring faith (and this was the great multitude of the people who were unable to support a mightier structure) ; to others he entrusted the entrances to the house, setting them to haunt the doors and guide the steps of those entering, wherefore they have not unnaturally been reckoned as gateways of the temple ; others he supported with the first outer pillars that are about the quadrangular courtyard, bringing them to their first acquaintance with the letter of the four Gospels. Others he joineth closely to the royal house on either side, still indeed under instruction and in the stage of progressing and advancing, yet not far off nor greatly separated from the faithful who possess the divine

[1] Eph. vi. 16 (inexact quotation). [2] Ps. lxxiv. 7.
[3] Cp. 1 Cor. iii. 12. [4] Isai. liv. 11–14.

64 vision of that which is innermost. Taking from the number of these last the pure souls that have been cleansed like gold by the divine washing, he then supporteth some of them with pillars much greater than the outermost, from the innermost mystic teachings of the Scriptures, while others he illumineth with apertures towards the light.

65   The whole temple he adorneth with a single, mighty gateway, even the praise of the one and only God, the universal King; and on either side of the Father's sovereign power he provideth the secondary beams of the light of Christ and the Holy Spirit. As to the rest, throughout the whole house he showeth in an abundant and much varied manner the clearness and splendour of the truth that is in each one, in that everywhere and from every source he hath included the *living* and firmly set and well-wrought *stones* [1] of men's souls. Thus he hath builded the great and royal house composed of all, bright and full of light both within and without; for not alone soul and mind, but even their body had been made glorious with the many-blossomed adornment of chastity and sobriety.

66   Now there are also in this fane thrones and countless benches and seats, as many as are the souls on which the gifts of the divine Spirit find their resting-place; such as long ago *appeared* to the sacred Apostles and those that were with them, to whom there were manifested *tongues parting asunder, like as of fire; and it sat upon each one of them.* [2]   But while in the ruler of all, as is right, the entire Christ hath taken His seat, in those who have the second place after him [this bounty] is proportioned to each one's capacity, *by gifts* of the power of Christ and *of the Holy Ghost.* [3] And the souls of some might be the seats even of angels, of those to whom the instruction and guarding of each several person hath been committed. But as to the reverend, mighty and unique [4] altar, what might it be save the spotless holy of holies of the soul of the common priest of all? [5]   Standing beside it on the right hand the *great High Priest* [6] of the universe, even Jesus, the only-begotten of God, receiveth with joyful countenance and upturned hands the sweet-smelling incense from all, and the bloodless and immaterial sacrifices offered in prayer, and sendeth them on their way to the heavenly Father and God of the universe; whom He himself first adoreth and alone rendereth to His Father the honour that is due; after which He also beseecheth Him to remain favourable and propitious towards us all for ever.

69   Such is the great temple which the Word, the great Creator of the universe, hath builded throughout the whole world beneath the sun, forming again this spiritual image upon earth of those vaults beyond the vaults of heaven; so that by the whole creation and by the rational, living creatures upon earth His Father might

70 be honoured and revered.   But as for the region above the heavens and the models there of things on this earth, and *the Jerusalem that is above,* [7] as it is called, and the *mount Zion* the *heavenly* mount, and the supramundane *city of the living God,* in which *innumerable hosts of angels in general assembly and the church of the firstborn who are enrolled in heaven* [8] honour their Maker and

---

[1] 1 Pet. ii. 5.   [2] Acts. ii. 3.   [3] Heb. ii. 4.
[4] μονογένης.   [5] Omitting τῆς ψυχῆς, with Schwartz.
[6] Heb. iv. 14.   [7] Gal. iv. 26.   [8] Heb. xii. 22, 23.

the Sovereign of the universe, proclaiming His praises in unutterable words of which we cannot conceive : these no mortal
man can worthily hymn, for in truth *eye saw not, and ear heard not,
nor did there enter into the heart of man* those same things which
71 *God prepared for them that love him.*[1] Of these things now in
part deemed worthy, let us all together, men with women and
children, small and great, with one spirit and one soul, never
cease to praise and acclaim Him who is the Author of so great
blessings to us; *who is very merciful to all* our *iniquities, who
healeth all* our *diseases, who redeemeth* our *life from destruction,
who crowneth* us *with mercy and pities, who satisfieth* our *desire
with good things ;* for *he hath not dealt with us after our sins, nor
rewarded us after our iniquities ;* for *as far as the east is from the
west, so far hath he removed our iniquities from us. Like as a
father pitieth his sons, so the Lord pitied them that fear him.*[2]
72 Let us rekindle the memories of these things both now and for
all time hereafter; yea, and let us keep before our minds night
and day, through every hour and, one might say, in every breath,
the Author of the present assembly and this happy and most
glorious day, even the Ruler of the assembly Himself; let us
cherish and revere Him with the whole power of our soul; and
now let us rise and beseech Him in loud accents, as befitteth our
earnest desire, that He would shelter and preserve us to the end in
His fold, and award us that eternal peace, unbroken and undisturbed, which cometh from Him, in Christ Jesus our Saviour
through whom to Him be glory for ever and ever.   Amen.

Imperial Ordinances.

5.   But come, let us now quote also the translations made from
the Latin of the imperial ordinances of Constantine and
Licinius.

   Copy of Imperial Ordinances translated from the Latin
tongue.

2   In our watchfulness in days gone by that freedom of worship
should not be denied, but that each one according to his mind and
purpose should have authority given him to care for divine things
in the way that pleased him best, we had given orders that both
to the Christians [and to all others liberty should be allowed][3]
3 to keep to the faith of their own sect and religion.   But inasmuch
as many and various conditions[4] seemed clearly to have been
added in that rescript, in which such rights were conceded to the
same persons, it may be that perchance some of them were shortly
afterwards repelled from such observance.
4   When I Constantine Augustus and I Licinius Augustus had come
under happy auspices to Milan, and discussed all matters that
concerned the public advantage and good, among the other
things that seemed to be of benefit to the many,[5]—or rather,
first and foremost—we resolved to make such decrees as should

---

[1] 1 Cor. ii. 9.   [2] Ps. ciii. 3–5, 10, 12, 13.
[3] Some words have fallen out of the text.   [4] αἱρέσεις.
[5] Lat. pluribus hominibus; the Gk. has ἐν πολλοῖς ἅπασιν (pluribus
omnibus).

secure respect and reverence for the Deity; namely, to grant both to the Christians and to all the free choice of following whatever form of worship they pleased, to the intent that all the divine and heavenly powers that be might be favourable to us and 5 all those living under our authority. Therefore with sound and most upright reasoning we resolved on this [1] counsel : that authority be refused to no one whomsoever to follow and choose the observance or form of worship that Christians use, and that authority be granted to each one to give his mind to that form of worship which he deems suitable to himself, to the intent that the Divinity . . . may in all things afford us his wonted care and 6 generosity. It was fitting to send a rescript that this is our pleasure, in order that when those conditions had altogether been removed, which were contained in our former letters sent to thy Devotedness, concerning the Christians, those things also which seemed to be wholly unfortunate and foreign to our clemency might be removed, and that now each one of those who were possessed of the same purpose—namely, to observe the Christians' form of worship—should observe this very thing, freely and simply, 7 without any hindrance. Which things we have resolved to signify in the fullest manner to thy Carefulness, to the intent that thou mayest know that we have granted to these same Christians free and unrestricted authority to observe their own form of 8 worship. And when thou perceivest that this has been granted unrestrictedly to them by us, thy Devotedness will understand [2] that authority has been given to others also, who wish to follow their own observance and form of worship—a thing clearly suited to the peacefulness of our times—so that each one may have authority to choose and observe whatever form he pleases. This has been done by us, to the intent that we should not seem to have detracted in any way from any rite [3] or form of worship.

9 And this, moreover, with special regard to the Christians, we resolve : That their places, at which it was their former wont to assemble, concerning which also in the former letter despatched to thy Devotedness a definite ordinance [4] had been formerly laid down, if any should appear to have bought them either from our treasury or from any other source—that these they should restore to these same Christians without payment or any demand for compensation, setting aside all negligence and doubtfulness; and if any chance to have received them by gift, that they should 10 restore them with all speed to these same Christians : provided that if either those who have purchased these same places or those who have received them by gift request aught of our generosity, let them approach the prefect of the district,[5] to the intent that through our kindness thought may be taken for them also. All which things must be handed over to the corporation of the Christians by thy zealous care immediately and without delay.

11 And inasmuch as these same Christians had not only those places at which it was their wont to assemble, but also are known to have had others, belonging not to individuals among them, but

---

[1] Omitting ἡμετέραν, with the Latin.
[2] Reading θεωρεῖς and inserting συνορᾷ, with Schwartz.
[3] τιμῇ : Lat. honori.
[4] certa forma, Lat. Eusebius has τύπος ἕτερος (cetera).
[5] Omitting the gloss δικάζοντι.

to the lawful property of their corporation, that is, of the Christians, all those, under the provisions of the law set forth above, thou wilt give orders to be restored without any question whatsoever to these same Christians, that is, to their corporation and assembly; provided always, of course, as aforesaid, that those persons who restore the same without compensation, as we have mentioned above, may look for indemnification, as far as they are concerned, from our generosity.

12   In all these things thou shouldest use all the diligence in thy power for the above-mentioned corporation of the Christians, that this our command may be fulfilled with all speed, so that in this also, through our kindness, thought may be taken for the common

13 and public peace.   For by this method,[1] as we have also said before, the divine care for us, which we have already experienced

14 in many matters, will remain stedfast . . . continually.   And that the form which this our enactment and generosity takes may be brought to the knowledge of all, it is fitting that this which we have written be set forth by thy order and published everywhere, and brought to the knowledge of all, to the intent that the enactment which embodies this our generosity may escape the notice of no one.

15   Copy of another Imperial Ordinance which he also made, indicating that the bounty had been granted to the Catholic Church alone.

Greeting, Anulinus, our most honoured Sir.   It is the custom of our benevolence, that we will that whatsoever appertains by right to another should not only not suffer harm, but even be

16 restored, most honoured Anulinus.   Wherefore we will that, when thou receivest this letter, if aught of those things that belonged to the Catholic Church of the Christians in any city, or even in other places, be now in the possession either of citizens or of any others : these thou shouldest cause to be restored forthwith to these same churches, inasmuch as it has been our determination that those things which these same churches possessed formerly

17 should be restored to them as their right.   Since, therefore, thy Devotedness perceives that the order of this our command is most explicit, do thy diligence that all things, whether gardens or buildings or whatsoever belonged to these same churches by right, be restored to them with all speed ; so that we may learn that thou hast yielded the most careful obedience to this our order.   Fare thee well, Anulinus, our most honoured and esteemed Sir.

18   Copy of an Imperial Letter, in which he commands the holding of a Synod of bishops at Rome on behalf of the union and concord of the churches.

Constantine Augustus to Miltiades bishop of the Romans, and to Mark.   Inasmuch as documents of such a nature have been sent to me in numbers by Anulinus, the right honourable proconsul of Africa, from which it appears that Caecilian, the bishop of the city of the Carthaginians, is called to account on many charges by some of his colleagues in Africa ; and inasmuch as it seems to me

---

[1] λογισμῷ.

to be a very serious matter that in those provinces, which Divine
Providence has chosen to entrust to my Devotedness, and where
there is a great multitude of people, the multitude should be
found pursuing the worse course of action, splitting up, as it were,
19 and the bishops at variance among themselves : it seemed good
to me that Cæcilian himself, with ten bishops, who appear to be
his censors, and such ten others as he may deem necessary to his
suit, should set sail for Rome, that there a hearing may be granted
him in the presence of yourselves, and moreover of Reticius and
Maternus and Marinus also, your colleagues (whom I have ordered
to hasten to Rome for this purpose), in such a manner as ye may
20 perceive to be in accordance with the most sacred law. Nevertheless, that ye may have the fullest knowledge of all these same
matters, I have subjoined to my letter copies of the documents
that were sent to me by Anulinus, and have despatched them to
your aforesaid colleagues. Which when your Firmness reads,
ye will gauge by what method the most careful investigation can
be made of the above-mentioned suit, and a just decision arrived
at; since it does not escape the notice of your Carefulness that the
respect which I pay to the lawful Catholic Church is so great, that
it is my wish that ye should leave no schism whatsoever or
division in any place. May the divinity of the great God preserve [1] you safely for many years, most honoured Sirs.[2]

21   Copy of an Imperial Letter, in which he gives orders for the
          holding of a second Synod for the purpose of removing all
          division among the bishops.

          Constantine Augustus to Chrestus bishop of the Syracusans.
Already on a former occasion, when some in a base and perverse
manner began to create divisions with regard to the worship of the
holy and heavenly Power and the Catholic religion,[3] in my desire
to cut short such dissensions among them, I had given orders to
the effect that certain bishops should be sent from Gaul, nay
further, that the opposing parties, who were contending stubbornly
and persistently together, should be summoned from Africa; that
so, in the presence also of the bishop of Rome, this question which
appeared to have been raised might through their coming receive
a right solution by means of a careful examination in every
22 particular. But since, as it happens, some, forgetful both of
their own salvation and the reverence they owe to their most
holy religion, even now do not cease to perpetuate their private
enmities, being unwilling to conform to the judgment already
passed, and affirming that after all it was a few persons who gave
their opinions and decisions, or that they were in a hurry to pass
judgment very speedily and sharply without having first accurately examined all those matters that ought to have been investigated; and since, as a result of all this, it has come to pass that
even those very persons, who ought to be of one mind in brotherly
concord, are separate from each other in a disgraceful, nay rather

---

[1] This is the reading of the Latin and some MSS. of Eusebius here
and also in § 24; 6, 5; in each case Schwartz reads the fut. indic.
[2] Gk. " Sir "; but the Lat. correctly gives the plural.
[3] αἵρεσις.

in an abominable, fashion, and give to those men whose souls are strangers to this most holy religion an occasion to scoff—wherefore it became incumbent upon me to provide that that which ought to have ceased by voluntary agreement, after the judgment already passed, may even now, if possible, be ended by the 23 presence of many persons. Inasmuch, therefore, as we have commanded that very many bishops from various and numberless places should assemble at the city of Arles by the Kalends of August, we have thought it good to write to thee also, that thou shouldest procure from the right honourable Latronianus, the "corrector" of Sicily, a public vehicle, and joining to thy company two others of those of the second rank,[1] whomsoever thou thyself mayest decide to choose, and, moreover, taking with you three servants who shall be able to attend upon you on the way, do thou be present at the above-mentioned place by that same day; 24 so that both by thy Firmness and by the unanimous wisdom of the others assembled, this quarrel also (which hitherto, by reason of certain disgraceful contentions, has maintained a miserable existence), when all has been heard that will be said by those who are now at variance among themselves, whom likewise we have commanded to be present, may, if only tardily, give place to a due state of religion and faith and brotherly concord. May the Almighty God preserve thee in good health for many years.

6.   Copy of an Imperial Letter in which grants of money are made to the churches.

Constantine Augustus to Cæcilian bishop of Carthage. Forasmuch as it has been our pleasure in all provinces, namely the African, the Numidian and the Mauretanian, that somewhat be contributed for expenses to certain specified ministers[2] of the lawful and most holy Catholic religion, I have despatched a letter to Ursus, the most distinguished finance minister of Africa, and have notified to him that he be careful to pay over to thy Firmness 2 three thousand "folles." Do thou therefore, when thou shalt secure delivery of the aforesaid sum of money, give orders that this money be distributed among all the above-mentioned persons 3 in accordance with the schedule sent to thee by Hosius. But if, after all, thou shalt find that there is aught lacking for the fulfilment of this my purpose in respect of them all, thou shouldest ask without doubting whatsoever thou findest to be necessary from Heraclides our procurator fiscal. For indeed when he was here I gave him orders that if thy Firmness should ask any money from him, he should be careful to pay it over without any scruple. 4 And since I have learnt that certain persons of unstable mind are desirous of turning aside the laity of the most holy and Catholic Church by some vile method of seduction, know that I have given such commands to Anulinus, the proconsul, and moreover to Patricius, the vicar of the prefects, when they were here, that they should give due attention in all other matters and especially to 5 this, and not suffer such an occurrence to be overlooked; therefore if thou observest any such men continuing in this madness, do not thou hesitate to go to the above-mentioned judges and bring this matter before them, so that (as I commanded them when they

---

[1] θρόνου.   [2] ὑπηρετῶν.

were here) they may turn these people from their error.　May the divinity of the great God preserve thee for many years.

7.　　Copy of an Imperial Letter, in which he gives orders that the presidents of the churches be released from all public services.

　　　Greeting, Anulinus, our most honoured Sir.　Since from many facts it appears that the setting at naught of divine worship, by which the highest reverence for the most holy and heavenly [Power] is preserved, has brought great dangers upon public affairs, and that its lawful restoration and preservation have bestowed the greatest good fortune on the Roman name and singular prosperity on all the affairs of mankind (for it is the Divine Providence which bestows these blessings): it has seemed good that those men who, with due holiness and constant observance of this law, bestow their services on the performance of divine worship, should receive the rewards of their own labours, most
2 honoured Anulinus.　Wherefore it is my wish that those persons who, within the province committed to thee, in the Catholic Church over which Cæcilian presides, bestow their service on this holy worship—those whom they are accustomed to call clerics— should once for all be kept absolutely free from all the public offices, that they be not drawn away by any error or sacrilegious fault from the worship which they owe to the Divinity, but rather without any hindrance serve to the utmost their own law.　For when they render supreme service to the Deity, it seems that they confer incalculable benefit on the affairs of the State.　Fare thee well, Anulinus, our most honoured and esteemed Sir.

The Madness of Licinius.

8.　　Such then were the gifts that the divine and heavenly grace of our Saviour bestowed upon us by His appearing, and such was the abundance of good things that the peace which came to us procured for all mankind.　And thus our happy state was celebrated with rejoicings and festive
2 assemblies.　Nevertheless the envy that hates the good, even the demon who loves the evil, could not endure the sight of what he beheld; as indeed that which had happened to the aforesaid tyrants was not sufficient even for Licinius, as regards sound reason.　He who had been deemed worthy of the principate in a state of prosperity, of second rank after the great Emperor Constantine, of a connexion by marriage and the most exalted kinship with him, ceased from the following of good men and zealously affected the evil manners and wickedness of the impious tyrants; and he preferred to follow the judgment of those whose end he had seen with his very eyes, rather than continue on terms of friendship and love
3 with his superior.　Filled, in fact, with envy of the common benefactor, he waged an impious and most terrible war against him, neither giving respect to the laws of nature nor

bestowing a thought on sworn treaties or ties of blood or
4 agreements. For Constantine, all-gracious Emperor that he
was, furnished him with the tokens of genuine good-will, did
not grudge him kinship with himself, and did not refuse him
the enjoyment of an illustrious union in the person of his
sister. Nay further, he deemed him worthy to partake of his
ancestral nobility and his imperial blood and origin, and
bestowed on him, as a brother-in-law and joint-emperor, the
right to a share in the supreme government : for of his bounty
he gave him the ruling and administration of no inferior part
5 of the peoples under the Roman sway. But Licinius pursued
an exactly opposite line of conduct : he was daily contriving
all kinds of devices against his superior, and inventing all
manner of plans to reward his benefactor with evil. At first,
indeed, he attempted to conceal the intrigue, and feigned
friendliness, hoping that frequent recourse to guile and deceit
6 would most easily secure his expectations. But God proved
to be Constantine's Friend and Protector and Guardian, who
brought to light the plots that were devised secretly and in
darkness, and confounded them.[1] Such power is there in
the great weapon of godliness to ward off the enemy and to
preserve its own in safety. Fenced verily with this, our
Emperor, most dear to God, escaped the plots of this ill-famed
7 master of intrigue. And he, when he saw that his covert design
was by no means going according to his wish (for God disclosed
every guile and wickedness to the Emperor whom He loved),
since he was no longer able to conceal himself, raised an
8 open warfare. And, to be sure, in his decision to make war
at close quarters upon Constantine, he was already hastening
to battle also against the God of the universe, whom, as he
knew, Constantine worshipped ; and so he designed an attack,
quietly and silently at first, upon his godly subjects, who had
never at any time done any harm at all to his rule. And this
he did, because his innate wickedness had perforce brought
9 upon him terrible blindness. Thus he neither kept before his
eyes the memory of those who had persecuted Christians
before him, nor of those whom he himself destroyed and
punished for the evil deeds they had pursued. But he turned
aside from the path of sound reason, and becoming altogether
mad, decided to make war on God Himself, as the Protector
of Constantine, instead of on him who was being protected.
10   First, *he drove* away every Christian from his palace ; thus
by his own act depriving himself, wretched man, of the
prayers *to God on his behalf*,[2] which after the custom of their
fathers they are taught *to make for all men*.[3] Then he
gave orders that the soldiers in cities were to be singled out

---

[1] Cp. Eph. v. 11–13.   [2] Cp. Dion. Al., *ad Herm.* (vii. 1 above).
[3] Cp. 1 Tim. ii. 1, 2.

and deprived of honourable rank, unless they chose to sacrifice
to demons.

And, moreover, these were but small matters when judged
11 by comparison with graver measures. What need is there to
mention singly and successively the things done by this hater
of God: how, to wit, this most lawless of men invented
lawless laws? In fact, with regard to those who were suffering
under imprisonment, he laid down a law that no one should
treat them humanely by distributing food, or have pity on
those who were perishing of hunger in bonds; and that no
one should be kindly at all, or do any kindly action, even
when they were moved by mere natural feeling to sympathize
with their neighbours. And of his laws this one at least was
quite openly shameless and the harshest of all, in its putting
aside of every civilized, natural feeling, by which also it was
enacted as a punishment that those who showed pity should
suffer the same as those whom they pitied, and that those
who humanely ministered should endure the same punishment
as those who were undergoing it, and be consigned to bonds
and imprisonment. Such were the ordinances of Licinius.
12 Why should one recount his innovations with regard to
marriage, or his revolutionary changes in respect of those
who were departing this life, wherein he dared to annul the
ancient laws of the Romans well and wisely laid down, and
in their stead brought in certain that were barbarous and
uncivilized, that truly were lawless and contrary to law; or
the countless assessments [1] that he devised to the detriment
of his subject peoples, and the manifold exactions of gold and
silver, the revaluations of land, and the lucrative fines of men
in the country parts no longer alive but long since departed?
13 And, moreover, as to the banishments that this hater of
mankind inflicted upon those who had done no wrong, the
arrests of noble and highly-esteemed men, whose wedded
wives he separated from them and consigned to certain
abominable members of his household for disgraceful insult;
as to the many married women and unwedded girls with whom
this drunken old dotard satisfied his soul's unbridled lust—
why should one enlarge on these things, when the outrageous
character of his last deeds show the first to be small and of
no account?
14 For example, in the final stage of his madness he proceeded
against the bishops, and deeming them opposed to his doings,
as being the servants of the supreme God, forthwith plotted
against them, not openly as yet (for he feared his superior),
but once more with secrecy and guile; and the most highly
respected of these, by the contrivance of the governors, he
put to death. And the manner in which they were murdered

---

[1] ἐπισκήψεις.

15 was strange and hitherto unheard of. For instance, the things that were done at Amasea and the other cities of Pontus outdid every excess of cruelty. There some of the churches of God were again thrown down from the top to the bottom; others they shut up, so that none of the accustomed worshippers might assemble or pay to God the service due 16 to Him. For he did not think that the prayers were offered on his behalf—such was the reckoning of an evil conscience—but had been persuaded that we did everything and suppli- cated God on behalf of the Emperor whom He loved. Hence 17 he hastened to vent his wrath on us. And in truth the sycophants among the governors, persuaded that they were doing what pleased the impious man, plied some of the bishops with penalties suitable for malefactors, and those who had done no wrong were led away and punished, without a pretext, like murderers. And some endured at that time a more novel form of death : their bodies were cut with a sword into many pieces, and after this cruel and most fearful sight they 18 were cast into the depths of the sea as food for fishes. There- upon the men of God began again to flee, and once more the fields, once more the deserts, glens and mountains received the servants of Christ. And when the impious man was thus successful in these measures also, he then conceived the idea of stirring up anew the persecution against all.

19   He had power to accomplish his purpose, and there was nothing to hinder him carrying it into effect, had not God, the Champion of the souls that are His own, foreseeing with all speed what would come to pass, caused to shine forth all at once, as it were out of deep darkness and most murky night, a great luminary and saviour of them all, leading thither *with* 9. *a lofty arm* [1] *his servant* [2] Constantine. To him, then, as the worthy fruit of piety did God vouchsafe from heaven above the trophies of victory over the wicked men ; as for the guilty one, He laid him low, with all his counsellors and friends, prone beneath the feet of Constantine.

2   For when Licinius had carried his madness to the uttermost, the Emperor, the friend of God, reckoning that he was no longer to be endured, summoned his sound powers of reason, and tempering the stern qualities of justice with humanity determined to succour those who were being evil intreated under the tyrant's power ; and hastened, by putting a few spoilers out of the way, to rescue the greater part of the 3 human race. For hitherto, when he employed humanity alone and showed mercy to him who was undeserving of sympathy, there was no improvement in Licinius : he did not give over his wickedness, but rather increased his mad fury against his subject peoples ; while as for those who were ill-treated, no

----

[1] Ex. vi. 1, etc.   [2] Ex. xiv. 31.

hope of salvation was left for them, ground down as they
4 were by a terrible wild beast. Wherefore, mingling a hatred
of evil with a love of goodness, the defender of the good went
forth, with that most humane Emperor, his son Crispus,
stretching out the right hand of salvation to all who were
perishing. Then, inasmuch as they had God the universal
King and Son of God, the Saviour of all, as their Guide and
Ally, the father and son both together divided their battle
array against the haters of God on all sides and easily won the
victory; for everything in the encounter was made smooth
5 for them by God according to His purpose. Yea verily, all
at once and in less time than it takes to say it, those who the
other day were *breathing* death and *threatening* [1] were no more,
nor was even so much as their name remembered; their
pictures and honours received a well-deserved disgrace; and
the things that Licinius had seen with his own eyes happen
to the impious tyrants of days gone by, these he himself also
likewise suffered; for neither *did* he *receive correction* [2] nor did
he learn wisdom from the strokes that fell upon his neighbours,
but pursued the same path of iniquity as they did, and justly
reeled over the same precipice.

Conclusion.

6   Thus was Licinius cast down prostrate. But Constantine
the most mighty Victor, resplendent with every virtue that
godliness bestows, together with his son Crispus, an Emperor
most dear to God and in all respects like unto his father,
recovered the East that belonged to them, and formed the
Roman Empire, as in the days of old, into a single united
whole, bringing under their peaceful rule all of it, from the
rising sun round about in the two directions, north as well as
7 south, even to the uttermost limits of the declining day. So
then, there was taken away from men all fear of those who
formerly oppressed them; they celebrated brilliant festivals;
all things were filled with light, and men, formerly downcast,
looked at each other with smiling countenances and beaming
eyes; with dancing and hymns in city and country alike they
gave honour first of all to God the universal King, for this
they had been instructed to do, and then to the pious Emperor
8 with his sons beloved of God; old ills were forgotten and
oblivion cast on every deed of impiety; present good things
were enjoyed, with the further hope of those which were yet
for to come. And, in short, there were promulgated in every
place ordinances of the victorious Emperor full of love for
humanity, and laws that betokened munificence and true
9 piety. Thus verily, when all tyranny had been purged away,

---

[1] Acts ix. 1.   [2] Zeph. iii. 2.

the kingdom that belonged to them was preserved stedfast
and undisputed for Constantine and his sons alone; who,
when they had made it their very first action to cleanse the
world from hatred of God, conscious of the good things that
He had bestowed upon them, displayed their love of virtue
and of God, their piety and gratitude towards the Deity, by
their manifest deeds in the sight of all men.

THE MARTYRS OF PALESTINE

Headings of sections in the Longer Recension.

(C)   On the confessors in Palestine, composed by Eusebius of Cæsarea.

(C, A)   The confession [a] of Procopius, in the first year of [b] the persecution in our days.

(C, A)   The confession [c] of Alpheus, Zacchæus and Romanus,[d] in the first year of [e] the persecution in our days [f].

(C, A)   The confession [g] of Timothy in the city of Gaza, in the second year of [h] the persecution in our days [i].

(C, g)   The confession of Agapius, the two Alexanders, the two Dionysii, Timolaus [k], Romulus and Paësis [l], in the second year of the persecution in our days in the city of Cæsarea.

(G, C, A, Lat.)   The confession [m] of Apphianus [n], [o] [p] in the third year of the persecution in our days [p] [q] in the city of Cæsarea [q].

(C, A)   [r] The confession of Ædesius [r].

(C, A)   The confession [s] of Agapius, in the fourth year of [t] the persecution in our days [u].

(G, C, A, g)   The confession [v] of [w] Theodosia, the virgin [x] of God [x], [y] in the fifth year of the persecution in our days [y].

(C)   The confession of Domninus, in the fifth year of the persecution in our days, in the city of Cæsarea.

---

[a] A : 'first martyrdom.'   [b] A : 'in.'   [c] A : 'martyrdom.'

[d] A adds : 'the martyrs of Christ.'   [e] A : 'in.'

[f] A adds : 'on the seventeenth of Dius.'   [g] A : 'martyrdom.'

[h] A : 'in.'

[i] A adds : 'on the twenty-first of Dystrus' [*i.e.* March—reading *Adar* for *Iar* (May)].   [k] So g, S.   C : 'Timothy.'

[l] So S and C (text, 3. 4).   C (here) : 'Plesius.'   g (here) : 'Plesius,' 'Publius.'   It seems that 'Plesius' stood in the title of the MS. of G, from which the Syriac version was translated.

[m] G, A, Lat. : 'martyrdom.'

[n] So (or 'Amphianus') G, A, Lat., g, S.   C : 'Epiphanius.'

[o] G, Lat. add : 'and Ædesius, brothers by the same mother.'

[p-p] A : 'on the second of Xanthicus.'   G : 'on the second of the same month, the second (*sic*) before the nones of April.'   Lat. omits.

[q-q] G, A, Lat. omit.

[r-r] G, Lat. omit : see note [o] above.   G, Lat., g, S have 'Ædesius.'   C : 'Alosis.'   A : 'The martyrdom of Ædesius, the brother of Mar Apphianus.'

[s] A : 'martyrdom.'   [t] A : 'in.'

[u] A adds : 'on the twentieth of Dius.'

[v] A, G : 'martyrdom.'

[w] A adds : 'the holy.'   g adds : 'the holy martyr.'

[x-x] A : 'of Christ the brave martyr of the true God.'   G, g omit.

[y-y] A omits.   G adds : 'the fourth before the nones of April in Cæsarea of Palestine.'   g adds : 'in Cæsarea.'

(C)   The confession of Paul, Valentina and Ennatha [a], in the sixth year of the persecution in our days, in Cæsarea.

(C)   The confession of Antoninus, Zebina, Germanus and Ennathas [b], in the sixth year of the persecution in our days, in Cæsarea.

(C)   The confession of Ares, Promos [c] and Elijah, in the sixth year of the persecution in our days, in Ashkelon.

(C, A)   The confession [d] of Peter, called [e] Abshelama, in the seventh [f] year of the [g] persecution in our days [g], in the city of Cæsarea.

(G, C, g)   The confession [h] of [i] Pamphilus, Valens, Paul, Seleucus, Porphyry, Theodulus [j], Julian and [k] five Egyptians [k], [l] in the seventh [m] year of the persecution in our days [l].

(C)   The confession of Hadrian and Eubulus, in the seventh year of the persecution in our days.

(C)   The confession of Peleus [n], Nilus, Patermuthius [o] and Elijah, in the seventh year of the persecution in our days.

(C)   The confession of Silvanus and his companions, in the eighth year of the persecution in our days.

---

[a] g : ' Ennatha,' ' Theê.'   C : ' Chōthō.'

[b] So S.   g : ' Ennatha,' ' Manatha,' Manetho,' ' Maratho.'   C (here) : ' Mannathus.'   C (in text, 9. 6) : ' Chōthō ' (= ' sister ').

[c] So S.   g : ' Promos,' ' Probus.'   C : ' Primus.'

[d] A : ' martyrdom.'   [e] A omits.   [f] g : ' sixth ' (?).

[g-g] A : ' our persecution.'   [h] G, g : ' conflict.'

[i] G adds : ' the holy and glorious martyrs of Christ.'   g adds : ' the holy martyrs.'   The order of the names varies slightly in the different authorities.

[j] C : Theophilus.

[k-k] G : ' the Egyptians who were with them.'   C : ' one Egyptian, in number eight.'   g adds : ' Elijah, Jeremiah, Samuel, Isaiah and Daniel.'

[l-l] G, g omit.   [m] g (in text) : ' sixth.'

[n] So g, S (cp. viii. 13. 5).   C : ' Paulus.'

[o] So g, S.   C (here) : ' Patrimithæus.'   C (text, 13. 3) : ' Patermithæus.'

L

(C)

Pref. Those holy martyrs of God, who loved our Saviour and
Lord, Jesus Christ, and *God who is over all* [1] and King of all,
more than themselves and their lives, and engaged in conflict
for religion, and were adorned with the martyrdom of confession, and accounted a horrible death more precious than
a fleeting life, and won all the garlands of victorious virtue,
offered up the glory of their wonderful victory to the most
high *God who is over all*,[1] because heaven was always with
them and they *walked with* [2] Him who granted victory to
their confession, and offered up praise and honour and majesty
to Father, Son and Holy Ghost. And the spirits of the
martyrs, counted worthy of the kingdom of heaven, are come
to the assembly of the prophets, and are precious.

2 So for our part, we who need the help of their prayers and
are commanded also in the book of the Apostles to *communicate in the commemoration of the saints*,[3] let us also communicate with them, and let us begin to describe their contests
against sin, contests whose fame is at all times on the lips of
every believer who knew them. But their praises were
declared, not by statues of stone, nor by pictures of mingled
pigments, nor by colours or images of lifeless terrestrial
things, but by the true word uttered before God. The deed
which was seen by our eyes added its witness. Let us therefore tell the clear signs and glorious manifestations of the
divine doctrine, and frame in writing an imperishable monument, and let us make their wondrous excellence a lasting
vision before our eyes.

REIGN OF DIOCLETIAN

S

Introduction

Pref.
303. It was the nineteenth year of the reign of Diocletian, the
month Xanthicus, or April, as the Romans would call it,
in which, as the festival of the Saviour's Passion was
approaching, while Flavian was governor of the people of
Palestine, a letter was all at once everywhere promulgated,
ordering the razing of the churches to the ground and the
destruction by fire of the Scriptures, and proclaiming that those

[1] Rom. ix. 5.   [2] Gen. v. 24.
[3] Rom. xii. 13 (reading μνείαις for χρείαις).

L 3　But I marvel at their all-enduring courage, at their confessions of divers kinds, their wholesome readiness of soul, the soaring of their mind, the boldness of their faith, the enlightenment of their thought, the endurance of their plight, the truth of their worship : how they fainted not in their minds, and their eyes looked upward, and they were without trembling 4 or fear.　Moreover, the love of God and His Christ had given them all-surpassing strength to conquer their enemies.　For they *loved God* the King of all, and they delighted in Him *with all* their *might*.[1]　And He rewarded them for their love to Him by the succour which He gave them; and He had a delight in them, so that they received power against those 5 that hated them.　And they used the words of that confessor who had witnessed before them, saying,

Who shall separate us from Christ ? Shall tribulation, or anguish, or persecution, or famine, or peril,[2] or sword ? Even as it is written,

For thy sake we are killed all the day long;
We are accounted as sheep for the slaughter.[3]

And again, says this martyr of God, exalting the endurance which is *not overcome of evil*,[4]

In all these things we are conquerors because of him who loved us.[5]

And he foretold that all evils are overcome by the love of God and proclaimed that all terrors and distresses are set at naught, when he said,

I am persuaded that neither death nor life . . . nor things present, nor things to come, nor powers, nor height, nor depth, nor any other creature, shall be able to separate us from the love of God, which is in our Lord Jesus Christ.[6]

6　At that time, then, Paul, who gloried in the power of his Lord,[7] was himself crowned with the victory of confession in the midst of Rome, the imperial city, because there he *fought* his *good fight*.[8]　And there, again, in that victory which Christ gave to the victorious martyrs, Simon also, the chief

---

S　who held high positions would lose all civil rights, while those in households, if they persisted in their profession of Christi- 2 anity, would be deprived of their liberty.　Such, then, was the force of the first document against us.　But not long afterwards we were further visited with other letters, and in

[1] Deut. vi. 5.　　　　　[2] Syr. ' death.' Cp. ii. 2, 6, note.
[3] Rom. viii. 35, 36.
[4] Rom. xii. 21.　　[5] Rom. viii. 37.　　[6] Rom. viii. 38, 39.
[7] Cp. 2 Cor. xii. 9 f.　　　　　　　　[8] 2 Tim. iv. 7.

L and first of the disciples, won the crown; and he suffered in
 7 like manner as our Lord suffered.   And as for other apostles
in other places—the end of their lives was by martyrdom.
And not only to the men of old was this grace given, but
also to this generation of ours was it given without stint.

 8   It is meet, then, that the conflicts which were illustrious
in various districts should be committed to writing by those
who dwelt with the combatants in their districts.   But for
me, I pray that I may be able to speak of those with whom
I was personally conversant, and that they may associate me
with them—those in whom the whole people of Palestine
glories, because even in the midst of our land, the Saviour of
all men arose like a thirst-quenching spring.   The contests,
then, of those illustrious champions I shall relate for the
general instruction and profit.

REIGN OF DIOCLETIAN

First Year (303–4)

Procopius.

(C, A, Lat., g)

1.   The first of [a] the martyrs of Palestine to be displayed
[b] was Procopius [b].   He was [c] in truth a man of God [c]; for
even before his martyrdom he had dedicated his life to
philosophy [d], and from a child embraced chastity of conduct
and a most rigorous mode of living; and he *buffeted* his
body [1] to such a degree that [e] it seemed [f] dead.   He had so
greatly strengthened his soul by the divine words that [g] even
his body was sustained by the strength of God [g]   His meat

---

a C, A add : ' all.'   b-b C : ' was called P.' A : ' P. was crowned.'
c-c Lat. : ' a man of heavenly grace.'   g omits.
d So g.   C, A : ' great austerity.'
e C, A add : ' even before his death.'   f Lat. adds : ' almost.'
g-g Lat. : ' he ministered strength by its nourishment even to his
body.'

S   them the order was given that the presidents of the churches
should all everywhere be first committed to prison, and then
afterwards compelled by every kind of device to sacrifice.

Procopius.

1.   So then, Procopius, the first of the martyrs in Palestine,
before he *had trial of imprisonment*,[2] and immediately on first
entering the governor's courts at which he appeared, when
ordered to sacrifice to the so-called gods, replied that he

[1] 1 Cor. ix. 27.   [2] Heb. xi. 36.

L   was bread, and his drink water; and these would be his only *food every* two or *three days*; and often he passed even a whole week without food.[1] Moreover,[a] from his meditation on the divine words he ceased not night or day. [b] Yet, as if inferior to the rest, he displayed a bountiful supply of gentleness and meekness as a proof of his character.[b] Though he was so deeply engaged in the study of the divine words,[c] he had no small knowledge of [d] this world.[d] Now Ælia [e] was the place of his birth, but he lived at Scythopolis [f], where he supplied [g] the needs of [g] the Church with three ministries : first as a reader, secondly as an interpreter of [h] the Syriac language [h], and thirdly ([i] though it was an office of special labour [i]) as a banisher of [j] demons. And when he was sent [k], with [l] his companions [l], from Scythopolis [m] to Cæsarea, from the very gates they brought him to the governor, and [n] before he *had trial of imprisonment and bonds* [n],[2] [o] immediately on his first entering [o], [p] he was urged by the judge, Flavian, to sacrifice [p] to the gods [q]. But, [r] bearing witness [r] with a loud voice, he said [s] that there is but one God only, the Creator and Maker of the universe. And the judge, smitten by the

[a] So Lat.; C, A, ' But.'

[b-b] So apparently Lat. (' Clementiæ autem et mansuetudinis tanquam ceteris inferior documentum sui præbebat copiam '). C, A : ' But (while C) he was so careful as concerning his deportment and virtuous manners (man. and modest dep. C) that by gentleness and meekness he surpassed (instructed C) all those of his own standing.'.

[c] A adds : ' which he had within.'

[d-d] Lat. : ' those things that are without.'

[e] A : ' Jerusalem.'   C : ' Baishan,' omitting the following clause.

[f] A : ' Baishan.'   [g-g] So g.   C : ' in the order of.'   A, Lat. omit.

[h-h] So g, Lat.   C, A : ' the Greek language into Syriac.'

[i-i] So apparently g ($\epsilon\iota$ $\kappa\alpha\iota$ $\pi\epsilon\pi o\nu\eta\mu\acute{\epsilon}\nu\omega\varsigma$). A : ' wherein he *laboured more abundantly*.'[3] C : ' which is also superior to the former.' Lat. omits.

[j] g (lit.) ' against ' : so C, Lat. Lat. (of whole clause) : ' adversus demones manus impositione consummans.'

[k] g : ' brought.'

[l-l] C : ' companion confessors.'   A : ' other companions.'

[m] C, A : ' Baishan.'   [n-n] So A, Lat., with S.

[o-o] So C, Lat., with S.

[p-p] C, A : ' the judge, whose name was Flavian (Paulinus, A), cried out, " It is necessary for you to sacrifice."

[q] g : ' demons.'   [r-r] C, S omit.   [s] Lat. omits.

S   knew one God and one alone, to whom was due such sacrifice as He desired. And when he was commanded to pour out a libation at any rate to the four emperors, he gave utterance to a certain remark which was displeasing to them, and so was straightway beheaded. For he made the following quotation from the poet :

[1] Cp. Philo, *D.V.C.* (above, ii. 17. 17).   [2] Heb. **xi.** 36.
[3] Cp. 1 Cor. xv. 10.

L stroke of the martyr's word [a], [b] assented to his proposition [b].
[c] Withdrawing his former order, he changed it for another,
saying that [c] he must sacrifice to the emperors, [d] who were
four in number [d]. But the holy martyr of God laughed to
scorn his words, and [e] made the following quotation from the
greatest poet of the Greeks [e] :

The lordship of many is no good thing; let there be one lord,
One king.[1]

And [f] because of this answer [f], which belittled the emperors,
by the order of the judge he was led to death, and being
beheaded the blessed one quickly discovered the [g] road that
leads upon the heavenly way.

2 It was the seventh day of the month of Dæsius [h] (which
the Romans call the seventh before the Ides of
7 June, 303 June) [h] in the first year of the persecution in
our days. This martyrdom [i] was the first that was con-
summated at the city of Cæsarea.

        *   *   *   *   *

[a] A adds : ' in his heart.' Lat. adds : ' and wounded by his conscience.'   [b-b] C omits.
[c-c] Lat. : ' betaking himself again to other arguments, that.'
[d-d] Lat. omits.
[e-e] So C, A (A adds ' Homer ' after ' from '). Lat. : ' quoted this
verse of Homer.'   g : ' uttered the saying.'
[f-f] So C. A, Lat. : ' with this word.'   g : ' forthwith.'
[g] C, A add : ' easy.'   [h-h] C omits. A omits the whole sentence.
[i] So A, Lat. : cp. S. C : ' confessor.'

S The lordship of many is no good thing; let there be one lord,
One king.[1]

2 On the seventh of the month Dæsius (the Romans would
call it the seventh before the Ides of June), on
7 June, 303 the fourth day of the week, this first sign was
accomplished at Cæsarea in Palestine.

Results of the Third Edict.

3 But after this, in the same city very many rulers of the
churches in the country contended with a stout heart throughout terrible torments, displaying to those who observed them
the spectacle of mighty conflicts; while others, whose souls
cowardice had numbed beforehand, readily proved weak at
the first assault; while of the rest, each underwent a series of
varied forms of torture : at one time it was lashes without
number, at another the rack, the laceration of the sides, and
unbearable fetters, the effect of these last being that, in the

[1] Hom., *Iliad*, ii. 204 f.

L *Zacchæus and Alpheus.*

(C, A, g)

5b At that time it happened that the festival of the year of
the vicennalia of the emperors was approaching; and an
amnesty was proclaimed for those at the festival who were
in prison. And before the festival the governor of the province came, and made enquiry concerning the prisoners who
were in confinement. And some of them, by the clemency
of the emperors, were released. But the martyrs of God, as
though they were worse than thieves and murderers, he
c treated shamelessly with tortures. Zacchæus, therefore, who
was a deacon of the church in the city of Gadara, was led,
like an innocent lamb from the flock, a with a heavy iron collar
on his neck [a]; and his acquaintances named him Zacchæus
by way of honour, calling him after the former Zacchæus,
because of the littleness of his *stature*,[1] and because b throughout
his whole life he was like him [b]. And coming before the
d tribunal [c] he [d] rejoiced in his confession for Christ's sake [d]. And
when he had spoken the words of God in the presence of the

[a-a] So A, g. C : ' for such indeed was he in his very nature.'
[b-b] So A, g. C : ' he led a strict life, and was more earnestly desirous
to *see* [1] our Lord than Zacchæus.'
[c] So g, A. C : ' judge.'
[d-d] g : ' remained unchanged in his faith in Christ.'

S case of some, they actually lost the power of their hands.
4 Nevertheless they endured whatever issue came to pass in
accordance with the mysterious decrees of God. Thus, in
the case of one man, others held him fast by both hands,
brought him to the altar, and let fall on it out of his right
hand the polluted and accursed sacrifice : then he was dismissed as if he had sacrificed. Another did not so much as
touch it, but when others said that he had sacrificed, he
held his tongue and went away. A third was taken up half-
dead and cast aside as if he were a corpse already ; yea, and
he was loosed from his bonds, having been reckoned among
those who had voluntarily sacrificed.   When yet another cried
out and testified that he was not yielding, he was struck on
the mouth and silenced by a large body of persons appointed
for that purpose, and forcibly driven away even though he
5 had not sacrificed. So much store did they set on seeming
by any means to have accomplished their purpose.

Zacchæus and Alpheus.

Therefore out of so great a number Alpheus and Zacchæus
alone were counted worthy of the crown of the holy martyrs.
These men after scourgings, scrapings and galling chains,

[1] Luke xix. 3.

L   judge he was delivered over to all the agonies of punishment,
and after the preliminary scourgings he had to endure grievous
scrapings. And after these he was again committed to the
prison, and there his feet were stretched for ᵃ a night and a
day ᵃ over four holes in the stocks.

e   And Alpheus, a lovable man, endured similar sufferings.
He was sprung of an illustrious family in the city of Eleutheropolis, and in the church of Cæsarea he was honoured
with the position of reader and exorcist. Now before he
became a confessor he was a preacher and teacher of the
word of God. And he used great boldness towards all men,
which thing was the worthy cause of his being brought to
f his confession for the truth. And because he saw that at
that time laxity and great fear had fallen upon all men,
and many were swept along, as it were, before the torrent of
many waters and were led ᵇ to the foul worship of idols, he
considered how he might oppose the torrent of evil by his
g fortitude ᶜ. And he, of his own will, threw himself into the
midst of the crowd of the torturers, and with words of warning
reproached those who from their fear ᵈ were drawn into error,
and turned them from the worship of idols, and brought to
their remembrance the words that were spoken by our Saviour
h about confession.¹ And when Alpheus, valiant warrior that
he was, acted thus with boldness, the soldiers arrested him,
and forthwith brought him before the judge. ᵉ Now he was
like a man full of the Spirit of God ᵉ : what expressions he
freely used with the utterance of a freeman, and with what
words of godliness he made answer, this is not the occasion to
i tell. ᶠ Because of this ᶠ he was sent to prison. And some
days later they brought him again before the judge, and
with grievous lashings they pitilessly tore his whole body,
while the fortitude of his mind stood erect against the judge,
and by his speech he resisted all error. And they tortured
him on his sides with grievous scrapings. But at length,
when he had wearied the judge, as well as those who ministered
to the judge's will, he was committed to prison with his
fellow-combatant, and there he was stretched ᵍ a night and a
day ᵍ on ʰ that instrument of torture, the ʰ stocks.

ᵃ⁻ᵃ So g, A. C : ' a whole day and a whole night.'
ᵇ So C. A : ' were falling headlong.'
ᶜ C adds : ' and check by his mighty words the terrible billows.'
ᵈ A : ' laxity.'   ᵉ⁻ᵉ So C. A omits. g omits ' like.'
ᶠ⁻ᶠ C : ' after this.'   ᵍ⁻ᵍ So A, S. C : ' a whole day and night.'
ʰ⁻ʰ So g, S. C, A add : ' wooden.'

S   after the agonies that ensued and other varied examinations
under torture, had their feet stretched for a night and a day
over four holes in that instrument of punishment, the stocks.

¹ Matt. x. 32 f.; Luke xii. 8 f.

L k   For the third time [a] the two of them together were brought before the judge; and he ordered them to sacrifice to the emperors. But they confessed, saying, " We know one God alone, King of all." And when these words were uttered [b], [c] by a sentence reserved for the worst criminals, they were beheaded; and [c] so they were numbered among the company of the victorious martyrs, and, as champions glorious and bright in their minds, were given the crown in the conflict of God [d]. And better than the whole course of their lives did they love the departure to Him in whom they made their confession.

But the day of their martyrdom was the seventeenth [e] of

17 Nov. 303   Dius ⟨that is, with the Romans, the fifteenth day before the Kalends of December⟩, on which day the confession of those of whom we have spoken was completed.

Romanus.

(C, A, g)

2.   And on the same day also Romanus suffered martyrdom at the city of Antioch. Now Romanus was a Palestinian, and he was a deacon and an exorcist [f] of the community at Cæsarea [f]. Like as Alpheus the martyr did [g], so the blessed Romanus was wont to deter [h] by rebukes those whom terror

---

[a] C : ' After three days.'   [b] C adds : ' before all the people.'
[c-c] So A; cp. S. C omits.
[d] C adds : ' for whose sake also they were beheaded.'
[e] So S. C : ' seventh.' g : ' eighteenth.' A omits the sentence.
[f-f] So g, S. C, A : ' in one of the villages (+ of the community [shultânâ] A) of (at, A) Cæsarea.' C adds : ' He also, therefore, was stretched upon the stocks. And.'
[g] C adds : ' at Cæsarea.'   [h] C, A add : ' from sacrificing.'

S   And on the seventeenth day of the month Dius (that is, with the Romans, the fifteenth day before the Kalends of December), when they had confessed one God alone, and Christ

17 Nov. 303   Jesus alone as King, as if they had uttered something blasphemous, they were beheaded even as the former martyr.

Romanus.

2.   Worthy of mention also is the treatment of Romanus at Antioch on the same day. Now this man, who was a Palestinian, and a deacon and an exorcist of the community at Cæsarea, came to Antioch at the very time the churches were destroyed. He saw numbers of men, and women and children as well, crowding up to the idols and sacrificing; and, deeming the sight intolerable, in his zeal for religion he advanced, and

L   was dragging down to the error of idolatry [a], putting them in mind of the fear of God. And he dared to go with the multitude [b] who were led into error by violence [b], and [c] there at Antioch [c] to appear, self-called,[d] before the judge. And when he heard the judge commanding them to sacrifice, and they in haste because of their fears were driven on [e] to sacrifice, this zealous hero could not support the grievous sight, and had pity on them as men groping in abysmal darkness about to fall from a precipice. So he made the doctrine of godliness to shine before them like the rising sun, as he cried out and said, "Whither are ye being led, O men? And are all of you descending to hurl yourselves into the abyss? Lift up the eyes of your mind on high, and ye shall know, above all the worlds, God and the Saviour of all [f] the ends of the world [f]; and do not abandon for error the commandment which was entrusted to you [g]: and there shall be manifested to you the godless error of the service of demons. And remember also the righteous judgments of God [h] who is
2 over all [h]." And when he had thus [i] cried out [i] to them with a loud voice and [j] fearlessly borne witness with courageous mind [j], by the command of the judge [k] who was in office there [k] the quaestionarii laid hold of him and ordered that he should perish by fire. For the [l] cunning judge [l] perceived that by the answers of the martyr many were strengthened [m]; and, [n] moreover, Diocletian, the chief of the emperors, was in the city. Forthwith [n] they led out the blessed one into the midst of the city of Antioch. And he had reached the place where he was to be executed, and the materials needed for the fire were prepared, and they were at pains to obey

[a] So g. C, A : ' demons.'   [b-b] A omits.   [c-c] A omits.
[d] So g. C, A omit.   [e] C adds : ' in their distraction.'
[f-f] A : ' men.'   [g] A adds : ' by your Creator.'   [h-h] A omits.
[i-i] So A, S. C : ' said.'
[j-j] So A; cp. S. C : ' and without fear and without trepidation stood there.'
[k-k] A omits.   [l-l] A : ' wicked man.'
[m] C adds : ' and he was inciting many to resist error.'
[n-n] So A; cp. S. C : ' because the servant of Jesus did these things where the emperors were, forthwith.'

S 2 crying out with a loud voice rebuked them. He was arrested because of his daring, and showed himself a most noble witness to the truth, if ever there was one. For when the judge sentenced him to death by fire, he gladly received the sentence with a bright countenance and most ready mind, and so was led away. Then he was bound to the stake and the wood piled up around him. But as those who were to kindle the fire were awaiting the word from the emperor, who was present,
3 he cried out, " Where is my fire? " On saying this he was

L 3 the command with speed. But the Emperor Diocletian, when
he learnt what was done, ordered that they should put back
the martyr from death by fire (for he said that death by fire
was too small a punishment for his presumption and per-
versity), and like a merciful [a] emperor he ordered a novel
form of punishment for the martyr, that his tongue should
be cut out. Nevertheless when his tongue, by which he
spoke, was taken away, his genuine love was not removed
from him [b], [c] nor was the tongue of his understanding silenced
from preaching [c]. And immediately he received from God,
the King of all, a compensation for the fight which he fought
in the hour of trial, and he was filled with power greater
than he had before. Then did exceeding wonder take hold
of all. For he whose tongue had been cut out, by the grace
of God forthwith spoke powerfully, and gloried boldly in the
faith, as though he were by the side of Him whose confessor
he was. And with radiant and joyful countenance he greeted
his acquaintances, and sowed the seed of the word of God
in the ears of all, and preached to all men that they should
worship God alone, and sent up supplication and giving of
thanks to God who doeth wonders. And these things done,
magnificently before all men did he bear witness to the word
of Christ, and by deed showed the power of Him whose
4 confessor he was. And when he had done this [d] for a long
time [d] [e] his feet were stretched over five holes [e] in the stocks,
and, by command of the emperors [f], [g] a noose was thrown
around his neck, even as he lay [g] [h] in his bonds [h] in the
prison, and he was strangled. And on the same day as the

[a] A : ' pitiless.'   [b] C : ' his God.'   [c-c] A omits.
[d-d] So C, g; cp. S. A omits.
[e-e] So A, g (S). C : ' he was again stretched.'
[f] So g. A : ' emperor.' C : ' governor and judge.'
[g-g] So g. C, A give the same sense.   [h-h] So A, g. C omits.

S summoned again before the emperor, to be subjected to a
somewhat novel punishment—inflicted on the tongue. The
cutting out of this he most bravely endured, thus showing to
all by his deeds [1] that of a truth a divine power is present to
lighten the sufferings and strengthen the will of those who
endure any hardship whatever for the sake of religion. Thus,
when the noble man learnt the novelty of his punishment he
was not dismayed thereat, but gladly put out his tongue and
offered it with the greatest alacrity in readiness for those
4 who were to cut it off. After this punishment he was thrown
into chains, and there suffered for a very long time. At last
on the approach of the twentieth anniversary of the emperor's
reign, when in accordance with an accustomed bounty liberty
was proclaimed for all who were everywhere in prison, he

[1] Or, ' by all his deeds.'

L   blessed martyrs who were the companions of Zacchæus he
5 was perfected in his confession.   And though it was at
Antioch that he fought and became a martyr, yet being a
Palestinian he may rightly be reckoned among the company
of the martyrs of this [a] our country.

SECOND YEAR (305)

The Fourth Edict.

(C, Λ)

3.   In the second year of the persecution the war against us
increased in intensity (the governor of the province of Palestine being Urban, who at that time had superseded the
governor Flavian), and imperial edicts arrived again for the
second time, [b] much worse than [b] the first [c].   [d] For the first [d]
gave commandment regarding the rulers of the Church of
God alone, that they should sacrifice.   But in the second
there was a grievous command, which compelled all alike,
that all the people in all the cities in a body—men and women
[e] and their children [e]—should [f] sacrifice and offer libations to
the lifeless idols.[f]   Such [g] were the commands of the tyrants
who in their madness desired to make war against God,[h]
the King of all.

> [a] A omits.   [b-b] C : ' in addition to.'
> [c] C adds : ' threatening persecution to all.'
> [d-d] C : 'For in the first he.'   [e-e] C omits.
> [f-f] C : ' sacrifice to the l.i., and a law was imposed upon them
> that they should offer libations to demons.'   A : ' sacrifice to the
> l.i.'   Cp. S.
> [g] C : ' For such.'   [h] A omits.

S   alone had his feet stretched over five holes in the stocks, and
as he lay therein was strangled.   Thus were his longings
5 satisfied and he was adorned with martyrdom.   And though
he was outside his own country, yet, being a Palestinian, he
may rightly be reckoned among the Palestinian martyrs.

The Fourth Edict.

3.   Such was the course of action in the first year, when the
presidents of the Church were alone menaced by the persecution.   But when the second year came round and, further,
the war against us increased in intensity (Urban being at
that time governor of the province), imperial edicts then
visited us for the first time, in which by a general ordinance
the command was given that in the several cities all the
people in a body should sacrifice and offer libations to the
idols.

L

Timothy of Gaza.

(C, A, g)

Now when these orders from the emperors were put into operation, the blessed Timothy was delivered up at Gaza, a city of Palestine, to Urban ᵃ when he was there ᵃ, and was unjustly put into bonds, like a murderer. But he was not bound for anything that was worthy of blame, for in all his conduct and life he was blameless. And when he refused to submit to ᵇ idol-worship, and did not worship dead, lifeless images (for he was in all respects a perfect man, and in his soul ᶜ knew his ᶜ God), and because of his temperance, ᵈ and on the score of his virtuous ways ᵈ, he had endured grievous sufferings, even before he was delivered up to the governor, from the inhabitants of the city, ᵉ and lived there subject to great insult, frequent stripes and afflictions.ᵉ For the men of Gaza were turbulent ᶠ and accursed ᶠ in their paganism. And when he ᵍ approached the governor's tribunal this champion of righteousness triumphed in all excellence of endurance. And angrily ʰ the judge ⁱ used against him grievous tortures, and ʲ showered upon his body ʲ unnumbered scourgings, and with fearful and indescribable ᵏ lacerations did he torture his sides. But amid all these sufferings the wonderful martyr ˡ strove like a warrior, and at last attained victory in his contest by enduring death by a slow fire. For the fire was ᵐ gentle and ᵐ slow in which he was burnt, so that his soul should not easily leave his body ⁿ and be at rest ⁿ. And there was he tried like pure gold in a ᵒ furnace of ᵒ gentle fire, and displayed ᵖ the perfection and genuineness ᑫ of his piety ᑫ towards his God; and was crowned with the crown wherewith the glorious conquerors

---

ᵃ⁻ᵃ A omits.   ᵇ C adds : ' the law of.'   ᶜ⁻ᶜ A : ' drew near to.'
ᵈ⁻ᵈ A : ' and his excellent deeds.'
ᵉ⁻ᵉ A : ' endured insult and frequent stripes.'   ᶠ⁻ᶠ C omits.
ᵍ C : ' they.'   ʰ A : ' cruelly.'   ⁱ A : ' wicked man.'
ʲ⁻ʲ A : ' tore his whole body with.'   ᵏ A : ' unhealable.'
ˡ C adds : ' of God.'
ᵐ So C, S. A omits.   ⁿ⁻ⁿ A omits.
ᵒ⁻ᵒ A omits.   ᵖ A inserts ' bravely.'   ᑫ⁻ᑫ A omits.

S

Timothy of Gaza.

Timothy at Gaza, a city of Palestine, having endured countless tortures was afterwards committed to a slow and gentle fire. By his endurance of it all he gave a most genuine proof of the genuineness of his piety towards the Divine Being, and thus carried off the crown that the conquering champions of religion wear.

L   of righteousness are crowned. And [a] because he loved God he received the reward that matched his desire—that perfect life which he desired—to be with God [a] the King of all.

And moreover with this valiant confessor, [b] at the time of his trial of confession [b] in the same city, Agapius the martyr and the admirable Thecla [c] of our days [c] were condemned by this governor to receive this punishment, namely, to be food for the wild beasts.

Agapius of Gaza, and others.

(C, g)

2   There was a festival of all the heathen assembled in their cities. This festival was also held at Cæsarea. For in the circus there was an exhibition of horse-racing, and a mad play was performed in the theatre, and it was customary that there should be foul and brutal spectacles in the stadium. And there ran abroad among all a report and tidings that Agapius, whose name we mentioned just now, and his companion Thecla, with the rest of the Phrygians, would be exposed in the theatre in the guise of martyrs, that they might be food for the wild beasts; for Urban the governor had granted this boon to the spectators.

3   And when the report of this was heard, it happened further that there were other young men, perfect in stature and strong in body, numbering six. And when the governor,

[a-a] A : ' by his stedfast conduct he received the excellent things that matched his God-loving desire, and, in exchange for the fleeting life of time, the perfect life with Christ.'
[b-b] A : ' on the same day.'   [c-c] A omits.

S   At the same time as Timothy, Agapius and the Thecla of our day displayed the most noble stedfastness and were condemned to be food for the wild beasts.

Agapius of Gaza, and others.

2   Who saw what followed, and did not marvel? Who even learnt it by hearsay and was not amazed? For indeed when the heathen were celebrating a general holiday and were holding some of their accustomed spectacles, it was noised abroad that, in addition to the other efforts made to please the people, those also who had lately been condemned to the wild beasts would exhibit their conflict.

3   As the rumour increased and spread to everyone, some young men numbering six (of whom one was a Pontic by race, named Timolaus; another, from Tripolis in Phœnicia, was called Dionysius; a third was a subdeacon of the com-

L   on his way to the theatre, passed through the midst of the city, these six men stood courageously before him, having themselves bound their hands behind them, and approached Urban the judge. And by the binding of themselves they signified in act that which should be done to them by others, as well as their exceeding great endurance and ready desire for martyrdom. And they confessed, crying out and saying, " We are Christians "; and they besought the governor that they too might be thrown to the wild beasts in the theatre, with their brethren, Agapius and his companions. For all this fortitude of Jesus our Saviour, which was in His champions, He displayed to all, abating the threats of the tyrants by the stedfastness of His champions. And He showed openly and clearly that neither fire nor steel, nor even savage beasts, availed to subdue His victorious servants; for with the armour of righteousness He girded them, and with victorious and invincible armour He strengthened them and
4 caused them to despise death. And when by this courageous conduct they had reduced on the spot the governor and his entire suite to a condition of amazement, the governor commanded that they should be committed to prison. There they were kept for many days. And, while they were there, Agapius, that humble and good man, brother of one of the prisoners, came from the city of Gaza, and frequently went to the prison to visit his brother; and because before he made these visits to the prison he had striven in many contests of confession, to the prison he went with confidence, and he was informed against to the governor as a man ready for martyrdom. And he was then delivered over into bonds to undergo another trial of confession.

And sufferings such as these Dionysius also endured; and this good reward was given him by the martyrs of God, in recompense for service to them. And when the governor

---

S   munity at Diospolis, whose name was Romulus; and, besides these, two Egyptians, Paësis and Alexander; and another who bore the same name, Alexander a native of Gaza), having first bound their hands, that they might signify their exceeding great zeal for martyrdom, ran up to Urban as he was about to go up to the sports, confessing themselves Christians, and showing, by their readiness to face everything terrible, that those who glory in piety towards the God of the universe do not cower even before the attacks of the wild beasts.
4 Having reduced on the spot the governor and his suite to a condition of no ordinary amazement, they were shut up in prison; but not many days after two others were added to their number, of whom the one—he too was named Agapius—had already on a former occasion made other confessions

L became aware of the recompense which Dionysius had received for the compassion which he had shown to the martyrs, he sentenced him to death. He also, then, was added to those who preceded him. They all numbered eight: Timolaus [a], a Pontic by race, and Dionysius, who was of the city of Tripolis, and Romulus a [b] subdeacon of the church in [b] the city of Diospolis, and two Egyptians, Paësis [c] and Alexander, and again another Alexander, and those two of whom we wrote that they were at last committed to prison. All these were March 24   delivered up to be beheaded together at the same time. And this event took place on the twenty-fourth of Dystrus ⟨the ninth before the Kalends of April⟩.

The Abdication.

(C)

5   And at that time there was a sudden change of the emperors, of him who was chief and emperor and of him who was honoured with the second rank after him. And those who laid aside their rule and empire and put on ordinary attire 6 and gave the empire to their colleagues, forthwith were divided from their love towards each other, and stirred up internecine war against one another. Nor was healing granted for the disease of their enmity until peace for us was extended 7 throughout the empire of the Romans. For, like a light,

[a] So g, S. C: 'Timothy.'
[b-b] So g, S. C: 'separated man (*prīqô* for *pdīqô*) of the church and.'
[c] So C, S. g: 'Plesius,' 'Publius.'

S and contended under fearful and manifold tortures; while the other, whose name was also Dionysius, was ministering to their bodily needs. So they all, numbering eight, were March 24   beheaded on a single day, at Cæsarea itself as before. It was the twenty-fourth day of the month Dystrus, the ninth before the Kalends of April.

The Abdication.

5   At that time there was a change in the rulers, that is to say, the highest of all and the second after him, who assumed the part of private citizens, and let public affairs fall into 6 disorder. But shortly afterwards the principate of the Romans was divided internally, and internecine civil war broke out; nor was the division, and the disturbance that ensued, healed, until peace for us had been secured throughout the whole of the world that was under the Roman principate. 7 For, like a light, peace rose upon all, as if out of a murky and

343

L peace rose out of its murky darkness; and forthwith the Church of the supreme God and the divine doctrine were spread throughout *the whole creation*.[1]

REIGN OF MAXIMIN DAZA (305–313)

THIRD YEAR (306)

Apphianus.

(G, C, A, Lat.)

4.   A terrible serpent and cruel tyrant took possession at that very time of his newly-attained [a] supreme [b] rule, and, the moment he did so, started as it were from [c] his hearth [c] to fight with God, by setting to work with greater spirit than his predecessors on the persecution against us. This was
2 Maximin. In truth [d] no small [d] confusion hung [e] over all the inhabitants of the cities; men [f] were dispersed, one to this place, another to that, zealously desiring to escape the evils which surrounded them.

In these circumstances, what word of ours could suffice to describe worthily the divine love of the martyr Apphianus [g]?

[a] C, A, Lat. omit.   [b] C, A omit.
[c-c] C, Lat. : ' his beginning.' A : ' the beginning of his reign.'
[d-d] So C, A, S (οὐ μικρᾶς). Lat. : ' great.' G : ' bitter ' (πικρᾶς).
[e] So G, S. C : ' fell.' A : ' raged.'   [f] C, A : ' many.'
[g] C : ' Epiphanius ' *passim.*

S black night, at that very time when the Roman Empire recovered its traditional concord, and became once more stable, harmonious and peaceful. But we shall give a more complete account of these matters at the proper time : now let us proceed with those events which followed immediately.

REIGN OF MAXIMIN DAZA

THIRD YEAR (306)

Apphianus.

4.   Maximin Cæsar, the moment he came to the principate, displayed to all the tokens, as it were, of his innate enmity with God and his impiety by setting to work with greater vigour than his predecessors on the persecution against us.
2 In truth no small confusion hung over all; men were dispersed, one this way, one that, seeking earnestly to escape the danger; and dire commotion universally prevailed.

[1] Mark xvi. 15.

L 3 In the life of the body he had not yet reached his twentieth year. As to his family, his people were persons of distinction in Lycia [a], who for wealth [b] and other dignities [b] held the first rank. Hence at the earnest wish of his parents he journeyed to the [c] schools at [c] Berytus for the purpose of study, and there amassed an equipment [d] of varied learning. But a narrative of these things would not be at all germane **4** to the present work. However, if we must place on record the marvellous conduct of that all-holy soul, it is a matter of wonder how in such a city he [e] was not overcome by [e] the society and intercourse of the young men, [f] while he adorned himself with the character of age, his conduct and habits settling into a mould of gravity [f]; how he was not seduced [g] by the full vigour of his body or [h] his companionship with the young; how [i] in his mind [i] he *made self-control* the foundation, *as it were*, of goodness,[1] and embraced absolute chastity and sobriety, [j] disciplining his own conduct gravely and in a manner becoming piety [j].

[a] g : 'Lydia.'   [b-b] C omits. A : ' of power.' Lat. : ' and dignity.'   [c-c] C, A : ' city of.'
[d] So G, C (reading *utdô* for *utrô* : W. K.).
[e-e] κρείττων ἐγίνετο (G) : so A, Lat. ; cp. S.
[f-f] So G. C, A differ slightly.   [g] C, A : ' conquered.'
[h] C, A add : ' led away by.'
[i-i] C, A : ' for himself '; lit. ' for his soul.' Lat. : ' *sibi*.'
[j-j] So G. A : ' in holiness, as is meet, disciplining well his life for piety.' C : ' bringing himself in purity, as is meet, to piety.' Lat. omits.

S   In these circumstances, what word of ours could suffice to describe worthily the divine love and boldness in confessing God of that blessed martyr, that truly guileless lamb, I mean Apphianus, who before the gates held up, for all in Cæsarea to see, a marvellous example of piety towards Him who is **3** God alone ? In the life of the body he was not as yet twenty years old. Now at first he had spent the greater part of his time at Berytus for the sake of secular Greek learning (for his people were in exceedingly affluent circumstances as regards this world's wealth). And, marvellous even to relate, though living in such a city, he rose superior to *youthful lusts*,[2] nor were his manners corrupted either by the full vigour of his body or his companionship with the young; he embraced sobriety, and discreetly, gravely and piously ordered and tutored his own conduct in accordance with Christian principles. **4** But if it is necessary to mention his native country as well, and so to honour it also as the place whence came this noble champion of religion, this too with good reason we shall do.

[1] Philo, *D.V.C.* (ii. 17. 16, above).   [2] 2 Tim. ii. 22.

L 5   But indeed after sufficient schooling he returned from Berytus to his parents'ᵃ hearth. But since he could not consort with his relatives because of dissimilar habits, he quitted the life there ᵇ unknown to his relatives ᵇ, with absolutely no thought for daily requirements, and, guided on his journey by the power of God, arrived at this city of ours with a faith ᶜ that was genuine and entire ᶜ, where had been prepared for him the ᵈ exceeding precious ᵈ crown of martyr-
6 dom. And when he had been in our company, and had received training in the divine studies and been instructed in the sacred Scriptures by Pamphilus the great ᵉ martyr, he acquired ᶠ from him ᶠ a moral state of virtue by no means ordinary. ᵍ Then, when he had by these means prepared for himself the perfecting of martyrdom, what an issue thereof
7 he displayed ! ᵍ ʰ Who was not amazed to see, who did not marvel to hear,ʰ the courage, the boldness, the constancy,

ᵃ So C, A.   Cp. Lat. (*patriam*).   G : ' father's.'
ᵇ⁻ᵇ So G.   C, A, Lat. omit.   ᶜ⁻ᶜ So G, Lat.   C, A omit.
ᵈ⁻ᵈ So G, A.   Lat. ' precious.'   C omits.
ᵉ C : ' perfect.'   A : ' holy.'   ᶠ⁻ᶠ G, Lat. omit.
ᵍ⁻ᵍ The text is uncertain. We follow Schwartz's emendation of G, which is supported by A, S.   G : ' Wherefore when he had by these means prepared for himself the perfecting of his martyrdom—what an end he displayed the following narrative will show.' Lat. : ' Whereby he made open for himself an entrance to the palm of martyrdom, as we shall now show.'   A : ' Whereby also he prepared the end of his excellent martyrdom : and, again, what a wonderful crown and good ending was made ready for him !'   C : ' Wherefore I have applied (prepared) myself to the martyrdom of Epiphanius, to tell it, if I am able, and what an end was his.'
ʰ⁻ʰ C : ' All the gatherings that saw him regarded him with amazement, and who to-day can hear of his fame without marvelling at.'

S 5 Well then, if anyone knows Gagæ, *no mean city* [1] of Lycia, it was thence that the young man came.
     After returning from his studies at Berytus, though his father held the first rank in his native land, he could not endure the society of his father and relatives, for they were not minded to live according to the sanctions of religion; but, possessed as it were by the divine Spirit, and, in accordance with an innate (nay rather an inspired and true) philosophy, he was filled with the thought of something greater than what the world counts glory, and utterly despised bodily indulgence. So he fled secretly from his family without a care for daily requirements; and with hope and faith in God he was brought by the guidance [2] of the divine Spirit to the city of Cæsarea, where had been made ready for him the
6 crown of martyrdom in the cause of religion. And when he had been with us, and with the aid of the divine Scriptures had acquired, as far as possible, a perfect moral state, and prepared himself with the utmost zeal by suitable studies—
7 what an issue thereof he displayed ! Who, indeed, would

¹ Acts xxi. 39.   ² Lit. ' led by the hand.'

L the self-control, the words addressed to the judge, the replies, the prudence, and, more than all these, the daring itself and the attempt [a] that breathed an inspired zeal [a] [b] and a strong piety towards God the universal King [b] ?

8 A second general [c] attack, then, was directed during the third year of the persecution of our day, and a rescript from Maximin [d] then for the first time [d] reached us, in which he gave the order that the magistrates in the several cities should make it their earnest endeavour that all the people [e] in a body [e] should sacrifice and pour libations to the demons. Forthwith [f] heralds in every city called men, and women and children too, to assemble at the temples of the idols; while the military tribunes and centurions went from house to house and from ward to ward making registers of the citizens : then they summoned each one by name and thus compelled him to do what was bidden. When all men, therefore, everywhere were thus overtaken by an unutterable sea [g] of troubles [g], Apphianus the all-holy martyr of God [h] did a certain thing which is beyond all words. Without anyone

a-a C, A : ' by which his zeal to God exhaled [the odour of sacrifice].' Lat. : ' with divine zeal.'   b-b C, A omit.
c C omits. A : *non liqu.* Lat. : ' passim.'
d-d G τότε. C : ' former ' (= πρώτων). A omits. S : τοῦτο πρῶτον.
e-e So G, S. C, A, Lat. omit.
f So G, Lat. So also C, A (reading *chṭīphô'īth* for *chphīṭô'īth* : W. K.).
g-g C, A omit.   h C, A : ' the Truth.'

S not be amazed to see again, who would not rightly wonder to hear once more, the courage, the boldness, the constancy, and, more than these, the daring and the attempt itself that evinced a zeal for religion and a spirit truly superhuman ?

8 For indeed a second attack was directed against us by Maximin in the third year of the persecution of our day, and a rescript from the tyrant then for the first time was published abroad, to the intent that the magistrates of every city should make it their earnest endeavour that all the people in a body at absolutely one time should sacrifice. Throughout the whole city of Cæsarea by the order of the governor heralds were calling up men, and women and children too, to the temples of the idols; and, in addition, the military tribunes were summoning every individual by name from the census list. And when men in every direction were thus overwhelmed by an unutterable sea of troubles, the aforesaid person, without anyone sharing in the secret of his intended action, eluded both us, who lived in the house with him, and the entire bodyguard of the governor as well, and fearlessly approached Urban as he was offering a libation. Seizing him undauntedly by the right hand, he not only stopped him forthwith from sacrificing, but also in truly persuasive tones and with, as it were, a divine assurance

347

L sharing the secret of his action—ᵃ he eluded even us who lived in the house with him ᵃ—he hastened to the ruler of the province himself.   Then coming up ᵇ all at once ᵇ, and escaping the notice likewise of the entire bodyguard of the governor, he approached Urban as he was offering a libation, and seizing him by the right hand not only stayed him from the idolatrous act, but also in a truly gentle manner and with a divinely-given assurance ᶜ exhorted him to cease from his error.   For, said he, it was not permitted that men should turn from the one and only and true God and sacrifice to 9 lifeless idols and evil spirits.   So then, it was God Himself who by means of the lad ᵈ refuted these impious persons ; ᵉ the power of ᶠ Jesus our Saviour ᶠ, that prompted him thereto, cried aloud ᵍ in the deed itself ᵍ, so to speak, that so far were His soldiers—at any rate those who were such in reality— from being won over by the opinions of atheists ʰ, that they not only despised the threats and every kind of death, but also showed so little inclination towards the worse course that they spoke freely to all with a noble resolution and fearless tongue, and desired to persuade, if that were at all feasible, even their persecutors to lay aside their ignorance, and come to know Him who is the Saviour of all and the 10 only true God ᵉ.   But ⁱ the demons' servants, that is, the

ᵃ⁻ᵃ So C, A, S.   G, Lat. omit.
ᵇ⁻ᵇ C, Lat. omit.   ᶜ C : ' gentleness.' A : ' mien.'
ᵈ (C) A add : ' Apphianus.'
ᵉ⁻ᵉ So G (Lat.).   A : ' It was for this that the victorious power of Jesus Christ our Saviour led the holy martyr forth, that He might show by the deeds done by his hand that His true soldiers despised not only the threats and tortures and every kind of death, and would not swerve from good to evil, with free knowledge and open mouth and courageous tongue they wished, if that were feasible, to persuade even their persecutors to lay aside their depraved error and to acknowledge the common Redeemer, the Saviour of all.' C : ' It was for this reproof that the power of Jesus led him forth from the house of his fathers, that he might reprove the works of uncleanness.   He despised the threats and every kind of death, and swerved not from good to evil, but spoke joyfully with pure knowledge and a tongue that uttered praise, as he wished, if that were feasible, to persuade even his persecutors, and he would teach them to lay aside their error, and acknowledge the common Redeemer, the Saviour of all and God.' S supports G throughout.
ᶠ⁻ᶠ Lat. : ' our Cross.'   ᵍ⁻ᵍ Lat. omits.
ʰ Lat. : ' impious men.'
ⁱ C, A add : ' when the holy martyr of God (martyr Apphianus, A) had so done.' Cp. S : ' whereupon.'

S exhorted him to cease from his error.   For, said he, it was not right that men should leave the one and only true God 9 and sacrifice to idols and demons.   Now, as it would seem, in this enterprise of the lad, the divine power that prompted him thereto cried aloud in the event itself, so to speak, that so far were Christians—at any rate those who were really

L soldiers who attended on the governor, as if a branding-iron [a]
had touched their senses, [b-b]rent him,[b-b] struck him on the face,
trampled him with their feet as he lay on the ground, [c-c]and
pounded his mouth[d] and lips until they tore them[c-c]. And
when he had undergone all this with the utmost bravery, the
dark recesses of the prison for a while received him.

11   On the next day, however, after a day and a night spent
there with his feet stretched on that instrument of punishment, the stocks, he appeared before the courts [e]. Then that
noble [f] governor [g-g]of the province,[g-g] Urban, gave a specimen
of his native [f] cruelty, [h-h]as if it were some good thing[h-h] : he
plied the martyr with every form of punishment, [i-i]giving
orders that his sides should be torn to the bone, even to the
very entrails, and that [i-i] stripes should be laid on his face
and neck—so many, indeed, that his face was disfigured and
it was no longer possible [j-j]even for his friends[j-j] to recognize
12 who he was. The veritable martyr of God, indeed, remained
like adamant, for he received still further strength both in
soul and body from the divine power which inspired him.

[a] Lat. : 'dart.'   [b-b] C, A omit.
[c-c] C, A : 'tore his mouth and lips with a halter.'
[d] Lat. : 'whole body' (σῶμα for στόμα).
[e] Lat. : 'the judges'; cp. S.   [f] C, A, Lat. omit.
[g-g] C, A omit.   [h-h] C, A : 'towards the lovely youth.'
[i-i] So C, A, and G (as emended by Schwartz). Lat. : 'so as to
lacerate . . . and gave orders that.'
[j-j] So C, A; cp. S. G, Lat. omit.

S such—from changing from that piety towards the God of
the universe of which they were once for all accounted worthy,
that they not only proved superior to the threats and the
punishments which ensued, but spoke still more boldly and
freely with a noble and fearless tongue, and exhorted even
their persecutors to lay aside, if possible, their ignorance and
10 acknowledge Him who alone is God. Whereupon (as might
have been expected after so audacious a deed) he of whom
we are speaking was torn by the governor's attendants as if
they were wild beasts; and having endured with the utmost
bravery countless blows over his whole body, was for a while
committed to prison.

11   There for a day and a night both his feet were stretched
on that instrument of torture, the stocks, and on the following
day he was brought before the judge. Then, when they were
for forcing him to sacrifice, he displayed every kind of endurance in the face of sufferings and terrible agonies : his sides,
not once nor twice but several times, were torn to the bone,
even to the very entrails; and so many stripes on face and
neck did he receive, that his swollen face could no longer be
12 recognized, even by those who had long known him perfectly
and well. But since he did not yield even before torments

L   In answer to the judge's many questions he made no further
confession than that he was a Christian; and when he next
asked who he was, whence he came, and where he was staying,
he confessed nothing, except that he was a slave of Christ.
The judge now became [a] infuriated; and, exasperated by the
invincible utterances of the martyr, he gave orders that they
should swathe his feet in linen cloths soaked in oil and set
them on fire.   And when the torturers carried out the order
and the martyr was suspended on high, it was a fearful sight
to see: his sides so rent, his whole body so swollen, and the
fashion of his face altered; and the fierce fire had burnt his
feet for so long, that the flesh [b] was melted and flowed like
wax, and the flame penetrated to the bones [c] as if they were
13 dry reeds [c].   But [d] the sufferer cared for none of these things [d].
For he had God who was within him for his helper, supplying [e]
[f] His succour and presence [f] as manifestly in the sight of all
as if it were a light for men to see.   Therefore the martyr
was possessed of greater courage and filled with more boldness
of speech.   So with a voice of exceeding great power he
spoke, and proclaimed his confession of the God [g] whose
martyr he was [g], and [h] bore witness while the power of Jesus
our Saviour was present with him and displaying these
marvellous spectacles [h] as in some mighty theatre [i].   For

[a] C, A add : ' more.'   [b] C, A add : ' of his feet.'
[c-c] So C, A. G, Lat. omit.
  [d-d] So G. Lat. (*quos omnes cruciatus . . . spernabatur*). C, A : ' in
all (every one of, C) these tortures (things, C) that were coming upon
him (+ while he was in great suffering, C) he was (became, C) like one
that had no suffering.'
  [e] So G, Lat. C, A : ' showing.'
  [f-f] So G; cp. A : ' the presence of Christ which strengthened him,
showed itself.' Lat. : ' strength to those who pray to Him.' C :
' Himself.'   [g-g] C, A, Lat. omit.
  [h-h] A and C differ from each other, and both are corrupt; but each
has a few words which agree with G. Lat. abridges.
  [i] So C, A. G omits. Lat. omits ' as in . . . theatre.'

S   such as these, the torturers, acting on orders, wrapped his
feet in linen cloths soaked in oil and set them on fire.   The
agonies which the blessed one endured from this, I believe
no words can express.   The fire, for instance, melted the
flesh and penetrated even to the bone, so that the moisture
of the body was melted away and oozed in drops like wax.
13 But since he did not yield even before this treatment, and
his adversaries were now worsted and all but despairing when
confronted with his superhuman endurance, he was again
imprisoned in bonds.   On the third day he was brought once
more before the judge, ånd when he had confessed to the
same resolve, although now half dead, was consigned to the
bottom of the sea.

L   ᵃ the oppressors of the martyr ᵃ were raging like ᵇ demons; they were pained to the heart, ᶜ as if they, and not he, were bearing the terrible sufferings ᶜ; they gnashed ᵈ their teeth; their minds were at fever heat ᵉ; while they endeavoured to force him to say who he was,ᶠ whence he came, and where he was staying, and to sacrifice and to obey the ordinances. But he looked intently upon them all, regarding them as drunkards ᵍ; yea, he did not even count them worthy of a reply, except that to their questions he made use of but one utterance—a confession of Christ ʰ and a testimony that he knew ⁱ His Father as God alone ⁱ. At all events, when his enemies were now worsted and despairing, the prison again received him; but on the following day ʲ he was brought before the ᵏ judge, and ʲ, having witnessed the same confession, was consigned by his order to the depths of the sea.

14   Now as to the events ˡ which followed, I know well that those who have not actually seen the thing will refuse to believe; for men naturally trust their ears less than their eyes. However, we are not thereby justified in consigning the wonder to oblivion; and every inhabitant of Cæsarea, ᵐ so to speak,ᵐ can testify to my account. At all events, persons of every age were represented at this marvellous sight.

15 For when they were throwing the man of God down into the

ᵃ⁻ᵃ G, Lat. : ' they.'
ᵇ C, A add : ' destroying.'
ᶜ⁻ᶜ So G, Lat. C, A : ' (+ and moreover it was, as it were, they themselves that were tortured, as he was, C) because of his endurance concerning the teaching of his Lord.'
ᵈ So C, A, Lat. G omits. C, A add : ' at him.'
ᵉ C, A add : ' against him.'   ᶠ C adds : ' whose son he was.'
ᵍ C, A : ' wicked demons.'   ʰ C, A add : ' that He is God.'
ⁱ⁻ⁱ G, Lat. : ' His Father and the Holy Ghost as God alone.'
ʲ⁻ʲ Lat. omits.
ᵏ C, A add : ' bitter and merciless.'
ˡ C, A : ' wonder.'   ᵐ⁻ᵐ So G; cp. S. C, A, Lat. omit.

S 14   Now as to what followed immediately it is not unlikely that those who have not actually seen it will refuse to believe it when it is told them; nevertheless, although we know this fact perfectly, we are not convinced that we ought not in every case to hand down the truth in an historical narrative, since also the incident was witnessed by practically every inhabitant of Cæsarea. At all events, persons of every age

15 were represented at this marvellous sight. As soon as they were seen to cast that truly sacred and thrice-blessed one down to the bottomless depths in the midst of the sea, all at once an extraordinary tumult and an upheaval agitated the sea itself and all the surrounding shore, so that both the land and the whole city were shaken thereat; and simultaneously with this marvellous and sudden shock, the sea

L deep of the [a] sea, his feet fastened with stones, at that moment an extraordinary tumult and a shock and an upheaval fell upon the sea itself [b] and all the surrounding shore [b], and an immense disturbance shook [c] the whole city; [c] and [d] simultaneously with this marvellous event [d], the sea cast up the dead [e] body of the divine martyr before the gates of the city, as if it were not able to bear it. In sooth the corpse presented a sinister sight as it lay at the very entrance of the city; [f] and it was a mighty shock which God stirred up to throw everything into confusion, and [f] to threaten all men with terrible wrath. And when it was told the inhabitants of the city what had happened, they all ran together [g] to the gates [g] to see, children, men, old men, and likewise women of every age, even [h] those who shunned publicity, and [h] those who, not yet being married, lived in the seclusion of their homes; and all, of either sex, [i] confessed the one and only God of the Christians [i]. Such, then, was the conclusion of the wonderful drama of Apphianus. [j] His memory

April 2 is celebrated on the second of the month Xanthicus, the fourth before the Nones of April [j].

5.   *   *   *   *   *   *   *

[a] C, A add : ' terrible.'   [b-b] So G, Lat., S. C, A omit.
          [c-c] C, A : ' also our city itself,' adding : ' And all men with (+ trembling and, C) fear had their hands spread out toward heaven; for they thought that the whole place, together with those that dwelt therein, would be destroyed that day.'
          [d-d] So G; cp. S. C, A, Lat. : ' at that time.'   [e] C, A : ' holy.'
          [f-f] C, A : ' that overwhelming (+ great, A) calamity of the earthquake (+ seemed like a message sent, C) from God.'
          [g-g] C, A omit.   [h-h] C, A, Lat. omit.
          [i-i] C, A : ' gave glory to the God of the Christians (+ alone, C), and with a loud voice confessed the name of (+ Jesus, A) Christ.'
          [j-j] So G (omitting ' the second '). C : ' on the second of Xanthicus, and his commemoration is kept on this day.' A : ' and his good memory is kept on the second of the month Xanthicus.' Lat. : ' who was crowned by martyrdom on the fourth before the nones of April.'

S cast up the corpse of the divine martyr before the gates of the city, as if it could not bear it. Such were the happenings

April 2 concerning the wonderful Apphianus, which came to pass on the second of the month Xanthicus, that is the fourth before the Nones of April, on the day of the Preparation.

Ulpian.

5.   About the same time and on the same days, at the city of Tyre a young man, named Ulpian, was shut up in a raw ox-hide along with a dog and that venomous reptile, an asp, and committed to the sea. He too had previously suffered terrible tortures and scourgings of the severest kind. Therefore in my opinion it is right that he also should be mentioned in the account of the martyrdom of Apphianus.

L

Ædesius.

(G, C, A, g)

2   And sufferings akin to his were shortly afterwards borne by
one who had a common mother [a], his brother, named Ædesius [b].
He truly, even before his brother's godly impulse, had been
before him in his devotion to philosophy. For indeed he took
part in all kinds of studies [c], and embraced not only Greek
education but also Roman as well; and had for a long time
enjoyed the instruction of Pamphilus. Moreover, after
[d] numerous confessions [d] and protracted harsh treatment in
prisons, he was first committed to the copper mines in Palestine. Then after suffering hardships therein,[e] he came to the
3 city of the Alexandrians. But he happened to be present
when Hierocles, who had under his own authority the government of the whole of Egypt, was passing sentence on the
Christians; and when he noted that he was exceeding the
laws of propriety by his offensive conduct towards the martyrs
of God, and was handing over God's holy virgins to brothel-
keepers for wanton violence and bodily insult, he could not
endure to look on such practices, and so set himself to do a
deed like his brother's.   [f] Filled, then, with divine zeal[f], he

---

    [a] So Arabic version (Violet, p. 31), g, and heading in G, Lat. (above,
p. 327, note [c]). G, S : 'father.'   C, A : 'father and mother.' Lat.
omits clause.
    [b] So G, S, Lat., g, Arab. vers. A : 'Hedesius.' C : 'Alosis.'
    [c] C, A add : 'of great thinkers.'
    [d-d] C : 'his admirable confession.' A : 'a first martyrdom.'
    [e] C, A add : 'and having been released.'
    [f-f] C, A : 'The zeal for God was kindled in him, and the heat thereof
burned within his members as in dry stubble (as a flame within him, A)
and with indignation.'

S

Ædesius.

2   And sufferings akin to those of Apphianus were shortly
afterwards endured by Ædesius, who was his brother not
only in God but also in the flesh, having a common father.
After innumerable confessions, and protracted harsh treatment in bonds; after sentences from the governor, which
included his assignment to the mines in Palestine; and after
conducting himself through it all as a philosopher, and in a
philosopher's garb (for assuredly he was more highly educated
than his brother, and began as a student of philosophy),
the last scene in his life took place at the city of the Alex-
3 andrians. There he noted the judge passing sentence on the
Christians, and exceeding the bounds of propriety by his
offensive conduct. At one time he would insult men of
grave character in various ways, at another hand over women
of the highest modesty and pure virgins of consecrated life

L advanced and put Hierocles to shame by word and deed [a] ;
for with [b] his own hand [b] he dealt him blows on the face,
threw him to the ground, and [c] as he lay there on his back [c]
kept hitting and warning him [d] not to dare [d] to act in a
manner contrary to nature towards the servants of God.
Much else did he say [e] ; and after enduring, in consequence,
with a stout heart the tortures that were inflicted on his
body, he was committed to the sea, and so won the death
that had been his brother's. But [f] it was at Alexandria, a
little while afterwards, that he emerged victorious from this
conflict. [f] Of the martyrs on the soil of Palestine the next,
after Apphianus, to advance into the arena was Agapius.

FOURTH YEAR (307)

Agapius of Gaza.

(C, A, g)

6. In the fourth year of the persecution in our day ⟨on the
twelfth day before the Kalends of December, that is⟩ on
November 20 Friday, the twentieth day of Dius, Maximin,
the chief of the tyrants, came to the city
of Cæsarea, and he boasted that he would display some-

---

[a] C, A add : ' of righteousness.' [b-b] C, A : ' both his hands.'
[c-c] C, A : ' when his guard were coming up (+ to help him, C).'
[d-d] C, A : ' Do not dare' (τολμᾶ for τολμᾶν).
[e] C, Lat. add : ' and do.'
[f-f] C, A : ' this servant of Jesus, yonder in the city of A. fought an
open conflict for His (the, A) truth, and yonder was he adorned with
the crown of victory.'

S to brothel-keepers for shameful insult. Thereupon Ædesius
took the same bold course as his brother, for indeed this
conduct seemed to him intolerable. He approached the
judge with confident assurance, and by his words and deeds
covered him with shame and dishonour. After enduring, in
consequence, diverse pains of tortures with a stout heart,
he was committed to the sea, and so won the death that had
been his brother's. But the events connected with him, even
as I said, took place on this manner a little while afterwards.

FOURTH YEAR (307)

Agapius of Gaza.

6. But to resume. In the fourth year of the persecution
against us, on the twelfth day before the Kalends of December,
November 20 that is, on the twentieth of the month Dius, on
the day before the Sabbath, a thing was
done in this same Cæsarea, in the presence of the tyrant

L thing new to all the [a]multitudes of spectators who were gathered together [a] [b] on his account [b]. For on that day
2 he celebrated the festival of his birthday. And it was necessary that when the tyrant was present he should provide [c] something more excellent than the usual programme.
3 What then should this new spectacle be, but that a martyr of God should be flung to be food for the wild beasts? For it was an ancient custom that when an emperor was present he should put before the spectators shows on a lavish scale [d] different from one another—in recitations, in listening to new and strange music, and [e] again also [e] in spectacles of all sorts of beasts and in the prowess of gladiators, in order that the spectators might have much pleasure and recreation [f]. It was therefore necessary that also at this festival [g] of the birthday of the emperor [g] he should do something great and special. [h] And in all former things which he had exhibited he had done nothing new; so—a thing dear to him and acceptable to wicked tyrants—a martyr of God was brought [h] into the midst, a man [i] distinguished for sobriety and forbearance of conduct [i]. [j] He was exposed as [j] food to [k] a wild beast [k] in the theatre. His name was Agapius, upon

a-a C : 'spectators who were gathered.'   A : 'multitudes in the theatre.'   S : 'multitudes (§ 1) . . . spectators (§ 2).'
b-b A omits.   c So A, S. C : 'display.'
d C adds : 'of sundry forms, and.'   e-e A omits.
f A adds : 'in the theatre.'   g-g A omits.
h-h A : 'as the former ones. At that time he had done nothing that was wrong, suitable to the honour of his festival; but now—as a wicked tyrant, a thing dear to him and agreeable—he brought a martyr.'
i-i So g. C, A : 'adorned with all righteousness and meekness (+ and chastity, A).'
j-j So C ('was flung'), g (περιεβάλετο : l. παρεβάλετο). A omits sentence.   k-k So g. C : 'wild beasts.'

S Maximin himself, who was lavishing upon the multitudes spectacles in honour of his birthday, as it is called, which
2 is truly worthy of being placed on record. Hitherto it was the custom that, when emperors were present, spectacles on a lavish scale should provide more excellent entertainments for the spectators than on any other occasion, and that new and strange shows should take the place of the usual programme. Sometimes it would be animals brought from India or Æthiopia or somewhere else; or perhaps men who amaze and divert the minds of the onlookers by a display of certain skilful bodily exercises. On that occasion also, since the emperor was providing the exhibition, it was absolutely necessary that in some way the lavish display should include some unusual and extraordinary
3 item. What, then, should this be? A martyr of our faith was brought into the midst, to contend on behalf of the only

L whom, with Thecla, sentence had been passed that they should be ^a food for ^a wild beasts. The fair name of Thecla
4 was mentioned in another narrative.¹ So then, they fetched the blessed Agapius, and brought him round in mockery in the midst of the arena; and a tablet with an inscription went before him, which bore no token of reproach save that he was a Christian. And a certain slave, a murderer who had murdered his master, entered ^b with the martyr of God ^c,
5 ^d and both alike received the same punishment ^d. ^e Very similar was this passion ^e to the Passion of our Saviour;² for one was a martyr for the God ^f of all, and the other was to die for the murder ^g of his master ^g. ^h And yet the same sentence for wrong-doing was passed on both alike! ^h Now this judge was Urban the governor (for he was still governor in Palestine); but ⁱ when Maximin arrived at the exhibition described above, as though to reward the prowess of Urban, he increased his power to do evil,ⁱ and he delivered the murderer who slew his master from death and exempted him from all tortures, while he gazed with joy on the martyr of

^{a-a} So A, S. C: 'devoured by.'   ^b A omits.
^c A adds: 'was condemned to be food for wild beasts.'
^{d-d} A: 'because the same sentence of death was passed on both alike.'
^{e-e} A: 'And here it is meet to observe the similarity of his judgment.'
^f A: 'his Master, the King.'   ^{g-g} A omits.   ^{h-h} A omits.
ⁱ⁻ⁱ A: 'the impious Maximin was more rabid in his wickedness than the evil Urban.'

S and true religion. This was Agapius, who, as we mentioned a little above,¹ was, with Thecla, the second to be given to wild beasts for food. He had also on other occasions, three times or more, marched from the prison with malefactors in the procession to the arena; yet from time to time the judge, after threats, had constantly put him back for other contests, whether from pity or in the hope that he would change his resolve. On this occasion, as the emperor was present, he was brought in. It might seem as if he had been kept of set purpose for that moment, so that in him also the Saviour's saying might be fulfilled, which by divine knowledge He spoke beforehand to the disciples, namely, that they *would be brought* even
4 *before kings for the sake of* their testimony to Him.³ So then, he was fetched into the midst of the arena, and a certain malefactor also, who, they said, was guilty of the murder of
5 his master. The murderer of his master was exposed to the wild beasts, and then thought worthy of compassion and clemency, almost like the notorious Barabbas of the Saviour's day;⁴ while the whole theatre rang with shouts and cries of approval thereat, since the assassin had been saved by the

¹ 3. 1.   ² Cp. Luke xxiii. 32, 41.
³ Matt. x. 18.   ⁴ Cp. Luke xxiii. 24 f.

L 6 God who was to be food for ᵃ bears and leopards ᵃ. Then, after they had brought him round ᵇ the arena ᵇ, the martyr Agapius was first asked if he would deny his God ᶜ and give up his resolve ᶜ. But ᵈ with a loud voice ᵈ he ᵉ testified and ᵉ said to the whole multitude. " Ye who behold this contest ᶠ in which I am engaged ᶠ; not for the sake of any trivial cause have I come to this conflict. For I am a witness to the true doctrine of God, and I bear witness to you all, to the end that ye may know ᵍ and worship ᵍ the one and only God,ʰ Creator of heaven and earth ; and all that has come upon me for the sake of this Name I accept with joyful mind. ⁱ For they have not brought me down here against my wish, but it is of my own free will that I stand even unto death. Moreover, for my faith I contend, that I may give courage to those who are younger than I, that they may despise death and follow eagerly after life, scorning Hades, so that they may arrive safe at the kingdom and, neglecting that which is mortal, may call to mind the life of the Life-giver, and fearing not the punishment which is but for a moment, may fear those flames of *fire* which are *never quenched*." ⁱ ¹

7 And when the martyr of God had said this, crying out with a loud voice ʲ and standing ʲ in the midst of the arena, ᵏ as one confident and fearless,ᵏ the wicked tyrant was filled with rage and anger and ordered the wild beasts to be let loose upon him. But he, ˡ full of courage and despising death, turned not to the right hand or to the left, but ˡ ran with a brave heart in front of the savage beasts; and a ᵐ savage bear ᵐ rushed foaming upon him and tore him with its teeth.

ᵃ⁻ᵃ So g, (A). C : ' savage beasts.'
ᵇ⁻ᵇ A : ' in mockery.'   ᶜ⁻ᶜ So A, S. C omits.
ᵈ⁻ᵈ A omits. Cp. S.   ᵉ⁻ᵉ So A ; cp. S. C omits.
ᶠ⁻ᶠ A omits.   ᵍ⁻ᵍ So g, A. C omits.
ʰ C adds : ' and the Dayspring that proceeds from Him and that you may know and worship the.'
ⁱ⁻ⁱ A omits. But S (' willing ') seems to echo the first clause.
ʲ⁻ʲ A omits.   ᵏ⁻ᵏ A omits.
ˡ⁻ˡ A omits.   g : ' recked not but.' Cp. S.   C : ' with swiftness of feet.'
ᵐ⁻ᵐ So g, C. A : ' ravenous wolf.'

S clemency of the emperor and thought worthy of honour and 6 freedom. On the other hand, the champion of religion was summoned first of all by the tyrant ; then, when asked with a promise of liberty to renounce his resolve, he testified with a loud voice that, not for the sake of some trivial cause, but of piety towards the Maker of the universe, was he about to bear courageously, with a willing and glad heart, whatsoever 7 they might inflict upon him. And having said this, he suited the deed to the word, ran straight in front of a bear that was

¹ Mark ix. 43.

L And ᵃ still breathing ᵃ he was again committed to prison. There he survived a single day, and ᵇ on the morrow ᵇ stones were fastened to him and his body was cast into the sea; but the soul of the blessed Agapius took her flight through the air to the kingdom of heaven, whither he was hasting, and was received to be with angels and multitudes of holy martyrs. ᶜ In such supreme victory, therefore, ended the conflict and the valour of Agapius.ᶜ

FIFTH YEAR (308)

Theodosia.

(G, C, A)

7. The persecution ᵈ against us ᵈ had already protracted itself ᵉ to a fifth year; it was the month Xanthicus, the second day
April 2 of the month; that is to say, the fourth before the Nones of April. And a certain maid from Tyre, consecrated and all-holy, who led a virgin life in the service of the Son of God, not yet full eighteen years of age, approached with kindly intention [certain] confessors of God ᶠ who were prisoners ᶠ, as they sat before the governor's courts and were

ᵃ⁻ᵃ So g, C, S.   A *non liqu.*
ᵇ⁻ᵇ So A, g, S.   C: 'afterwards.'
ᶜ⁻ᶜ A : ' Such was the valiant conflict of the renowned Agapius.'
ᵈ⁻ᵈ C, A : ' in our day.'
ᵉ So C, agreeing in sense with S (παραταθέντος). The single MS. of G which remains has the imperfect, ' was being protracted ' (παρετείνετο). An emendation, involving a change of only one letter (παρετείνατο), brings it into accord with C.   ᶠ⁻ᶠ So G, A; cp. S.   C omits.

S let loose upon him, and most cheerfully offered himself to it for food.   After the beast had done with him, he was taken up still breathing and cast into prison.   There he survived a single day, and on the morrow stones were fastened to his feet and he was sunk in the midst of the sea.   Such was the martyrdom of Agapius.

FIFTH YEAR (308)

Theodosia.

7. Now when the persecution had already been protracted up to a fifth year, on the second of the month Xanthicus, that
April 2 is, the fourth before the Nones of April, on the very Lord's Day of our Saviour's resurrection, once more at Cæsarea, Theodosia, a virgin from Tyre, a faithful and most grave maiden not yet full eighteen years of age, approached certain prisoners when they, for their part too, were confessing the kingdom of Christ and were seated before the court of justice. This she did with kindly intention, and also to make the

358

L just about to appear before the judge;[a] and requested them to remember her when they had reached *the goal*.[1]

2   But when she had done this, soldiers[b] seized her away, as if she had perpetrated something lawless and profane, and brought her immediately to Urban.[c] For at that time he was still in charge of the government of Palestine. But some feeling, I know not what, came over him, and he was filled immediately with rage and fury, as if the maid had done him the greatest injury. So he ordered her to sacrifice, and when he saw [d] her refuse [d], then the more did this man, who was likest a wild beast, ply her with fearful tortures upon the sides and breasts [e]; yea, the pitiless one drove [f] into the very bone and entrails [f]; so perseveringly did he punish the girl, who received his tortures in silence. While she yet breathed he asked and exhorted her to sacrifice. But she opened her mouth, [g] gave him a keen, earnest look with her eyes [g], and with a gentle smile upon her face (she was then in the full bloom of her beauty) said [h]: "Why dost thou err, O man? . Dost thou not know that I fare now in accordance with my prayers [i], since [j] I have been judged worthy to join the company [k] of the martyrs of God?"[1]

a C, A add : 'and saluted them.'
b C, A : 'quaestionarii.'   c C, A add : 'the governor.'
d-d C : 'that though she was a girl she refused like a heroine to obey the imperial command'; A : 'that the heroine refused to,' etc.
e C, A add : 'with cruel combs.'
f-f C, A : 'so that her entrails were seen; and her ribs were scraped.'
g-g C, A : 'raised her eyes and looked.'
h C, A add : 'with a loud voice.'   i C, A add : 'at thy hands.'
j C, A add : 'I rejoice greatly that.'
k C, A : 'the fellowship of the sufferings.'
l C adds : 'For it was for this very reason that I stood up and spoke with them, in order that by some means or other they might make me their fellow-sufferer, so that, even in the kingdom of heaven, I with them might receive a portion'; and then proceeds with A : 'Because while I was remote from their afflictions I could have no fellowship in their salvation. And see at this present time how, on account of the recompense to come, I now (A omits) stand before thee with great pride (stand and with all my soul confess God, A) because I have found the means to approach (+ my God, even, C) before those righteous men (those confessors, A) whom but a little while ago I besought to be my advocates.'

S natural request that they should think of her when they were
2 come to the Lord. But when she had done this, soldiers seized hold of her, as if she had wrought something profane and impious, and brought her before the governor. And he (seeing he was filled with madness and likest a wild beast in his rage) immediately inflicted fearful and most horrible tortures upon her sides and breasts, yea even to the bone itself; and while she yet breathed—her face, for all her

[1] Cp. Phil. iii. 14.

L And he [a], since he perceived that he was become a laughing-stock to the girl, and being no longer able to torment her with greater tortures than before, condemned her to [b] the depths of the sea.

Leaving her he came to the other confessors on whose account the girl had fared as we have stated, and committed them all in a body to the copper mines in Palestine, sparing them further words or violence. For she [c] who was *the champion of them all* had *taken upon herself* their sufferings [d]; [1] by her firmness and strength of soul she had unnerved the savage judge, and thus had him turned into a coward to face those who came after her. It was the Lord's day, on which these events took place at Cæsarea, in the said month and in the year we have mentioned.

Domninus and others.

(C, g)

3 Urban was governor of Palestine, and it was the fifth [e] day of Dius ⟨as the Romans would say, the Nones of Novem-
November 5 ber⟩. So from day to day he was renewed in his wickedness, and year by year he made himself ready with crafty devices against us; and how many sufferings he caused on the single day which I have mentioned I am about to relate.

[a] C : ' the wicked judge '; A : ' the wicked man.'
[b] C, A add : ' be cast into.'   [c] C, A : ' the (this holy, C) girl.'
[d] C, A add : ' as it were on a shield.'   [e] So g, S.   C : ' first.'

S sufferings, lit up with joy—he ordered her to be cast into the waves of the sea. Then from her he turned to the other confessors, and committed them all to the copper mines at Phæno in Palestine.

Silvanus.

3 Afterwards, on the fifth of the month Dius, or, as the Romans would say, on the Nones of November, at the same
November 5 city, Silvanus (who became a confessor while still a presbyter, to whose lot it fell not long afterwards to be honoured with the episcopate and perfected by martyrdom) and his companions, after giving a most noble display of constancy in defence of religion, were condemned to work in the same copper mines by the same governor, after he had given orders that first of all the ankles of their feet should be disabled by hot irons.

[1] Dion. Alex., in vi. 41. 18 above.

L 4 On that day, then, which we have mentioned a certain man adorned by his whole manner of life and proficient in the knowledge of medicine—now he was a youth, of great stature and comely; and he was distinguished for the holiness of his life, for his pure soul and for sobriety. His name was Domninus, and he was well known to all the men of our day who suffered martyrdom. This man, before his perfecting in martyrdom [a], had been tortured in the copper mines; and because of his constancy at the martyrdom itself he was condemned to the flames as his punishment.

And when the judge, clever in his wickedness (though it is not right to call those clever who glory in the savagery of their harshness), had turned from this martyr he lighted upon three youths [b] in the prime of their bodily strength, comely [b], and goodly [c] to look upon [c], and in their souls distinguished for the courage with which they worshipped God. That the people might enjoy themselves, he [d] condemned them to single combat at boxing [d]. And again, turning from these, he gave over a [e] grave and saintly [e] [f] old man [f] to the wild beasts for food. And he turned again with rage and came upon others, [g] persons who had reached the full estate of manhood [g], and ordered them to be castrated, making them eunuchs. And leaving these also he came to Silvanus (who was destined afterwards to become a martyr of God) and his companions, and condemned them to the mines at Phæno. Again, turning from these he came to others whom with tortures he shamefully entreated. Nor did the fury of his wickedness slake itself with men, but he threatened to torture

[a] So g. C : ' confession.'
[b-b] So g. C : ' comely and beautiful in the stature of their bodies.'
[c-c] C omits. 　　[d-d] So g, S. C : ' sent them to the ludus.'
[e-e] So g, S. C : ' distinguished and godly.'
[f-f] g : ' presbyter. 　　　　　　[g-g] So g, S. C omits.

S *Domninus and others.*

4 And at the very time when these were sentenced, he gave over for punishment by fire a man who was distinguished for innumerable other confessions. This was Domninus, very well known to all in Palestine for his extraordinary boldness. After him, the same judge—for he was a clever inventor of evil, and skilled in making novel attacks upon the doctrine of Christ—invented punishments against the godly which had never been even heard of : three he condemned to single combat in boxing; while Auxentius, a grave and saintly old man, he gave over to the wild beasts for food; others again, persons who had reached the full estate of manhood, he castrated and condemned to the same mines; while others again he shut up in prison after severe tortures.

L women also, and delivered three maidens to [a] licentious
brothel-keepers [a]. Others [b], again, he [c] shut up in [c] prison.
And all those things which we have described did this mad
judge in a single hour.

Pamphilus.

(C, g)

And, when those things which we have described were
ended, Pamphilus also (a name dear to me), the heavenly
martyr of God, holy in all things, and adorned with all graces,
was put to the test in the conflict of his confession.   Of all
the martyrs of our time he was the most illustrious by reason
of his philosophic life and his consummate learning in things
5 divine and human.   This man, adorned with every adornment, was first tested as to his wisdom by Urban in question
and answer.   But at last he attempted to force him by
threats to sacrifice to dead images, and when he ascertained
by trial that he could not be persuaded by words, and saw
that he paid no heed to threats, he plied him with grievous
tortures, and grievously lacerated his sides.   But he could
6 not intimidate him as he imagined.   Then the evil judge
bethought himself that if he [d] assigned a place to [d] the victorious
martyr in the prison among the confessors already mentioned
he might subdue him.

[a-a] So g. C : ' fornicators to suffer bodily shame.'
[b] g : ' other women.'   [c-c] So g, S.   C : ' committed to.'
[d-d] Or ' bound ' (reading *nachbsheh* for *nachshbeh*).

S   *Pamphilus.*

Among these last was Pamphilus, of all my companions
the one whose memory to me is dearest, the most illustrious
5 of the martyrs of our day for every kind of virtue.   Him
Urban first tested in the knowledge of rhetoric and philosophy,
then afterwards tried to force him to sacrifice ; and when he
saw that he refused and paid absolutely no heed to his threats,
he at last became savage and ordered him to be punished
6 with severer tortures.   Moreover, when that wild beast was
almost drunk with the tortures which incessant, stubborn
scraping inflicted upon the sides—and yet he only brought
shame upon his own head in the presence of them all—he
assigned to Pamphilus also a place among the confessors in
prison.

L   *The End of Urban.*

(C)

7   As to this harsh judge who used all these wicked devices
against the confessors of God, what sort of requital and
punishment shall he receive? This indeed will be easily
discerned from what we are writing. For suddenly and
immediately and not long after, because of his daring cruelty,
the righteous Justice of God visited him and took grievous
and bitter vengeance upon him. And he who was seated
aloft upon a tribunal in his pride and attended by his escort
of military, boasting and exalted as præses over all the
province of Palestine, in a single night by this same Justice
was stripped of all his state and, as it were, deprived of all
his dignities. And in this our city, in which he committed
all those wicked acts described above, by a sentence of
Maximin, an impious man like himself, he was delivered up
to a miserable death. But first the measure of his shame
and humiliation, worse than all deaths, was filled fully.
ᵃ Poured into his ears before his death, he received reproaches
from the women and foul taunts from the mouths of all.ᵃ

a-a The text of C seems to be corrupt. See S.

S   *The End of Urban.*

7   Now as to the requital which he will receive from the
divine Justice for his savagery against the saints—so infuriated
was his conduct towards the martyrs of Christ—this will be
easily discerned from the events that formed its prelude in
this world. Immediately, that is to say, not long after his
daring cruelty to Pamphilus, the divine Justice visited him
as he was still holding the post of governor. And all in a
moment he who yesterday was seated aloft as judge upon a
high tribunal, who was surrounded by the usual escort of
military, who was præses of the whole province of Palestine
and shared the company and table of the tyrant himself, as
a dearest friend might do, was stripped in a single night by
this same Justice and deprived of all his dignities. She
poured upon him dishonour and shame in the presence of
those who had formerly regarded him with admiration as a
ruler;[1] she showed him in the character of a craven and
coward, uttering womanish cries and entreaties, to the whole
people over which forsooth he had ruled; and she placed at
Cæsarea itself a harsh and most cruel judge, even Maximin
(of whom Urban used to boast proudly that he held him in

[1] ἄρχοντα.

L So by these things we may learn that this was a foretaste of
the punishment of God which is reserved for him at the last
for his wickedness and pitilessness towards the servants of
8 God. But we have narrated these things rapidly for those
believers, of whom some still remain to our time, omitting
the narrative of many sufferings which he underwent, so that
we may set down these things briefly and in few words as a
record for those who come after us. But a time may arise
when we shall treat of the fates and downfall of the wicked
men who made war upon our people.

SIXTH YEAR (309)

Confessors from the Thebais.

(C, g)

8. Up to the sixth year of the persecution in our day the
storm raised against us still blew. Now great multitudes of
confessors were in the mines which were called the Porphyry
Mines, in the region of the Thebais which is at the side of
Egypt; and because of the purple marble which was in that
region the name was given also to those who quarried it, so
that they were called Porphyrites. This name, then, came
to be applied to those large multitudes of confessors treated
as convicts throughout the whole land of Egypt. For there
were at that place one hundred martyrs all but three. And
these confessors—men, with women and children—were dispatched to the governor of Palestine, whose name was Firmilian, who at that time had succeeded to the province of
Urban. Now he was a man far from peaceable. Indeed in
ferocity he surpassed his predecessor, for he had been a soldier
in the wars, and he was experienced in war and bloodshed.

S especial affection because of his treatment of us), so that he
passed on him the sentence of death, after covering him
8 with shame for the offences of which he was convicted. Let
us say so much in passing. A suitable time may, however,
arise when we shall treat at leisure of the end and downfall
of the wicked men who were pre-eminent in making war on
us, that is to say, Maximin himself and his accomplices.

SIXTH YEAR (309)

8. Up to the sixth year the storm against us blew incessantly.
Before this, indeed, the mine in the Thebais, that derives its
name from the porphyry stone which it produces, had an
exceedingly large multitude of the confessors of religion. Of

L   Now there is a certain great and populous city in the land of Palestine, and all its inhabitants are Jews. It is called Diocæsarea [a]. And to that city Firmilian the governor went, and brought thither the whole assembly of those hundred confessors. This was a great sight, worthy of being recorded in writing. But the Jews watched that amazing contest and surrounded the court of justice on all sides. To their own reproach their eyes looked upon these things, while the whole body of confessors with great confidence and unbounded courage confessed the Christ of God. But the Jews, to whom Christ was proclaimed aforetime by the prophets, and whose fathers had waited for Him, did not accept Him when He came. And these Egyptians, who of old had been enemies of God, these confessed God the Lord of the universe [b] and the Dayspring that proceeded from Him [b] with joy in the midst of their sufferings. And these Egyptians, who from their fathers had learnt to worship idols alone, by reason of the excellence [c] of their intellect were at that time striving hard in order that they might not worship idols. But the Jews, who were always accused by the prophets for worshipping idols, stood around, seeing and hearing, while the Egyptians renounced the gods of their own fathers and confessed [d] the God [d] who was also the God of the Jews, and witnessed for Him whom the Jews had many times renounced. And they were the more agitated and rent in their hearts when they heard the heralds of the governor crying out and calling the Egyptians by Hebrew names and making mention of them under the names of prophets. For the herald, when he cried out to them, called saying ' Elijah,' ' Isaiah,' ' Jeremiah,' [d] Daniel,' and other similar names, which their fathers had selected from among the Hebrews, that they might call their sons by the names of prophets. And it came to pass that their deeds were in harmony with their names. And at the men and at their names, at their words and at their actions, the Jews were greatly amazed, while they themselves were despised for their wickedness and apostasy. And I myself believe that these things did not happen without the will of God. Nevertheless, after this testing they were

---

[a] So g. C : ' in Syriac Lud, but in Greek Diocæsarea.'
[b-b] Perhaps an interpolation; cp. 6. 6. But see S : ' and Christ.'
[c] Or ' discrimination.'   [d-d] g : ' our true God.'

S   these one hundred men, all but three, together with women and mere babes, were despatched to the governor of Palestine. And when they had confessed, on Jewish [soil], the God of the universe and Christ, the ankles of their left feet, sinews and all, were destroyed by hot irons; while their right eyes, membranes, pupils and all, were first cut out with swords, and then the whole organ destroyed to the very roots by hot

L   deprived of the use of their left feet, by hot irons applied to
their hams, and, moreover, their right eyes were ᵃdug outᵃ with
the sword and then finally destroyed by fire.   And it was
not only men who endured these sufferings, but also the
very children, and many women.   And afterwards they were
committed to the copper mines to see hardships there.

Palestinian Confessors.

(C, g)

2   A little while after, those three Palestinians also who, as
we mentioned a little above,[1] were given for a season ᵇ to
fight in single combat at boxing ᵇ, endured similar sufferings,
because they would have nothing to do with the allowances
from the treasury, and would not submit themselves to the
exercises and training which were necessary for the business
3 of a gladiator.   They endured much ill-treatment which it is
beyond our powers to describe; and at the end of all their
sufferings they underwent this cruel punishment.
4   And others, because they assembled together for prayer and
were constant in reading the divine Scriptures, were taken at

ᵃ⁻ᵃ So g, and C, as emended by Violet ('ōqrîn for 'ōvrîn).
ᵇ⁻ᵇ So S.   C : ' at the ludus.' Cp. 7. 4.

S   irons.   And all this was done by the order of Firmilian (who
was sent there as governor in succession to Urban) as if in
obedience to an imperial command.   And then he committed them to the mines in the province to be worn out
with toil and suffering.

Palestinian Confessors.

2   But it would seem that it was not enough to behold with
one's eyes the terrible sufferings of these alone; for there
were also those Palestinians who, as we mentioned a little
above,[1] were condemned to fight in single combat at boxing.
Since they would have nothing to do either with the allowances
from the imperial treasury or with the necessary exercises for
3 the boxing match, they had for this reason to appear, not
before procurators alone or even governors, but before
Maximin himself.   There they displayed a constancy in confession of the noblest kind, by their valiant bearing of hunger
and endurance of scourgings, and suffered a like fate to those
already mentioned, together with other confessors who were
added to their number, at Cæsarea itself.
4   On the heels of these came others, who were taken at the
city of Gaza because they assembled together for reading the

[1] 7. 4.

L the city of Gaza and endured the like sufferings in feet
and eyes as did their companions; and others again stood
firm in even greater contests than these, and after they had
suffered in feet and eyes were tortured also with terrible
scrapings on their sides.

Valentina and Ennatha.

(C, g)

5 And again, when he turned from these he came to judge
one who, though in body a woman, was yet in the strength of
mind which she possessed a man. In manner of life also she
was a maiden; and being unable to endure a threat of
fornication which she heard with her ears, she straightway
spoke violent words against the tyrant emperor, because he
had entrusted the government to a vile and wicked judge.
For this, therefore, first of all he marred her whole body with
stripes, and then she was ᵃ raised aloft on a gibbet ᵃ and her
sides lacerated. This was done, not once, but twice or three
times in a single hour, and long and often, till those who
lacerated her were wearied and collapsed. But these assailants
were succeeded by others, who by command of the rabid
governor grievously tortured her. For these judges were
barbarians in manners and enemies in heart.

6 But while this furious judge was racking the girl with his
tortures it came to pass that a voice, from the midst of the
crowd of men who stood before the governor, cried out in
complaint, saying, " How long dost thou lacerate my sister

ᵃ⁻ᵃ So S.   C: ' raised aloft.'   g: ' fastened to a gibbet.'

S divine Scriptures; of whom some endured the same sufferings
in feet and eyes as did the former persons; others even
greater, for they underwent the most fearful trial, being
tortured on their sides.

Valentina and another.

5 Of these there was one, in body indeed a woman, but in
mind a man. Unable to endure a threat of fornication, she
made a disparaging remark as to the tyrant who would
entrust the government to such cruel judges. First of all
she was scourged; then, raised aloft on the gibbet, she had
her sides lacerated.

6 But as those whose task it was plied the tortures incessantly
and severely at the judge's command, a voice from the midst
of the crowd cried out to the judge: " And how long dost
thou torture my sister so cruelly? " It came from another
woman, far surpassing those vaunted champions of liberty

L   so cruelly and unmercifully ? " It came from another girl, in body mean, but strong in soul, and possessed of a great mind which gave strength to the meanness of her body, who could not endure the wickedness and mercilessness of what was being done to her sister. But when the wicked Firmilian heard he was bitterly enraged and ordered the girl who complained to be brought before him. Her name was Valentina.
7 And they lifted her up and brought her into the midst of the judgment hall. But she took refuge in the august Name of Jesus. And then the murderous judge in his wrath commanded her to sacrifice. But the girl Valentina despised even the voice of the ferocious one. Then he commanded those who ministered to his will to seize the girl by force and take her to the side of the altar, that she might defile herself with the sacrifice. The noble girl, then, in that time of alarm, displayed the fortitude of her mind ; for she kicked at the altar with her foot, and overturned it, ᵃ together with
8 the offering which lay upon it, in the fire ᵃ. But because she had done all this without fear, the judge was enraged like a wild beast, and ordered her to be tortured without mercy with combs, so that never before had anyone been so terribly combed ; and I believe that had it been possible he would have glutted himself on the girl's flesh.

But when his madness was satiated by the sight of blood, and he had learnt by deed and word how divine is the

ᵃ⁻ᵃ So g. C : ' and scattered the fire which had burned upon it.'

S   among the Greeks, who could not endure the mercilessness, the cruelty, the inhumanity of what was being done. Like the former, she had taken upon herself the burden of virginity ; in body altogether of a mean appearance, and contemptible to look upon, but on the other hand strong in spirit and possessed of a mind greater than her body. The judge was stung to the quick and ordered the woman to be seized on
7 the spot. She was then haled before them all ; and when she had acknowledged the august name of the Saviour as that of her Guardian, they at first tried to persuade her by words to sacrifice, but on her refusal dragged her by force to the altar. She, however, was true to her own self : she kept to her former zeal, kicked at the altar with an intrepid and resolute foot and overturned everything connected with it,
8 together with the fire that lay thereon. The judge was enraged at this like a wild beast, and first of all inflicted such tortures on her sides as he had never done to anyone before. One might almost say he had a craving to glut himself on her raw flesh.

But when his madness had come to be satiated, he bound them both together, this woman and her whom she called

L   unconquerable power which arms and strengthens even little
    girls with surpassing fortitude, then he bound the girls both
    together, Ennatha [a] and Valentina, and condemned them to
    death by fire. The name of the former was Ennatha [a], and
    her father's house was in the country of Gaza, and the other
    belonged to our city of Cæsarea. With her also many were
    acquainted, and her name was Valentina.

Paul.

(C, g)

9   Now after this Paul, a confessor, was brought forward to
    the conflict; and he also strove bravely. And in that hour
    he was condemned by the impious judge to be crowned, and
    received sentence of decapitation by the sword. And when
    he was at the place of his departure, where the blessed one
    was to pass from this life, he requested the executioner who
    was about to cut off his head to have patience with him for
10 a brief space of time. And when the executioner granted
    him this desire, with sweet and resonant voice, first of all,
    he offered up praise and worship and honour and prayer to
    God who had accounted him worthy of this victory; and then
    he besought God for the tranquillity and peace of our people,
    imploring Him to bestow deliverance upon them with all
    speed; and after this he *prayed for* the *enemies*,[1] the Jews

[a] So g. C : *chāthā* : error for *'ennāthā.'*

S   her sister, and condemned them to death by fire. Of these
    the former came, it was said, from the country of Gaza; as
    for the other, it should be known that she belonged to Cæsarea,
    and that many were acquainted with her, her name being
    Valentina.

Paul.

9   But how can I worthily recount the martyrdom that
    followed, of which the thrice-blessed Paul has been accounted
    worthy? He was included with these women at the same
    time in a single sentence of death; but at the actual moment
    of perfecting he requested him who was just about to cut
10 off his head to grant him a brief space of time. Having
    obtained this, he first with a clear, resonant voice besought
    God in prayer for the reconciliation of his own people, loudly
    imploring Him the while to bestow freedom upon them with
    all speed; then he desired that the Jews might be brought

[1] Matt. v. 44.

L (for many of them at that time stood around him); and
proceeding further in his intercession, he also prayed for the
Samaritans, and for those among the nations who were in
ignorance—he prayed that they might *come to the knowledge
of* ᵃ *the truth* ᵃ [1]; nor did he leave unheeded those who sur-
11 rounded him : for them also he prayed. Oh, unspeakable
guilelessness !—for the judge also who sentenced him to
death, and for all rulers in every place did he pray; and not
only for them, but also for the executioner who was about
to cut off his head. And while he made supplication to God
the executioners heard him with their own ears, praying for
them and earnestly entreating God that He would not reckon
12 to them that which they did to him; [2] and as he prayed for
all men with a voice of yearning he brought the whole multitude of spectators who stood around him to sadness and
tears; and then he voluntarily bowed his body and stretched
out his neck to be severed by the sword. On the
July 25 twenty-fifth of Panemus ⟨that is, the eighth before
the Kalends of August⟩ was the contest of this victor finished.

ᵃ⁻ᵃ g : ' God '; cp. S.

S to God through Christ; after that, he went on to request
the same boon for the Samaritans also; moreover, he
entreated that the Gentiles who were in error and ignorance
of God might *come to the knowledge* [1] of Him and receive the
true religion; nor did he leave unheeded even the motley
11 crowd that was then standing around. After all these he
besought the God of the universe—oh great and unspeakable
forbearance !—on behalf also of the judge who had assigned
to him the penalty of death, and of the supreme rulers, and
of him too who was about to cut off his head, in his hearing
and in the hearing of all present, entreating that their sin
12 towards him might in no wise be reckoned to them.[2] These,
and such as these, were the prayers he uttered with a loud
voice, so as almost to draw tears of pity from them all, as
for one unjustly put to death; then, as the custom is, he
arranged his own garments and offered his bare neck for the
sword to cut off. Thus was he adorned with a divine martyr-
July 25 dom, on the twenty-fifth of the month Panemus,
that is, the eighth before the Kalends of August.
And such was the issue that befell these persons.

[1] 1 Tim. ii. 4; 2 Tim. iii. 7.   [2] Cp. Acts vii. 60.

L   *More Egyptian Confessors.*

(C)

13   But ⟨no⟩ [a] long time had elapsed after those things
which we have related, when from the land of Egypt another
company of martyrs of God—the second—in number one
hundred and thirty, were sent to our country; and once
more all these endured the same afflictions in eyes and feet
as did the former martyrs.[1] Then some of them were sent to
the mines in Palestine, and some of them were handed over
to the judges in Cilicia, to be chastised with wicked and
shameful sufferings.

A Respite and the Fifth Edict.

(C)

9.   But the fire of persecution lessened a little towards us,
the sword having been satiated with the blood of the holy
martyrs, and a short relief and calm restrained the persecution
of our days. But the scourge of God fell heavily on Maximin,
the wicked tyrant, to punish all the evil deeds, wherein—to
teach him—he had as demonstrators and prompt ministers
the governors of the districts, and the dux who was the chief

[a] So S.

S   *More Egyptian Confessors.*

13   But no long time had elapsed when a second band of
Egyptians, those marvellous champions in the confession of
Christ, one hundred and thirty of them, endured in Egypt
itself at the command of Maximin the same afflictions in eyes
and feet as did those others [1] a short while ago. They were
sent away to the aforesaid mines in Palestine; but some
shared the lot of those under sentence in Cilicia.

A Respite and the Fifth Edict.

9.   These brave deeds on the part of the magnificent martyrs
of Christ were followed by a lessening of the fire of persecution,
which was being quenched, as it were, by their sacred blood;
relief and liberty were now granted those who for Christ's
sake were suffering affliction in the mines of the Thebais;
and we were just about to regain a breath of pure air, when
some agitation (I know not how) caused him, to whom had
been assigned the authority to persecute, to be inflamed

[1] § 1.

L   2 of the army of the Romans. And, on account of those things
which happened, they were urging the curators of the cities
and the duumvirs and the registrars that they should build
with speed what was fallen of the idol temples, and ⟨that
they should take care⟩ that all the men with their wives
and children and slaves, even babes at the breast, should
offer sacrifice and libations to demons and that they should
compel them even to taste the sacrifices; and it was ordered
that every article which was bought in the market was to
be defiled by libations and sprinkling of the blood of the
3 sacrifices. When these things, then, were thus done, these
acts were abominated even by the unbelieving heathen. So
a mighty storm and tumult, the like of which had never been
before, distressed all of us in every place, and the souls of
all were set in distress and vexation. But, because of these
happenings, the divine Power inspired His own with such
courage as would enable them to spurn the threats of the
judges and scorn their tortures.

S   2 once more against us. At any rate, all of a sudden an edict
of Maximin was again published against us everywhere;
and the governors in each province and, moreover, he who
was placed in charge of the troops, urged by means of proclamations, letters and public ordinances the curators,
together with the duumvirs and registrars in every city, to
put into execution the imperial edict. This ordered that
those idol temples which had fallen should be rebuilt with
all speed; that care should be taken that all the people in
a mass, men with their wives and households, even babes at
the breast, should offer sacrifice and libations and taste
with scrupulous care the accursed sacrifices themselves; that
the articles for sale in the market-place should be defiled by
the libations from the sacrifices, and that guards should be
posted before the baths in order to defile with the abominable sacrifices those whose custom it was to cleanse them-
3 selves therein. While these orders, then, were thus being
carried into effect, our people once more fell a prey, as was
natural, to grave anxiety, and the unbelieving heathen found
fault with the absurdity of what was done, on the ground
that it was harsh and unnecessary (for to their mind the
thing was disgusting and burdensome). A mighty storm
brooded over all in every place, but again the divine power
of our Saviour inspired its champions with such courage
that they needed neither inducement nor urging to spurn
the threats of these mighty persons.

L   *Antoninus and others, and Ennathas.*

(C, g)

1   But some men, servants of the people of Christ, who were
in bodily stature mere youths, but their souls were armed
with the worship of God, came of themselves, and when the
governor was offering libations to idols in the midst of the
city, all at once they rushed forward at him, and cried out
to him to cease from error, For, said they, there is no other
God save one, the Maker and Creator of the universe. And
when they were asked who they were, they confessed them-
5 selves Christians. No sooner had they said the word than
they received sentence of death. And readily and unim-
peded they journeyed to Him whom they had confessed.
The name of the first was Antoninus, and the second was

November 13   called Zebinas, and the name of the third
was Germanus. It was on the thirteenth of
the month Dius ⟨on the Ides of November⟩ that this was
done.

6   Now they had a fellow-traveller [1] in that same hour,
Ennathas [a], a virgin of her Lord, a pure and brave girl who
came from the city of Scythopolis [b]. But she had not done
what they had with whom she was joined as confessor; for
7 they forcibly brought her from Scythopolis [b], and she endured

[a] So S.   C has here ' a sister ' (*chāthā*), and in the title of the chapter
' Mannathus.'   g : Ennatha, Manetho, Maretho, Manatha.
[b] So S, g.   C : Baishan.

S   *Antoninus and others, and Ennathas.*

4   In fact three of the faithful combined together, rushed
forward at the magistrate as he was sacrificing to idols, and
cried out to him to cease from his error. For, said they,
there is no other God save the Maker and Creator of the
universe. They were asked, of course, who they were; and they
5 boldly confessed themselves Christians. Thereupon Firmilian
broke out into a passion, and without even first inflicting
tortures upon them, condemned them to capital punishment.
The eldest of these was named Antoninus; the next, who
came from Eleutheropolis, was called Zebinas; while the

November 13   name of the third was Germanus. It was on
the thirteenth of the month of Dius, on the
Ides of November, that their execution was carried out.

6   Now they had a fellow-traveller [1] that same day, Ennathas,
a woman from Scythopolis; who also was adorned with the
chaplet of virginity. She had not done what they had, but
7 she was forcibly dragged and brought before the judge, after

[1] *I.e.* to heaven : see § 5 (L); 1. 1 (L); 11. 20.

L   insult and grievous scourging at the hands of the judge before she was sentenced. But one of those who were set over the markets of the city was the originator of the evils. His name was Maxys; and he proclaimed himself to all to be worse than his name, for he stripped that blessed one, so that she was covered only from the loins downwards, to the intent that he might gaze on the rest of her limbs with lascivious eyes. He led her round the whole city, she being beaten, the while, with
8 thongs. Then he brought her to the tribunal of the governor. There she boldly confessed the Christian faith; there too she displayed her courage and stedfastness under all kinds of tortures, and was committed by the governor to be burnt in the flames.

But this judge day by day carried further his hardness of heart and displayed his lack of mercy and his brutality. He transgressed the laws of nature, in that even on the lifeless bodies of the Christians he showed his spite, and with threats
9 forbade them to be buried. And as concerning the corpses of the girl of whom we have spoken and of those who on the same day were perfected in confession, a further order was given that they should be left to wild beasts to devour, and be guarded carefully night and day that they might be devoured by birds. And the guards were attending from

---

S   scourgings and terrible insults which one of the military tribunes stationed in the neighbourhood had the audacity to inflict upon her without even the consent of the superior authority. His name was Maxys, a person worse than his name might indicate. While brutal in all other respects, he was of an exceedingly violent disposition and a truly terrible character in every way, bearing a bad reputation among all who knew him. Now this fellow stripped the blessed one of all her clothing, so that she was covered only from the loins to the feet and the rest of her body was bare. He then led her round the whole city of Cæsarea, and thought it a great thing to beat her with thongs as she was dragged
8 through all the market-places. Moreover, after all this she displayed the most courageous stedfastness also before the governor's tribunals, and was committed alive to the flames by the judge.

He also carried his rage against the godly to an inhuman length, and transgressed the laws of nature, in that he was not ashamed to grudge even burial to the lifeless bodies of
9 the holy men. Certainly, he gave orders that night and day the corpses should be carefully guarded in the open air as food for wild beasts, and one might see for many days no small number of men attending to this savage and barbarous decree. On the one hand they kept watch from afar,

L afar to this barbarous decree and taking care that the corpses of the confessors should not be stolen by us. Beasts of the field, therefore, and dogs and the fowls of heaven were tearing
10 to pieces human flesh hither and thither, so that even in the centre of the city bones and entrails of men were found. And all were clothed with mourning for these things; for never before had the like evil deeds been done. And even upon those who were alien from us in our faith there came great distress and sorrow at those things which their eyes
11 beheld. For there lay before the gate of the city the terrible spectacle of human corpses devoured by wild beasts.
12 But when for many days things had proceeded in this fashion, a marvellous and incredible thing took place in the midst of the city. The sky was clear and the atmosphere bright. Then all at once a great number of the pillars of the porches of the city let fall as it were drops, like tears,[a] and the market-places and streets, though not a single drop had fallen from the sky, were sprinkled and moistened with water. And the story was on everyone's lips that the stones wept and the earth shed tears. For [they said] that the sense-less stones and the impassive earth could not endure this foul and cruel deed; and tears [a] which flowed from stones, and the earth which without rain shed from its body as it were

[a] C : ' blood ' (*dmô*' for *dem*'*ó*').

S as if it were a matter worthy of care, lest the corpses should be stolen; on the other, wild beasts, dogs and birds of prey
10 scattered human limbs hither and thither; indeed the whole city on all sides was strewn with the entrails and bones of men, so that nothing had ever appeared more dreadful and horrible, even to those who formerly hated us; although they bewailed not so much the misfortune of those who were the object of all this, as the insult to the nature which they
11 themselves shared with all. For there lay very close to the gates a spectacle which nothing ever told [by men], nothing ever heard on the tragic stage, can equal : not only in one spot was human flesh being devoured, but it was scattered in every place. Certainly, according to the statements of some, even within the gates were seen whole limbs and pieces of flesh and certain portions of the entrails.
12 When this state of affairs had continued for very many days, the following marvellous thing took place. It was fine weather, the sky was clear, the condition of the atmosphere very calm. Then all at once the greater number of those pillars throughout the city which support the public porches let fall drop by drop as it were tears, and the market-places and streets, although no rain had fallen from the sky, were moist, sprinkled with water, I know not from what source.

L **13** tears, rebuked all those who were without God. And perchance it may seem, to those who did not see with their own eyes ª that which we have written, that this is a fable ª foreign to the truth. God forbid; yea, the truth of this matter which we have committed to writing was seen by those who were present at the time; some of whom remain to this day.

Such then was the consummation of those holy martyrs of God, whose contests and strivings against error were accomplished before our eyes.

Ares, Promus and Elijah.

(C, g)

10.   On the fourteenth day of the month Apellæus ⟨that is,
December 14 the nineteenth before the Kalends of January⟩ certain martyrs of God, Egyptians, were seized at the gates of the city of Ashkelon.ᵇ And because, when they were asked who they were, they confessed that they were Christians, and because they confessed that they were on their way, and had ᶜ set off ᶜ from their own country for the purpose of bringing food to the confessors in Cilicia, they were brought to the judge as traitors ᵈ. Now the guards of

ªª Lit. ' the things that we have written—who suppose that what I have put into writing is a fable.'

ᵇ g adds : ' Filled with a godly zeal they were wont to enter the prisons, and visit and heal the holy martyrs who were enduring conflicts for Christ.'

ᶜᶜ So g. C : ' come.'   ᵈ So g. C : ' malefactors.'

S So that immediately the story was on everyone's lips that the earth, unable to endure the wickedness of these deeds, had mysteriously shed tears; and that, as a rebuke to the relentless and unfeeling nature of man, stones and lifeless
13 matter bewailed what had taken place. I know well that my *word* will seem, perchance, *idle talk*,[1] and a fable to those who come after us, but not to those who have had its truth accredited on the spot.

Ares, Promus and Elijah.

10.   Now on the fourteenth of the following month Apellæus
December 14 (that is, the nineteenth before the Kalends of January), once more certain Egyptians were seized by those who searched such as would pass in by the gates (they had set off for the purpose of ministering to the confessors in Cilicia), and received the same sentence as those whom they meant to help, being deprived of the use

[1] Luke xxiv. 11.

L the gates of the city, who seized these martyrs, were barbarous [a] and savage [a] men; and they brought them before
Firmilian the governor (for he was still over the people of
Palestine), and he passed a cruel sentence upon them. On
some he gave sentence that they should have their eyes and
feet made useless by fire and iron, on some that they should
be given over to death by the sword. Regarding one of
them, whose name was Ares, his confession was perfected
by a fierce fire; and Promus [b] and Elijah were beheaded by
the sword.

SEVENTH YEAR (310)

Peter Abshelama.

(C, A)

2   On the tenth day of the month Audynæus ⟨that is, the
fourth before the Ides of January⟩, Peter who
January 10   was called Abshelama, a well-known confessor [c]
of the kingdom of God [d], appeared [e] at the city of Cæsarea [e].
Moreover, so valiant was he in his contest for [f] the worship
of [f] God, and so glorious in the conflict of his confession that
he astonished even the judge himself and greatly amazed
those that were beside him. But much did they beseech
him to have pity on himself and to spare his body [g]. However, he paid no heed to any of their words. And those who

---

[a-a] So g. C omits.
[b] So S. g: 'Promus,' 'Probus.' C: 'Primus.'
[c] A: 'martyr.' S: 'ascetic.'   [d] A: 'Christ.'
[e-e] So A, S. C omits.   [f-f] A omits.
[g] C adds: 'and to preserve himself from the evils that hung over him.'

S of their eyes and feet; but three of them displayed in Ashkelon, where also they had been imprisoned, a marvellous
example of bravery, and gained a martyr's end in divers
fashions. One of them, named Ares, was committed to the
fire; while the others were beheaded. These last were called
Promus and Elijah.

SEVENTH YEAR (310)

Peter Abshelama.

2   On the eleventh day of the month Audynæus (that is, the
third before the Ides of January), at the said
January 11   Cæsarea, Peter an ascetic, called also Apselamus,
from the village of Anea in the neighbourhood of Eleutheropolis, gave by fire, like the purest gold, the proof of his faith
in the Christ of God by a noble counting of the cost. For

L   were around him—not only those who knew him, but even
those who knew him not—urged him, and one after another
entreated him, and besought the blessed man, as it were for their
own lives. But some of them confirmed his good resolve,
while others by their words suggested weakness, and urged
him to spare his youth and person. Those who were like-
minded with him called to his remembrance the hell to come;
others sought to terrify him with the present visible fire.
Some would put him in fear of the mortal judge; others
reminded him of the Judge of all judges. Some would have
him fix his gaze on the life that is temporal; others persuaded
him to gaze upon the kingdom of heaven. *Those on the right
hand* called upon him to turn to them; *those on the left* [1]
persuaded him to gaze upon earthly things. But this youth
was glorious in person, valiant in soul [a], strong in body; and
being such [b] an one [b], he gave *proof* of his purity, like *gold,
by* furnace and *fire*,[2] and preferred the confession of our
Saviour to the life of this passing time.

3   Now on one and the same pyre was yoked [c] with him a
certain person of the Marcionite error, who called himself
a bishop. And he gave himself up to this as though forsooth [d] in his [e] *zeal* for righteousness—but he was not *in the
[f] knowledge of the truth* [f] [3]—[g] and suffered martyrdom by fire
along with this martyr of God [g].

But this holy martyr of whom we have spoken came from
the village of Anea [h] in the neighbourhood of Eleutheropolis [i].
And in this consummation of which we have spoken he strove,
and was crowned in the contest for the glorious *righteousness* [j] [4]
of the martyrs of Christ.

[a] C adds : νεανίσκος (transliterated).   [b-b] A : ' a champion.'
[c] Reading *'ethkden* for *'ethkren* (C) and *'ethkāvān* (A).
[d] So A; cp. S.   C omits.   [e] C omits.
[f-f] C : ' true knowledge.'
[g-g] A : ' which is with the holy martyrs of God; and was burnt
with fire.'   [h] So A, S (§ 2).   C : ' Aia.'
[i] C, A : Beth Gobrin.   [j] C : ' victory.'

S   though the judge and those around him besought him many
times to have pity on himself and to spare his youth and
bloom, he paid no heed, but preferred the hope he had in the
God of the universe to all things, even to life itself.

3   With Peter too, Asclepius (accounted a bishop of the
Marcionite error), in his *zeal*, as he thought, for piety, but
not that piety which is *according to knowledge*,[3] nevertheless
departed this life on the one and self-same pyre. Such,
then, was the course of these events.

[1] Cp. Matt. xxv. 34, 41.   [2] Cp. 1 Pet. i. 7.
[3] Rom. x. 2; 1 Tim. ii. 4; 2 Tim. iii. 7.   [4] Cp. 2 Tim. iv. 8.

L   *Pamphilus and his Companions.*

(G, C, Lat., g)

11.   The present opportunity indeed summons us to record and
present to the eyes of all the great and famous spectacle of
Pamphilus, ^a the holy martyr ^a, and those wonderful ^b men
who were perfected with him and displayed in divers manners
  b conflicts for religion.   Certainly, while very many ^c known to
us contended valiantly in the persecution ^c, ^d the conflict
which we beheld, whose story we are now to tell, was without
parallel in our experience ^d, comprising as it did, all in one,
every kind of bodily age and mental development, with
differences of life and conduct, and is adorned with manifold
forms of tortures and the varied crowns of perfect martyrdom.
  c For among ^e the Egyptians ^e who were with them one might
see certain young men and mere boys; others in adolescence,
among whom also was Porphyry; ^f on the other hand ^f,
men who had reached the height of their vigour both in
body and mind, even one whose memory I fondly cherish,
  ^g and his companions, and ^g Paul of Jamnia, and Seleucus
and Julian, the last two having come originally from the land
of the Cappadocians.   And of their number were even those
who were adorned with the holy crown of a hoary and ripe
old age, Valens, a deacon of the church of Jerusalem, and
he who proved true his name, Theodulus.
  d   Such, then, was the diversity in age to be found among
them.   On the other hand, they varied in mental development.   Some still had the uninstructed and simple mind of
a child, others were altogether of a sturdy and weighty
character, and among their number were men by no means
ignorant of sacred learning.   But in all was to be found, as a
natural quality, bravery of a surpassing and valiant order.
  e   Yet, like a luminary which shines by day among the glittering
stars, conspicuous among them all in dazzling splendour was
my master (for it were not right that otherwise I should

---

^{a-a} Lat. omits.   ^b C adds : ' and brave.'
   ^{c-c} C, Lat. : ' contended valiantly (were distinguished, C) in the
persecution known to us ' (cp. G, MS. p.).
   ^{d-d} Lat. follows G, MSS. w, o, which give bad sense.   C has a feeble
paraphrase.
   ^{e-e} Lat. : ' those.'   ^{f-f} Lat. omits.   ^{g-g} Lat. omits.

S   *Pamphilus and his Companions.*

11.   Of a truth the present opportunity summons us to record
the great and famous spectacle of those who were perfected
in the company of Pamphilus—a man whose memory is
thrice dear to me.

379

L   style the marvellous and truly blessed Pamphilus). For he
had embraced in no ordinary degree those studies by which
the Greeks set great store; and in those connected with the
divine doctrines and the inspired Scriptures he had so trained
himself that none of his contemporaries [a] (to use a true, if
somewhat bold, expression) [a] could be affirmed to have done
the like. But he was possessed of something more advantageous than all this, which came to him naturally, or rather
had been given him from God, intelligence and wisdom.

f   [b] Such were they all, then, in matters that concern the
mind; but in manner and sphere of life the greatest differences, once again, were to be found amongst them.[b] For
Pamphilus traced his descent [c] according to the flesh [c] from
a noble stock, and played a part with fame and distinction
in the public affairs of his own country, while Seleucus had
been honoured in a most notable way with positions of high
rank in the army; others belonged to the middle and ordinary
class in life. [d] The group which they formed contained even
slaves.[d] For [e] the attendant in a governor's household was
[f] of their number [f], as also was Porphyry,[e] who outwardly
was a servant of Pamphilus, but in affection [g] differed nothing
from *a brother*,[1] or rather a veritable son, and never failed
to imitate [h] his master [h] in everything.

g   How else could it be? Nay, were one to say that they
comprised a complete [i] model [j] on a small scale [j] of a community in the Church, it would be no bad shot at the truth.
For, among them, Pamphilus had been deemed worthy of the
presbyterate, Valens the diaconate; others had been allotted
the rank of the regular public readers; Seleucus, long before
his end came by martyrdom, was distinguished for confessions
made while most stedfastly enduring scourging, and he
accepted bravely the loss of his military rank; and the
remainder, over and above these, in the person of catechumens
and faithful, completed the rest of the resemblance, under a
small image, to a church of countless numbers.

h   This chosen band of martyrs [k] we beheld, its marvellous
character, the number and quality of those who formed it.
And although as regards numbers it was not large, [l] still it
lacked nothing of what is to be found in groups of humanity.[l]

[a-a] C omits.   [b-b] C omits.   [c-c] C omits.   [d-d] C omits.
  [e-e] Lat. : 'also Porphyry was brought into their number from the
governor's house.'
    [f-f] C : 'called with them to this honour.'
  [g] C adds : 'towards God and his admirable confession.'
  [h-h] C : 'his foster-father' (*mrōbiōneh* : error for *mōreh* ?).
  [i] Lat. omits.   [j-j] C, Lat. omit.
  [k] C adds : 'all of them.'   [l-l] C omits.

---

*   *   *   *   *   *

[1] Cp. Philem. 16.

L As, for example, in a many-stringed lyre formed out of diverse strings, high and low, slackened, taut and medium, yet all disposed agreeably to the musical art, in the same way also in their case young and old were found together, slaves and freemen alike, learned and unlearned, ^a obscure (as it seemed to most people) and famous ^a, faithful and catechumens, as well as deacons with presbyters; and these all, being struck in diverse fashion as if by the hand of a single all-wise Musician^b, the Only-begotten, the Word of God, severally displayed, by their endurance of tortures^c, the excellent power that was in them, and gave forth ^d in their confessions ^d the clearest ^e of tuneful harmonics and concordant ^e sounds before the courts of justice, leading up to one and the self-same close. ^f For in the perfect close of martyrdom they rendered a most devotional and skilful melody to the God of the universe.^f

i Moreover, the number of the men is worthy of great wonder, significant, as it was, of a prophetic and apostolic gift. For it so happened that ^g they were twelve in all^g, ^h the number (so tradition assures us) of the patriarchs ^h, prophets and apostles.

k Nor must we omit those brave acts of great endurance on the part of each in turn : the laceration of the sides, ⁱ the friction of the lacerated parts of the body by a woven cloth of goat's hairⁱ, the barbarous scourgings, the manifold tortures applied one after the other, ^j the terrible and insupportable rackings with which the soldiers in attendance, at the order of the judge, stretched the hands and feet^j, and strove by force to compel the martyrs to do something forbidden. Why need we tell of the ever-memorable ^k utterances ^l those divine men ^l made, wherein with bright and smiling countenances they answered the judge's enquiries, recking not their sufferings, but laughing bravely in the very face of torture, ^m and with earnest deportment bantering his questions ^m? Thus, when he asked whence they were, they omitted to tell him their earthly home, but declared what was their true city, saying that they were from ⁿ Jerusalem. Their meaning was, of course, to indicate the heavenly city of God, towards m which, indeed, they were hastingⁿ. ^o And other remarks also of a like character they made, passing the understanding and

---

^{a-a} C : 'famous and obscure.' ^b C omits.
^c Lat. adds : '*i.e.* confession.' ^{d-d} Lat. omits. ^{e-e} C omits.
^{f-f} C omits. ^{g-g} So G; cp. S. C omits.
^{h-h} C : 'like the.' Cp. S. ⁱ⁻ⁱ C omits. ^{j-j} C omits.
^k C : 'divine.' ^{l-l} C : 'they.' ^{m-m} C omits.
ⁿ⁻ⁿ C : 'Jerusalem above, which is in heaven, and confessing that to it they were hasting again' (πάλιν for πόλιν). ^{o-o} C omits.

S i They were twelve in all, having being accounted worthy of a prophetic, or even apostolic, gift and number.

*   *   *   *   *   *

L   beyond the ken of those who had not tasted of sacred things, but very clear to themselves alone and to those who were of the divine faith.[o] At this especially the judge was convulsed with anger and downright rage, and, [a] being at his wit's end [a], contrived devices [b] of various kinds against them, that he might [c] not be worsted.[c] Then, when he had given up hope, he at last permitted each one to carry off the prizes of victory.

   [n] And the manner of their end was varied also : two of their number, who were catechumens, were perfected in the baptism by fire; another was delivered up to suffer after the manner of the Saviour; [d] while my dear friend and his companions put on, as their rewards, crowns differing the one from the other [d].

   [e] So much, then, would one say in mentioning them in a somewhat general manner. But were one to go through each case in turn, he would rightly call him blessed who was the 2 leader of the company. This was Pamphilus,[e] a man verily dear to God, and [f] in truth dear and friendly to [f] all, [g] one true to his name [g], the ornament of the church of Cæsarea, since, being a presbyter, he conferred honour on the chair of the presbyters, alike adorning and being adorned by his ministry there. [h] Even in other respects [h] he was verily divine and [i] partook of divine inspiration, for he was distinguished all his life long for every virtue; who, while he bade a long farewell to luxury and superfluity of riches, 3 devoted himself entirely to the word of God. In fact he [j] gave away [j] what came to him from his fathers, and distributed it all among the naked, the maimed and the poor, while he himself lived in poverty, pursuing divine philosophy with the most persistent self-discipline. He came from the

---

[a-a] C omits.
   [b] C : 'cruel scourgings.'   [c-c] C : 'accomplish his desire upon them.'
   [d-d] Lat. : 'but my dear friend was wreathed with divers rewards.' C omits.   [e-e] C : 'But Pamphilus.'
   [f-f] C : 'a peacemaker among.'   [g-g] C omits.
   [h-h] C : 'In his general conduct too.'   [i] C adds : 'at all times.'
   [j-j] C : 'sold ' (?).

S   2   Their chief, and the only one adorned with the rank of the presbyterate at Cæsarea, was Pamphilus, a man distinguished all his life long for every virtue, for his renunciation and scorning of this passing life, for the sharing of his goods with the needy, for his contempt for worldly expectations, for his philosophic manner of life and self-discipline. But he was especially distinguished above all our contemporaries for his most sincere devotion for the divine oracles, for the unwearying and patient industry he bestowed on his self-imposed tasks, and for the help he gave to his relatives and 3 all with whom he came in contact. The rest of his good

L city of Berytus, ª in whose schools he had been brought up
in early manhood ª. But when ᵇ his understanding had
advanced into that of a full-grown man ᵇ, he passed from ᶜ these
to the study of the sacred ᶜ Scriptures, and assumed the
manner of life of an inspired ᵈ prophet, ᵉ proving himself a
true martyr of God, even before the final close of his life.

4 Such, then, was Pamphilus.ᵉ But the second after him to
advance to the conflict was Valens, adorned with old age and
the gray hairs that become sanctity, and a venerable and
holy old man even to look on; ᶠ versed, moreover, in ᶠ the
divine Scriptures, ᵍ if anyone was. In fact he had so laid
up the memory of them in his heart, that his repetition of
what he remembered of the sacred teaching ʰ lacked nothing
of the text when read.ᵍ Yet, for all this, he was a deacon of

5 the church of Ælia ⁱ. The third to be numbered among them
was Paul, a man ʲ most hasty in action and ʲ *fervent in spirit* ᵏ.[1]
He came from the city of Jamnia ˡ and was well known,
inasmuch as ˡ even before ᵐ his martyrdom he had sustained
the conflict of confession by enduring the branding-iron.

ᵃ⁻ᵃ C : ' where he had increased in stature and learning together.'
ᵇ⁻ᵇ So G (emended), Lat., (C).
ᶜ⁻ᶜ C : ' human wisdom and embraced the divine.'
ᵈ C : ' heavenly.'   ᵉ⁻ᵉ C : ' and was crowned with martyrdom.'
ᶠ⁻ᶠ C : ' Nor were these his sole title to honour, but there was his
knowledge of.'
ᵍ⁻ᵍ C : ' For his memory was a complete treasury of the Scriptures,
so that he could repeat the Scriptures of God by rote, like one in
whose memory the whole Scriptures were stored.'
ʰ Lat., G (MSS. w, o) : ' disciples.'
ⁱ C : ' God ' ('*ālōhô*' for '*ālēiā*').   ʲ⁻ʲ C omits.
ᵏ C : ' the Spirit of God.'   ˡ⁻ˡ C omits.   ᵐ Lat. : in.

S deeds, the fruit of his virtue, would require a longer recital,
and we have already on a former occasion committed them
to writing in three memoirs, in a work whose special subject
is his life. We refer to that work those who are eager to
know these additional facts. Let us now pursue the history
of the martyrs in their order.

4 The second after Pamphilus to advance to the conflict
was Valens, adorned with the gray hairs that become sanctity.
He was a deacon of the community at Ælia, a most venerable
old man even to look on, and versed in the divine Scriptures,
if anyone was. In fact, he had so laid up the memory of
them in his heart, that any passages whatsoever repeated by
him from memory wanted nothing of the text when read, of

5 any Scripture one might choose. The third, Paul from the
city of Jamnia, most hasty in action and *fervent in spirit*,[1]
was well known among them; since before his martyrdom
he had sustained the conflict of confession by enduring the
branding-iron.

[1] Acts xviii. 25; Rom. xii. 11.

L   When these had languished ᵃ two years in prison, the occasion of their martyrdom was the arrival of Egyptians;
6 who with them also were perfected. ᵇ These men had brought down those that were suffering affliction in the mines of Cilicia ᵇ as far as the places assigned them, and were returning to the home country. And then they were questioned by the guards at the entrance to the gates ᶜ of Cæsarea as to who they were and whence they came. When they concealed nothing of the truth, but declared themselves Christians, they were seized after the manner of malefactors caught in the
7 very act. They numbered five. Brought before the ruler, they spoke boldly in his presence, and were immediately thrown into chains. But on the day after, which was the sixteenth of the month Peritius, ᵈ but according to the Romans

February 16 the fourteenth before the Kalends of March,ᵈ these same persons were brought before Firmilian,
8 together with Pamphilus and his companions. And he ᵉ tested the Egyptians alone ᵉ ᶠ first of all, harassing the men with all kinds of tortures.ᶠ Bringing, then, their spokesman into the midst, he asked him who he was ᵍ; then, when he

> ᵃ C adds : ' about.'
> ᵇ⁻ᵇ Lat. : ' But these men, after so suffering exceeding affliction in the mines, had come ' (cp. G, MSS. w, o).
> ᶜ C, Lat. : ' gate.'   ᵈ⁻ᵈ C omits.
> ᵉ⁻ᵉ G (MSS. w, o), Lat. : ' only tested the E.' C omits ' alone.'
> ᶠ⁻ᶠ G, Lat. : ' before the (πρὸ τῶν for πρῶτον) tortures, exercising the men in every manner.'
> ᵍ So C, S. G, Lat. add : ' and whence he came.'

S   After these had languished two entire years in prison, the occasion of their martyrdom was, once more, the coming of Egyptian brethren, who with them also were perfected.
6 These men had escorted the confessors in Cilicia as far as the mines there, and were returning home. In like manner they too were questioned, just at the entrance to the gates of Cæsarea, as to who they were and whence they were coming, by the guards, who were men of barbarous character. They concealed nothing of the truth, and, like malefactors caught in the act, were arrested. The men numbered
7 five. Brought also before the tyrant, they spoke boldly in his presence, and were immediately shut up in prison. But on the following day, which was the sixteenth day of the

February 16 month Peritius (the fourteenth before the Kalends of March, according to the Romans), these same persons were brought before the judge, by order, along with
8 the aforesaid Pamphilus and his companions. He made proof of the invincible constancy of the Egyptians first of all, by all kinds of tortures and by inventing novel and varied contrivances. Having harassed the spokesman of them all

L had heard, instead of the man's proper name, that of some prophet—for this ᵃ was what the rest as well did ᵃ : in place of the names belonging to idols which their fathers had given them, they called themselves after the names of prophets; for instance, ᵇ you might have heard them ᵇ giving themselves the names of Elijah and Jeremiah and Isaiah and Samuel and Daniel, ᶜ and thus manifesting, not only by actual deeds but also by the literal sense of the words they used, *the Jew which is one inwardly,*[1] and the genuine Israelite ᶜ—when the judge had heard, then, some such name from the martyr's lips, not understanding the force of what was said, he next

9 asked him what his city was. But the martyr ᵈ let fall a second expression in harmony with the former one ᵈ, saying that Jerusalem was his city—meaning, to be sure, that one of which it was said by Paul, *But the Jerusalem that is above is free, which is our mother,*[3] ᵉ and, *Ye are come unto mount Zion, and unto the city of the living God, the heavenly Jerusalem.*[4]

10 ᶠ This was the one he meant. But the other had his thoughts fixed on this world here below, and enquired closely and carefully as to what city it was, and in what part of the world it was situated ᶠ; and indeed applied tortures ᵍ as well,

---

a-a Lat. : ' was done before (πρό for πρός) other things.'
b-b C, Lat. omit.   c-c C omits.   d-d Lat. : ' said.'
e C adds : ' whom we acknowledge as the holy Church.'
f-f C : ' But the governor was painfully inquisitive about this.'
g C : ' to them the combs and the branding-irons.'

S with these trials, he first asked him who he was; then, when he had heard, instead of the man's proper name, that of some prophet—for this was what they all did : in place of the names which their fathers had given them (names, perhaps, belonging to idols) they called themselves by others; for instance, you might have heard them assuming names such as Elijah and Jeremiah and Isaiah and Samuel and Daniel, and thus manifesting, not only by deeds but by the literal sense of the words they used, *the Jew which is one inwardly* [1] and the genuine and pure *Israel of God* [2]—when Firmilian had heard, then, some such name from the martyr's lips, not understanding the force of what was said, he next

9 asked him what his city was. But the martyr let fall a second expression in harmony with the former one, saying that Jerusalem was his city—meaning, to be sure, that one of which it was said by Paul : *But the Jerusalem that is above is free, which is our mother,*[3] and, *Ye are come unto mount Zion, and unto the city of the living God, the heavenly Jerusalem.*[4]

10 This was the one he meant. But the other had his thoughts fixed on this world here below, and enquired closely and

[1] Rom. ii. 29.   [2] Gal. vi. 16.
[3] Gal. iv. 26.   [4] Heb. xii. 22.

L ^a to secure a confession of the truth ^a. But our martyr, ^b though
his hands were wrenched behind his back and his feet crushed
by certain machines ^b, ^c stoutly affirmed that he had spoken ^c
11 the truth. The judge next put the same questions to him
again and again as to what and where situated the city of
Jerusalem was which ^d he had mentioned; and he ^e replied
that it was the country of ^d the Christians alone ^f. ^g For,
said he also, none others save they alone had a share in it,
and ^g it lay towards the East and the light itself and the
12 sun. So he continued thus to utter wisdom even again after
his heart, not heeding those around who plied him with
tortures; nay, he did not seem even to perceive the agonies,
as if he were a person without ^h flesh and ^h body. The judge,
on the other hand, ⁱ was puzzled and ⁱ shook with impatience,
thinking that the Christians had perchance established for
themselves a city somewhere at enmity and hostile to the
Romans; and he was much occupied in urging his tortures
and discovering the said city and enquiring into the country
13 in the East. But when he had even still further lacerated the
young man with scourging, he discovered that he could not

^{a-a} C omits.
^{b-b} G (MSS. w, o): 'though he was wrenched.' Lat.: 'while he was
being examined.'
^{c-c} C : 'confirmed his previous words and spoke.'
^{d-d} C : 'was said to belong to.'
^e G (MSS. w, o), Lat. add : 'only.'   ^f G (MSS. w, o), Lat. omit.
^{g-g} C : 'he replied.'   ^{h-h} C omits.   ⁱ⁻ⁱ C omits.

S carefully as to what city it was, and in what part of the world
it was situated; and then applied tortures as well, to secure
a confession of the truth. But our martyr, though his hands
were wrenched behind his back and his feet crushed by certain
strange machines, stoutly affirmed that he spoke the truth.
11 The judge next asked him again and again as to what and
where situated that city was of which he spoke, and he replied
that it was the country of the godly alone. For, said he,
none others save they alone had a share in it, and it lay
12 towards the far East and the rising sun. So he continued
thus to utter wisdom again after his own heart, in no wise
paying heed to those around who plied him with tortures;
nay, he seemed not even to feel the agonies, as if he were
without flesh and body. The judge, on the other hand, was
puzzled and shook with impatience, thinking that the Christians had certainly established a city somewhere at enmity
and hostile to the Romans; and he was much occupied in
discovering it and enquiring into the said country in the
13 East. But when he had still further lacerated the young
man with scourging, and punished him with all kinds of
tortures, he perceived that his persistence in what he had

L be changed in what he had formerly said; so he condemned
him to death by decapitation.

[a] Such, indeed, was the drama which this man's story
affords.[a] The rest of the Egyptians, too, the judge exercised
with similar conflicts and dispatched in like manner.

14 After that, he went from them to [b] the companions of [b]
Pamphilus. It was impressed upon him that as a matter of
fact they had already on a former occasion been tried with
numerous tortures. And reckoning it absurd to inflict the
same torments on the men and spend one's labour in vain,
he put this only question to them : if they would even now
obey; and on hearing from every one the final [c] word of
their witness, he gave sentence against them and similarly
inflicted the punishment of decapitation.

15 The last word had not left his lips when a certain lad,
an attendant belonging to Pamphilus' household, came forward and shouted out from somewhere in the midst of the
crowd of those who surrounded the court. He cried [d] with a
loud voice, demanding the bodies for burial. Porphyry was
the blessed one, a true nursling of Pamphilus, not full [e]
eighteen years old. He was skilled in the art of penmanship,
and for sobriety and manners was beyond all praise, [f] as we
might expect from one trained under such a man. Learning [f]
the sentence against his master, he shouted aloud from the

[a-a] C omits. [b-b] Lat. omits. [c] C omits.
[d] C adds : ' again.' [e] C omits.
[f-f] C : ' This youth, then, who was trained . . . man, when he
learned.'

S formerly said could not be changed; so he condemned him
to death by decapitation.

So great, then, was the drama which this man's story pro-
vides. The rest, too, the judge exercised with similar sufferings and dispatched in like manner.

14 After that, he became weary and recognized that the men
were being punished to no purpose; and, his lust being
satiated, he proceeded to the companions of Pamphilus. It
had been impressed upon him that already on a former occasion they had shown under torture that their zeal for the
faith might not be changed : so he asked them if after all
they would even now obey, and on receiving from every
single one of them this answer and this alone—the final
word of their confession as martyrs—he inflicted the same
punishment on them as on the former persons.

15 When this had been accomplished, a lad who was a servant
belonging to Pamphilus' household, learning the sentence
against his master, shouted out from the midst of the throng
a request that the bodies should receive burial. Such an
action might have been expected from one who had received

L midst of the throng a request ^a that the bodies should receive
16 burial ^a. But the judge, who was not a human being, but a
wild beast or more savage than any wild beast, neither
admitted the reasonableness of the request nor made allowance for the young man's age. And when he heard ^b him
confess himself ^b a Christian, waiting to hear no more he
ordered the torturers to use all their strength against him.
17 And when the marvellous youth refused to obey the order
to sacrifice, he commanded that they should torment him
^c and tear his whole body ^c to the very bone and the recesses
of his bodily organs, as if he were made, not of human flesh,
but rather of stone or wood ^d or some other lifeless material ^d.
When this, however, had gone on for a long time, he recog-
nized that his efforts were to no purpose, ^e for the noble
martyr's body had become almost incapable of speech and
18 lifeless ^e. But the judge, ^f whose mercilessness and inhumanity
knew no respite ^f, ^g ordered that his sides, already skinned
by the tortures, should be still further rubbed and scraped
with hair-woven cloths; then, as if he had had enough and
taken his fill of madness, he ^g gave sentence that he should
be cast into a slow, smouldering fire. So this man, then,
who ^h was the last to enter ^h the arena, before Pamphilus was
perfected, ⁱ anticipated his master in release from the body.ⁱ

S 16 a real education and training under so great a man. But the
judge, who was not a human being but a wild beast or more
savage than any wild beast, neither admitted the reasonableness of the request nor made allowance for the young man's
age. He asked him but the one question, and when he
heard him confess himself a Christian, he was as if wounded
by a dart, and, swelling with rage, ordered the torturers to
17 use their whole power against him. And when he saw that
he refused to obey the order to sacrifice, he commanded him
to be torn without respite to the very bone and the inmost
recesses of his bodily organs, as if he were made, not of human
flesh, but of stone or wood or some other lifeless material.
When this, however, had gone on for a long time, he recognized that his efforts were to no purpose, for the lad's body,
worn out with the tortures, was incapable of speech and
18 sensation, nay, almost completely lifeless. But [the judge],
whose mercilessness and inhumanity knew no respite, gave
sentence that he should be committed immediately, just as
he was, to a slow fire. And so this man, who was the last

L 19 One might behold, then, Porphyry, like a conqueror [a]in the sacred games [a] who has triumphed in every conflict, his body [b]soiled with dust[b], yet withal of a cheerful appearance, and advancing on the way to death with a stout, exultant[c] heart,[d] truly filled with the divine Spirit. And[e] he was clad, too, in the garb of a philosopher with his mantle thrown about him like an ordinary cloak. With his gaze fixed on high, and despising all this mortal, human life, he advanced to the pyre with soul unmoved. [f] Now although the flame was already near him[f], he[g] gave directions to his friends as to his affairs with undisturbed and sober consideration, as if he had nothing to trouble him, [h] and up to that moment still kept his countenance cheerful and unchanged. But when the farewells to his friends were fully said,[h] he then hastened to God. In fact, as the pyre was kindled from a distance all around him, he drew in the flame with his mouth from this side and from that, to speed his steps upon the journey that lay before him. [i] And this he did, calling on no other save Jesus.[i]

20 Such was the contest of Porphyry. Now the messenger that brought the news of [j] his perfecting [j] to Pamphilus was

a-a C omits.　　　b-b C : ' weak.'　　　c C omits.
d C adds : ' without fear.'
e C adds : ' when he came to the place of execution.'　　f-f C omits.
g So C, Lat., S. G (MS. p) : 'the hero.' G (MSS. w, o) : 'the blessed one.'
h-h C omits.
i-i C omits.　　　j-j C : ' all that had been done to Porphyry.'

S to enter the arena, received his release from the body before his master according to the flesh was perfected; while those who had eagerly sought the earlier conflicts had still 19 to linger. One might see, then, Porphyry, like a conqueror in the sacred games who has triumphed in every conflict, his body soiled with dust, yet withal of a cheerful countenance, advancing on the way to death after such sufferings with a stout, exultant heart, and truly filled with the divine Spirit Himself; clad in the garb of a philosopher with only a mantle thrown about him like an ordinary cloak, he gave instructions to his friends as to his wishes with sober consideration, beckoned to them, and even at the stake preserved still a cheerful countenance. Nay more, as the pyre was kindled from the outside at a considerable distance all around him, he drew in the flame with his mouth from this side and from that, and most nobly persevered in silence up to his latest breath, after he had uttered a single cry as the flame first touched him, when he called on Jesus the Son of God to help.

20 Such was the contest of Porphyry. Now the messenger that brought the news of his perfecting to Pamphilus was

L Seleucus, and he was deemed worthy ª straightway ᵇ to share ᶜ the lot of the others ᶜ.   Certainly, the moment he announced the end of Porphyry and saluted ᵈ one of the martyrs with a kiss ᵈ, he was apprehended by the soldiers and brought to the governor.   And he ᵉ, as if so to hasten his steps that he might join the travellers ᶠ in front of him ᶠ, ordered that he

21 should undergo the penalty of decapitation.   Seleucus came from the land of the Cappadocians, and had a most brilliant reputation in the army, and, ᵍ of those who were promoted among the Romans,ᵍ had attained to no small honour.   Moreover, in stature and strength of body, in size and excellent vigour, he greatly surpassed the rest; his appearance by itself made him the cynosure of every eye, ʰ and his whole form excited admiration for its size and goodly proportions ʰ.

22 Indeed, at the beginning of the persecution he was distinguished in the conflicts of confession for endurance under scourging, but after his departure from the army ⁱ he became a zealous follower of the religious ascetics ⁱ, and ʲ displayed himself a true soldier ʲ of Christ; after the manner of a

ª C adds : ' by God.'
ᵇ Lat. omits.   C : ' as a reward for his tidings.'
ᶜ⁻ᶜ C : ' the martyrdom of Pamphilus.'
ᵈ⁻ᵈ Lat. : ' the martyrs with one kiss.'   Cp. G (MSS. w, o).
ᵉ C : ' Seleucus himself.'   ᶠ⁻ᶠ C omits.
ᵍ⁻ᵍ C omits.   ʰ⁻ʰ C omits.
ⁱ⁻ⁱ C : ' on account of his faith, his zeal now suffered him not to abstain from good works.'   For ' religious ascetics ' Lat. has ' those who exercised themselves in piety.'
ʲ⁻ʲ C : ' he earnestly desired to serve in the beloved ranks.'

S Seleucus, a confessor who had served in the army; and as the minister of such a message was deemed worthy straightway to share the lot of the others.   For the moment he announced the end of Porphyry and greeted one of the martyrs with a kiss, he was seized by certain soldiers and brought to the governor.   And he, as if so to speed his steps that he might join the travellers in front of him on the road to heaven, ordered that he should undergo the penalty of decapitation

21 immediately.   Seleucus was from the land of the Cappadocians, and belonged to a picked band of young men in the army; and of those who held positions of rank among the Romans had attained to no small distinction.   For in stature and strength of body, in size and vigour, he so greatly surpassed his fellow-soldiers, that even his appearance was a matter of common talk, and his whole form excited admira-

22 tion for its size and goodly proportions.   Indeed, at the beginning of the persecution he was distinguished in the conflicts of confession for endurance under scourging, but after his departure from the army he became a zealous follower of the religious ascetics, and, like a father or pro-

L   guardian [1] [a] or trustee [a] he cared for destitute orphans and unprotected widows and those oppressed by poverty and sickness; and like a [b] father or protector took on himself the pains and sufferings of all the outcasts [b]. Hence, as might have been expected, he was accounted worthy of the martyr's perfecting, by God who delights in such things rather than

23 in sacrifices [c] with their smoke and blood [c]. He was the tenth champion, along with those mentioned, to be perfected on one and the selfsame day; whereon, as it seems to me, thanks to the martyrdom of Pamphilus, a mighty gate to heaven was duly opened, and the way to the kingdom of God [2] became easy and freely bestowed [d] for others too [d] in his company.

24   In the steps of Seleucus came Theodulus, a venerable and godly [e] old man, who had been accounted worthy of the highest position in the governor's household [e] on account of his character and age—for he had lived to see the third generation—and, still more, for the good-will he ever bore to his superiors. [f] Now he also [f] had done a similar action to that of Seleucus, and had saluted [g] a certain martyr with a kiss [g].

a-a C omits.
b-b C : 'guardian and burden-bearer, and as it were a compassionate father he tried to heal their diseases.'
c-c C : ' and burnt offerings and sweet incense.'
d-d So C, S.   G, Lat. omit.
e-e C : ' man.   Now he was the oldest servant of the governor, and by them all was highly favoured.'
f-f C : ' When his master had heard that he.'
g-g C : ' the martyrs, he had no mercy on him.'

S   tector, showed himself, as it were, a guardian [1] or patron of destitute orphans and unprotected widows and the outcast poor and sick. Hence, as might have been expected, he was accounted worthy of the martyr's wonderful calling, by God who delights in such things rather than sacrifices with their

23 smoke and blood. He was the tenth champion, after the aforesaid, to be perfected on one and the selfsame day; whereon, as it seems to me, thanks to the martyrdom of Pamphilus and the man's worth, a mighty gate was opened, and the way of entrance into the kingdom of heaven [2] became easy for others too in his company.

24   In the steps of Seleucus came Theodulus, a venerable and godly old man, who belonged to the governor's household and had been honoured by Firmilian above any in his house, both on account of his age—he had lived to see the third generation—and also for the good-will and right faithful conscientiousness he ever bore to them. Having done a similar action to that of Seleucus, he was brought before his

[1] ἐπίσκοπος.   [2] Cp. 2 Pet. i. 11.

L So he was brought before his master, whom he infuriated to anger more than did the others, and received the same martyrdom as the Saviour in His Passion; for he was delivered to the cross.

25   After these, as there still lacked one to complete the number twelve in the ranks of the said persons, Julian came to complete it. He had arrived that very hour after absence from home, nor had he even as yet entered the city, when he heard the news from someone, and hastened immediately, just as he was after his journey, to see [a] the martyrs. And when he beheld the bodies of the saints lying prone on the ground, filled with joy he embraced each one [b], saluting them all with
26 a kiss. But while he was still so engaged [c], the [d] ministers of murder [d] having seized him brought him before the governor, who [e] by a deed worthy of his principles committed him also to a slow fire. Thus verily Julian too—bounding and leaping and with a loud voice rendering [f] thanks to God who had thought him fit to receive such blessings—was received up into [f]
27 the choirs of the martyrs. Now he also was a Cappadocian; and as to character [g], full of piety, [h] full of faith [h]; a meek

---

[a] Lat. : ‘hear.’   [b] C adds : ‘with heavenly love.’
[c] C adds : ‘and was weeping because he had not suffered martyrdom with them.’
[d-d] C : ‘quæstionarii.’   Lat. : ‘lictors.’
[e] G (MSS. w, o), Lat. : ‘But the impious man.’
[f-f] C : ‘rendered . . . thought him worthy of this, and his soul was received up to the Lord with.’
[g] C : ‘his soul.’   [h-h] C omits.

S master, whom he infuriated more than did the former martyrs, and received the same martyrdom as the Saviour in His Passion; for he was delivered to the cross.

25   After these, as there still lacked one to fill up the number twelve in the ranks of the aforesaid martyrs, Julian came to complete it. In fact, he had just arrived after absence from home, and had not even as yet entered the city, when he heard the news and hastened immediately, just as he was after his journey, to see the martyrs. And when he saw the tabernacles of the saints lying prone upon the ground, filled
26 with joy he embraced each one, and saluted them all. While he was so doing, the ministers of murder were at their work again, and having seized him brought him before Firmilian; and he by an act worthy of himself committed him also to a slow fire. Thus verily was Julian too—bounding and leaping and with a loud voice giving great thanks to the Lord who had thought him fit to receive so high an honour—counted
27 worthy of the martyr's crown. Now he also was according to the flesh a Cappadocian; and as to character, most pious,

L   and gentle person; in ^a other respects ^a a good man, and
breathing the sweet savour of the Holy Spirit.

   ^b Such was the band of fellow-travellers, who ^b with the
blessed Pamphilus were counted worthy of the perfecting of
28 martyrdom.   For four days, indeed, and as many nights at
the command of Firmilian the all-holy bodies of the martyrs
of God were exposed as food for carnivorous wild beasts.   But
when nothing drew nigh to them—no wild beast, ^c no bird, no
dog ^c—^d thanks to a dispensation of God ^d, they were found
safe and unharmed, and receiving the honour and care due to
the dead were buried in the accustomed manner.   Placed in
splendid church buildings and in sacred places of prayer,
they were given to ^e the people of God that they might honour
them in unceasing remembrance.

Hadrian and Eubulus.

(C, g)

29   When the perfecting of Pamphilus and the martyrs who
suffered with him was proclaimed on everyone's lips, Hadrian
and Eubulus hastened from the country of Batanæa, as it is
called, to Cæsarea, to visit the rest of the confessors.   And
when they drew near to the gate of the city of Cæsarea they

a-a C : ' all well doing.'   b-b C : ' And he.'
   c-c So G. S. G (MSS. w, o), Lat. add : ' nor anything else.'   C.
omits.
   d-d C : ' without permission of the governor.'
   e C adds : ' their brethren.'

S   faithful and sincere; in all other respects a good man, and
breathing the Holy Spirit Himself.

   Such was the band of fellow-travellers, companions of
Pamphilus, counted worthy to enter together upon martyr-
28 dom.   By the command of the impious governor their sacred
and truly holy bodies were kept for four days and as many
nights as food for carnivorous beasts.   But when by some
miracle nothing approached them—no wild beast, no winged
creature, no dog—they were found again unharmed, thanks
to a dispensation of the providence of God; and receiving
the care due to the dead were buried in the accustomed
manner.

Hadrian and Eubulus.

29   Now while the commotion concerning these men was still
on everyone's lips, Hadrian and Eubulus arrived at Cæsarea
from the country of Batanæa, as it is called, to visit the rest
of the confessors.   They too were examined at the gate as
to why they had come.   Then, having confessed the truth,

L were examined as to why they had come. Then, having spoken the truth, they were brought before Firmilian. And he made no delay, but first of all ordered that they should be scraped on their sides, and tortured them in a special way, 30 as if they were enemies and among foes. And not satisfied with this he condemned them to be food for wild beasts. After an interval of two days Hadrian was thrown to a lion

March 5 on the fifth of Dystrus ⟨the third before the Nones of March⟩, and valiantly perfected his conflict. When he had been torn by the beast[a], at last he was dispatched with a sword. And Eubulus on the second day

March 7 thereafter, the seventh of Dystrus ⟨the Nones of March⟩, when the judge had again and again made efforts regarding him and said, " If thou sacrificest to demons, thou shalt be liberated in peace," scorning the whole course of this transitory time, preferred on his part the life eternal to this unreal and transitory life. Then he was thrown to a lion, and after he had been mangled[b] by the lion, he suffered like his predecessor[c]. Now he was the last of the martyrs at Cæsarea to [d] *set his seal* to the conflicts [d]. [1]

*   *   *   *   *   *

[a] C : ' beasts.'   [b] C : ' eaten.'   [c] So g, S.   C : ' predecessors.'
[d-d] So g, S.   C : ' fulfil his conflict.'

S they were brought before Firmilian. And he on the spot, once again without delay, condemned them to be food for wild beasts, having previously inflicted numerous tortures on 30 their sides. So then, after an interval of two days, on the

March 5 fifth of the month Dystrus, the third before the Nones of March, being the birthday of the goddess whom the city of Cæsarea worshipped as Fortune, Hadrian was thrown to a lion, then dispatched with a sword and so perfected.

March 7 Eubulus after another day's interval, on the Nones themselves, that is the seventh of Dystrus, was long entreated by the judge to offer sacrifice and so enjoy the liberty they think they can give. But he preferred a glorious death for religion to this transitory life; and after being thrown to the wild beasts, like his predecessor, he was sacrificed. Thus did the last of the martyrs at Cæsarea *set his seal* to the conflicts.[1]

31 But it is right further to mention, at this point in my record, that not long afterwards the heavenly Providence visited those wicked rulers, including the tyrants themselves. He who had behaved with such violence against the martyrs of Christ—Firmilian himself and no other—endured the supreme penalty in common with the others, and ended his life by the sword.

[1] Cp. *Mart. Pol.* Insc. 1 (iv. 15. 3 above).

L   *Peleus and others.*

(C)

13. On the nineteenth day of Gorpiæus ⟨that is, the thirteenth
before the Kalends of October⟩, in the wonderful
September 19 conflict of the martyrs of God, a great spectacle
was assembled at Phæno in Palestine. And all the champions
were perfect men, in number about one hundred and fifty.

S   *Things omitted.*

12. Such were the martyrdoms accomplished at Cæsarea during
the entire period of the persecution. But as to all that
happened in the subsequent interval to the presidents of the
churches; how the divine Justice condemned and appointed
them to the oversight of camels, as their proper charge, a
creature without reason, to whom nature has given the most
crooked of bodies, instead of being pastors of the reasonable
sheep of Christ, over whom they had not presided according
to law, and how she sentenced them to be obliged to attend
on the imperial horses; all the insults, indignities and tortures
that these same persons had to endure at the hands of the
imperial procurators and rulers, who from time to time were
in office, because of the sacred vessels and treasures of the
Church; the lust of power, moreover, that possessed the
many, the rash and unlawful ordinations, and the schisms
among the confessors themselves; all that the young agitators
eagerly devised against the remnants of the Church, heaping
fresh innovations on what were still novelties, adding with
an unsparing hand to the misfortunes of the persecution, and
building evil upon evil—all this I purpose to omit. For I
judged their tale unsuitable for me, inasmuch as I shun and
avoid such matters, as indeed I stated also at the beginning.[1]
But rather *whatsoever things are honourable* and *of good report*
(as the Holy Scripture says) and *if there be any virtue and
praise*,[2] these I deem it most suitable to say and write and
place before faithful hearers in my account of the wonderful
martyrs. And I purpose to adorn the conclusion of the entire
work with the ensuing peace which dawned upon us from
heaven.

Peleus and others.

13. A seventh year of the conflict against us was nearing its
end, and our affairs having taken a quieter and more peaceful
turn—a state of things which continued until the eighth

[1] viii. 2. 2, 3.   [2] Phil. iv. 8.

L   Many of them—over a hundred—were Egyptians. These had first their right eyes and the sinews of their left feet destroyed by branding-irons and the sword, and afterwards they were given over to the mines to dig copper. And the Palestinians also endured the like sufferings as the Egyptians. But all of them together were assembled at the place called Zoar, like a church consisting of many persons, and there was a great crowd with them, who had come from other districts to see them. And there were many others, who ministered to them in those things of which they had need, and visited them in love and supplied their wants, and were ministering all day in prayer and the ministry of God and in teaching and reading; and all the afflictions that befell them they counted as pleasure, and they spent all that time as though in a festive gathering.

2   But the hater of God and wicked envier could not endure these things, and immediately there was sent against them a Roman general, called a dux. And, to begin with, he divided them one from another, and some were sent to Zoar, an evil place, and some not; some to Phæno where the copper is

3 dug, and others went to other districts. After that they picked out four of those in Phæno who were of special excellence, thereby to terrify the rest. And when he had brought them to the test, and not one of them was dismayed, the unmerciful judge, considering that no punishment was as bad as that of fire, handed over the holy martyrs of God to that death. And when they were brought to the flames, they threw themselves into them without fear, dedicating themselves, as a thing more *acceptable* than any incense or oblations, and *presented* to God, the King of all, their *bodies*,[1] a peace-offering, better than all sacrifices.

S   year—in the neighbourhood of the copper mines in Palestine no small number of confessors was gathered together, who used great boldness, so as even to build houses for church assemblies. But the ruler of the province (a cruel and wicked person, as bad a man as his acts against the martyrs proved him to be), having come to stay there and learning the manner of their life, communicated everything he thought fit to the

2 emperor in a letter that was meant to slander. Next came on the scene the superintendent of the mines, and acting, apparently, on the emperor's orders he divided the body of the confessors, assigning to some a place of abode in Cyprus, to others in Lebanon, scattering some here and some there in the districts of Palestine; and ordered that they all should

3 be oppressed with various kinds of labour. After that he picked out those four who seemed most like their leaders, and sent them to the officer in command of the armies in

[1] Cp. Rom. xii. 1.

L   Now two of them were bishops, Peleus [a] and Nilus, and
two were picked men of the laity, Patermuthius [b] and Elijah;
all of them Egyptians by race. They were pure lovers of
that high philosophy which comes from God, and they brought
themselves like gold to the fire that they might be purified;
and He who *giveth power to the faint and to* them that suffer
affliction *increaseth strength,*[1] counted them worthy of the
heavenly life,[2] and assigned them a place in the assembly of
the angels.

EIGHTH YEAR

Silvanus of Gaza and others.

(C)

4   This blessed Silvanus came from Gaza, and he was one of
the veteran soldiers; but having attained (?) freedom regarding his manner of life he made himself *a good soldier of Christ.*[3]
For he was a meek man in every respect, and clear-minded,
and simple and pure in his faith.   Being a presbyter at the
5 city of Gaza, he there lived a beautiful life.   And because the
contest for life was proclaimed against the soldiers of Christ
he, an old man, of venerable mien, went down to the arena,
and then, in his first confession, was resplendent in the

[a] So S; cp. viii. 13. 5.   C : ' Paulus.'
[b] So S.   C : ' Patrîmuthæus.'

S   that quarter. These were Peleus and Nilus, Egyptian bishops,
a presbyter also, and in addition Patermuthius, whose devotion
for everyone made him universally well known. Having
asked without success for a denial of their religion, the
commander handed them over to be perfected by fire.

EIGHTH YEAR (311)

Silvanus of Gaza, John the Egyptian and others.

4   There were others again to whose lot it fell to inhabit a
separate district there by themselves, such confessors as had
been released from service in the works owing to age, or
because they had been maimed, or on account of other bodily
infirmities. Their leader was a bishop Silvanus, who came
from Gaza, a marvel of devoutness and a true pattern of
5 Christianity. This same man was distinguished, from the
first day of the persecution, one might say, and all throughout
it for confessions in every kind of conflict. He had been
preserved to that moment, to *set the* final *seal* [4] on the whole
conflict in Palestine.

[1] Isai. xl. 29.   [2] Cp. 2 Thess. i. 5.
[3] 2 Tim. ii. 3.   [4] Cp. *Mart. Pol.* Inscr. 1 (iv. 15. 3 above).

L presence of a multitude of Cæsareans, being examined by scourging. Having manfully suffered thus, he strove in a second contest, enduring scrapings on his sides, old man as he was, like a youth. Then in a third contest they sent him to the copper mines, and during a long life he gave to view great proof of himself. He was deemed worthy of the ministry of the episcopate, and also in this, his priestly life, he was gloriously resplendent.

* * * * * *

S 6 Now with him were also a large number of Egyptians, among whom was John, who surpassed all the men of our day in excellence of memory. Though he had on a former occasion been deprived of his vision, his confessions, in which he was distinguished, cost him, as they did the others, the further loss of a foot under the branding-iron, and his sightless orbs had to endure the same burning by fire : to such lengths of mercilessness and want of feeling did the executioners 7 carry their savage and inhuman conduct. And though such was his character and such his life of discipline, why need one wonder thereat, since that did not appear so marvellous as his excellence of memory ? For, aided by a soul filled with light and an eye of the mind most pure, he had *written* whole books of the divine Scriptures *not in tables of stone*, as the divine apostle says, nay, not even on skins of animals nor on paper which *moths* and time *destroy*,[1] *but in tables that are truly hearts of flesh*,[2] so that he brought forth at will from his mouth, as from some treasury of words, a passage, now from the law and the prophets, now from the historical books, or again from the Gospels and apostolic writings. 8 For my part, I confess that I was amazed on a certain occasion when first I beheld the man standing in the midst of a large congregation and reciting certain portions of the divine Scripture. As long as I could only hear a voice, I thought that someone was reading, as is customary in the assemblies; but when I came quite close and saw what was happening— the others all standing round with sound eyes, while he was using the eyes of the mind alone and simply uttering his words as some prophet might have done, and far surpassing those endowed with bodily soundness—then I hardly knew how to glorify God enough and to wonder. And to my mind the facts afforded a clear and certain proof that the true man is to be found, not, as men suppose, in the body that they see, but only in the soul and mind, since he shows the superior excellence of the power that is in him even when the body has been maimed.

[1] Luke xii. 33.
[2] 2 Cor. iii. 3 : but Schwartz adopts the reading of the A.V., ' fleshy tables of the heart.'

398

L 9 And on the fourth day of Artemisius ⟨the fourth day

May 4 before the Nones of May⟩, the great gate of heaven was fully opened to him, and with a multitude of martyrs the blessed one was taken up, and not alone, for a great multitude of brave men followed with him. For all at once an impious order was issued, and it was decreed that those who were shattered by age or sickness in the mines, and those who were unable to work, should be put 10 to death with the sword. The martyrs of God—forty all together in number—were decapitated on a single day. Now many of these were Egyptians, but their chief and leader was this martyr, this bishop of martyrs, Silvanus, a truly blessed one, dear to God.

But since we have reached this point in our record we shall make known to you that not long afterwards God took vengeance on those wicked rulers, and they suddenly received the punishment of their sins. For he who like a terrible beast was stirred up to savagery against those confessors of God endured a terrible penalty; and, by command of him who held the temporal authority, perished in fashion as a savage beast, and all the rest died by various kinds of death and received righteous punishments for their offences.

Conclusion.

(C)

11 Those things, then, that were accomplished in the entire time of the persecution among the people of Palestine we

---

S 9 But while the said persons dwelt in the place assigned them and performed their wonted round of fastings, prayers and the other exercises, God, yea God Himself, deemed them worthy to receive the perfecting of salvation, extending His right hand in answer to their prayers. On the other hand, the bitter foe determined to kill and remove from the earth as annoying him those whose quiet arming against him by 10 prayer to God he could no longer endure. And God also permitted the accomplishment of this his endeavour, so that at the one time he might not be hindered from the wickedness he purposed, and they might at length receive the prizes of their varied conflicts. So then, forty save one were decapitated on a single day by the order of that accursed Maximin.

*   *   *   *   *   *

Conclusion.

11 These, then, were the martyrdoms accomplished in Palestine in eight entire years, and such was the persecution in our

L have written and made known. And all these were the blessed martyrs of God who were of renown in our time; men who declined the temporal life and counted the worship of God of more honour than aught else, and received from God the hidden hope of good things unseen by bodily eyes.[1]

* * * * * *

Oh, the blessed confessors of the kingdom of Christ, who like gold were tried in the excellency of their righteousness, and attained the heavenly life of the angels [2] by the contest in which they stood fast, and *obtained* the promises of hidden good which is *the prize of the high calling!* [3] For *eye hath not seen nor ear heard, neither hath entered into the heart of man, that which God hath prepared for those that love Him.*[4]

Here end the chapters of the narrative of the victories of the holy confessors in Palestine.

S time, which, beginning with the destruction of the churches, increased greatly as the rulers made fresh attacks from time to time; wherein the diverse and varied conflicts of those who contended for piety produced in every province an innumerable multitude of martyrs, in the regions extending from Libya and throughout all Egypt and Syria and the countries of the East and *round about to* the parts in the

12 region of *Illyricum.*[5] For indeed the countries beyond these said places, all Italy and Sicily, Gaul and all that lies towards the setting sun as far as Spain, Mauretania and Africa, had not endured the conflict even two entire years—the first two of the persecution—when God bestowed on them with all speed His visitation and peace, the heavenly Providence thus

13 sparing the single-heartedness and faith of these men. Certainly, that which had never been recorded in the annals of the Roman government from the beginning, now for the first time took place in our day contrary to all expectation. For the Empire was rent in twain in respect of our persecution: the brethren who dwelt in the aforesaid part enjoying peace, while those in the other part of the world endured countless

14 conflicts. But when the divine and heavenly grace manifested for us too its kindly and gracious visitation, then verily even the rulers of our day, those very persons by whose means hostile measures had long been prosecuted in our time, changed their minds in a most marvellous fashion and gave utterance to a recantation. Thus by kindly edicts and humane ordinances on our behalf they quenched the fires of persecution against us. The recantation also must be placed on record.

* * * * *

[1] Cp. Rom. viii. 24, 25.
[2] Cp. Matt. xxii. 30; Mark xii. 25; Luke xx. 36.
[3] Phil. iii. 14 (Peshittâ).   [4] 1 Cor. ii. 9.
[5] Rom. xv. 19.

THE APPENDIX TO BOOK VIII

BUT the author of the edict, after such a confession, was immediately, though not for long, released from his pains, and so departed this life. It is recorded that this same person was the prime author of the calamity of the persecution; since long before the movement of the other emperors he had used force to turn aside [from the faith] the Christians in the army—and, first of all, those in his own house—degrading some from their military rank, and heaping the most shameful insults on others; and since he was already threatening others even with death, and, finally, had stirred up his partners in the principate to the general persecution. It is not possible to pass over the ends of these same emperors in silence.

2 Four, then, had divided the supreme power between them. Those who were the more advanced in age and honour retired from the principate not two whole years after the persecution began, as we have already stated, and passed the remainder of their existence like ordinary, private citizens. The end

3 of their lives fell out thus. The one who had attained the chief place in honour and age fell a victim to a prolonged and most painful infirmity of the body; while he who held the second place to him ended his life by strangling: suffering this fate, in accordance with a certain demoniacal prediction,

4 for the numerous crimes he had perpetrated. Of those after them, he who held the last place—the same who was the originator,[1] as we stated,[2] of the whole persecution—suffered the fate which we have mentioned above;[3] but he who ranked next before him, that kindest and mildest of emperors, Constantius, passed the whole period of his principate in a manner worthy of his high office, and in other respects displayed himself in a most beneficent and favourable light to all; yea, and he held himself aloof from the war against us, and carefully preserved his God-fearing subjects from injury and harsh treatment; neither did he pull down the church buildings or employ any other additional new device against us at all. So he has had as his reward a truly happy and thrice-blessed issue of his life; for he alone met with a favourable and glorious end while he was still emperor, with a lawful son, in all respects most prudent and godly, to succeed him

5 in the office. He from the very first was proclaimed by the

---

[1] ἀρχηγόν.   [2] § 1.   [3] *Ib.*

armies most perfect Emperor and Augustus; and he set himself
to be an emulator of his father's piety towards our doctrine.
Such was the issue which befell, at different times, the lives
6 of the four men of whom we have written above.   Of these
same persons, he of whom we spoke a little while ago alone still
remained,[1] and, in conjunction with those who subsequently
were admitted to the principate, openly placed before all the
aforesaid confession in the document which was set out above.

---

[1] ἐτὶ λιπών : but we should require λειπόμενος to give the above sense.

S.P.C.K. Translations

Select list. The full list will be sent on application.

The Greek Fathers

ST. BASIL : ASCETIC WORKS. W. K. L. CLARKE. 12s. 6d. net.
ST. DIONYSIUS OF ALEXANDRIA. C. L. FELTOE. 4s. net.
DIONYSIUS THE AREOPAGITE : THE DIVINE NAMES AND THE MYSTICAL THEOLOGY. C. E. ROLT. 7s. 6d. net.
DOCTRINE OF THE TWELVE APOSTLES, THE. C. BIGG and A. J. MACLEAN. 3s. 6d. net.
EUSEBIUS : THE PROOF OF THE GOSPEL. W. J. FERRAR. 2 Vols. 20s. net. (Not sold separately.)
HIPPOLYTUS : PHILOSOPHUMENA. F. LEGGE. 2 Vols. 20s. net. (Not sold separately.)
ST. IGNATIUS : EPISTLES. J. H. SRAWLEY. 4s. net.
ST. MACARIUS : FIFTY SPIRITUAL HOMILIES. A. J. MASON, D.D. 15s. net.
MACARIUS MAGNES. T. W. CRAFER. 7s. 6d. net.
PALLADIUS : THE LAUSIAC HISTORY. W. K. LOWTHER CLARKE. 5s. net.
PALLADIUS : THE LIFE OF CHRYSOSTOM. H. MOORE. 8s. 6d. net.
THE LIBRARY OF PHOTIUS. J. H. FREESE. Vol. I. 10s. net.

Latin Fathers

ST. AUGUSTINE ON THE SPIRIT AND THE LETTER. W. J. SPARROW SIMPSON. 5s. net.
ST. BERNARD : CONCERNING GRACE AND FREEWILL. WATKIN W. WILLIAMS. 7s. 6d. net.
MINUCIUS FELIX : THE OCTAVIUS. J. H. FREESE. 3s. 6d. net.
NOVATIAN : ON THE TRINITY. H. MOORE. 6s. net.

By A. SOUTER

TERTULLIAN : ON PRAYER, ON BAPTISM. 3s. net.
TERTULLIAN : AGAINST PRAXEAS. 5s. net.
TERTULLIAN : CONCERNING THE RESURRECTION OF THE FLESH. 12s. 6d. net.

Liturgical Texts

ST. AMBROSE : ON THE MYSTERIES AND ON THE SACRAMENTS. T. THOMPSON and J. H. SRAWLEY. 4s. 6d. net.
THE PILGRIMAGE OF ETHERIA. M. L. McCLURE and C. L. FELTOE. 6s. net.
BISHOP SARAPION'S PRAYER-BOOK. J. WORDSWORTH. 2s. 6d. net.
THE SWEDISH RITE. By E. E. YELVERTON. 8s. 6d. net.
TWENTY-FIVE CONSECRATION PRAYERS. ARTHUR LYNTON. 7s. 6d. net.
SERVICE BOOK OF THE HOLY ORTHODOX CATHOLIC APOS-TOLIC CHURCH. 20s. net.

Oriental Texts

THE ETHIOPIC DIDASCALIA. By J. M. HARDEN. 9s. net.
ST. IRENAEUS : THE APOSTOLIC PREACHING. (Armenian.) J. ARMITAGE ROBINSON. 7s. 6d. net.

Lives of the Celtic Saints

ST. BERNARD : ST. MALACHY OF ARMAGH. H. J. LAWLOR. 12s. net.
THE LATIN AND IRISH LIVES OF CIARAN. R. A. STEWART MACALISTER 10s. net.
ST. DAVID. A. W. WADE EVANS. 7s. 6d. net.
ST. PATRICK. NEWPORT J. D. WHITE. 6s. 6d. net.
THE LIFE OF ST. SAMSON OF DOL. THOMAS TAYLOR. 5s. net.

Select Passages

ANTE-NICENE EXEGESIS OF THE GOSPELS. HAROLD SMITH. Vols. I.–III. Each 7s. 6d. net.

DOCUMENTS ILLUSTRATIVE OF THE HISTORY OF THE CHURCH. B. J. KIDD. Vol. I. To A.D. 313. 7s. 6d. net. Vol. II. A.D. 313–461. 10s. net.

Jewish Texts

By R. H. CHARLES

THE BOOK OF ENOCH. 3s. 6d. net.
THE BOOK OF JUBILEES. 4s. 6d. net.
THE TESTAMENTS OF THE TWELVE PATRIARCHS. 3s. 6d. net.
THE ASCENSION OF ISAIAH. Together with "The Apocalypse of Abraham" in one volume. 4s. 6d. net.

JEWISH DOCUMENTS OF THE TIME OF EZRA. (The Assuan Papyri.) A. E. COWLEY. 4s. 6d. net.
THE WISDOM OF BEN-SIRA (ECCLESIASTICUS). W. O. E. OESTERLEY. 3s. 6d. net.
THE APOCALYPSE OF EZRA (II. ESDRAS). G. H. BOX. 3s. 6d. net.
THE APOCALYPSE OF ABRAHAM. G. H. BOX. With "The Ascension of Isaiah" in one volume. 4s. 6d. net.
THE BIBLICAL ANTIQUITIES OF PHILO. M. R. JAMES. 8s. 6d. net.
THE SIBYLLINE ORACLES (Books III.–V.) H. N. BATE. 3s. 6d. net.
THE LETTER OF ARISTEAS. H. ST. JOHN THACKERAY. 3s. 6d. net.
THE THIRD AND FOURTH BOOKS OF MACCABEES. C. W. EMMET. 3s. 6d. net.
THE BOOK OF JOSEPH AND ASENATH. E. W. BROOKS. 3s. 6d. net.
SUKKAH, MISHNA AND TOSEFTA. A. W. GREENUP. 5s. net.
THE SAYINGS OF THE JEWISH FATHERS (Pirke Aboth). W. O. E. OESTERLEY. 5s. net.
TRACTATE BERAKOTH (Benedictions). A LUKYN WILLIAMS. 6s. net.
TRACTATE SANHEDRIN: Mishnah and Tosefta. HERBERT DANBY. 6s. net.
KIMHI'S COMMENTARY ON THE PSALMS (Book I, Selections). R. G. FINCH. 7s. 6d. net.

SELECT PASSAGES ILLUSTRATING MITHRAISM. A. S. GEDEN. 3s. 6d. net.
SELECT PASSAGES ILLUSTRATING NEOPLATONISM. E. R. DODDS. 5s. net.
PISTIS SOPHIA. GEORGE HORNER. Introduction by F. LEGGE. 16s. net.

Texts and Editions in the Original

S. AURELII AUGUSTINI EPISCOPI HIPPONENSIS DE CIVITATE DEI CONTRA PAGANOS. Libri XXII. J. E. C. WELLDON. In two Volumes. 42s. net.
CHRISTIAN INSCRIPTIONS. H. P. V. NUNN. 1s. net.
ITINERARIUM REGIS RICARDI. M. T. STEAD. 1s. 9d. net.
LIBRI SANCTI PATRICII. NEWPORT J. D. WHITE. 6d. net.
PSALTERIUM IUXTA HEBRÆOS HIERONYMI. J. M. HARDEN. 10s. net.
SELECT PASSAGES ILLUSTRATIVE OF NEOPLATONISM. Greek Edition. E. R. DODDS. 4s. 6d. net.
SELECTIONS FROM THE "HISTORIA RERUM ANGLICARUM" OF WILLIAM OF NEWBURGH. 1s. 3d. net.
SUKKAH. A. W. GREENUP. 2s. 6d. net.
THE BOOK OF AMOS. T. H. ROBINSON. 2s. 6d. net.
THE CODE OF HAMMURABI. PERCY HANDCOCK, M.A. 1s. net.
THE EPISTLE OF BARNABAS. T. W. CRAFER. 6d. net.

S.P.C.K., LONDON